Natives and Exotics

Natives and Exotics

WORLD WAR II AND ENVIRONMENT IN THE SOUTHERN PACIFIC

Judith A. Bennett

University of Hawaiʻi Press
HONOLULU

Printed in the United States of America

14 13 12 11 10 09 6 5 4 3 2 1

Library of Congress Cataloging-in-Publication Data

Bennett, Judith A.
Natives and exotics : World War II and environment in the southern Pacific / Judith A. Bennett.
p. cm.
Includes bibliographical references and index.
ISBN 978-0-8248-3265-0 (hard cover : alk. paper)—
ISBN 978-0-8248-3350-3 (pbk. : alk. paper)
1. World War, 1939–1945—Environmental aspects—Oceania. 2. Oceania—Environmental conditions. 3. Natural resources—Oceanic—History—20th century. 4. Human ecology—Oceania—History—20th century. 5. Nature—Effect of human beings on—Oceania—History—20th century. 6. Oceania–Social conditions—20th century. 7. United States. Army—History—World War, 1939–1945. 8. United States—Relations—Oceanic. 9. Oceania—Relations—United States. 10. World War, 1939–1945—Political aspects—Oceania. I. Title.
D767.9.B46 2009
940.53'1—dc22

2009000222

University of Hawai'i Press books are printed on acid-free paper and meet the guidelines for permanence and durability of the Council on Library Resources.

Designed by University of Hawai'i Press production staff
Printed by The Maple-Vail Book Manufacturing Group

To the memory of my maternal grandfather, Godfrey James Collins, "D" Company, 25th Infantry Battalion, 1st AIF, who served at Gallipoli during World War I and on garrison duty in Australia in World War II.

To my uncles who served in World War II: the late Ashley Collins, in the 11th Infantry Battalion, AIF in Australia, so keen to serve that he subtracted a year from his date of birth; the late Noel Collins, Light Anti-Aircraft Regiment at Milne Bay, Papua, and then the 1st Australian Parachute Battalion in the Pacific and Singapore; Eric Collins, Leading Aircraftman, in the Philippines; and Mervyn Collins, who served six years in the AIF in the 1950s.

And to Heather's lost "malini," Wayne (Ab) Abbey, submariner, U.S. Navy, and to all the other mothers' darlings the war took away.

Contents

Acknowledgments / ix
Currency, Measurement, and Place-Names / xiii
Abbreviations / xv
Preface: Was the Environment a Stage or an Actor? / xix

Prologue The Great Ocean: How Others Tried to Ride Its Waves / 1

Part I Encountering Pacific Environments

1. Imagining Landscapes / 11
2. Peopling the Southern Pacific / 28
3. Diseased Environments / 49

Part II Using Indigenous Resources

4. Local Resources: Living off Land and Sea / 75
5. Taking Stock: Building for Battle / 97
6. Resources for the Metropole: Trade for the Periphery / 115
7. The Human Resource / 133

Part III Exiting Environment, Leaving Residues

8. Paying for the Damages / 157
9. Close Out: Quitting the Islands / 179
10. Leavings on Landscape / 198
11. Legacies and Visions / 219

Part IV Embodying War's Environment

12. Remembering Place: The Use of Souvenirs / 243
13. Places of Memory, Sites of Forgetting / 268
Conclusion / 291

Notes / 307
Bibliography / 393
Index / 425

Acknowledgments

Many have assisted with the production of this book. Sincere thanks to many friends, colleagues, supporters, scholars, war buffs, librarians, curators, and archivists for help, advice, hospitality, and encouragement—Tim Bayliss-Smith, Mary Braun, Barbara Brookes, Tom Brooking, John Broadbent, Fred Brooks, Steve Bullard, Les Carron, L. L. (Bill) Callow, Lin Chapman, Kathy O'Connor, Julie Cronin, Paul D'Arcy, Robert Desowitz, the late Reece Discombe, Bronwen and Charles Douglas, Philip Endean, Simon Foale, David Friswell, David Gegeo, Karen-Ann Gegeo, Bruce Harding, Cathy Hermes, Christina Hellmich, Jo and John Herlihy, Ulrike Hertel, David Hilliard, Dolores Ho, Stephen Innes, Janey Jackson, Christopher Johnson, Russell Johnson, Stephen Jones, Windsor Jones, Kehaulani Kauanui, Jean Kennedy, Laura Kessel, Mecki Kronen, Virginia Krumholz, Ismet Kurtovich, the late Bob Langdon, Fanaafi Aiono-Le Tagaloa Sr., Fanaafi Aiono-Le Tagaloa Jr., Kristen Mable, David and Gundi McKean, Natalie Mahony, Ewan Maidment, Alex Maravel, Mac Marshall, Jocelyn Maughan, Sharon Dean May, Clive Moore, Karen Nero, Dorothee Pauli, Karen Peacock, Brian and Liz Ponter, Dorothy Prince, Joseph Sanchez, Bunny Schlaffer, Mark Seymour, Barry Shineberg, Takashi Shogiman, Peter Stanley, Ewan Stevenson, Annie Stuart, Tony Sweeney, John Spurway, Peter Stanley, Jim Tedder, Andrew Thornley, Tauga Vulaono, Sandy Walker, Anni Watkins, Alfred Weinzierl, Mary Wolfskill, and Elizabeth Wood-Ellem. And thanks to Khyla Russell for her generous assistance with copying records in the United States and England and her support in places distant from Te Wai Pounamu (the South Island).

Special appreciation goes to Gavan Daws, Ian Campbell, Hank Nelson, Ken Inglis, Neil Clayton, and the press's readers for their valuable comments on all or substantial parts of an earlier draft. All its errors and imperfections are mine, not theirs.

This book owes much to the History Department, the Division of Humanities, and the University of Otago, Dunedin, New Zealand, for funding support with various research grants, a publication subvention and their endless patience in the writing of a war book that took longer that the war itself!

I extend my gratitude to the Macmillan Brown Centre for Pacific Studies in 2003 for a fellowship for research and writing of chapters of this book. Thanks too to St John's College, Cambridge, for an overseas visiting scholarship in early 2007, which enabled me to tie up some loose ends in this research as well as starting a new project.

Thanks to research assistants who sorted some of the data into categories at the start and assisted with interviews and tables—Jane Adams, Karyn-Maree Piercy, Eleanor Cottle, and Aaron Fox. Thanks to Bill Mooney, formerly in the Department of Geography, for his patience with my motley collection of "maps," which he made presentable; to Kyle Matthews for sorting all things to do with electronic files and my occasionally wayward computer; and to Frances Couch, who put the bibliography in order.

I extend my appreciation to the following repositories for the use of their records: In the USA: National Archives and Records Administration, San Bruno, California, and College Park, Maryland; Judge Advocate General's Archives and the Library, Navy Yards, Washington, D.C.; American Museum of Natural History, Ohio State University Archives; in England: Rhodes House, Oxford, University of Cambridge Library, Cambridge, and School of African and Oriental Studies, London; in Fiji: National Archives, Suva; in Solomon Islands: National Archives of Solomon Islands, Honiara; in New Caledonia: Territorial Archives, Noumea; in Australia: Australian National Archives at Canberra, Sydney and Melbourne, Australian War Memorial, Australian National Library, Canberra; and in New Zealand: Archives New Zealand, the National Library of New Zealand, the Parliamentary Library, Wellington, Army War Memorial Museum, Waiouru; and the University of Auckland Archives.

I am grateful for permissions given to use reproductions of photographs from the National Archives of the United States, the Australian War Memorial, the National Archives of New Zealand, the Archives of New Caledonia, and the Apia Museum, Samoa. I am especially thankful to individuals who have allowed me to use their photographs. Thanks to the Oregon State University Press for permission to use the map of New Caledonia in *Natural Enemy, Natural Ally*, by Richard P. Tucker and Edmund Russell, 2004. Some parts of chapter 3 first appeared in my "Malaria, Medicine, and Melanesians: Contested Hybrid Spaces in World War II," *Health and History* 8: 1 (2006): 27–55. In chapter 5, I have also drawn on sections of my "Local Resource Use in the Pacific War with Japan: Logging in Western Melanesia," *War and Society* 21: 1 (May 2003): 83–118.

My thanks go to the University of Hawai'i Press for the editorial advice provided and for the support of Masako Ikeda, the acquisitions editor.

While mostly research is fun, writing can be challenging, especially sometimes when it had to take second or third place to the teaching timetable and other university work. When I hit a wall and things got tough I was thankful for the memory of a beloved friend and Pacific historian, the late Dorothy Shineberg, whose spirit I often felt walked alongside me. Thanks too to my former supervisor, longtime mentor, and friend Murray Chapman, who taught—and still continues to teach—his students the virtue of perseverance.

Currency, Measurement, and Place-Names

In most cases, units of weight, distance, area, and currency are given as in the sources. In most of the western Pacific the currencies were based on the pound. Twenty shillings (20/-) made a pound (£1), twelve pence (12d) made a shilling (1/-), so 240d made a pound. The Tongan pound was on par with the Australian pound. From 1932, Australian £1/5/- or 25 shillings equaled British Sterling £1 or 20 shillings.

US$1 = 6/1 (rounded in most places to 6/-); 50 cents = 3/-; 10 cents = 7d.
A£1 = $3.26; 10/- = $1.63; 5/- = 82 cents; 2/6 = 41 cents; 6d = 8 cents.[1]
Depending on location, conversion rates sometimes differed slightly.

C. F. P. Colonies Françaises du Pacifique.
In 1944, 50 francs C. F. P = One American dollar = 6 shillings
200 francs C. F. P. = One pound Sterling or Australian £1/5/-.

Generally, all the Allies except the French used the Imperial measures of weight, area, volume, and distance. Metric measures, especially in relation to timber volume, have sometimes been included for clarity for non-Imperial systems readers since the metric system is now current in much of the Pacific and its neighbors. Japanese measures have been converted to Imperial for simplicity.

M/t is an abbreviation of one measurement ton, or 40 cubic feet. Americans used the measurement of the short ton (2,000 lbs.) and British, Australians, and New Zealanders used the long ton (2,240 lbs.). For timber, board feet superficial feet or feet board measure. This measurement is one foot long, one foot wide, and one inch thick.

Before the war the northeast of the island of New Guinea was known as the Mandate of New Guinea or, more commonly, New Guinea under Australian jurisdiction. The southeast was a territory of Australia known as Papua. The western portion was Dutch New Guinea. During the war, under a joint administration the entire eastern portion was known as New Guinea, but I use the two names where such distinction assists the location of events. After the war, it was called the Territory of Papua and New Guinea (TPNG), which became Papua New Guinea (PNG) at Independence in 1975.

Abbreviations

AG	Attorney General
AIF	Australian Imperial Force
AJ	*Agricultural Journal*, Fiji
AMF	Australian Military Forces
AM	Kippenberger Military Archive, Army Museum Waiouru, New Zealand
AMNH	Division of Anthropology Archives, American Museum of Natural History
ANC	Archives of New Caledonia, Noumea
ANGAU	Australian New Guinea Administrative Unit
ANU	Australian National University, Canberra
ANZ	Archives of New Zealand, Wellington
ANZAC	Australian and New Zealand Army Corps
AR	Annual report
AWM	Australian War Memorial, Canberra
BDU	Bomb Disposal Unit
BEW	Board of Economic Warfare
BSIP	British Solomon Islands Protectorate
CB	Construction Battalions (Seabees)
CDC	Commonwealth Disposals Commission
CF	Confidential file
CFCs	Chlorofluorocarbons
CO	Colonial Office, Britain
Coy	Company (Australian military)
CP	Council Paper
CRE	Command Royal Engineers
CS	Colonial Secretary
CSR	Colonial Sugar Refinery

CSO	Colonial Secretary's Office
CWA	Chemical warfare agents
DC	District Commissioner
DDT	Dichlorodiphenyltrichloroethane
DEET	N, N-Diethyl-meta-toluamide
DO	District Officer
DNA	Deoxyribonucleic acid
EA	External Affairs
FEA	Foreign Economic Administration
FLC	Foreign Liquidation Commission
FMF	Fiji Military Force
FNA	Fiji National Archives
GO	Governor's Office, American Samoa
HC	High Commissioner
HMAS	His Majesty's Australian Ship
HP	Haddon Papers, Cambridge University Library
JAG	Judge Advocate General
KC	King's counsel
LCVP	Landing craft for vehicles and personnel
LST	Landing ship for tanks
MBL	Macmillan Brown Library, Christchurch, New Zealand.
MP	Minute paper
M/t	Measurement ton (40 cubic feet)
NAA	National Archives of Australia
NASI	National Archives of Solomon Islands, Honiara
NARA	National Archives and Records Administration, College Park, Maryland, U.S.A.
NARA SB	National Archives and Records Administration, San Bruno, California, U.S.A.
NCO	Non-Commissioned Officer
NGFR	New Guinea Forests Reports
NLA	National Library of Australia, Canberra
NLNZ	National Library of New Zealand, Wellington
NZEF	New Zealand Expeditionary Force
PCB	Australian Production Control Board
PIM	*Pacific Islands Monthly*
PIR	Pacific Islands Regiment
PM	Prime Minister
PMB	Pacific Manuscripts Bureau, Canberra
PNG	Papua and New Guinea

POW	Prisoner of War
PX	Postal exchange and canteen
RAAF	Royal Australian Air Force
RC	Resident Commissioner
RG	Record Group
RH	Rhodes House, Oxford
RNZAF	Royal New Zealand Air Force
Seabees	CBs; Construction Battalions
Sec.	Secretary
SF	Secret file
SFNH	Société Francaise des Nouvelles Hebrides
SIDF	Solomon Islands Defense Force
SILC	Solomon Islands Labor Corps
SOAS	School of Oriental and Asian Studies, London
SoPac	South Pacific (U.S. abbreviation)
SOS	Secretary of State
SOS SPA	Service of Supply, South Pacific Area
Stg	Sterling (pound)
SWPA	Southwest Pacific Area
TNA	National Archives of Great Britain, Kew
TNT	2,4,6-Trinitrotoluene
TPNG	Territory of Papua and New Guinea
USCC	United States Commercial Company
V-J	Victory over Japan
WPA	Western Pacific Archives, Library, University of Auckland
WPHC	Western Pacific High Commission
WPHC BSIP	Western Pacific High Commission, British Solomon Islands Protectorate Series
WPHC CGEC	Western Pacific High Commission, Gilbert and Ellice Crown Colony
WPHC NHBS	Western Pacific High Commission, New Hebrides, British Service, Office of the High Commissioner
WPHCTS	Western Pacific High Commission, Tonga Series, Great Britain. Agent and Consul Tonga.

Preface

Was the Environment a Stage or an Actor?

When I was a small girl in Brisbane, Australia, we had on a sideboard at home a metal ashtray with a little silver airplane supported aloft. It was made of one big bullet and two little ones. I knew bullets were dangerous because my father had told me so, and anyway, I had seen cowboys in the Hollywood movies felled with great dispatch by bullets just like these in six-shooters. Yet my family seemed unperturbed at its being in the house. This ashtray with its bullet airplane forever flying above transient hills of cigarette ash furthered puzzled me because my Uncle Eric had brought it home "from the war in the islands." A mysterious event in a mysterious place. Among family photographs, I also pondered a picture of another uncle standing beside a tall, gaunt man, both smiling at the camera. "That is Uncle Noel in uniform and that is his friend Syd who survived Changi as a prisoner of war of the Japs." Just who were these "Japs"?

Of such small percepts of World War II the building of a concept comes, though new experiences constantly modify the structure. Years on, I visited yet another uncle in Lae, New Guinea, and saw remnants of whole hospitals that, so I was told, the Americans had simply abandoned. I wondered why such waste in a country so in need of medical equipment. More years had gone by when I sat in a high school common room, a big tin-roofed shed with leaf and canvas walls, at Alotau, Milne Bay, in Papua doing lesson preparation for the next day. The headmaster and schoolboys were leveling ground to pour concrete for a basketball court. Two boys walked in, presented me with two soil-encrusted hand grenades they had dug up, and asked what we should do with them. I cannot recall my response other than to get them and me out of there fast! And a year later, Okada-san, a gentle Japanese, appeared to seek vainly for the bones of his father killed in battle with the Australians at Milne Bay.

What I saw in the Territory of Papua and New Guinea, and later in the Solomon Islands and Tonga, made me wonder what impact this sudden foreigners' war had on the environment and its native inhabitants and how thousands of military personnel reacted to them. Here, I try to provide an answer. My field, or should I say my ocean, of history has been for many years focused on the Pacific, and, given the huge corpus of operational histories of World War II in that vast area and the strategic battles the Allies won there, I hardly need to explain why I have chosen it as a time and place of significance. Were I to exclude military history, I could analyze the impact of the war in terms of social, economic, and political factors on the inhabitants; these are not incidental considerations, as will be seen. To go to the heart of the relationship between human beings and their surroundings, we need to consider these older conceptual categories in light of the significance of the environment, even when it was, for a time at least, more of an imagined and later a remembered landscape, and the central role it played in the lives of the other actors in this great war. To achieve that, I approach the war in the southern Pacific islands through the lens of environmental history. This research attempts, then, to take into account the social, economic, and political dimensions of environmental issues.

J. R. McNeill reminds us that in regards to twentieth-century wars, and certainly World War II, the ecological shadow of preparing and supplying the waging of industrialized war fell heaviest on the protagonists' homelands.[1] I know of no reliable calculation of, say, the amount of carbon dioxide and other greenhouse gases cast into the atmosphere in producing war matérial and waging war, but it certainly added substantially to the total of the Industrial Revolution in the nineteenth century. In terms of specific locales, I also have no doubt that the cost to the environment and resources of the United States and Japan, for example, was greater than those of the Pacific islands.[2] This study, however, is not an exercise in comparisons or relativities, but an assertion that the islands are important in themselves, with their own environmental rights and responsibilities, not just as means to the ends of other peoples and their states, including global superpowers.

In *Natural Enemy, Natural Ally*, the first collection of essays to address the interactions between war and environment in 2004, Richard Tucker and Edmund Russell argue that this aspect of environmental history has been largely ignored because that subdiscipline has its roots in the history of conservation, which has "focused attention on civilian rather than military affairs."[3] This may be true for the American school, which, in its moral concern for the future of the environment originating in the work of G. Perkins Marsh, John Muir, and Henry David Thoreau, was galvanized into being with the appearance of Rachel Carson's *Silent Spring* in 1962 and the rising concern for life on the planet. But as John Mackenzie argues, not only is the concern for the environment much older, but also a variety of European historians have concentrated on colonial activities in several regions, revealing how imperial ideologies and technologies interacted with environment and introduced major changes, planned and unplanned.[4] Imperialism is no stranger to war in imposing its way. Even so, few of its historians have concentrated on the specific relationship between war and environment, probably because most such "little wars" involving limited technologies did not leave massive direct damage on landscape.[5]

I argue that war is a significant force in environmental change in two major respects: First, it causes a range of changes in the landscape—which, for most islanders, includes the sea—and its several interrelated ecologies, including human populations, which I see as elements of the environment. Secondly and more subtly, war contributes to altering human perception of the environment by the ideas it generates in its human participants, both military and civilian, along with the demonstrated effect of their actions. Military historians know that the environment where war is waged is pivotal to operations, and so strategists and tacticians consider such things as weather, tides, and terrain in planning campaigns. Despite this, few military historians portray the environment as an active agent in conflict or address the environmental consequences of war.

I also analyze the nature of the damage war caused and how it was dealt with in the islands. Because of the perceptible and lingering damage to humans and their environment caused by more recent wars such as the Vietnam and Gulf wars, scientists, lawyers, and the military are considering the scale of damage as well as how to measure it and, more important, if and how it can be rectified. The more perplexing issue of who is responsible for rectification also is central.[6] This process was underdeveloped during World War II and, though the Allies came up with a variety of ways of compensating for damages, actual losses incurred on battlegrounds were excluded. They considered this collateral damage and inevitable in war. A few colonial governments felt it prudent to pay *ex gratia* payments to their subjects because, unlike foreign armies, these administrations remained in the islands. But, as indicated, these were mainly monetary compensations rather than rectification. The only other making good was to remove, or more commonly hide from view, the detritus of war's dangerous material. Some of that has a nasty tendency to come eventually to the surface, and none of the protagonists is keen to accept responsibility more than sixty years later.

Environmental history, despite its concern with the environment as an actor, still keeps focused on human beings. Without them there would be no history. Like the compass needle, the environmental historian flits across, hovers over, and sometimes fixes on particular arcs in the great circle of life, but always her north is people and their stories. I am interested in the cattle tick, not as the entomologist is, in its life cycle, its host, and habitat, but on how these insects have influenced the way humans behaved in their environment in wartime New Caledonia. In the area of material culture, I am interested in the souvenir and the war memorial not simply as objects, productions, structures, and artistic representations by the human species, but also and centrally because they both trigger and signify stories about people in place. People, places, and perceptions are at the core of this study.

The war in the southern Pacific islands revealed and reinforced fundamental patterns in the use of, interactions with, and attitudes to the environment as well as catalyzing change. As part of a larger process, it was more than that, however. An intrusive act, it was an expression and extension of imperialism, both offensive and defensive, as well as imperialism's failed diplomacy and hubris. The process of warring was the distillation, the concentrated essence of all exogenous influences that had impinged on this environment since Europeans first espied the Great Ocean "upon a peak in Darien"[7] and sailed its vastnesses to discover for themselves what the native peoples had found thousands of years before. Though there had been earlier European harbingers, the period of more continuous intrusions of exotic strangers among the native inhabitants began in the late eighteenth century in the wake of Captain James Cook, who put so many islands on the West's maps and revealed the resource potential of several.

Wartime observers often commented, we shall see, on the region's wilderness, of islands or large areas of them as imagined absences, revealing few signs of a humanized or cultural landscape. They saw not with indigenous eyes or those of the prehistorian or, in less deep time, of the forest botanist, for the native inhabitants had made some enormous changes to their environment. Those the first Europeans met had been no ecological "noble savages" any more than they were uniquely savages, noble or otherwise. In the earliest days of their colonization of their oceanic world about forty thousand years ago, incoming peoples in western Melanesia as well as ancestral Polynesians from about three thousand to twelve hundred years ago, had used its natural resources sometimes unwisely, endangering or even eliminating some species, especially birds. They introduced exotic species of food plants and animals and with them certain unwanted cargo, such as the Polynesian rat (*Rattus exulans*). Over thousands of years, these settlers cleared and burned vast areas of primary forest and created grasslands or secondary forests. By gardening on hillsides, they induced landslips and silting of valleys, lakes, and lagoons, but they also often created productive landscapes for themselves. Hard lessons of scarcity, famine, and death taught them to husband resources and conserve for the future, though some did better than others, since near-fatal reduction of fauna along with forest and soil depletion occurred in some islands, most commonly those with a limited range of habitats and resources in cooler latitudes, or those extremely distant from other islands.[8]

Once the second wave, the Europeans and some Japanese, arrived in the Pacific, they made even more rapid environmental changes, first as resource raiders of the seas and land, exploiting the regions' whales and seals, as well as tortoiseshell, pearl shell, bêche-de-mer, sandalwood, coconut oil, and feathers. From the 1850s through the 1890s, beyond Australia and New Zealand, Europeans crossed the beaches to settle, transporting their landscapes of plantation agriculture, farming, and pastoral industries, with their associated animals and plants as well as continental diseases, the last triggering a massive drop in microbially naïve native populations until about 1920.[9] Perhaps the most fundamental and lasting change, however, was ideological: the beginnings of commodification of resources—land, labor, and produce of land and sea. Most of these goods variously circulated in indigenous societies prior to this, but within social relations that bound related groups together in a network of patronage, competition, reciprocity, affection, and shared values. Paradoxically, whether a high chief leading seven thousand in Hawai'i or a "big-man" with a hundred followers in the New Hebrides, those who distributed most among supporters and kin were deemed the wealthiest and the most honored. In spite of this, gradually the native people both willingly and unwillingly became involved in this resource commodification process, when, for example, Hawaiian high chiefs and New Hebridean big-men became middle men in organizing labor to collect sandalwood, for a large slice of the goods or cash the white man offered.[10]

With these contexts of deep history and exotic intrusions in mind, I examine the multifaceted interactions of the environment with the military and their activities during World War II in the southern Pacific islands where the main operations against Japan were launched. I have used a problem-centered approach, focusing more thematically on how the military dealt with the environmental realities when they arose throughout the war and how such processes affected or reacted with the environment. There is a natural progression of challenges particular to various phases of the war and their demands on the environment, along with its effects on people, their perceptions, and their behavior. I have addressed these issues serially, though their sequence inevitably overlaps because of the mobile nature of the front. Thus the discussion is not a straight chronological narrative and there is little reiteration of operational details except where appropriate, such as the events of the American landing at Tarawa.

Human beings are a species and certainly a natural resource. They are part of the biota that interacts with other living organisms and with the abiotic or nonliving environment. With the addition of energy originating ultimately from the sun, these form an ecosystem, its scale depending on perspective, whether local, regional, or even global. Studies of ecology focus on physical, chemical, and biological interactions. But there is another intangible element when humans make up part of an ecological system. Certainly, they have certain biological characteristics and behaviors, even if cloaked in culture that is formed and performed in human societies. Even so, unlike most other living things in such ecological systems, all viable humans can envisage the future and recall memories of the past that are not solely necessary for their biological survival. They attach meanings to places and to objects associated with occurrences in such places, a process irreducible to a direct chemical or biological ecological interchange, unless we analyze the neural and synaptic processes within the brain. In some cases, instinct is surely part of such mental processes, as in many other organisms. But human beings also have complex belief systems, capacities of imagination and creative thought, and emotions such as sympathy, hubris, hate, and love. Agreeing with Donald Worster, I see this area of ideology, human perceptions, and feelings as a valid level for analysis in any environmental history.[11] This ecology of the heart is, for humans caught up in war, both their strength and their weakness.

Such human characteristics are something nation-states and military commanders have to understand in order to shape and command behavior in the battlefield, where men unnaturally and often continually expose themselves to possible death and commit what in peacetime would be mass murder. Thus, part I of the book opens with what the men going to war expected their new environment to be in terms of its insular geography and climate and its human population, and how they and their commanders coped with the reality. Even these commanders were unprepared for much in the new environment, including tropical diseases. The link between these exotic humans and the smallest of endemic organisms, bacteria and viruses that cause disease, is analyzed along with how these, as well as unfamiliarity with operational conditions in tropical swamps and forest, affected both physical and mental health and thus performance. In the battle with endemic disease, military manipulation of the ecology became a primary weapon, since several infections, mainly mosquito-borne, had no completely preventive drug or fully curative medicine.

When large numbers of human beings interact with an unfamiliar environment far from their homeland on islands they have little formal political control over, several factors that are not specifically environmental become braided with their behavior in natural systems. As a species, human beings are political animals, so questions of power, authority, and control on several interfaces—between the occupying military and colonial administrations, between the colonial administrations and metropolitan governments, and between, on the one hand, administrations and the indigenous people and, on the other, the military and the people—constantly arose in attempts to marshal local resources for the war effort, both in the islands and for Europe and the United States. Here too, long-term economic and political motives for the postwar world constituted a hidden agenda that sometimes sat uneasily beside the most urgent common strategic goal of winning the war. These political threads are woven into the warp and woof of the interactions between the environment and humans throughout the book, but most markedly in parts II and III.

Armies from distant places certainly utilized local resources such as vegetables, fruit, and timber. The Americans recognized the vital role of such supplies in the war effort worldwide when they set up a wartime authority known as the Board of Economic Warfare (BEW). Coordinating the systematic use of local resources involved significant interaction by the military with local administrations and people and raised questions of ownership. While historians have discussed military exchanges for fresh food and native labor because of their influence on native social attitudes, there are silences regarding other local resources, such as timber and fish. Nevertheless, local resources alone could not sustain temperate climate armies for any extended period, a reality the Japanese soon confronted. As I discuss in part II, to fight and win by application of maximum force, armies needed to have constant supplies of matériel from their distant homelands. Such massive incoming resources, seemingly limitless in the case of the Americans, made a deep impression on the indigenous people, particularly in more isolated western Melanesia. They also witnessed the novel uses to which the Allies put local resources such as coral and timber. Their environment had afforded them life-giving resources, but before the war, if they knew anything of rest of the world, it was usually just a minute glimpse of modernity, like Plato's shadows flickering on the cave's wall. Consequently, they were curious and attracted to the new, to the humanity that the incoming troops represented and to the convenient, to their food, dress, devices, and routines. Unless the military or the colonial administrations could keep up the supply of goods that the islanders valued, their active assistance in the war effort, particularly as carriers to the Allied troops, would have been less forthcoming, as it became with the Japanese when they had nothing to offer in exchange except brute force. For their part, islanders, with their intimate knowledge of their own environment, gave valuable information and support to the armies of both sides. Of course, the meaning they took from these varied interactions and the way the military utilized resources was not necessarily what the exotic occupiers or even the colonial administrators might have expected.

In part III, I address the exit of armed forces and the material legacy they left on the environment, as well as less tangible influences among the islanders, such as food preferences. In attempting to dispose of the matériel they had brought with them, the military faced similar geographic and climatic constraints to when they had arrived, but a different order of urgency. As armies demobilized, maintaining surplus equipment became almost impossible. The enforced speed of disposal meant a loss to their owners, but some gain to those few administrations, missions, and commercial operators, as well as local people on the spot. Much was simply abandoned, including dumps of munitions—a process that seemed wasteful to returning Europeans and even to their metropolitan public, but to the islanders it was, at least in western Melanesia where dumping was greatest, a baffling process.

Since the early years of the conflict, the military and some administrations had sorted out payments in cash and war surplus for environmental damage, including destroyed crops and trees the islanders valued, inflicted outside the operational zone. Despite this, some islanders and European settlers did better from this than others, with the equity of outcome falling victim not only to economics of the metropolitan governments, but also ultimately to power politics on a regional and global scale. The war brought more than foreign matériel to the islands. Living organisms came with human carriers or their heavy equipment, finding congenial niches in the wake of mobile armies and often making their presence felt in the environment years after war ended. There was no compensation for this delayed war damage any more than there is likely to be for what is now appearing as sunken ships break up and corroding containers of biological warfare compounds are discovered. On the wider canvas, the changes the war brought in world geopolitics saw a re-evaluation by colonial powers of their role in the Pacific. Although policies were far more developmental of people and resources than before the war, they were framed, as ever, within the colonial vision of their own strategic interests.

In part IV, the focus returns to humans' perceptions of environment and the meanings they attached to it because of the events they experienced there. For young men, the novel, if trying, environment they encountered was something they attempted to convey to loved ones by sending souvenirs home as symbols of how they dealt with the alien and as messengers of future hopes. Through shared experiences with comrades in particular battle sites, the environment wrote its text on their hearts. They in turn wanted to mark their histories on place, to inscribe meaning on what before had been to them just another nondescript corner of a foreign land. Nowhere is this more telling and more poignant than in the fighting men's desire to memorialize their dead, an emotion bereaved families and friends at home shared, with local and domestic sites becoming special and indeed sacred places within the respective environments.

The conclusion considers the main themes in the context of subsequent developments as well as the persistent vision of the southern Pacific islands' environment as means to the strategic ends and even the fantasies of greater nations in the neighborhood. Yet for all this regional focus, the islands were and are "a part of the main,"[12] because, as well as the war's direct impact, they and their peoples have to deal with the legacy of its prodigal panoply of manufactured, fossil-fueled technology that has contributed to global warming.

Prologue

The Great Ocean: How Others Tried to Ride Its Waves

Before Japan came into World War II by attacking the naval base at Pearl Harbor in the U.S. territory of the Hawaiian Islands on 7 December 1941, the actions of the future Allies in relation to the Pacific islands revealed one aspect of their perception of the islands that was to remain constant during and after the war. Although defended, lost, fought over, and regained, relatively few of the islands of the southern Pacific had been coveted by the United States, Australia, New Zealand, or even Japan as ends in themselves or even for their known resources, as useful to the war effort as some proved to be. In their view, the islands were largely means: bridges, barriers, bastions, and occasional bargaining chips. As means, the interests of their native peoples and of their environment in these scattered archipelagoes remained secondary to the desires of the contending Pacific powers, just as they had always been.

In the late eighteenth and early nineteenth centuries, the settlement of eastern Australia was assisted by knowledge of the islands that European explorers such as Cook, Bougainville, and Vancouver had provided. As bridges and refreshment stops, they lessened the occurrence of scurvy (vitamin C deficiency) on long sailing voyages taking the "eastern route" and, for a time, were offshore sources of valued food items, such as pigs, for the nascent British penal settlement of 1788 at Port Jackson (Sydney). With the influx of settlers, including convicts, to temperate Australia and, by 1840, of free settlers to New Zealand, neo-Europes were being created and the Great Ocean was being crisscrossed by commercial and imperial interests. By the 1800s, Britain's rivals had feared she would block their access to the Pacific and its rim countries and be able to launch campaigns from Australia, for example, against the Spanish in South America, using the islands as bases. Thus oceanic islands became increasingly significant. The imperial powers completed their carving up of the Pacific in the late nineteenth century, motivated by pressure from isolated Australasian colonies, which feared invasion should Britain's rivals annex island bases, and also motivated by national hubris, such as France's rush to claim New Caledonia, soon designated a convict depot. Avoidance of possible war over these minor territories played a part too, as was the case in 1899, when Britain, the United States, and Germany bargained rather than battled over Samoa, Solomons, and New Guinea, balancing "winnings" with adjustments to British-German lands in Africa. The last colonial territorial reassignment followed World War I, when Germany lost her holdings.[1] Thereafter, disputes among the powers as regards the Pacific ceased for more than a decade.

The pattern of islands as means to ends was reasserted in the 1930s when commercial aviation became feasible. Claims to mainly uninhabited islands, such as Canton, suited to either seaplanes or airfields, came forward from the United States, which wanted a trans-Pacific aviation monopoly, and from Britain, supported by New Zealand, since some of the islands were close to her possession of the Cook Islands. From 1935, President Roosevelt of the United States was also interested in some form of American control in New Caledonia to ensure the U.S. monopoly. Britain opposed this monopoly, and New Zealand saw itself a beneficiary of competition, but preferred a British airline.[2] Gathering war clouds meant these territorial claims were laid aside.

Political and military observers in the United States, Australia, and New Zealand, however, had long believed Japan was likely to expand from the Chinese mainland and eventually turn to Southeast Asia for further expansion, but the timing was uncertain. With Vichy-controlled French Indochina occupied by Japan by 1941, objections to American airfields in the South Pacific vanished. Before Japan attacked Pearl Harbor, the Americans, with the hurried assent of colonial governments, began building airfields across the southern Pacific islands to create an "air ferry" route in the hope of maintaining links with the U.S. territory of the Philippines via Australia, avoiding tiny U.S.-held islands near the Japanese mandate of Micronesia. In these islands Japan continued airstrip construction begun in 1939. Meanwhile, New Zealand, on behalf of Britain, was making preparations to defend British territory in the South Pacific, while Australia assisted its neighbor New Caledonia to entrench the De Gaullist Free French, who were antipathetic to the Axis powers and unsupportive of Japanese ambitions in Southeast Asia.

Across the vast Pacific Ocean, the islands were of strategic value in the defense of the United States, Australia, and New Zealand, and, in Micronesia, possible bases for a southward offensive by Japan. If and when war broke out, all the Allies preferred to fight the enemy on other peoples' lands and seas, thus preventing the Japanese from becoming entrenched in their homelands and preserving their environments and peoples from the depredations of invasion. The Allies saw the islands as a protective arc, fanning out across the seas from these three countries, the first line of defense from the northern invader. Just as they were to be for the Japanese, the Pacific islands were bastions and bridgeheads to a greater goal.

This was to remain a constant of strategy, diplomacy, and politics during and after the war.

The engagement that exotic military forces brought to the southern Pacific environment began far away. The Pacific War originated in hubris and the desire for other countries' resources. In the 1930s, Japan's military clique had gained increasing political influence and had silenced most opposition. Japan hungered for autarky, but those taking power saw empire as the key to this goal. Having already annexed Korea in 1910, Japan in 1931 began eating into Manchuria and China, but this alienated the United States and her allies, who gradually invoked trade sanctions from 1939 to 1941. Japanese planners believed their colonial resources, including those of Southeast Asia, would be funneled to the European war, frustrating Japan's ambitions in China. In addition to the loss of their manufactured exports, Japan saw itself as the victim and therefore sought to consolidate its sparse resource base with the mineral, timber, and productive wealth of Southeast Asia, which France, the Netherlands, Britain, and the United States held as colonial possessions. Japan's leaders enunciated their vision of a Greater East Asia Co-Prosperity Sphere, which really was to be a Japanese prosperity sphere, threatening those with vested interests in the region. The United States, rich in resources and manufacturing, nonetheless imported 60 percent of the world's rubber as well as 45 percent of its chromium, 40 percent of its tin, and 36 percent of its manganese. In the 1930s, for example, 90 percent of the crude rubber and 75 percent of the tin the United States needed came from the rest of Southeast Asia, not from the American Philippines.

Increasingly during the Depression, Japan suffered from economic nationalism and resultant trade barriers put in place by many countries, including its best customer, the United States. This reinforced the Japanese militarists' ambitions and their drive to find new sources of raw materials and markets. Although the United States, with considerable commercial investment in Southeast Asia, desired unfettered access to its primary materials, it preferred the European colonial powers to Japanese hegemony, a hegemony that seemed inevitable as both France and Holland were invaded by Japan's ally, Germany. By August 1941, the U.S. government had frozen Japan's assets in America and joined Britain and Holland in an economic embargo.

In an attempt to draw the United States into a naval battle on its own terms, Japan's sudden, sharp, and stunning attack on Pearl Harbor and America's Pacific Fleet on 7 December 1941, along with the cataclysmic fall of British Singapore in February 1942, served to extend Japan's battle perimeter on yet another front, reaching east and south over a vast ocean. America's determination to fight, with major military headquarters in Australia and New Caledonia as well as Hawai'i, seems not to have been anticipated by Japan. Japan's strategic vision then aimed to secure its lines of communications in and with resource-rich Southeast Asia by a series of fortified bases in the central, south, and southwest Pacific, as well as Southeast Asia itself. These bastions-cum-forward military bridgeheads, however, were vulnerable to the vagaries of distance and Japan's dependence on its conquered satellites for primary materials. Add to that the fact that Japan alone had no more than 10 percent of America's industrial potential and the odds seemed stacked against its long-term success. It was to be a victim of its own propaganda and the split between army and navy strategists in trying to hold this huge area from the Asian mainland to New Guinea, across to the Gilberts and north to the Aleutian Islands, while trying to manage China. For a country dependent largely on imported crude oil, Japan had reeled under America's embargo in mid-1941 following the takeover of French Indochina. By 1942, Japan was getting 40 percent of the production from the captured oil fields of the Dutch East Indies and British Borneo. Although Japan was able to hold them until 1945, its ability to ship the oil back to Japan declined along with its technical capacity. The amount that reached Japan fell in 1944 to only 5 percent of the production and none in 1945. Without oil for fuel, the industrial base and transportation networks of Japan's industries and military campaigns collapsed.

The United States had embraced a twin strategy of isolating Japan and its army. Its tactics were to destroy the lines of naval communication and supplies and to bypass significant concentrations of enemy troops, leaving them to "wither on the vine," then attack pivotal bases ever closer to Japan. By late 1943, with U.S. attacks on their shipping, the many units of Japanese forces scattered over the southern Pacific theaters were isolated, though determined to honor their commitment to their emperor and the military virtue of fighting to the death (*gyokusai*).[3]

Thus hunger for resources brought war to the Pacific. The search for resources, including local people, in the lands conquered by the Japanese or occupied by the Allies meant the environment of the southern Pacific islands came under more intense pressure, as well as economic scrutiny, than most of its prewar colonizing powers had managed or wanted to achieve.

Before the war, the island administrations resembled medieval fiefdoms, tending to stay behind imagined walls of nationalist metropolitan differences. In spite of their minuscule size and the vast distances and poor communications within and between their scattered archipelagoes, it rarely had occurred to their metropolitan colonial overlords that since there were common needs and challenges facing them, a common, shared approach could achieve economies of scale and concomitant benefits for not only the small number of settlers and foreign sojourners, but also the island people. Several administrators on the spot saw the potential of cooperation in training native medical practitioners for the region, for example, but winkling agreement to budgetary spending from their metropolitan superiors was a tortuous process. Part of the reason for this was British colonial orthodoxy that colonies had to pay for themselves and, more importantly, the stultifying effects of the Great Depression, which from 1929 eroded the economic base of territories dependent on commodity prices of products such as copra. Although within administrations a governor or high commissioner could have significant influence, frequently supported by district officers in the field, plans for innovation often fell prey to transfers and retrenchment. Add to that the intricate micropolitics of small administrations, and the impetus for significant change was often too diffuse to be effective.[4] The crux of the problem was that the powers saw these southern island dependencies as largely insignificant to their greater imperial and foreign policies and, with a few exceptions such as Nauru and Ocean Islands with their rich phosphates, New Caledonia's nickel, and Fiji's sugar, also of little importance in metropolitan economic calculations. Their small land masses and their distance from markets were a barrier to commercial exploitation. Had they been larger and closer to major powers and markets, their post-European ecologies would have been even more altered, as were the Hawaiian Islands, for example.

In addition to the gap between the vision of in-field administrators and metropolitan governments, there was also considerable unevenness in colonial knowledge of the environment of the different archipelagoes. Resource research and development were minimal or absent in many potentially valuable fields.[5] For example, whereas the French in New Caledonia knew much about its mineral potential, they seemed content to cordon off the indigenous people into reserves in the hope of making the island a French settler colony, yet by the 1930s the conservative French settlers' numbers stagnated, along with their backward agricultural and pastoral industries, as they struggled to grub a living from the poor soils of La Grande Terre. Along with those in the Solomons, the prewar administrators of Papua and New Guinea had concentrated more on basic administration and tax collecting and less on development of resources. Except for copra and some gold and rubber exploited for the benefit largely of the colonizers, Papua's and New Guinea's " natural resources . . . were relatively unknown, poorly plotted and controlled."[6] When war came, some district officers had excellent knowledge of specific regions, but much of the assessment of resources vital to the war effort was on the spot, often not far from the front lines.

Because of the existing prewar environmental knowledge and the scattered nature of the islands, metropolitan governments deemed the southern Pacific islands to have very limited economic potential, but they were perceived as important strategically, which is why most had been annexed. Those who had ringside seats understood this far better than did distant Europe. The war, of course, both confirmed and reinforced the "yellow peril," which the Australians, with their seven million clinging to a massive continent of fragile fertility and their extended, exposed northern coastline, had feared since the nineteenth century. To a lesser extent, the war did the same for American strategists who had watched, since the early twentieth century, Japan's sun rising along with the size of its navy.[7] For the British, possessions east of the Suez proved harder to hold than they had anticipated. The fall of Singapore early in 1942 proved that.

Beyond the islands, the idealistic but vaguely worded Atlantic Charter of 1941 and the emerging values of the United Nations awakened imperial powers to their obligations to develop and assist their dependent peoples. Britain had already decided in 1940 to modify its tenet that colonies must be self-funding, admitting development assistance as a principle and a boost for its own commerce. Appreciations of the same spirit found expression nearer the islands. Australia and New Zealand in 1944 were concerned that the United States, ensconced in a series of military bases in the South Pacific, might not go home after the war, so it proposed alternative regional arrangements in their Canberra or Anzac Pact, which emphasized, *inter alia*, the duty to assist their dependent peoples. Implementing much of this had to wait, of course, for the war to end.

War thrust a tsunami of superlatives on the warm tropical beaches of the southern Pacific islands. Exotic waves had ebbed and flowed across these shores before, but for its intensity and scale relative to its duration, the war swept in a mighty deluge. From late 1941 to 1945, the largest number of exotic men landed there than at any other comparable period. Many islands' population doubled, tripled, or quadrupled almost overnight. On a few small atolls, troops outnumbered natives by ten to one. The amount of matérial these men, and this war was a very male enterprise, brought with them was the greatest ever seen and probably exceeded the mass of all imported goods of the previous 100 to 150 years. The distances traveled by men and materials to reach the battleground were often the longest that any military force had ever to traverse. Many islands were the most isolated in the world—with vast expanses of sea between them and far from centers of population. And they were the least developed. The built environment was negligible, particularly in the west islands, with infrastructure confined largely to a few wharves, a couple of warehouses, short filaments of roads wisping out tentatively from small port towns to jungle dead ends or looping back to their beginning, and only a couple of rough airstrips. Most of the native inhabitants lived entirely by subsistence horticulture, and near the sea by inshore fishing, with some men intermittently earning cash by indentured labor on plantations and mines or by selling their copra and shell. Most of these native people were Melanesians and, in terms of familiarity with the wider world, among the least sophisticated; most were illiterate. So the engagement the invading armies had with the environment was direct, virtually uncluttered by modernity's layers of structures and a familiar cultural patina. For these exotic young men, mostly from temperate lands, this was the wildest and weirdest environment they had ever encountered. It soon made demands on them, physically and mentally. More Japanese, for example, were to die from disease than from the enemy's armaments. Of all the theaters of World War II, combat fatigue came to the Americans the most quickly in the western Pacific battlefields, and postings of more than a year, even in benign rear bases, severely reduced morale and mental stability.

Regarding the native peoples, whether near the front or rear bases, there had never been anything before of such strangeness and magnitude. The rapid creation of military cities brought the most concentrated nodes of communications and new knowledge exchange ever witnessed in the region. In inland New Guinea's fastnesses, there were villagers who had never seen their neighbors a valley away, let alone parties of Australians or Japanese in battle array suddenly reconnoitering their homeland. Even Christian Tonga, with its own monarch and constitution, had never before beheld so many foreign men, white and black, clustered on Tongatapu, with more than forty warships crowded into the harbor. Industrialized war fought by more than two million exotic troops flooding onto their soils and traversing their seas was a unique experience for Pacific islanders. For all involved—the Japanese arrayed against the Americans, Australians, New Zealanders, their respective local supporters, and villagers—one of the biggest events of human history was being enacted on some of the world's smallest islands in its largest ocean. This concatenation of superlatives rapidly engulfed the natural environment and people, to recede almost as quickly four years later, leaving lingering traces wherever it touched.

PART I

Encountering Pacific Environments

CHAPTER 1

Imagining Landscapes

> The soldiers wrote home that Hollywood producers were responsible for a great fraud.
>
> Victories in battles win wars. . . . What is possible will depend firstly on geography, secondly on transportation in the widest sense, and thirdly on administration. Really very simple issues, but geography I think comes first.
>
> —General Bernard Montgomery

Most Pacific islands were little-known to their wartime invaders. In films and fiction, the South Seas had been fantasized paradoxically as both free from and in need of the constraints of "civilized" societies, not only socially, but also environmentally. The Pacific islands largely lacked the physical structures and transformed landscapes that the invaders believed were technological markers of their own civilizations, but they were little prepared for this. An alien environment and the exigencies of war forced the invaders to recalibrate their mental pictures of imagined landscapes.

Dreaming Islands

For most in the Pacific War, the battleground was unfamiliar. Unfamiliarity left spaces for speculation. Beginning with the eighteenth-century European explorers' accounts of "discovery" of the Pacific Islands, an exogenous parade of commercial, evangelical, and intellectual entrepreneurs peddled their versions of islanders, causes, and schemes, whether as critiques of their own societies or for investment, conversion, and colonization.[1] Because of such selective representations, to many outsiders these faraway islands had become a hotbed for their dreams, fantasies, and fears.

By the nineteenth century, Western intellectual writing about tropical landscapes and people revealed a duality of the paradisiacal and potentiality on the one hand, and the pestilential and primitive on the other.[2] What few specifics Allied servicemen knew of the Pacific islands originated largely from film fantasy or the Hawaiian tourist industry's publicity.[3] For most, in darkened movie theaters across the United States of America, Australia, and New Zealand, from the days of silent pictures, filmmakers repeatedly supplied electric shadows of an imagined Pacific, such as *Hurricane* (1937), with Hollywood star Dorothy Lamour. Early docudramas, such as *Cannibals of the South Seas* (1912), left a less alluring impression.[4] These built on works of fiction, the popular press, and travel books that romanticized the exotic, if not the scandalous.[5] For the few that read them, anthropological tomes hardly provided a corrective, since most focused on "traditional" cultures, eschewing any taint of modernity such as the cash economy, Christianity, or colonial administrations. Museums with South Seas artifacts echoed cultures frozen in this same anthropological timelessness.[6] Mission publications and native converts on deputation work gave some Australians and New Zealanders a more sober perspective.[7] Since Australia administered eastern New Guinea, the island's people rated a mention in some school geography books.[8] But for most, their notion of the region was based on few hard facts.[9] So the dominant tropes in the average Allied serviceman's imagination were twofold: lush South Seas landscapes with golden beaches, peopled by olive-skinned natives with hula girls in sarongs or grass skirts, compliant and welcoming; more distantly, in dense, humid jungles, savage headhunters and cannibals threatened strangers.

Japanese South Sea dreams in film and fiction were less concerned than Westerners with an escapists' world of sensuality than with establishing their presence, couched within patriotism. They portrayed natives as not especially intelligent but capable of learning from them about the dangers of being undefended against Western imperialism. Some showed natives as welcoming the Japanese presence and cooperating in "developing" their islands' resources. Japanese policies in their Micronesian mandate from 1920 reinforced these assumptions, with an influx of thousands of Japanese migrants and heavy initial subsidization creating economic growth that outstripped that of other island colonies. Honed in Manchuria, Japan's assimilationist policies were founded on a belief in the superiority of their race and civilization.[10]

Even at the highest level, much was vague about the southern islands. When the war began, the Japanese navy had anticipated fighting America in the seas around the Philippines or Guam once American naval forces had regrouped in Hawai'i. But General Douglas Macarthur, U.S. supreme commander of the Southwest Pacific, based himself in Australia, not Hawai'i. In mid-1942, the battles of the Coral Sea and Midway weakened the Japanese navy. Their army had been expect-

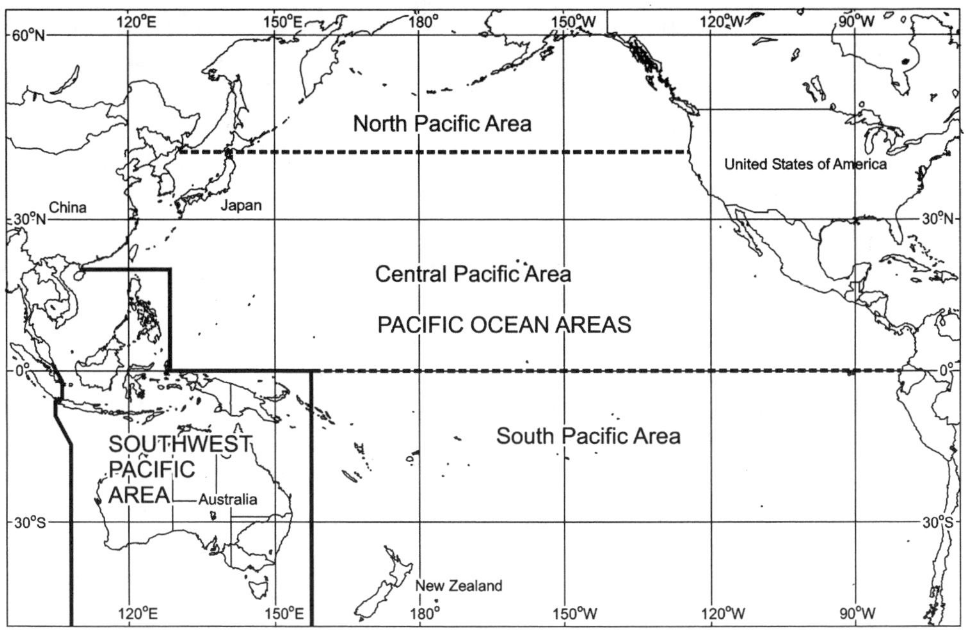

Map 1. Command areas, Pacific Ocean.

ing to fight in Micronesia, not in New Guinea and the Solomons. Japanese command assumed that this area was like China or Southeast Asia—an easy climate and a region rich in agriculture and natural resources.[11]

The Allies too were not well-prepared for the environment. With the European war underway for two years in December 1941, they had conditions there in mind—not trackless rain forests, a few towns looking to the sea with little port development, or small atolls dotted across a huge ocean.[12] As one soldier put it, "[a]ll our armed forces' training was based on the assumption that action would be in 'civilized' countries with cities, towns and villages linked by roads and rail."[13]

In war, those who had captured the lay of the land on maps had more chance of holding it. Although better informed than the Japanese, the Allies had poor maps, particularly of the Southwest Pacific. Exploration of New Guinea represented the writing of colonial power on landscape, but as late as the 1930s explorers in the Australian possessions were ineffective cartographers. Maps of Dutch New Guinea on the scale 1:1,000,000–1:250,000 existed, but the Australians in the east had "nothing but sketch maps."[14] In May 1942, Allied mapping agencies met in Melbourne under the command of the American chief engineer. Allied command gathered information from colonial administrations, supplemented by former residents and ships' captains. This, combined with a hotchpotch of old and new military maps and hydrographic studies, produced terrain studies, with details of vegetation, climate, anchorages, landing grounds, trails, river crossings, swamps, sunrise, sunset, moonrise, rainfall, population, languages, supplies, acceptable trade goods, and so on. Though not always totally accurate, these texts were valuable for operations.[15] Moreover, by late 1942 the Americans, unlike the Japanese, were able to reconnoiter the south Pacific to assess resources.[16] The first Japanese Solomons' study only appeared as their army was retreating.[17]

Terrain studies described the environment, but understanding how to fight in it was another thing. In 1942, most Japanese commanders in Melanesia had served in China and Malaya with limited knowledge of trackless tropical forests, while the infantrymen had to learn in the field.[18] The Americans lacked both trained manpower and equipment but rapidly switched to war mode during 1942.[19] For most of 1942, Allied marines and infantrymen learned jungle fighting on the spot. Some of Australia's only conscripts in the militia who fought at Kokoda had very little training. By late 1942 the AIF had learned lessons from Kokoda and the Buna-Gona campaigns in New Guinea and had taken the advice of the members of New Guinea Volunteer Rifles, incorporating these into

Figure 1. Various types of food plants obtainable "in the jungle" displayed at jungle living course, Combat Training Center, Santo Espiritu, New Hebrides, c. 1943 (EX. 111-SC-332672, NARA).

tactical manuals and training within Australia.[20] U.S. land forces trained in rear areas such as American Samoa, Fiji, and New Hebrides, but some, especially the Guard divisions, were poorly acclimated to the jungle, unlike, say, New Zealanders who had trained with Fijians in Fiji's hinterland.[21] By 1944 at Higaturu, former district officers with jungle skills, as members of the Australian New Guinea Administrative Unit (ANGAU), trained elements of the American 38th Infantry Division and other Americans in the field, enabling them to deal with the land and its people.[22] The Allies also gave men guidebooks for finding jungle foods, which the Japanese seemed to have lacked.[23]

Reality Checks

As the Kokoda campaign had shown, the reality of terrain and climate dispelled dreams of an easy locale. Other realities of distance and extended lines of communication soon became crucial. After their 1942 naval reverses and the retreat from Guadalcanal in early 1943, the Japanese recognized that it was a "a great mistake to make operations in such remote and solitary islands."[24] Within the Solomons, by 1943 they could not maintain their troops because of shipping losses. By early 1944, Rabaul on New Britain was isolated, part of the MacArthur-Nimitz island-hopping strategy.[25]

What the invaders found in this alien environment surprised and sometimes disappointed them. What they failed to find often caused their demise. Believing basic infrastructure was in place, they hoped to ride around on cars and bicycles, only to find roads "were just a dream."[26] At first, Japanese troops could sing,

> Push on into the jungle,
> Bananas, papayas and coconut milk
> Enjoy the taste of bounteous nature.[27]

But even fruit proved scarce. New Guinea did not export food crops; those grown were for subsistence and natives needed them. Lush jungle growth did not equal abundant food. The Japanese soon perceived New Guinea as a "green desert."[28] Starving men determined to kill Americans, if only to "get their good food."[29] Fighting desperately on Guadalcanal in December 1942, as his comrades died of malnutrition and malaria, First Lt. Akogina recorded, "I killed some ants and ate them, really tasted good."[30] As another noted, just before he died, "There is no sympathy in the jungle."[31]

The environment threatened strangers. In late 1942, the moss forests of the Owen Stanley Ranges in Papua, at six to eight thousand feet, provided camouflage for the Horii detachment from aerial observation, but

> the jungle became thicker and thicker, and even in midday we walked in the half light of dusk. The humidity was almost unbearable. The surface of the ground was made up of decayed leaves and was covered with thick growth of soft, velvety moss. We felt as if we were treading on some living animal.[32]

Their enemies were as apprehensive. When A. J. Traill of the AIF arrived, he recorded,

> So this is New Guinea. Waving palms certainly, but where are the dusky maidens, dancing on the beaches? Beaches? None. Just the damp uninviting jungle reaching down to the water's edge—nay, stretching into the very water itself. The white man's grave wading out into the sea to meet one.[33]

Yet many saw the beauty of their new surroundings.[34] At Verahui, Guadalcanal, an American journalist noted, "Beach beautiful beyond description . . . more South Sea-ish than a Dottie Lamour set."[35] New Guinea could appeal to the eye, but rarely to the rest of the senses: "In scenery and shades of color she is paradise; in climate and impenetrability, a green hell."[36] The dank smell of decay and, on battlefronts, rotting corpses assailed the nostrils. Unseen danger played on soldiers' fears:

> . . . deep among the Jungles there, by tracks of moonless gloom,
> The nightmare creatures crawl and creep, like Messengers of Doom,
> Dark forms among the shadow ways, ugly and undefined,
> And dark as are the thoughts, the Jungles of their minds.[37]

Fear of enemy and environment coalesced. Even sixty years after the war ended, Americans attributed their slaughter of surrendered Japanese on Guadalcanal to revenge for mutilation of U.S. Marines but explained more generally that "on that remote island, full of malaria, mosquitoes, bugs, ants and crud, we lived from one day to the next."[38]

Yet without the enemy, the Allies found the west Melanesian environment "almost entirely devoid of the works of man," lacking a historical landscape, and thus uncivilized.[39] Espiritu Santo in the New Hebrides was a "steaming wilderness."[40] New Guinea seemed barely inhabited. "I guess we're all very glad Tojo [Japanese planes] can't drop any of his pills on our beloved Australia. . . . Anyway he is only blowing up jungles here; not cities."[41] Another Australian who could not have known then that New Guinea's landscapes were being humanized thirty-five to forty thousand years ago, noted,

> In New Guinea there was nothing, bar traces of coconut plantations on the coast and a tiny native population, even the best of whom . . . were practically as they had always been. In the wild, jungle-clad and largely unexplored mountains there were no roads, no towns and few signs of any people whatsoever.[42]

Amid this emptiness, the occasional sign of place marked by a familiar house style briefly uplifted the spirits of Allies and enemy alike.

> When viewed from the deck . . . its [Espiritu Santo's] beauty is profound, but once disembarked the traveler finds instead of beauty . . . dense jungle . . . malaria ridden swamps . . . dengue . . . hookworm . . . and the omnipresent rain and heat. Occasional oasis of cultivated plantations with the planters homes . . . relieved the bleakness [*sic*].[43]

With the remnant Horii detachment retreating from the Owen Stanley Ranges to the north Papua coast, in 1942 Japanese journalist S. Okada rejoiced when he saw:

> The radio operator's dwelling at Soputa stood in a coffee plantation. It was a nice little hut, a heavenly sight for our eyes. To us who had lived most of the time in jungles, it was as cheering as light in a painter's studio.[44]

Even the grid of plantations became depressing to men who lived for months among them: "Wherever we looked or journeyed it was Palms, Palms, Palms."[45] There were but few places in New Guinea, such as Wau's fertile valley, where white miners and native gardening had created more reassuring landscapes.

> The rich soil of this garden-like part of the valley was full of yam, taro and the ubiquitous sweet potato. . . . Above ground the banana palms, laden with green and golden fruit, stood in crowded groves, overlooked by stands of mature, bulbous paw-paws. It's a pity that it wasn't like this all over but once outside the civilized part of the valley, the jungle reverted to its normal savage tangle.[46]

To men who had experienced battle, French New Caledonia was "civilization," for it boasted a major port town, but to troops fresh from home camped in "la brousse" (the bush), the island disappointed:

> Here we were at last, on a sub-tropical island surrounded by a reef and mosquitoes. It is nothing like the romantic tropical islands one reads about. No

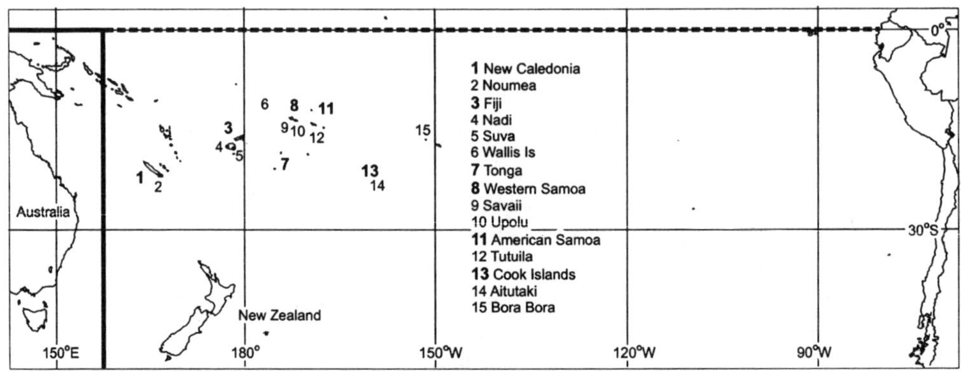

Map 2. South Pacific command area.

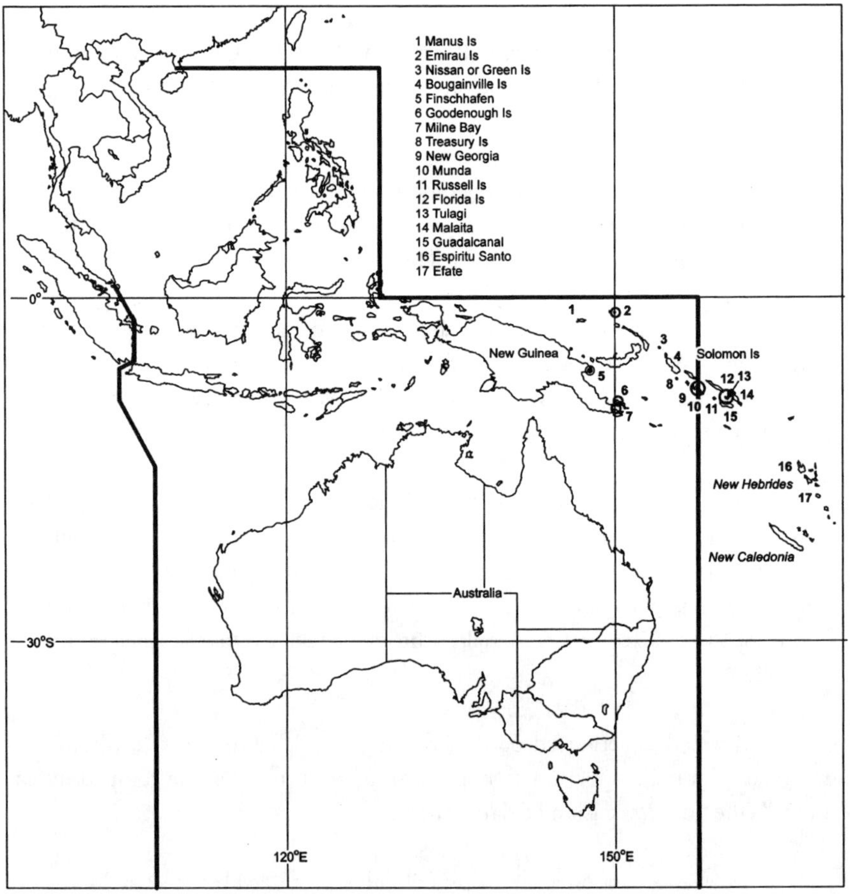

1 Manus Is
2 Emirau Is
3 Nissan or Green Is
4 Bougainville Is
5 Finschhafen
6 Goodenough Is
7 Milne Bay
8 Treasury Is
9 New Georgia
10 Munda
11 Russell Is
12 Florida Is
13 Tulagi
14 Malaita
15 Guadalcanal
16 Espiritu Santo
17 Efate
New Guinea
Solomon Is
New Hebrides
New Caledonia
Australia
0°
30°S
120°E
150°E

Map 3. Southwest Pacific command area.

> swaying palms, clear sleepy lagoon or dusky hula girls. Instead there are steep rugged hills and mountains, very scraggy vegetation, primitive buildings, dusty roads and last, and the worst, thousands of ants and mosquitoes. When I look back and remember all the glorious and glamourous descriptions I have read about the South Sea Islands it is a great disappointment to see the actual thing.[47]

Allied forces garrisoned in Fiji, Tonga, and Samoa generally found the islands pleasant. The chains of small tidy coastal villages interspersed with food gardens spoke of domesticated landscapes with named sites of "some event in recorded history or . . . age-old legends."[48] Aitutaki, Cook Islands, seemed like Hollywood's South Seas with its "lagoon, swaying palm trees, moonlight nights of dreamlike serenity, an ideal climate."[49] Servicemen in American Samoa first thought it a "paradise," but as they neared the end of their first year's service, for many whose visual memory of the Pacific originated in the Hollywood film, it became "Alcatraz in Technicolor."[50] On isolated bases, bored men grew tired of the rainbow sunsets, blue seas, and golden beaches: "It is amazing how this beauty can enthrall for a moment and then the reality of stagnation sets in and shakes us so badly."[51] Even away from battle, scenery was not enough.[52]

Reading and Writing Environment

Whether scenic or not, in operations the environment was crucial. Much of the Pacific was ocean and demanded understanding from those who sailed and assailed across her. With fossil fuels and great engines, modern navies had overcome dependence on wind power to ply the Pacific, but not all had learned that "tide and time wait for no man." Though the Americans counted the capture of Tarawa in the Gilbert Islands from the Japanese in late 1943 as their first successful amphibious assault on a coral atoll at Betio, it was at the cost of over 1,000 dead and 2,200 wounded of the 5,000 American marines who landed on the first day.[53]

Local residents, including Lt. Commander G. Heyen of the Royal Australian Navy and Major F. Holland, a former headmaster for twenty years on the island, who kept records of the tides, assisted with "Notes on Tarawa" and charts for the navy authorities in Hawai'i planning "Operation Galvanic."[54] This expert "Foreign Legion" calculated how much water would be on the atoll's apron reef, six hundred to one thousand yards from land around the supposed time of the landing. The consensus was there would be perhaps five feet on the reef's seaward side, allowing an LCVP with a draft of three and a half to four feet a clearance of up to eighteen inches—how far it could proceed across to the beach at Betio would depend on the lagoon bottom. The "Foreign Legion" warned there could be a one-

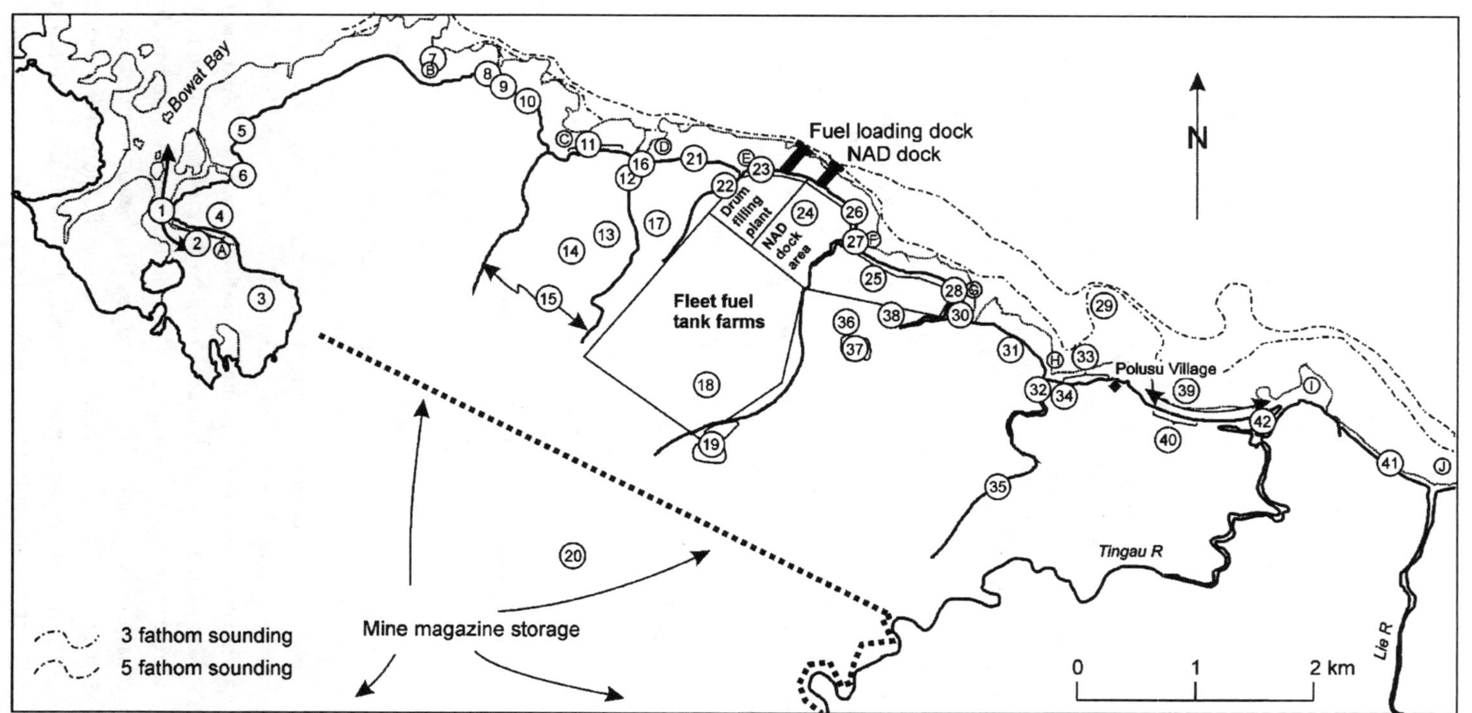

Map 4. Western section of Manus Base, Admiralty Islands, 1945 (based on map in RG 313-58-4316, NARA SB).

1. Small boat landing
2. Water depth 9' to 15'
3. Possible small boat haven
4. Gently rolling area suitable for development
5. Graded track or road along beach
6. Possible small boat (?) entrance
7. LST can be brought within 250' of beach road at this point. Only one LST can be accommodated
8. Mangrove
9. Road is now behind mangroves
10. Beach only averages about 15' to 20' between "B" and "C"
11. No beach
12. Sago swamp with beach 30' to 50'
13. Highland with rain forest and undergrowth
14. Dense rain forest, rugged, cut up by drains or small streams
15. Rivers appear to be all-year water supply
16. Sand bar, ford, very narrow
17. Clearing with logs lying on the ground, rough hill country
18. Secondary growth with four interspersed clearings of about one acre each. Good dry land (---) cover for camouflage
19. Clearing to river is indicated
20. Rough terrain cut by draining valleys, appears suitable for erection of magazine
21. Coconut trees along beach "D" to "X". No entrance through the coral here. Beach 20' to 30' wide. Narrow belt of swamp behind beach road
22. Clearing, dry area, logs visible
23. Landing for LCT (?). Space of 300' over coral
24. Inrim plantation. Road located within 100' of beach. Upraised coral 60' to 80' wide. The small (-) 15 x 20' between road and beach (---) fuel loading pier. Area behind (--) 150' swampy during wet season. Plantation area all rolling hills cut by the radiating shallow drains from high point. Uniform slope from coastal flat to high point of 200'. Coastal flat is 300' to (-) in depth
25. Plantation continues from "F" to "G", narrow belt of sago swamp behind coastal flat. It is a dry area, gently rolling rising to 30' before reaching belt of sago swamp
26. Possible best pier site
27. Small landing craft passage into river mouth at "F"
28. Small landing craft can approach to 150' of beach in channel 200' wide at "C" and "H". Rain forests and slope immediately behind beach. River about 60' wide at "M" in well-defined canyon. Clearing along canyon for one mile upstream
29. Dangerous coral heads
30. Small patch of coconuts
31. House 20' x 20'
32. Banks are swampy on both sides of river
33. Landing beach for LST, entrance as indicated
34. Beach 50' wide fringing with coconuts for one-half distance from "H" to Polusu River
35. River appears to be all-year water supply
36. Nose of hill half plantation and half rain forest. Ht. 120'
37. Sago swamp in clearing
38. Stream drain
39. LST and LSI landing beach. Sand beach overshelving coral 50' to 60' wide
40. Rain forest
41. From "I" to "J" there is a good beach. It is a coastal levy about 80' wide. Immediately behind it Sago swamp cut by tidewater drain. An underwater obstruction exists at "I"
42. This area practically isolated by swamp and lagoon

foot variation, however, highlighting the hazard of a "dodging tide" that ebbed and flowed unpredictably at neap tides.[55] Holland had expected the landing to be on the 15th of November, but to synchronize the complex operation, which involved a massive flotilla and air support, U.S. Admiral C. Nimitz scheduled the landing for the 19th of November (20 November, local time), with the moon in its last quarter. Holland was alarmed when he learned it was to be on 20th. He claimed he had said that "3 to 4 feet of water" would be on the reef for "about 4 hours, but only 1 or 2 feet during the high water neaps" and that "neap tides would be at their very lowest in the lagoon, on the 19th and 20th."[56] After witnessing a rehearsal of an amphibious landing on Efate, Holland again warned of a possible neap tide of two feet on Tarawa, contradicting what the biographer of the commander of the northern attack force, Admiral R. Turner, states was Holland's earlier support for the predicted four to five feet.[57] Yet Holland pointed out in the document "Notes on Tarawa" that there was "sufficient warning."[58] Certainly, even three feet would have been fatal to surmounting the reef with the LCVP. Holland accompanied the armada and again warned Admiral H. W. Hill, commander of the southern attack force, against landing when the tide would be at its lowest because landing craft would be unable to clear the reef.

Holland's was not the only voice. The U.S. navy historian S. M. Morison mentions that Heyen, a former Tarawa resident, had also warned Admiral R. Turner about the nature of the Tarawa neap tides and that they sometimes were "dodging tides," very low or high.[59] In other words, the two leading commanders knew the risk, but Turner decided to proceed for other tactical considerations including even worse conditions likely later in the month, and Hill, so Holland recalled, stated that he expected four feet because his "luck" had never deserted him.[60]

It did, for the tide was a low dodging one, as Holland had predicted, yet some retrospective calculations labeled it "anomalous." So thousands of men waded into enemy fire from stranded landing craft while their Amphtracs crossed the reef but proved fragile under intense Japanese fire and of limited use in ferrying them in.[61] The U.S. force also had underestimated the strength of the Japanese positions, expertly constructed under layers of coconut logs. This error compounded the poor judgment, because the Japanese fought tenaciously. The U.S. forces learned much from their mistakes, but could have made better use of the data at hand. Although this bloody island saw four thousand Japanese killed, for the consumption of the stunned American public mourning its own, command misunderstanding of the atoll environment was represented for years as a result of "the sudden shifting of the wind,"[62] although when Philip Mitchell, high commissioner and Fiji's governor, visited Tarawa soon after the battle he recorded, "I met no one who had heard of the change of wind reported in Washington."[63] Later, the cause became the "capricious tide" and, more truthfully, a "failure of reconnaissance."[64]

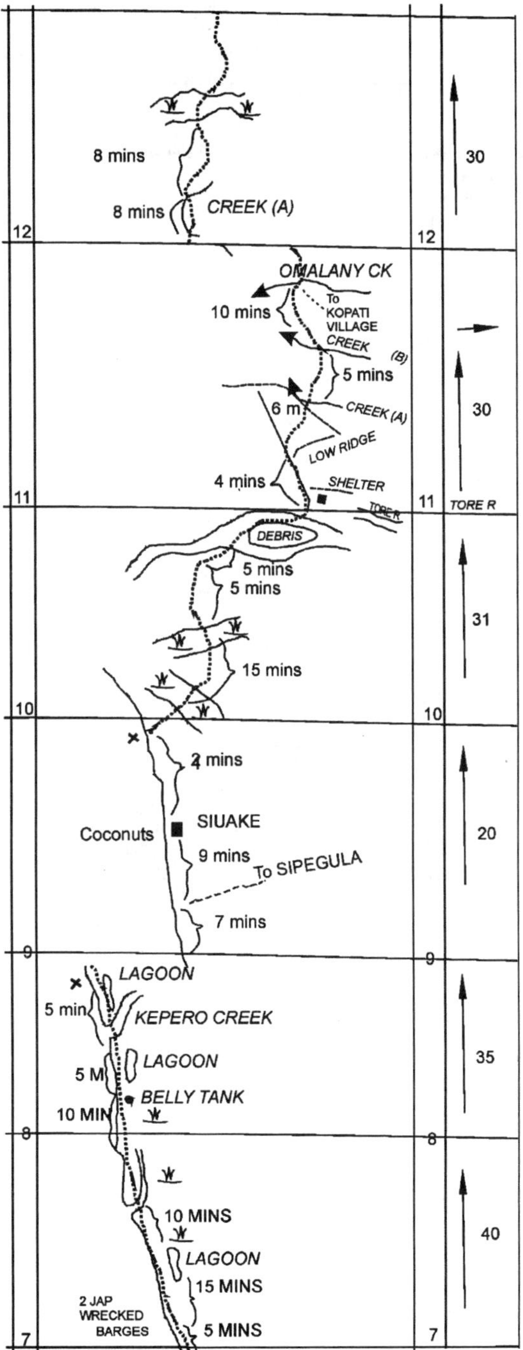

Map 5. Field sketch for section of west Bougainville (based on map at 7/9/99, (613/7/8), LS, AWM 54, AWM).

Creek A log crossing. Swamp very muddy water knee deep; overhanging branches 2'6" above water. Water ankle deep along remainder of track. Vegetation; wild bananas. Visibility 10 yds. Mosquitoes very bad.

The right track is very hard to find. Though it follows a low ridge to X. Guide necessary. Creek A 5 yds W 1' D muddy bottom. Creek B 6 yds W 1'6" D muddy bottom. OKALANTA CK 10 yds W 2' D. Very muddy bottom; visibility 10 yds.

TORE RIVER 30 yds W moderate current knee deep in morning waist deep in afternoon. Swamps very muddy knee deep. Overhanging branches 2'6" above water. Level. Guide necessary along this ill-defined track. Ground subject to flooding and very muddy. Visibility 10 yds

SIPEGULA is a village inland – inhabited. SIUAKE is deserted but recognized by clump of coconut trees. Track X is believed to be unknown to Japs therefore extreme caution necessary to keep well off beach before reaching turn-off. Is very hard to pick up.

KEPERO Creek 10 yds W 3' D. Log crossing poor flow. Walking on beach very heavy. Lagoon X approx. 200 yds long 120 yds wide slightly brackish; known as TOKORO.

Track on water's edge; very heavy walking. Beach steep; creek of a reddish colour poor flow 8 yds W 3' D.

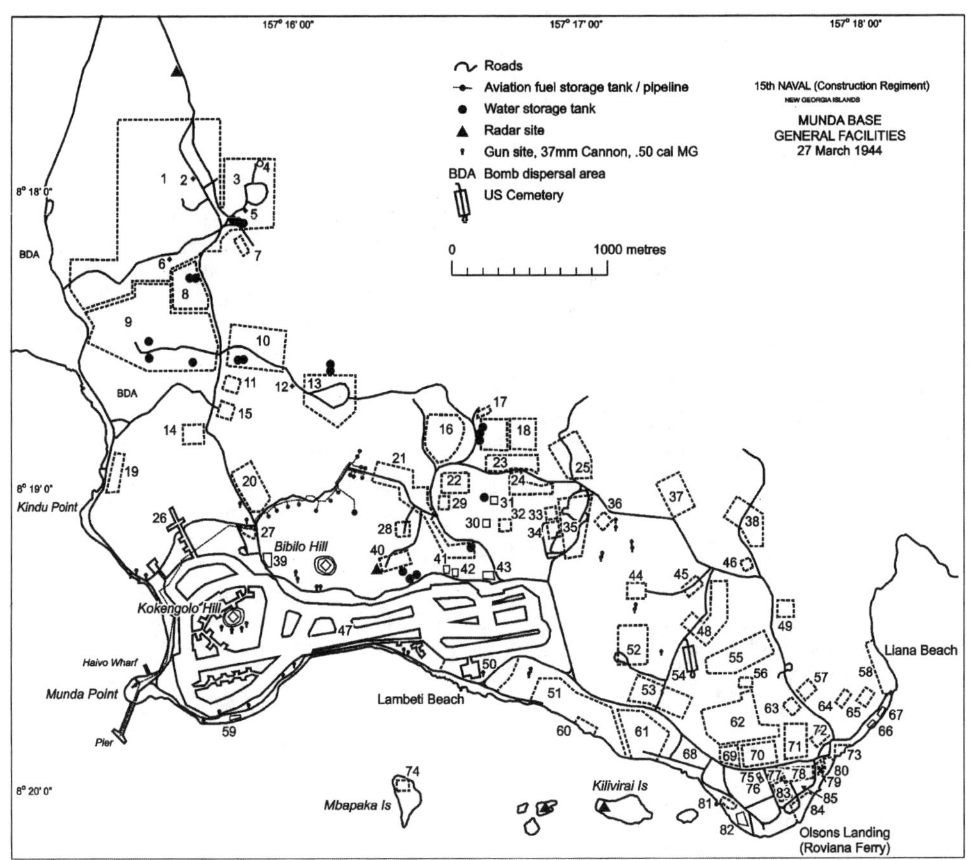

Map 6. Munda Base: general facilities, 1944 (based on map in RG 313-58-3401, NARA SB).

1. Camp 3&5 under canvas, XIII Air force
2, 5, 6, 11. 75 Kw Generators
3. Camp – canvas 73rd NCB Camp Williams
4. 73rd N C B sawmill
7. Acorn 25 Camp (canvas) No 4.
8. Camp (canvas) PATSU 1-1,12, No 2
9. Vacant camp, 24th N C B
10. Acorn 25 Camp enlisted men
12. Advanced Naval Base Hospital
13. Army special Service Div
14. Acorn 25 Transportation
15. Camp (canvas) 361 (?) Inf.1+2 Batt.
16. Camp (canvas) 7? AAA Gun Bn & Fleet Air Wing
17. Camp (canvas) Air Command, Munda,
18. Camp (canvas)
19. Central Ordnance area.
20. Camp (canvas) Naval Base H Q
21. Camp (canvas) ?
22. Camp (Canvas) Navy ? No 5
23. Camp (canvas) Sparks: Eng & Flight crew, Navy
24. Camp (canvas) 318th Mech & Engineers
25. Hardstands (for airplane)
26. Aviation Gasoline Tank Farm
27. 319 Light Control Camp (canvas)
28. Jan (?) Company (?) Control.
29. Radio Munda and Command Centre
30. Photo laboratory, 903 Airbase Security Bn
31. ? Signal Command
32. 15 Naval Construction HQ
33. Service Command
34. VI Island Command Camp
35. 938 CA Battalion
36. 36 Ind.
37. 350 Eng'rs Reg't 1st Bn
38. 73rd N C B workshops
39. Camp (canvas) 192 Field Art.
40. WI Maintenance Unit
41. 548 Bomber Ordnance
42. Naval Motor Pool.
43. 334 Truck Company Quartermaster
44. 221 Quartermaster Salv. & Repair.
45. 172 Inf Service Co
46. Pontoon Assembly Dock
47. Runway extended from 3000 to 8000 ft & taxiways
48. 328 Av. Eng's Bn
49. 472 Eng'r Maintenance 1st Plat.
50. Ready Bomb area (37mm)
51. Camp (canvas) 47th NCB
52. 44 Base Hospital Malaria Control
53. Eng'r Depot Serv. Command
54. Camp – Canvas SCAT enlisted men
55. Camp 595 Field Art.
56. 'A' co 374 AAA searchlight
57. 23rd Med Supply Depot
58. Camp Boat Pool
59. Skeet range
60. Camp (canvas) 205 AAC Camp.
61. Camp (canvas) Naval Base Service Unit.
62. Camp Canvas AA Gun BN Batt. 'A'
63. New Zealand Coast Watchers
64. Island Stockade
65. Crash Intelligence
66. Radio Munda
67. Recreation area
68. Service Command Storage
69. Ordnance Dept
70. 106 Ordnance
71. 2561 (?) Ordnance
72. No designation
73. 656 Q M Bakery
74. 'E' Battalion AA area
75. 250 PRO
76. 453 APO (Post Office)
77. PX (Canteen store)
78. HOQ Co Service Command
79. Q M Reefers (Refrigerated Units)
80. Q M Laundry
81. Salvage Yard
82. Navy Supply
83. Service Communal Quartermaster storage
84. 'K' Co, 24th Inf
85. CWS(?) Signal Depot

But, unlike such sea-borne invasions, most ground fighting in the southern Pacific theaters was in small-scale encounters between patrols or with men guarding perimeters.[65] Their perceptions of environment depended on their mission and any layers of meaning the military presence had already placed on the land. When Salvation Army padre Albert Moore, running a tea canteen on the Kokoda Track in early 1945, pointed out the beauty of the setting sun in the Owen Stanley Ranges to the Australian infantrymen,

> One lad turned away saying, "Mr Moore you look through different eyes to what we do." It was not theirs to see the beauty of it, they only know the blood and sweat and mud of it all . . . unless one lived through those tragic days of '42 with Australians on the Trail, then one could never realize just the reason, why, to many Australian lads, New Guinea is a ghostly experience that will haunt them for the rest of their days.[66]

The military gaze was highly selective when operations depended on it, permitting no interest in the scenic landscape. Surveys for bases concentrated on aspects of terrain useful in operations, either offensively or defensively, as the small slice of the perimeter of the U.S. base on Manus reveals, reflecting its mission as a major naval and air base from March 1944.

For the patrol leader field sketching a path though enemy territory, potential tactics within the terrain were the focus. In these texts of military landscapes, streams were obstacles or fresh water; wetlands were swamps that hindered progress; flora were possible camouflage, canopy, a hideout, food, a barrier to vision or visibility, or a landmark. Local names were recorded. In a land where local guides, if available, had no idea of mileage other than "long way lik lik" (not too far) or "close up" (near), which could mean a hundred yards or four miles, distance was measured in average walking time of a kitted soldier. But, as the dense jungle ensorcelled some, more subtle disorientation crept in:

> in a dripping land of harsh and frightful ranges . . . [t]ime replaces distance and the first became a tiny arc with the man on the spot the only person who could say what it was like there. Maps became largely redundant.[67]

Like all invaders, however, the military tried to put new labels on "otherwise nameless places" to own them.[68] This may have helped disenchant and acculturate the strange environment, but it was dangerous. Given that all extant maps had local place names (or misheard variants) and that the Melanesians knew them as such, commanders decided that indigenous names were to stand. Yet here and there, new names prevailed, at least for the duration. Invariably these allied "cultural features" were new texts on the landscape or apparently unnamed places.[69] The AIF's veterans named the bridges they built in New Guinea after Middle Eastern and European places: Barani, Bagush, and Athens.[70] The King George cricket field of the Europeans at Tulagi, Solomon Islands, soon became Halsey Park to the Americans.

American "cultural features" sprung up rapidly. The U.S. Seabees and army engineers set many records for airfield construction.[71] They also did much to change the environment. Around bases, large-scale clearing occurred—partly to provide a field of fire, to prevent falling branches or fronds from cutting telephone wires, and to rid the area of mosquito-breeding sites (see chapter 3), but also to make bases appear more like a home. Most American bases had the essentials and often had more than those of their allies who, because of limited heavy equipment, tended to fit themselves around and in the jungle rather than obliterate it.[72] The Munda base, which was by no means the largest American base, had facilities for offense, defense, and maintenance of health and morale. In rear areas where men had time on their hands, bases became more elaborate than their mission warranted. By early 1944, with the Japanese on the defensive, U.S. command began emphasizing conservation to reduce costs of shipping and materials, prioritizing the mobility of forward bases. Yet even on bases nearer the front, extras soon began to be justified as morale building. On Manus in late 1944, the malaria units complained that native laborers needed for antimalarial work were being diverted to build a museum, chapel, and clubs.[73]

Such "touches of Americana" inscribed the familiar on island places.[74] The alien tropical landscape became more a lived-in environment. With the exception of a few uninhabited atolls, however, the islands were already peopled. For all the military men, much of what they found in the physical environment had almost uncanny parallels in the social sphere. Just as these exotic newcomers wrought transformations on their surroundings, so too did they among the local people, altering many aspects of their lives.

CHAPTER 2

Peopling the Southern Pacific

> The islands are divided into two large racial groups: on the west are the islands of Melanesia [comprising] Solomons, New Hebrides, New Caledonia and Western Fiji Island. On the east and south are the Polynesian groups of New Zealand, Bora Bora, Tongareva [Penrhyn] and the eastern islands of Fiji. Melanesians are a dark skinned, bushy-haired type with a very primitive civilization while the Polynesians have a lighter skin and, in general, have found the ways of Western civilization more acceptable than their Melanesian neighbors to the west.

For the invaders, another means of coming to terms with their new environment was to find a shared humanity among its peoples. Hollywood ideas about natives rested on a foundation of the newcomers' racial attitudes and limited knowledge. South of the equator, battles were fought in Melanesia, with Polynesia's islands behind the operational area. Melanesia, Polynesia, and Micronesia were names given by outsiders to areas that to them had some kind of racial uniformity. Though there are some common cultural characteristics within these locales, their boundaries are porous and many societies defy these foreign normative labels. For all their imperfections, however, these convenient names have persisted. By coincidence, the geography of conflict was to mirror the invaders' racial geography.

Portmanteau Bigotry

All the Allies, like the Japanese, came from societies where racism was entrenched. Both white Americans and Australians as well as New Zealanders had by the 1920s, if not well before, laws preventing the migration of Asians into their countries. The actions of the Japanese from Pearl Harbor onwards only confirmed the racial stereotypes the Allies held. But racism was not directed solely against Asians. Australia had most of the Aboriginal people on "outback" reserves or working as cheap labor on sheep stations. Unable to marry each other or "white" Australians without government permission, these voteless, "protected" people often had their children removed for "their own good," to be brought up by white people or institutions. Australia had held Papua from Britain since 1905 as a colony and New Guinea as a mandate from the League of Nations from 1920. Protective and paternalistic in Papua, Australia's policies in New Guinea supported the white-run plantation and mining industries' need for cheap indentured labor, though little native land was alienated. Most of the small white population in both dependencies regarded the Melanesians as primitive and of limited potential. In white settler society New Zealand, the state discriminated far less against Maori than was the case with the Aboriginals, but Maori remained on the rural power periphery. New Zealand, as colonial administrator since the late nineteenth century in the Cook Islands, Nuie, and Tokelau Islands, was largely benign. As the mandatory power in Western Samoa from 1920, it faced resistance from the Mau movement until the mid-1930s, when some rapprochement emerged. Native Americans, like Maori and Australian Aboriginals, had suffered huge land losses when the Europeans colonized. In the South Pacific, the American navy had paternalistically governed eastern Samoa since 1900, protecting its lands from alienation and foreign investment. Many white Australians had very little experience of Aborigines, just as many white Americans had of African Americans. Like the New Zealanders, few knew much about their countries' Pacific territories.[1]

Servicemen who had never seen brown and black people before, however, still knew what to call them. To many Australian soldiers, the Papuans and New Guineans were likeable "boongs" or "coons"—terms redolent with pre-existing racist connotations or emphasizing physical markers of race, such as "blacks," "darkies," "fuzzies," and "fuzzy-wuzzies."[2] Few Australians expressed negative opinions of the men's appearance: "The fuzzies are just as they were depicted in some of the books. . . . Small of stature black as ink with bushy fuzzy hair." Some had "marvelous physiques, muscular with large white teeth."[3] More condescendingly, one remarked that the "boongs" were "as a funny as a bagfull of monkeys."[4] The Japanese too commonly used terms—"dojin" and "domin"—to describe Melanesians as "natives" in the most derogatory sense.[5]

In the United States, "Negroes" suffered discrimination in public facilities. Racism took an institutionalized form in the American forces. African Americans were in segregated units and camp areas; most served in the Quartermaster units and Construction Battalions. Similar racism was evident in Americans' underlying wartime assumptions about Pacific "natives" and their selective gaze in their visual record. For publicity, photographers were to record U.S. personnel overcoming difficult conditions: "before and after pictures of construction areas are good stuff, and a background of jungle or curious natives adds to the general interest." As well, pictures of "men showing natives how work should be done" were wanted, and so we see many such instructive representations of American know-how, as well as photographs contrasting modern weapons to spears and arrows, the American medical teams treating the local people, and picturesque scenes of native dwellings.[6] Aimed at maintaining national morale, these representations were fed into magazines such as *Life* and *National Geographic.* These reflected a patronizing tolerance and the assumption that American civilization was vastly superior, no less a colonial mentality than among the administrations of the Pacific islands.[7] This was most marked for western Melanesia: "The population of . . . northwestern Melanesia present[s] no serious problems to an occupying force. . . . In the hinterland primitive natives carry on their customary existence."[8]

Appreciating Melanesians

Both the Allies and the Japanese needed and appreciated Melanesians' help, but they feared the Melanesians could betray them. With few entrenched loyalties, the natives in New Guinea sometimes did; harsh retribution often followed.[9] Nonetheless, the AIF respected those in the Pacific islands regiment for their skills in jungle fighting and as "scouts and guides. They were the navigators, the eyes and ears of our patrols."[10] Since the survival of New Guinea and possibly Australia depended on it, ANGAU's former government officers dragooned thousands of New Guineans into working for the AIF and on plantations for the war effort. Although some fled the horror of war and conscription, most stayed to work for the Allies.[11] In the difficult New Guinea topography, these carriers of supplies and wounded won enduring admiration from the Australian soldiers and public.[12] Americans shared this view:

> the men were very surefooted, but there were times . . . that one of them would lose their footing. Remarkably, that individual's concern was the safety of the litter and my well being. . . . Those men may have been from a simple culture. They certainly didn't live according to our standards, but they were loyal and faithful to us. There was no reason in the world why they should not have deserted. . . . Their pay for the devotion they showed us . . . was simply subsistence of rice, bully beef, hard tack and . . . trade tobacco.[13]

Because Allied forces in New Guinea depended on ANGAU to organize labor, they rarely had extended contact with laborers, a constraint determining their behavior toward native people. The Americans needed Allied support, local labor, and resources because their supply lines were stretched more than seven thousand miles and shipping was scarce. Moreover, except for American Samoa, American forces were in the colonial territory of their allies. Their commanders ordered that the forces treat the natives with respect to keep them "on side."[14]

The Americans valued the Melanesians' ability to work.[15] For all their usefulness as labor, a U.S. captain at Milne Bay, Papua, deemed them

> mainly aboriginal in type. A little work has been done among them by the missionaries, but they are not a class of people with whom one would associate.... They are friendly ... and reasonably intelligent—given their background.[16]

The Japanese said much the same: New Guineans were represented as "obedient, gentle and friendly" but of "low intelligence."[17] They were honest, but primitive and lazy.[18] Americans found the Melanesians—the "Charlies"[19]—could be "good, steady workers," if supervised.[20] But they were "indolent."[21] An American medical man judged Bougainvilleans "the most primitive. . . . They had very low intelligence and a high incidence of malaria, pot belly, and poor teeth."[22] The Utupuans in the eastern Solomon Islands were "friendly" but "lazy and un-industrious and live from day to day."[23] Yet close working relationships between Solomon Islands laborers and American units on Russell Island refined generalizations, but confirmed older colonial representations:

> The Choiseul natives are ... less intelligent and less imaginative.... They will do the assigned tasks well but lack initiative. At the other extreme are those from Malaita, who are exceedingly ingenious and very aggressive ... they bully the natives from the other islands ... so much so that it was never possible to combine the Malaita natives ... with natives from other islands. If such a thing were done there was apt to be trouble, with the Malaita natives passing all of the heavy or dirty work to the Santa Isabel or Choiseul natives.[24]

Few made such nice distinctions. The New Hebrides native "in his savage state is war-like and treacherous. When civilized, he makes a good and sometimes intelligent worker," but they were "all more or less lazy"[25] while their life was "less rich than some of the other islands of the Pacific."[26] Though they regularly characterized Melanesians as a "crummy lot" and "dumb and ugly," most ordinary U.S. ranks got along well with them, and the local people appreciated this.[27]

Throughout western Melanesia, combat personnel rarely had time for prolonged socializing, and the language barrier barred sophisticated exchanges.[28] Moreover, colonial officials in the military in New Guinea and the Solomons controlled labor and often relocated thousands of village people out of the battle zones for protection. Even behind the lines in mid-1943, in Espiritu Santo and Efate, contact was reduced to prevent disease infection from the natives and sustain the labor supply to planters whose copra and coffee fed into the war effort.[29] Some historians see this as colonial policy to prevent the egalitarian Australian soldiers and the open-handed Americans from "spoiling" the natives at a time when hierarchies needed to be stable for the war effort. "Spoiling" was common, but it sometimes backfired, causing some Americans to agree with the colonial administrators.[30]

Few servicemen knew civilian Melanesians as rounded human beings. When they did, it tended to be behind the lines when work was routinized. On the Russells, for example, "American enlisted men who have worked regularly with native crews have developed strong friendships with the natives . . . and treated [them] with more friendship and more laxity than do the white officers of the Solomon Islands Labor Corps."[31] U.S. fisheries expert Wilbert Chapman worked on boats with Solomon Island men and respected their different personalities and abilities.[32] Charles Crary of the American army, waiting for months near the Waria River to go into action, spent his time with the people in villages and hunting. Understanding pidgin English (*tok pisen*), he found his companions kind and intelligent. Two AIF wireless operators at an outpost at the Lakekamu River, Papua, grew to like the English-speaking Peter, who as a carrier had been flogged by ANGAU for desertion. They even wept when they said their goodbyes.[33] By late 1943, their supply lines cut, lonely Japanese in the Murik area of New Guinea formed friendships with the local people and their children, who "brought some joy into their lives," and started a school to occupy their time.[34] None of these interactions occurred under combat. What enabled these relationships was the rare extended contact, not the passing acquaintance of people trading curios and fruit, or weary troops offering cigarettes to the stoic carriers they passed on a jungle pad.[35]

In rear bases, contact was less constrained but officials sometimes discouraged it to rationalize the labor supply, such as in Fiji, where labor was needed for the army, to assist the Americans, and to keep Fiji's cash as well as subsistence economy functioning. Moreover, to avoid incidents, colonial officials placed villages and "notorious" parts of Suva off-limits and sent many young Fijians back to their villages.[36] At the front, the New Zealanders admired the fighting qualities of the Fijians and worked easily in integrated units with them;[37] many Americans who saw the "tall, straight clean-cut" Fijians in the Solomons felt the same and invited them into their "chow" line, although African Americans were not welcome.[38] Yet Admiral A. W. Fitch, the commander of Allied air forces, refused to have respected Fijian Major Ratu Lala Sukuna in his quarters on Espiritu Santo.[39] Fijians at the front, assessing comrades as fighters, thought the African Americans units such as the 93rd were "black bastards"[40] and the Malaitans "stupid little savages."[41] In

Fiji, when Maori with the New Zealanders went into the Suva Everyman's Club, the Americans objected, wanting "whites" only and leasing the entire building to achieve it. As a New Zealander noted, the "'good ole boys' from the South also objected to being in the same company as our Maori troops and obviously considered them as 'Nigrahs.'"[42] For the newcomers, Fiji was a liminal place.

Preferring Polynesians

The Allies found the Polynesians' ways more socially agreeable than the Melanesians'. The Allied gradient of racial and cultural markers coincided with the gradient from rear bases to operational areas. Greater Polynesia was behind the lines, away from combat. Along with the French in their Polynesian territories, officials in the Samoas, Cook Islands, and Tonga did little to keep the military men apart from the people. Attitudes to Polynesian interaction with the African American servicemen, however, were overlaid with concepts of racial hierarchies. The commander of the Samoan defense group, Major General Charles Price, did not want African Americans in his command because of the danger of intimacy between them and the "primitively romantic" Samoan women. Their union with whites had resulted in "a very high class half-caste," Price noted, while white mixture with Chinese produced a "very desirable type," and union between African Americans and "Melanesian [*sic*] . . . produces a very undesirable citizen." To protect the Samoans, Price suggested sending the African Americans to Micronesia, where "they could do no racial harm."[43] After only a day in Samoa, two African American units were redeployed to the Ellice Islands. Others in power agreed with Price's views. Unofficially, the New Zealand administrators of the Cook Islands requested the removal of the nine hundred African Americans from the bases there.[44] American domestic racism was brought to the Pacific; the lighter-skinned the natives were, the higher they rated in intelligence and even humanity. Many Americans thought the Polynesians were racially superior to the Melanesians, with Samoans "perhaps the finest physical specimens of the race . . . intelligent and amiable, love to sing and dance."[45] For New Zealanders, too, the Samoans were "well built and really a fine race" who "spoke fluent English," while the Tongans "appeared quite like our NZ Maori, especially the women, the men appeared to be very fine types."[46] The Americans considered them "hospitable and peace-loving" and "industrious and intelligent," adding that "kindness to women was a distinguishing mark to ancient Tongan society."[47] Cook Islanders were "intelligent and generous," their "girls lovely even by Hollywood standards."[48]

Yet other considerations could compromise this. Some Polynesian Wallisean were found to have a high level of TB, filariasis, leprosy, and dengue fever when the Americans arrived, partly because of the neglect for years by the

Figure 2. In iconic "grass skirt," young Samoa Siva dancer gives substance to Hollywood's elusive South Seas dream, entertaining the marines, Apia, c. 1943 (courtesy of Apia Museum).

French.[49] Many marines there were from the southern United States, and a Yankee marine soon found that he, in being civil to the Walliseans, was labeled a "gook lover."

> The word "gook" alone was a label of derision on anyone with dark skin. The same people who had such a dislike for these dark skinned natives did not mind at all to trade a can of "tinny cow" or "tinny beef" for a little sex. . . . This island had been occupied . . . since May 28, '42 and there were a few babies . . . with white skins. . . . The women . . . were very well covered, unlike the ones we had seen in the Hollywood movies.[50]

Several factors combined to enable the occupiers to become acquainted with the Polynesians. On most bases there were a large number of servicemen relative to the population, they stayed in one place for long periods, several were in remoter parts of the islands on outpost duty, and the local people usually were involved in working for the occupiers. As in the Cook Islands, many spoke some English. Some American Samoans had enough English to make racy remarks to newcomers, such as "push push Malini."[51] Men had time for socializing at kava ceremonies, feasts, and local performances, as well as "smokers" (boxing matches), dances featuring "hula," and movies.[52] Relations with the local people soon became more intimate. Commanders who considered sexual virility a mark of "good soldiers and sailors" turned a blind eye to preserve the sanity of bored men.[53] As one American medical officer commented on Aitutaki, "[t]he native girls were of a fairly high type and I think that helped the morale a great deal."[54] On the Reef Islands, eastern Solomons, three U.S. wireless operators dealing with isolation soon found the "bare-breasted daughters" of these Polynesians made "up on kindness for what they lack[ed] in clothing."[55] Many young Tongan and American Samoan women established relationships with the powerful strangers, believing they were bringing wealth and status to their families.[56] American troops and marines (*malini*) cohabited with *vahines* (women) in local *fales* (houses) they set up or rented.[57] At the time, "[r]omances were many and temporary,"[58] but for married women they often came with social costs, as divorces increased.[59] American medical officers noted, regarding their fight against venereal disease among servicemen in Samoa,

> Professional prostitution is uncommon on the island, but the warm reception rendered US servicemen by civilians and the somewhat promiscuous habits of the Samoans remain a barrier to completely effective control.[60]

Commandant Moyer in American Samoa in mid-1942 predicted that "the inevitable biological consequences will become apparent during the next year."[61]Any arrangements that were more than brief encounters between an American and a Samoan woman were couched as "the custom of 'Samoan marriage' which was popular at that time."[62] Similar arrangements developed in Bora Bora, Aitutaki, Penrhyn (Tongareva), and even on Wallis Island. Yet not all relationships were sexual. Many young men became friends with families whose matrons knew

> how to administer to a lonesome kid, how to talk to him, listen to him, draw him out, show her maternal sympathy, do little sewing jobs for him, laugh and talk with him, fix up his soul so he could go to his barracks in the evening and fall asleep more tranquilly.[63]

Nature's Demographics

The war brought more than two million servicemen to the southern Pacific theaters, effectively doubling the known population of the island world.[64] Transient as it was to be, compressed in the short time frame of four years, this was the greatest influx of male newcomers to the region ever. The Americans were the most ubiquitous, with the AIF concentrated in New Guinea and the smaller force of New Zealanders on Fiji, Tonga, and New Caledonia early in the war and later mainly in the Solomons. The Japanese forces, including Korean and Chinese as well as captive Indians as laborers, were confined to New Guinea and the western Solomons.

While thousands of the Allies died in Melanesia, some left a significant reproductive legacy in Polynesia, adding another layer to the human lineages. Most military fathers were Americans. Figures are not precise, but since colonial administrators and the military were observing, they are reasonably accurate. In Western Samoa, "half-castes from marines" numbered between 800 and 1,600.[65] In American Samoa there were about 1,000.[66] In Tonga there were "numerous American babies."[67] Even though on Penrhyn, "every girl over fourteen years and nearly every married woman had a soldier lover,"[68] overall in the Cook Islands, where about 1,600 men were stationed, such children were not numerous. There were about 50 on Aitutaki.[69] This seems also to have been the case in Fiji, Wallis, and the Gilbert and Ellice Islands. Governor Philip Mitchell in August 1944 sought maintenance for local women pregnant by U.S. men in Fiji, but when he enquired of the Colonial Office regarding the legalities, he found that American servicemen had immunity in non-American courts. The American Congress, however, decided in June 1942 that deductions from the pay of the serviceman for maintenance could be enforced, but the original action had to begin in a Fijian court.[70] Since the Colonial Office's enquiry to the Home Office took an astonishing eleven months to be answered, any paternity proceedings were impossible because the "putative fathers" had left Fiji.[71] In the New Hebrides, neither the military nor the administration seemed particularly concerned about the few children fathered mainly by African Americans.[72] In the Polynesian bases, such as Tonga, the Cooks, and American Samoa, discreet arrangements were made for men to pay to support the children while they were in residence, although in American Samoa occasional written agreements were used as a basis for maintenance.[73] In the Cooks, relatively few women made claims.[74] When they did, the "GIs involved paid up like gentlemen" and set aside $300 for a trust fund for their children.[75]

Some women sought abortion. In Western Samoa, the infant mortality rate in 1943 suddenly shot up by 42 percent.[76] Most children, however, were absorbed into the mother's extended family, the pattern since the first outsiders came to this great ocean world.[77] By 1945, additions to the gene pool had a larger effect in American Samoa. Some chiefs sought to redefine Samoan identity. They argued that the prewar blood quantum of three-quarters Samoan blood as a prerequisite for land and title holding be reduced to one half:

> The Armed forces left here in Samoa so many children without fathers. No effort has been taken to provide support from the fathers of those children. The mother is able enough to support such a child. . . . Is this father an innocent

> man, or a criminal? No, this father was a soldier fighting for the good cause of freedom, but through nature, the child was given birth. Samoa will never, in time to come, be pure Samoan.[78]

The military forbade marriages of servicemen with island women "to discourage romances from going too far."[79] The logic of the military and racial categorization did not follow the contours of the human heart. Ships and men eventually sailed away from Bora Bora and all the island bases:

> Goodbyes are always difficult and we kept them short. Many natives were there lining both sides of the Landing.... Several of the native girls clutching infants, were weeping piteously. Nobody felt like talking.[80]

"Feelings of affiliation"

In Melanesia the search for affiliation[81] and women was more difficult. Except for organized social events and legal brothels in Noumea, men wanting female company had to make their own contacts. Carrying Hollywood images of Dorothy Lamour in a sarong or Princess Luana in a grass skirt, servicemen registered their disenchantment when confronted with the reality.[82] Nowhere was this greater than in western Melanesia, as their drawings show. Even meeting native women was challenging. Relocated populations in combat zones or refugees were more interested in survival than conviviality. Except in a few societies, sex-starved soldiers ran the risk of confronting the woman's machete-wielding clansmen. Aided by anthropologist F. Williams, Allied guidebooks, such as *You and the Native*, and ANGAU instructed troops to leave women, possessions, and gardens alone because of fear of alienating communities needed as allies.[83] In Wau, for example, one AIF man "made it with a native girl" and was packed off to Australia.[84] In the Solomons, the U.S. Navy declared villages on Florida off-limits when villagers complained about sailors "worrying" the women.[85] African Americans in the Seabees and Quartermaster's Corps sought women near Sattelberg and Wareo, New Guinea, in mid-1944, but the village leaders "told them to get out."[86] In villages around Port Moresby, the women were "afraid of them," and local men complained.[87] Some Americans, mainly African Americans, propositioned local women in the New Hebrides and there were a few reported cases of rape and bestiality.[88] Tales circulated that African Americans were hanged for rape—they certainly were for raping white military nurses, with one sentenced to life imprisonment for raping a civilian in Dutch New Guinea. African Americans had such a bad reputation for pestering Australian nurses near Port Moresby and Buna hospitals that pickets were posted, while at Torokina, a fifteen-foot fence was erected around their quarters.[89] Near the hospital at Rouna Pass in Papua, John Laffin recalled, "I saw two negro soldiers shot dead by the side of this road in 1943, executed on the spot by military policemen for raping an American nurse."[90] Annoying nurses in New Guinea was not confined to African Americans, as "white troops" sometimes prowled around their quarters.[91] Considerably more African Americans than whites were charged with rape and related offenses in New Caledonia, but this probably says more about white commanders' racist attitudes than the criminality of African Americans, who made up only 10 percent of the American forces.[92] Yet at the legal brothel, Madame Benitier's Pink House, U.S. commanders refused African Americans access. They sought French support for a separate establishment with Kanak women for the African Americans, but the French refused, advising the Americans to import "Negresses" from their homeland.

Most of the Allies—of European extraction—found Melanesian women generally unattractive; the women in Santo's Suranda brothel, as in Noumea's, were

Figure 3. As the Americans saw the ladies of Melanesia (RG 313-58-3283, NARA SB).

Figure 4. New Zealand soldiers consider "the lure of the islands" and the New Caledonian reality (AAACF 898, NCWA 280, Archives New Zealand).

mainly from Marseilles or Indochina.[93] As an Australian medical officer in New Guinea noted, "the 'Mary' of these parts is not the dark beauty of a tropical isle that 'Smiths Weekly' sketches would lead one to believe."[94] Another was more direct: "Saw a few boong 'Marys' today. All were smoking pipes or newspaper cigarettes and gabbling like mad."[95] More disparagingly, one commented, "how anyone can have relations with them, talk about stink."[96] Their betel-nut red or black-stained teeth did little to add to their appeal.[97] The New Zealanders' comment that a young woman on Pinipel, near Nissan Island, "was downright handsome for a Solomon Islander" reveals more about their aesthetics than it does of "Little Nell," as they called her.[98] Japanese troops too tended to leave the local women alone to avoid conflicts.[99] The Japanese at Rabaul had their own "comfort women," many forced into sexual slavery from China and Korea.[100] Isolation could alter racial preference, however. When the war was going their way, the Japanese received offers of

Memo From Australian and American Troops on Melanesian Stations

FIGURE ON LEFT: Hullo! I'm the Islands Girl as the writers and illustrators depict her. Who are you?

DITTO ON RIGHT: Oh, I'm the Islands Girl as she is!

Figure 5. Allied views of the New Guinea woman (*Pacific Islands Monthly*, Oct. 1942, 14).

women from New Britain communities, although "[s]ex with them was somehow strange. But when you are away from Japan for so long, even black women were women."[101] This was not a singular opinion. In the Milne Bay District, particularly in the Trobriand Islands, where brown-skinned girls have considerable premarriage freedom, some of the seven thousand American and RAAF servicemen based there in mid-1943 paid them for sexual services.[102]

In this theater, however, servicemen most sorely missed the company of their own women. The few white women there, American navy nurses, as officers could only fraternize with American male officers, a fact deeply resented by the ordinary ranks. In such rigidly hierarchical forces, African Americans could never date these white women.[103] Australians, who were more egalitarian in their armed forces, were less exclusive and their "sisters" (nurses) much closer to the front in New Guinea than their American counterparts.[104] Unlike Americans, they were not regularly quartered inside barbed-wire enclosures to protect them from their countrymen.[105] Yet when eight New Zealand nurses came to Guadalcanal amid the Americans in early 1944, a New Zealand soldier remarked, "God help them . . . there is to be a body guard of 14 men for them. They need it."[106]

Bringing Home to Them

Missing their women and all they represented, the men measured time in two ways: first, in months since they had last seen a white woman.[107] Their silence about local women confirms that these did not rate highly as potential sexual or romantic partners. Working at Manus Island in the RAAF, Arthur Gately noted that "two American Red Cross girls drove up in a jeep. . . . I was standing nearby; the closest I have been to a woman near on seventeen months. Their voices sounded as smooth as silk."[108] For one New Zealander his tour in Melanesia meant,

> Prickle heat twice, rheumatics for 3 months, soars [*sic*] on legs, one tooth out, two filled, Doubies [itch] once (six weeks) but what has it done to us physically and mentally that can only be told when once we have been home? 18 months today since I saw a white woman, one year & one week today since I last talk[ed] to an English speaking woman.[109]

Another asked sardonically in a letter from the front, "What are these women they talk about? Are there really beings other than men?"[110] Australian A. Long, as he was admitted to a hospital, noted, "Nursing sisters here are the first white women I have seen for over 6 months but I would sooner see Thel [his wife] than anyone else."[111] Married for thirteen years, he constantly looked for her letters.

The men's other marker of time's passage was letters received and sent.[112] "Someday, when this war is over, maybe some person will ask what was the mainstay of the soldiers in the tropics. The answer from one and all of us, would be 'letters.'"[113] American poet Karl Shapiro knew their power:

> war stands aside for an hour and looks at our
> Faces of total absorption that seem to have lost their places.
> Demobilised for a moment, a world is made human,
> Returns to a time that is neither the present or then.[114]

Letters reveal that men in combat lived between two social times and landscapes—where they were fighting their war and where they came from. The alchemy of memory transformed vicarious experience conveyed in letters into a living, imagined landscape of the domestic and the familiar. Once the first year of the Pacific

War passed, the Japanese there had very few letters in an alien environment. Yet their thoughts often turned homewards. One pilot sailing from Rabaul composed a still-popular ballad, expressing his longing for the "mountains and rivers of home," his affection for an island girl, along with readiness to die in battle.[115] Tamura Yoshikazu at Wewak, New Guinea, in March 1943 confided to his diary, "The Empress' birthday has passed and canola flowers should be flowering at home.

Figure 6. Signpost, U.S. camp, New Caledonia, 1944 (Album, Elmer J. Williams, 1Num 12 y, Collection, Archives of New Caledonia)

I have not received any letters since I left home and that makes me feel very sad." At Madang in mid-June 1943, the Japanese army was out of food when two "sea trucks" entered the harbor. The men rejoiced that they would have more food and "we'll be able to send some mail." But when American planes bombed the vessels, "the soldiers . . . watching screamed loudly and burst into tears."[116] With little hope of their letters getting out and no consolation from home communications, isolated pockets of Japanese had only diaries as confidants, the society of suffering comrades, and the hope that if death found them, they would die bravely for their emperor.[117]

About 75 percent of Americans wrote one or more letters a day.[118] Away from combat, letters from those in garrison units were expansive; their discourse was more touristic, long on detail of the food they ate, the movies they saw, the places they were stationed, and the activities they found to occupy them, such as shell collecting. Many sent snapshots of their great overseas adventure, following the Kodak culture.[119] In this capturing of images of place, photographs also staked out their possession, albeit temporary, of their surroundings.[120] Behind the lines in New Caledonia, Elmer Williams' four hundred photographs attested to this. His picture of the signposts near his camp indicates that imagined home places loomed large.[121] These men lived between two landscapes—their home place and "their" island; the familiar and the foreign.

For men at the battlefront, however, fear soon swamped any illusion of adventure tourism. They used the domestic to make both the foreign and the fear bearable. James Donahue, on Guadalcanal in November 1942, noted,

> Today we are happy. We received mail . . . it was too dark to read them. I was afraid I would get knocked off before morning and then not read the letters. I saw it happen before. . . . Gee, Cassie is swell.[122]

When R. Catteley wrote from the horrors of the Kokoda Track in 1942 he briefly described the country and the incessant rain but reminded his mother to "keep the Sydney and other news up to me here . . . while I'm badly situated."[123] Also in the Owen Stanley Ranges under mortar fire, A. Long noted in his diary, "Received 2 letters . . . I hope Albert is quite well again and Dad has got over his fall."[124] Farm boys commented on the cycle of the agricultural year at home—tree pruning, fruit picking, potato planting, sheep shearing, the lambing season, as well as the price of eggs and land.[125] W. Olsen asked his girl, "Are the roses still in bloom Joey?" and, after wondering why the Japanese would want such an awful place as New Guinea, he told her of how they would spend a night out in Sydney: "The night skies would be glowing with a million tiny specks of life. They won't explode into death, those heavens . . . only peace and you beside me, Joey." He wrote of plans for building a home.[126] A. P. Pirie of the AIF told his eighteen-year-old sweetheart, Melva, "We can't stop thinking of home. . . . Your snaps are almost worn out as I have looked at them so often." To his mother: "Don't grow rusty in your cooking Mum as I'll be looking forward to an extra special meal one of these days." Recuperating from fighting and struggling to keep sane, he admitted to Melva, "Having a bit of trouble with my nerves . . . never could have survived New Guinea without you."[127] To his sister, H. Dunkley confided, "It's good to get mail in this hell hole, where either nothing happens or too bloody much. No sweet moderation about this game at all."[128]

Some things were too awful to be told. Jack Browne, on patrol in the Owen Stanleys, noted in his tiny diary in September 1942,

> Will be lucky to get out of this . . . tracks terrible, nothing but mud. Mountains high and hard to climb . . . artillery opening up enemy quiet. Received a letter from Sally. God bless her—if she only knew what a man is going through. Raining now. Now we have them [Japanese].[129]

Traumatized by months and even years of battle, some began to find that the longed-for letters reflected an increasingly unreal world going about its pleasures: "Sort of makes me feel apprehensive at the thought of going back to this strange civilization. . . . So do me a favour, Darling? Don't mention dances in your letters."[130] Any hint of domestic betrayal hit men hard. When AIF men read of industrial action delaying their supplies by the "wharfies" (longshoremen) at home, they reacted bitterly to an Australia that seemed uncaring. But more dreaded and demoralizing was no mail and the "Dear John" letter.[131]

Recreating the familiar was another way men coped with war in strange places. The U.S. command understood that morale in the Pacific islands was the lowest of any theater,[132] and since good morale meant less likelihood of neuroses, they provided comforts. Entertainers visiting Allied bases included movie stars and singers, such as Carole Landis, Frances Langford, and Patty Thomas, who brought a touch of feminine glamor to the men, and comedians like Jack Benny and Bob Hope, who could make them laugh.[133] Families sent their own care packages of local papers and magazines to sons, brothers, and lovers.[134] His girlfriend sent a "weird nightgown" with his high school colors to nineteen-year-old marine Lee Edwards from Denton, Texas, who, as he did at home, found a pet kitten to care for.[135]

Men also recreated the feasts of family such as Thanksgiving and Christmas, bringing the symbols of faraway places into the new environment.[136] Even near battle, they trimmed their Christmas "trees" and often decorated their tents.[137] It was not possible to escape into the peace of the season and memories of home for long, however. "Santa Claus" came around one camp on Guadalcanal in a jeep

Figure 7. Private Lee Edwards in nightgown sent by his girlfriend, putting cat out before retiring at Pavuvu, Russell Islands, February 1945 (EX. 127-GW 1149-111575, NARA).

with a band of carolers, with someone on the end of a rope dressed as "Tojo," but it cheered the men.[138] Church services brought comfort to many:

> The service was brief and ended with the sweet melody of . . . "Silent Night." As we stood together and the cadences of the voices of the small group mixed with the sound of the rain on the canvas above us, there was a moment of sadness of separation from loved ones at home.[139]

Perhaps to save the men from thinking too deeply, ribald humor typical of young and often battle-weary men came to the rescue. The wry Australians gathered at their mess in the heat for an unimpressive Christmas meal of meat and old potatoes, and when the YMCA leaders asked "what carol they would like, someone yelled out 'Carol Landis'!"[140]

Figure 8. Carole Landis, Jack Benny, Martha Tilton, and Larry Adler visit the only "drugstore" on Green Island, August 1944 (EX. 80-G-247191, NARA).

The Australians and New Zealanders admired American logistics on such comforts, including magazines, Coca-Cola, beer, ice cream, and the service radio Mosquito network.[141] Movies were a big part of entertainment that also brought something of home to the Pacific bases, whether of places known to the Americans or of the remembered happy experiences familiar to the Australians and New Zealanders who had watched the Hollywood "flicks" with their families or girlfriends.[142] The last thing the men wanted to see were war films, while "sob stories" or tragic romances rated low because they made them think too much about what could go awry in relationships. Rather, they favored cartoons, comedy, light romance, and musicals.[143]

When South Seas genre films appeared on the screens, however, "hoots and jeers" echoed across the tropical night.[144] In July 1944 on Nissan Island, off Bougainville, the Seabees viewed "White Savage," starring Maria Montez as Princess Talia, set in a "forbidden island paradise."[145] Robert Conner wrote sardonically to his wife,

> it gave me a most vivid description of life in a South Seas Island. It must really be nice to be on one of them with all those beautiful princesses and most appetizing fruits. Some day we must take a cruise out in that vicinity.[146]

Another film, "White Cargo," set in the generic tropics and starring Hedy Lamarr as the siren Tondelayo, did the rounds of the bases.[147] A New Zealander on Guadalcanal found a mirror for his anxieties, as it

> shows how a man will go wrong, will rot in the tropics and how the black natives look white as time goes on. If you tried to explain what the tropics do to you . . . well others would laugh but White Cargo shows what happens and how.[148]

The soft Polynesian South Seas were not quite the paradise of Hollywood fantasy, but few came away thinking its islands or people inhospitable or uncivil. For those who experienced Melanesia's humid heat, rain, and jungles, had seen comrades blown to pieces, or had suffered its endemic diseases, the tropics were so potent an environment that men even feared the dissolution of their identity. For all that, once the Japanese ceased to be a threatening element of that environment, the Allied soldiers' perceptions began to shift to an aesthetic appreciation of landscape. On 10 August 1945, hearing that the Japanese Imperial Army was about to surrender, the AIF war diarist in Wewak recorded, "Next morning, the mountains and jungle slopes suddenly became scenery and spring was in the air."[149]

Hollywood had created in the minds of most Allied troops an imagined but bifurcated South Seas, both paradisiacal and scandalous. Encounter with the environment replaced the dream, with the tangible realities of geography, climate, and native people; for some, in the heart of the Melanesian jungle, the menace of the enemy, sickness, and discomfort were infinitely more compelling than its supposedly "uncivilized" inhabitants. Yet for the Allies, with movies screened at bases almost every night, Hollywood also contributed to conjuring the landscapes of home and the familiar amid the ubiquity of the alien. When opportunity allowed, men went further than simply viewing remembered places and tried in their new environment to emplace the signs of home—an ordered base habitat with clubs and theaters, celebrations of the feasts of family, and the invocation of old familiar names. All warriors need something to fight for and something to go back to. So, even on the battlefield, the Allies maintained the precious link with their own domestic environments in the States, Australia, or New Zealand through correspondence with loved ones, transcending distance to create, even if fleetingly, a fusion of times and places, past and present. After almost two years of battle, the Japanese found their enemies were strangling their vital connection with home. Increasingly disarmed, both mentally and materially, the Japanese Imperial Army faced an intransigent environment, which was to kill more of them than their enemies' guns.

CHAPTER 3

Diseased Environments

Germs are as dangerous as bullets.

For more than a century to about 1920, most of Oceania had suffered depopulation as a consequence of introduced continental diseases.[1] Ironically, this took indigenous population pressure off land and coastal maritime resources, but in some areas Europeans, their animals, and crops soon filled some of the vacated niches. Western Melanesia, however, though vulnerable to introduced disease, had remained a bulwark against European settlement because the people had their own stealthy allies: endemic diseases that were not readily susceptible to Western medicine. European settlers were rarely more than 7,300 amid more than 1.5 million Melanesians.[2] Here, from New Guinea to the Solomons, the Japanese and the Allies fought major battles.

Most who went to war were the fittest of their generation, but the Allies were fitter. The Japanese came either from units in China and Southeast Asia in 1942 or, from 1943, from Japan. The former consisted of healthy specimens, but the army, on a poorer diet than the navy, suffered from low thiamin intake. The latter consisted of many conscripts and former rejects, some with tuberculosis.[3] Bullets, bayonets, and bombs would reap a harvest of dead and wounded, but bacteria, viruses, and parasites endemic in the environment were far more successful in finding human targets.

When the armies came to the tropical Pacific, they tried to control disease medically through drugs and by manipulating the ecology, including the human population, to reduce the habitat for disease carriers. It was never a fixed ecology, for the presence of tens of thousands of troops drastically altered it and created the potential for disease carriers to flourish more than ever before.

Host and Habitat

To the invaders, the southern Pacific environment and peoples were alive with infections, as the U.S. Standard Operating Procedure warned:

> The target for the operation in an area where flea, louse and parasite infested native population . . . is a seed-bed of disease. Fly-borne and water-borne intestinal diseases are likely to be the most immediate disease hazards. Native food is contaminated. . . . Dengue fever and mite-borne typhus are potential dangers.[4]

As much as the threats of a strange, primitive environment, this representation of the natives as a "seed-bed of disease" remained a dominant trope in American medical thinking.

Not all diseases were deadly, but all were debilitating. Insect vectors, primarily mosquitoes, spread the most dangerous from human hosts. Mosquitoes, established in several habitats, required water for their larval form to develop. There was rarely a water shortage in the larger islands, but most species thrived best in the wet season from about November to May.[5] All American bases were in areas where annual rainfall exceeded 100 inches, with a relative humidity of 80 percent and, for most, an average temperature range of about 70° to 90° F, conducive to mosquito breeding.[6] Stagnant and sluggish waterways were ideal sites for many, while others deposited their larvae in small containers such as coconut shells and plant axils. Geology, soils, and the topography influenced mosquito breeding and could provide advantages. Coral atolls and coralline foundation to light soils, such as Emirau and Stirling Islands, drain rapidly, unlike heavier clayey soils. Exposure to breezes often reduced mosquito numbers. Cyclonic winds and rain sluiced waterways and lessened larval populations.[7] But conflicting invaders could rarely locate their base and battle sites to maximize such advantages of climate or terrain.

Mosquitoes and Malaria

Australian entomologist and physician Colonel Neil Hamilton Fairley condensed the bitter truth about malaria: "From remotest times war and malaria have been loyal allies."[8] In the Pacific, malaria "caused more than five times as many casualties as did combat."[9] It was endemic west and north of Buxton's line—170 degrees east longitude and 20 degrees south latitude, including New Guinea, the Solomon Islands, and New Hebrides.[10] It takes four forms, which reflect the effects of specific parasites in the blood: *Plasmodium falciparum*, *P. vivax*, *P. malariae*, and

P. ovale. The last two were medically insignificant, unlike the vivax type (formerly called benign tertian malaria, as the common pattern was recurring fevers in a three-day cycle). In non-immunes, vivax malaria causes intermittent high fevers alternating with chills, profuse sweating, bad headaches, often with abdominal pain and respiratory problems, and extreme weakness. It destroys red blood cells and, even if treated, usually reoccurs. Untreated, falciparum malaria (formerly called malignant tertian) is more severe and often fatal. Female mosquitoes of the genus *Anopheles* transmit the *Plasmodium* parasites from the infected host to an uninfected one. Within the vector mosquito, the sexual stage of the parasite occurs.

Malaria was an enormous challenge because it and its mosquito vectors in the Pacific had been poorly studied. Before the war, for example, in the Solomon Islands researchers had identified only thirty species of mosquitoes; by the end of the war, U.S. entomologists had identified seventy species on Guadalcanal alone.[11]

Combatants were ill-prepared for malaria. In the early campaigns not only were equipment and trained personnel lacking, but also commanders did not realize malaria's dangers. One on Efate, New Hebrides, when instructed on malaria discipline by the first malaria units, snapped, "We are out here to fight troops, and to hell with mosquitoes."[12] The Americans revised their thinking when rates in April 1942 reached over 2,600 per 1,000 per annum,[13] with a similar epidemic pattern on Guadalcanal in November, a few months after the United States established a beachhead there.[14]

The Australians and the Japanese fared no better. After the Japanese failed to reach Port Moresby at the battle of the Coral Sea (April–May 1942), they began a two-pronged assault at Buna-Gona on the north coast of Papua and at Milne Bay in the east. The Australians established a base at Milne Bay in June but the north coast was undefended. On 21 July 1942 the Japanese from Rabaul came ashore at Buna and Gona. Of Major General Horii's South Seas Force of 13,500, about 3,000 began the initial push south in late August to cross the Owen Stanley Range on the Kokoda Trail, an indeterminate "native pad," in mountainous, wet terrain.[15] Fed on polished rice, within five weeks of their landing half were suffering from beriberi. An advance Australian force went north from Port Moresby to defend Kokoda, only to be forced back. Reinforced, the Australians retook Kokoda in November and advanced north.

A simple environmental chance contributed to the AIF's victory. Port Moresby, in the rain shadow, was relatively dry midyear and malaria less common; moreover *Anopheles punctulatus* did not breed in the high altitudes of the Owen Stanley mountains south of Kokoda, so no malaria suppressants were issued and few cases occurred. Coastal Buna and Gona were in swampy plains where malaria was hyper-endemic. Already infected, the Japanese, with lax malaria discipline, soon succumbed on the coast and in the mountains. In combination with U.S. forces, the AIF won the battle of Buna-Gona, but the Americans, with little malaria discipline, also suffered. The malaria- and beriberi-ridden Japanese South Seas Force was in disarray, dying by the hundreds. When the AIF had pursued the Japanese to Buna, its malaria rates climbed. By early 1943, the 7th Australian Division had suffered 2,500 killed in action, 2,500 wounded, and 6,500 sick, 6,000 with malaria. Other AIF units meanwhile had arrived down the coast at Milne Bay to forestall the Japanese in late August and repelled them by early September. Again, malaria control was minimal. Cases peaked at 1,000 a week in December 1942, with a rate of 4,200 per 1,000 per annum and a third of the AIF having been treated for the disease.[16]

This alarmed Allied command. AIF commander General Sir Thomas Blamey, aware of the worsening situation, supported sending a delegation including Colonel Fairley to Washington and London in September 1942 to seek supplies of mosquito netting and the insecticide pyrethrum, scarce because of the European war. It also sought synthetic antimalarials—atebrin[17] (Atabrine) and plasmoquine—since the quinine source in Java had fallen to the Japanese.[18]

Elsewhere, there were fears that malaria was spreading. Australia north of 20 degrees south latitude had malaria foci, though the scattered nature of settlement limited its severity. Refugees from east New Guinea had created a pool of infection in Cairns, Queensland, where the vector *Anopheles farauti* was present. Concentrations of Australian troops training there precipitated an epidemic in June 1942. The military removed them to *Anopheles*-free Atherton Tableland and concentrated on eliminating mosquitoes from Cairns, where troops embarked for the north. Infected troops returning from New Guinea to Australia subsequently were repatriated to areas beyond the *Anopheles* zone.[19]

Such epidemics interested the Americans because of the toll the disease was taking on their forces.[20] In the first eighteen months of the campaign, led by Fairley, the Australians cooperated with the Americans headed by Dr. James A. Shannon in America and by Lt. Fred Bang in New Guinea, researching malaria's epidemiology and the optimum dosage of the malarial suppressant atebrin, which had become standard for the Australian forces in December 1942. By May 1943 Fairley's work had convinced the AIF generals, and malaria discipline became part of routine orders, although the most effective dosage was still uncertain. Fairley headed an army laboratory in Cairns in mid-1943 using AIF volunteers for malaria research.[21] About the same time, the United States malaria field control organization became fully operational. In the Southwest Pacific command, divided medical authorities hindered effectiveness, whereas in the South Pacific the joint services' malarial organization under one commander performed better[22] (see Map 1). Similar units were developed in the Australian forces in May 1942.[23]

Manipulating Environments

Military transformation of the environment created an initial population explosion of mosquitoes. Bomb craters, borrow pits, trenches, miles of ruts made by vehicles, and streams blocked by logging operations provided perfect breeding conditions for mosquitoes, especially the common vector *Anopheles farauti*, while the high human numbers supplied an enormous source of blood meals. An entomologist in the New Hebrides calculated that 90 percent of all breeding came from military activity.[24] In New Guinea, clearing of vegetation for installations expanded the habitat for the common vector *Anopheles punctulatis*, which favors sunlit breeding areas,[25] yet on Guadalcanal it thrived in conditions "almost the reverse of those found in New Guinea."[26]

Malaria units manipulated the environment to control mosquito-borne disease. Where possible, they located camps far away from breeding sites, which in operational conditions was problematic. The pivotal strategy was to eliminate the breeding habitat. Engineers devised drainage systems and filled in swamps. Dynamite and Bangalore torpedoes unblocked waterways. Streams were dammed and then released to flush out stagnant, larval waters; flumes were installed to sluice out coastal backwaters with constant tidal flow. Units cleaned weeds from sluggish water and applied larvicides such as diesel and insecticides such as Paris green (arsenic and copper compound). To reduce larvae, the military introduced minnows of *Gambusia affinis*, native to Central America, with little thought of effects on native species.[27] The scale required in New Guinea was prohibitive, and often the native fish ate them. One scientist, however, believed that these were far less harmful to aquatic life than oil and insecticides, but few looked beyond military necessity.[28]

Education reinforced military discipline. To persuade men to use their mosquito nets, keep their skin clothed, and apply repellent, units campaigned with lectures and films, such as *Winged Scourge*. They displayed posters that caricatured the Japanese as vile mosquitoes, simultaneously dehumanizing them as mere insects while demonizing the mosquito enemy.[29] Around camps, entomological surveys mapped and targeted areas of high larval population. To control "man-made malaria," sanitation and malarial units policed the trashing of water-holding receptacles, filled holes, and disc-harrowed miles of vehicle ruts around camps, ammunition dumps, and tank farms.[30]

As well as the remaking of the external environment, the men's internal chemistry changed with the taking of malaria suppressants. Many believed stories of atebrin's debilitating effect on sexual potency; others feared the yellowing of their skin from the dye indicated liver damage, though neither belief was correct. At first many pretended to swallow the dose or otherwise avoided it. In the wake of epidemics, officers supervised the dosing of men, which improved their health.[31]

Malaria and the Native Body

To the Americans, the twin strategy of controlling mosquitoes by environmental and insecticide interventions and suppressing the parasite by drugs was not the total solution, however. In the New Hebrides, the Solomons, and New Guinea, "natives are . . . to be feared as a seedbed of malaria."[32] Before the Guadalcanal landing in August 1942, the American command realized this, yet they judged the "gravity of the tactical situation required all available troops on the firing line." So with British help, they recruited Melanesians, bringing their infected bodies into the camps.[33] For more than six months, Guadalcanal demonstrated the usual battlefield conditions of

> troop mobility and dispersion necessarily based on tactics and not on sanitary conditions; a great deal of vital nocturnal activity; difficult logistics . . . enemy action . . . and combat tension when the chief concern is not malaria control but immediate life and death.[34]

In New Guinea this remained so for much of the war at the front as the AIF pushed north against the Japanese. Native laborers simply could not be segregated, because they were taking supplies to the front and carrying out the wounded, in tandem with troops.[35] Natives also served alongside the Australians and the Americans as guides, soldiers, intelligence agents, and coast watchers.[36]

Once the AIF secured an area, malarial discipline became more regularized at bases. But ANGAU, from prewar experience, treated only acute cases of malaria among laborers and refused to dole out suppressants for fear they would reduce the natives' semi-immunity once dosing ceased. They did not dose villagers because children could fail to develop this semi-immunity.[37] ANGAU was less concerned about the "seedbed" of the native body, depicting it more as a "reservoir" they could control and segregate. By 1945, routine orders stated, "Patrols should not camp in native villages as the primitive native sanitary arrangements will probably endanger the health of the troops."[38]

In the South Pacific command by mid-1943, with the Japanese no longer on Guadalcanal, the U.S. Malaria Control Units attempted to ameliorate the problem of infected Labor Corps men in proximity to their troops by administering atebrin to them. When surveys showed high levels of infection in November 1943, plans were also made for massive therapy of villagers near camps.[39] Villagers, used to the successful injections to heal yaws before the war, willingly submitted to American blood tests.[40] As in New Guinea, they had greater parasitemia rates, reflecting the higher incidence in infants and children than adults and probable selectivity in hiring fit young men as laborers.[41]

Because so little was certain about atebrin dosages to effectively suppress malaria, the Americans were underdosing their men as well as the natives. Until early 1943 medical officers dosed at from 0.4 grams to 0.7 grams at various intervals in a week. The commoner dosage of 0.4 grams gave only partial protection. Once the dose increased to 0.6 grams in January 1944 the malarial rate dropped dramatically. A few months later, the AIF enforced a 0.7 dosage in New Guinea for troops.[42] Separation, suppressants for laborers, and insecticide spraying of huts did not fully safeguard troops. Moreover, separation was difficult because the U.S. service command wanted native labor near to save on transportation, the Malaria Control Units wanted them at a safe distance, and often the colonial authorities did not want them beyond their oversight. In Guadalcanal four labor camps were within one mile of forty thousand U.S. troops, and it was thought that *Anopheles* might fly that far.[43] Although orders were given to remove these camps in January 1944, flooding and costly road construction delayed the removal until August. Consequently, for almost two years after the Americans landed in August 1942, the proximity of the native labor from at least December 1942 meant the "seedbed"

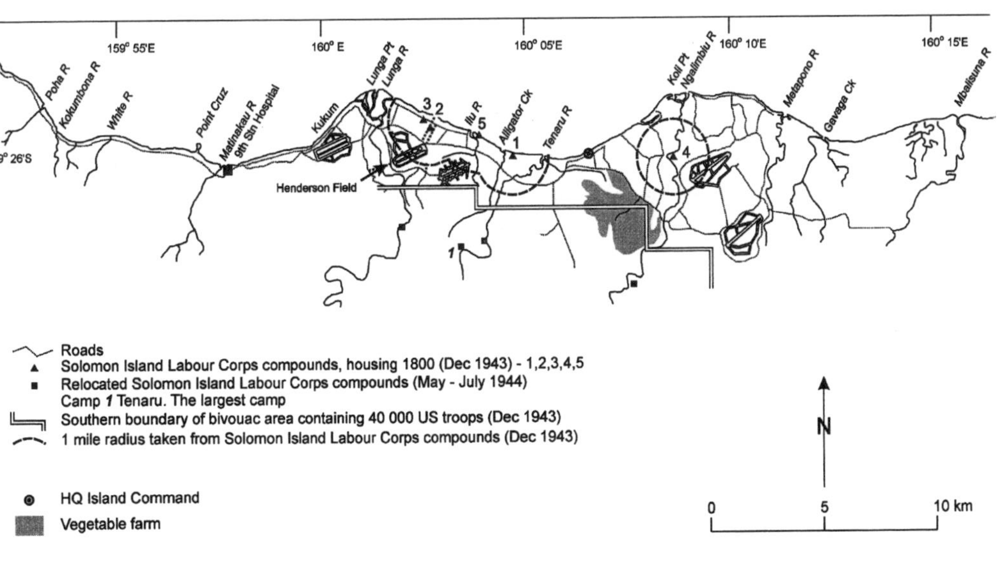

Map 7. North Guadalcanal SILC compounds relative to troop bivouac area, 1943 (based on maps in RG 313-58-3441 and RGF 313-58-3401, NARA SB).

was ever present, though here and elsewhere laborers were confined to their own camps at night, from 1700 to 0700 hours.[44]

In the New Hebrides, the Malaria Control Unit in September 1942 had been alarmed that Melanesians were scattered among various military units that had landed on Santo Espiritu in May, the beginning of the dry season, predicting that when the rains came, "these heavily infected natives will produce a malaria rate of alarming proportions."[45] By mid-December, laborers had been consolidated into three camps, where they were supervised, checked for malaria, and put on atebrin. There was no epidemic, as occurred initially on Efate and Guadalcanal. By early 1943 this regime also applied to nearby plantations, where Melanesians and Tonkinese laborers were heavily infected. A year later, native villagers in troop training areas were included, each receiving 0.6 grams a week of atebrin. Among the hundreds treated, there was a noticeable decrease in the virulent *Plasmodium falciparum.*[46]

In the Efate base, a year after the major epidemic, the labor camp was removed from troops at Riserville, where the staff administered suppressants and sprayed with insecticides.[47] At the New Hebrides bases by 1944, the command banned Melanesians and Tonkinese from the movies because they were malaria "seedbeds."[48] So great was the risk to personnel that the legendary labor supervisor Major George Riser recommended that Sergeant Edward F. Power be awarded the Legion of Merit "for his skill and patience in his handling and care of the natives, endangering his own health by living right in camp with the natives."[49]

By mid-1943 the Malaria Control Organization had the ear of U.S. command. Orders were explicit:

> In every base consider the question of proximity to mosquito-breeding area. One mile is the minimum distance which is reasonably safe, two miles is preferable. Experience has shown that the same holds true for native villages in the South Pacific, as these are prolific sources of infection. If the site of a native village is the only one suitable for the base, the village should be moved.[50]

What the Allies could not avoid near the front line was the close proximity of seeded natives, Japanese, prisoners, and their own infected troops. As the Solomons campaigns moved west to the Russell Islands and Munda in 1943, malaria infection rates began to decline. On the east New Guinea islands, improved malaria control and medication plus the absence, removal, or containment of native populations near camps meant the rate of malaria infection among Americans was far lower than initially on Guadalcanal.[51] For example, the British supervised the labor corps camps on the Roviana lagoon islet of Hombu Hombu, off shore from the Munda base.[52] Laborers were ferried away from Munda for the

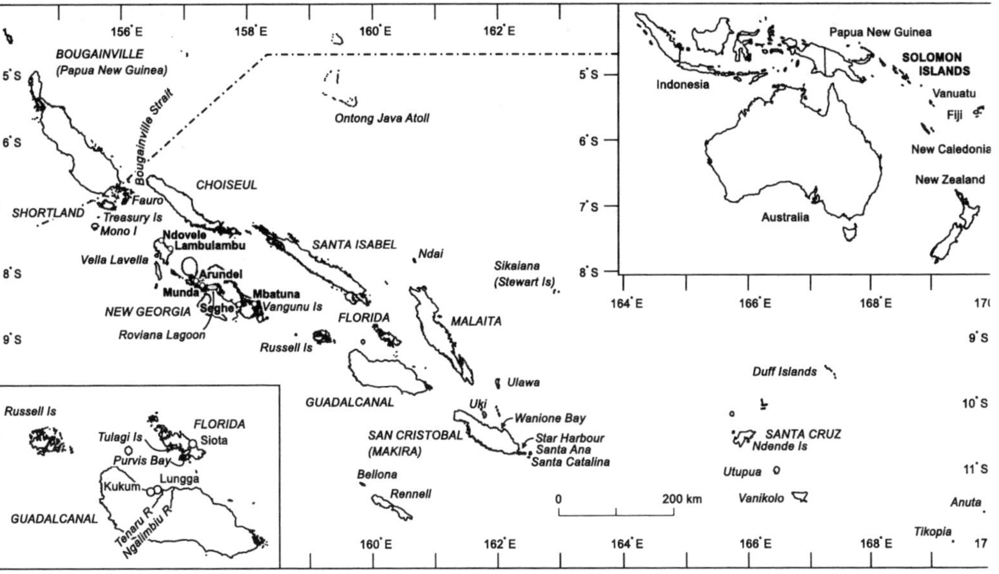

Map 8. Solomon Islands.

night.[53] The entire population of Emirau, New Guinea, was removed before the Americans occupied it.[54] Prior to their occupation of Nissan, the Americans required ANGAU to relocate twelve hundred debilitated people to Aola, Guadalcanal, where they suffered from influenza, dysentery, pneumonia, and depression, with more than 150 deaths in 1944. This was an indication of what displacement could do to weakened communities in spite of U.S. rations, supplementary gardens, and a resident medical officer.[55] On Manus Island, malaria units recommended the relocation of a village of 245 people on Ponam islet to protect the U.S. Seabees (Construction Battalions) there because the troops had malaria. But ANGAU argued that these Melanesians were fishermen who would starve if they were placed on Manus. ANGAU, moreover, could not find a healthy site for them. At Ponam, the Malaria Control Unit found some *Anopheles punctulatis moluccensis*, which were soon eradicated by larvicides. Tests, however, showed that it was the troops that were the "seedbed," not the Melanesians. Brought forward from other bases, the Seabees were "so highly seeded" that they were a threat to the natives until put on a strict regime of atebrin.[56] These Seabees believed they were about to be sent home and did not want the characteristic yellow skin stain, so they had ceased taking the suppressants.[57]

In New Guinea, native labor was pivotal to Allied success.[58] Because the Australians often lacked heavy equipment, they relied on labor for drainage works.

Both allies employed Melanesians because "[t]he natives are accustomed to the terrain and they do the work much more rapidly than the Marines."[59] More important, "they are more willing than American troops to wade through swamps and water holes."[60] U.S. Malaria Control Units in all Pacific theaters consisted of about 10 percent native labor and they were at the front line in mosquito control.[61] At war's end, in spite of this contribution, the American cost accountants weighed the value of Melanesian labor to all units and found it wanting because

> infected native laborers were the major factor in epidemic malaria and that they were responsible for a far greater loss of man-hours among the troops because of malaria than could be gained by their presence as laborers.[62]

In the demanding terrain of their tropical battlefield, the Australians would have disagreed.

Japanese Victims

Malaria could be an ally. The Allies understood that

> Malarial discipline is an offensive weapon of great power. In exact proportion to the superiority of our troops' malarial discipline over the enemy's, so we decrease sickness and increase our reliable manpower and fire power. Malaria under these circumstances fights for us and against the enemy.[63]

Although data on Japanese malaria rates are incomplete, they indicate what Allied observers had witnessed: high malaria rates often resulting in death, especially in combination with other medical conditions. In the Bismarck Archipelago and the Solomons, the Japanese malaria rates in February 1943 reached 1,637 per 1,000 per annum and were climbing. Around Rabaul in the same month it reached 2,053 per 1,000. These were no greater than what the AIF and the Americans had suffered initially. The significant difference during 1943 and 1944 was to be not only the failure of Japanese medical systems when the Allies were streamlining theirs, but also the collapse of Japanese logistics as Allied strategy isolated the enemy. Few Japanese vessels reached the islands with medical supplies.[64] Moreover, they had relied more on quinine in combination with atebrin, rather than atebrin alone.[65] When Java fell to the Japanese this was "a blessing in disguise" for the Allies because atebrin was superior to quinine as a suppressant and was an eradicant for *falciparum.*[66]

Among the U.S. forces, the early infection rates had been high, though the mortality rates were low. In the army alone, a total of 410,727 cases of malaria occurred outside the United States; of those, 219,937 were in the Pacific theaters. Of that number there were 157 deaths or 0.07 per 100. The AIF's mortality rate was 0.05 per 100. No New Zealanders died of malaria.[67] In New Guinea, 10 percent of Japanese died from malaria.[68] Clearly, the odds were in the Allies' favor.

Miscalculating Malaria

Entomologists and malaria units were "dealing with a dual ecological problem—with a parasite and its environment on the one hand and an insect and its environment on the other."[69] Malariologists thus needed to know how the drugs affected the internal human habitat of the parasites. Some Americans believed that prolonged use of malaria drugs might be a danger, so they endeavored to perfect environmental controls to eliminate the disease. A mistake in the campaign against malaria was the policy of "demalarialization," which was practiced not only when units left the malaria zone, but also within that zone when malaria rates had become low.[70] On Efate, when rates fell from 2,600/1,000/annum in April 1942 down to 144/1,000/annum, they withdrew atebrin, but reinstated it when the rate climbed to 521/1,000/annum in November.[71] What was being demonstrated was that *P. vivax* could be suppressed by atebrin (although doses lower than 0.6 grams weekly sometimes meant a "breakthrough"), but it was no cure. On the other hand, by 1944 researchers found it did eliminate the most dangerous form of malaria, *P. falciparum*, providing there was no reinfection.[72] For men returning from the war, *P. vivax* relapses were common for years until the men were treated with more effective drugs. Along with prolonged suffering, the costs of this premature demalarialization were high—more than 295,000 lost man-days.[73]

Efforts to control contact with the native "seedbed" of malaria infection had been useful. Certainly the hope had been to prevent initial infection, but this was impossible in operational zones and difficult even where malaria control was efficient, as the folly of the "demalarialization" in malarial zones proved. Military camps experienced some illicit movement of natives bringing curios and fruit to trade while troops visited villages and exposed themselves to infective "seedbeds." Moreover, dosing laborers and villagers with atebrin was largely useless because it did not act on the gametocytes, the stage of the parasite in the blood that is taken up from humans by the mosquito to reproduce in its body, to pass on the parasite to another human host. The gametocytes in humans are not affected by quinine or atebrin alone. *Falciparum* gametocytes, even if all the other stages of the parasite in the blood are destroyed by drugs, remain infectious to mosquitoes for several weeks, but their infectivity is destroyed by plasmochin. This was a rationale for continued plasmochin use by Australians after the Americans stopped using it for their troops.[74] Thus while atebrin suppressants alone relieved natives (and troops) of proneness to attacks of *vivax* malaria and "cured" *falciparum*, it did not prevent the spread to other hosts of the parasites that caused these infections—to do that all vectors would have to been eliminated.[75] To control the potential infectiousness of the Melanesians in late 1943, the American units began giving thousands of laborers and villagers mass dosages of atebrin (0.3 grams for seven days), followed by plasmochin at the rate of 0.020 grams for five days, reducing the gametocytes dramatically. Yet between 0.5 and 2.0 percent of these laborers still showed malaria parasites in blood smear tests, compared to between 7 and 11 percent before treatment. The dosage then became a suppressant at 0.1 grams daily.[76] Apparently, thereafter only those who showed positive for malaria parasites in the blood were put on the atebrin/plasmochin regimen.[77]

While Melanesians on atebrin certainly felt better, some evidence suggests that this decreased their natural semi-immunity. Once they ceased taking suppressants, this immunity or antigen level in time was usually regained, but they may have paid the price with increased and more severe attacks of malaria in the interim.[78] This was important to the Australians, because of long-term implications. Believing that only acute cases should be treated, ANGAU would not dole out suppressants to carriers or villagers, as coastal Melanesians had considerable natural immunity. ANGAU also knew that:

> Natives, particularly native children, cannot be treated with continuous suppressive atebrin, partly because of administrative difficulties and partly because the resulting interference with the development and maintenance of the immunity that will result.[79]

Yet when using ANGAU's laborers, the Americans insisted they take suppressants and, because the Americans were in overall command, ANGAU agreed. In the Solomons and New Hebrides, American practice also prevailed. Interference with native immunity was of no concern to the Americans.[80]

Filariasis and Dengue Fever

In much of Polynesia the major endemic threat to occupying troops was filariasis (*mumu* or "big-leg"), which was not fatal but was potentially debilitating and disfiguring. Symptoms include fever, swellings, and dull aching of the genitals and the extremities. Lymph glands near the affected areas become sore and swollen. In American Samoa the American medical authorities initially had been complacent about filariasis because there had been virtually no serious cases among navy personnel who had administered the island since 1900. Even Europeans of more than thirty years' residence did not suffer chronically from the disease. Before the war few navy men had close contact with villages because they were confined to their base area, unlike the bivouac arrangements of wartime. And when infection was confirmed, American command initially hid the fact.[81]

Filariasis was hyper-endemic in Samoa, where 24 percent of Samoans carried the parasite *Wuchereria bancrofti* that causes the disease. Initially, the medical teams did not understand that the mosquito carrier was a diurnal biter. The most common vector mosquito there (and in much of Polynesia) was then identified as *Aedes scutellaris pseudo-scutellaris*, the intermediary in transferring the parasites from infected Samoan hosts.[82] Up to 23 percent of mosquitoes that the American entomologists surveyed in villages carried the parasites. Successive bites were needed to create a population of breeding parasites in humans, so men in regular contact with villages were most likely to be infected.[83]

Just as in Samoa, entomologists in New Hebrides and the Solomon Islands learned much about filariasis disease vectors in the field. They concluded that *Anopheles punctulatis farauti*, a nocturnal biter, was the main one, infecting 22 percent of natives. Relatively lower rates of troop infection may have been due to antimalaria measures against *Anopheles*.[84] Native infection rates for filariasis ranged from 20 percent on Bora Bora, Society Islands, to 39 percent on Emirau Island, New Guinea, so the potential threat to the military was geographically extensive.[85]

Another mosquito, *Aedes egypti*, which bred around dwellings in water containers, was the main vector in the South Pacific for dengue fever—a virus that induced symptoms of high fever, headache, generalized aching, nausea, anorexia, and depression. Though mortality was low, morbidity could be extremely high.[86] It reached epidemic proportions in early 1943 among the troops in Espiritu Santo, Efate, New Caledonia, Fiji, and Tulagi-Florida in the Solomons. In the Santo epidemic about 25 percent of the military suffered, with a loss of eighty thousand man-days.[87] The military's tin can dumps, stored tires, and sagging tents provided perfect nurseries for *Aedes* in the wet season.[88] In New Caledonia, the main breeding places were in Noumea's "medieval plumbing system with open drains," cisterns, water-filled barrels, and goldfish ponds, as well as vases on graves.[89] In New Guinea, research showed that *Aedes scutellaris* that bred in coconut shells, empty cans, and the axils of plants was also a vector, yet relatively few troops became infected. Like *Aedes egypti*, it was a diurnal biter.[90] The vector mosquitoes of filariasis and malaria were believed to have a flight range of 100 to 200 yards, while the carriers of dengue had a maximum range of about 330 yards, so removal of indigenous hosts a mile from camps and drainage considerably reduced infection rates.[91]

If men were diagnosed early, nursed, and rested, most recovered from dengue. Treatment for filariasis throughout the Pacific, however, was evacuation of personnel to the States. Unlike malaria, there was then no prophylactic to suppress parasitic multiplication. Control work on filariasis did not start until late 1943. Part of the campaign, as with other mosquito-borne diseases, was the representation of villages and natives as "seedbeds of infection," to be avoided.[92] In American Samoa, for example, the filarial infection rate was "as high as 50 to 70 percent in some of the units," and similar patterns prevailed in parts of Western Samoa.[93] The military evacuated 1,265 infected men from Tutuila between October 1942 and June 1943. Jungle training for the U.S. Marines in Malaeimi Valley, started in late 1942, was discontinued because of infection rates. In Western Samoa rates were lower because most troops were camped by the airfield, with Samoans excluded and mosquito control enforced. About 10 percent mixed with Samoans in villages or in the town of Apia.[94] In all, 350 men contracted the disease and were repatriated in fourteen months. The American medical teams had

> discovered that it was important to keep natives away from the Army camps and the Army personnel away from the villages during the day. Native crews, working in Army camps in the day time, were probably the greatest factor in spreading disease.[95]

Although patients recovered in America, the attrition rate was alarming.[96] But on some isolated bases such as Bora Bora and Aitutaki, where the tedium threatened men's sanity, local commanders ignored prolonged social interactions with the local people, although by early 1944 on Aitutaki, only uninfected laborers were allowed to work in the camps.[97] What was most disturbing to virile servicemen, however, was that lymph gland swelling characteristic of the disease often affected the scrotum. Men believed filariasis would make them sterile and impotent, a cause for anxiety, with some developing a "castration complex."[98] These fears were just as marked on Wallis Island base, where American personnel were "jammed on a . . . Island approximately 34 square miles, populated by 5000 preindustrialised unhealthy natives and filth." The marines' "illicit fraternizing" was thought likely to result in 30 percent infection if their tour of duty was longer than six months.[99] This epidemiological implication was not well-understood until February 1944 when the rotation of personnel increased so that men did not serve in hyper-endemic regions for more than six months.[100] Where the military had the alternative of separating men from the native "seedbed," it did so. Laborers found to be heavily infected with filariasis were usually repatriated or moved to distant camps. In mid-1943, infected Walliseans laborers were returned home from New Caledonia despite the need for workers.[101] Though filariasis never became a major problem for troops on Solomons' bases, by early 1944 infected natives near camps were evacuated.[102]

"Malaria control" included mosquito vectors, as well as rats and mites that carried scrub typhus. It was a massive exercise; in the South Pacific theater alone, more than 4,500 men worked on control, which cost the Americans an estimated $8,754,672 yearly in salaries and equipment. One accountant calculated that the cost of not doing malaria control would have been about $17,920,000 per year. Many would consider this an underestimate.[103]

Scrub Typhus

Before the war, relatively little was known of scrub typhus (*tsutsigamushi* fever) in New Guinea, the Solomons, and as far east as Santo.[104] Mites, the *Trombiculae* spp., could be the host for *Rickettsia* spp. that carried the diseases. *Tombiculae* had not been well-studied, but rodents, marsupials, and birds were hosts. *Tombiculae* were thought to hatch from eggs laid in the soil. They then clung to warm-blooded animals that went past, including human beings, and entered the skin, sucking bodily fluids. Engorged, they dropped to the ground, then developed and laid eggs, and the cycle would repeat. If they carry *Rickettsia*, the infection in humans causes high fever, headache, rash, toxemia, disordered mental states, and sometimes coma and death.[105]

Typhus was most common in New Guinea. When the AIF crossed the Owen Stanleys in late 1942 to pursue the Japanese to Buna-Gona, typhus death rates reached 10 percent. The Americans experienced one of the worst outbreaks when they set up camp on Goodenough Island in late 1943. Of seventy-five cases, more than 25 percent were fatal.[106] Men feared scrub typhus far more than malaria. Although it did not incapacitate as many as malaria or dysentery, it was a problem because of its severity. It put huge demands on medical resources because the sufferers needed intensive care for up to six weeks—consequently patients were often airlifted to Australia or specialist nurses were flown in. Nursing, maintenance of bodily fluids, and management of complications made up the treatment, but death often resulted.[107]

The U.S. Typhus Commission conducted much research, but during the war it found no cure or vaccine. To control the disease, researchers tried to understand its epidemiology. It occurred in widely scattered localities under field conditions, with no seasonal variation. Areas of kunai grass, forest margins, and abandoned plantations seemed the most favorable habitats. Some areas were a continuing problem; some were a problem for a short time. Foci of infection at Finschhafen induced high mortality of 35.3 percent, yet in Dutch New Guinea at Biak and Oti Islands morbidity was high but fatalities only reached 0.5 percent. For any incoming unit the most vulnerable time was when they first arrived in "primitive areas."[108] After a month the infection rate usually dropped dramatically. Apparently, the mite's habitat was so transformed by then that it had left or died out.[109] Control units instructed men not to sit on logs or the ground.[110] Burning of grass and vegetation for camps sites was helpful, as was spreading sand or creosote on the floor of tents. Ridding the area of rodents reduced incidence. A repellent, N,N-Diethyl-meta-toluamide (DEET) applied to ground sheets and clothing proved highly effective and remained so, even after successive washings.[111]

War Hero or Lesser Evil? DDT

DEET was one of several compounds tried in the war against insects. A new device greatly assisted: The aerosol freon container ("bomb") that propelled insecticides in a fine mist enabled each man to spray his quarters and tent. From early 1943 they began to arrive from the United States and, used in conjunction with pyrethrum, were a major asset against mosquitoes and flies.[112] The most publicized "war hero" in 1944 was dichlorodiphenyltrichloroethane (DDT), as Edmund Russell shows.[113] Although experts in the Pacific found it highly effective as a residual and broad-spectrum insecticide, many believed that atebrin was the key contribu-

Figure 9. New Guinea laborers dusting grassy swampland with DDT, 18th Australian Anti-Malaria Control Unit, Dumpu, December 1944 (Australian War Memorial Negative No. 061440).

tor to Allied health in relation to malaria. Certainly, on Guadalcanal malaria was under control by the time DDT appeared.[114]

Different regimes and means of DDT application were tried. Early experiments on Santo revealed the toxicity of the high concentrations resulting in "the complete destruction of plant and animal life."[115] But at the time, DDT seemed the lesser of two evils—the loss of human life or the loss of biota on some faraway island. The standard concentrations were 5 to 10 percent in solution for spraying from planes and 5 percent inside structures where the mosquitoes lit. Its spread on water was superior to diesel, though in New Guinea the effectiveness of aerial spraying of the jungle was about one week, so it was targeted around new bases or perimeters where access was difficult.[116]Although in Santo the American malaria units carried out the first applications of residual sprays on native quarters in June 1944, before their own military structures were treated, no studies were made to measure longer-term effects on the Melanesians.[117]And it is to be wondered what large-scale dusting of DDT in powder form with talc over large areas at Dumpu, for example, had on the New Guineans involved.[118]

Dermatitis and Dysentery

The Allied troops were susceptible to other ailments. Troops stressed in the humid heat, often not able to wash their persons or clothing properly, were prey to an array of fungal and parasitic skin infections, accounting for almost half the AIF's and 20 percent of American admissions to hospitals. Dermatological afflictions including "Atabrine dermatitis" were detrimental to morale and wore men down, some to the point of being invalided out.[119]

More dangerous was dysentery. Caused by the *Shigella* bacilli, it spread through contamination with infected fecal matter via contact, water, or flies, as it did along the Kokoda Trail, with the Japanese dying in hundreds and Australians debilitated.[120] But the Allies, using sulphaguanidine ("sulfa") drugs and better sanitation, such as long-drop latrines, largely contained outbreaks.[121] This was not the case for Melanesians in New Guinea. The *Shigella* bacilli were there before the war, but it is likely that the most severe form, *Shigella dysenteriae* (Type 1) was introduced in wartime by either the Australians (from the Middle East) or the Japanese or both. Isolated inland populations in 1943 were similar to the island Pacific of a hundred years earlier in their lack of exposure to introduced diseases. Thus their experience of coping with new epidemics was limited. Population numbers are incomplete, so it is difficult to assess the disease's severity. But Bryant Allen and John Burton believe that the epidemic carried off between 2.5 and 5 percent of the people in the inland Aitape region and the highlands of New Guinea. Around Aitape, the death rate in certain areas was far higher because of the stress of battle conditions, marauding Japanese, and malnutrition. ANGAU could do little to assist until the Japanese surrendered.[122]

Out of the conflict zone, the highland New Guinea people were largely "uncontrolled" by the Australian administration, so controlling disease by Western biomedicine was a daunting task. Despite this, ANGAU established more than fifty basic hospitals by 1944, with ten in the Bena (highlands) area alone, treating dysentery with drugs and nursing.[123] As with malaria, where regimenting the native people could confine diseases, contagion was less likely. The United States, for example, dealt effectively in 1945 with an influenza epidemic that eventually infected almost all of the 264 native laborers, including Gilbert and Ellice Island Dock Company at the Florida Islands base. A "working quarantine" prevented the infection from spreading. Although eleven cases of pneumonia developed among the native laborers, there were no deaths.[124]

Venereal Diseases

Venereal diseases came to the Pacific Islands with the first Europeans and Asians, long before the war. Sexual encounters between servicemen and women (or men) were a concern because venereal disease could disable a fighting force, especially as the "miracle" antibiotic penicillin only came into general use in late 1944.[125] Military medical control of venereal disease was rapid and effective. Unlike the first exotic strangers in the pristine Pacific, few servicemen were diseased when they arrived, as regular inspections precluded this.[126] The cline of military incidence of these diseases generally went from relatively high in the east, where there was no combat, to very low in the operational zone.

But there were local variations. Although Fiji was well behind the lines, the military, as well the Fijian leaders and the colonial government, placed severe strictures on relations between the troops and local young people, especially women. Fijian police removed to the rural districts certain women who were likely to fraternize with the Allies in the capital, Suva.[127] Those who did consort with the Americans, so Ratu Lala Sukuna claimed, were "either half castes or pure Polynesians with a sprinkling of Fijians."[128] As in Tonga, chiefs kept women of rank away from unwanted contacts.[129] Military regulations kept servicemen out of native "encampments" except on supervised visits, forbade them consorting with local women, and imposed off-limits sanctions to seedy parts of Suva. Sexual interactions near the camps around Nadi, Viti Levu, occurred to a limited extent with Indian women. Fijian "waitresses" for the military were also involved, often with the connivance of their male relatives. Gonorrhea rates among the Fijians increased with the arrival of the troops, but syphilis was confined mainly to the Indians, because Fijians, like Samoans, mostly had cross-immunity as a result of previous yaws infection. American medical teams regularly inspected these women and notified the colonial health officer who treated them. If positive, they were confined to Suva hospital, where, undaunted, some still went about soliciting customers from the ward veranda![130] The American medical teams represented such local women as "seedbeds" of venereal infection. In spite of the dubious legality of forced inspection of suspect women in all islands, it was common practice, sanctioned by the colonial authorities. At Noumea's Pink House, which is said to have provided 24,000 man visits, the women were regularly checked, as were males before admission.[131] Newly arrived troops at smaller bases such as Penrhyn were prevented from mixing with women for five days to see if they were infected "to safeguard the villagers from venereal infection."[132]

On Bora Bora and Aitutaki, a U.S. surgeon commented, "The Polynesians are not an immoral people—rather they should be considered amoral," with sexual freedom before marriage. The Americans on Bora Bora found "themselves in high favor with these Polynesian beauties," yet even six months after occupation gonorrhea rates remained low. An epidemic occurred, however, in early 1944—the result of men being allowed to make weekly visits to Tahiti and overnighting at Raiatea, where the French were lax in their controls. Men were also munching sulfa tablets "like candy" as a prophylactic, reducing its effectiveness as a curative and necessitating use of the new but scarce drug, penicillin.[133] Men finagling plane flights were especially vulnerable; one infected marine based in Samoa "admitted having intercourse in both Aitutaki and Tahiti. He does not know the name or the address of the girl in either place."[134]

On Wallis Island the American command regarded the people as "indolent"[135] and infected with "tuberculosis, yaws and filariasis among other diseases." Medical officials checked every native on Wallis, removed lepers to Nukuatea Island, and posted "signs outside fales where reside tubercular, leperosy and other communicable diseases [*sic*]," warning American visitors,[136] but sexual liaisons still occurred.[137]

This trade in sex was not a major issue in western Melanesia since closeness to battle, guarding of women by clans, and removal of the villagers to safe areas all contributed to keeping contacts minimal, though covert visits by U.S. personnel for sexual purposes to the Polynesian Rennell Island in the Solomons occurred.[138] Trobriand women in Papua, known for their sexual freedom, fraternized with troops from the American outpost at Kiriwina, which left many of the population with gonorrhea.[139] In western Melanesia generally, however, few VD infections among U.S. personnel were contracted from the local people. Most were syphilis, originating in Australia or New Zealand when men were on leave or through ongoing homosexual activity in Melanesia, particularly among African American troops.[140]

Homosexuality, although considered to be a mental disease, was a punishable offense, as there was "no place in the service for the homosexualist, the panderer or the pederast,"[141] with a court martial or dishonorable discharge the outcome. A few psychiatrists preferred to ignore it, but that did not prevent VD from spreading.[142] Homosexuality was more common in the armed forces, including the marines, than the command would admit. In New Caledonia in August 1943, when a party of about thirty homosexual navy officers and enlisted men spilled out from the officers' mess into the Rendezvous Café in Noumea, where presumably others noted their behavior, the resulting court of enquiry was terminated as "it was felt to be in the best interests of the [U.S.] government," though an "informal administrative investigation" found several counts of "oral coition" and "sodomy." Those involved opted for dishonorable discharge.[143]

Milieu, Morale, and Mind

For most men, lack of congenial female company and surroundings depressed morale. After the AIF 7th Division veterans from the Middle East arrived in New Guinea in May 1942, they complained of lack of home leave, to which their Australian militia compatriots countered, "they saw towns, good meals, women and beer and all we have seen is jungle, Japs and natives."[144] For the Americans, "[d]uty on an isolated island in the Pacific appeared to be as great or even greater cause for the precipitation of psychiatric breakdown as actual combat conditions."[145] Morale basically depended on affiliation, unity within units, food, shelter, health, and a manageable environment. Without these in fair measure, men on rear bases for more than a year or two often became dispirited.[146] On the battlefront, if morale weakened, the chances of combat fatigue increased. Forty percent of the casualties among the marines and then the army suffered from "Guadalcanal neurosis" during the early months after their landing in 1942, induced by battle confusion, malaria, and environmental stress.[147] But more was to come with mass combat fatigue in the U.S. Army operation against the Japanese at Zazana, south New Georgia, by the 43rd, the 37th, and 25th Divisions between 30 June and 22 September 1943. Their ally, the British believed that these men of the 43rd, "with little aptitude and less training for such fighting" were unevenly matched against the Japanese, who then were "the finest bush fighters in the world."[148] In all, 2,500 Americans were admitted to hospitals suffering from "war neurosis." Of a total strength of 12,000 in the 43rd, it contributed 80 percent of all cases, mainly from the 169th Infantry in the first month of the campaign. These high figures demanded explanation. Both the 43rd and the 37th Divisions were inexperienced and lacked orientation:

> A soldier needs to know what is going on, what is expected of him, what he may expect to encounter, and must have a definite objective or goal. Without these, he is an automaton, with no personal interest in the efforts of his unit.

They landed in swampy, thick jungle, a wilderness in stark contrast to the domesticated, controlled environments of their homeland, to be targeted by mobile Japanese patrols. Leadership at both the company and platoon level was poor and units were unaware of their goals. They were rattled by jungle noises, especially at night,

> the whispering breezes through the trees, the crackling limbs, the whistling birds, the clatter caused by land crabs . . . are often misinterpreted as indicating that the enemy is near and danger is present. The failure of the soldier to recognize these sounds will result in wild, fantastic misconceptions . . . this caused men to break, screaming and running from imaginary danger.

The psychiatrists concluded that 50 to 60 percent of cases were men suffering from combat fatigue rather than neurosis. Removal and rest would cure this transient state that had "infected" poorly led young men. The rest were marginal, needing more treatment, but only about 2 to 3 percent suffered from true war neurosis.

In contrast, a mere 6 percent of the 25th Division had combat fatigue. This division had been "blooded" in combat on Guadalcanal. In spite of a lowered combat efficiency of 40 percent because of reduced fitness from malaria infections, this experience had prepared them better for fighting as a unit and for the natural environment than the other divisions.[149]

Japanese medical opinion held, perhaps disingenuously, that their men, convinced that death in fighting for the emperor marked the zenith of their spirituality, suffered far less from combat fatigue. Their greatest fear was not exposure to battle and hardship, but to surrender, which they considered dishonorable. Hence, once defeated, their tendency was to commit suicide and, if possible, kill the enemy in doing so.[150]

Disease: Enemy and Ally

The war in the southern Pacific was a war of strategies and operations, but for the invaders from temperate lands, it was also a war of morale. A significant contributor to that was good health. Tropical island environments pose several disease hazards. Allied victory in part lay in the poor health of the Japanese, notably the army fed on refined rice. As General MacArthur and Admiral Nimitz believed, the Allies only had to isolate the enemy from its supply lines and it would "wither on the vine." After the early phases of the campaign at Tulagi and eastern New Guinea, "the old triad of malaria, dysentery and beri-beri" took its toll of the Japanese. On Guadalcanal alone, the Americans estimated that of the 42,000 Japanese who fought there, fewer than a quarter were evacuated, about the same number were killed or died from wounds, and a shocking 20,000 died of disease and starvation as opposed to 1,500 American dead.[151] For the Allies, in Polynesia the major endemic threat was filariasis, not a fatal complaint, but in western Melanesia, malaria and other diseases proved as dangerous as Japanese bullets, though superior logistics advantaged the Allies.

Here, diseases that threatened the Allies and flourished in the "native seedbed" were associated with a "primitive" people in a primeval environment. Even on Polynesian Wallis Island, the Americans equated disease and ill health with indolence and backwardness. In the South Solomons (Bougainville and Solomons) command, the American historian commented on medical corps' success against malaria and also noted, "Isolation of our troops from contact with natives effectively prevented contraction of other diseases common among the native people."[152] Medical men and entomologists saw themselves as containing malaria and other diseases by an ecological approach, controlling the embodied source, vectors, and habitat. But, except for ANGAU in New Guinea, where Australians, unlike the Americans, were not going home, Allied military concern with the health of the natives was transient, intended only to protect their own men and create goodwill to gain labor and local resources. Australia had surrendered considerable sovereignty to the Americans under the unity of command, so against their better judgment regarding malaria suppressants for Melanesians, ANGAU conformed to American wishes.[153] The silence of the archives speaks of no American concern with the long-term impact of such medical regimes and DDT spraying on the people.

Especially in the western Pacific, attempts to eradicate disease vectors involved reorganization of the natural environment. Here and there, the invaders did major reconfiguration of the topography by the infilling of swamps, permanently reducing mosquito breeding grounds. More commonly, changes were less permanent: the opening of coastal lagoons to sea tides, networks of drainage, clearing of banks of streams, disc plowing ruts, spraying of miles of jungle fringe with DDT, burning off of undergrowth, killing of animals such as rodents and bats, and adding an exotic fish species. The Allies sited labor compounds well apart from camps and moved entire villages. Briefly, at great cost, they reordered and in their own eyes redeemed an environment they read as "primitive" and unimproved.[154] They took pride in lowering malaria and other disease rates. The medical units conflated people and place into a congruous epidemiological, if not pathological, text. For a time, near their bases, they cured and controlled a primitive people who were "seedbeds of infection," believing such people to be "an expression of their environment."[155] Realistically, the Americans knew that though they had won the medical battle, it had been merely a holding operation. As the Florida Islands' bases closed, the malaria unit officer noted, "Within a very few weeks the above-mentioned bases will have reverted to their primitive state and will again be highly malarious."[156] In the invaders' eyes, just as the jungle growth soon covered the relics of bases, so too would the people return to their previous disease-ridden existence, the thralls of their environment.

PART II

Using Indigenous Resources

CHAPTER 4

Local Resources

Living off Land and Sea

While aerial battles over New Britain Island are increasing in intensity the Japanese troops are going about their daily routine with perfect composure . . . vegetable patches are seen side by side with air-raid shelters. These vegetable gardens are being cultivated by our own soldiers during their leisure hours to attain self-sufficiency in food. Besides such miniature farms full-scale farming is also being undertaken with remarkable success.

—Radio Tokyo, Feb. 1944

In 1943, THE Great White Father decided that his warriors in the Pacific needed fresh fish to supplement their normal diet of Spam, Vienna sausages, New Zealand lamb and K rations.[1]

—Wilbert Chapman

Allied logistics for medical supplies saved thousands of lives. To provide these and other necessities, one ton of shipping space (seventy cubic feet) per month was needed to supply one soldier.[2] So, to save space on the extraordinarily long hauls across the Pacific, protagonists needed to utilize as many local supplies—food, timber, and labor—as they could, as near as possible to concentrations of troops. In terms of the prior experience of most natives, the military marshaled and utilized all three in novel ways. The Allies had to negotiate for them with both metropolitan governments and administrators while not alienating the people. The Japanese had only the islanders to deal with, but they understood that appropriating resources could create foes where they needed allies. Both sides, to retain the goodwill of the islanders, had to assist with supplying the goods they valued. Some islands supplied products needed for the metropolitan war effort, so the laborers involved also needed incentives. Colonial administrations best mediated military demands on the environment's resources. For those islanders under the Japanese, there was no such agency to consider their interests.

Feeding Fighters

The natural world is fundamental to military forces because those with adequate food are more likely to win. Unprecedented distances between production and consumption, lack of storage facilities, and a tropical climate that rapidly rusted and rotted containers plagued provisioning. Though America's vast industries produced good dry and canned rations, fresh food was expensive to ship and of variable quality. War in the south needed food from the south. Initially, the Japanese were expected to supplement their food locally, but once their supply lines were cut, they had to rely completely on food at hand.[3]

Planners realized the food's importance. U.S. Rear Admiral Richard E. Byrd led a team to the Pacific to report on "defense installations"[4] and also recommended an "increase in the agricultural production of the islands," provision "for exporting surpluses," and "a supply of trade goods for sale to natives."[5] Consequently, the American Office (later Board) of Economic Warfare (BEW) began surveying in December 1942. To manage the resources of indigenous people, Douglas Oliver, an anthropologist in Bougainville before the war, was appointed deputy director of the South Pacific Project, heading a team of agriculture and fisheries specialists. They visited Pacific bases, Australia, and New Zealand and proposed vegetable-growing projects. In New Zealand, a joint purchasing board took responsibility for supplies.[6]

The major suppliers of fresh vegetables, fruit, meat, and diary products to the Americans in the southern Pacific were New Zealand and Australia under reverse lend-lease.[7] The original lend-lease arrangement started with American aid to Britain and indirectly the British Commonwealth in March 1941, before the United States entered the European war, in return for payments deferred until after the war and for the lease of naval bases in British colonies in the Atlantic and Caribbean. Lend-lease applied to de Gaulle's Free French forces in Europe in November, but legal uncertainties in the New Hebrides saw the Condominium excluded. Once the Pacific War started, the United States extended lend-lease to Australia and New Zealand. Tonga was not in the Commonwealth and was excluded. The U.S. Foreign Economic Administration (FEA) administered this program and reverse lend-lease or reciprocal aid when these countries supplied services and goods, such as food, to the United States. Not all Australasian fresh vegetables and fruits, however, reached the battle areas, and when they did, some were often in poor condition.[8]

Nonetheless, by 1944 the American serviceman was the best fed in the world, the envy of the Australians and New Zealanders.[9] Each American was getting an average of 38.4 pounds of fresh vegetables and fruits, 31.6 pounds of fresh meat, 4.4 pounds of butter or substitute, cheese, and miscellaneous items (excluding eggs) per month. Nutritional deficiencies had emerged before 1944 and rations were adjusted.[10] For maximum nutritional value for the sick and front-line troops, fresh vegetables needed to be produced close to hand.

The BEW found some island commanders and local people had taken their own initiatives to produce fresh food for the forces. Everywhere, the American presence stimulated cash cropping but stressed local subsistence. Thus the BEW faced a range of garrison and operational situations, organizing expertise and supplies, but hindered by the lag between requisitioning and delivery as well the challenges of changing troop concentrations and competing native subsistence needs.[11]

Allied Farms on Rear Bases

The BEW faced political intricacies in the southern Pacific with four foreign colonial powers: Britain, France, New Zealand, and Australia. Not all their territories had the same resources or needs. Not all were absolute possessions. Tonga was a kingdom, under the protection of Britain, so negotiations went on at two levels, Tonga's government and the British High Commission in Fiji. The navy considered small unit gardens in July 1942, because "the production of native farmers was not dependable." The typical vegetables Tongans grew—yams (*Dioscorea esculenta*), taro (*Colocasia esculenta*), and cooking bananas (*Musa* spp.)—were not appealing. Ignorant of their productivity, the Americans had a poor opinion of the Tongans'

> methods of farming. The main reason being that they have none. After crops are planted and given a start, they grow wild until harvest time. The land is never turned except in small holes where single plants go.[12]

Moneymaking opportunities for Tongans so drew them away from their own gardens that Queen Sālote had to intervene to maintain subsistence production on Tongatapu. The government nevertheless developed a farm at 'Atele, established a central buying agency, fixed prices, and retained export fruit for the military, producing about £4,700 worth of vegetables. The navy abandoned unit gardens in favor of crop rotation in a bigger area. In August 1942, with Tonga's agreement and local labor, it began cultivating three hundred acres at Vaikeli, the government experimental farm. When the BEW mission visited, one hundred acres were under crops and had produced more than $7,000 worth of vegetables. The local commander improvised a dairy herd and a chicken farm to supply the military hospital. As the American garrison reduced in January 1943, the navy transferred Vaikeli to the New Zealanders.[13]

Unlike Tonga, Fiji's mixed population already grew some typical Western market or "truck" vegetables and fruits. Producing extra since 1939, once the Americans arrived in May–June 1942, the Department of Agriculture encouraged Indians, Fijians, and Chinese, through growers' co-operatives, to grow more. To assist, the FEA provided new seed varieties and indemnified the department for losses if the Americans reneged on contracted plantings. By mid-1943, at peak demand, a monthly average of 1,552,460 pounds went directly to the military. In November, the FEA set up a twenty-five-acre experimental farm at Namaka in west Viti Levu. A few months later, the army quartermaster, using Indian labor, took over the farm and extended plantings to forty acres. Fiji soil supplied all the vegetable and fruit needs of the island's troops, with surpluses, including canned pineapple, going forward in 1944–45. Moreover, manufacturers met all American soap and sugar needs, which saved shipping.[14]

In American Samoa, some units had obtained seeds from home and made small "victory gardens."[15] There and in Western Samoa from March 1943, FEA negotiations and the delivery of gardening supplies took almost a year, by which time the need had lessened with the reduction of the garrisons.[16]

Meanwhile, Western Samoans made money selling fresh produce, especially fruit. Moreover, because most men in American Samoa worked on "defense works," the military administration had to import local foodstuff from Western Samoa while ordering its people to cease retailing foodstuff to military personnel. Encouraging women and children to plant food crops, it instructed Western Samoan workers to bring taro to eat. In exchange for taro, American Samoan storekeepers offered excess stocks to buyers in Western Samoa, to the annoyance of the New Zealand administration because of taro shortage there.[17] On Aitutaki, Cook Islands, to prevent famine after the Americans left, the administration allocated one day a week for compulsory planting of "native foods," which the Americans endorsed. American personnel were also not permitted to purchase imported food from traders.[18]

Farming on War's Periphery

Across the Pacific, five systems of farming under the FEA operated (see Table 1):

> (a) organised military personnel operating farms under FEA supervision, with native hand labor; (b) the same method, but with military prison labor; (c) individual military units operating their own gardens with FEA assistance; (d)

Figure 10. Solomon Island laborers harvesting radishes at service command farm, Ilu, Guadalcanal, 1944 (EX. 342-FH-3A43728, NARA).

> groups of native farmers under contract with Army QM[Quartermaster]; (e) groups of native farmers under contracts with FEA for resale of produce to Navy.[19]

The largest production came from gardens closer to operations where needs were greatest. New Caledonia, Efate, and Espiritu Santo (see Map 11) always were behind the lines, while Guadalcanal (see Map 7) became so in early 1943. In New Caledonia, French farmers were familiar with preferred military crops, as were the few settlers in the New Hebrides. New Caledonian farmers produced about 1,500 tons of coffee annually, which went to the Americans, supplying about half of what was needed, along with all the New Hebrides coffee. A typical military garden grew corn, chinese cabbages, cucumbers, cantaloupes, eggplant, lettuce, okra, green beans, green onions, sweet peppers, radishes, watermelons, pumpkins (squash), and tomatoes, with potatoes and cabbages from cooler New Caledonia. In the operational areas of New Georgia, Torokina on Bougainville, and Manus Island, gardens were often at the periphery of battle.[20]

In 1944, American farm production amounted to approximately fifty million pounds, worth about two million U.S. dollars, though detailed statistics were not

TABLE 1. Production U.S. Military Farms

Location	Maximum Acreage	Approx. Period of Operation	Maximum Output in Pounds, p.m. except #	System
Fiji: Namaka	28→40	Nov. 1943–Aug. 1944	3178	a→d
Fiji: Viti Levu		c. May 42–Sept. 45	4,251,063	e
Tutuila	5			a
Aitutaki	1	April 1943		c
Wallis	7			c
Tonga	100	Oct. 1942–Jan. 1943	13,360 +*	a
# New Caledonia: St. Louis, Paita, La Foa, Bourail	885	July 1943–Sept. 1945	369,840	d
Dumbea, Porte la Guerre	20	Ditto		a
Ouaco	500	Ditto	147,082	e
Nakety		Sept. 1944–Sept. 1945		e
New Caledonia	100	July 1943–Aug. 1945	12,000	b
#Efate: Army	52	May 1943–?	19,872	** a/b
#Efate: Navy	68		50,535	e

(Continued on next page)

always available. Regarding shipping space, a telling statistic was that the islands' farms in late 1944 supplied the equivalent of 52,080 cubic feet per month (exclusive of Fiji farmers' crops of about 12,000 cubic feet). In some places however, the amount produced via FEA projects relative to *all* food consumed was not great, but it was a considerable proportion of the fresh produce. Over the war years, New Caledonia produced only about 10 percent of all the food requirements of the army of 65,000 there, but the island was close to New Zealand, which furnished the bulk of fresh foodstuffs. This was particularly so in 1944–1945, when it produced more than 1,292,622 cubic feet monthly when shortages had developed globally

TABLE 1. *(continued)*

Location	Maximum Acreage	Approx. Period of Operation	Maximum Output in Pounds, p.m. except #	System
#Espiritu Santo	197	April 1944–?	68,703	a
#Guadalcanal	2102	Oct. 1943–Sept. 1945	911,982	a
Guadalcanal	70	May 1943–Aug. 1945	?	c–FEA
Kolombangara	25	Jan. 1944–?	?	a
Russell Is.: Navy	12	? –Sept. 1945	?	e
#Bougainville	600	April 1944–Nov. 1945	55,275	ac
Admiralty Is.	200	April 1944–?	?	A

Sources: Rose, Report on Agriculture Project, 18 Aug. 1942–25 Jan. 1943, F. A9, RG 313-58-3394, NARA SB; Tahiti Survey, 15 May 1943, FEA Resume of current activities by Subject, Dec. 1943, Oliver, Summary, South Pacific Project Report, First Quarter 1944, Bishop, FEA Activities in British Pacific Island Colonies, 10 Oct. 1944, NARA RG 169; Fiji Islands, July–Aug. 1944, Entry 427, RG 407, NARA; *AR, Department of Agriculture,* 1942–1945, Legislative Council, Fiji, 1942–1946; Naval Base Aitutaki, 10 Apr. 1945, Entry 178, RG 313, NARA; AR Department of Agriculture, 30 June 1943, Box 20 (v. 9712) F. A9, RG 313-58-3440, NARA SB; FEA in South Pacific Project, Third quarter 1944, Sept. 1944, Entry 217, RG 234, NARA; Final close out Report on the South Pacific Command, 30 June 1946, Entry 44463, RG 338, NARA; Service Command Bougainville, Dec. 1944, Entry 427, RG 407, NARA; HQ SOS SPA, Organizational history, c. Apr. 1944, Entry 44463, RG 338, NARA.

Notes: Key: See above text at footnote 19.

*Cannot be calculated accurately because some measured in bunches and ears.

** From early 1943 the Condominium government was initially the lead agency in association with the U.S. forces and FEA. By early 1944 the Condominium had withdrawn.

Averaged monthly production for period July–September 1944.

because of scarcity of refrigerated shipping and the long war, its damage to productive lands, and loss of labor.[21]

Local people traded significant quantities. Once fighting ceased on Guadalcanal and Tulagi, villagers sold produce at the camps, with prices set by the military. New Zealanders on maneuvers in New Caledonia traded with the Kanaks. On Aitutaki, an islanders' committee dealt directly with the American quartermaster for foodstuffs. American boats in the New Hebrides went to Nguna and Tangoa twice a week to collect villagers' produce.[22] On Santo in 1944–1945, "[e]very Tuesday natives from miles around, sometimes numbering 200, bring their produce (mainly bananas) to Point Annand for sale . . . at controlled prices and a regular market has developed."[23]

In New Guinea, men in the stretched lines along the Kokoda Track and the Buna campaign of 1942 suffered privation and monotony in their diet, as did the native carriers, one third of whom became too ill to work.[24] As one major general dryly remarked, "Bully beef, biscuits, rice, tea and sugar, dried fruit, dried milk and salt may appear a lot but they have their limitations."[25]

Considerable Australian fresh food was shipped to New Guinea, most commonly vegetables that kept well and that were scarce. The most popular was the staple potato, along with onions, carrots, rutabagas (swedes), parsnips, tomatoes, and citrus fruits as well as cargoes of cabbages and cauliflower for hospitals. Food in the battle zone generally had to be canned or dried to last, and much of it was carried in or dropped from planes. The army considered increasing production in north Queensland (Map 13), but shipping would still be required. Although New Guinea gardens could not produce the thirty tons of food the AIF consumed daily, they could supply hospitals and convalescent depots. The army's farm platoons and companies did the growing with ANGAU labor, after mechanical clearing and plowing. These units established farms mainly in New Guinea. By September 1943 in Papua near Port Moresby, the 3 Australian Farm Coy had eighty acres, each producing eight tons a year for hospitals. By early 1943, at the 2/9th Battalion Australian Hospital at "17 Mile," located that distance from Port Moresby, Chinese liberated from the Japanese were growing vegetables for the patients.[26] A large farm started in December 1942 by ANGAU was at the "12 Mile" outside Port Moresby, near the U.S. Farm Coy one. When the U.S. withdrew in late 1944 ANGAU took this over. In November and December 1944, the 12 Mile farm produced 71,301 lbs. of fruit and 80,064 lbs. of vegetables—about thirty-three tons monthly.

The AIF dietitians in 1944 eventually recognized the heavy work load on native labor and increased the ration to three pounds of meat and one pound each of sugar and animal fat per week, much of which, like the regular army rations, came from Australia.[27] ANGAU had about 30 one-acre outstation gardens to supplement laborers' rations. In early 1943 ANGAU also worked with U.S. Air Transport command on a garden at Bena Bena, with produce being flown out, mainly for the command.[28]

Food was not the only agricultural consideration. Coffee production at Sangara, except for the short Japanese occupation, went to the Allies throughout the war.[29] In the eastern highlands of New Guinea, the prewar administration's farm at Aiyura had started coffee and cinchona plantings for quinine in 1937.[30] Although suitable for cool-climate crops, there was "no good land transport" from Aiyura to troop concentrations, so cinchona dominated, with seven hundred pounds of bark produced in 1944.[31]

Abandoned local gardens in the Wau valley provided food for the AIF, as did introduced crops like chokos (*Sechium edule*) and pumpkins, rampant in the prewar miners' gardens. In September 1943, the army made its first New Guinea garden near the administration's garden, producing twenty thousand pounds a month (7.5 tons per acre per annum) or 920 rations per day from fifteen acres plus thirteen acres of native gardens. Potatoes (*Solanum tuberosum*) grew at this elevation. The army trucked or flew Wau food to Allied bases in the Markham area. In 1944, two farms at Nadzab and Malahang near Lae supplied troops with two to five hundred cases of tomatoes monthly. Late in 1945 at Lae, the army experimented with rice growing to feed labor while ANGAU extended a prewar project in the Mekeo area of the Gulf district.[32] Overall, the army's north New Guinea farms were producing about 380,000 lbs. of vegetables and some fruit per month in the first half of 1945.

The Australians contracted with local residents for food. The most successful operation was about seven miles from Lae at Busu River, where Rabaul Chinese resettled by ANGAU grew vegetables. Because of scarcity, ANGAU generally discouraged villagers from trading their food.[33] But discouragement did not mean enforcement. Near Nadzab,

> these villages have been providing troops with native foods and fruit, which has caused a drain on their supplies. This was unavoidable, owing to the shortage of [ANGAU] staff to supervise matters of this kind.[34]

In some places ANGAU was able to oversee fresh food collection, working through the village headmen. In 1944, for example, villages in the Lae region as well as Karkar and Manam Island filled weekly barges sent by the army.[35]

Melanesians produced few surpluses of staples;[36] the climate and lack of preservation militated against it. In peacetime extra vegetables rotted or were fed to the pigs, transforming carbohydrates to protein in a more storable form. Fruit, however, growing in abandoned gardens was often surplus. In the forward areas, thousands of displaced Melanesians were unable to make proper gardens. What they could most offer, besides curios, was fruit, bartered for canned meat and ship's biscuits, which had the advantage of being storable and provided protein and carbohydrates, often as lacking in their diet as much as fresh fruit with vitamins and minerals were in the Allies':

> they bring . . . fresh fruit, grass skirts, combs, baskets, etc., for which we gave them cigarettes, bully beef or army biscuits, often referred to as dog biscuits. We are glad to get rid of them.[37]

TABLE 2. Production Australian Army Farms, New Guinea (not Papua)

Location New Guinea	Maximum Acreage	Approx. Period of Operation	Maximum Output p.m.
Lae: Malahang	60 acres	May 1945	80,000 lbs. (estimate)
Wau	31+	Feb. 1945	90,000 lbs.
Bulolo (fruit)	?	Feb. 1945	8,000 lbs.
Erap, Nadzab	75	May 1945	100,000 lbs. (estimate)
Madang	40	Feb. 1945	30,000 lbs.
Aitape	?	May 1945	15,000 lbs. (estimate)
Torokina, Bougainville	70	May 1945	60,000 lbs. (estimate)
Jacquinot Bay, New Britain	A few acres	Feb. 1945	?

Sources: Brigadier to 'Q' Branch, 1 Oct. 1945, Cleland to HQ, 21 Sept., AWM 54, 337/7/1, AWM; Sunderstrom, Review of Farms in First Army Area, Feb. 1945, Kjar, Farms-General Policy, 14 May 1945 and enclosure, AWM 54, 337/7/10, AWM.

Outside the battle zone, in the Mekeo region, barter rates were a tin of bully beef and two packets of biscuits for a stalk of bananas (about one hundred), and two tins beef or a quart of kerosene (for lanterns) for a large stalk (two hundred).[38]

Although the shortage was not critical, there was often insufficient fresh food. A diet lacking fresh fruit, vegetables, and milk combined with a relatively high carbohydrate and protein intake—often overcooked—was believed to be the cause of increased "dento-oral" disease among the men, exacerbated by damp toothbrushes and negligence.[39] Produce from small gardens on Aitutaki, even when supplemented with "bananas and a few oranges," was not enough to prevent mild deficiencies, so the Americans took multivitamin tablets.[40] Those who benefited most from local and imported fresh vegetables were the sick near the forward areas.[41]

Not all gardening succeeded. Soils were frequently deficient in nitrogen and phosphate, and many temperate-climate vegetables failed. However, New Zealanders, led by the padre J. W. Parker at isolated Boguen in New Caledonia, managed to grow a one-acre garden in early 1943 to feed their hospital patients until trading arrangements with local French farmers improved the diet for patients and staff, who had been getting 90 percent of their food from American cans.[42] Close to the fighting at Torokina, Donald Jackson, an Iowa farm boy, found himself running a garden of three acres. He coped with the lack of a "gardening season," the malnourished state of his Bougainville laborers, insect infestations, and crop experimentation with some success:

> I had fed endive (chicory) to every enlisted man on the base, including hospital patients. Some had never seen this curly and slightly bitter leaf, but after a few remarks about rabbit food they ate it hungrily.[43]

The worth of these military gardens was greatest in areas where the size of the occupying forces and relocation of the civilian population meant that large-scale trading was out of the question. On Guadalcanal a hospital dietitian noted, "It must be said that the produce of the Island Farm was of inestimable value. . . . Native foods were seldom, if ever, used."[44]

Supplementary Proteins

To assist hospitals at Dumbea, New Caledonia, the American army quartermaster established a poultry farm of 3,600 chickens in April 1943 to supply eggs and meat. In Fiji, the Americans with the Department of Agriculture set up a piggery at Lami, near Suva, fed with mess scraps. In Fiji and New Caledonia, the open and black market in beef sold to Americans caused significant reduction of cattle herds.[45] Aggie Grey in Western Samoa gave Americans a taste of home with her hamburgers, made with meat from Reparations Estates' cattle and "elsewhere," with condiments like ketchup bartered for curios from cooks on American ships.[46] Nearer the front, self-help was common. On Makira (San Cristobel), Fijian troops, investigating a rumored Japanese landing in June 1943, stole pigs from the natives.[47] The Americans in the Russell Islands slaughtered 1,200 cattle on Levers' plantations. The Japanese and the Americans helped themselves to Burns Philp Co. Ltd.'s cattle on Tetepare Island, as did the Australians at Milne Bay. During operations near Lae, New Guinea, in September 1943, Jack Craig's unit came across a Lutheran mission station and noted,

> Chasing chicken for the pot and "ratting" the veg[etable] garden. We were told not to touch the livestock or veg, but what's to do when there is nice fat chicken running all over the bloody place owned by a bloody Hun and we so hungry?[48]

If soldiers were determined to steal food, civilians had few options. On Funafuti in the Ellice Islands, the people, fearing invasion by the Japanese in August 1942, consumed their chickens and most pigs, which left them short of stock.[49] The Japanese plundered "every corner of Melanesia."[50] Following Japanese depredations, the 1st Battalion Fiji Defense Force camped on Nggela in the Solomon Islands. A villager noted little difference in outcomes;

> they start to cut down ngali nut trees betel nut trees breadfruit trees and then they went into our garden and did bad damage with harvest and foods. . . . From that time the Fijians soldiers and we the native we rushed between ourselves to get foods in the gardens. Their officer tried to stop them but invained [*sic*]. In that season of the year we nearly lost all our foods.[51]

Japanese Subsistence

Although Japan's knowledge of New Guinea was limited, it planned to develop local resources to support its occupation. With a civil administration (Minsei-bu) in Rabaul under the navy, and several commercial planting, tuna fishing, milling, and minor manufacturing companies, various initiatives involving local labor began in early 1942. The result was good returns of coffee, cocoa, beans, tobacco, and vegetables including rice in 1942–1943, assisting the almost 100,000 Japanese and foreign workers. But in mid-1943, supply lines were collapsing to American submarines, and Japan was well on the defensive in Micronesia. By early 1944, the Allies had isolated Rabaul and Japanese units throughout the New Guinea islands.[52]

For the Melanesians, the retreat of the Horii detachment from Kokoda in late 1942 was a stark preview of what famished men would do. As the Australians passed Japanese dead, villagers along the path

> keep saying Good one no doubt meaning they are glad we have freed them from the Japs evidence of who's [*sic*] cruelty to them can be seen on every side, ruined gardens and starving women and children. These scenes move me greatly and tears come to my eyes.[53]

Before they became desperate, most Japanese bartered or purchased both labor and food from the people.[54] Near Kavieng, Taketoshi Nagaoka found that by mid-1944,

> The natives had become shrewd and it was not easy to trade with them. Bananas were scarce and 15 cigarettes were required for a single bunch. Papaya was more plentiful and 10 cigarettes would buy about 2 good-sized ones.

Figure 11. Japanese kitchen, Rabaul area, New Britain. This was probably taken before mid-1943 as tuna fish and squid are featured, indicating Japanese fishing boat involvement (Courtesy of Alfred Weinzierl).

By 1944, some islanders were too sick to labor for the Japanese. To survive, they made small gardens deep in the jungle. Where the bombs fell, some foraged wild food; some stole from one another; a daring few stole from the Japanese.[55] Especially on Bougainville, where the Japanese had effectively doubled the prewar population of forty-five thousand, many people succumbed to illness because of malnutrition.[56] Fighting inland from Wewak-Aitape, Australian B. H. Macdougal in May 1944 noted the state of the Japanese: "this living off the land is not all it's supposed to be, this fact being exemplified when one sees the few prisoners that are taken."[57] In a pathetically ironic inversion, civilization's thin film dissolved: A few Japanese slaughtered and ate their own and hapless Melanesians, whom many of both sides had considered cannibals and savages.[58]

The Japanese made demands on local fauna, but a certain repugnant ecological balance emerged. In 1944–1945 their raids around most of coastal mainland New Guinea, its northern islands, and parts of the western Solomons stripped villages of their domestic pigs, chickens, and garden produce.[59] At Rabaul they ate dogs. On the Gazelle Peninsula "the most favored food of the soldiers were toads, lizards . . . they reached more than a metre long—and snakes."[60] Wild pigs fared better, as the islanders could not fence their gardens in the disorder, so the animals foraged at will.[61] In the battlefields, dogs "have been better fed and stronger than in peace time, due to having eaten dead Japs."[62] Wild pigs did the same.[63] And, at Cape Endaiadere where the 18th Brigade of the AIF had defeated the enemy,

> mounds of old coconuts were about the place. We were told not to disturb them. Under each was at least one dead Jap. There were many rats here. I saw one about 14 inches long. They looked obscene, probably because we knew what they had been feeding on.[64]

Unlike the Allies, whose gardens were supplementary, the Japanese from mid-1943 became dependent on their immediate environment. Command's official dictum of "cultivat[ing] vegetables and fruit trees" for some of their provisions[65] extended to "self-support."[66] They boiled seawater to collect salt and demanded that villagers manufacture coconut oil for their cooking. After their retreat from Guadalcanal, the Japanese collected seed material. On Karkar Island, north of Madang, they planted gardens of "Kong Kong" taro (*Xanthosoma sagittifolium*); on Simberi Island off New Ireland they used local people to plant about thirty acres of tobacco and rice and thousands of pounds of sweet potato, and to make sago (*Metroxylon sagu*) on Tabar Island. The Japanese forced Chinese traders on New Hanover to make gardens for them.[67] At Murik in New Guinea in 1944, the Japanese grew wetland rice and other crops with local labor.[68] Sometimes they commandeered local gardens. On Vanga Vanga in the Solomons, they planted beans and Chinese cabbage among native vegetables. In barren areas how the Japanese fertilized gardens may be surmised from their use of nightsoil on Nauru and Ocean Islands.[69] On fertile Bougainville, they planted hundreds of acres, some of the best being in Buin. Paw paws (papaya), sweet potatoes, beans, pumpkins (squash), marrows, cucumbers, chilies, peanuts, and cantaloupes all flourished, along with the introductions of eggplant, cabbage, and new varieties of sweet potato. Yet by April 1945, across the Bougainville Strait on Fauro, they remained confined, eating the last of a planter's cows and villagers' pigs. Their commanders forbade fishing with scarce grenades. Even their taro and greens were insufficient to feed them. All they had to barter with were promises or threats.[70]

In the rich volcanic soils of Rabaul's hinterland each man had to cultivate about 598 square yards (0.12355 acres or 500 square meters). In about four square yards grew greens including a fast-growing, edible chrysanthemum (*Chrysanthemum coronarium*), similar to Japanese *shungiku*; in the rest grew staples such as rice, sweet potato, or tapioca (cassava) with plantings of eggplant and onion, probably negi (*Allium fistulosum*). By early 1945 the Japanese had cultivated around ten thousand acres near Rabaul. Insects infested the rice, but the Japanese stoically ate the lot. Without chemical sprays, they attempted to control a sweet potato worm by digging a channel around the garden, filling it with gasoline, and igniting it. They found new sources of food, unused by the natives: the tap root of the papaya and bamboo shoots, boiled and flavored with certain ashes. Unable to feed pigs adequately, they commandeered them or bartered with the people using goods looted from Rabaul's stores. More successful with chickens, they kept these mainly for eggs. By the end of the war there were about 70,000 chickens for a force of about 89,000, excluding about 20,000 auxiliary civilians.[71] Another food item was the "demdem" or giant African snail imported from Palau. A few became 200,000 within a year and these soon became two million, "which almost solved

Figure 12. Japanese navy pilots working in gardens near Rabaul, probably wearing flying goggles to indicate their status (Courtesy of Alfred Weinzierl).

the question" of a protein source.[72] Troops fished with explosives and harvested fish when Allied bombs hit the sea, or they forced villagers to do so. From 1944, they had neither quinine nor synthetic antimalarials, so they tried different tree bark and papaya leaves, with little success. They used sulfa from volcano craters for skin treatments as well as improvising salves from toads and plasters from the gum of certain trees. Their daily routine was three hours for "self support," construction of the fortress, and military training respectively. As Allied bombing increased in 1945 the ratio became 2: 3.5: 3.5.[73] After the surrender, the Japanese at Rabaul appeared "well fed and in fairly good health" and, as prisoners, tended their gardens while awaiting repatriation.[74]

Aware of the value of these gardens, the Americans and the RNZAF had experimented with dropping various chemicals and bombs. Because pilots could not always tell a Japanese garden from a Melanesian one, local people already struggling to feed themselves often had their gardens bombed.[75] The Allies considered using ammonium thicyanate, a defoliant, but this was most effective on crops as roots formed—which was impossible to ascertain from the air. Spraying with diesel oil and gasoline was tried from May 1944, "without any spectacular results." Incendiary gasoline (napalm) bombing was used, but the fuel would often not ignite. Other chemicals were considered but rejected for fear that the Japanese would accuse the Allies of chemical warfare. By mid-1945 the RNZAF regarded gardens "an unprofitable target" because they were then too small and scattered.[76]

Correcting Great Tragedies

When the Japanese imperial forces captured Rabaul in February 1942, its hedges of red hibiscus, the "South Seas Camellia," caught the eye of journalist S. Okada, as he admired the town's orderly layout. By late 1943, Allied bombs had devastated "the beautiful seaside town," and Okada mourned the loss.[77] Beauty and its loss touched the hearts of men, even in war. In the midst of the killing, gardening was a creative act. Gardens nurtured not only the body, but also the spirit. Intuitively, war-weary young men responded. On Kolombangara in early 1944, gardening on the abandoned Japanese airfield,

> 2nd Lt. W. O. Sabel is in charge, and has working for him a number of colored enlisted men and a dozen natives. Tomatoes were doing exceptionally well, and were the pride and joy of a young colored corporal, a former country agent, who tends the plants lovingly and, in his own words "expects to get enough data from them to write a master's thesis." (In this connection, a heartwarming by-product of all the garden projects is the enthusiasm and renewed interest in life shown by so many farm-boy G. I.s detailed to work in the gardens).[78]

For the invaders, gardens like those back home impressed some familiarity on an alien landscape, orderliness in the disordering environment of war. Flower gardens meant even more; they asserted the cycles of life, resonating home and peace. In 1942, the Australian nurses, dealing with ten medical patients to every one battle casualty from the Kokoda campaign, found solace for themselves and those around them, when they

> made a garden and rockery around the sisters' mess, and ferns, balsam, zinnias and croton bushes with bright coloured leaves flourished in the heat and rain. Orchids and staghorns were tied to the posts supporting the grass roof, and the atmosphere was cool and attractive.

Allied nurses started flower gardens around the hospitals in New Guinea and soon had their patients helping—for many, a part of their healing. Australian officers of the Salvation Army who had been up the lines knew the significance of having gardens around their Red Shield rest areas and canteens at base.[79] The New Zealand 2nd casualty clearing station west of Point Cruz, Guadalcanal, had an impressive flower garden by late 1943 that "appeared to delight" the patients.[80]

Warriors carried their domestic environment and its beauty in their minds. Corporal V. O. Hunt arrived at Milne Bay in October 1943. Sent to Dutch New Guinea in July 1944, then to Noemfoor, he witnessed the suffering the Japanese had inflicted on their laborers and he endured successive bombing raids, but his thoughts were of the future: "they (Tojo) had me out of bed at 5 am this morning. . . . Good ground plenty of coral mixed in with chocolate rock, must grow some flowers." In April 1945, suffering from exhaustion, malnutrition, and sores that refused to heal, Hunt was finally evacuated after two and a half years of fighting. In a Sydney hospital he knew he had reached home. "Now I am in bed looking at flowers, clean wards, real nurses, and a bed. The food's delicious. My God, thank God. Will see Gwen and the babies Sunday."[81]

In Troubled Waters: Fishing

Not simply food, but a varied diet contributed to troop morale, especially of the sick. Fish was excellent food for hospital patients. The AIF's fishing operations in New Guinea were small but focused, with specialized units in early 1944 replacing the Army Transport Unit in Port Moresby in providing for hospitals. The 1 and 2 Marine Food Supply Units were based respectively at Yule Island, west of Port Moresby, and at Salamaua near Lae. They worked closely with Melanesians, using traps, long lines of six hundred fathoms with one hundred hooks on each, trolling, and beach and trawling nets. As soon as they were caught, the fish were gutted,

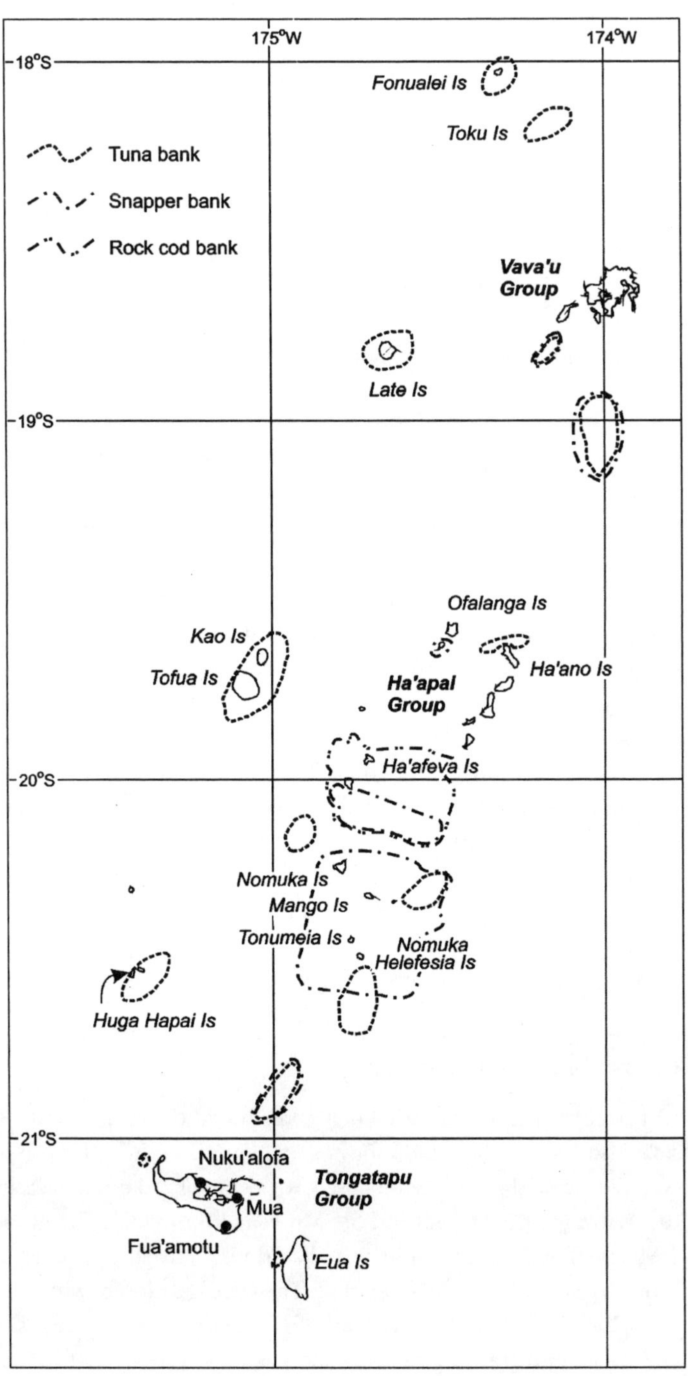

Map 9. Tonga Islands fishing grounds (Based on map in RG 313-58-3394, NARA SB).

cleaned, and refrigerated for the hospitals, with excess given to service units.[82] The Terrain Studies suggested how others could get a supply: "Fish are plentiful and can be obtained in large quantities by the use of dynamite. The average catch from one plug of dynamite is . . . about 150 lbs."[83] This was successful, as one Australian wrote home: "Our food has been supplemented by a few meals of fish obtained by methods peculiar to the Army—you'd know about this, Uncle."[84]

In the South Pacific, the FEA became the facilitating agency to provide fish for the Americans. They were not the first. In July 1942 the navy investigated possibilities in Tahiti with French support to supply the Bora Bora base, but this never eventuated. The commander then requested fishing equipment since most of the islanders bought their fish in cans from Chinese traders.[85] In Tonga, American command in September 1942 worked with the motorized cutter *Hokelau* to survey fishing grounds, guided by expert Tongan fishermen. Although there was "no Fishing industry of sufficient importance to be classified as commercial fishing," the survey confirmed an abundant supply. The idea was abandoned, however, because of the lack of a suitable vessel with refrigeration.[86]

New Caledonia with its huge troop concentrations was next considered. After investigations in November 1942 by the American Joint Procurement Board in Wellington, plans were made, but they were suspended when the FEA took over the islands area in early 1943. Meanwhile, the New Zealand force had made arrangements with villagers to trade Spam for fresh fish for their hospital at Gomen, while men of the 23rd Battalion got their own with gelignite.[87]

The FEA had no South Pacific fisheries specialists. It drew upon domestic experts, such as Reginald Fiedler, chief of the Division of Fishery Industries. Following the survey in December 1942, the plan was to design kits for fishing littoral species along shore as well as for pelagic and demersal species. Yet fear of attack and shortage of vessels and knowledgeable fishermen made deep-sea fishing unlikely. Fiedler sought advice from Australian scientists, testing a kit in Port Moresby. Despite this, the FEA purchased forty kits modeled on gear used in New England in the United States and sent them along with American experts to each base to advise on their use.[88] Lessons taught by the Australians and local fishers in Tonga were lost on the FEA.

Fishing for Potential

In his South Pacific survey, Fiedler refueled at the airfield in Canton, an Anglo-American condominium where there was an American garrison that could benefit from a fishing kit.[89] Fielder proposed a wider agenda. He wanted the army to do the fishing; if this was not possible and Gilbert Islanders had to be employed, then they should be employed by the Americans

> so that the fishery will be considered an American fishery and not a British one ... the Island will be under joint American and British jurisdiction for ... fifty years ... because of conflicting claims to ownership.... I understand that our claim to the Island is based on old whaling explorations ... we should make an effort to continue this claim by the establishment of an American industry.... Furthermore, the fishery explorations of men attached to your Division may reveal the presence of large schools of fish offshore which might form the basis for a fish-canning or freezing industry ... after the war. Therefore, if we establish a fishery now we should have a prior interest in fisheries in that area.[90]

When the advisor, Wilbert Chapman, arrived he studied the fishery and the politics. The American forces there were not interested in fishing and the British were reluctant to allow them to direct the Gilbertese workers. Chapman decided to use the Gilbertese on the beach purse seine with an American to collect the catch for the messes. This worked, as the "natives know very well the way to operate the seine, know where to fish and when to go."[91]

After Chapman reached Noumea in November 1943 he found that Oliver had obtained an aging trawler with refrigeration added, the *Crystal Star*, later joined by two similar vessels, to fish on a larger scale. A month later, he surveyed south New Georgia waters and advised the FEA that two of the vessels could be better used there with an estimated catch of about ten tons a week, enough to give each serviceman one weekly meal of fish.[92] Unsurprisingly, in New Caledonia he had found that the Fiedler kit designed for the northern hemisphere environment "had to be modified in the light of local experience" and conditions. The deep seines for example, had to be cut and re-hung by the local French fisherman to half their original depth. The seine's use was restricted anyway, as coral ripped it.[93] Other modifications were needed. The trawlers had caught plenty of fish but often had engine trouble. Some of the fish was useless even with chilling after it was left on board too long. Some collected from local fishers had been dynamited, and the kidneys of such finfish often were pushed into the broken flesh, giving it an unpleasant taste. Mess cooks did not like the labor of preparing fish.

Before any changes could be implemented, the vessels and Chapman went to the Solomons, but French fishermen took on the job, under FEA supervision. Their main ground was from Boulapari northwards. Paid by the pound at rates the government set, they were to catch, chill, and get the catch to trucks for the "fish house" in Moindou, where the Melanesians cleaned it. The Americans again demonstrated their ignorance not only of the local environment, but also of local cultures, when they installed processing tables that were never used because the Melanesians worked squatting, not standing.[94]

During the trawler trials in New Caledonia, the distribution of fishing kits to units had been sidelined. By May 1944 with these vessels gone, the FEA resumed kit distribution as well as overseeing local fishing contractors, though the purchasing agency was the United States Commercial Company (USCC). The fishing was successful, producing in February 1945 about 64,400 lbs., but the veterinarians found problems with hygiene at Moindou. When the army refused to take the responsibility, the USCC cancelled the contracts.[95]

The gap in supply was filled from two sources. First, the trawlers had returned from the Solomons in late 1944 and fished for the army quartermaster, making large hauls around the Loyalty Islands. They concentrated on line fishing, especially near the Isle of Pines. Although catches were good, "some of these fish were unfit for human consumption at times."[96] By May 1945, trawler fishing ceased.[97] More significantly, New Zealand supplied four thousand pounds of frozen "high quality filleted fish for use in the hospitals" weekly from February 1945. Being frozen, these could "be transported throughout the entire South Pacific area,"[98] so there was no reason to persevere with the New Caledonian fishery.

After the trawlers had gone north, in April 1944 the *Crystal Star* fished around New Georgia and the *Jack Cam* around Guadalcanal. Briefly at Munda, the *Olga Star* went on to Green Island (Nissan). All fished with considerable return in spite of mechanical troubles, catching around 1,017 lbs. a day.[99] Chapman admitted he had known little about these waters when he started

> plying his trade . . . with a crew made up of equal parts of white Americans, who knew less than he about fishing around the coral reefs, and black Melanesians, who fortunately for the success of this venture, knew all there was to know about such activities.[100]

He relied on his five Solomon Islanders from New Georgia. Despite difficulties with the old trawler and drunken white crewmen, they regularly supplied fish for Munda. In the western Solomons, Chapman distributed kits to isolated units who had relied on explosives. Yet this sometime director of the School of Fisheries at the University of Washington also resorted to dynamiting to obtain a catch.[101] Elsewhere the army and navy units used the kits, but "due to the westward movement of combat activities fishing kits were transferred westward."[102]

By late 1944, the FEA had surveyed most central and south Pacific fishing grounds outside the combat area. Chapman in 1943–1944 visited practically every American-occupied island from Hawaii to Nissan. These surveys assessed potential stocks for both military use and the American domestic market. Although stocks were high, especially of pelagic species such as tuna and albacore, the lack of any commercial fishery and large refrigerated vessels precluded immediate exploitation.[103]

Being able to sustain supplies of nutritious food from America, Australia, and New Zealand was fundamental to Allied success. Its lack undermined the Japanese. A captured Japanese understood this when he saw food supplies awaiting distribution on Guadalcanal:

> To realize that these potatoes had to be brought all the way across the Pacific Ocean from the American mainland. . . . And with that, I suddenly got a feeling of how that distant country America had come right here.[104]

Local vegetables, fruit, and fish made a significant contribution to food variety and thus to the health and morale of front-line troops and the sick. Regarding fisheries, had the FEA been more attentive to local environmental knowledge, as Chapman had with his Gilbertese and Solomon Islanders and the AIF with the New Guineans, they may well have been able to catch even more.

The Allies, nonetheless, achieved their immediate goal of feeding their troops well. For them, their influence was to be more enduring than their ephemeral farms because of the resource information they now had. The Americans especially had gained access to southern Pacific lands and seas that had been beyond their peacetime reach. For the islands and people concerned and often employed, they witnessed both Allied and Japanese agriculture on a semi-industrialized scale, far greater than existing patterns of horticulture. Unlike prewar experience especially in western Melanesia, these new crops were not exported to unknown shores but were utilized directly, as was timber.

CHAPTER 5

Taking Stock

Building for Battle

> [T]he country is largely undeveloped, reef rimmed, heavily forested islands, devoid of roads and port structures.

> Don't waste these natural materials and, above all, don't "overgraze the range." The bamboo, cane saplings, grass and Naiouli bark represent resources that must be carefully preserved for the permanent population. . . . Each island has its own special materials and methods; take advantage of them and—when in Fiji do as the Fijians do.

Food was essential for all combatants, but so too was shelter. In the Pacific theaters, most shelter and infrastructure had to be built from scratch. Allied engineers reconnoitered the environment and found resources at hand, often learning their characteristics as they went along. Aggregates—gravel, sand, and coral—were needed for roading, runways, in-fill, and foundations. Timber too was a necessity, not only for building and dunnage, but also for containers to ship matériel forward. Since both aggregates and timber were bulky and took up shipping space, the more supplied from the local environment, the better.

Great Empty Pits

Engineers with geological expertise applied their knowledge of aggregates to Pacific settings. Before they entered the war, the American engineers Svendrup and Parcel of St. Louis began constructing airfields for the "ferry route" across the Pacific, but they found no gravel and scoria on coral atolls.[1] They utilized the very substance of such atolls—coral. Most used was live, blasted away from its foundations in the reefs and lagoons and dredged up to be crushed and compacted into a surface for runways. If stabilized by being moistened with water or sealed, coral made a hard surface.

Some concept of the scale comes from Midway Island in 1939–1940. The dredges raised 1,970,730 cubic yards at a cost of $491,791 for the runway. As well, blasting for the seaplane base of 1,460 square feet and for a channel in the reef removed 2,527,355 square feet of coral. Once the war started, another 1.25 million cubic yards were dredged. In the Cook Islands on tiny Penrhyn's Motukohiti district, a coral runway 7,000 feet by 300 feet needed one million cubic yards of fill.[2] This and the adjacent Omoka district held two-thirds of Penrhyn's population of six hundred. Elsewhere in the lagoon, "[t]o provide filling for the Runway etc., the American forces have completely removed one small islet and part of another and what was once land is now part of the lagoon."[3] On Funafuti, Ellice Islands, where the Americans extended the Te Buabua channel in 1943 for shipping access with 472,599 cubic yards dredged, the engineers deposited the fill on shore.[4] Excavated borrow pits from which dead coral was excavated filled with seawater to become fetid swamps, making eight of Funafuti's precious 260 acres useless. Here, where the land-to-population ratio was precarious, the permanent loss of the *babai* pits for growing *pulaka* (*Cyrtosperma chamissonis*) as well as coconut-bearing land under airstrips worried administration and people.[5]

Figure 13. 73rd Seabees using "Carry-alls" to spread crushed coral on new runway, Munda, New Georgia, August 1943 (EX. 342-FH-3A43672, NARA).

Once the battles began few records were kept, but the volume used was vast because airfields and roads needed resurfacing regularly.[6] In the Russell Islands and the Munda bases, these borrow pits pockmarked areas adjacent to roads, because the roads needed surfacing.[7] On Guadalcanal's extensive roads and runways, the demand was ongoing, so the main borrow pit at Kukum had to be reserved solely for airfield maintenance.[8]

In New Guinea there was "ample sand and gravel in most localities," though the gravel was "poorly graded" and often required crushing.[9] American geologists discovered the younger coral typical of atolls was localized. At Finschhafen, Madang, and Hollandia, the older, uplifted, weathered coral often had high clay content and was unsuitable as foundational material. So base facilities were either moved to higher ground, or rock, riprap (crushed stones), and corduroy roads of logs were used as foundation.[10]

In the operational zone the Americans rarely considered compensation for aggregates. On Guadalcanal, the departing Americans asserted, "It is felt that in no case was any compensable damage done because the various pits are located on hills which were not cultivated or in other waste areas." Yet the same could not be said regarding, say, the villages and Methodist mission station around the Roviana lagoon, New Georgia, or Lever's plantations on the Russells. Even so, the American forces often considered that they had "improved" these islands, thus administrations and islanders were in their debt.[11] Beyond the combat zone, however, in Western Samoa and New Caledonia, the Americans accounted for aggregates via reverse lend-lease to the New Zealand government or by direct payment to French owners respectively. In Fiji, a joint government and military committee controlled the allocation of construction materials, with reverse lend-lease apparently operating.[12]

Strange Forests

American engineers reckoned that to establish a Pacific base, about 30,000 board feet (70 cubic meters) of timber per 1,000 men were needed during the first three months of occupation, with about 4,000 (9.3 cubic meters) per month to continue until completion.[13] Utilizing local timber, however, posed problems. Heavily forested islands had timber of highly variable quality and quantity, and were usually difficult to access. Before the war, other than limited indigenous use, the timber had little commercial appeal. Lack of infrastructure, along with distance from world markets, kept demand low. Only a few high-value timbers had received attention. From Fiji to New Guinea, most of these—kauri (*Agathis* spp.) and some New Guinea "walnut" (probably *Dracontomelum magniferum*), *Callophyllum* spp., and *Terminalia* spp.—went to Australia. Fiji annual exports before the war were about 725,000 board feet of kauri, a quarter of the cut, while exports from the Solomons never exceeded 2.4 million board feet (5,600 cubic meters).[14] From the 1920s, some New Caledonia kauri went to Australia.[15] With world trade upset in 1940–41, New Guinea experienced a brief, unprecedented boom with 7.5 million board feet (17,500 cubic meters) of "walnut" exported to America for furniture manufacture.[16]

No detailed prewar colonial surveys of timbers existed for the New Hebrides, the Solomons, or even smaller Western Samoa. The Australians in New Guinea had carried out a couple of limited botanical surveys, but specific information was lacking, the Forestry Department having just been set up in 1938 with two foresters. Although the British knew more about Fiji species, the stock levels had not been assessed, as its department was also new. In New Caledonia, several botanists had surveyed the forests, but there was no stocking detail and no forestry department.[17] Timber properties were little known. Even the fiber stress of the common coconut was uncertain. Moreover, in a cline going from west to east, species became fewer in number and were rarely in concentrated stands as in more temperate areas, but stocks were greatest in the west.[18] So, where the battles raged, there were ample local timbers. What was known came from the experience of a few sawmillers, since the business on these islands rarely paid high returns and all territories imported construction timbers.

The BEW initially sought timber for crating military farm produce. Before the war, Western Samoa and Fiji had imported wooden shooks to make cases for banana export. Tonga and American Samoa had little timber to spare and imported much. None were getting their usual supplies from North America such as Douglas fir (Oregon pine) and redwood, nor were they getting Australian hardwoods, so the BEW worked with the administrations to expand local production for military and civilian use.

Meanwhile, New Zealand, the FEA, and military timber specialists carried out surveys.[19] Before the survey was complete in Western Samoa, American millers had already started logging on Upolu in August 1942, extracting more than a million board feet in a year from three hundred acres of the Crown or Reparation Estates, near Mulifanua. They found suitable building timbers—mainly *mamalava* (*Planchonella samoensis*), *mamala* (*Dysoxylum samoense*), *tamanu* (*Calophyllum spectabilis*) and *malili* (*Terminalia richii*). The administration's estates had the only other mill, mainly for local demand. Timber produced was costly due to low stocking levels, but wartime economies were relative. For well-forested Savaii's rough terrain, the FEA planned to provide equipment, transportation, and expertise, with the administration supplying labor. But by the time the New Zealand forester submitted his report, the forces had little need of timber, so the scheme lapsed.[20]

In Fiji, the BEW worked closely with the American army, utilizing existing operators, assisting with roads, and maintaining equipment. Even so, in times of peak transshipment, lack of dunnage in Suva and Lautoka caused water damage to cargo piled on the ground until a local mill at Vatia Point supplied 100,000 board feet in late 1943. With extraction regulations suspended, production doubled from prewar years, reaching 3,050,000 cubic feet in 1943, apart from 5 to 10 million lineal feet of round timber (poles) the military cut with payments to the Fijian owners.[21]

In the New Hebrides, the FEA supplied portable sawmills for crate making, but the military diverted these to Efate and Santo, where some settlers also supplied milled timber. The U.S. Army provided heavy equipment to the Aneityum Logging Company, which had purchased timber rights from the local people, to extract kauri timber for New Caledonia as well as plywood in Australia, totaling more than 2.1 million board feet.[22] In New Caledonia by early 1943, the Americans urgently needed timber because supplies from North America and New Zealand were scarcer. Although the broken mountain valleys made access difficult, the Americans arranged contracts with French landowners to mill about three million board feet in the Nepui Valley. The FEA came later, concentrating on milling for produce crates. Its forester, Major W. Tilton, carried out surveys for the army, and in early 1944 the FEA handed its mills to the army, which already had several operating, the largest being the French sawmill at Plum, Baie des Pirogues. Here, the kauri and *Callophylum* spp. from Aneityum and pine (*Araucaria cookii*) from the Ile des Pins were milled at about 15,000 board feet daily. With Tilton in charge of army timber activities, the FEA's role became advisory.[23]

Wharves and bridge pilings required durable timbers. Local knowledge indicated that the most durable timbers, resistant to rot, borer, and worm, were *Vitex cofassus* spp., *Afzelia bijuga* (*Instia bijuga*), and *Pterocarpus indicus* in eastern New Guinea and the Solomon Islands, as well as *Metrosideros* spp., in the Milne Bay district of Papua.[24] As New Britain had good stands of the hardwood *Eucalyptus deglupta,* Japanese milled these from early 1942. In the New Guinea hinterland, near the mining settlements of Wau and Bulolo, there were substantial stands of the pines *Araucaria cunninghamii* and *A. klinkii,* but lack of roads for much of the war meant limited utilization.[25]

Except for the few export timbers and the locally used hardwoods, little else was known. When New Zealand forester C. T. Sando reported on Guadalcanal in October 1943 in conjunction with the FEA, he noted, "About forty different kinds of millable sized timber trees were seen but, unfortunately, it was not possible to identify many as no botanical literature was available and, at the time of my visit very few trees were bearing flowers or fruit."[26]

Lack of knowledge of timber properties frustrated the Allied timber men and made for uneconomic use of the resource, but sustainability and combat needs remain eternal adversaries on any battlefield. Although myriad fungi and insects attacked most unseasoned and untreated timbers, reducing their useful life to months, construction did not need to be permanent, so local timbers sufficed.

Getting Timber in Combat Zones

When the Japanese invaded New Guinea and the Solomons, their command expected self-sufficiency. In 1942, their commercial companies operated a sawmill in New Britain, but the military controlled most.[27] Although utilizing local materials, the Japanese did not make their bases on the scale of the Americans, concentrating by mid-1943 on underground structures.[28] Given the severity of Allied bombing, they would have had a constant need for construction timber. Of about forty small mills on the Gazelle Peninsula, nineteen survived Allied bombing, so the AIF used them to construct internment camps.[29]

In the combat zones of western Melanesia, any ideas the BEW had about assisting civilian needs were subsumed to military necessity. When the Japanese

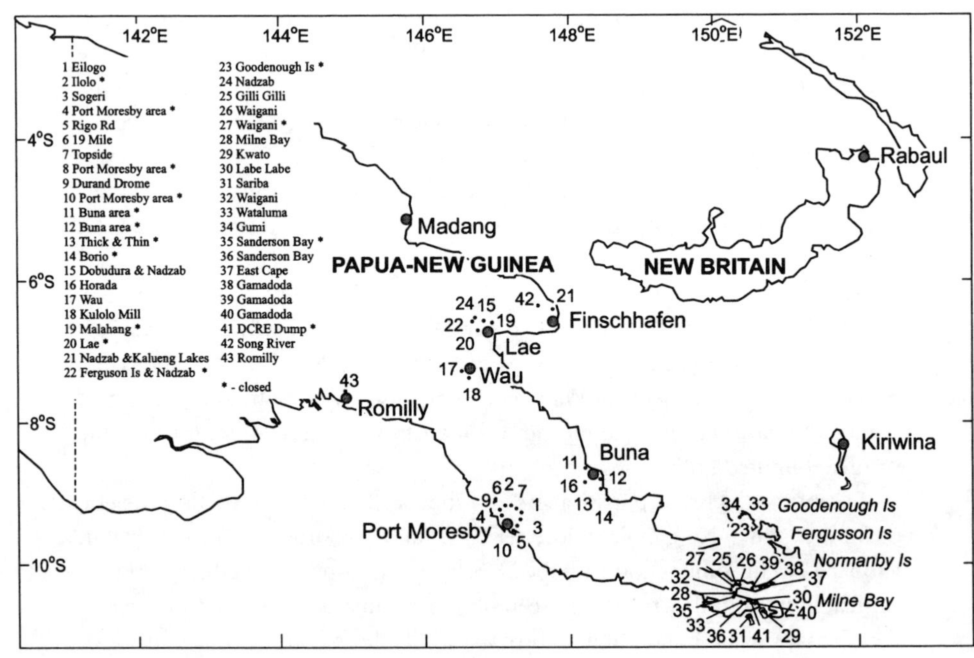

Map 10. Sawmills in Papua and New Guinea, March 1944 (based on McAdam, 10 Apr. 1944, Entry 305H, file 348, RG 77, NARA).

occupied the Solomons' capital of Tulagi in May 1942, the British administration went into hiding until the Americans landed on Guadalcanal in August. So, while the fighting continued, arrangements for timber utilization were ad hoc, though the administration maintained that the trees belonged to the landholders. Because Melanesians fled coastal battlefields, finding owners of trees was difficult. With little regard to ownership, the Americans and New Zealanders logged areas close to camps and bases. No count of timber felled began until about November 1943, and even then the Allies cut thousands of unrecorded poles and small trees. They felled thousands of coconut palms for construction and clearing for installations. On northern Guadalcanal alone, non-combat activities destroyed more than 116,500 coconut palms. As in other operational areas, most belonged to plantation companies or missions, but Solomon Islanders lost palms too.[30]

The situation in New Guinea differed from the Solomons. In the initial stages of the fighting, log extraction and milling were uncoordinated. The AIF commandeered civilian mills, five of which were producing about 188,000 board feet (438.6 cubic meters) monthly by December 1942. Landing in Papua from mid-1942, the Americans brought in sawmills and used Australian ones. The push north put more pressure on timber supplies. Though the Australians kept rough production tallies in Papua from about December 1942, the Americans did not. Preoccupied with airfield building, the American engineers sought Australian help to obtain timber.[31]

Both armies liaised with ANGAU. By March 1943, the AIF operated six mills: two in Milne Bay, two near Port Moresby, one to the southeast at McDonald's plantation, and one at Wau. ANGAU and the AIF operated one in the Gulf district near Port Romilly, and the American engineers had two near Port Moresby and one at Horada near Buna. ANGAU expanded its sawmilling by midyear, operating two commandeered mills in Milne Bay at Kwato and Labe Labe. Official production had reached 499,500 board feet (1,165.5 cubic meters) monthly in March. Demand was almost double this and estimated to climb to about 1,539,200 board feet (3,591.5 cubic meters) a month for the year June 1943–June 1944. Milne Bay, for example, was short of timber piles and construction timbers when the Americans set up their base there in mid-1943. Yet production at Port Romilly in the Papuan Gulf had to be reduced because there were insufficient boats to carry milled timber to Port Moresby. The Americans wanted ANGAU to provide labor for timber production as well as to rationalize operations.[32]

When operations began in New Guinea, Australia had supplied hardwoods while American ships brought in Oregon pine. To relieve demand on Australian forests and to reduce the shipping space, both allies wanted greater utilization of New Guinea timbers, but the lack of information, infrastructure, and logistics was hindering this.[33] Desperate for coordination as well more systematic assessment and exploitation of reserves, the Allies called a conference in Melbourne on 29

July 1943. Representatives of both forces, ANGAU, and relevant government departments created a timber organization headed by New Guinea's former chief forester, Major James McAdam. He was to organize surveys of possible logging areas, "all information pertaining . . . the milling of such timber," advise on equipment, supervise the running of the Australian mills, and "maintain records of the quantities of timber milled by both . . . forces."[34]

Recalled from Britain, reinforced army forestry units arrived in New Guinea in May 1944 where they were joined by the 2/1 Forestry Company in early 1945. Their task was logging and milling. As well, the 1 and 2 Survey Companies were formed under the command of W. T. Suttie, with a technical unit based in Australia for testing and classification of timbers. The survey companies were to locate, measure, record, and map forest reserves for possible military use. By the time these units arrived, the front had moved north, so they were based around Nadzab, inland from Lae.[35]

Timber Production and Policy: Papua and New Guinea

Major McAdam commanded the headquarters unit, 1 Command Royal Engineers (CRE), organizing a count of sawmill production, equipment, location, and capacity. He calculated output at 10,488,768 board feet (24,473.7 cubic meters) for the period ending 31 March 1944.[36] This does not include production before mid-1943 because several units, mostly American, had left, while certain inaccessible areas had not been included. McAdam also found that "[i]nformation regarding the operation of the Allied forces has been difficult to obtain. Some units felt that a directive from higher authority was required before the information could be made available."[37]

When asked to provide data, the Americans thought this a preliminary to compensation claims against them. Negotiations at command level decided that any claims would fall under reverse lend-lease.[38] The American planners admitted the value of such records, as they provided "an orderly basis for submitting requisitions . . . for overseas shipment of lumber" and "for allocating engineering sawmilling effort."[39] To assist the Americans, the Australians made their records available. From late 1944 the records collated by CRE seem more reliable, though there were units that fell outside the count. McAdam, for example, did not know Manus' production during the war. Between December 1944 and July 1945, about 3,346,806 board feet (7,809.2 cubic meters) of local Manus timber was produced, a third of it by the RNZAF, who had come from Guadalcanal to run mills. Seabee units produced the rest. CRE ceased formal counting in November 1945, but subsequent to January 1946, platoons of the 2/2 Forestry Company working on Bougainville and New Britain milled 1,286,208 board feet (3,001 cubic meters) of timber.[40]

Even this does not reflect the full extent of logging. A total of 71,778,749 board feet (167,483.7 cubic meters) for the period from about mid-1942 to January 1946 is a count based on monthly production averages to about mid-1943, then on more detailed data until the beginning of 1946.[41] In the light of American reticence until late 1944, this is conservative. As late as June 1944, some of the Australian units too, particularly the RAAF, were tardy with "authentic" figures.[42] Piles for wharf structures usually were not included.[43] Moreover, the figure of 71,778,749 board feet was milled timber, not volume in log. In most mills that operated to late 1944,[44] recovery was low; "between 30 and 50%." Again, the American sawed volume did not stand up beside the low log volume, at least for 1944.[45] In view of these factors—volume in piles, low recovery rates, and underdeclaration—the in-log volume was probably close to 120 million board feet (about 283,168 cubic meters) felled by the Allies. Moreover, thousands of coconut palms were just sawed into lengths and not counted.

McAdam's concern for timber tallies had a wider purpose. Unlike her allies, Australia had an enduring interest in New Guinea. Seen as a buffer to northern invasion, its strategic potential was obvious. After the Australian public saw touching newsreels of wounded Australians being assisted by native carriers, they too appreciated the contribution of Melanesians.[46] At the Melbourne conference in July 1943, McAdam voiced what was to become a keystone of Australian policy:

> The lands and forests of the Territories are owned by the native peoples, and although the Administration had the right under the Timber ordinances . . . to acquire by purchase from the native owners timber and land for forestry purposes, actually very little timber has been so acquired. Most of the areas . . . purchased are under sawmilling operations. The bulk of the army's new sawmilling activity will broach native timber. Although very little appears possible in the way of adjustment at the present time, it will be necessary to collect and preserve records of all these operations so that eventually equitable recompense can be made to the owners for our use of their timber.[47]

Before the war, when the government occasionally required the felling of trees for a public purpose, it paid compensation to owners, but in wartime the demands for timber and clearance were extraordinary.[48] In declaring this principle, McAdam deserves credit for taking his responsibilities so seriously, for a year later it became part of the orders guiding the AIF's commander-in-chief, General Sir Thomas Blamey.[49]

Logging often hurt local communities. ANGAU was worried in mid-1944 when the 2/2 Forestry Company took over a mill on Karkar Island from an army park detachment, because a man, Grouch, with prewar experience left with the detachment. ANGAU had supported his attachment because he made loggers "conscious of the importance of preservation of Galip trees," valuable to Melanesians as a source of the canarium almond (*Canarium* spp.).[50] Directives soon went to all Allied units to consult ANGAU for this information, stating, "It is desired that native food trees not be utilized for sawmilling or construction purposes except in cases of emergency."[51] ANGAU had raised consciousness, and by November 1944 the American navy on Manus ordered that all food-bearing trees—"coconut, breadfruit, sago, nipa palm, mango, New Guinea almond, pandanus, fig, galip, okari, talisa and areca (betel nut)"—were to be preserved wherever possible.[52]

ANGAU's concern was warranted. After the 2/2 Forestry Company left Karkar, it went to Aitape still logging the canarium tree, remarking how easy it was to cut.[53] Most logging units generally took the easy option in the field, particularly near the front. Although the Australian forestry companies had been directed that timber production was to be "on a sound reafforestation basis" to protect the reserve,[54] once again the reality of battle conditions prevailed. Where they did not, the reality of logging and milling in a wartime tropical forest did:

> The logs had been skidded through mud deep enough to completely engulf them; rocks were embedded in the bark, and log washing facilities were inadequate and unsatisfactory. Shrapnel was encountered in a great many logs and rarely detected before being struck by the head saw. Saws ran hot; new teeth became dulled often on the first log sawed after filing; the timber cut considered of some of the hardest and stringiest in the world . . . logs were far from cylindrical in shape, having spray butts and often surface irregularities that made the logs extremely difficult to turn in the carriage . . . the loggers often worked in a deluge of rain in mud to their knees. "Cats" [Caterpillar tractors] bogged down above their tracks . . . and slabs had to be continually layd [*sic*] in the skid roads to keep them passable. Creek crossings were numerous and water in the magneto and other parts of the "Cat" motors was an unending source of trouble. Splay rooted trees made the use of "spring boards" essential, and thickly hanging vines made falling extremely hazardous.[55]

Applying peacetime's counsels to the exigencies of war was unrealistic, but McAdam's survey companies came closer to achieving the ideals of modern forestry. Instructions to them in November 1943 highlighted this:

> Complete surveys will be made, and detailed records will be kept in such a manner that they can be passed over to the civil administration when a change from a war footing to civil control is implemented.[56]

Their primary task was finding viable stands of timber for immediate needs. These demands, however, eased with the shrinking Japanese perimeter. By war's end the companies had covered a huge area on the mainland coast and the islands of Milne Bay, Manus, New Britain, and Bougainville. Much of this work was done by strip surveys. Even when the Americans supplied aerial photographs that enabled the surveyors to match tree type to canopy appearance and habitat in the aerial photograph with locations on the ground, footwork in arduous jungle conditions had to be done for accurate mapping. The companies relied extensively on Melanesians for carriers, for strip cutting parties, and for climbing trees. Lieutenant L. T. Carron also taught six Melanesians to identify trees from the photographs.[57]

The survey companies assembled a catalogue of photographs from which they mapped more than 30 percent of eastern New Guinea's vegetation on a scale of 1:63,360. As the war ended, the companies had checked more than a quarter of these mapped areas on the ground. They also carried out botanical surveys, assembling several dozen area collections to send to the Commonwealth Scientific and Industrial Research unit in Australia for identification, and they prepared timber samples for testing. In all, more than 1,500 specimens had been collected. Botanists had studied 620, listing 295 separate species. That collection was to become the basis of the postwar herbarium at Lae. This work continued until the end of the war until it was curtailed in October 1945 by demobilization.[58]

Cutting British Afterthoughts

During 1943 various units commenced milling on north Guadalcanal. By September there were six mills operating, three by the U.S. Air Force, one by the Service Command (a Seabee unit), and the one by the RNZAF. These were milling about 200,000 to 250,000 board feet (466 to 583 cubic meters) weekly. Trees milled were, according to the Americans, "mahogany, rosewood and teak"[59]; in fact, mostly *Calophyllum* spp., *Magnifera solomonensis*, and *Pometia pinnata*, *Vitex cofassus*, as well as *Pterocarpus* spp., *Terminalia* spp., and *Porinarium* spp. Three other mills that had been operating there were moved to the New Georgia Islands. Various Seabee units, the U.S. aviation engineers, and the 3rd Marines, as well as the forestry engineers operated in the Guadalcanal floodplain and cut about half the total output from about March 1944 when mills numbered eight until early 1945, with the New Zealanders cutting most of the rest. Their No. 2 mill, five miles up the Tenaru (Ilu) River, opened in August 1944. The FEA had ordered $200,000 worth of sawmills by 1944, supplying five to the American army.[60]

Sawmills followed the need for base construction and crating. In October 1943, near Munda, New Georgia, the first mill operated by a Seabee unit commenced work, with another finishing the logging in February 1945. In late 1943 the New Zealanders ran one at Kohinggo, west of Noro passage. A year later there were American mills on Roviana Island at Gega, two at Dobelie on Vella Lavella, and another at Lambulambu. A small one operated at Seghe. The Americans also cut about 20,000 board feet (46 cubic meters) in log from the area to tow to Mbatuna's Seventh-day Adventist mission mill. In April 1944 there were two operating in the Russell Islands with two more of the 1st Marines being set up.[61] The output of some seems to be unrecorded. At war's end, however, the American material salvage units counted 30,000 board feet of "mahogany" in the Russells, some being used for crating to Guam.[62] One of the largest sources of timber in the west was Stirling Island, Mono, where the Seabees milled more than 3 million board feet (7,000 cubic meters).

Production figures for the Solomons are subject to similar caveats as the New Guinea statistics. For example, an experienced miller from Fiji calculated in August 1945 that the timber cut from northern Guadalcanal was about 9 million board feet. This approximated the American statistics of 9.9 million board feet (23,100 cubic meters) cut at three American mills plus 280,000 (about 653 cubic meters) in log. This total, however, was for the period March 1944 to September 1945. American records from about April 1943 to February 1944 for Guadalcanal indicate another 1,524,964 board feet (3,558.2 cubic meters) milled—a grand total of 11,424,964 board feet (26,658.2 cubic meters), not counting at least 280,000 board feet (653.3 cubic meters) in whole logs for the later period only. But local timbers had been used increasingly since about August–September 1942 when the Americans landed on Guadalcanal and the Florida Islands, and no records have been found to April 1943. Sawmills operating in the Florida Islands, Russell Islands, New Georgia, and Stirling Islands recorded production of 9,222,046 board feet (21,761 cubic meters), a conservative amount as it covers only December 1943 to May 1945. Thus from the Solomons' forests the Allies alone removed at least 20,647,010 board feet (about 48,722 cubic meters) in milled timber.[63] In many places uncounted logs were felled to make bridges. The real total, if poles, firewood, and milling loss were included, would be far greater, probably double the 20.6 million board feet of milled timber.[64]

In the Solomons, the administration's request to the military to keep returns of cut timber came as an afterthought. Its small numbers—a dozen or so amid the American military forces of 200,000 by early 1944,[65]—the lack of a British military presence, as well as the typical confusion of war, saw native timber rights sidelined. Nonetheless, the Americans generally kept their own records for planning. Experience elsewhere indicated there were likely to be claims for trees cut and possible reverse lend-lease charges. What seems to have stimulated the high commissioner in Fiji to instruct the Solomons' administration to seek extraction statistics, however, was a New Zealand request in late 1943 to assess the forest resource to supply its domestic needs, as it had sent hundreds of prefabricated buildings to New Caledonia.[66] The Solomons resident commissioner received directions from Fiji in January 1944, indicating that keeping a record of trees felled had not been a priority.

> With regard to the timber cut for milling purposes, the question of compensation to the owner of the land from which the trees have been taken and are being taken will inevitably arise sooner or later. Possibly such payments may have been made by the Protectorate government and treated as Reciprocal Aid [reverse lend-lease] . . . if not already in operation, a system of records in respect of all timber should be instituted forthwith.[67]

This was too late. There were no detailed figures before mid- to late 1943. And who would do the counting thereafter? The British had no army alongside the Americans, let alone forestry units as the Australians were to have by early 1944. A year later, the Solomons' administration conceded that it was "more convenient, and perhaps more politic, to treat timber removal as war damage."[68]

British tardiness was not solely because of battle conditions, for in the New Hebrides the same attitude pervaded the British administration. Two days after the High Commission's secretary had raised the issue of compensation for trees in the Solomons, he remarked to the resident commissioner in the New Hebrides, "Presumably payment for the trees cut is being made to the natives or other owners of the timber lands being worked."[69]

In the Solomons, the use of local timber stimulated interest in its commercial potential. Word had traveled fast, as indeed did samples of the timber. Airmen, impressed by the quality of "mahogany" on Guadalcanal, loaded up two flitches, 12 feet by 12 inches by 12 inches, onto a C-47 aircraft and flew them to home to New Zealand to panel their commanding officer John Adams' parents' home.[70] Even before the war ended, hopeful logging interests, including service personnel, as well as the New Zealand government were sounding out the administration. The British, aware of deficiencies in their nascent prewar forest policy, thought a forest survey and legislation were needed before any commercial development could proceed, so they sent forester F. S. Walker to do this.[71] Just before the Japanese surrendered, Walker on Guadalcanal reported,

> A considerable number of logs are being transported to Kukum landing base, ostensibly for shipping aboard. Some three loads a day are rumoured to be going out this way. Species include Pometia pinnata (Island ceder), Terminalia sp., Palquium sp., Canarium grandistipulum (nut trees) among others. . . . This removal of logs would hardly appear to be necessary military requirements

> nor classifiable as war damage. . . . The Ngali nut tree is being felled indiscriminately . . . [it] is a valuable food here, whose felling in New Guinea is illegal.[72]

This "furniture" timber was going on order to Honolulu buyers, but complaints to the U.S. command stopped it.[73]

Walker also noted the felling of trees of value to Solomon Islanders—the canarium almond (ngali/nari nut).[74] He spoke to the American commander, who ordered such felling to cease, and planned to discuss this with the high commissioner.[75] The administration's records are silent on the cost to the local people, as no specific claims for tree damage have emerged since the war.[76] Yet in 1946, the Americans, vigilant for compensation claims for "damage to timber trees" as they "closed out" their north Guadalcanal base, admitted,

> The natives have complained that many almond nut trees, used by them for food, were destroyed, however, it is felt that no considerable additional damage could be considered because of the variety of the trees cut.[77]

Walker's intervention had come too late with war's end in sight and the imminent American departure. In his botanical research from June 1945 until late 1946, however, he was able to draw on the preliminary work of three New Zealand foresters done in 1943–45. Walker also had access to American aerial photographs to identify forest types, but detailed mapping of the Solomons' forest on a scale resembling that done in New Guinea remained beyond his brief and budget.[78]

Non-Timber Products

The forest is more than timber. In the Solomons, the administration paid the people for sago leaf for the military. In some Melanesian areas the sago palm grew wild. Often the processed pith was a famine food, such as on Malaita or in the Morobe area in New Guinea, and a staple in a few areas such the Gulf District of Papua and the Shortland Islands. To maintain the supply for food and building panels, the people planted suckers when palms were cut down. For panels, leaves were attached around a stick about three to six feet long and pinned with a small twig. The panels were then placed overlapping on the frame--the smaller the distance between each consecutive panel for roofing, the less likely leaks were and the more durable the shelter, though these did not last more than about four years. Leaf houses were cool, "cheap, serviceable, and withal quite satisfactory for storage."[79] The Allies used such buildings, as well as their prefabricated frame structures with leaf roofs. Areas outside the battle zones often produced the panels, with significant cash flowing into distant villages. Malaita, Makira, and parts of the Floridas provided great quantities of panels to the Guadalcanal camps, the standard price being 25 shillings per 1,000 fathoms.[80] Milne Bay villagers also did well out of leaf making for the Americans, though not all their fellows were so fortunate.[81]

In parts of New Guinea where sago was an emergency food, an emergency existed because the conflict had deprived the people of their normal sustenance. ANGAU was torn between military necessity and civilian need. Around Lae from October 1943, the demand for leaf panels or *maratta* for the camps was so great that the supply was almost exhausted. So were the villagers, because for months ANGAU had required them to make panels up to three days a week. The Japanese earlier had taken great quantities, then ANGAU labor continuously cut the fronds, which "either kills the palm or ruins it for food purposes." When ANGAU ordered this stopped to save the remnant, the "dejected, undernourished, and impoverished population" feared this would mean the cessation of their ANGAU-supplied rations. It did not.[82]

Other local materials were used. Samoans built *fales* and the Fijians built *bures* of reeds and thatch for the troops. Bamboo made all kinds of temporary structures.[83] In Serua, Viti Levu, the district officer infused a "missionary spirit" among the people to gather the bark of the *vau* (*Hibiscus tiliaceus*) for camouflage netting to cover almost eighty acres.[84] An American officer in the chemical warfare service had ideas of using "shoot rope" or derris, the New Guinea fish poison vine, as an "agent for future toxic warfare."[85] At Buna in 1942, the Australian engineers improvised with bark as lashings for bridge building because stocks of metal fasteners had not arrived.[86] With supplies closed from the Dutch Indies, ANGAU urged people on Sud-Est, Rossel, and Misima Islands to tap copel gum, "to make paint for battleships against the Japs." Paid a stick of tobacco for every six pounds, women and children, cut off for months from trade supplies, gathered more than twenty-two tons in a few weeks.[87] Pacific forests and their peoples provided much for a war that was not theirs.

Benefits to the War Effort

New Guinea's timber contribution to the war effort was considerable; the Americans estimated it at about a third of the timber used. The picture becomes complex because of the use of American imported timber by Australian units and vice versa, the varying needs over time, and because Southwest Pacific command included Australia, New Guinea, and the Netherlands Indies.[88] Overall, New Guinea's contribution was at least a third and no less than a quarter. Who cut it? On the mainland the Americans felled and milled about 63 percent, the AIF about 20 percent, ANGAU about 12 percent, and the RAAF around 5 percent. What was this worth? In terms of ship-carrying tonnage the production of 71,778,749 board feet (167,483.7 cubic meters) from New Guinea saved about 204,857 tons; in terms of cost of freight from Australia, it saved about A£3,072,847; in terms of cost of the equivalent volume in Australia, it saved another A£1,707,142.[89] For the United States, it would have been higher because of the greater distance. Based on pricing before the war, however, costing for reverse lend-lease for the Americans was to be averaged for all timbers, from the best furniture timbers at 2s 6d per 100 board feet to the most common at 10d. The Allies set the price at one shilling (12 pence). So at one shilling per 100 board feet, the Americans, if they had used all this timber, would be debited about A£35,889, were reverse lend-lease accounting to prevail.[90]

The contribution of the Solomons' timber resource was proportionately as great, as were the losses. In Fiji, the New Zealand engineers reckoned that the use of local timber reduced their costs by one-sixth. In these rear areas—Samoa, Fiji, New Caledonia, and the New Hebrides—the total timber cut probably reached a very conservative 14 million board feet, a considerable saving in shipping space to the Americans. Engineers estimated that when demand was greatest, military mills in the South Pacific command were producing one million board feet a week.[91] With the exception of the Solomons, reverse lend-lease, rentals, and compensation reimbursed owners who gained a new appreciation of the cash value of their resource, but the question of cost to the local ecology simply did not arise.

Consequences to Ecology

For military construction, the immediate environment was scoured for aggregates and timber. The scale of this remained localized, while most "high" islands were far less labile than small atolls. On the larger islands, with or without human intervention, the land's surface and vegetation constantly change under the influence of heavy rain, earthquakes, volcanic activity, tsunamis, and sometimes cyclonic winds. These forces did not disengage for the duration. Near Aitape, Australian gunner Flew recorded a landslip upriver that had blocked the water flow until it burst through and rushed down to where

> A couple of sections of the M G bn [machine gun battalion] were camped on an island about 10 yards from us. The island was swept away. Their screams . . . as it gradually went tree by tree were terrible, more so because we could do nothing to help them. Insects and snakes went up the trees with them. I went up the side of a mountain but it was dangerous with crashing trees.[92]

Throughout much of western Melanesia, under soaking rains from the trades or the monsoon, sides of hills regularly collapse into the valleys; rivers flood and change course overnight. A gravel bank can be swept away faster than any engineers can dig it out. It can build up just as rapidly. Certainly, over hundreds of years, humans gardening in Melanesia have changed forest and soil composition,[93] but for the short period of the war, human-induced change of topography was minuscule.

Whether or not damage was done to the localized forest ecology, the answer can only be equivocal. In most areas the stocks and nature of the forest had been largely unknown, so losses were hard to gauge. Some areas, however, were logged to the point of exhaustion, especially smaller islands since these were more accessible by sea. For example, by mid-1944 Seabee units on Stirling Island, where three million board feet had been milled, were complaining that logging timber was running out. In Papua, islands in Milne Bay such as Rogeia and Sariba lost their big trees. Parts of the Trobriand group were logged out. Such clearance of tropical forest induced succession patterns that created a different ecology. U.S. troops camping in the Yahoue basin in New Caledonia upset the French because they had cut down trees and damaged the watershed. In Fiji, logging probably intensified erosion and leaching of soils, though no assessment followed.[94] In the Solomons and New Guinea, Melanesians had complained about losing food trees, and administrations made efforts to prevent this. In some areas where many trees were felled, the administrations considered it detrimental because of the impact on humans or to future logging plans, but the impact on the forest ecology was irrelevant.

More enduring modification of the environment, however, was largely out of sight. No thought at all was given to the impact of underwater explosions on the reefs. Reefs take centuries to build up from minute living organisms piling themselves on and in the dead, solid remains of others. As well as excavating fill for construction, the Allies blasted channels for shipping access from one end of the tropical Pacific to the other.[95] Rottman in 2002 observed that "reefs around many atolls and adjacent to islands are still gouged and scarred from rampant dredging, blasting and drag-lining."[96] Massive killings occurred of coral and associated organisms as well as fish that depended on this habitat; one can only surmise the extent of the ecological impact, but measured by effects on the human species, it left depleted food sources in some atoll lagoons and possibly contributed to outbreaks of ciguatera poisoning. Even after ten years, where wartime blasting had occurred in the Cook Islands there was undernourishment of the people because of reduced seafood. Certainly, blasting of reefs, opening of passages, and reconfigured shorelines have changed current flows and increased erosion on labile atolls, often to the detriment of their inhabitants.[97]

The extreme circumstances of war caused the invaders at times to "overgraze the range," just as the Australians had done in the Morobe District with sago leaf and the Americans with mining coral on small atolls. Even as peace came, the most vulnerable felt the unkindest cut. Tarawa and Betio had lost practically every coconut and the main structural timber, pandanus (*Pandanus* spp.) or screw pine, to battle damage.[98] To add to injury, the Americans had cut and shipped large quantities of pandanus wood from the rest of the tiny Gilberts to their new territory, the Marshall Islands, and "made a bad situation worse for the people." At least this palm took only three years to grow to maturity, and the British administration worked hard to encourage replanting.[99] On north Guadalcanal, as the war ended, a logger bewailed the wastage of forest: "only certain species have been removed, leaving large quantities remaining, but which . . . would not be a commercial proposition." Here, even during the war, military loggers gave up trying to get timber on the coast between the Berande River and Henderson airfield as the shrapnel-riddled trees were too dangerous to mill.[100] Just as it had on the human population, the war had set its seal on the land above and below the high water mark, but its magnitude depended on the viewer's lens.

CHAPTER 6

Resources for the Metropole

Trade for the Periphery

> Now a second discovery of the South Seas has come.... As stubbornly as one small island after another has been assaulted and finally captured from the Japs, so island by island, reef by reef, plantation by plantation, the islands have entered into the consciousness, into the planning, into the council tables of the world. The calculations of the agricultural expert intent upon provisioning ships and armies on the spot, bring volcanic soil and coral atoll into the Ministries of Agriculture in London and Washington, the echoes in Moscow and Chungking. The men in the Ministries have to know about your soil on which you produce your bananas, sugar and pineapples.
>
> —Margaret Mead

> Money is a valueless token of remuneration for services if inconvertible to articles of utility or desirable value in a native, not European sense.

While before the war, the southern Pacific Islands were rarely major global primary producers, the loss of production and access elsewhere during the conflict gave increased significance to what their environments could offer. Islanders, the human resource, needed recompense for their labor, and so the goods they valued had to be supplied. Wartime colonial administrations thus had a double mission: to assist the military to obtain resources such as timber, fresh food, and labor while looking to the future. Wary of American ambitions in the region, they strove to protect the interests of their people and their metropolitan governments to ensure that resource exports were maintained equitably. As well as sustaining production, administrations also needed to ensure that the incentives of manufactured goods remained available or the people would not do paid work or sell crops to obtain them. Because of the dislocation of civilian supply lines, the military and their metropolitan governments assisted where possible because they were beneficiaries, especially of islanders' labor.

Copra and Sugar

Soon after war began in Europe, the South Pacific felt its effects. The islands' main exports were copra, sugar, rubber latex, shell, and—west of the Andesite line, from New Guinea, Fiji, and New Caledonia—minerals. The Depression had kept the price of inferior "South Seas" copra particularly low from 1929 for almost a decade, and several territories were almost completely dependent on copra exports. In the western Pacific, from where most of the copra went to Britain and Europe, copra-dependent colonial administrations were in dire straits when British vessels became German targets in the Atlantic and neutral shipping costs skyrocketed.

Pacific administrations considered possible solutions. Because of British and Australasian support for Charles de Gaulle's Free French, schemes to export copra had to include the French territories. Overall annual South Pacific production was about 220,000 tons, excluding American Samoa, which exported to America. America was, however, an unlikely potential market for others because its imports came from its colony, the Philippines, and it imposed protective tariffs against others.

South Pacific colonial representatives sought guaranteed purchase from the Ministry of Food, which worked to obtain resources for Britain and to stimulate empire trade. Colonial administrations devised a "pooling scheme" and a Pacific marketing board so that some copra from each territory would receive a guaranteed price. Yet despite tinkering with prices, quality, uses, stockpiling arrangements, and reduced rentals on leased plantations throughout 1940–1941, all plans ultimately depended on shipping. Though initially keen, Australia cooled to the scheme. One of the region's major commercial companies, Australia-based W. R. Carpenter and Co., established a crushing plant in Vancouver that could absorb the better, hot-air-dried copra that New Guinea produced. Most of the copra destined for Australia went to Lever Brothers' Sydney soap factory and later to manufacture glycerin for explosives. Some went to Mexico and Singapore for transshipment to Britain. To equalize returns for its New Guinea copra from these markets, Australia in mid-1941 set up its own pool.

By September 1941, as Dutch shipping faltered, exports from their Southeast Asian territories declined, increasing the demand for Pacific copra. Once Japan invaded Southeast Asia, this skyrocketed. The arrangements for the WPHC territories, Fiji, and Tonga came under the Ministry of Food, as some of the oil from the copra was destined for Britain via Canada. The Pacific Copra Marketing Board folded, but Fiji extended its own board to stabilize prices for the ministry and producers. Elsewhere, production control boards were set up to buy copra, with former merchant companies sometimes acting as commission agents, an unpopular change since it reduced profits. Canada wanted copra from the Solomons, Fiji, and Tonga at £18 a ton, rather than the £7 offered by the three major South Pacific merchants: Burns, Philp and Co. Ltd., Carpenters, and Morris, Hedstrom and Co. America was anxious to secure copra directly. With Japan's advance to Rabaul and the Solomons in early 1942, however, production declined.[1]

In peacetime, the sugar from Colonial Sugar Refining Company's (CSR) Fiji refinery had gone to Britain. During the war, as property of the British Ministry of Food, it went mainly to New Zealand, Canada, and the United States.[2] The CSR complained of the loss of some of its Fiji Indian labor to the Americans. But the greatest loss of labor to overall export production was from the Fijian population who joined the army and provided labor for American needs, such as stevedoring. Unlike the tenant Fiji-Indians, the Fijians owned the lands that provided subsistence. Copra production was a sideline or work they did periodically on European-owned plantations.[3]

This was the pattern in most of the Pacific; islanders as producers or laborers were the backbone of the copra industry. As prices rose, the demand for copra increased, but other higher-paying war work had greater appeal. In some places such as Aitutaki, copra production ceased when the able men and many women worked for the Americans.[4] A complicating factor was the shortage of trade goods, an outcome of the large trading firms' reduction of stocks when copra prices fell in 1939.[5] Because most Pacific islanders were not a savings-oriented people, money was useful as a means to immediate social ends. Theirs was an economy of sociality, not capital. If money could not be spent, then it was less desirable.[6] Though a shortage of consumer goods was an issue initially when Japan entered the war, the established trading companies eventually supplied a considerable quantity in non-operational areas. What profits they lost in copra they recouped in increased retail sales to well-paid islanders.[7]

In the South Pacific, the BEW hoped to channel copra to America. It seemed unaware that the old commercial companies knew the business better than newcomers. The output of French Polynesia, New Caledonia, and the New Hebrides, beyond the reach of the British Ministry of Food, went mainly to the United States from late 1942, however.[8] The FEA played a significant role in developing and shipping up to 52,000 long tons in 1943, whereas production had been 32,000 before the war. Removed from alternative employment, the Tahitians made the most of high copra prices. And, after the Americans withdrew, the New Hebrides' production increased in 1944. By 1945, however, the New Caledonian merchants complained of the tardiness of American shipping and wanted Australia to take small lots.[9] On the outlying British dependent islands, such as Rotuma, the northern Tongan islands, and Fanning Island, the High Commission had managed to have the copra shipped until mid-1943. By 1944, most available copra was being shipped from Apia and Tongan and Fijian ports, in addition to Papeete, largely without FEA intervention. Despite FEA encouragement, planters and administrations were reluctant to expand production, lest in committing to America's market they would lose when the Philippines were again exporting.

The FEA was anxious to get the Solomons producing. In the expectation that the military would soon allow resumption of copra production in mid-1944, BEW's Douglas Oliver tried to convince Resident Commissioner Noel to agree to export via the USCC to America for "the manufacture of synthetic rubber, plastics, insecticides . . . as well as for soap." Oliver even tried to persuade his superiors to pressure the British using the lever of reverse lend-lease arrangements, contrary to policy for the "South Pacific project."[10] In Suva, High Commissioner Mitchell was annoyed with Oliver's proposal, confiding to Noel in July 1944,

> I believe that FEA (which is the name under which our old friend Oliver and his gang now go) has elaborate plans for exploiting all sorts of articles of strategic importance to the Pacific. Up to the present, however, all that they have succeeded in doing is to fail to grow vegetables, and I do not seriously expect much to come of the new scheme.[11]

Oliver had proposed to Noel that "co-operation from the United States Officers would be more readily forthcoming if they knew that the copra was going to the United States." As Mitchell pointed out to American command, such a deal was beyond their control, because the destination of South Pacific copra purchased by the Ministry of Food was a matter of high policy set by the Joint American-British Authority in Washington.[12] There was already an agreement that the ministry controlled copra from British territories, "cooperating with the governments of Australia and New Zealand."[13] Even so, exclusive of Australian-controlled New Guinea copra, South Pacific exports to the United States amounted to 90 percent of production, a dramatic contrast to the prewar figure of 3 percent.[14] This outcome was what the FEA had hoped but, excluding the French territories, it had less to do with FEA's intervention and more to do with strategic necessity, Allied production policy, efficient production boards, and the established commercial companies' networks.

Minerals for Armaments and Food

The Americans, however, were quite capable of gaining considerable knowledge about a country's resources. Nowhere in the South Pacific was this truer than in

New Caledonia. An elaborate reporting system collected intelligence on economics, politics, psychology, subversive activity, as well as the geology and meteorology. Several of these categories furnished weekly information, its assemblage viewed with suspicion by the French administration, which feared a U.S. takeover as the war drew to a close.[15]

To the Americans, New Caledonia was of major strategic importance because of its geology and location, an importance that only increased as it became the largest U.S. military base in the South Pacific. The armaments of modern war require nickel, chrome, and iron ore—all found in New Caledonia. Before the war, the New Caledonian economy depended on nickel exports to France, Germany, and Japan, but the European war left only Japan as a market. Before Japan went to war, the Free French and their Allies tried to construct plausible excuses to refuse it nickel, particularly after the June 1940 armistice between Vichy France and Germany. Australia agreed to purchase the nickel to keep the Free French New Caledonian economy viable, as commerce with France had ceased. By August 1940, Australia was thus denying Japan nickel from New Caledonia, its only potential major source. Australia continued to give economic aid to New Caledonia as well as continuing airfield construction started in May 1941. As part of the communication lines between Australia and North America, it would have been a rich prize for the Japanese, so after the Pearl Harbor bombing the Allies garrisoned the island. As the Japanese advanced south and captured Rabaul, so grave was the threat that Australian commandos prepared to destroy mines and installations. This receded in mid-1942 when U.S. victories at the battles of the Coral Sea and Midway checked Japan's progress.[16]

Most of the island's mineral production went to America. What displeased the Americans was that Australia controlled the nickel supply because of prior deals to support the Free French. Australia sold it to Canada, which sold it to the United States via the USCC. Another frustration to the Americans was that a major chrome producer, the British-owned Société Le Tiébaghni, controlled purchases via the London parent company, which charged a commission and did not guarantee payment in American dollars. The Americans tried to negotiate a new contract for the chrome to go directly to them, but they failed. The importance of this nickel and chrome can be seen by considering that before the war none of New Caledonia's nickel output (in ore and matte) of 8,341 short tons went to the United States. By 1943, U.S. imports amounted to 7,315 short tons from Canada, with 2 percent being New Caledonia's indirect contribution. U.S. imports of New Caledonian chrome increased from 17 percent to 23 percent. The rest of the metal exports went to U.S. allies.[17] No matter how great American interest in postwar economics was, however, the object was always the defeat of the enemy, so supplying allies was crucial. In New Caledonia, the BEW, the U.S.

Service of Supply, and the French worked closely with the Société le Nickel to maintain production.[18]

All this revolved around known mineral resources. The Americans, however, were seeking further deposits, though to what extent they shared information with the French is unclear. The U.S. Corps of Engineers established a geology subsection in March 1943 to advise on water supplies, aggregate pits, and construction. Soon after, the Metal Reserves Corporation, a U.S. government agency, was seeking increased quantities of "strategic minerals," so the geology section expanded. Their first survey began in August 1943 in New Caledonia. With information from the Kanaks and French engineers, they examined oil seeps and rock formations, finding deposits of quartz in the northeast. They investigated deposits of mercury, nickel, and copper and located high-grade magnesite in the northwest. They found deposits of barite, but, as they had with the magnesite, the BEW decided market conditions did not "justify the development of the deposits."[19]

The geologists carried out investigations on Espiritu Santo in New Hebrides in 1943–1944. Headed by Major B. Geiger, three expeditions found traces of lead, silver, and gold. Geiger concluded, however:

> terrain is so difficult that very high class ore would have to be found in considerable body to warrant working. . . . Opinion based on years of successful mining operations lead me to believe that a 99-year mineral right to the entire island is not worth $100,000, excluding what coral is used for roads and possible quarrying for concrete aggregates.[20]

On Guadalcanal and the Florida Islands, geologists conducted surveys in April 1944. Hopes of gold had brought the Spanish to the Solomons in the sixteenth century, but they never found any. Later prospectors did, and by the late 1930s the Australian-based Theodore group, which had a mine in Fiji, was mining in the Gold Ridge on Guadalcanal. Although the Americans examined this, their main interest was the south or weather coast. With 100 porters, they went up all the major rivers, but failed to report any sign of copper, which is now known to be in the central area. They found coal near the coastal village of Mbiti, and had they been less secretive, they may have learned that the British had done so long before. On Hanisavo in the Florida Islands they found traces of manganese.[21]

Months later, High Commissioner Mitchell learned of these expeditions and advised the secretary of state for colonies:

> There are various comments which might be made on the action of the American Command in instituting an investigation of this nature in British territories without previous consultation with us; but I do not think that . . . it would

be reasonable to object to a Commander in so primitive a place giving directions that search should be made for minerals or any other natural products that might be of assistance to him.[22]

The secretary of state was concerned with how such surveys might affect the Melanesians in this "primitive" place, and rightly so, because their perceptions of who owned "natural products" were not the same as an occupying army or a colonial administration.[23] His other concerns were whether or not such activities were only "limited to work on behalf of the United States Forces" and if they intended to pass their results over to the British, who were about to commence the first of several natural resource assessments in the Solomons.[24] Resident Commissioner Noel reassured his superiors that Geiger intended to hand on survey reports for the Solomons. Four years later in 1948, the U.S. State Department, when asked for the reports, claimed Geiger did not submit any but at least forwarded a topographical map and six geological sections.[25]

What command did, so too did some servicemen. On Guadalcanal, marine patrols took time out to pan for gold.[26] Bulolo, New Guinea, had been the site of a prewar gold-dredging operation. When the AIF arrived, men of the light aid detachment

devoted most of their spare time to prospecting for the still plentiful gold in the Bulolo and its tributaries. . . . With their wonderfully equipped workshops they were able to fashion crucibles, furnaces and other paraphernalia needed for the processing of gold.

They shaped the gold into tools, blackened them and hid them in their toolboxes to ship home. Once ANGAU found out, they policed the gold fields to protect the absent civilians' claims.[27]

Phosphate was a more vital mineral than gold to the Australians in the war. Australia and New Zealand have very poor soils, deficient in phosphates. Yet they were producing significant food for the Allied forces. By 1944 more than 10 percent of Australia's and nearly 20 percent of New Zealand's meat production went to the American forces alone. Supplies of cheap, high-grade phosphates from the atolls of Nauru and Ocean (Banaba) Islands, mined by the British Phosphates Commission, suffered from German raider ships and then Japanese control from August 1942 until late 1945. Judicious stockpiling initially had helped Australia and New Zealand. Local low-grade rock phosphate, such as from Clarendon, New Zealand, was mined. Australia and New Zealand obtained 250,000 tons from Makatea in the French Society Islands and 210,000 tons from the Red Sea in mid-1943, but faced difficulties with labor and shipping respectively. When the French decided in

1942 to impose a duty on phosphate export on the pretext of falling revenue, Australia and New Zealand reminded them of the £150,000 they had spent aiding the Free French, and Australia threatened to remove price controls from its exports to Tahiti. Meanwhile, Australia and New Zealand succeeded in getting some supplies under lend-lease from Florida in the United States by late 1943. In New Zealand, the amount of grassland top-dressed with super phosphate in 1944–1945 was 10 percent less than 1938–1939.[28]

The reduction of prewar supplies meant that New Zealand and Australia had "mortgaged the fertility of their soil by maintaining maximum production regardless of their inability to put anything like the required quantities of fertilizers." They and the Phosphates Commission requested the Joint Chiefs of Staff for an early occupation of the islands, because, although they had suppliers of phosphate elsewhere, shipping remained a problem.[29] The Americans had occupied many of the Gilbert Islands in late 1943, but Nimitz refused to sacrifice more American lives and waited for Nauru and Ocean Islands to "wither on the vine." Wither they did, when, five days after Japan surrendered, Lieutenant Commander Suzuki Naoomi murdered 140 Banabans. Some four hundred Nauruan lives were lost to starvation and about thirty to Allied bombing when the phosphate mining plant and Japanese airfield constructions were attacked. Without American support, the Australians could not reoccupy the islands until after the surrender.[30]

Supplying the Human Resource

None of the island resources needed in metropolitan areas could be obtained without local laborers, be they Melanesians or immigrant Asians. These laborers needed their basic needs met and, in the BEW's view, "fictitious needs" created if they were to continue producing and working for the military.[31] Consequently, administrations and the military were concerned with the supply of both imported consumer goods—such as petroleum, paper, and canned food—and "trade" items. The description "trade" implied goods that were originally bartered, the mode of exchange when the first Westerners came to the Pacific. They had to have been goods the islanders wanted or there would have been no exchange for, say, sandalwood, bêche-de-mer, copra, or labor. As Westerners became settlers and colonizers in the late nineteenth and early twentieth centuries, elements of the cash economy emerged in cross-cultural transactions, particularly in the plantation sector. Over the decades, "trade" items of inexpensive "common quality" became everyday necessities for most islanders.[32]

In the southern Pacific, only Australia was sufficiently industrialized to produce most of the consumer goods for the region, yet it had to make some rapid transitions to supply its own needs.[33] On the region's eastern periphery, of course, was the United States, and the BEW and later the FEA believed America had a part to play in supplying the area. Initially in September 1942, the U.S. Navy had focused on "notions, cloth and other trade goods" to encourage the islands' labor supply, but the BEW saw part of its role as expediting imports of all goods.

Most dependencies had some reserves when Japan entered the war. They saw their regular shipping diverted or commandeered by the Americans, so sometimes they had intermittent deliveries. In late 1942, the BEW visited most archipelagoes, gathered lists from merchants and governments of "such trade good needs as can not be supplied through the normal channels," and sent them to Washington for exporters.[34] By early 1943, the BEW assisted lend-lease negotiations with Fiji, dealing with the most efficient colonial administration in the southern Pacific outside the battle zone. The administration had a thorough grasp of the country's needs, ordered goods from the United States procured by the USCC, and distributed accordingly, early instituting price as well as import and export controls and licenses.[35] Tonga introduced similar controls. Ineligible for lend-lease, Tonga's requirements were added to Fiji's. Fiji and Tonga also obtained essential goods from Australia, New Zealand, and Canada. For the BEW, New Caledonia was more of a problem. Still recovering from the Vichy–Free French debacle, the loss of contacts in France and Indochina, and a shortage of staff, the administration initially deferred to the powerful merchant syndicates to order goods via BEW.[36]

In New Caledonia imports came mainly from Australia, the United States, and New Zealand, with goods being distributed to retailers by quota, reducing the monopolistic power of the main prewar companies. Few price controls operated and inflation resulted. In the New Hebrides Condominium, controls on prices, imports, and exports prevailed by late 1943. As usual, the French and the British opted for different suppliers, despite a supply board formed in 1943 after a year of infighting. The WPHC and Fiji established an agency in Sydney under a former official from the New Hebrides, so the needs of the Condominium were well-understood. Enduring differences persisted, however, as the French were trying to find an alternative to the Australian trading company Burns, Philp, which had a retail store in Vila and opened a new one on Santo in 1942 to profit from the huge native wage bill. Thus the French resident worked mainly through the FEA and the BEW to order U.S. goods, so by 1943–1944 the Condominium was well-supplied.[37] For essential goods, the British territories under Fiji's mantle, as well as the French (after November 1942), could obtain these by means of lend-lease if merchants could not obtain the goods at a better price by direct import.[38]

Politics of Procurement

The role of the FEA as major go-between did not continue long. Fiji could get much of what it needed from America via the British Supply Mission in Washington, but until the second half of 1943 it had to balance this with the FEA's ability to get shipping to Fiji and the British western Pacific territories. At that time too, Australia and New Zealand, without consulting the U.S. government, co-operated in a supply arrangement with the South Pacific countries, including American Samoa. What they could not supply was sought elsewhere. For example, in early 1945, Australia's drought had meant it could not provide New Caledonia's rice requirements, so the United States was asked to.[39]

Australia and New Zealand had strong claims to commercial expertise in the region. Before the war, even with the inclusion of the French possessions, they had about 35 percent of the export business to the area. Most of their major trading companies better understood their customers and had more established connections than the American suppliers. Moreover, the lists the FEA had submitted to Washington had been poorly prepared, and deliveries lagged. There were other considerations besides Australasian commercial know-how. Australian and New Zealand officials were aware of talk among American personnel of the United States taking over islands it had garrisoned. Roosevelt long had wanted New Caledonia as an airplane stopover, and its minerals would be a bonus. In late 1943, when New Zealand finance officials stopped off in New Caledonia, they noted, for example, the proprietary attitude of the Americans, who suspected New Zealand of seeking iron ore supplies.[40]

In January 1944 tensions between Australia and New Zealand and their ally America had reached a climax with the formers' Canberra Pact, which, inter alia, declared the South Pacific region except American Samoa off limits for America once peace prevailed. America reacted negatively to this bold southern "Monroe doctrine," but the alliance endured and ultimately the Americans achieved the ring of security they so wanted with their control of Micronesia. Historians have seen Australia as the prime mover in this assertion of Australasian interests,[41] but New Zealand had also become suspicious of American intentions.

This was demonstrated in the Cooks where the United States had bases at Aitutaki and Penhryn.[42] Although the resident judge had agreed to a procedure for assessing claims, the New Zealand government in September 1943 refused to allow the Americans to pay compensation for damages, lest it imply some postwar claim. In relation to commerce, the government monitored the activities not only of the U.S. commanders there, but also of the BEW when Oliver paid a flying visit in March 1943. Despite welcoming access to American suppliers for the local traders, the New Zealand government was concerned about proposed transactions by

Aitutaki women to send mail orders of $3,000 to the States for clothing. New Zealand also feared that the U.S. Navy would undercut local traders by selling goods to islanders and that servicemen would remit orders to America for them. Commanders of both bases, however, appeared to want simply to motivate islanders to work, so they cooperated with officials, much to the relief of the New Zealand investigator.

> I . . . was soon convinced that he [Col. Stafford] had no interest in post-war aspirations of the US in the area under his command; he was obviously concerned only with his own immediate job. He evinced little interest in the visit of Dr Oliver and his Mission—seeming to regard the leader as rather an impractical visionary.[43]

The degree of New Zealand anxiety can also be gauged by comparison with the French attitude on Bora Bora. Here labor shortage came in the train of lack of incentive for the people to work. So the American base commander, Ostrom, obtained sixty workers by selling goods from the commissary to the value of $200 monthly. Montgomery Ward catalogues from America, like the dollar, circulated freely and the Americans ordered dresses, lingerie, shoes, and toys at the request of the local people. All this and never a whisper of protest from the French authorities![44] Similarly, in Wallis, where its tiny administration's loyalty to Vichy saw it isolated until the Americans arrived, the need of the islanders for basic "trade" goods had become so urgent that the military sold supplies to the Burns, Philp's trader to retail.[45]

Yet in Western Samoa, the New Zealanders were more tolerant of American influence, though they handled the compensation issue themselves. The administration's controls on currency exchange and imports were minimal. Price control was flexible and inflation resulted by late 1943, but with no ill effects on the Samoans,[46] who enjoyed the easiest and most profitable war of the entire Pacific. Most exports were controlled under arrangements with the UK Ministry of Food, but in spite of better prices, the volume of copra, cacao, and bananas dropped as American demand for labor climbed.[47] Nonetheless, the administration's Reparations Estates, with some labor from New Zealand's Tokelau atolls, maintained more than half of the normal copra output during 1942–1943. Increased rates of export duties in 1942 cleared an estimated government deficit. Dollars freely circulated, wages increased by 60 to 80 percent, and 2,600 men on Upolu worked for the Americans, with many women doing laundry—their demand for charcoal irons jumped from nil in 1939–1941 to 2,345 in 1942![48] Americans paid monthly wages of more than $40,000. Imported store goods climbed dramatically and included "expensive American toilet preparations, model frocks, canned fruits, soups, vegetables, poultry, olives."[49] After April 1943, to restrict remittances and to save shipping space, the administrator and the BEW curtailed some U.S. imports: "cordials and other beverages, fruit juices, musical instruments, furniture, trunks and suitcases, glass and china ornaments," but other "fancy lines" continued.[50] Despite the BEW's organizing orders for projected needs, there were others more pivotal to obtaining goods from the States. Morris, Hedstrom was able to find American suppliers for his Samoa's stores at cheaper prices than from New Zealand. The New Zealand administration did not move to closely control the economy until early 1944, when the U.S. impact was lessening,[51] because of "fear of political repercussions should the introduction of import control result in a diminution in the availability of supplies."[52]

New Zealand had faced political disfavor from the Samoans before. In the late 1920s and early 1930s, the Mau movement opposed the mandate New Zealand held under the League of Nations. A peaceful protest in 1929 saw seven Samoans, including chief Tupua Tamasese Lealofi, shot by New Zealand police. Several Mau leaders, including part Swedish/part Samoan Olaf Nelson, were heavily involved in trading and business. Some historians see the Mau as being manipulated by men such as Nelson to win greater commercial power. In the war years, the New Zealanders believed that the Samoans owed them no loyalty and kept leading Samoans, such as Nelson's daughter Calmar Nelson Meyer, under surveillance.[53]

Figure 14. Samoan workers being paid by the United States, Apia, 1943 (courtesy of Apia Museum).

If New Zealand restricted Samoa's supplies of imports, there could be unrest. New Zealand thus allowed Australia to continue its prewar dominance of imports because the people got better goods, such as better-keeping flour and superior beer, at lower prices. The Fiji-based trading company Morris, Hedstrom and Co. found Australian goods to please the Samoans, as did Burns, Philp, whose reduced income from copra was offset by high turnover at its Apia and Pago Pago stores.[54]

Antipodean opposition to America became more pronounced. By late 1944, the FEA complained that it was unable to devise a satisfactory procedure for "preparing and presenting island requirements in cooperation with Australia and New Zealand." It believed Australia was unwilling to cooperate to "provide equal access to South Pacific markets to American importers" and prohibited the re-export of U.S. lend-lease goods to the islands.[55] In 1945, U.S. economic strategists concluded that

> on the economic level, there has been a marked tendency on the part of Australia, N.Z., and the British colonies to unite in an effort to improve their trade relations in the Islands in order to counteract likely U.S. expansion of influence.

They also noted that the metropolitan French were reasserting control, ending the Indian summer of the autonomists' dalliance with the United States.[56] But in New Zealand's case, at least in Western Samoa, it had been prepared to ride out the American occupation, preferring to placate the Samoans rather than asserting tighter control.[57]

Seeking "Trade"

When the war began, in a gradient from east to west across the southern Pacific, the diversity and value of desired imported goods were greater in Polynesia than in the islands "on the line" and in Melanesia. By coincidence, the operational Pacific frontier generally followed the cline of this geography of "civilization"—the people who had the longest exposure to outsiders and their goods generally were in rear bases while those with the least, with the exception of the environs of established ports such as Rabaul and Port Moresby, were in or near battle zones. Within western Melanesia another gradation of consumer geography ran roughly from the coast to the inland. In May 1943, Michael Leahy, a gold prospector in prewar New Guinea, offered terse directions to the military:

> Trading in New Guinea could be roughly divided into civilized, semi-civilized and uncivilized . . . the whole of the coastline can be considered civilized and

> under [government] control . . . cash, if there is somewhere to spend it, tobacco, newspaper (for rolling cigarettes), matches, razor blades, calico, and small beads will be found convenient trade for buying native food, paying carriers . . . etc. Inland civilized areas would take the same plus salt.
> Inland Semi-civilized:
> Steel: Hatchets, ½ and ¾ axes, knives up to 16" and plain blades (instead of stone axes). Shell: Goldlip (8" in diameter minimum), Bailer, Green Snail, Diwara or Tambu, or White Gum will take care of pig buying, casual laborer's pay, large quantity of native food, etc., depending on the areas. Small cowrie shells . . . salt, if natives have been in contact with whites for some time, otherwise small beads, dry colored powder such as red ochre . . . and matches . . . for purchasing natives foods, paying carriers . . .
>
> Tambu or Diwara shell "worked"; that is, the conical end ground off and the white shell sewn on to strips of fibre, or threaded on to strips of cane, will be . . . good trade for almost any part of the semi-civilized or uncivilized parts.[58]

Leahy was right. When the U.S. construction engineers were building an advance base at Bena Bena, L. J. Svendrup had to employ 1,900 "inland semi-civilized" highlanders. Too inaccessible for heavy machinery, here the engineers used the 1,900 to clear the airfield and then compact it with bare feet.[59] Bena was no Samoa. Neither Yankee dollar nor Australian pound had any value to highlanders. They prized gold-lip pearl shell. The U.S. supply section obtained 700, but another 1,000, the balance of the order, was wanting until the Australian Intelligence Bureau assisted.[60] In this region—Mt. Hagen—and in "some districts of Central New Guinea" the bailer shell, found in the Torres Strait, was also highly valued "when cut up" into desired shapes. Leahy scotched American suggestions to manufacture "counterfeit money" in the form of beads, which he insisted was never "money" anyway, but "trade," though he conceded they might appeal to the "primitive" natives.[61]

Lack of "trade" goods was more acute near the front, where the need for labor was vital. Thus ANGAU, at least until mid-1943, had a tremendous task supplying "trade," as it needed incentives for labor not only for the military but to keep copra and rubber plantations of the Australian Production Control Board (PCB) in Papua functioning. The old trading firms had left the country and, even in secured areas, were likely to be more trouble than help. For the first two months of 1942, when the AIF supplied plantations and native trade stores, it obtained supplies with the help of the Department of External Territories in Australia. After that, the purchase and consignment of this "trade" became ANGAU's responsibility. In the second half of 1943 the PCB took control of supplying "trade," except where

Figure 15. Laborers from Fergusson Island buying rami (calico or cloth) with earnings from war work on Goodenough Island, 1944 (R. Emerson Curtis, *Walkabout,* 1 Dec. 1944, 20).

operational conditions saw ANGAU as the more appropriate body. Needs in operational areas always had priority because men's lives depended on it.

Getting pearl shell was a relatively simple task since most of it could be obtained outside the conflict zone. What was needed for "trade" among the "civilized" where stores could function extended Leahy's basic list and included razor blades, flageolettes, Jew's harps, mouth organs, whistles, cricket balls, bats, fish hooks, diving goggles, adzes, hatchets, needles, signet rings, umbrellas, pipes, scarves, handkerchiefs, cloth, cotton blankets, small beads, enamel ware (plates, mugs, and basins), lanterns and, of use for the locals' American laundry service, charcoal box irons.[62]

Buying by the Department of External Territories in Sydney was not a success. The Australians failed to utilize the knowledge of "trade" goods possessed by companies such as Burns, Philp Co. Ltd. Perhaps because the "trade" was seemingly in such simple, cheap, and almost childish goods, the authorities believed any official could manage procurement. There were structural problems too. The prewar trading companies had bought their supplies cheaply in bulk from several sources overseas, but wartime import controls initially favored dependence on Australian manufacturers even though they had never been major suppliers. When they could supply goods, the cost was too high, even though the PCB did not "operate for profit." So vital was native labor, price was not an issue to the Australians in operational areas, but elsewhere it was to the native purchaser. "Twist" tobacco, mainly from America as before the war, matches, and cloth were usually procurable, but other items were far less so once the accumulated stocks of the old trading firms and diverted cargoes in Australia had been bought up by the Department of External Territories. Even with 36,000 native men under indenture in early 1944, some officials were not taking seriously the true value of "trade" items to the war effort and thought, for example, that Jew's harps were too trivial to motivate a search for overseas suppliers. Their one success to that time was finding cricket bats in India for 7/-, compared to 40/- in Australia.[63]

The implications were alarming for ANGAU as administrator supporting the military and plantations, more of which were becoming available for production. As well as natives' wages in hand, a backlog of wages of £152,000 when the Japanese invaded was due. Trade sales figures to mid-1944 represented "a monthly turn-over of £8373 against a monthly wage earnings of about £23,000, so that the unexpended wealth of the native community" was bound to "rapidly accumulate." The outcome was obvious, for there was a limit to how long ANGAU's power to conscript indentured labor could prevail once the war was ending.

> Trade must be available when the above monies are paid, otherwise the native returns to his village without value for his services and the natural reaction is dissatisfaction and the spread of discontent.[64]

What frustrated the PCB was that they were aware that the Dutch in western New Guinea and the Americans had found supplies of "trade," while the Department of External Affairs generally failed.[65] Some improvement came in late 1944 as the Australian government set up procurement contracts overseas,[66] but this explains why the British in the Solomons and the Gilbert and Ellice Islands—where trading companies had also departed—kept their options open with the FEA or its parent body, the BEW.

In the Gilbert Islands the people had suffered under the Japanese occupation and were soon bereft of imported goods. Hence when the Americans arrived in late 1943 there was a backlog of demand. These atoll dwellers had very different needs than say, highlanders of New Guinea. For example, about 1,300 square yards of sail cloth, 12,150 board (superficial) feet of canoe timber (redwood), and 5,000 fish hooks were needed for the 7,600 people on Aranuka, Makin, Abemana, Butaritari, and Tarawa for a four-month period. Tobacco was desired—about 2,500 lbs. A clean people, their soap needs for the same period were a phenomenal 15,400 lbs. (about seven long tons) but almost certainly included estimates for doing American laundry! The U.S. Navy furnished rations of white rice, canned meat or fish, hard biscuit, sugar, tea or coffee, and salt to the new labor corps, as well as relief K and C rations to displaced communities short of local food.[67] In anticipation of the American occupation and the "stimulation of labor," the British administration had sent orders for trade goods via Hawai'i in September 1943. Thereafter most were ordered along with Fiji government requirements through the BEW from America or via the High Commission office from Sydney. By mid-1944, native co-operative societies were retailing these goods at far cheaper rates than had the prewar commercial companies.[68]

In the Solomon Islands, the major supplier of trade goods remained the FEA until mid-1945. Oliver had negotiated with Resident Commissioner Noel to get goods into the hands of the native labor corps and others who had earned cash.[69] As part of the WPHC's territories, the Solomons obtained some trade goods from Australia early in 1944, but these had been "bought up by goods-hungry natives almost immediately after having distributed throughout the Protectorate."[70] Thereafter the Australian government, in difficulty with New Guinea, could not guarantee supplies, but Noel reminded the FEA that the administration still retained this option.[71] Goods ordered from America through the FEA arrived in May, June, and July in such quantities that the FEA and the resident commissioner had trouble housing them, and much was lost to breakage and pilfering until a new warehouse was completed in August.[72] From May 1944 to February 1945 proceeds of sales already amounted to $140,000 of goods ordered worth $350,000, so most of the needs of the labor corps, casual workers, and those receiving back wages had been met. The high commissioner's preliminary inquiries with established trading companies regarding their return to the Protectorate in late 1944 had alarmed Oliver, who thought that if the American trade goods were transferred to such companies, America would be subsidizing their profits "in an area towards which US commerce itself has some ambitions."[73] Oliver saw no reason to continue to import American goods at cost once normal trading resumed. Moreover, the resident commissioner opined that, as the war went northwards, the FEA was focusing more on Micronesia. By midyear the FEA phased out its work in the South Pacific, most goods then being sourced from Australia.[74]

More starkly than in peacetime, the war revealed the interconnections that Pacific islands, even atolls such as Nauru, had with the great land masses and their peoples. What their environment provided reached out to the Allies' homelands. In return, goods manufactured from the resources of distant environments flowed into the islands, reinforcing patterns begun when the first white men crossed the beaches. Customers, consumers, producers, and disparate environments were braided together, and the military mind quickly perceived such global implications. Local input in the form of the human labor resource was needed for the military and for production, but they had to have incentives to work, so "trade" and consumer goods were essential, just as they were to keep the copra, sugar, and nickel coming to the Allies. From pearl shell and pipes to petroleum and paper, these goods originated in distant places. When old suppliers failed, others had to be found or the war effort would suffer. With Southeast Asia, the northwest and some of the southwest Pacific sealed off for four years, the lines of trade, supply, and communication reconfigured, which was a challenge to the old order. The "men at the Ministries" wanted to know a good deal more than simply the agricultural potential of these islands for immediate and possible postwar needs. The United States, via the FEA/BEW, its geologists, and intelligence network, made the most of its virtually unfettered access to information about the southern Pacific's resources, but in so doing often raised the hackles of other colonial powers that had their own visions of the future and incurred their restrained, but resolute, resistance.

CHAPTER 7

The Human Resource

> This is not their war. They do what their white friends ask willingly; they watch his activity without curiosity; then, the demands of the moment fulfilled, go contentedly back to their daily rounds.

Labor was essential to the war effort. The Americans calculated that to keep one man at the front, whether employed "combatantly or logistically," ten more were behind, servicing his needs.[1] Local substitutes reduced expenditure for transport, training, upkeep, and pensions. Though colonial governments understood the military's need for labor, this did not constrain their long view of sustaining the islands' populations, many just recovering from considerable loss to introduced diseases in the previous 80 to 150 years. Thus, they sometimes competed with the military for directing labor though usually retaining responsibility for them. Several administrations perforce became recruiters, a role in peacetime that most eschewed. How labor was recruited and utilized varied, and was most contested in the operational area. How the parties involved viewed this also varied. Unlike other local resources exploited by the Allies, the human resources were less predictable and attached their own meaning to their experiences. That meaning remains diverse, but not immutable.

Wartime and Regimentation

By 1942, many islanders had become used to working for Europeans who had begun to settle in the tropical Pacific in the late nineteenth century. Their plantations needed labor, as did their mines. In the early twentieth century, trading produce, rather than laboring on other people's plantations to obtain trade goods, proved more congenial for Polynesians. Other islanders with less choice were coerced into or offered indentures overseas. During the labor trade, thousands of Melanesians were initiated into the cash economy, working in Queensland, Fiji, New Caledonia, Samoa, and Hawai'i in the second half of the nineteenth century and at home in the next. Colonial governments, entrenched by 1900, needed revenue and supported the capitalistic mode. Most introduced taxes, which encouraged cash cropping or laboring on plantations.[2] Many communities also worked to underwrite their churches. Islanders thus had incentives for undertaking barter and cash-based economic activity.

These, nonetheless, were insufficient to attract the numbers Europeans needed. From the late 1800s they introduced indentured Asian labor mainly to Fiji, New Caledonia, and the New Hebrides. The Depression eased the demand, though mining in New Caledonia and New Guinea still employed thousands.[3] With war, all protagonists urgently needed labor and, in the Allies' case, paid more than ever before.

War workers fell into four categories that sometimes overlapped: Soldiers, labor corps, laborers in essential industries, and casual laborers. Islanders generally were more coerced to work the closer they were to operations. On the Melanesian front, the sociopolitical units were small and independent of each other, with their identities expressed through connections to specific locales. This obviated concerted resistance not only to the colonials' enemy, but also to colonial demands. Yet the invaders introduced novel manpower concentrations, creating the milieux for the sharing of ideas on an unprecedented scale. Generally, the length of experience that most western Melanesian peoples had with global forces was about 100 to 150 years less than that of Polynesians. To the exotic combatants, they were battling in what they considered the most primitive part of the Pacific.

Marshalling for Combat

When the European war began, Pacific administrations established home guards of Europeans and native police. The Fiji Defense Force's territorial unit expanded to an effective force under the guidance of the New Zealand Army, responsible for Fiji's defense as part of the British Empire. In September 1942, after the Americans had assumed command of the South Pacific, the governor of Fiji, Sir Philip Mitchell, considered local defense and a Fijian-Tongan unit for overseas operations. He offered to organize commandos as well as a labor corps for service in the Solomons.[4]

Urged by their chiefs, some Fijians had offered to serve in 1940, but they volunteered by the hundreds in 1942. Fiji's persuasive recruiter of men, Ratu Lala Sukuna, was a public servant and decorated World War I veteran, with degrees from Oxford and the Middle Temple. He grasped the global as well as the local implications of service: "*Eda na sega ni kilai na i taukei kevaka e na sega mada ni dave e liu na noda dra*" ("Fijians will never be recognized unless our blood is shed first"). Few Fijians perceived Britain as an oppressive overlord; most perceived it as a chiefly protector of their interests against the multiplying migrant Indians. The Indians, almost half the population of 183,000, were less complaisant.[5] Though they donated to "patriotic" funds, few volunteered for service, demanding the same wages and conditions as the white soldiers.[6] From early 1942, the Fiji Military Force (FMF) expanded to commando units and four infantry battalions. At its peak in August 1943 it, with two battalions of labor corps, consisted of 6,371 Fijians, 264 Indians, 1,070 Europeans, and 808 members of the NZEF. In all, 11,000 men passed through the FMF.[7] Fijians made up the bulk of the fighting units. Their New Zealand officers found that Viti Levu Island gave its own lessons:

> The main training took place in the surrounding bush-clad hills, some of the most rugged in Fiji. The locals excelled in this environment and it was a complementary learning experience for both the Fijian recruits and the New Zealanders.[8]

Neighboring Tonga, with 33,000 people, offered men and money. Under a treaty of friendship, Britain was responsible for Tonga's defense. When Britain went to war the Tongan parliament declared war on Germany and, by 8 December 1941, on Japan. Once Britain was at war, Queen Sālote called for men for the Tongan Defense Force (TDF). Almost every male in the kingdom volunteered, along with twenty-six local Europeans, with the queen's consort and premier Tungī Mailefihi as colonel-in-chief. For the first year the men took no payment. At full strength, the TDF numbered two battalions or 2,000 men, 12 percent of Tonga's male population. Privates received five pence a day, and most served as coast watchers and gun crews. A proud force, they walked out of camp when enlisted New Zealanders failed to salute their officers. Only Sālote's intercession brought them back. When the Americans assumed defense responsibility in March 1942, the Tongans took over garrison work. Except for fifty men who trained in Fiji, the TDF became a labor force of more than eight hundred, working on stevedoring and construction. A platoon of twenty-eight went with the Fijians to the Solomon Islands; a second fought on Bougainville with the Americans, several receiving awards for valor from the British and Americans.[9] These few served well, as did those at home, but by late 1943 the force was virtually demobilized,[10] its " principal disappointment has been that it was not used overseas."[11]

Some islanders went to battle; others found the battle came to them. When the Japanese landed in the Solomons, Martin Clemens, district officer, was on Guadalcanal spying. After the Americans landed his Melanesian police acted as scouts. Clemens wanted a battalion of Solomon Islanders trained by the New Zealanders.

The New Zealand commandos did their best with about 200 Malaitans, but the Americans pressed to use these men before their training was finished. Paid £1 or $3.24 a month and given uniforms and rations, many were unsure what they were getting themselves into. Compared with the Fijians' months of preparation, their less than two weeks' training in January 1943 was scant, and, except for about twenty-five eventually attached to the Fijian force, they tended to "go bush" under fire or skive off to collect discarded Japanese gear. Their New Zealand officers saw them as small and primitive, more useful as scouts and porters, an opinion soon shared by the Americans.[12] When trained by district officers, however, the men in the Solomon Islands Defense Force proved their worth as guerrillas. A group of about sixty-eight from the western islands led by Donald Kennedy killed more than a hundred Japanese, captured several prisoners, assisted with coast watching, and saved several crashed Allied airmen.[13] And the sole Solomons' hero to be acknowledged in the American record, Sergeant Major Jacob Vouza, a former policeman, did not betray Allied positions to the enemy though tortured by the Japanese.[14]

The Australians formed the Papuan Infantry Battalion in June 1940, later to become the Pacific Islands Regiment (PIR). Consisting of 300 when the Japanese invaded, it peaked at 2,500 in March 1944. Overall, 3,500 men in three PIR

Figure 16. Solomon Islands Defense Force, passing out parade, April 1946, at closing of Guadalcanal base (290/48/02/07, RG 338, NARA).

battalions served, after five weeks' basic training. As well, over 3,000 police and 955 medical orderlies served ANGAU.[15] The PIR "fought in every campaign waged by the Australians in New Guinea except Milne Bay." Like the Australians, they had both weaknesses and strengths as fighters.[16] What made them different, however, was that the war provided weapons and opportunities for some to take revenge on former enemies or to rape women of foreign clans. Many saw their participation as an entrée into a more equal relationship with the white man, a view not all their Australian officers appreciated, even when New Guineans received bravery awards. They organized demonstrations against what they saw as discriminatory treatment in rations, uniforms, pay, and pensions. General Blamey, appreciating their role, lobbied Canberra for improvement. With the war's end near, wages went from 10/- a month to 15/- for privates after one year's service, with £1 a month after two years' service, being retrospective for six months, while death and disability were compensable. Instead of lap-laps (wrap-around skirts) of prewar times, men were issued shorts and shirts.[17]

Most native troops had the advantage of environmental knowledge, which they could use to frighten and kill those less at home in what to outsiders was a jungle wilderness. Clemens' Solomons' scouts "demonstrated a superior knowledge of woodcraft."[18] Coast watcher H. E. Josselyn's SIDF men had "infinitely better eyesight" than the European.[19] When the Japanese snipers camouflaged themselves with leaves, the Melanesians recognized that the species was not typical of a vegetation zone or that leaves were wilted or unnaturally placed.[20] The New Guineans and Fijians knew high islands' forests well. AIF officers considered the PIR "natural experts in jungle warfare . . . and few Australians ever reach their individual standards."[21] The Fijian commandos were "among the greatest bushmen in the world."[22] Their ability to move stealthily through the jungle, especially at night, dispatched many Japanese, but they scored a proportionately larger number of friendly-fire casualties from Allied sentries mistaking them for the enemy. Their allies admired their prowess and affability. From a culture of social hierarchies, they carried the honor of their chiefs and *vanua* (land). Sefanaia Sukunaivalu won the highest British military award, the Victoria Cross, on Bougainville.[23] By contrast, the Tongans were less skillful in distinguishing disturbed vegetation because they came from low islands with little dense forest.[24] Yet in their home environment, the seaward-looking Tongans proved "especially adept at spotting mines" in the ocean.[25]

New Caledonia's French were less forthcoming with native units. In January 1943, they allowed the Americans only 204 Kanak guides for maneuvers. Besides their rate of 5 to 25 francs a day—depending on their skills—and rations, quarters, and medical care, the men received a monthly family allowance: 195 francs for a wife and 90 francs for each child under sixteen.[26] Kanaks and Loyalty Islanders had already enlisted in the Pacific Battalion, and a few score had been sent to Africa and Europe. By mid-1943 they numbered 1,039, mostly in New Caledonia employed as labor for French officers. Those on Wallis Island, under the incompetent resident Dr. Mattei, were noted for their brutality.[27]

In the New Hebrides, events without overtook inertia within. The Vichy versus Free French issue preoccupied the administration until its resolution in September 1940, when some European settlers volunteered for service. Blandy, the British resident commissioner, believed the "local natives would be useless . . . to face the fire of modern weapons."[28] Nevertheless, after the Australians established a flying boat base at Vila, Governor Luke of Fiji and High Commissioner Sautot met with them in June 1941 to formulate plans to train two forces: a garrison unit of "local non natives" as officers, with "natives as privates" and a volunteer defense corps from "other non natives." For months, the "impractical" requirement for men to swear allegiance to both the king and de Gaulle stalled the plan.[29] Even as the Japanese advanced, by March 1942 the defense force numbered only 130. Should the Japanese invade, the 30-man AIF saw their own role as a guerrilla unit; the role of any local force still remained unclear. The native defense force's training was underway before the Americans under General Rose arrived in March, and it continued until May, but they were diverted to unloading American ships. With the Americans in charge, the AIF departed and training ceased. Rose asked that New Hebrideans be posted at Big Bay to guard against Japanese infiltration. About 270, mainly from Malekula, went to this "notoriously unhealthy" area and became demoralized, and in late 1942 they returned to Vila where some were trained to use firefighting equipment. The Americans used some to train combat troops for bush conditions and to assist in "close-up" operations. The fractious European volunteer force disbanded in December 1943.[30]

In Nuie and the Cook Islands, defense corps formed in 1941–42, with privates getting 3/- daily.[31] In August 1939, Western Samoa had raised a local defense force of 175, for "guarding internees, protecting public buildings and utilities, and manning defense and coast watching posts." When the Americans took over, this unit came under their control.[32] Although the administration declined Samoans for overseas units, many European residents, part Samoans, and Samoans, like several Cook Islanders, Nuieans, three Tongans, and a Tahitian, joined in New Zealand. About 110 islanders served as part of Company D ("Ngati Walkabout") of the New Zealand Maori Battalion.[33] In American Samoa the prewar Fitafita guard expanded to 500 men in February 1941, while a battalion of around 500 formed part of the U.S. Marine Corps Reserve. Recruits were paid 70 cents a day, with a uniform allowance of $5.00. After four months, their pay was raised to $1.00 a day. Proud of their status, when disciplinary infringements resulted in public humiliation, some reservists, rather than shame their *nu'u* (village), killed themselves.[34]

Figure 17. Mrs. Eleanor Roosevelt with Major General C. Price, reviewing Samoan marines, Tutuila, August 1943 (EX. 80-G-81393, NARA).

Mustering Labor

The nearer the front, the greater the need for discipline, so governments formed labor corps. When Governor Mitchell had suggested that Solomon Islanders assist the Americans, Vice Admiral Ghormley demurred, fearing they would desert. Mitchell believed once "they were in uniform and serving in an organisation" with experienced supervisors, they "would not be inclined to run off from their jobs . . . if forces of the enemy were also present on the island." The Americans agreed and implementation began for Fiji and the Solomons.[35]

In Fiji, the urgency of reassigning American cargoes to forward areas and constructing bases prompted Mitchell to consider conscription, but he decided persuasion was the better inducement.[36] As before the war, the commercial firms had recruiters "round up labor from the villages whenever men were needed to work a ship." By September 1942 this system faltered because the men were unused to the "continuous, uninterrupted labor the new situation had imposed on them," so a labor battalion became essential. Major Ratu Lala Sukuna led the recruiting: "all the islands responded to his appeal." In October 1942 the First Battalion Fiji Labor Corps began working in Suva, with another underway for Lautoka. With former stevedores and with their Fijian recruits assigned to their own chiefs as NCOs, the corps expanded. The "call of duty," reinforced by the highest remuneration rates in the British Pacific territories—at 2/- a day for privates, 1/6 for a wife or dependent mother, as well as sixpence a child (up to three children)—was "an inducement to some of the men." In January 1943 the First Battalion was at full strength of 1,263 and the Second Battalion soon numbered 850. The Americans appreciated these men who worked alongside them, learning to use labor-saving machinery. Labor costs per measurement ton fell from seventy-five cents under the commercial firms to an average of thirty to forty-five cents.[37] Elsewhere, in the American hospitals, laundries, and gardens, about a thousand Indians found casual work, taking their labor from the sugar company, CSR. But the increasing cost of living meant Indian growers suffered greatly when cane prices lagged, resulting in a seven-month strike in 1943.[38]

Australian prime minister John Curtin knew the Fijians' reputation and wanted 500 for New Guinea, but Mitchell refused. Of the total indigenous population of 98,000 in January 1943, 22,800 Fijian men were between eighteen and fifty, with 6,000 either in the services or the labor corps and another 1,500 needed to complete the unit's establishment. Moreover, there were "Fijians in essential civil industries . . . and engaged in food production" so that the "manpower situation is . . . near breaking point."[39] A year later, however, when pressures had lessened, Fiji provided 400 men for a dock company for Bougainville.[40] To assist the American withdrawal in December 1945, a second dock company of 270 went to Guadalcanal, encouraged perhaps by the American goods their predecessors had brought home.[41]

On Guadalcanal after the American landing in August 1942, Martin Clemens had recruited labor. By December, the Americans noted:

> we have 490. This number is not as impressive as it sounds. 150 are needed to lay mats for the Air Corps. One day in seven or 1/7 of the strength must be given a staggered Sunday off. Carrying parties to flank an outpost position absorbs 100 to 150 more. Washing parties for hospital laundries absorb up as high as 30 per day. There is a certain sick rate. The natives frequently wander into the bush for several days before returning. This may be as high as 5 or 10 a day. Yesterday's figures netted me 180 laborers for beach work out of 490.[42]

By February 1943, the Solomon Islands Labor Corps (SILC) numbered 1,200, mostly from Malaita, a source of about 68 percent of labor before the war.[43] Working cargo and airfield construction, these reduced "the number of combat troops who would otherwise have been necessary to perform these laborious tasks." Under Captain G. Trench, district officer, six hundred carriers took supplies to forward areas.[44] Former planters became officers in the SILC, while district officers recruited. By July 1944 the corps numbered 3,700, but the cumulative total was around 8,000. Monthly wages were £1, double the prewar wage, and more for higher ranks. The administration set one-year contracts, but even this undermined subsistence on north Malaita, where 90 percent of able-bodied men were recruited, though several were permitted to return home on compassionate grounds to assist families.[45]

Throughout 1943 on Guadalcanal and Nggela, American units competed for labor. From a command viewpoint market forces were hardly an efficient basis for allocation: "Every native . . . used unofficially puts one more soldier or marine on the docks loading ships or laboring in the ration dumps." Command issued directives to forbid the hiring of casual labor and inducements of goods in lieu.[46] Both occurred; about 10 percent of the U.S. native labor force in March 1944 was casual. So that "gardens can be maintained," no extensions of contracts were permitted before repatriation.[47] Solomon Islanders, encouraged by American ratings, believed such restrictions were the machinations of the parsimonious British to deprive them of American largesse and wages. Malaitans on Guadalcanal, concentrated in large numbers in one area for the first time in their factional, combative history, attempted to strike for better wages.[48] Their negative opinion of the "government" was confirmed when, while prioritizing passenger space on vessels returning to their islands, officials destroyed some of their American goods. Yet five years later, one district officer noticed much American material in some of the villages whose men complained loudest.[49]

For Solomon Islanders, working for the Americans was attractive if outside the combat area. They joined the labor corps to make money, obtain novel goods, and see the wonders of American military society. Many signed on for second contracts with bonuses. Some, such as the north Guadalcanal people, could access the camps because they lived nearby, often earning more through casual work and trading artifacts or fruit than those in the SILC.[50] Starved for trade goods, even distant Santa Cruz sent more than two hundred laborers when shipping allowed in 1945.[51] Further east, several Tikopians set off to work for the Americans in the New Hebrides. One canoe with sixteen on board washed ashore on Vanikoro, the fate of the other unknown.[52]

Although the administration contained wage inflation, thereby incurring indigenous opprobrium, the United States benefited under reverse lend-lease. The contribution of the SILC alone amounted to 2,591,272 days, worth £103,489 ($334,994) in wages to Solomon Islanders, exclusive of rations.[53] Had U.S. ratings worked these man-days, the wages would have been more than twelve times as high, at least $4,318,800.[54] Costs of their training, outfitting, food, transportation, and benefits would have multiplied this several times.

Gilbertese also worked for the Americans. After the Tarawa landing in November 1943, the Americans desperately needed labor, if only to bury the thousands of rotting dead. They agreed with the British that a labor corps would prevent units competing for workers, freeing the military for other tasks.[55] The Americans wanted 1,300—of the scattered population of 3,000. The British resident commissioner Fox-Strangeways, with "little regard to family life," cobbled together groups from around the atoll, led by anyone with a modicum of English, using their own tools, with rudimentary instructions in hygiene and protection from air attack. "In these unfavourable and uneconomic conditions the men worked cheerfully and well and . . . did creditably."[56] By late December they numbered more than a thousand. The wage scale was 2/- daily up to a week, by the month £2, except where doing "abominable work under severe conditions (such as shoveling liquid corpses)," when the pay was £3. But to prevent neglect of children, the women laundresses who received 15/- a month per customer had a limit of four customers,[57] still earning as much as the men.

The British meanwhile formalized a labor corps of 1,675, consisting of companies of 200 to 300 in platoons of twenty-five, including four NCOs and a cook.[58] These were "drilled, trained, and equipped" by late January 1944 and were eligible for pensions.[59] Their wage was £2/5/- a month for privates, up to £6 for a warrant officer. They received uniforms and rations as well as the usual weekly allowances of tobacco, matches, soap, salt, sugar, and tea or coffee. Led by New Zealanders, in late 1944 they numbered about 2,000. The Americans so valued them, they requested a unit for the Solomons. When 400 Gilbert and Ellice Islanders left for Guadalcanal in August 1944[60] Mitchell advised the Americans to keep

> this unit separate as far as possible from the British Solomon Islands Labor Corps as it will be composed of Polynesians [*sic*] of a much higher level of civilization and will not mix well with Melanesian and more primitive, Solomon Islanders.[61]

Under the 4th Special U.S. Naval Construction Battalion, this dock company became proficient with loading machinery, although 90 percent of them had never handled cargo before. When they departed in October 1945, the U.S. command judged them "far superior to the Solomon Islands natives," as they had set port records for unloading.[62]

In New Guinea, labor was essential because most fighting was inland. In rugged terrain, supplies in and wounded out would determine operational success. ANGAU, in charge of recruiting, faced a conflict because "all the native administration" was "subordinated to operational purposes."[63] Initially, no more than 25 percent of adult males from any village were to be recruited.[64] ANGAU evacuated

Figure 18. Gilbert and Ellice Islands dock workers attached to American forces, loading a truck, Guadalcanal, c. 1944 (290/48/02/07, RG 338, NARA).

more than 60,000 villagers from battle zones and allocated emergency rations, providing basic medical care in fifty-three field hospitals. With power to conscript from mid-June 1942, ANGAU officers obtained the laborers' consent via suasion or force—a contrast to the administration's protective prewar role. In October 1942 the total labor force attached to the military, with those working on plantations for the PCB, was 7,914; early in 1943 it was 18,446. Often employed in nonessential services such as officers' messes, numbers reached 30,000 by September 1943, climbing to more than 45,000 in mid-1944. About 15 percent were on plantations and about 1 percent on coastal vessels. Former crew from the Papuan Gulf District captained luggers: "That they should do so well witnesses to their courage and skill with these boats—an opportunity engendered by the war—and not lost!"[65] Many laborers were on short-term contracts. "Shy" Bougainvillean women, for example, provided 5,400 "woman days" of labor to make American gardens at Laruma Road in early 1944.

To Allied thinking, the logistics of fighting in New Guinea made the conscription limit of 25 percent derisory. In many villages ANGAU conscripted 80 to

Figure 19. Bougainvillean woman and child carrying box of lettuce from military garden, April 1944. Note the pipe-smoking by both (EX. 111-SC-254141, NARA).

100 percent of the fit men and even the unfit. Not all became carriers, but many who did faced battle conditions. Laborers in the earliest campaigns were chronically underfed except where concerned ANGAU officers "scrounged" extra food. Some had worked a year without one rest day. ANGAU knew this was driving men too hard. Diet and conditions improved by 1944 with wages at minimum of 10/- a month (increased in 1945 to 15/-). In some isolated areas where trading was impossible, pay was in goods.[66] America's exit from New Guinea meant a loss of machinery, so labor demand remained. Coercion of recruits and beatings for deserters continued, though some officers connived to prevent excessive recruiting by "masterly inactivity."[67] When the war ended, thousands of conscripted men and others stranded behind enemy lines had not been home for three years. Treatment of forced labor was even worse under the desperate Japanese; they, for example, conscripted 2,000 New Britain laborers to support their landing at Buna. As the

tide of war turned against them they beat or killed any who disobeyed.[68] Many New Guineans suffered pitifully for being across the path of great armies.

Behind the lines, the New Hebrides Defense Force became effectively a labor unit. The administration conscripted labor for the Americans to build airfields in 1942. Wages set by the administration in July 1942 were at one shilling for an eight-hour day for a three-month contract. The ability of the Seabees to reconstruct their environment amazed the people, so curious men offered themselves to the Americans, in part because an anticolonial cult on Tanna, centered on the elusive Jon Frum, predicted America's coming.[69] On Santo, however, where efficiency in cargo handling mattered, the Americans found "they were not good workers, did not learn readily and possessed low vitality."[70] By then, the Americans were recruiting and setting up labor camps, but the official wages for this labor corps generally were followed. Some, however, received around 50 cents (3/-) a day, plus extra rations for casual work.[71] Competition drove up wages. To control this and to encourage coffee growing and copra making, the administration in April 1943 set casual rates at 5.5 pence or 7 cents an hour (about 4/- a day) and overtime at double rate. With powers of conscription, sometimes the administration pressured men to work on unpopular activities, such as logging for the Aneityum Logging Company because the Americans in New Caledonia needed more timber.

In New Caledonia, the Americans in mid-1942 requested a "port company" "so that combat units could be freed."[72] The French responded that only 4,930 able Kanak men were available and already about 3,400, or 70 percent, were working away from home, compared to 20 to 25 percent before the war. They allowed them only 950, as labor was also needed for seasonal work, especially the coffee harvest.[73] By late 1942, 500 had signed on, receiving 20.50 francs (46 cents) daily. The administration ran Camp Joe Louis at Montravel, with expenses reimbursed by the Americans. Trained by the Americans as winch operators, hatch tenders, and jitney drivers, the Kanaks "performed well and damage to cargo was amazingly slight." The Americans thought the French supervisors "low grade," failing to promptly pay wages and supply rations. Unrest ensued until January 1943, when the Americans took over quartering, feeding, and payment of the Kanaks while the French nominally controlled discipline and hygiene. Responding to American demand, the French extended contracts from three to four months, but refused re-enlistment as detrimental to "the economic life of the families." Supplied with free uniforms, bedding, mess gear, sports equipment, and, at minimum cost, cigarettes, the Kanaks also could view weekly movies.[74] In New Caledonia, where forced labor had been used before the war for public works, this was an entirely novel experience.[75]

New Caledonia's labor requirements could not be met. Casual American employment such as laundry work drew some away from agriculture. The French conscripted Kanaks for public works so heavily that 200 at Hienghene rioted in November 1942. A casual labor pool at Dumbea helped the Americans. As the Japanese threat began to recede early in 1943, more than 250 civilian workers worked on Noumea's docks, the Americans rejecting some because they carried filariasis. Short of mine workers, the French imported about 200 Wallis Islanders.[76] The Americans objected because Walliseans were "the lowest and dirtiest," infected with filariasis, so they repatriated them.[77] Some remained and worked in the Baie des Pirogues sawmill.[78] On Wallis Island, the Americans thought the "gooks"[79] were "lazy, unreliable and not enthusiastic over work." At 20 cents a day, the 250 Wallis workers were among the lowest paid in the South Pacific, though the Americans opined they would work no harder for $1.20![80]

In the larger French territories, however, there were other resources. In New Caledonia the war isolated about 9,000 Javanese and 4,000 Vietnamese.[81] Most were indentured mine and farm laborers, though about 1,000 had completed their indentures before the war and worked freely. Conditions in the mining industry were oppressive. Women were subject to sexual exploitation and suffered. Wages were about $5.50 a month, though they increased to about $6.00 in 1944. A few hundred laborers defaulted on their indentures and found employment with the Americans, to the disquiet of the administration. Led by communists, mine workers went on strike several times from 1943 to 1945, appealing to the Americans, but it was in American interests to keep the mines producing. In the New Hebrides, 2,000 Vietnamese were working on plantations. Many contracts expired during the war, but the administration enforced extensions. When the Vietnamese went on strike because of a rice shortage on Santo in May 1945, the native police killed two workers. The Americans helped restore peace and sold rice to solve the ration problem, but they remained aloof from Condominium politics.[82]

The Americans were less aloof from events that could undermine their war industries. In 1943–44 the Dutch wanted their Javanese laborers returned to assist in the re-establishment of Dutch authority in the East Indies. Both the New Caledonian French and the Americans, in need of nickel, refused, as mining employed more than 2,350 workers, with 1,330 in agriculture and the rest in essential industries.[83]

American pragmatism applied to its own territory. When a thousand contractors began building the Tutuila base in 1940–41, more than 1,500 Samoans worked for them, each paid $40 monthly, double the prewar rates. But once Japan entered the war "all able bodied Samoans were called to assist in construction of defenses."[84] Any "not employed were forcibly recruited to work for the Navy in loading and unloading ships."[85] In all, 2,500 Samoan men, almost 20 percent of the population, worked for the military, deceasing to about 700 by 1945.[86] Here and in Western Samoa men worked on construction and stevedoring, and many women did American laundry.[87] By 1942 the daily male wage of $3.20 (19/5) in American Samoa was more than three times as high as its neighbor, so many Western Samoans crossed to the American territory. American Samoans could not believe such wealth was possible. Western Samoans prospered too, working for the Americans initially at 4/-, increased in late 1943 to 5/-, for laborers on an eight-hour day.[88] Labor was so willing that when the Americans arrived, the New Zealand administration did not need to organize a labor corps, allowing the marines' brigade quartermaster to hire. American heavy equipment compensated for many of the administration's normal labor needs. The Americans, for example, built the transinsular Upolu road in 1943. The monthly wages bill was between $45,000 and $65,000 for the 1,500 to 2,600 Samoans, with daily wages ranging from the basic 5/- to as high as 16/- and 18/- for skilled workers. Perhaps the best indicator of the Western Samoans' experience was their response when the administration tried to raise a labor corps in September 1943 for the forward area. Few were interested because the wages offered were judged insufficient.[89]

When in November 1943 the army took the control of labor from the marines, they decided that wages should be charged under reverse lend-lease. While New Zealand wanted to control the Samoan labor, it was worried that this reverse lend-lease costing would become an excuse for the Americans to have some claim on the islands, and they preferred a charge to direct expenditure. A new army commander was unaware of the policy change, and soon afterward the Americans left.[90]

Tiny Tokelau largely escaped the war, although there were seaplane alighting areas on the lagoons and a small American garrison at Atafu from 1944. Some worked for the Americans on a barter basis, since there were no stores. Anxious for trade goods, fifty Tokelauans answered Western Samoa's call for workers on their Reparation Estates, but because of "diet difficulties," recruiting ceased.[91]

In the Cook Islands, at Penrhyn and Aitutaki bases, men from throughout the Cooks worked on three-month contracts. At Aitutaki, at the height of construction, 400 islanders worked for the Americans at a daily base rate initially of 3/- but soon 4/- to 5/- (65 to 82 cents) depending on tasks. Women did laundry until the Americans installed a steam laundry to get them back to the gardens to feed their families. Because of the phosphate demand and cessation of Vietnamese migration, from 1943, more than 485 Cook Islanders, including about 70 wives, went to French Makatea to work.[92]

To the south, the Tonga Defense Force was effectively a labor corps. Others worked for the Americans too, including men from the northern islands, hired via a government labor bureau that later transferred recruitment to the Americans. Under Sālote, aiming to maintain Tongan integrity amid the "invasion," the government exercised strong wage controls, the daily rate remaining about $1. The

Americans cooperated, but prices for local products went as high as the market would pay.[93]

High prices for local products caused difficulties on Bora Bora. When the Americans arrived in February 1942 they had problems finding male workers among the population of 1,200. Instead, the local women worked as laundresses and made souvenirs to sell. Their newfound income was soon spent at the Chinese traders' stores, but these could not replenish stocks. So Commander Ostrom used the navy's commissary to bargain for sixty male workers by selling "canned goods, bulk rice and flour" to the value of $200 monthly. In some places, setting up a reciprocal relationship by trading "trinkets, clothing, cigarettes, chewing gum, tools, knives" meant the Americans did not always pay cash wages.[94]

Waging of War

Unlike trees and aggregates, human beings can think, and their behavior is shaped by society, its institutions, and the environment. Although war exposed islanders to unique circumstances, often varying spatially as well as temporally, these social and environmental constants remained foundational. In the western Pacific, the Allies benefited from the indenture system. The institution of the plantation had conditioned recruits to the work routines the Allies expected, and if they resisted, similar punitive clauses or worse were invoked nearer the front. In the east, the hierarchical nature of Polynesian societies meant that men followed respected leaders and conformed to group expectations; as long as the chiefs supported the cause, their people would too. And their chiefs, including Sālote and Sukuna, while invoking traditional values to rally their people, looked to the future. Even more ancient Polynesian values of adventure, descent linkages, and pride in their islands moved dozens of Cook Islanders, Samoans, and other Polynesians to enlist alongside their *teina* or younger brothers in the Maori Battalion in New Zealand.

Even so, islanders were not Allied thralls. They resisted actions that attacked their dignity. Courage and discipline were valued culturally, so they responded constructively, even proudly, to being attached to Allied armies. But when those organizations broke their own mores by relegating "expert" jungle fighters to bare-chested auxiliaries in lap-laps, the New Guineans objected, just as the Tongans resented enlisted New Zealanders treating their TDF officers as inferior. The first of the SIDF missed the combat training the Fijians had, so many deserted. Kanak laborers in New Caledonia protested poor conditions; the New Hebrideans circumvented wage regulations. Where there was choice, as with the Western Samoan workers, low remuneration was no compensation for the risks of the forward area, so they declined. As much as they dared in the lands of alien peoples, some New Guinean conscript labor ran away from the ill treatment some ANGAU and Japanese meted out; some SILC men organized strikes when exposed to battle conditions and low wages. In Fiji, New Caledonia, and New Hebrides, Asian workers used the emergency to try to extract better conditions and wages from their masters.

Whispers from colonial and military archives murmur of island women becoming a significant proportion of the casual work force. In the Gilbert and Ellice Islands they had wage parity with men. Yet authorities were quick to assign them unpaid subsistence work to free up male labor. Except for migrant Asian women, many experienced paid labor for the first time and had buying power, formerly a male prerogative. How this altered their self-perception is unclear, but it initiated many into the cash economy, even if only ephemerally.

For many, then, wages were a measure of their worth in the white man's cash-oriented and racially categorized society. In much of prewar western Melanesia, the introduced economy had been poorly diversified while highly regulated conditions kept wages down. The low Depression wages changed when the war came, as there was not only increased demand, but also competition. Melanesians had an

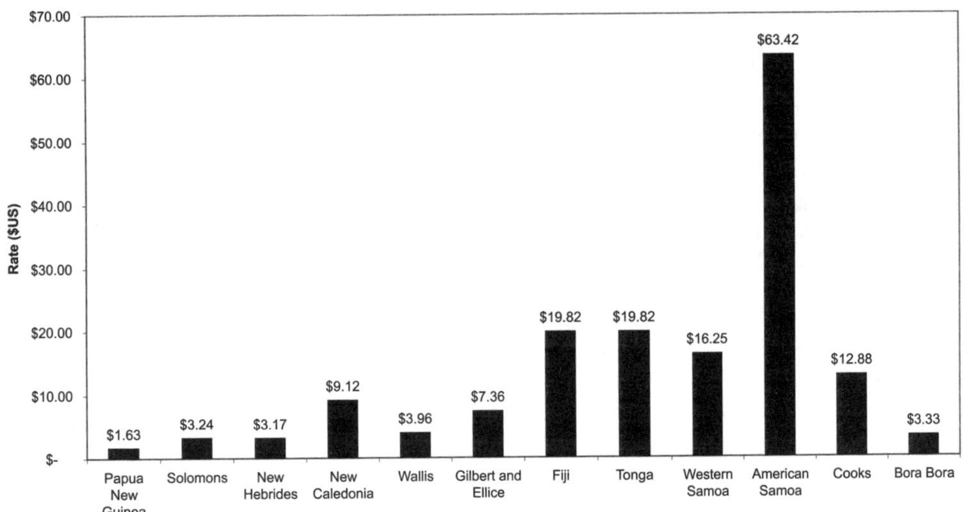

Figure 20. Wartime monthly wages for unskilled labor in the southern Pacific (Bora Bora rate is an estimate based on value of the navy's commissary supplies made available for the workers to purchase, but was probably a little higher).

idea of what the Allied infantryman earned, but not that many were earning more money than they had in their homelands before the war. The numbers of exotic servicemen were extraordinary—in the Solomons in early 1944, they outnumbered the people two to one. With little else to tempt their pockets and dollar bills literally rotting in their wallets,[95] servicemen paid high prices for limited goods and services. Moreover, the failure of the "recovery" units of the U.S. Quartermaster Corps to fulfill their mission supplied surplus goods to the people.[96] In war, islanders thus perceived a new type of white men: wealthy, open-handed, and more egalitarian than the prewar colonials. They noticed too the U.S. colored troops seemed better off materially than they. They concluded that if they were doing similar jobs, they were worth the same.[97] Economic relativity based on domestic productivity was beyond their contemplation.

Yet, although wages were higher than before the war, most administrations kept them modest in contrast to the Americans, who emerged as a generous people, having passed on bonuses in gifts and discarded items. For example, six thousand people on Nggela each had an American stretcher bed and mosquito net.[98] Melanesian social memory still recalls American generosity, logistics, and material wealth.[99] One astute visitor noted,

> What we are witnessing in the Solomons is the rise and fall of a great civilization. The islanders will remember these war years as a fabulous Golden Age which vanished almost as soon as it had begun. . . . From Lunga to Torokina [bases] the Solomon Islands are a chain of highly civilized . . . and wealthy European communities.[100]

To societies valuing patronage, this potential source of wealth sparked attempts to press the Americans to remain.[101] But the great mobile towns, which embodied a successful complex web of inter- and intracommunications as well as the technical knowledge of the West, were suddenly dismantled, their inhabitants returning to their metropolitan preoccupations. As the ships took the armies home, dreams of this utopia faded, with lingering hopes retreating to scattered attempts at political change, but more commonly to "cargo cults" and nostalgia.[102] Some appeared simply puzzled as to why such technological power revealed in war had not been seen before and used for their benefit. To outsiders they seemed dispirited, as J. M. Clift noted on Guadalcanal:

> They seem to have lost what little vim they had. Perhaps the magical equipment and organization of the Americans brought home to them the primitiveness of their existence. The little things that made up their contented lot appear to have lost their value. They seem to be adrift . . . on the sea of time.[103]

Of more enduring significance though, was the abolition of indenture during or soon after the war in all territories; global scrutiny, the labor movement, and economic recovery blew it apart and asserted the dignity of the worker.[104] Striving for better wages during the war and demanding wage parity with the European to fight at its beginning, however, were two different scenarios. When the threat was greatest, the Indians in Fiji missed an opportunity to create a respected place within the community because they put provisos on their military participation. Failing to take the tide at the flood, they long remained in a political backwater. Yet exploited Indian tenant farmers in Fiji's sugar industry as well as Asian laborers in the French territories took the pressure off native communities, enabling them more easily to contribute to the war effort without jeopardizing their families' livelihood. Lacking this Asian labor subsidy, military and colonial coercion of, say, the Fijians and Kanaks could have been of a similar order as on the New Guineans.

Everywhere, the U.S. commanders followed their own agenda: maximize the native resource where most needed; what happened thereafter was of little moment. Had the Americans had their way in the Solomons in 1943, for example, labor would have been conscripted. The British realized the negative effects this would entail, believed that numbers in the SILC were near the maximum, and preferred trade inducements.[105] They, like other colonial administrations, tried to stabilize the people's subsistence and the wage structure because they would remain after the armies had left. Paternalistic it was, but for many islanders the presence of the colonial wartime administrations often ameliorated excesses that the military believed expedient. So long as administrations could muster labor, the military had no desire to undermine them and create another foe, though the Americans came close to doing so with many New Caledonian French who feared American annexation. And in extreme conditions, "realism" prevailed.[106] Fearful that Australia would succumb to the Japanese, ANGAU invoked labor conscription. The inevitable legacy was ill will among their subjects. Even in American Samoa when the military feared the worst in early 1942, it too coerced labor. Only the subsequent inflow of wealth and opportunities and absence of battle left a positive memory for Samoans.[107] Though generous, the Americans were no fools. To what extent they used the "mean" colonials as scapegoats to avoid greater indebtedness under reverse lend-lease in higher wages is unclear. But when they had nothing to gain, they did not consider paying disproportionately high wages on isolated islands such as Wallis and Tokelau, where there was no competition for the fixed labor supply and/or little for the people to spend money on. Both the military and the administrations thus had economic agendas for the islanders.

Most Polynesians had plenty to spend their money on. Church collections soared and savings bank deposits increased—for the duration, at least. Within the Samoas, *malaga*, or intervillage visiting and feasting, increased along with massive exchanges of fine mats and competition to provide superior entertainment. In Tonga, Fiji, and the Cook Islands, as well as the Gilbert and Ellice Islands, people early offered funds and men for Britain. Western Samoa paid for a Spitfire airplane[108] even though "Samoans ever since 1920 have been conscious that because of the Mandate they are not British; they regard themselves as a separate nationhood."[109] These contributions reasserted cultural values of reciprocity and solidarity that, with some accommodation as well as resistance, had survived the coming of Europeans and comparatively benign colonial governments. Many leaders in these archipelagoes had secondary education, a rare few had tertiary qualifications. Much of the population of Fiji, Samoa, and Tonga was literate; many could also speak English.[110] This, along with their large sociopolitical groups and retention of most of their lands, gave them a positive view of themselves and their culture. The war provided new opportunities to reinforce this. As well as employment, well-equipped Americans offered entertainment, gifts of "surplus," and medical care in rear bases for islanders, setting up reciprocal patterns familiar to the Polynesians.[111]

The islanders embraced all these, yet as the war receded, they largely returned to their own preoccupations. In Tonga by 1945, "the older customs of the island [were] being revived."[112] The Gilbertese, confident of their own ways, glided gracefully into acceptance of British administration in spite of their wartime preference for the Americans.[113] The Fijian chiefly elite had won more control over their communal affairs from the British in 1940, slowing the drift toward individualism, but, as Sukuna realized, wartime experiences meant that "the Fijian was beginning to learn what to do in order to keep his place in the surge of civilization."[114] Wartime Indian political and economic agitation reinforced the barrier between them and the Indians. The Western Samoans resumed their perennial demands for independence,[115] politics having "hibernated" for the duration; after all, those who joined the New Zealand army did so for Samoa.[116] For the American Samoans there was "no real breaking away from the roots of their mores and lore."[117] Although some wanted more of the wartime opportunities, the domestic job market shrunk with peace. Politically, they puzzled over their constitutional status with the United States but wanted a continuing joint relationship.[118] On Aitutaki, wartime's carnival atmosphere faded after the American dollars were spent and people reluctantly faced the reality of living off their own local resources. But there and on Rarotonga, American influence combined with discontent among local growers, negative experiences of the Makatea workers, and continuing union connections in Auckland coalesced in a labor movement that from 1943 to 1947 articulated both industrial and political demands New Zealand soon took seriously.[119]

In western Melanesia, although their soldiers and laborers had made a huge contribution to the war effort, wage scales were lower than in much of the South

Pacific command. For the Melanesians, there was some counterweight not just in gifted goods but also in altered self-image. Yet it was a bifurcated and contradictory image. Through their participation in the war, many now began to glimpse a new kind of civilization: modernity and greater possibilities than before, with themselves as competent actors in it, with moral equivalence to the Europeans and not just *bois* (boys) or *buskanakas* (bushmen).[120] ANGAU trained some in practical nursing, as drivers, wireless operators, and, in 1944, as schoolteachers. A few received commando training in Australia.[121] Soldiers who could wield an Owen gun and outwit the enemy, coast watchers who could succor crashed airmen, men who could captain coastal vessels, laborers who could lug the wounded over New Guinea mountains and operate winches on Noumea's wharves, rediscovered some of the self-confidence that colonialism often suppressed. In war, these natives not only were masters in their environment, they also had mastered elements of the invading culture. The resource had found itself resourceful. And there were many Allied troops who shared that opinion, particularly the Australian soldiers who lauded their help as fighters and stoic carriers. Even though the Americans considered them "generally quite primitive," Melanesians had been "of great value."[122]

But these armies vanished and had no more need of them. In fact, as Marty Zelenietz notes, the Americans barely mentioned them in their subsequent published operational and popular accounts.[123] Although most Melanesians had proved adept in this ephemeral war society, it also showed many a part of themselves that was unsettling: their own cultures, ancestors, and big men had been unable to produce the Allies' unity of command, material culture, and colossal power to alter landscape and lives.[124] At the micro level of internal politics, some groups with a growing island-based consciousness formed in the plantation culture found that the war challenged their nascent localized identity. Prewar Malaitans, for example, had a reputation for their aggression, hard work, and intelligence.[125] In the war, as in peace, they remained simply laborers who, except for their solid work in the SILC, were otherwise undistinguished. Yet, coming from the stereotypically reserved, unindustrious society of Guadalcanal, war hero Jacob Vouza received medals and adulation from both the Americans and the British. Furthermore, villagers in southwest Guadalcanal had proved adept fighters, picking off isolated Japanese patrols. The supposedly docile, Christianized western Solomon Islanders also produced an effective guerrilla force, again recognized as such by the Allies.[126] So the war stimulated Malaitans, some challenged by U.S. servicemen such as John Burke (see chapter 12), to reflect on who they were as a people. Most diverse Melanesian groups, however, lacked cohesion and could not gather momentum for systematic change, but thousands mixed with formerly unknown groups and began to understand they were all living in the one island or archipelago. Very few Melanesians in New Guinea, the Solomon Islands, New Hebrides, and

New Caledonia had secondary or technical training; a mere handful had Western tertiary education. Some had only a smattering of mission primary schooling and few spoke English or French fluently. Consequently, access to literacy and thus modernity was constricted. So, with few alternatives, most returned to old preoccupations. More questioning Melanesians, however, sought the means to connect with the power of the stranger through their own multitudinous epistemologies. To realize this, some reformulated their mythical pasts; some blamed their condition on the colonial masters and diverted old values along novel trajectories to resist; and others, borrowing elements from the Allied sociomilitary template, endeavored to create a hybrid "new way" within the colonial order.[127]

PART III

Exiting Environment, Leaving Residues

CHAPTER 8

Paying for the Damages

> Let the government or whoever is responsible re-dig our pits, we did not destroy them.
>
> —Karotu

> [T]he Pacific Islanders are generally in the fortunate position of being able to repair their gardens and houses without any great difficulty.

To survive in their environment, human beings need food and shelter. In war, these necessities, the resources to provide them, and humans themselves often are damaged or destroyed. Victims look for compensation to assist recovery. The concept of compensation is embedded in Pacific island societies, perhaps most clamorously in Melanesia. In Western jurisdictions, the law of torts enables victims to seek a remedy. To keep the continued goodwill of islanders, the Allies took compensation seriously, and colonial administrations generally tried to facilitate compensation to assist rehabilitation. The process was often tortuous, but it injected considerable cash or goods into the economy. Equity of outcome, however, was determined by the entangled politics of the powers' relationships among themselves and even within their different territories, the administrations' assessment of needs, fiscal resources, and postwar objectives, as well as the expectation that the aggressor would contribute to reparations.

Maintaining Friendly Relations

In January 1942, the U.S. Congress defined America's responsibilities. Public Law 393 aimed to "provide for the prompt settlement of claims for damages occasioned by Army, Navy, and Marine Corps forces in foreign countries" "for the purpose of promoting and maintaining friendly relations," for claims up to $1,000, later amended to $2,500. By April 1943, local claims commissions could consider claims of up to $5,000. Claims exceeding this had to be certified to Congress by the secretary of the navy. These commissions, of one to three commissioned officers, proceeded fairly informally. The statute of limitations was one year, though there were sometimes retrospective variations.[1]

Financial Fiji

Until the United States entered the war, the colonial powers were solely responsible for dealing with the consequences of war preparation in their territories.[2] The Fijian government was the first to pay compensation in 1938, after it resumed land for airstrips at Vucimaca in east Viti Levu and Cawa in the west.[3] The declaration of war in September 1939 saw legislation guaranteeing compensation for land, crops, and housing affected by military occupation.[4] By October 1941, anticipating Japanese invasion, the Americans began building airstrips for the "air ferry" routes to connect America and Australia.[5] The government declared five square miles between the Nadi and Sabeto (Malika) rivers on Viti Levu reserved for "military purposes," securing the perimeters of the airstrip being constructed in cooperation with the Americans.[6]

Fiji's capital, Suva, required fortifications since it was on the main trans-Pacific shipping routes, although the natural features of west Viti Levu and its drier climate provided better sites for airfields and bases[7] (see Map 13). Once Fiji became a forward base for the assault on the Solomon Islands during 1942–1943, the 20,000-strong American force required more land near Nadi, most of which was leased to Fiji Indian tenants. Besides "large areas" of Fijian land, five villages also were resumed in the five-square-mile zone.[8] The Colonial Sugar Refinery Company (CSR) also lost significant acreages of cane land.[9]

Though the government paid the Indians for the costs of relocation and for improvements destroyed, as well as £8 to £10 an acre for loss of the use of productive land, getting more lease land was problematic. Officials in early 1942 struggled to process claims from often destitute tenants. Concerned with the pro–Indian Home Rule propaganda circulating, the government settled most claims within six months of resumption.[10] Fearing further problems, the government convinced the Americans that evacuating residents from the five-square-mile zone was unnecessary and would reduce the supply of fresh farm vegetables.[11] Indians' and Fijians' cultivations suffered, however, as U.S. military units crisscrossed their lands despite government complaints. By the second half of 1943 most of these claims had been processed to the value of about £98,000, including more than £10,000 to CSR.[12] Although strained, the relatively buoyant Fiji administration compensated claimants, but it perhaps created the impression that the British government—in the guise of the WPHC—would do the same elsewhere.

Small Satisfactions in Tonga

Tonga was not a British territory, but had been its protectorate since 1900, and the British consul there was answerable to the governor of Fiji. Tonga's defense, initially the responsibility of New Zealand, went to the Americans in May 1942. They built a refueling base, supporting operations south of Fiji and the Samoas. Overall, about 8,600 American personnel occupied Tongatapu until late 1943.[13]

The Americans in June 1942 agreed to:

> Pay compensation for the use or occupation or for the damage or destruction of all improved or personal property belonging to the Tongan government, or to the inhabitants of Tonga . . . by reason of the activities of the United States Forces provided that there shall be no obligation to pay compensation for damage caused by enemy action or by the United States Forces when engaged in conflict.[14]

A joint compensation board worked well with one officer from the navy commission and the Tongan superintendent of police advising on local matters, such as setting payments for loss of plants (Table 3) and rentals.[15]

The everyday settlement of claims fell to a navy commission and an army commission.[16] They settled about half "out of court," often with war surplus. Most claims were under $200.[17] The navy commission completed its work quickly, but was reconstituted in late 1944 when Premier Ata announced 16 December as the closing date for all claims. As Tonga was ineligible for American lend-lease arrangements,[18] the government claimed $35,000 for "damage" to piers and roads—beyond the consideration of the commission but maybe as an offset to U.S. demands for payment for equipment they were to abandon.[19] The Americans assigned infrastructure, including the Yellow or American pier at Nuku'alofa, a new water supply, and some roads to the government, so this may have finalized claim settlement.[20]

Assessing American Samoa

American Samoa was America's possession, so compensation was less urgent. Although under a navy governor in peacetime, once the 2nd Marines Brigade arrived in January 1942, its Commander Larsen became governor during the emergency,[21] when "private property was appropriated whenever and wherever needed for the

TABLE 3. Compensation Payments for Valuable Plants in Tonga, October 1942

Plant	Rate	Tongan Pound	U.S. Dollars
Bananas		1 shilling	16c
Breadfruit		10 pence	13c approx.
Coconuts	Per tree	4 shillings	65c
Corn		1 penny	1c approx.
Hiapo, old *(Broussonetia papyfera)*		1 penny	1c approx.
Hiapo, young (paper mulberry, bark used to make ngatu or tapa cloth)		1/2 penny	0.5c approx.
Kape (kape kape, similar to taro-*Alocasia*)		4 pence	7c approx.
Kava *(Piper methysticum)*		7 shillings, 6 pence	$1.22
Kumala (sweet potato-*lpomoea batatas*)		3 pence	4c
Manioc (Cassava)	Per plant	6 pence	8c
Orange tree	Per tree	4 shillings	65c
Pawpaw (Papaya)		1 penny	1c approx.
Pineapple		1 penny	1c approx.
Plantatain		9 pence	12c
Sugar cane	Per "hill"	9 pence	12c
Talo *(Colocasia esculenta)*		3 pence	4c
Tava tree (*Pometia innata,* green-skinned fruit, like lychee)		2 shillings	33c
Ufilei (small vairiety of yam)		4 pence	7c approx.
Watermelon		1 shilling	16c
Yam (*Dioscorea* spp.)		8 pence	11c approx.

Sources: Olsen to Commanding Officer, 1 Feb. 1943, Box 1, F. L0, L10, & L13, RG 313-58-3394, NARA SB.

war effort . . . without the negotiation of leases or purchases."[22] There was hardship, as Mrs. Tasi explained when she lost land for the Leone airfield.

> I have no objection—I realize the importance of the work . . . but because of my not knowing where I could find any kind of support for my six children and myself, who is a widow, I do certainly hope that I will get some kind of consideration [*sic*].[23]

"Consideration" took various forms. When a platoon of the 7th Defense Battalion first arrived near Pago Pago in March 1942, it lacked rations, so a local chief, T. M. Emeleo, often gave its men food, allowing them to use a local "hall as a billet." Although he made no claim, when the battalion installed its water supply it also ran seventy-five feet of extra pipe to take water to the chief's yard for the village.[24] Often, release from lease payments came about in much the same way—several Samoan leaders received the novelty of electric power supply.[25]

The standing claims commission of two navy members and chairman, Chief Justice Arthur A. Morrow, was set up in August 1945. In 1946 it heard 206 claims.[26] To examine claims on site, village by village, was slow, as the high chiefs of Leone complained in 1948.

> Our coconut plants which are our chief means of living and main export were cut down merely for the clearance of target ranges, etc. Yet, we made no objection. Why? Because we were willing to assist the US government . . . in Samoa most of our claims have not yet been touched nor investigated [*sic*].[27]

Claims for loss of valuable trees and crops were paid according to a schedule (see Table 4) at a higher rate than in Tonga.

The commission continued until the signing of the peace treaty with Japan, but ceased when the navy left in July 1951 and the Department of the Interior became the administering authority. Its successor, the war damage commission headed by Morrow, resumed in January 1952. The administration notified Samoans that they had only one year from the signing of the peace treaty in April 1952 to lodge more claims, but they extended this until late 1954.[28]

Some claims were extravagant. Maisu Pasine asked for $825,790 for damages to land he held as *matai* (extended family or *aiga* head), but he signed a release for only $325. Some realized that any claim over $1,000 had to go to the U.S. Congress, so they accepted payments that were less than demanded. Most seemed happy to accept, and while only a few were settled for the full sum claimed, the process appeared fair.[29]

Table 4. Recommended Scale of Compensation Payment by the Claims Commission, American Samoa

Plant	Value US $	Plant	Value US $
Avocado tree	$3.00	Mulberry plant *(Broussonetia papyfera)*	$0.25
'Ava plant' *(Piper methysticum)*	$4.00	Milo *(Thespesia populnea)*	$3.00
Banana tree	$0.50	Nonu tree *(Morinda citrifolia)*	$0.50
Breadfruit tree	$3.00	Oli'oli tree *(Cyathea spp)*	$0.25
Cocoa (cacao) plant	$6.00	Orange tree	$2.00
Coconut tree	$5.00	Pandanus (fine)	$1.00
Cucumber plant	$0.50	Pandanus (plant)	$0.50
Fetau tree *(Calophyllum inophyllum)*	$2.25	Pandanus (tree)	$0.25
Giant taro plant	$0.50	Papaogo tree (*Litsaea* spp.?)	$0.25
Guava tree	$0.50	Papaya plant	$1.00
Ifi tree *(Inocarpus fagifer)*	$1.50	Pineapple plant	$0.25
Kapok tree	$1.00	Poumoli tree (*Flueggea flexuosa*?)	$1.50
Kava tree *(Pometia pinnata)*	$2.00	Reed plant (single)	$0.10
Lemon tree	$4.00	Reed plant (bundle, bed, hill)	$0.25
Lime tree	$4.00	Sugar cane plant (thatch)	$0.25
Malama tree (*Dysoxylum samoense*?)	$0.25	Sugar care (edible)	$0.50
Mango tree	$4.00	Taro plant	$0.25
Manioc tree	$0.25	Tapioca plant	$0.25
Melon plant-water	$4.00	Toi tree *(Alphitonia zizyphoides)*	$1.00
Moso'oi plant *(Cananga odoratum)*	$0.25	Yam plant	$1.00

Sources: Recommended scale of payment, enclosure, Afao village, no. 1, 1953, War Damage claims, RG 284, NARA SB.

New Zealand's Cautionary Compensation

New Zealand's relationship with its American ally was premised on an experience in the 1930s when the U.S. attempted to claim for airfields uninhabited Pacific islands, some under New Zealand sovereignty or claimed by Britain, in order to guarantee American control of trans-Pacific commercial aviation.[30] New Zealand was thus wary of giving the Americans any foundation for postwar claims to bases constructed in its territories. In Western Samoa, American marines arrived in early 1942, with base construction underway in April on north Upolu. By agreement, the New Zealand administration worked with the forces, negotiating leases and the relocation of 1,200 Samoans from the airfield base at Fale'olo. For each acre of the land at Satapuala and Satuimalufilufi, the administration gave them 1.25 acres of government land, as well as paying compensation, but some Samoans objected to the loss of lands, the locus of their identity. Although the administration jollied them along and the war lent urgency, the issue persists today. The Americans began to reduce their base in February 1944, with lend-lease supplying the administration's construction materials' requests.[31] They settled claims for personal injury, with the administration taking responsibility for those arising after the Americans withdrew.[32] Aware of the Samoans' questioning of colonial control and talk of Americans taking over, the administration claimed nothing for the use of lands, roads, harbors, and buildings, thus eliminating any basis for the Americans to remain.[33]

New Zealand proved careless in the Cook Islands. The administration authorized American bases on Aitutaki and Penrhyn, with the destruction of thousands of coconuts and other crops, but they neglected to make a formal agreement. Before the main force left in late 1943, the commander wanted to settle all claims. After the native land court judge had assessed claims for the Americans to pay, the New Zealand administration realized that there was no guiding agreement. Claims amounted to £1,613/10/1 on Aitutaki and £6,894 on Penrhyn, where 16,400 coconut palms were destroyed, along with rentals for land remaining occupied or in use as an airfield.[34]

New Zealand was alarmed to realize that informal documents exchanged in August 1942 implied use of native lands for the "duration of the present war, plus one year following the war." New Zealand, Australia, and the French were by then fearful that the Americans would stay on in the South Pacific after the war.[35] The New Zealand administration decided to meet all claims of the islanders and not present them to the Americans because:

> To lodge such a claim would merely serve to consolidate the interest of the United States Government and indeed put them in a position to claim some

> right to use these facilities in the post war period. As well as derogating from the sovereignty of the New Zealand Government of the Cook Islands the effect of such claims might be construed as giving some title to the United States Government which should be avoided.[36]

New Zealand did not claim under reverse lend-lease and by 1946 had compensated Cook Islands claimants.[37]

Friction in the French Territories

The Americans arrived on New Caledonia in March 1942, with Japan advancing, so "material was installed without formalities."[38] By August, claims emerged and so required a commission, which comprised three navy officers.[39] Claims from the agricultural and pastoral sector often came in the first instance to the director of the veterinary service, Dr. Jean Verges. A significant one centered on the American introduction of the cattle tick, *Boophilus microplus* (see chapter 10). Verges had warned against this as early as June 1942 when the American army was importing horses from Australia, but Verges was ignored. The French, dissatisfied with the naval claims commission consisting solely of American assessors, requested that Verges "represent the Colonial Government . . . to fix the damages . . . to farmers and cattle raisers caused by American troops." Major General Patch agreed that Verges could be called as a witness in assessing values, but no more.[40] Governor Montchamp insisted that Verges and a government agriculture officer should be part of the commission, preferring the New Zealand practice of a mixed commission of their officers and the French. Eventually in May 1943, the Americans complied and Verges plus two other French representatives with three navy officers presided over the commission's deliberations.[41]

The commission paid claims up to $1,000 and later $5,000, charged to reverse lend-lease accounting. Although there was no formal agreement for the French Pacific, an agreement between the Free French National Committee and the United States signed on 1 January 1942 addressing lend-lease pertaining to North Africa became the basis for operations elsewhere, reinforced by a local understanding in September between the New Caledonia administration and the Americans. The revised agreement of April 1945 for French Bora Bora, regarding lease renewals and French retention of installations, had set up a commission to settle compensation disputes, with no mention of lend-lease or reverse lend-lease. As there was no specific agreement, the governor of New Caledonia, Tallec, would not agree to a local arrangement for New Caledonia and stated that he had no authority to do so for the Society Islands because its administration was answerable to the Ministry of Colonies in Paris. Understandings were exchanged for the

Pacific soon after the bombing of Pearl Harbor, however, as to who retained sovereignty, postwar possession of installations, and rentals. By 1946, the Americans intended that materials that had been allocated to the French under lend-lease would offset claims.[42]

America forgave the French empire its high lend-lease debts, provided that France took responsibility for unsettled damage claims.[43] New Caledonia gained tons of plant sold for $425,000, around a third of their original cost. As stated in the original U.S.-French understandings of January 1942, the Americans handed over their infrastructure at a cost of three million dollars. Elsewhere in the French Pacific at Bora Bora and Wallis Island, rentals were settled to mutual satisfaction, with no recorded claims.[44] In addition, the French owed Australia £790,000, which Australia forgave to foster trade relations.[45] A congenial arrangement to cancel the eighty million francs owed to New Zealand by the French Pacific was the provision of accommodation for the New Zealand legation in Paris and scholarships for New Zealand students in France.[46]

Confusing Condominium

For all its frictions, the compensation process in New Caledonia was simple in comparison to the Condominium of the New Hebrides. In the New Hebrides, three systems of government operated: the French, the English, and the Condominium. A joint court consisted of British and French judges with a neutral president and an executive government composed for some purposes of the French and British resident commissioners, while for other purposes the French and British nationals remained under the jurisdiction of their respective national authorities. The British resident commissioner was subject to the British high commissioner in Suva and the French resident commissioner to the French high commissioner in Noumea. There were about 200 British nationals, 800 French, and 2,000 Asians, mainly Tonkinese (Vietnamese). About 40,000 Melanesians were effectively stateless.[47]

In early 1941, the RAAF had established a flying boat base on Efate on land leased from French residents holding registered titles. The compensation assessment commission of judges of the joint court assessed losses such as coconut trees and paid compensation as well as rental, passing costs on to Australia.[48] Soon after the Americans arrived on Efate (March 1942) and Santo (June 1942), the French and British commissioners attempted to agree on the legal status and powers of America with regard to its bases, leasing land, and compensation, drawing up a draft agreement in July 1942. Until January 1944 this ran to about ten drafts with several amendments, but, constantly referring to their home governments, the three failed to agree, and the agreement was never ratified. In December 1943, the

British secretary of state urged an ad hoc agreement.[49] As High Commissioner Mitchell pointed out to Shaforth, deputy commander, South Pacific:

> Such an agreement would . . . quite satisfactorily meet the situation, whereas if the matter has to be referred to London and Washington the result is likely to be an immense amount of labour for all of us which I cannot regard as likely to have much effect on the defeat of the Japanese![50]

By early 1944 Americans thought it was too late because they were beginning to withdraw.[51]

This spawned difficulties. Because the United States had only de facto status under the constitutional arrangements of the New Hebrides, it was not able to make legal leases, a situation further confounded by irreconcilable differences between British and French lease laws. No debits and credits could come under lend-lease and reverse lend-lease. Moreover, on Santo there were no publicly registered lands, merely claims by settlers. Since land boundaries were hazy, cross-claims for compensation could arise.[52] By 1943, local regulations had been modified to protect American property rights, but there was Condominium concern that Melanesian rights might suffer. The British legal adviser concluded that only sale or grant by a native needed joint British and French approval. Leasing could not be made because under the law, the Melanesians lacked any nationality and America had doubtful legal standing. The two commissioners compromised: The U.S. authorities were to approach the district agent in the area for permission to use native land for a fixed term, and he then checked to see if the natives agreed. If they did, he then submitted it for consideration of the two resident commissioners who then advised the Americans.[53]

Leases with settlers were even more problematic, as "they stand completely outside Condominium law and no Court or machinery adopted by consent, exists for settlement of differences."[54] The Americans, nonetheless, persisted in trying to arrange them with the French settlers, but many refused because of an automatic renewal clause with no set termination date. Eventually the American forces, building the South Pacific's largest naval base at Luganville, Santo,[55] proceeded with little "finesse and tact" toward civilians, causing "considerable damage to property." Until mid-1943, they often simply occupied the land.[56] The Americans delivered letters to the owners or managers of many of the twenty-five properties involved, mainly on Santo, telling them that their lands would be needed, "with a copy to the French or British local official," to harvest crops, remove animals before a given date, and to submit claims.[57] Even the British resident commissioner thought them unnecessarily destructive of French property.[58]

Consequently, by May 1943 many Santo planters had become "definitely antagonistic to the Americans." The Americans contemplated installing a military government because they felt the administration could not control the civilians,[59] while the administration complained that the Americans frequently exceeded their legal powers.[60] The establishment of an American civil affairs office in June 1943 and the appointment of more competent administration officials improved relations, but the legal uncertainty continued to create "endless complications."[61]

When valuing destroyed crops there were problems with the meaning of "replacement value." Payments varied from 75 cents to $5.00, but most were in the range of $3.25 (A£1) for each bearing tree, a rate similar to American Samoa but higher than Tonga and New Guinea.[62] Some claims however, stalled in December 1943, when the French set a value on trees in excess of American calculations.[63] Settlers were accused of being unduly "claims conscious," though the Americans admitted that

> severe damage and great hardship have been inflicted upon the civilian population. In some cases, plantations have been entirely taken over, and the owners and their families have been forced to move elsewhere.[64]

An army claims officer heard claims monthly and those worth less than $5,000 were settled quickly.[65] By 30 June 1945, claims amounting to $1,214,330.22 had been lodged, and of this $94,243.04 had been approved, but most of these claims were in excess of $5,000 and so had to be forwarded to Washington, D.C. After 30 June 1945, there was a flood of claims as the European war ended and evacuation by the Americans seemed inevitable. A policy change allowed claims amounting to $79,534.48 to be paid "in consideration of the leaving of buildings or other items of excess property." Eventually, $100,000 in claims were settled this way.[66]

The Condominium had claims for damages to its property leased to the Americans, but without a reverse lend-lease agreement "it seemed politic not to make such claims," and the administration anticipated that American surplus would provide sufficient compensation.[67] In late 1944 the administration released the Americans from all such claims, but some individual ones were still pending.[68] What of these? Under a policy directive in February 1943, the Americans settled the claims of certain Santo lessors with surplus buildings, plant, and vehicles.[69] Regarding the Santo tenants of the Société Francaise des Nouvelles Hebrides (SFNH), the U.S. judge advocate general ruled it was an agency of the French government and that claims were to be credited against improvements the Americans had made on Santo.[70] In May 1946, the French settlers' claims fell under the agreement with the Americans wherein the French metropolitan government accepted responsibility for compensation in all French territories in return for the cancellation of lend-lease debts owed America. Yet in 1951 the French rescinded this for the Condominium, wanting a joint agreement for settlement with Britain. Britain declined as it did not consider the French settlers their responsibility. The final claims amounted to 500,000,000 Pacific francs, but French authorities in Noumea calculated a more realistic 10,000,000 francs or about $215,000. The matter eventually concerned the government of France, which finally in 1956 settled most of the claims of SFNH, though funding some from the New Hebrides' budget.[71]

Melanesians and a British settler were also successful. Two claims of less than $300 were brought on behalf of several Melanesians, including Chief Kalsakau, for crops and trees lost when the Americans built a road across their land. These were passed on to the British under the January 1946 statement by High Commissioner Grantham to the Americans that Britain would take responsibility for claims by British subjects. The British resident commissioner investigated and, with slight adjustments, paid them, including those of New Hebrideans, charging them to the British Colonial Office.[72]

Another claim via American legal channels reached the high commissioner in 1952. The Hills had first lodged it with the U.S. Army claims officer in 1943 for damages to their Efate property, but they added to it as damage mounted in 1944. This claim for $10,310 was included with the French settlers' and so by 1951 Mrs. Hill, a British subject, feared it would be refused like the Santo French claims, and so she requested British compensation. Two years later she received $2,404 or £stg 858/18/9 as settlement.[73]

In spite of these tortuous cases, the war financially benefited the New Hebrides. The planters did not have to face combat. By 1942 they had a guaranteed good price for their copra and other produce in Australia and America, which pulled them out of the Depression doldrums.[74] The Condominium in late 1941 recorded a surplus of £stg10,000; by the end of the war it had risen to £stg129,000.[75] The Americans believed their coming had boosted the economy,[76] a view the British high commissioner shared:

> many of these planters prospered from the illicit sale of liquor to the US Forces and from huge profits from mushroom, laundry and restaurant ventures. . . . Since the war, most of them have benefited to a great extent from American property abandoned on their plantations . . . the value of the properties has appreciated considerably, due to the road construction.[77]

Replanting Atolls: Gilbert and Ellice Islands Crown Colony

The same could not be said for some atolls in the British Gilbert Islands and Ellice Islands Crown Colony occupied by the Japanese, whose viciousness increased as their situation worsened. Most Europeans had fled or died at their hands. The

Japanese occupied Butaritari (Makin), Tarawa, and Abemama in the Gilberts, which the U.S. forces recaptured in 1943, building a base on Tarawa. On Ocean Island (Banaba) and Kuria there was also much damage. On both Banaba and Nauru, the British Phosphate Commission eventually lost all its mining and port infrastructure.[78] Before they attacked the Gilberts, the Americans had set up bases in the Ellice group on Funafuti, Nukufetau, and Nanumea. With a population of about 34,000 islanders on only 262 square miles, life was not easy, especially during drought.[79] Before the war, land disputes were so clamorous that resettlement had been planned. The major staple was a root crop, *pulaka* (*Cyrtosperma chamissonis*), but to grow it, pits had to be dug to tap the fresh water lens on the seawater. These *babai* or *pulaka* pits were then filled with humic matter. Passed from generation to generation, they represented not only livelihood, but also enormous labor, as it took three years to dig through coral to prepare a pit and bring the crop to maturity. In the Gilberts alone, airfield construction, fortification, and bombing destroyed 2,000 pits and 60,000 coconut palms, a major food and shelter source and the only cash crop. In March 1943, compensation seemed necessary where the Americans were occupying Funafuti, as the people had lost 4,500 palms and 400 *pulaka* pits, seven-eights of their total.[80] District Officer Harry Maude realized lives would soon depend on it once the "dollar prosperity" vanished.[81]

The British Colonial Office had considered compensation as a charge under reverse lend-lease prior to the devastation of Tarawa by the Japanese and the American landings in November 1943. Some in the administration thought that after the war, captured Japanese assets could provide compensation. Long before Japan was to surrender, however, the Gilbertese on Tarawa and Butaritari in April–May 1944 had asked the open-handed Americans to rule them instead of the austere British. The American commanders explained that such high policy decisions were beyond them.[82] These movements were soon to abate, but Mitchell feared their significance and in June 1944 he advised the Colonial Office, "In view of the political difficulties . . . some announcement must be made at once." He proposed the people be informed that the

> British government accepts responsibility for compensation for all native land taken for use of allied forces and for native crops or other property destroyed. . . . Accordingly Government will for the present act as if such land and the crops on it were leased to Government by owners and will pay rent for it on a basis to be agreed with owners. Government will also institute at once a full enquiry into extent of private claims and damage so that compensation can be calculated at a later date when final settlement is possible.[83]

The secretary of state agreed in light of the "peculiar conditions" and the "political considerations" to take "immediate action," but not for missions and commercial companies.[84]

"Immediate" is a relative term in the Pacific. In April 1945 a British officer began a survey of claims. For replanting coconuts, digging of pits, and smaller items such as the loss of fish traps, Britain authorized payments of more than £105,000 between 1947 and 1950—about £15/12/- per head, equivalent to more than seven months' wages for a laborer. The High Commission, anxious for self-sufficiency and copra production for cash, paid not on claims but on trees or crops replanted by a set date.[85] By 1950, the people, with this spur, had achieved much reconstruction. In Nauru and Ocean Islands the wealthy British Phosphate Commission soon rebuilt new infrastructure, but as with the missions received no compensation.[86] As a consequence of the sale of Japanese assets in British Southeast Asia in 1953, the Gilbert and Ellice Colony administration received £100,000, which recouped much of its rehabilitation expenditure on islanders—some token, if enforced, compensation from Japan, but no one compensated for damage to the lagoons and land in the battlegrounds.[87]

Sorrowing Solomons

Such British magnanimity may have had an unforeseen impact for the Solomon Islands protectorate. In a letter of August 1944 to Admiral Newton, deputy commander, South Pacific command, Mitchell focused on commercial matters. Almost incidentally he stated,

> I should add that responsibility for all claims for war damage in the Solomons lies, of course, on the British government, and there is no question of any claim against the United States. I have not yet had instructions from London as to how this very complicated matter is to be dealt with.[88]

Hardly a binding agreement, it was a statement fixed upon by the American command.[89] Where their forces had expelled the Japanese, their policy was not to meet any claims arising for "damages or rentals or port charges." Their lawyers, however, believed that once the planters returned and counted their losses, they or the British authorities might seek a waiver of the one-year statute of limitations and redress for certain types of damage. For example, the military's slaughter of Levers' cattle on the Russell Islands to supplement their ample rations was not due to combat necessity. This the Americans understood,[90] secretly collecting information regarding possible damage done by their forces to refute "claims in their entirety and not as an admission of liability."[91] The Americans realized how fortunate they were and acknowledged—though never to the British—that "the United States has undoubtedly been saved large sums of money in the processing and payment of claims which would have been compensable under existing [U.S.] legislation."[92]

Why did High Commissioner Mitchell give such an assurance? First, he had accepted British Colonial Office statements in 1943 and 1944 that Pacific claims would fall under reverse lend-lease or reciprocal aid "pending post-war settlement."[93] Second, by June 1944, Mitchell knew that Britain was concerned with the parlous state of the Gilbert and Ellice Islanders and may have assumed the same concern would extend to the Solomons.

A week after he gave his assurances to Admiral Newton, Mitchell, "captivated" by the American command,[94] visited Hawai'i, where the admired generals entertained him.[95] Other factors could have contributed to his sanguine view. Most non-native civilians had fled the Solomons in the face of invasion. Although some islanders were displaced, this was localized mainly to the Shortlands, south New Georgia, Nggela, and north Guadalcanal, since all the military airfields and most installations were built on flat coastal land held by governments, missions, or planters. Except for a few in the eastern Solomons where there was no war damage anyway, almost all expatriates were out of the county. Unlike most of their counterparts in the New Hebrides, they had been unable to keep watch on their properties and confront the military, though some claimed unsuccessfully for losses from the government's scorched earth policy.[96]

There was little clamor for redress from Solomon Islanders. Those displaced, once the fighting had passed, received emergency aid from the Allied forces and the administration.[97] As many Solomon Islanders benefited materially from American gifted war surplus as had lost houses and gardens. Although the war was traumatic for those hiding in the hills and swamps, most of the population and their subsistence were not severely affected, unlike atoll dwellers in the Gilberts and Ellice group. Certainly wild pigs, fish, timber, and aggregates were taken virtually ad lib by the military. Claims generally were made after the war when the sense of urgency had passed and the Americans had gone.[98] The resident commissioner had objected to the Americans concerning their bombing and strafing of Laulasi village, Malaita, outside the combat zone on 7 August 1942, with twenty-two killed, eleven wounded, and possessions destroyed.[99] If a claim had been lodged, successive researchers have not found any American record of it, though the Laulasi people still seek compensation. On Guadalcanal, some complained to the Americans about felling their valuable ngali nut trees. Several Solomon Islanders also registered unspecified claims with a value of A£50,429 in 1947–48 when the British Colonial Office finally sent a commissioner to assess damage, subsequent to questions in the British parliament. The Europeans were not reticent about their losses, claiming A£3,080,000 of which A£1,475,425 was recognized by the assessor.[100] On their 62,000 acres of plantations, there was 20 to 25 percent damage and "universal deterioration."[101]

In January 1946, Mitchell's successor, A. H. Grantham, had reiterated assurances to the Americans. A formal agreement followed in May by which the protectorate government accepted responsibility for damage done under American occupation.[102] There were two expatriate wartime claims that gained some attention, however. Bishop Baddeley put his directly to the Americans. The navy had occupied Melanesian Mission land and buildings, felling their trees at Siota and Purvis Bay, Florida Islands. As naval historian John Burke recorded,

> This American occupation resulted in the complete destruction of a number of the buildings. . . . The Cathedral Church was turned into a warehouse. The mother of pearl was gouged out of the altar . . . part of the cathedral itself was used for a latrine . . . and all the buildings were so used that when I saw the property two months after the last of our forces had left, it was apparent that the entire station of Siota would have to be rebuilt.[103]

In October 1945 and again in January 1946, the bishop claimed £4,000.[104] Meanwhile, as the U.S. authorities countered, about "$4000 worth of lumber, roofing, paper and wire screen" had been donated to the mission along with various engine parts and five hundred books. They had sold Quonset huts, engines, and other goods to the mission at a good price and "further co-operative action" was in the offing.[105] No more was heard from the bishop.

Facilitated by the BEW's Douglas Oliver in late 1943, U.S. South Pacific command requested logs belonging to the Vanikoro Timber Company. They reached a verbal agreement with Resident Commissioner Noel but decided not to act when they realized that the logs were rotting.[106] The company's £4,765 claim against the government lodged in January 1945 failed, since under the Defence (Compensation) Regulations of 1942, it had to be lodged within six months of the date of requisition and only applied to the use of "land, vehicles, vessels and aircraft," not "goods."[107]

After the war the protectorate government sought compensation from Australia for constructing Japanese prisoner-of-war camps in the Shortland Islands, reasoning that the "natives will no doubt expect compensation for damage to their lands and forest products."[108] Ironically, the high commissioner did not apply this logic regarding resource loss to the United States. Businesses, missions, native people, and small European planters submitted their war damage claims to W. Ramsey Main, appointed commissioner in 1947–1948. Upon receipt of his report in 1948, High Commissioner Freeston[109] and the Colonial Office disregarded actual losses and used "economic need" as a measure, reasoning that the big companies had made money in the war and thus had capital, the missions had received renewed support from overseas churches, and that by 1948 the natives had recovered anyway. Because their meager "one man commission" in the Solomons[110] could not assess native claims in detail, to give planters compensation would not be fair to the native claimants. They would, so the Colonial Office opined, be better served if compensation went into some overall assistance for economic recovery, since a per capita grant could decrease the incentive to resume production, as had happened in the Australian territories.[111] Moreover, any compensation would be "a further burden on the United Kingdom taxpayer."[112]

The High Commission announced in August 1949 that no compensation would be paid in the Solomons (as well as the Gilbert and Ellice Islands), which meant that many prewar interests never returned. In 1954, £500,000 realized from the sale of captured Japanese assets in British Southeast Asia went into general Solomons' revenue, including a scheme to sustain commerce through trade goods outlets.[113] The planters and businesses tried to access these funds, but the government reasoned that they were "not derived from any interest held by the Western Pacific High Commission" and thus had to be spent for the widest "moral and social aspects of rehabilitation."[114] Except for emergency rations to a few Solomon Islanders, no islander or European was ever compensated individually for property or resource loss by the Japanese or the Americans.[115] Some have not forgotten, as Gideon Zoloveke revealed in 1987.

> What did we get from the war, from our friends who came here to fight? My goodness, they were "fully insured," everything—families at home, everyone got something, but for us nothing.[116]

The British government had stated that war damage compensation in these colonies would depend on the amount of indemnity Japan paid.[117] America called the tune in the postwar world and befriended Japan to win an ally against the Communist Soviets and China, so they did not exact reparations, though overseas assets already had been forfeited. The settlers in the Solomons, in comparison to their counterparts in the New Hebrides and New Guinea, lost enormously.[118] Had they been aware of the high commissioners' agreements at the time, the broken planters and aggrieved Solomon Islanders probably would have concluded that Mitchell's concession to his American friends had done them a disservice.[119]

Paying Back: Papua and New Guinea

Marty Zelenietz has noted that while America had the Marshall Plan for Europe, "[n]o such plan benefited the war-ravaged people of Melanesia."[120] True of America, it was not true of Australia, which compensated the New Guineans and embarked on a development program in a country that, unlike Europe, had little of modernity to reconstruct. As Hank Nelson, one of the few historians to consider this, has stated, "it was an extraordinary policy and an even more extraordinary application of a policy."[121]

In the midst of the most intense jungle fighting of the war were villagers, whose experience of the outside world was largely of Christian missions, plantations, a few mines, and the patrolling district officer. For most, modernity's flag bearers were the copra boat and traders' drab stores. Thousands remained beyond the reach of the administration. For many, war remained a mysterious but awful event. As it advanced, about 15,600 men were laboring under indentures and were left stranded. After the few white settlers fled or were killed by the Japanese, there were cases of lawlessness, with some Melanesians attacking their old tribal enemies and looting European property. Both sides conscripted Melanesians as labor, often under duress; both executed those they considered traitors.[122] The people suffered, especially in places where the Japanese, trapped and left to "wither on the vine" from mid-1943, preyed on them and their resources. Those Australians who

Figure 21. "Fuzzy wuzzy" Papuan bearers carrying wounded Australian soldier, Kokoda Track, Owen Stanley Range, August 1942, taken by Damien Parer (Australian War Memorial Negative No. 013286).

knew the people realized that the "fight is ours, not theirs."[123] Yet the Melanesians often offered assistance to the Australian military, especially from mid-1942 on,[124] but their "loyalty [was] of a personal nature, not to the abstract 'Crown' or government," while many saw the Australian soldiers as a kinder people than the prewar colonials. For the pragmatic majority, as Japanese maltreatment intensified, so did local collaboration with the Allies.[125]

Carrying supplies and Allied wounded, New Guineans earned the gratitude of the AIF and the Australian public, who viewed the touching visual images of their efforts, eloquently recorded by award-winning filmmaker Damien Parer.[126] These carriers entered Australian social memory as the "Fuzzy Wuzzy Angels"[127] and their country became

> a place known intimately to practically every Australian . . . and the natives of the Territories by their assistance to the allied cause against the Japanese aggressor have earned from Australia and its people the right to expect much greater interest and assistance than have been given . . . in the past.[128]

Australian policy was that the people should be compensated for their losses,[129] irrespective of who caused the damage, and all should be compensated except those who "had voluntarily assisted the enemy with a knowledge that it was wrong to do so."[130] To establish the extent of loss and schedules of payment, the Australian government appointed three assessors: Judge J. V. Barry, KC, the anthropologist Ian Hogbin, and a district officer and member of ANGAU, J. Taylor.[131]

The Barry report reflected a legal and humane assessment of damage. From January until late April 1945 the commissioners visited all districts as well as the Solomon Islands, observing and consulting widely with ANGAU and former administrative personnel, as well as planters and missionaries. They first addressed losses arising from "[t]he natives and ourselves during the war." The focus fell on wartime labor demands and the suffering of villages robbed of able-bodied men, which reduced food production and disrupted family life and marriage patterns.[132] At peak recruitment for the AIF and ANGAU, 45,203 were under indenture in mid-1944. In early 1945 there were 35,000 under indenture to the AIF alone; many had been away from home for three years, and those stranded had been six years absent. The Barry report echoed ANGAU: The conscription of natives reflected badly on the administration, the reverse of its prewar role of safeguarding villagers from excessive demands of labor recruiters.[133] The commissioners "calculated that the Japanese had plundered over 100,000 pigs, the common measure of Melanesian wealth." Many villagers near the battle zones could make only small gardens hidden in the bush. Even these were sometimes raided by Japanese or bombed by the Allies. Many perished from malnutrition and illness, especially on Bougainville and New Britain. In disturbed areas the birth rate dropped. When Allied bases were built, ANGAU and the AIF evacuated the people, to their bewilderment. Away from their home environment, they often became sick. Moreover, "thousands of native-owned trees [were] cut down" as well as sago palms destroyed to "make room for military camps," thus reducing food supplies after the fighting ended.

Payments were based on prevailing values. Loss of life fell into two categories—that arising directly from the conflict and that resulting from disease. The commissioners' knowledge of Melanesian economics and society was evident. Compensation for the loss of a male aged between fifteen and fifty ranged from £20 to £60 because these were their most productive years. "In New Guinea all save children of the most tender years contribute labor towards the maintenance of the household," so if a child under seven died as a result of the war, £5 would be paid (1⁄12 of the adult male maximum); if the child were between seven and fifteen, 1⁄3 would be paid or £7 to £20 depending on various factors. Incapacity saw compensation in the form of pensions ranging from 2/6 a month for a person under age seven to 10/- to 30/- for an adult between fifteen and fifty, with adjustments as time passed and age changed. Pensions were allocated at a rate of 100, 75, or 50 percent, depending on the nature of the injury.

They set payments for loss of chattels including livestock, food plants, and valuable trees as well as communal property. If communal land was damaged, loss could be calculated by the value of taro that could have been grown. An acre could produce four tons of taro, which was valued at £4 a ton. So an acre of potential garden land lost to, say, an airfield or bombs would be worth £16. If the land was taken out of use permanently a higher rate prevailed. Timber felled was reckoned at ten pence per hundred superficial feet, as paid by millers before the war. Payment for communal property was to go to the village treasuries to be set up as part of a new system of native councils suggested by Hogbin based on ones in the Solomon Islands.[134] Savings banks were to be established because many were unfamiliar with money, and:

> Evil social consequences may result from the natives possessing large sums of money which they can neither spend nor deposit safely. Gambling for example has markedly increased.[135]

The Australian government accepted the report and increased some payments. From 1946, as the civilian administration began to reassert itself, district officers patrolled areas touched by the conflict. They assessed myriad claims up to 1960 fairly accurately, as several knew the prewar condition of the villages. Over 140,000 were accepted,[136] though Melanesian opportunism sometimes emerged;

> the number of bicycles claimed to have been either lost, damaged or appropriated by the Japanese, for which the compensatory rate was [A]$30 [A£15], seemed in some regions to have been multiplied by memory.

During the war a dysentery epidemic had hit the people of the central highlands badly, and so the Australian government allocated £254,000 to assist. Since it was impracticable to compensate for deaths with money because the highlanders were unfamiliar with cash, the Australians funded health education and medical personnel. Near Port Moresby, the big coastal village of Hanuabada, wrecked by wartime activities, was to receive £130,000 for reconstruction, but the final cost was £180,000. Another £50,000 was allocated to compensate for airfield construction and loss of soils.[137] The amount allocated for milled timber was £10,000. The Australian government's overall compensation package for all damage and deaths came to £2,207,547 by the 1960s, exclusive of the funds for the dysentery epidemic, the reconstruction of Hanuabada, soil, and timber compensation. The total A£2.7 million was an enormous per capita sum for a population of around one million then counted by the administration—the majority of whom were outside the conflict zone. This amount appears to be the highest per capita compensation paid to any South Pacific island people.[138] This was, moreover, separate from expenditures of more than A£1.4 million on wartime relief for 61,000 evacuees and postwar administrative spending, which was far greater (and became increasingly so) than before the war when total yearly grants from Australia had never exceeded £60,000.[139]

Beginnings and Endings

Australia's motives were twofold: "as a measure of justice and as a method of restoring confidence in the Administration."[140] The Australians appreciated that damage to their territories had "saved their mainland property owners loss."[141] Ironically, this generous policy carried out in the face of critics at the time, including the white settlers who saw their labor supply as being "spoiled,"[142] has been largely forgotten.[143] This hiatus in social memory may be explained by Australia's failure to provide demobilization pay to the carriers and its tardiness in paying pensions to native soldiers and police.[144]

The white settlers also received compensation. Australia's War Damages Commission, through the National Security (War Damage to Property) Regulations, a scheme of compulsory insurance for property owners, came into operation in early 1942 and was extended to New Guinea settlers, even though they had never paid premiums. Where the AIF commandeered plant, buildings, and standing timber, they paid, though ultimately the Australian taxpayer footed the bill.

The commission extended payments in January 1945 for consequential loss such as weed infestation of plantations.[145]

The European settlers, missions, and commercial interests claimed about A£9 million, and by early 1948 £5 million had been approved as the commissioners inspected properties. Despite this, many planters found that their subsistence in Australia ate into these payments. Radical Australian policies abolishing indenture, increasing the native wage, coupled with spare cash in indigenous hands and lack of spending outlets, induced a postwar labor shortage.[146] These did not help struggling planters to re-establish. For such people, compensation could never cover the loss of a way of life. The Chinese community, however, benefited by being on the spot to start trading, some counterbalance for their sufferings under the Japanese.[147]

In much of the eastern South Pacific, the Americans or the colonial governments compensated islanders for loss of resources. Even in the Condominium's fractious politics, the outcome, if protracted, was similar. An anomaly in the British Pacific, only Cinderella Solomon Islanders totally missed compensation, as did the expatriate community there and in the Gilbert and Ellice group. In the battle zone, Australia's compensation of New Guinea's affected peoples was the largest undertaking of all and the most costly, alerting them to the cash potential of their environment's resources. Japan lost only its confiscated overseas assets to compulsory but minor reparations in the islands, but it managed to provide some in the 1950s to certain Southeast Asian governments because it needed their raw materials and markets.[148]

Wars fought in other people's backyards cost much in blood and treasure to marshal men and matériel. Even so, as the Australians acknowledged, forward island bridgeheads and bastions as operational loci, while straining national economies, protected the protagonists' domestic infrastructure, environment, and resources, including civilian populations, from major damage. For all the compensation and transfer of goods, the price paid by most in the conflict zone was far higher at the time and in war's lingering legacy in the islands.

CHAPTER 9

Close Out

Quitting the Islands

Until the 1950s, the only profitable post-war business conducted in New Guinea was buying and selling junk.

More of the industrialized world's goods came into Melanesia, Micronesia, and southern tropical Polynesia in the four years from 1942 to 1945 than in the preceding one hundred.[1] Except for some local resources such as timber and food, every item needed for warfare had to be brought in. The protagonists drew on the economies of home, colonies, and allies to supply these from distant lands. In perilous times few questioned the necessity of this long ecological shadow. To homeland populations and their economies making their sacrifices, however, intimations of waste of resources at the front could be demoralizing. While American industry turned from a peace to a war economy, military planners saw resource conservation as significant for civilian morale and waging war. As the front moved on, but particularly when peace came, the disposal of war's vast matériel posed as many difficulties as had its assemblage. Environmental factors remained pivotal agents and pressed heavily on colonial administrations as much as the military in their endeavors to dispose of war's vast apparatus.

Works of War

In war there is an inevitable tension between conservation and waste. As Admiral Halsey observed,

> large reserves of men and material are necessary to insure the application of overwhelming strength when and where needed; this principle of reserve automatically makes war an uneconomical and wasteful business, but those disadvantages must be accepted.

In the rear, reserves had to be dispersed, away from enemy attack, and maintained ready for action. Between the fighting front and the reserves, there were forward areas, near enough to supply operations. Forward areas had to be mobile, and structures had to be "limited to essentials." The balancing of "a high degree of striking mobility," with supplying forward areas and dispersed rear bases, required constant recalibration with the shifting front, a challenging operation in the Pacific where distances were great and islands scattered.[2]

When war's juggernaut halted in late 1945, the whole Pacific Ocean area (excluding the Hawaiian islands) held 8,938,400 m/t of American matériel alone, valued at $3,712,852,000.[3] All Allies faced the task of "rolling up" equipment, clearing the land so it was habitable, and "closing out" their bases. Colonial governments were involved because they were often the purchasers of war surplus and recipients of scrap. And the inhabitants had to re-establish themselves on lands littered with war's detritus.

Redeployment and Conservation

When the conflict began, the United States had little appreciation of what the Pacific islands, up to seven thousand miles away, would be like. Geared to operate in more developed theaters, such as Europe,[4] their engineers had to adjust: "The thing that we had better remember when organizing a South Pacific base is to send everything. . . . The only thing you get out there is coconut trees and sand."[5] They soon learned to remember and, by late 1942, most forward bases were better supplied and rear bases far more so. Inefficiencies, however, emerged as the war continued because base construction had been as much for defense as offense, based on the premise of Japan's advance south—"each anchorage, base, and airfield aiming at becoming a small Oahu." Following Allied successes in the battles of the Coral Sea, Midway, and Guadalcanal, in rear bases it "was time to curtail further construction and development and utilize the men and materials for construction where it is urgently needed."[6]

Within the strategy of mobile base organization from early 1943, Nimitz cautioned,

> While we accept the principle that war is wasteful and is uneconomical in the extreme, we must constantly remain on the alert to stamp out any unnecessary employment of either men or materials.[7]

As the Japanese were pushed back into defensive positions in Southeast Asia and Micronesia or isolated in New Guinea, Allied matériel went forward. The military also salvaged useful material for return to the United States: tires and tubes, gas cylinders, metal drums, and cases, as well as non-ferrous metal and steel.[8] Even empty beer bottles went home.[9] Conserving unused scrap cost, as commanders soon recognized. On Wallis Island, the ninety tons of scrap on hand in late 1944

> would, considering its intrinsic value, not justify the expense involved in loading and shipping. About five days would be required to load it by natives. It consists of old machinery, old chains, motor blocks and pieces difficult to date. If it has no strategic or utilitarian value, it is suggested it be . . . dumped at sea.[10]

Though some was dumped, assemblage often continued, but legislation effective in December 1944 disallowed return to America (except for re-export), creating an expanding backlog by mid-1945.[11]

Throughout 1944, construction units had packed useful equipment for forward redeployment.[12] In rear bases such as Tutuila, locating materials was sometimes difficult, as "the undergrowth had completely covered them."[13] But considerable quantities were shipped during 1944–45, which left Tutuila less littered at war's end.[14] Once operations centered on the Southwest Pacific area, the commanders called for inventories of supplies in the South Pacific Command, resulting in the "Transco Agreement" for "the transfer of service units, overhead personnel and excess supplies and equipment" in January 1945. As the Americans pushed to Japan, the forces shipped 2,474,737 m/t to the Southwest Pacific, mainly north of New Guinea. From mid-1945, the predominantly naval surplus in the South Pacific was initially consolidated at three centers: Noumea, Santo, and Guadalcanal.

There had been constant redefinition of what was salvageable.[15] Certain surplus was sold locally, initially by the FEA, but later by the army and the navy, each with its own procedures.[16] Island administrations were buyers. For example, Fiji's supply and production board, set up in 1943, received and allocated U.S. surplus plus returned reverse lend-lease supplies. Its "economic and orderly disposal" impressed the Americans, as shown by their ready acceptance of the board's lend-lease accounting.[17]

Shifting Policies, Shifting Commissions

A major shift in American disposals policy occurred in mid-1945, when war's end neared. As reserves, the mission of the South Pacific bases ceased after they had contributed to the Philippines' offensive in late 1944, with material mainly from the Southwest Pacific, and the Okinawa assault in April 1945, supplied by the South Pacific. Roll-up, commenced in March 1945, accelerated in the South Pacific and Mid-Pacific commands.[18] From mid-1945, redeployment and conservation were subject to "port capacities to load out, shipping, port capacities to receive, and determination of definite destinations for this material" in forward areas or America's west coast. Because commanders repatriated personnel not required at the front, there were fewer to decommission and pack equipment. There was less need to redeploy certain equipment, such as munitions, to the Southwest Pacific. Much had deteriorated anyway, and its reshipment was hazardous.[19] Matériel sent forward from hasty roll-up elsewhere was often in such poor condition that it had to be scrapped. Consequent to Japan's unexpected surrender in August 1945 and the volume of equipment readied for invasion, the Americans reduced the categories of material to be repatriated. While both scrap and surplus accumulated, units awaited directions. Belatedly, the American government realized that its policy of January 1945 deprived it of construction equipment, steel, and non-ferrous metals useful for rehabilitation. So, material salvage units, established in early 1946, were sent to make assessments.[20] Meanwhile, the plan to dispose of as much surplus as possible locally prevailed.

In January 1945, the United States had set up a surplus property board to administer the new Army-Navy Liquidation Commission as it carried out its disposals, but it was some time before the commissioners assumed duties in the South Pacific.[21] Meanwhile, the lend-lease surplus property division in the New Caledonia Island Command arranged the sale of surplus property,[22] but

> Aside from native chieftans [*sic*], who possess little besides coconut trees, the market for sales of surplus in the islands of SoPac is limited to the French in New Caledonia, New Zealand (providing imports are allowed) and the few British, American and Dominion companies trading in the islands; Australia might also be a market.[23]

This division, however, sold goods up to the value of $25,225,031. The commanding general of the South Pacific Base Command assumed its duties in September 1945, pending the arrival of a field commissioner of the Army-Navy Liquidation Commission. From 1 November 1945, this commission became the Foreign Liquidation Commission (FLC) under the State Department, with maximum capacity to deal with foreign governments but minimum experience with disposal. The FLC initially focused on the sale of fixed installations, while the commander of the South Pacific, with military boards at various bases, continued disposing of scrap and salvage, excepting aircraft and ships.[24]

Dispose or Destroy

The simultaneity of peace had meant all equipment in the South Pacific, New Guinea, and Australia suddenly became redundant, and it pronounced surplus in

October 1945. This represented about 12 percent of the total in the entire Pacific Ocean area, excluding ships. Categories of matériel to be dumped or destroyed expanded.[25] Boards formed in October were to

> have full authority to recommend destruction and abandonment of excess property . . . determined to have no commercial value or that the cost of its care handling and disposition would exceed the estimated proceeds. Excess property will be included in this category when in the opinion of the unit (a) no local market exists or proceeds of local sales will not cover sales costs, (b) sale "where is and as is" to purchasers in other areas not practicable, (c) cost of packing handling and shipping will exceed proceeds of sales in other areas, (d) storage for future use or sale is not practicable in virtue of reasons such as (1) absence suitable storage facilities, (2) inevitable deterioration, (3) cost of placing in storage estimated to exceed possible future value, (4) cost of maintaining in storage will exceed future value. . . . Local boards shall act promptly . . . but should lean towards recommendation for destruction or abandonment in borderline cases.[26]

Geographic and climatic factors were implicit in the conditions permitting "destruction and abandonment," but limited manpower was significant also, as by

Figure 22. Dumping surplus at sea off Guadalcanal (390/18/17/7, RG 112, NARA).

December 1945, 90 percent of all navy personnel there on V-J day had left.[27] Disposal at the Solomons highlights this and the elasticity of the accounting process. From Guadalcanal's invasion in August 1942, "vast stores had been brought to the island with questionable records of their quantities and placed in widely separate depots, warehouses and camps." By August 1945, there were "approximately" 241,642 m/t still there. Yet the first full inventory was not completed until January 1946, when considerable matériel had already been disposed of, for example, to Christian missions.[28] The Russell Islands base shipped matériel to Guadalcanal for consolidation, but much already had been abandoned when the Russells were reduced to garrison status. Before the material salvage unit arrived in the Solomons in August to collect matériel for Manus, Guam, and Pearl Harbor bases,[29] complaints emerged about disposals in the Russells:

> Captain Beattie was responsible for the unfortunate destruction of a great amount of materials. . . . This includes almost all the supplies and mechanical equipment of an Advanced Base Construction Depot. Most of this material, some new some used, was dumped into the coral pits. . . . These pits . . . were carefully covered with coral, which was used to camouflage them.[30]

Colonial officials found that other disposal techniques left even more challenges.[31] Before the war, Levers operated copra plantations on the Russell Islands, their main wharf being at Yandina. The British wished to reconstruct this in 1948, but encountered "a pile of bulldozers and other vehicles driven off the face of the wharf by United States troops on evacuation. This pile fouls the approach to the wharf and efforts to shift it have proved unsuccessful."[32]

This was not isolated dumping. The Solomons' government, in search of trucks, investigated a dump on Treasury Island (Mono) of

> American matériel, included much much-needed lorries, was buried in this dump. I am advised that such equipment buried in the ground is likely to be in a good state of repair. Some equipment has appeared on the surface. . . . I saw two tyres which looked as if they had just come out of the shop. They had, however, been deliberately mutilated, presumably by the Americans . . . a previous Administrative Officer . . . actually saw this equipment being buried, and most of it was brand new.[33]

In the New Hebrides, the British resident had tried "to treat with the American forces prior to their departure for certain surplus material" but had failed.[34] The navy and marines on Efate "had little or no proper responsibility or accountability and had given away considerable property."[35] Moreover, early in 1946, the military dumped motorized vehicles, cranes, lighting plants, and Quonset huts in the sea at "Million Dollar Point."[36] In Tonga, the Americans offered certain surplus for sale but the government declined, some say on the advice of the crown prince, who thought the occupiers would abandon it. They did—in the sea or in flames![37]

So extensive was the waste that some servicemen notified the U.S. Congress. An inquiry headed by Senator Mead ensued, but the justification echoed in the Congress was that the cost of upkeep and return to America was greater than the matériel's worth. Senior officers then were instructed to be present when matériel was to be classified, but this was often too late, since these directions came in January 1946.[38]

Throughout the humid tropics, destruction of equipment had been justified by deterioration due to climate and wear and tear. Lack of personnel because of demobilization and the cost of shipping also meant much potentially valuable matériel was not salvaged. Obsolescence was another factor. The War Department did not want old matériel that would "hamper research and development aimed at the . . . production of more efficient and more modern weapons and equipment."[39] Another concern was flooding of the market with cheap war surplus. For the Americans the buoyancy of the war-based economy was a dominant political concern, even if its disposal policy left it short of some vital materials.[40]

Colonial Opportunities

The FLC opened for business at Noumea on 1 November 1945. The military consolidated excess matériel there and in American Samoa.[41] Noumea had excellent infrastructure, much from American wartime construction. Moreover, New Caledonia's drier climate enhanced storage of surplus far more than the equatorial humid tropics,[42] so Noumea was the last extraterritorial base in the South Pacific theater to close down.[43]

The FLC favored sale by bulk purchase, but initially "no one was interested."[44] Although the small WPHC dependencies lacked capacity to absorb bulk purchases, administrators were aware that the tropical environment was their ally because of the expense of maintaining surplus. The British and other administrations bided their time.[45]

Prior to January 1946, American refusal of foreign currencies delayed some sales in the South Pacific, but arrangements such as balancing of food purchases from New Zealand after V-J day, when reciprocal lend-lease ceased, against equipment sales to New Zealand made transactions easier. The French colonial government allowed civilians to purchase minor surplus while potential buyers were becoming familiar with procedures. When the services released surplus for the FLC throughout late 1945 and 1946, governments, commercial companies, missions, and individuals began purchasing. In May 1946, the Americans in New Caledonia compensated for war damage claims and reverse lend-lease debts by assigning about $3 million worth of fixed installations to the French. In mid-1947, as well as smaller sales to French citizens and other governments, the New Caledonian administration bulk purchased army and navy property for $425,000. On Bora Bora, under the lease conditions, the French received fixed installations costing $2,203,148. They purchased all moveable equipment for a modest $75,000.[46] In Fiji, the Americans achieved a bulk sale to New Zealand of moveable items at Nadi airbase for $230,000. Because both New Zealand and America had contributed to the airfield's construction, its ownership was not settled until 1948, when the Americans declared it abandoned.[47]

New Caledonia and Fiji, unlike Guadalcanal, were more accessible to outside buyers as well as local interests. By May 1946, of matériel inventoried on Guadalcanal in January, only 7 percent had been sold, with about 24 percent destroyed or abandoned and 69 percent sent elsewhere. The original value of the 58,831 m/t destroyed or abandoned material was $19,888,587. Excluding the sale of rations to W. R. Carpenter Company Ltd. and signal equipment to the Dutch, the 16,980 m/t sold produced $91,951 for the American treasury. The Fijian government had bought several Quonset huts, and 10,600 steel drums went to trading firms. The Catholic mission purchased building material, medical and school supplies, and vehicles.[48] The Methodists paid $3,000 for 150 tons of medical gear, receiving a gift of "two tons of toilet rolls."[49] New Zealand also made selective purchases. The Solomons protectorate bought "all improvements, steel and wooden buildings, rough construction including plumbing, water and electrical systems" north of coastal Highway 50 for a length of three miles—the site of Honiara, the new capital.[50] The FLC offered the administration the remaining "Camp Guadalcanal," including office equipment, fourteen jeeps, twenty trucks, heavy equipment and all spares, two refrigeration units, two cub piper aircraft, six generators, a large crane, an oceangoing steel tug, and an engineering workshop. The British valued this at about $200,000. They reckoned the worth at about $70,000 under "present conditions" and received a bargain when the liquidator settled for $33,000.[51]

Rebuilding an administrative center was also on the minds of the British in the Gilbert and Ellice Islands. They were keen to purchase surplus from Betio (Tarawa) and Funafuti. What was not needed might be useful in Fiji. They purchased huts at Betio for $2,500 and offered $5,200 for equipment, including a ten-bed hospital and generators at Funafuti.[52] After the Americans accepted this, the remnant Betio garrison prepared to depart in December 1946, with most equipment "about to be burnt destroyed or dumped." Calculating the value at around $20,000, the high commissioner in Suva made a bid of $10,000.[53] The administration did not want it all but knew that the FLC preferred bulk sales, accepting that "whether we want it or not we shall have it all on our hands for ever more."[54] A Philippine interest made a counteroffer for the Betio surplus, valued at $1,666,086, reconditioned some machinery, and commenced to ship it out. The FLC withdrew its offer because no contract had been signed and reoffered the surplus to the administration. The administration's advantage was that if the FLC did not accept its consideration, the Americans or another buyer would remain responsible for clearing all matériel from the atolls. Finally, the FLC and the High Commission agreed on a price of $10,000, less the value of any equipment the Filipinos had taken. The final payment was $6,019 (£1,805), a bargain considering that the Filipinos had reconditioned the machines. The British now had the basis to rebuild their administrative centers.[55]

Geography, climate, distance, and time worked against the FLC. By April 1946, South Pacific installations for which there was no buyer, such as roads, airstrips, and campsites to the value of $51,103,000 were abandoned, with the sale of another $37,492,000 worth unlikely. Token garrisons still provided communications for shipping and aircraft returning to the States, but "roll-up" was ending, airplanes were fewer, and airstrips and wharves were deteriorating, making visits more difficult for the commissioner and prospective buyers.[56] Lacking competitors, the New Zealand administration at Aitutaki, Cook Islands, bought two aircraft runways, surplus equipment, and some boats valued at $205,573 for $28,000, which the liquidator thought fair, "taking into consideration its condition and the daily increasing cost of such equipment brought about by the maintenance of a garrison, whose mission, apart from custodianship, is actually completed." At Tutuila, surplus offered as minimum $1,500 lots attracted few local buyers, but the New Zealand administration and dealers in Western Samoa took much worth about $1,370,000. Local people with American friends had already relocated small items such as tires before they were dumped into the sea. Remaining scrap went to dealers at $20 a ton, providing all was removed from the site.[57]

The FLC had little work in the New Hebrides because before 1946 much matériel had been dumped, while a "considerable amount of moveable property" went unofficially to civilians. White planters claimed surplus left on their lands, selling to dealers who on-sold in Australia, Tahiti, or New Zealand.[58] As the matériel on land went, some turned to Million Dollar Point. Diver Reece Discombe hauled up five hundred tires from a hundred feet of water. He salvaged and reconditioned a dozen bulldozers and sold them in Australia. He also stripped the sunken *President Coolidge* of scrap, including two fifteen-ton brass propellers.[59]

Pressure to finalize disposal intensified as Americans became critical of huge military budgets in peacetime. Even in its reduced state in October 1946, the army's base at Noumea cost $1,500,000 a month to run. Balance that cost with the likely return from equipment deteriorating in storage along with competing production by a reviving civilian industry at home and the ledger pointed to abandonment. President Truman ordered all surplus declarations completed by 1 July 1947. Even so, the procedures demanded that some local authority accept responsibility or at least agree to the inevitable.[60]

New Guinea: America Disposes

Battles create far more scrap than rear bases. The zone of engagement stretched from New Guinea across the Bismarcks into the Solomons as far south as Guadalcanal and, on the northern boundary of the South Pacific Command, arched into the Gilbert Islands and the central Pacific's Ellice Islands. Though concentrated around key strategic areas, the conflicts left behind mountains of metal and munitions. On atolls such as the Gilberts, the scrap was less able to be lost to view; on the rugged terrain of the high islands, forests soon camouflaged abandoned equipment and their seas hid war's lost armadas.

In New Guinea, the difficulties attending disposal in the South Pacific were more acute. General MacArthur decided to withdraw most of the Americans from the Australian territory in the last quarter of 1944 to reinforce the thrust to the Philippines. The Australians were left to mop up in New Guinea and along the Solomons' border. Suspicious of possible postwar American intentions and anxious that its own army reassert Australia's status in the eyes of the indigenous people, the government agreed.[61] To the Australians, the Americans

> had shipped to northern bases the more important items of equipment. . . . Other goods were transferred to the Australian Services . . . the US Forces had adopted something approaching a scorched earth policy; M.T. [mechanized transport] had been wrecked, water-craft sunk, machinery sprayed with acids or cut with oxy-acetylene torch and then bull-dozed into the ground, whilst other action of a like nature was rampant.[62]

The AIF fought in New Guinea for another year. When the war ended they had more reasons than most to want to go home because unlike their allies, many of their volunteer infantrymen had already fought Germans in the Middle East.[63] So getting Australian troops home quickly was politic. The surrender of 150,000 Japanese in early September to 85,000 Australians meant the AIF, ANGAU, and the Australian government were preoccupied with their repatriation and investigations of war crimes. Most troops were home by early 1946. At the end of 1946, when all but 500 war criminal suspects had been repatriated to Japan, the AIF had fallen to 338 men, guarding the Japanese and disposing of munitions.[64] Unlike the

American forces in the South Pacific, there was not even the pretense of the AIF making inventories of surplus. For ANGAU and its successor provisional civilian administration, the focus was the survival and compensation of the territory's war-damaged peoples. These immediate needs often competed with the longer-term goals of re-establishing and extending the infrastructure.

When the war ended, American army surplus in New Guinea was much greater than the navy's, the reverse of the pattern in the South Pacific command. In mid-1945, the army-navy liquidation commissioner had estimated surplus in New Guinea at about 609,819 m/t of army matériel, of which 160,000 m/t were in Dutch New Guinea. The navy's surplus was 138,000 m/t (exclusive of about 390,000 m/t at Manus), of which about 48,000 m/t were in Dutch New Guinea.[65] After war's end, the liquidator's task exceeded his capacity to perform his inspection and selling functions. Commissioner Frederic Butler had jurisdiction over the vast area of the South Pacific as well as the Southwest command. In the South Pacific he had some support at Noumea, but in New Guinea the rapid decline in air transport made his mission almost impossible. He relied heavily on officers involved when the army and navy in the Southwest Pacific had been the disposals agency before the FLC came into being, but these were being demobilized. These agencies had already engaged in negotiations with prospective buyers and had contracts approved. Matériel was offered on an "as-is where-is" basis, with rejects to be sold as scrap or dumped, in accordance with the October 1945 directives. The navy, with FLC approval, sold most of its property in both New Guinea and Australia for $18 million to the Dutch as a bulk sale. The army also sold its fixed installations at Hollandia to the Dutch and the FLC contracted with them for those at Biak for $1.4 million, plus moveable property to the value of about $4.6 million.[66] Buyers on the spot made smaller deals: Bishop Scharmach purchased building materials for $57,780 to rebuild the Catholic mission near Rabaul.[67]

The Americans wanted to sell remaining surplus in New Guinea to the Australians, but as the war ended, a General Purchasing Agency agreement prevented this in Australia itself, probably because of likely distorting economic effects. Another impediment was that the Americans in mid-1945 already had a huge surplus in Australia and no ships to move it. In New Guinea, by late 1945 the FLC had contracted with the Australians for the sale of heavy engineering equipment for $1 million. Yet there was still a tremendous amount of surplus left—about 157,000 m/t that had a depreciated book value of about $67 million, with more than two-thirds of it in the Australian territories.[68]

Anxiety about American surplus in New Guinea grew with time. The climate was a relentless destroyer of military equipment. Even where surplus had been maintained while stored for as little as six months, "the deterioration has of necessity been severe." By mid-1945, some already had been stored for two years.[69] The best the Americans could do, after the Dutch and Australians had bought what they wanted, was to sell the rest "on a junk basis for $50 a ton."[70]

Even so, the American liquidator's work in New Guinea virtually ceased by 1946. Except for the Manus base valued at $15,955,000, which closed in September, America was little concerned about the fate of residual equipment.[71] Most moveable Manus matériel, costing the Americans more than $104 million, was sold to the United Nations Relief and Rehabilitation Administration (UNRRA) and Nationalist China, with small lots to Australia, the Netherlands East Indies, and New Zealand and some shipped to American territories, such as Guam, by mid-1947.[72] Once Manus closed, the liquidator had little chance of visiting former bases and seemed satisfied that the U.S. treasury had obtained roughly forty cents on the dollar on bulk sales to the Dutch and Australians.[73]

Australia Disposes

For Australia there could be no such finality because the Territory of Papua and New Guinea (TPNG) was its dependency. In late 1944 and early 1945, as the bulk of the American force moved north, what it did not remove or dump passed to the Australian forces under lend-lease. When the war ended, this equipment, along with the Australians', generally was left with little recorded location. In June 1945, the Australian Commonwealth Disposals Commission (CDC) began work in the TPNG. Until the Japanese capitulation, however, the AIF's commander-in-chief, Thomas Blamey, was uncooperative regarding stocktaking of army equipment, as he was reluctant to downsize while war was still being waged.[74] Blamey's attitude and Prime Minister Chifley's demand for rapid repatriation of Australian forces in New Guinea were the first of many obstacles the CDC faced.

After reaching a confused Port Moresby, any ideas the commissioners might have had about following the Australian procedure of holding departments compiling lists of surplus for the commission to sell by tender vanished. No one had any idea of the amount of surplus and no troops were available to "list material littered over hundreds of miles." The AIF was preoccupied with the transition to a provisional civil administration, which was completed in late June 1946. As a temporary expedient, in August the commander of the 8th Military district made a "blanket" declaration to authorize the disposal of "all Army stores, vehicles, water-craft, equipment, etc., located within Papua and the Territory of New Guinea for which no Army records are held . . . it applied to all AMF, British, New Zealand, American and Japanese goods and had a retrospective effect."[75] Some useful American equipment remained. In the St. Matthias group, for example, there were

> two sealed airfields and enough crated supplies to build and maintain a tent and quonset city: one-hundred thousand-bed hospital complete to the last detail, generating plant, vehicles, bulldozers, building material, refrigerators and utensils down to bandages, scalpels, crockery, stainless steel cups, cutlery and milk jugs.[76]

One difficulty with possible utilization, as in this case, was that many of the U.S. bases were not in centers of high population and some of the equipment required specialized maintenance, unlikely to be available in the immediate postwar period.[77]

Valuers went to the centers of surplus: Port Moresby, Finschhafen, Milne Bay, Aitape, Wewak, Lae, and Rabaul, as well as Dobodura, Torokina, Jacquinot Bay, Kavieng, and Emirau and Mussau Islands. Care of surplus devolved to the district officers, but they had little chance of guarding equipment scattered over areas as large as one hundred square miles while attending to other administrative duties. In areas with sea access, pilfering occurred, mostly by opportunistic Europeans.

The environment hindered the commission's task. Deteriorating equipment became lost in the re-establishing overgrowth. "[A]t some places flood waters had been responsible for completely covering equipment with silt, including motor vehicles over the bonnets." Around former bases, roads dissolved in the rains, wooden bridges decayed and metal ones often were washed away. Wharves rotted or collapsed in high seas. Subsistence and accommodation for the commissioners and buyers were basic, to say the least. Practically everything needed for the job had to be brought in. Access often was on foot. Matériel in Milne Bay, for example, was scattered along the forty miles of coast and inland in places to four miles. Often staff members endured seasickness and cramped conditions amid copra, rats, bilge, and cockroaches on small coastal vessels to reach distant dumps. Malaria eradication had ceased, so staff members became ill and returned to Australia. Few could be persuaded to replace them.

Following Australian policy, the provisional administration and the PCB, vital to the functioning of the plantations, had priority for surplus disposal. Their purchases amounted to more than a million pounds, but some proved in excess of needs so were passed back to the commission, realizing about £370,000. Lack of administrative personnel, planning, and transportation hindered potential utilization. The commission next offered surplus to missions, local industries, traders, and planters to encourage economic rehabilitation. Considerable surplus also went to UNRRA. Only then did the commission offer matériel to Australian government departments, such as the Post Office in TPNG.[78] By October 1946, bases still had considerable "residues." These were sold by auctions at Lae, Rabaul, Finschhafen, and Milne Bay, while bids for salvage of more distant bases were accepted. Since there was little available transport, the commission arranged for boats to take them and buyers there.

The commission made agreements for specific materials, as well as selling salvage rights by area, with no royalties levied on tonnages. By late 1946 the auctions returned £400,000. In subsequent months sales diminished, so the commission declared all surpluses liquidated. Any still-to-be-declared surplus seemed insufficient to justify the organization's continuance, and with the approval of the Australian prime minister, it became the responsibility of the provisional civil administration in July 1947.[79] The commission's sales had recouped more than £2 million for the Australian government. The Department of Supply and Shipping in Australia regarded this as "an outstanding achievement,"[80] but others were to become less sanguine.

A Climate of Corruption?

When the provisional administration replaced the CDC, its disposal methods were little different. By the second half of 1948, problems emerged, made more pressing by the American renunciation in June of residual rights in its matériel, including that on Manus. At least 5,000 tons of scrap there attracted dealers making illicit collections. They were evading the export regulations for non-ferrous metals to be sold in Australia by placing cargoes in bond and later re-exporting to countries where they could get better prices. Closer inspection of licenses solved this. The biggest headache was the area salvage rights, mostly issued by the CDC before mid-1947, many of which had no close-off date. Rights holders who had often paid only a token amount for licenses speculatively sold them. Scrap still littered large areas, as dealers targeted specific salvageable items and left the rest. Annoyed private landowners commenced action to recover rents from the government for storage. Lack of staff for surveying, pricing, and supervision hindered finalization.[81]

When the minister for external affairs, Percy Spender, visited the territory in 1950, he heard such negative reports that he wanted a public Royal Commission of Inquiry to investigate the CDC. A preliminary internal inquiry revealed that cases attracting the most attention pivoted on the sale of salvage rights by area and speculation in rights dealing. Various administrative departments, well after salvage rights allocation, decided they might have been able to use some items salvaged.[82]

The CDC could not have foreseen this demand. Its faults were procedural: It should have set reserve prices, worked on a royalties basis for non-ferrous metal, set target dates for removal, and been more definite about the timing of a particular auction at Milne Bay. But the inquiry revealed no corrupt dealings. The commissioners had carried out their duties as well as possible under difficult circumstances. And, as one senior official in the Department of External Affairs pointed out, the prime minister could have obviated all these problems in 1945 had he been advised to retain soldiers for salvage work. The provisional administration was part of the problem, as it had been "shortsighted" regarding possible needs and likely appreciation of, say, scrap cast iron.[83] This was not the fault of the CDC, but of the Australian government's poor planning. The subsequent performance in relation to disposals by the provisional and then the permanent administration was little better than CDC's, as it continued to labor under the Australian government's failure to set target dates for clearance. Unsurprisingly, the minister decided not to proceed with a Royal Commission. In TPNG, Australia had failed to realize the greatest windfall that had ever come its way.

Gilbert and Ellice Islands

A vast amount of the equipment left on these atolls was useless to the administration, so they began to dispose of it. By early 1948, only one buyer, a Mr. Martin from Melbourne, had bought scrap from Funafuti and inspected surplus there and at Betio. He put in a bid for £3,620, but the high commissioner hesitated, hoping for a better offer. Meanwhile, the government shipping agent, Morris, Hedstrom and Co., brought some gear to Suva, on-sold to Martin's successor Mitchell, acting for his principals, L. and M. Newman and M. Tatchell. Mitchell submitted a new offer of £5,000 for the remainder on Betio and Funafuti, which, in the light of further deterioration, the administration accepted, subject to satisfactory cleaning up. Mitchell revoked his offer, but it passed to the Union Manufacturing and Export Company (UMEC) in August 1948. Though this company soon took away the most valuable items, by the end of 1951 much scrap remained. The administration had enforced their contract for Betio, but Funafuti remained uncleared. The best the administration could do was to force the company to renounce title there, but it claimed the rights had been transferred to yet another company. Thereafter, odd lots were taken off the islands, some illegally, but the residue remained an ugly reminder of war. Even so, the administration had obtained from the Americans most of what it needed for its buildings and furnishings. Having paid about $17,700 (£5,307) for this and the remaining U.S. surplus, while recouping all $25,000 (£7,500) from sales to dealers, the administration, it seemed, could tolerate some untidiness.[84]

Solomon Islands' Scrapping

In the Solomon Islands, throughout 1946 the FLC declared fixed installations at Tulagi, Guadalcanal, and the Russells abandoned.[85] As commercial interests trickled back, picking their way amid their ruined plantations, they wondered who had title to the buildings on their land, as these were not really "fixed." U.S. Navy hydrographic surveyors, still in the protectorate in 1947, assured the resident commissioner that except for the property they were using, America had abandoned all else. This spurred the administration to seek tenders to collect scrap and advise of any useful equipment found for its reconstruction program. The high commissioner hoped to have private contractors negotiate directly with the liquidator, but he refused, wanting a bulk purchase by the administration. Potential buyers received little guidance from the liquidator regarding ownership of material because equipment already declared surplus or abandoned was intermixed with unknown volumes "of unspecified and unidentified material" in the jungle.[86] The high commissioner sought clarification of ownership of these "residuals," eventually obtaining American assurances of abandonment in early 1949.[87]

When the price of brass on the world market began falling in mid-1949, the High Commission quickly opened the tendering process. The contract went to L. and M. Newman (later South Pacific Traders) for the rights on Guadalcanal above the low-water mark, including brass, paid by the ton, and to other non-ferrous and ferrous metals at a fixed sum of £30,000. From December 1949 to October 1951, the company paid the government royalties worth more than £80,000 on more than 2,200 tons of brass. Their extended contract ended in October 1953.[88]

The Solomons' government had drawn this distinction of rights to scrap from below the low-water mark because it was uncertain of its position. In British law, all material dumped at sea within the three-mile territorial limit became the Crown's, but the administration sought assurance from America regarding its sunken ships. The Americans treated the ships as any other scrap but awarded the *John H. Couch* to a Philippines dealer in March 1953, which they admitted was a mistake. The British Foreign Office conceded this exception. So by 1953, title to all American property, including wrecked ships, was the administration's.[89]

When in 1949 the administration had first called for tenders for Guadalcanal, it hoped dealers would collect all scrap (except explosives) in specific areas. The original requirement seemed to have frightened off most dealers, and the High Commission soon softened the terms to leaving "the said area in reasonably good order and condition," observing that:

> Government as present owners must in the end pay for the removal of any useless scrap . . . and I see no objection to leaving it where it lies unless this actually impedes employment or economic factors.[90]

Compromise had other benefits. In a time of limited shipping, scrap exports filled empty ships, enabling the administration to import large items from Australia for modest rates.[91]

With a new tender accepted in 1953, the administration became more specific, emphasizing the environment's utility, safety, and, at least to European eyes, aesthetics:

> (a) Where the scrap is impeding or likely to impede industrial or agricultural development, total clearance will be required; (b) Where the scrap is an eyesore and may be a public nuisance, such clearance as may be necessary to remove the eyesore or nuisance will be required; (c) Where the scrap is in isolated unused areas, only such minimum clearance as may be necessary to render the scrap safe against accidents, such as collapse of a scrap head, will be required.[92]

Scrap had been a major contributor to protectorate exports in the late 1940s, declining to about a tenth in value in the early 1950s. In one of peacetime's ironies, a Japanese salvage company made the last major collection below the high-water mark on Guadalcanal in 1960, when scrap amounted to more than £82,000, or almost 5 percent in value of exports, though minor export from other areas continued until the late 1960s.[93] These revenues were small recompense for a war that had taken much more from the embattled islands and the people.

In all this administrative thinking, the islanders rarely feature, though there were precautions for their safety and revenue earned assisted them indirectly. Even so, they made the most of opportunities, helping themselves to matériel, such as Marston matting, the premier fencing material from New Guinea to Tonga for decades. Most village pastors call people to church by banging on wartime oxyacetylene cylinders. Dumps of forty-four-gallon drums were scoured for fuel.[94] On Abemama in the Gilbert Islands, the people "acquired" much surplus, such as beds, stoves, and tools, only to have these seized and destroyed by nervous American officers when a commander was scheduled to visit in mid-1944.[95] In some places, local peoples' souvenirs were sometimes props for nostalgia, but predominantly they salvaged anything for which "a domestic use" could be found.[96] Women jangled "with bracelets wrought from the metal of crashed Zeros."[97] Following the marines' example, men gathered gold from Japanese teeth to sell. Local contract gangs, hired by dealers to collect scrap, did well from war's waste.[98]

Uninvited, a foreign war had brought tons of military paraphernalia to the southern Pacific, with limited benefit to the islanders. Modernity's potlatch impressed, but it created enduring misconceptions of supply, demand, and costs. It fed Melanesians' hopes of "Amerika" supplying cargoes of unlimited goods.[99] Unaware of the Allies' bookkeeping, many resented colonial rulers who somehow persuaded the Americans to bury matériel or seemingly give to the administration goods the islanders thought would be theirs. Social memory for some even

Figure 23. A sample of modern war as it came ashore in LST 399 at village, Mono Island, October 1943 (200646, RG 80, NARA).

had the colonial government spitefully dumping American equipment because "it manifested the rivalry of the American nation [*sic*]."[100] For them, the war had lifted a veil briefly on another world of plenty and, for some, horror. But this powerful world lay beyond their grasp.[101]

Certainly, surplus assisted some colonial governments, but often it was merely a replacement for infrastructure war destroyed. The price was often higher than they paid the liquidators; fouled anchorages delayed reconstruction in several ports. Much has been made of the benefit bestowed on far-flung islands in constructing airfields, wharves, roads, and even towns. Honiara, a larger Luganville, and Noumea emerged from wartime bases, but Rabaul and most other New Guinea towns were flattened.[102] Some airfields did survive or were resurrected decades later; others became the building pads for schools and other public facilities or straight stretches of road.[103] Most became tangles of weedy species struggling on compacted coral or concrete that had obliterated productive land. A few roads survived, often less for economic than for political reasons, such as the transinsular road on Upolu.[104] On high islands, roads needing a huge work force to maintain quickly returned to the jungle except near the few towns where the colonial establishment followed a truncated wartime template. Wharves, bridges, and telegraph poles rotted within a few years.[105] As ever, the natural environment of the tropics proffered no surrender, assaulting the built environment.

Although peace's spur was less compelling, the roll-up process was governed by the same enduring strictures that had made war so costly: distance, location, and climate. Like military operations, disposing of war's detritus became braided with the politics and economics, not only of Allied governments, but also of the colonial administrations and their subject peoples, who had to live with the conflict's equivocal legacy in their islands. Some, such as Fiji's administration, maximized opportunities, and others, such as Australia in New Guinea, dissipated possibilities. Even the victors who nostalgically returned "to glory" amid the places where they had fought and saw their companions die came away unsettled at the waste and wasting of resources, as the forest reclaimed their frail structures, rain rusted mighty machines, and their many lost dead dissolved into the earth.[106]

CHAPTER 10

Leavings on Landscape

Isle of beauty, azure seas and skies,
Of tropic's verdant growth which given time
Will tirelessly enclose the ravages of men and war,
For time wins in the end: there is no end to time.
—Oliver Gillespie

While damage to the built environment and the human species received attention during and after the war, damage to the wider ecology largely went unnoticed. Where it was, it was tolerated as a normal by-product of war, not especially problematic. In some cases, the scale of damage is elusive because colonial administrations were not able to immediately assess this, so it did not become manifest until the war was long over. Often allies were secretive about possible damage, lest they be held to account after the war or simply because they wanted to leave as quickly as possible. Moreover, there was little if any measurement of prewar conditions, so changes in the ecology were almost impossible to gauge. Except where colonial officials knew of dangerous pests that wartime traffic could introduce, it was only when the changes reached a scale large enough to endanger human well-being that they were noticed. Often the threat of damage from hidden explosives and even chemical weaponry was not appreciated until these armaments were discovered, often by accident, years after the armies had left.

A Little World

Nowhere is ecological change more observable than on small atolls, the most labile of all island environments. What was known of their war-transformed ecology in the Pacific was a response to earlier interference by bird hunters with a more pristine state. In the early twentieth century, Western millinery fashions demanded feathers and bird skins, so Japanese poachers raided atolls, including Midway Island, and severely reduced the bird population.[1] Conservation glossed political and strategic motives, but the outcome was that the United States surveyed the considerable bird populations of Midway and other atolls.[2] Such data enabled postwar scientists to understand the war's impact, and what they tell us can be extrapolated to other islands. As war threatened, the United States built an airfield near Midway's cable station and installed a garrison. To zoologist Harvey L. Fisher, war's negative avian impacts resulted from construction, from everyday disturbance of the breeding grounds, and from predator introduction.

Construction flattened almost the whole island's surface for roads, an airfield, storage, and buildings. Ground- and burrow-nesting birds suffered, as did the species that had nested in the few native trees (*Scaevola*), though some sheltered in the introduced Casuarinas near the cable station. For about eighteen months, construction went on day and night, so diurnal as well as nocturnal birds suffered, their eggs destroyed by bulldozers. Albatrosses and other species tangled in fences, barbed wire, overhead wires, and watchtowers. Foxholes, pits, and gun emplacements trapped albatrosses, shearwaters, tropic birds, and petrels, which starved to death.

Great flocks of sooty terns and the red-tailed tropic birds collided with planes in the air. Again and again, ground-nesting birds would return instinctively to former nesting grounds that had become tarmac and would be destroyed as planes came and went. Frustrated ground crewmen pummeled many to death. Hundreds of birds perished under the wheels of jeeps and trucks. The fifteen thousand humans crowded on an atoll of two square miles stressed the survivors, while their eggs were constantly gathered to feed bored, hungry men.

Another blow was the accidental introduction of the rat (*Rattus rattus*) in 1943. Partly controlled by baits from 1945, the survivors still ate eggs and raided nests. Their numbers increased as the garrison pulled out, since the men were killing the rats for their own protection, not the birds'. On the side of the birds was the extension of the land made by infill from reef blasting.[3]

Other atolls, such as Funafuti, Nanumea, and Nukufetau in the Ellice Islands, infilled and flattened for airfields, did not have huge bird populations, since people had long lived there. But like Midway's birds, humans could not be sustained by the tarmacs as they had been formerly. On the Ellice airfields, coconuts planted in the compacted coral never again thrived.[4] The "ravished desolation" Betio (Gilbert Islands) suffered to both land and lagoon was huge. Its inshore fisheries were ruined. Yet in war's stark ecology, by the early 1950s, new coconut planting on the former Japanese-built airstrip did exceedingly well compared to the coastal fringe. It was the site of mass burials of Japanese; "fast acting fertiliser" came from their bodies.[5]

Figure 24. Two weeks after the landing at Betio on Tarawa, the damage on land and in the lagoon areas is clear. The main landings were to the point closest to the viewer and on the left coast where the vessels are, as the shell damage to area indicates. Traces of barriers to landing in the lagoon laid by the Japanese are still present. The Japanese constructed the airfield, which the U.S. renamed Hawkins Field (EX. 342-FH-3A 43460, NARA).

On high islands such as Guadalcanal, the fauna suffered along with humanity from bombing and artillery fire. Bored men on the north coast took pot shots at crocodiles, birds, and flying foxes to pass the time. But such destruction was localized and there was still ample forest refuge for animals and bird life to shelter in.[6]

In the earlier discussion of the use of aggregates, the resulting borrow pits were noted. Such remaking of the landscape was typical of any base establishment.[7] The Munda base map shows how extensive an average sized U.S. base for sea and aircraft was (Map 6). Munda's coralline stratum remains dotted with pits from the construction. Where vegetation and topsoil has been stripped from such coralline substratum and compacted for roads and airstrips, neither the vegetation nor the soil has yet recovered. Overall, only about eleven square kilometers of the Solomons' 28,000 square kilometers is in this state from the war.[8] In the Trobriand Islands "[s]everal thousand acres of garden land" were compacted for American airstrips and ancient stone works were destroyed.[9] Emirau lost its best garden land under tarmac.[10] Two village sites and gardens were lost to the Fale'olo airfield in Western Samoa. Near Suva, the New Zealand engineers changed the Walu Bay coastline by excavating tons of soapstone and rock to install gasoline storage tanks at Sealark Hill, dumping the spoil into the sea. So extensive was the spoil that there were worries about its becoming "more and more conspicuous to a prospective enemy plane."[11] The Americans did much more with extending the airfields in west Viti Levu, constructing jetties, tank farms, and wells.[12] How the changed shoreline and hillside affected the ecology is anyone's guess.

Overall, the impact of artillery and bombing on soils was rarely intensive because the war occurred on a moving front. Where Americans constantly shelled a small mangrove islet off Tulagi for target practice, it disintegrated.[13] Excluding areas of compacted coral, most atolls, if uninhabited, forgave even major disturbance since, as is common in tropical soils on high islands, the reassertion of hardy pioneer vegetation and its decay gradually rebuilt the humic layers and thus soil fertility. On Shaggy Ridge in New Guinea, the site of a major battle between the AIF and the Japanese, a veteran commented seven years later:

> The entire ridge was blasted bare of vegetation, but today the foliage and kunai [grass] have covered much of the scene, and the mass-grave of the Japs killed there are not to be found [*sic*]. Nor could I distinguish the once important features.[14]

Seeing the Sea

In the conflict zones those most affected, the illiterate Melanesians, rarely recorded perceptions of their changed environment. What survives in social memory relates more to people than place. In the west, the people witnessed the sinking of many ships. This must have had a dramatic impact on maritime resources, especially along the littoral. Some idea of its scale can be gained from the sinking of a troop transport when the Americans fought the Japanese off Tulagi in 1942. The wreck was both a provider and destroyer of resources, as a Nggela man testified.

> It carried the Marines. This transport was sank opposite Idale. Lots of things were washed ashore such as cornbeef, C rations, canvases, medicines, life floats, full of all sorts of things, blankets, hand grenades, axes, shirts, towels, mail bags full of calico. Two weeks we did not eat a native foods for the course of the European foods washed ashore. Lots of women were dislike the smell of oils. Always they like to vomit. . . . Men and women swim to sea to get things which were adrift. But what can you see. The oil covered their faces heads and all over their bodies. When we came ashore we cleaned out the oils. The shells, clams, crabs in the sea died ashore in the course of the poison of the oil [*sic*].[15]

Like the Solomon Islanders, most humans tend to be anthropocentric and only consider the sea's dead when laid before their eyes. The war harvest of marine life was most observable among the whales. While war reduced the global prewar kill rate of about 40,000 annually, the slaughter did not cease. The need for war food took an uncounted toll, and many died as a result of combat.[16] Young pilots found whales an easy mark on which to try out their bombing skills.[17] Many "valiant attacks have been made upon 'submarines' which in reality were whales or blackfish." Radar on ships and submarines could not easily distinguish these great beasts with "considerable 'hull' " from enemy submarines, so they were shelled with depth charges. When oil ruptured from their bodies surfaced, inexperienced observers convinced themselves they had scored an enemy hit, even though it did not smell of diesel. Eventually command sent out directions to highlight the difference in profile from a submarine.[18]

Around their bases the U.S. laid mine fields, from Bora Bora across to the Solomons. The whales' curiosity often drew them to these objects. In Tongan waters, the humpback whales come to give birth in the southern winter months. By August 1943, of 550 mines laid, 33 exploded:

> Several of these were caused by whales contacting the mines or floats. Several whales have been noted floating off the harbor and on the reefs. It is expected that during the month of September when the run of whales usually takes place, many more mines may be set off.[19]

This prediction proved accurate, as noted two years later: "For months after the fields were laid, explosions were seen almost daily. . . . Quite a number of dead whales have floated into the harbor."[20] Whale mortality was never calculated, but as Kurk Dorsey has noted, "it is hard to conclude that the years of war for people were years of peace for whales."[21]

War did provide relief from the exploitation of most deep-sea species and shellfish, however. Trochus shell used for buttons could not be exported, so reefs remained unfished. In New Caledonia they had not been touched for five years.[22] This was good for the fishery, but merchants grumbled that shells had grown too big for button manufacture.[23]

Exploding Deposits

Unlike in the sea, war's impact on terrestrial sites was more likely to attract the attention of land-bound human beings. Thousands of tons of munitions were hauled to the Pacific islands during the war. Beyond the combat zone, munitions were stored at the perimeters of airfields and docks, awaiting transshipment. When the war ended, these and secret chemical weapons were not the sort of surplus the returning ships wanted as cargo. Munitions were dumped on a huge scale on land and sea, an unwelcome inheritance for the people and colonial administrations.

Wherever possible, the Allies stored munitions away from living areas. In rear bases where existing port facilities were near residential areas, explosions were catastrophic. On the Noumea Nickel dock, the ignition of explosives and fuel was a fatal combination in November 1943 when at least eighty-seven died, thirty-five of whom were never identified.[24] One of the largest ammunition dumps in the South Pacific was near Henderson Field, Guadalcanal, holding bombs for operations up the Solomons chain to Rabaul. Bombing Rabaul, between mid-February to mid-May 1944, the Allies dropped at least 7,410 tons of bombs.[25] By April, as airfields to the north were closer to the target areas, Guadalcanal ceased as a base for bombing operations and became a supply and transshipment area. Even so, the dump still covered eight hundred acres and held 20,000 tons of "[g]eneral purpose bombs, fragmentation bombs, depth bombs, pyrotechnics, aircraft gun ammunition, bomb fuses, and miscellaneous inert equipment." Despite numerous regulations about the stacking and storage of munitions and the construction of roads and revetments, manpower shortages resulted in shortcuts.

The greatest threat to safe storage was the nature of the climate, terrain, and vegetation. At Banika in the Russells in October 1945, more than 4,000 tons of ammunition exploded. The cause was uncertain, but a lack of safe distances between clusters of munitions and the heat of the sun on certain types of bombs were contributing factors. On north Guadalcanal, flat areas, part of the great northern flood plain, were poorly drained. Though the U.S. engineers had successfully drained other dumps, near Koli and Carney airfields, Henderson was little better in 1943 than when it had been the only dump in 1942. Unless sufficient dunnage had been laid down, the lower levels of ammunition sank into the mud. But the greatest safety threat was the "fire hazzard" [*sic*] of grasses, especially in the drier months.[26] The difficulty was cutting the tough grasses to the recommended two inches over an area of more than a square mile. Since Japanese bombing had started grass fires, safety experts in September 1943 highlighted such dangers. Their fears became reality in November when a fire broke out at Hell's Point ammunition dump, between the Ilu and Tenaru rivers, and the same day another burned the Henderson dump to the east of the airfield. Explosions killed two soldiers, with fifteen patients in an adjacent hospital presumed dead, as little trace was found of them. Explosions continued for several days, scattering ammunition with each blast. The unstable Hell's Point dump was put off-limits except to more dumped ammunition.

Lessons had not been learned, because on 26 June 1944, the Sun Valley dump of five hundred tons of condemned ammunition and explosives blew up. Storage boxes had rotted away and contents had scattered. Inquiries failed to produce a specific cause—self-ignition and sabotage were possibilities, a concern since this dump was not far from another full of serviceable material.[27]

In rear bases, the military honed their skills with practice aerial bombing and artillery exercises. Sometimes these projectiles had warheads that failed to explode; planes crashed in the jungle with cargoes of bombs embedded beneath the fuselage. When these areas were to be frequented by the forces, bomb disposal units defused or detonated munitions. Other than assembling some scattered dumps

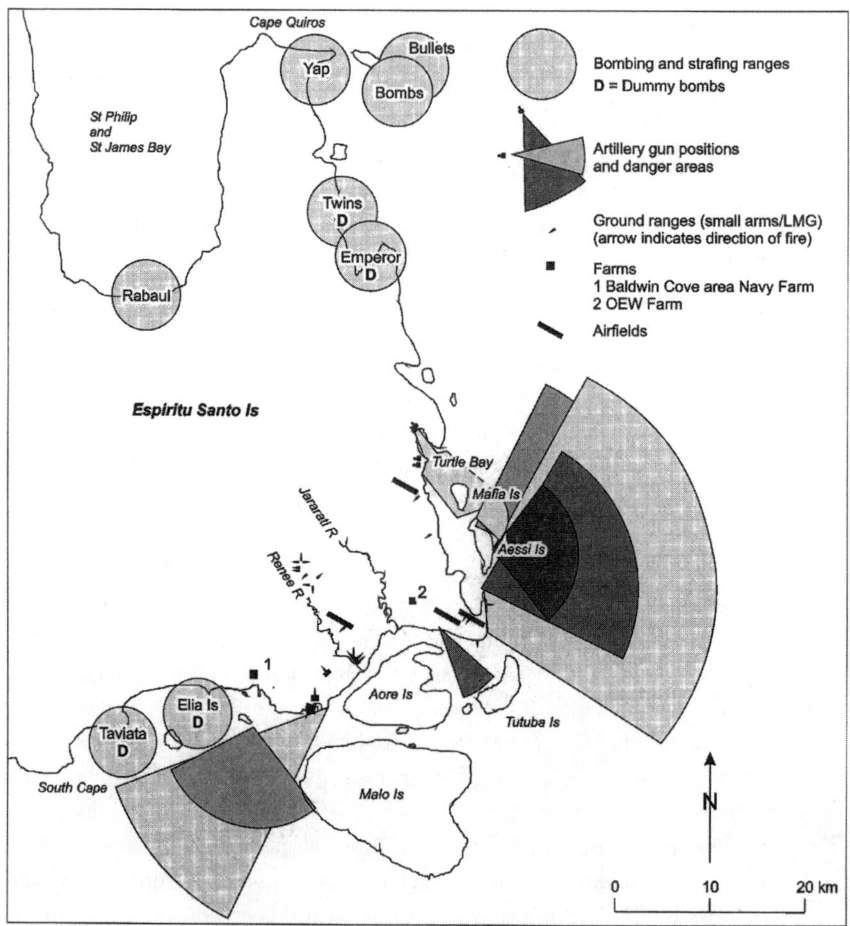

Map 11. Ranges for live and dummy bombing practice, Santo Espiritu, January 1944. Note also the military farms (based on map RG 313-58-3500, NARA SB).

in areas preparatory to dumping in the sea as the war drew to a close, however, the Allies did not clean up the thousands of tons of munitions that peppered the jungles and beaches.[28] In the Russell Islands alone the U.S. forces left at least five dumps of various munitions around Banika Island and dumped TNT in a swamp on Karamola Island.[29] The Japanese left their own dumps, mainly in the western Solomons. As the Americans found, one of the most dangerous was a large quantity of munitions dumped off the Gizo wharf when the Japanese fled. In the seas, Allied sweepers collected their own mines laid down to prevent the passage of enemy vessels, but often missed enemy mines.[30]

Even dumping at sea was not a perfect way of ridding the land of munitions. In theory, unwanted munitions were to be dumped in 50 to 120 fathoms, ten miles or more out from land.[31] In February 1945 defective bombs that had been dumped "off Koli Point" in Guadalcanal floated to the surface.[32] In Fiji, off Savuna Reef, Moturiki Island, soon after the war, ammunition and surplus bombs were dumped and supposedly exploded, yet several bombs later surfaced nearby.[33] Throughout the war the United States dumped defective ammunition, but with the end in sight, disposal speeded up in all bases. After V-J day, South Pacific command estimated that at least $20 million worth of ammunition had been dumped or burned by March 1946, over half of this at the Noumea base and the rest on Guadalcanal and Espiritu Santo. Smaller bases such as Munda were not part of this total. In addition, "certain obsolete or useless, heavy ordnance items were abandoned or destroyed also" to the value of more than $7 million.[34] In the New Guinea islands, the Australian army made Japanese captives dump their arms and ammunition at sea.[35] In the sea or on the land, if munitions were out of sight, they soon were out of the minds of departing armies.

"Tabu—Dangerous Duds"

For those who remained, the most warning they were given were such cryptic words as these on the signs posted around the dumps on Guadalcanal in 1946. Never mind that few Solomon Islanders could read and even fewer would have known what "dud" meant.[36] As the last of the U.S. forces prepared to leave, the resident commissioner accepted this complacently, absolving Britain's ally from responsibility for dangerous material, just as he had for war damage claims.

> all reasonable precautions appear now to have been taken in the interests of safety to the public, including the native population. Presumably the area can never be really safe for many years to come, but I am satisfied that no more can be done now.[37]

By 1944, the British had decided to build their new capital at Honiara, and soon after V-J day they planned its construction around the core of American Guadalcanal installations. With clearing for building sites, ammunition surfaced. The administration called on a bomb disposal officer from the HMAS *Culgoa* in 1948, who managed to clear two hundred hand grenades, mortar bombs, and various large- and small-caliber shells from Honiara, but this was just a beginning. The resident commissioner estimated that across the protectorate there were 12,500 acres that needed intensive examination for munitions, so he requested an Australian bomb disposal unit (BDU) and agreed to pay the costs.

Australian units were very busy in TPNG into the mid-1950s, when the civil administration took responsibility. With the exceptions of major, visible dumps, the BDU had to rely on local residents to point out the locations of explosives. Any one area could be cleared, but months later, as people made their gardens or when planters cleared undergrowth, more munitions would appear. In some areas local people had limbs blown up or worse when they burned off undergrowth to make gardens. Some concealed the munitions because they wanted to use these in fishing, but the careless lost hands.[38]

The BDU had discovered some dumps secreted by the Americans. One of the largest they detonated was at Torokina, Bougainville, where 4,000 tons were cleared.[39] On Manus, the BDU found that Americans had thrown at least two hundred magazines of 40mm Bofors and 20mm SAAs "over a steep embankment into a small ravine." Part of the embankment collapsed, covering the ammunition, which soon became overgrown. Collection by local laborers and the army was extremely hazardous because the munitions had to be dug out.[40]

When in 1950 a combined Australian navy and army BDU arrived on Guadalcanal, once overflowing with military surplus, it faced transport problems and poor messing arrangements, as well as bickering between the respective senior officers. Concentrating initially along the north coast, the BDU cleared the Sun Valley dumps. At Henderson's airfield it found that the U.S. forces had bulldozed munitions in. They excavated almost 20,000 projectiles, and more remained. The Hell's Point dump, covering at least one hundred acres and holding about 15,000 tons of munitions, was eight miles east of Honiara, but about a mile away from Tenaru Catholic mission and school. The BDU cleared grass and began stacking a thousand tons of the munitions for removal. In June 1951, a bomb exploded, killing a Solomon Islander, injuring another, and causing a fire, which detonated and scattered ammunition. The Solomon Islanders refused to work unless they were paid more danger money, and transport remained minimal, so work slowed.[41] After this, any informal arrangements of South Pacific traders' scrap collectors working alongside the BDU ceased because the commander suspected the collectors had left "a lot of loose cordite" around after taking the brass shells.[42] Under a new

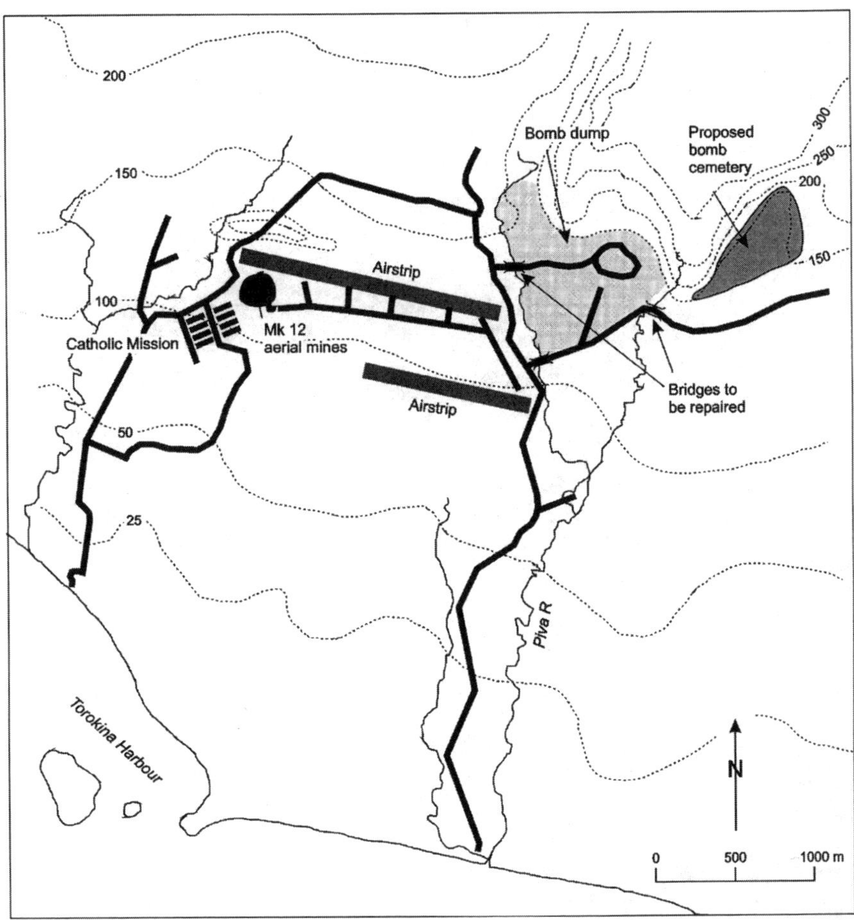

Map 12. Plan for location of Australian Bombing Disposal Unit's consolidation of unused explosives, Torokina, Bougainville, March 1947 (based on map, MP742/1/0, Item 11/1/1113, NAA).

commander, in spite of the resident commissioner's concerns, local brass collectors returned.[43]

Others rummaged around the dumps. Some Seventh-day Adventist boys at Betikama School financed their fees with the sale of brass from shells, and in 1949 the headmaster had paid for a tractor the same way, fueling it for years with gasoline salvaged from abandoned forty-four-gallon drums.[44]

Different commanders gave the resident commissioner conflicting advice: to close Hell's Point dump off permanently and, in mid-1952, to make smaller stacks of about two hundred tons, to lessen the chance of a major explosion and then dump each of these at sea—if the unit could get suitable vessels. The resident commissioner worried about mounting costs. With little progress on Hell's Point by early 1953, the BDU calculated that about a fifth of the volume had been removed and that another six years would be needed to complete the process. Because of the needs of the western district and the possibly interminable operations in one location, the resident commissioner closed off Hell's Point.[45] Despite this, in mid-1954 the administration decided that once the worst dumps were cleared from the Munda area, work in New Georgia would have to cease because the lack of local transport and high costs relative to "the wide dispersion of the remaining ordnance and the number of local residents who are affected by it."[46] Hell's Point would remain "dangerous for all time" in an area increasingly settled by Solomon Islanders.[47]

At the Solomons' independence in 1978, Australia assisted in munitions disposal with the training of a team of islanders and visits by specialists. Yet periodically old munitions explode as forest is cleared in former combat zones.[48] Localized Melanesian conflicts from the late 1980s have even seen the excavation of old armaments for militias. No combatants escaped the domestic burden of their wartime armaments, however.[49] In Queensland, Australia, recent environmental audits have revealed dumps of Allied munitions in areas used for World War II maneuvers across the state. Toxic dumps litter America, including uncounted radioactive material originating in World War II. Each combatant has its hidden dumps, often coming to light as more intense settlement spreads into formerly "safe," isolated areas.[50]

Toxic Ghosts

A passive threat awaits wandering people in the Rabaul area. Miles of old Japanese tunnels are likely to collapse and people will fall into pockets of bad air.[51] Man-made chemicals are also a danger. Wartime chemical agents were little publicized, nor was their disposal. In 1942, Australia had no capacity to produce chemical gases for warfare, but Britain sent supplies and expertise.[52] The U.S. South Pacific command had chemicals stocks in Hawai'i, Tonga, Canton Island, New Caledonia, New Hebrides, and the Solomons. In the Southwest Pacific including Australia, U.S. stocks were held in Australia and at Finchhafen, New Guinea. U.S. command planned to use chemicals such as the blistering agents H and L, mustard gas, and Lewisite gas if the Japanese used them, but most Allied commanders, having seen their effects in World War I, eschewed them.[53] Although the Japanese employed both chemical and biological weapons in China and Manchuria, there is no evidence that they used them in the Pacific or held stores south of the Philippines.[54]

The environment affected chemical weapons. Gases did not behave in the forested, humid tropics in the same manner as in other theaters, such as the North African deserts. The "strange climates and topography" seemed uncooperative because the dense forest canopy and understory proved a barrier that affected the gas flow and the timing of the detonation of the explosive.[55] Consequently, the Allies conducted experiments to remedy this. The Australians were unwilling to experiment in New Guinea due to "political reasons" and the unsuitability of the terrain,[56] but they did so on Brook Island, in the Great Barrier Reef of north Queensland.[57]

Another question was how such persistent gases affected human skin "under conditions of high temperature and high humidity." As Lt. Col. F. S. Gorrill from Britain, commander of the Australian Chemical Warfare Research and Experimental Section, already knew in 1943 from tests in India, skin was four times more sensitive in the tropics than in a temperate climate.[58] He headed tests in north Queensland on more than two thousand poorly informed AIF volunteers, often at the cost of their lingering suffering. Several men were on Brook when it was gassed by the RAAF, once with ill-fitting gas masks and once without. Sworn to silence, their subsequent claims for compensation denied by the Australian and American authorities, their story was little known until a TV journalist, Bridget Goodwin, made it public in 1989.[59] They were not the only victims. One of the Brook men, T. Mitchell, noted that as well as tethered goats, mice, guinea pigs, and rabbits, "[a]mong the birds wiped out was a scrub fowl a mound building bird that had been there since the beginning, the gas got every living thing even some of the trees." He added that, as in all wars, there were no "Greenies" to prevent such extirpations.[60]

Many chemical weapons were abandoned locally. Since the 1970s more intensive human use of Australia's marine environment has exposed dumped conventional munitions and chemical warfare agents (CWA).[61] Containers of mustard gases were found on Guam in 2004 and on Banika in the Solomons in 1991. In an attempt to win Pacific support for operations of its controversial chemical incinerator on Johnson Atoll, the United States, for the first time, took responsibility for the Solomons and sent a team to remove around one hundred unstable shells of the gas, of which 75 percent were still full.[62] It is likely that more such weapons remain.

Other toxic agents threaten the fishery. Seepage of oil and heavy metals from sunken wartime vessels is likely as corrosion increases, though generally oil damage is temporary and mainly confined to crustaceans and mollusks, depending on spread area and dispersal rates.[63] Small Pacific countries cannot deal with such problems. Pleas by the Solomons' prime minister Ulufa'alu in 1997 to former protagonists to assist with about 111 ships and 1,450 fighter planes sunk in Iron Bottom Sound have been ignored. In spite of a South Pacific Commission survey, details of munitions on board are elusive and thus so are their likely toxic effects. As in Truk (Chuuk) lagoon, ships may have had cargoes of depth charges, which, as casings deteriorate, could leak ammonium picrate and powdered aluminum and poison fish stocks.[64] Legal liability would be difficult to establish since ownership of these vessels passed to the state where they are, but the moral obligation for remediation for the common good is hard to deny since the islanders did not invite such threats to their environment.[65]

Wandering Weeds

More mobile threats came with war. Weeds, or, as humans anthropocentrically define them, plants in the wrong place, favor conditions that mirror their place of origin. If they have less competition in their new site, they thrive. Generally, those that flourished in the Pacific came into areas where human activity had disturbed vegetation. In war, such activity was both extensive and intensive, with clearing for camps, airfields, tank farms, ammunition dumps, and roads. Most exotic plants were accidentally introduced and rarely noticed at the time. Although a few were from the Old World tropics, most were native to the American tropics and most had naturalized in Hawai‘i before the war. The westward and northward flow of the U.S. forces mirrors the direction of these plant invaders.

Attached to the trouser cuffs of personnel, ruderal plants such as the tropical grasses *Cenchrus echinatus, C. browni, Paspalum conjugatum,* and the burred shrub *Triumfetta semitrilobata* found their way to several islands.[66] Others were carried in packing material or soil attached to machinery such as bulldozers. The shrub *Sida acuta* (broom weed) was noticed in the east of Fiji where the U.S. had occupied "dry areas and poor pasture." In the Solomons by 1947, the government agricultural officer noted it was doing well where troops had been stationed.[67] In the dry pastures of west New Caledonia the prickly pea, *Mimosa invisa* (giant sensitive plant), seems to have been introduced deliberately as a forage plant in 1942. A weed shrub, *Flemingia strobilifera,* was noted in 1947 as rapidly spreading in disturbed areas. The Americans had brought this along with *Euphorbia heterophylla* and *Kalachoe.* Floral transfers went the other way too. Some soldiers in New Guinea collected seeds of impressive flowering plants to send home to their wives.[68]

F. Fosberg records that in Micronesia not only did new weeds come in from distant places, but also introduced species located on one island were carried to others. In all, about 135 species seem to have come to the Micronesian islands most affected by the war and soil disturbance. Those commonly found on and around former airfields include the sunflowers *Conyza bonariensis, C. canadensis, Tridax procumbens, Eclipta alba,* and *Sonchus oleraceus* and the grass *Eragrostis poaeoides,* so they may have been attached to the wheels of planes. Where supplies were stored and unpacked, the grasses *Chloris inflata* and *Tricachne insularis* were common.[69] *Pluchea indica* and *P. ororata* took hold on several islands as they did in U.S. base areas on Penrhyn, the Cook Islands, and Santo and Efate, New Hebrides.[70]

More aggressive was "mile-a-minute" or "American rope" (*Mikania micrantha*), believed to have been deliberately introduced by the Americans as a quick camouflage plant. Native to South American rainforests, *Mikania* found a perfect habitat in the western Pacific, where a related less vigorous variety was already established in Fiji and possibly Samoa before the war.[71] During the war or soon after, "American rope" was noted not only in the Solomons and New Hebrides, but also in the Ellice Islands and American Samoa, where it was "growing rapidly over the scars of battles and old camp sites."[72] A perennial vine with heart-shaped leaves, it can reproduce by seeds that cling to clothing. As well, it can reproduce vegetatively and grows about fifteen inches (30 cm) a day, quickly climbing up saplings and eventually deforming their growth or smothering them. By now, it is a major weed pest in many Pacific islands and a particular nuisance in western Melanesia, where poor logging practices encourage its spread.[73]

The Japanese seem to have brought relatively few new species with them, probably because of the decreasing number of their ships and planes that survived the U.S. blockade in 1943 and their lack of earthmoving equipment. Moreover, many of the Old World "weeds" had already arrived in New Guinea long before the war. Nonetheless, *Chromolaena odorata,* with its hooked clinging seeds came with the Japanese and established at Rabaul, Vanimo, and Lae in New Guinea, as well as Rota in the Marianas. An invasive species of cleared forest and disturbed land, it continues to spread.[74]

Creeping Blights

The Japanese did not stop at floral introductions. In northern New Guinea and adjacent islands, when ANGAU officers on patrols in 1943–1946 moved into areas formerly occupied by the Japanese, they found another more enduring exotic: The giant African snail (*Achatina fulica*). This snail can grow up to eight inches but commonly is three to four inches long at maturity. Feeding on decaying vegetation, they consume practically any greenery near the ground. They have an enormous reproductive capacity as hermaphrodites that breed by cross mating, producing usually four batches of about 150 eggs a year and living five to six years. One gravid individual could produce eight million in progeny.[75] At Hansa Bay, between Wewak and Madang, the ANGAU officer recording claims for war damage compensation in November 1946 reported that "the Japanese Snail pest is in great numbers. It is thought however, the pest has not made great progress since November 1945." He went on to say that the natives were frightened of it.[76]

They had every reason to be so. Recorded as "causing alarm" in New Ireland, the snails were advancing south from Kavieng in mid-1946,[77] and were noted in New Britain a few months later at Rabaul and environs, where they seemed "to tackle any kind of vegetable."[78] By December there were great populations at Kavieng, Madang, and Rabaul. With no apparent natural enemies, "incredible numbers" were taking over an area of two square miles at Hansa Bay.[79] Yet in early 1947 at Kavieng, their spread seemed to have slowed and they were not readily seen in the daytime, as they were nocturnal feeders.[80] By 1951 they had so decreased around Kavieng that more vegetables could be grown and that "huge piles of moribund shells" were found.[81] A pattern began to emerge of a sudden efflorescence in one area, then a slowing and leveling off period of varying years and then a decline, but with colonies in new locations bursting forth in full vigor.[82] In the Kokopo district in mid-1947, they were numerous around Kabunga plantation, consuming taro and sweet potato.[83] By 1948 the administration sent in entomologists to seek some biological control to replace expensive baits or hand collecting. Meanwhile, there were reports of its almost getting to the United States on shipments of scrap metal from New Guinea. The Americans, alarmed at the snail's depredations in their new territory of Micronesia, sent entomologists to its east Africa homeland to find some natural predator.[84]

The ANGAU officer at Hansa was correct in calling it the "Japanese snail pest." In New Britain an Australian soldier, M. K. Carter, noted that the productivity of the Japanese gardens in the Rabaul-Keravat region made them "nearly self-sufficient. Unfortunately, they brought in the Giant African Snail to supplement their diet, and these large, ugly things multiplied."[85] Although the prewar Japanese government had recognized its danger after its introduction in about 1935, their successful measures to eliminate it from Japan did not include Okinawa. In the late 1930s Okinawa settlers in Micronesia had brought the snail to cultivate for medicinal and food purposes, but it had escaped and was colonizing several Micronesian islands as the war began.[86] The malacologist Albert Mead believed the Japanese introduced it from Singapore or Malaya,[87] but according to one Japanese in New Guinea,

> it became known that in a certain unit, edible snails which had been brought in from Parao [Palau/Balau] island increased to about 200,000 within a year and were cooked tastefully [*sic*]. Accordingly, these were distributed to all units. Shortly after, the number amounted to one million.[88]

Not simply a predator of plants, the snail is now known to carry three important pathogens: *Phytopthora nicotianae, Phytophthora colocasiae*, and *Phytophthora palmivora*. These fungus-like organisms cause disease in several horticultural plants. The latter two pathogens thrive in warm tropical regions.[89] Still a pest in New Guinea and the adjacent islands, the snail's march across much of the Pacific continues. It has colonized Hawai'i, and more recently an outbreak occurred in north Queensland.[90] From the 1950s, attempts to control it with the exotic predator or cannibal snail *Euglandina rosea* and a flatworm have seen some diminution of numbers, along with the unplanned extinction of native snails, for example in Tahiti and Hawai'i.[91]

Native food supplies faced another mobile pest. In Bougainville, as the war ended, a leaf blight caused by *Phytophthora colocasiae* severely affected taro, another blow to a war-weakened people.[92] It spread down the Solomons chain, killing lowland taro.[93] Many Bougainvilleans believe it was an effect of the occupation, either because of Japanese bombs or of U.S. diesel oil dropped on Japanese gardens. Their explanation is an example of "colliding ecologies," for the Western interpretation of environmental damage does not tally with theirs.[94] Jerry Packard's research suggests it was present on New Guinea and the islands for some years before the war, originating in Southeast Asia, but increased in severity from 1948 on and spread into areas such as Buin in Bougainville. It could have come with a variety of taro brought to the Shortlands by the Japanese troops, but the evidence is slight. Packard, however, did not consider the possible role of the African snail, which spreads *Phytophthora colocasiae* to new areas. More recently, the blight has appeared in islands east of the Solomons, with a major outbreak in Samoa in 1993–1994, necessitating research into resistant varieties of taro.[95]

Another pest did not emerge until the late 1970s. On Guam, observers noted the extirpation of birds and most forest vertebrates. At first blamed on disease and then pesticides, the cryptic culprit turned out to be *Boiga irregularis*, the brown tree snake. Native to coastal northern Australia, the Moluccas, all of New Guinea, and most of the Solomon Islands, recent scale counts point its origin to Manus Island. In 1944–46, tons of heavy equipment were moved forward from the Manus base, probably with snakes curled up inside. Of low vagility and only moderately fecund, it moved northwards across Guam from the port of entry. It slowly multiplied exponentially, having no predators and a plentiful food supply of introduced species such as the skink (*Carlia fusca*), along with small birds, eggs, and bats. It is now a pest on a massive scale, not only by direct extirpation but also in its cascading effects, since, in killing frugivores such as birds and bats, it prevents the forest from regenerating, as there are no seeds spread and little pollination. Moreover, the mildly venomous snakes invade houses, bite infants, and crawl along power wires causing power failures, which upsets the human population. On several occasions only vigilant quarantine officers stopped its migration on airplanes to other islands such as Hawai'i. Attempts to exterminate it on Guam have failed.[96]

Defending the Colonies

With the exception of live munitions, the hazard of other dangerous matériel and pests did not register with colonial officials during or soon after the war, because they knew nothing of threats such as chemical weapons dumps and the brown tree snake. Other dangers known to the colonial administrations, however, were unacceptable, even in war's emergency. The British in Fiji and Tonga and the French in New Caledonia nevertheless struggled to convince the Americans of this.

Based on prewar thinking, the British believed it was possible for the malaria vector mosquito, *Anopheles*, to pass from the area where it was endemic, west of Buxton's line, into islands to the east of 170 degrees east longitude and south of 20 degrees south latitude.[97] Before the war, Fiji had developed effective quarantine methods of fumigation to deal with possible mosquito introductions on ships, and officials were preparing to deal with a regular commercial airlink.[98] With the war, however, the sheer magnitude of traffic meant problems with control, all the more so because of the unity of command under the Americans and the inevitable braiding of civilian and military interests. All ships passing from the malaria zone eastward where they would dock were required to undergo fumigation in Fiji. In mid-1942, however, the U.S. Navy requested that the Australian government order Burns Philp's *Morinda* off the New Hebrides–Australia run to detour to Tonga for the navy to collect bombs.[99] In Tonga, the British consul, Armstrong, requested the American commander carry out "anti-malarial precautions" in front of Tonga's chief medical officer and to keep the ship half a mile off land until this was done, since *Anopheles* could possibly cover a shorter distance and infect Tongans.[100] The navy preferred advice from its own doctors and loaded the cargo, giving insects ample opportunity to go ashore.[101] The objections of Governor Mitchell of Fiji subsequently reached the commander of the South Pacific, Vice Admiral Ghormley.[102] His advisors pointed out:

> In general the local rules of quarantine and measures laid down at ports of those islands have been evolved by study of experts. These rules of local health officials have been effective for decades in preventing the introduction of malaria.[103]

While Ghormley agreed, the campaign against malaria in the operational zone so preoccupied American officials that they took their time in developing processes to "deinsectisize" ships and planes going from western Melanesia to the south and east. Mitchell meanwhile applied to the Colonial Office's new development and welfare fund for mosquito control and began more intensive methods in Fiji to eliminate breeding sites, draining and spraying with larvicides and insecticides.[104]

Ghormley's successor, Admiral William Halsey, supported this.[105] By early 1943, effective American aerosol Freon "bombs" filled with pyrethrum for interior spraying were in use, though sometimes they were not activated until after the doors of arriving airplanes had been opened! Throughout 1943 and 1944 the American military improved its procedures. Thus on ships, as well as spraying cargo holds with pyrethrum, the crew checked deck cargo for water pools and oiled these with kerosene or diesel while screening fresh water tanks.[106]

British colonial officials had urged such precautions even as the war broke out, having before them the example of the introduction of the *Anopheles gambiae* and malarial parasites from Africa to Brazil in 1930 and their costly elimination.[107] Even so, since the mid-nineteenth century there had been many times that, for example, *Anopheles farauti* in the New Hebrides could have passed by ship to nearby New Caledonia as a vector to spread malaria parasites from New Hebridean migrant labor, so the French were largely unperturbed. This mosquito failed to establish there, but there was no guarantee that it and other *Anopheles* might not do so elsewhere.[108] Nonetheless, Tonga and the islands to the east remained malaria-free, probably more because of their unsuitable habitat than by the tardy response of the Americans, spurred eventually to act by the persistent Fijian government.

Ticks and Lorraine's Cross

In New Caledonia, the French, however, were more concerned about other exotics. Since the 1890s they had established quarantine regulations to ensure that pests, including the cattle tick (*Boophilus microplus*), were not introduced.[109] As an epidemic in a completely susceptible population of cattle, tick fever induced by the blood parasites *Babesia bovis*, *Babesia bigemina*, and *Anaplasma marginale* may cause death rates approaching 90 percent, especially if the "virgin" cattle are one of the *Bos taurus* breeds that evolved in Europe, away from the tropical tick fever parasite. After the parasites "settle in" to a new environment, disease rates fall as a result of immunity developing in survivors and their progeny and a possible reduction of virulence of the parasites. Once this has happened, combined mortality and morbidity rates may be of the order of 5 percent. When the breeds are *Bos indicus* (originating in Asia and Africa), disease caused by tick fever is much less severe. Fortunately, all animal species other than cattle are strongly resistant to tick fever parasites and never experience disease. *Boophilus* occasionally mature and lay eggs after growing on horses, sheep, deer, goats, and dogs. Females engorged with their host's blood fall off and lay thousands of eggs on the grasses where larval ticks hatch and attach themselves to new and preferred cattle hosts.

Even without infection with the blood parasites and resultant fever, tick-infested cattle experience irritation and blood loss ("tick worry"), soon lose condition and milk production, and often die, most commonly when herds have not been exposed to the ticks before and ticks are not controlled by chemical dipping. *Bos taurus* breeds are far more susceptible to tick worry than *Bos indicus.*[110] New Caledonia had *Bos taurus* herds, so veterinarians remained cautious about animal and fodder introductions from Australia and other infected areas, lest they carry the tick.

In June 1942, New Caledonia's chief veterinary officer, Dr. Jean Verges, was alarmed when he learned the U.S. Army had begun in May to import mules from Panama as well as horses from Australia for its cavalry. Although the first horse shipments had been from tick-free Melbourne in southern Australia, Verges voiced his concerns about the possible importation of livestock disease, citing the colony's quarantine regulations to the chief of staff of the American forces, Colonel E. B. Sebree. Sebree apologized and agreed to work with the Free French authorities in the future. Despite this, in July the first of several shipments of horses came in from tick-infested Brisbane. Verges went on board the ship and saw the ticks, as did the U.S. Army veterinarian.[111] The U.S. Army had not sought the advice of experienced Queensland quarantine officers or had the animals inspected and treated for tick eradication prior to embarkation.[112] Verges demanded access to the herds at Dumbea for a full inspection, but the Americans refused and continued to import horses until November 1942.[113]

Just as Verges had feared, in early 1944, the tick pest was noticed in the southern west coast area, in St. Louis, Paita, and Magenta, near Dumbea where the horses had been concentrated, with the cattle on V. Fayard's property said to be the first affected. Fortunately, although the tick survived on the temporary horse host, the parasites did not. In the Dumbea valley alone by the end of 1944, about a thousand cattle had died as a result of "tick worry."[114] The French government established a cordon marked by the Tontouta River around the infected area to control all movement of cattle from south of this line to areas north.[115]

But this was an inauspicious time for a cordon sanitaire. Legal and black market cattle were being moved around the land and slaughtered for the troops. Moreover, before the cordon was set, French farmers had unwittingly taken cattle north and across the mountain chain to the east coast. Wild cattle and deer also carried the tick, and U.S. maneuvers constantly destroyed fencing.[116] Verges initiated an education campaign and dipping of cattle, to little avail.[117] Fearing damage claims, the Americans initially denied responsibility, which was ludicrous. Their intelligence network reported regularly on all matters in the French territory, including the spread of the tick.[118] They began their own investigation in August 1944, but the French were never privy to the findings reported in January 1945.[119] Lieutenant C. G. Fredine, a parasitologist, collected evidence from shippers, horse dealers, hide importers, Australian customs officers, Panama officials, scientific personnel,

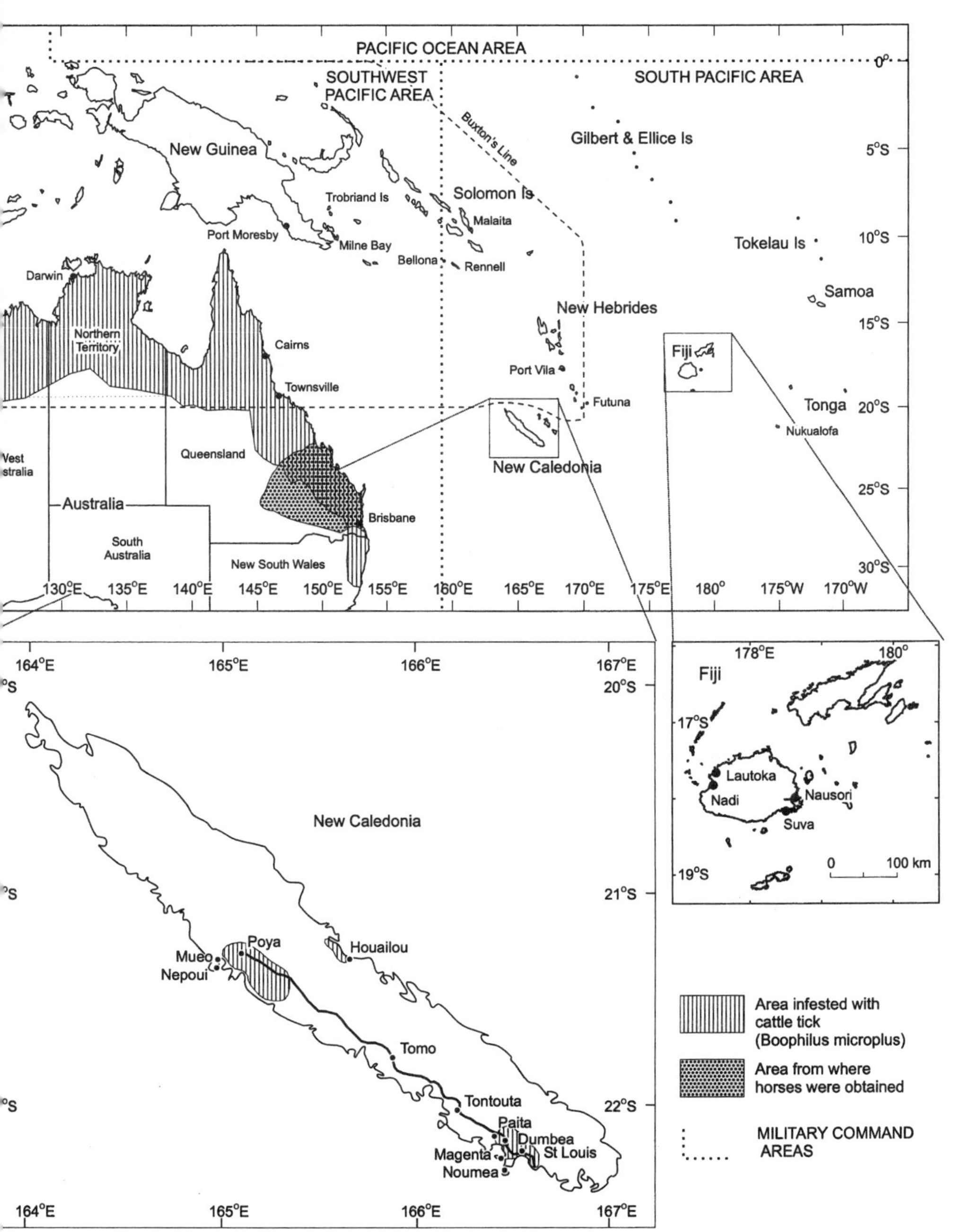

Map 13. New Caledonia, Buxton's line, and cattle tick spread.

and army officers as well as the French authorities and farmers. Fredine concluded that the ticks came from Australia on the untreated imported horses, were not in New Caledonia before this, and that no tick fever was present.[120]

U.S. command had set regulations in July 1944 whereby all animal introductions had to be quarantined by the army veterinarian, and finally, in February 1945, instructed that all animal imports be cleared with the civil administration. This was their first effective recognition of French authority, in the face of their objections not only to the horses, but also U.S. importation of pet dogs, cats, and birds.[121] The Americans conceded that if they had been responsible for introducing the tick it was under wartime emergency.[122] Despite French claims about continuing damage caused by the tick, as the war ended the diplomats had to resolve the issue. New Caledonia owed vastly more to the United States on lend-lease than the United States owed it. By agreement, in May 1946, the U.S. and the French governments used lend-lease accounting to absorb the cost of claims, including the tick infestation.[123] New Caledonia had done well in terms of tons of plant sold cheaply and infrastructure worth $3 million handed over by the Americans, but no one had accounted for all the decades of cost that the control of the tick through regular application of chemicals would require. For example, between 1944 and 1953 alone, the tick-control campaign cost the government of New Caledonia about 11.5 million francs CFP or about $2.3 million.[124]

As in New Caledonia's case, much of the immediate, apparent damage caused by the war received some kind of compensation, except for damage in the unfortunate Solomon Islands. Recompense for ecological damage is hard to calculate and was not a real issue in the war. More controllable, quarantine is difficult to achieve even in peacetime; it was an illusion in wartime. The diplomatic Mitchell in Fiji won American support to control mosquitoes, but the Free French remained suspicious of America's imperial ambitions in New Caledonia, discouraging American cooperation on animal quarantine. More generally, islands in the great ocean may have been bastions for defense, but plants, animals, and organisms slipped in amid the myriad interstices of mobile men and materials and the depleted capacity of colonial administrations. War's remains of dangerous armaments, however, were something that the combatants knew about and chose to leave. These were a heavy burden for peoples beginning their tentative journey to self-government and a continuing danger enclosed in the land and seascape. If recent discoveries of conventional and chemical weapons and the corrosion of sunken ships are any indication, more time may be needed to defeat such persistent "ravages of men and war."

CHAPTER 11

Legacies and Visions

> [W]hat the war provided was like a huge theatre . . . we gained new perceptions. . . . The conflict also brought into our backyard all the heavy equipment of war as well as various good things and the infrastructure that makes life more convenient.

> The Government considers that, before the war, not sufficient interest was taken in the Territory [of Papua and New Guinea]. . . . It is determined that natives will no longer be exploited. Apart from the debt of gratitude to the native soldiers and faithful "fuzzy-wuzzies," Australia is fully conscious of her duty to further native advancement, by providing facilities for better health, better education, greater participation in the wealth of their own country, and eventually in the government.

Historical interpretations of the impact of the war on the Pacific Islands center on the sociopolitical. They range between the extremes, on the one hand, of indigenous resistance and rejection of colonialism[1] and, on the other, relief and return to acceptance of the old certainties of colonial control—albeit with regional variations.[2] Much of the impetus for change in fact came from the colonial powers.[3] Both the process of war and the altered global geopolitical balance brought ideological shifts that motivated colonial governments to look more closely at the islands' environment in the search for resources to underwrite new development policies.

Little consideration, however, has been given to the effects of the war on islanders as a part of their environment. Did the war alter their perceptions of their environment, its resources, their use, and of its ability to afford them a satisfying livelihood in the face of new wants? To what extent did this influence their response to colonial plans and processes to increasingly exploit local resources?

From the Ground Up

For islanders the soil was their most important resource. Where adequate land existed for the old methods of horticulture to feed the indigenous people, little impetus for change emerged. Variants of swidden cultivation with a bush or grass lands fallow for ten to fifteen years were efficient and productive so long as population did not increase suddenly. Extra fertilizer was not added.[4] Prior to the war, South Pacific administrations had done scant horticultural research. The U.S. Navy administration in American Samoa had set up an experimental farm in 1932, but its greatest success was distributing improved varieties of tropical fruits.[5] Tonga was much the same, but was planning research on new crops and pastures when war began.[6] Early research in the Solomons had focused on plantation cash crops. The administration planned to "put native agriculture on a better basis" in 1940 and 1941, seeking funds from Britain under its Colonial Development and Welfare Act, the first development spending for colonies.[7] With a considerable migrant population, Fiji and New Caledonia were different. Fiji was more advanced in research, as the Americans realized when they sought to harness local production.[8] The French farmers in New Caledonia growing coffee and mixed crops, as well as raising cattle, had survived the Depression and the reduction of Indochinese indentured labor, but they were not progressive. By 1942 they were barely producing enough for the domestic market. Many cultivated areas had reverted to pasture and mechanization was unknown.[9]

Consequently, military farmers had little prior knowledge of local conditions. As in most of the humid tropics, they found that once they cleared the land,

> a considerable decrease in fertility took place, resulting from rapid sheet erosion. . . . It is estimated that per acre production [on Guadalcanal in 1945] is about ½ of what it was in early 1943, whereas twice the amount of fertilizers are necessary.

The Americans had access to prewar soil surveys of the Guadalcanal plains, done by Levers Plantations,[10] but they claimed that in relation to their wartime farming, "since this was uncultivated land at the outset, no damage can be said to have been done to it," just as they thought no damage was done to "waste" land by their borrow pits.[11] Soil surveys there in 1947 indicated that in the former American gardens, soils were less rich in nitrogen than those uncultivated nearby.[12] Had they returned entirely to fallow, nutrients would have gradually built up, but the soils in nearby areas under coconuts before the war lacked both nitrogen and phosphorus and a wartime survey supported this.[13] Despite this, significant areas of plains had good soils and just as they appealed to the military for agriculture, they also attracted the postwar colonial administration because of proximity to Honiara, the new capital. This area around Ilu became the focus of experimental cattle raising and intensive agriculture, including the takeover of the U.S. rice-growing project, which could only succeed with applications of fertilizers and irrigation.[14]

Military farming provided a model for some. As part of a new political order under a social movement called Maasina (Brotherhood) Rulu or Marching Rule, some Malaitans made large-scale gardens to provide for bigger village communities, but the order faltered as quarrels divided settlements.[15] In parts of northern Papua and New Guinea, army farms may also have accelerated interest in cooperatives and "kampani" rice-growing projects. These largely failed because of pests, lack of economies of scale, and an unrealistic "cargo-cult" ideology. Exposure to the growing of coffee at Aiyura during the war, however, certainly provided Australian gold miner Jim Leahy with the knowledge to plant this crop commercially in the eastern highlands in the late 1940s, and it went on to become a major export earner.[16]

Occasionally, the war saw new food-producing regimes imposed on communities with lasting impact. Fearful of a breakdown of order in the wake of the retreat of the colonial power in early 1942, ANGAU imposed on the people of Vanatinai (Sud-Est) Island in Papua the increased planting of starchy crops in 1944, as well as consolidated settlements on the swampy coast. Health seems to have suffered. The people's former mixed and semiwild food diet was much richer in vitamins and minerals, while their new villages left them more exposed to *Anopheles* and malaria.[17]

In Fiji, war's demands left herds diminished and the arable land in need of fertilizers, allocated in wartime to the military farms and the sugar industry. Weeds had invaded many areas because men worked elsewhere for more return. Erosion increased under more intensive farming. It took some years for the herds to recover.[18] In New Caledonia probably the greatest potential for change was war surplus machines to continue the mechanization of production, but without technical expertise and cheap labor, agriculture slowly drifted into stagnation,[19] with the pastoral sector laboring under the American-added burden of the tick pest.

Not all the knowledge of garden production in a challenging environment gained during the war endured. The Australians and Americans were beginning to accumulate data on the suitability of different vegetable strains to varying conditions.[20] On Guadalcanal, the departing Americans congratulated themselves on their legacy: "A definite benefit can be derived by the Island because of the experimentation of varieties and methods which were undertaken by the project."[21] Even so, there were not going to be twenty to sixty thousand invaders to consume these novel vegetables. The Americans do not seem to have given any details of production for the Ilu area to the British. Moreover, what the British in 1949 had started as a project to encourage native settlement and agriculture on the Guadalcanal plains faltered with the realization that American methods could only work at great cost and energy input. That cost did not include damage from cyclones, floods, and consequent soil loss, which subsequently frustrated the area's commercial use until oil palms were grown as a resilient monoculture from the 1960s.[22]

Elsewhere there was some local interest in new crops that were easy to grow. On Kolombangara and Ranogga, people today still grow watermelons that an American, William Sabel, introduced. On Bougainville the Japanese introduced a new variety of sweet potato.[23] In Fiji and New Caledonia, American tastes consolidated an existing trend. The American Samoan naval administration concentrated on growing "truck" crops at its experimental farm for navy personnel and used this to instruct students from the vocational school, including ex-servicemen, encouraging them to try such crops on their own land. In the New Hebrides, the administration freely distributed seeds in 1944 and urged the people to keep some of the harvest for seeds or to buy them from traders. With missionary support, the people sustained interest in these for their own consumption into the late 1940s, thus varying their diet.[24] American preference for such vegetables may have made them prestige foods.

Military farming introduced the islands to their first large doses of chemical insecticides and fungicides. Before the war, for economics more than conservation or organic farming, the controls of coconut pests were biological or human labor. In American and Western Samoa, as the military absorbed labor during the war, hand picking of the coconut pest, the rhinoceros beetle, ceased, and it multiplied greatly.[25] Common military farm poisons used were copper oyxchloride (Cuprox), colloidal and flowers of sulphur, and white oil (as a spreader) for fungi; arsenate of lead, nicotine sulphate, copper carbonate powder, Paris Green (a copper acetoarsenite—$C_4H_6As_6Cu_4O_{16}$), and derris (Rotenone) for insects. To control the recalcitrant green vegetable bug (*Nezara viridula*), the Australians introduced parasites (ichneumon wasps). Understanding DDT's short-term potency at least, the Australians eschewed it in their farms because of "world wide lack of accurate knowledge of its true role in pest control" and because it killed beneficial insects.[26] What was available went to malaria control. Aerial spraying methods developed by the Americans, however, were used as the war ended and in peacetime to spread DDT over American Samoa to kill filariasis-carrying mosquitoes.[27] From what we now know from Rachel Carson's *Silent Spring*, fortunate was the agriculture and associated biota of the other colonial dependencies whose similar enthusiasm for the chemical was limited by lack of suitable aircraft. DDT, though, was to return in vast quantities by hand spraying of houses in the 1960s, as administrations and the World Health Organization made futile attempts to eradicate malaria. Another "war hero," the Freon aerosol can, was a marvelous weapon against insect-borne diseases, but its proliferation worldwide, with other CFCs, in time helped to deplete the ozone layer. Yet, unlike DDT's dangers, this was not understood until the 1970s.[28]

From Islands' Forests

On land too, the Allies had used local timber supplies to supplement imports, focusing attention on western Melanesia's forests and intensifying administrative concern for the future timber resources of the smaller South Pacific islands. Wartime utilization also showed that in spite of the difficulties of terrain, modern equipment like portable sawmills, tractors, jiggers, and sky lines could achieve an output far in excess of prewar logging ventures. Initial interest in the forests faded as more established producers restarted their export trade, wartime facilities disappeared, and the territories' administrations concentrated on basic infrastructure. The extent and potential of the resource, however, were more widely known. Not only had thousands of military men gained practical logging experience, but also information assembled from loggers, botanists, and timber testers became available, such as J. H. Kraemer's *Native Woods for Construction Purposes in the Western Pacific Region*, published by the U.S. Navy in 1944 (a standard reference into the 1970s), and W. N. Sparkhawk's *Notes on Forest and Trees of the Central and Southwest Pacific Area.*[29]

With the postwar thrust for development, the utilization of forest resources was a prime objective. This thrust accelerated in the early 1960s as the United Nations pressured for a timetable for independence for both Papua and the New Guinea Trust Territory and the Solomons. The Solomons had established a forestry department in the late 1950s, just as its counterpart in TPNG was beginning to expand the surveys and botanical data obtained during the war under James McAdam. Commercial exploitation in the Solomons had to wait on the forest survey and legislation that took more than fifteen years. In TPNG most output of sawmills in the 1950s, with the exception of a joint plywood venture at Bulolo, was, as in the Solomons, for reconstruction. Large-scale extraction and log export did not eventuate until the 1960s, when a timber-hungry Japan began to dominate the market and colonial authorities offered favorable conditions.[30]

In Fiji, the war emphasized the limited control the forestry department had, since the ownership of forests other than mangroves remained with Fijians. The administration in the 1950s saw that a productive forest estate promised an economic contribution to future governments, but it had to lease it piecemeal for reforestation, a slow process that did not gather momentum until the 1960s. In the New Hebrides, deep suspicion of governments kept control of the resource with local landowners.[31] Elsewhere, the forests were really only sufficient to serve part of local needs, though some reforestation occurred on a minor scale.[32]

A more subtle outcome of wartime logging at least for western Melanesia was a raising of local consciousness of the worth of trees. Though Melanesians valued various species as food, medicine, firewood, and canoe timbers, house construction was generally with slender poles and thatched leaves. Yet they understood the potential of their trees as they snapped up surplus American milled timber for building.[33] In PNG during the war, the amount extracted as milled timber only was more than 71.7 million board feet, or averaged over four years, about 18 million board feet annually, far in excess of the pre-1941 boom maximum of 7.5 million board feet. In Solomons, the ratio was similar. At 20.6 million board feet of production of milled timber, the annual cut was more than 5 million board feet, more than double the highest prewar export figure, and those figures were of log volume exported, with a 20 to 30 percent loss in milling. Significantly, unlike the sporadic prewar peaks, these figures represented sustained production over time and over a much wider geographical area. Moreover, compensation in PNG provided a notion of what a tree was worth in cash. Except for the few places where commercial logging had existed before the war, though, this was less so in the Solomons, which had not received any compensation. A gradual realization emerged, nonetheless, that several timber species were valuable. Why else would airmen smuggle them onto planes and sailors ship them back east? In many areas, a notion of their cash value among Melanesians began at this time and reinforced existing knowledge in Polynesia.

Regaining Control of Older Resources

The war induced a transition in the beneficiaries of more established resources. The plantation economy in western Melanesia had been in the hands of expatriates, but the war added the nails to its coffin made in the Depression. Although copra prices recovered, much of the ownership began to leave expatriate hands, particularly in the Solomons. Exposed to global scrutiny, the colonial governments dealt a blow to the planters by removing the indenture system, giving workers better wages and bargaining power. Rise in postwar demand for copra and rubber coupled with newly available highland labor postponed expatriate retreat in TPNG until the late 1960s, however. Overall, plantation production gradually moved into native control.[34]

In American Samoa the administration had organized the collection and marketing of copra from 1903, with solid gains to native growers. Wartime production boards in several other territories had a similar effect. In Fiji, the farmers' cooperatives organized by the wartime administration worked well, laying the foundation of the formal cooperative movement in 1947. Cooperatives in the Gilbert and Ellice Islands saw the power of trading companies decline, which meant better profits from copra and lower prices for trade goods.[35]

The Last Frontier: Fisheries

War used the resources of both land and sea. Inshore areas of some atolls suffered from blasting to clear reefs and to obtain coral fill, lessening the food supply, but the scale is difficult to assess because prewar colonial knowledge of fisheries was poor.[36] With the exceptions of the French in New Caledonia and the Japanese in Micronesia, and mainly Indians and a few Japanese in Fiji, colonial administrations and settlers before the war had done little to expand the potential of the sea. Only the Japanese in Micronesia developed commercial, deep-sea fisheries in the Central and South Pacific.[37] This "neglect" had been a blessing, for where Western economic development theories came into vogue after the war,[38] the indigenous fishery universally declined. About a dozen prewar settler fishermen around centers such as Rabaul, Suva, Noumea, and Papeete had some form of refrigeration on vessels or shore.[39] Japanese fishermen outside Micronesia had been interned when the Pacific war began.[40] Lack of commercial exploitation, however, in no way reflected the importance of the fisheries and shellfish beds to riverine and coastal dwellers. Fish in the indigenous diet was significant, often vital, but few outsiders had studied this.[41] Hence, Wilbert Chapman's success at finding dozens of formerly unidentified species in New Georgia waters.[42] Cash-strapped colonial administrations had taken more interest in pearl shell, trochus shell, and bêche-de-mer fisheries to gather export duties. If the study of fish for food did not feature in the agenda of colonial administrations, even less did the fish habitat.[43]

The Americans in the South Pacific began to change that. Wilbert Chapman had done his surveys well. He also had details of the Japanese prewar tuna fishing.[44] As the war was ending, Chapman, armed with data, saw the huge potential of the pelagic fishery:

> tuna occurs in heavy commercial abundance in all waters of the Pacific bounded by the tropics of Cancer and Capricorn. In the case of the bluefin tuna and albacore, the area extends to the Washington coast on the American side to Hokkaido on the Asiatic coast. In the case of the Australian tuna (*Thunnus maccoyii*), the area extends to Queensland and the North Island of New Zealand . . . no food resource of equal quantity has been made available to our nation since the opening of the Middle West to agriculture. The crux of the matter . . . is how we are to secure the privilege of exploiting this resource for our fisherman.

Chapman urged a congressional committee to negotiate with the British and French for access to colonial ports and bait taking even though he believed the U.S. fisheries would not fully utilize the area for twenty-five years. A prescient man, he advised, "Foresight now will secure to us a rich resource in the future" and to act before American influence in the Pacific, in the form of naval bases, will "wither on the vine when peace replaces war in the Congressional and public minds."[45] The Americans, however, did not maintain their South Pacific bases and found enough tuna in the central Pacific and close to their west coast, protected by President Truman's extension of the U.S. territorial limit in 1948 to include their continental shelf.[46] The islanders long had known their inshore fishery, but until the 1960s, few understood the commercial value of what was beyond, and indeed behind, the Western world's preference for property rights to only the three-mile limit.

Tasting Change and Changing Tastes

Fish was a regular item in most coastal islanders' diet and they soon took to it in tins. Since the 1880s indentured labor and government employees, such as police, in most islands had eaten salted or canned meat or fish and white polished rice as part of their rations.[47] Associated with the powerful white man, imported, storable food such as canned meat and even sweet condensed milk already had a certain cachet for those who could sell their copra or labor for cash.[48] The war experience reinforced this. Particularly in the Solomon Islands and New Hebrides, where Allied occupation was comparatively long, the informal trade relationships that developed around souvenirs and local produce were creating new wants and "fictitious needs" in the Melanesian consumer.[49] The people had sampled

> many types of tinned canned goods, American clothing, combs, cigarettes, cloth, scissors, jewelry, and a host of other items common to everyday American life . . . will they ever again to work . . . for tobacco, cloth, and a rice-and-fish diet which was their pre-war lot[?][50]

Further west, where men had mainly worked on plantations in Papua and New Guinea and the western Solomons, ANGAU rations supplied 5 percent of the population while the military's bartering introduced many to canned bully beef (corned beef) and white rice, a marked difference from the predominantly vegetable diet, a dietary trend with slight variations that has grown since.[51] A similar pattern of introducing families to new foods prevailed in the New Hebrides and New Caledonia.[52] In the Gilbert and Ellice Islands, where most males at some time had worked on the plantations in the Phoenix and Line Islands or in the phosphate mine on Ocean Island,[53] wartime ruin of the *pulaka* pits and coconuts brought

Figure 25. Gilbertese children sampling Spam, November 1943 (EX. 111-SC-182993, NARA).

about "the inevitable introduction of the 'spam economy.'"[54] This was no transient taste. These atoll dwellers underwent a major dietary shift, with a nutritionist in 1949 noting, "Since the recent war, imported foods have come to more and more into fashion, particularly in the six islands in the Colony which were occupied." The combination of American money and high copra prices "have provided people with means to buy them."[55]

Food is not simply nutrition; food can represent power. Food can be produced, bought, exchanged, and consumed as a marker and affirmation of identity and social worth. The New Zealanders joked that "when the Yanks landed, the infantry went ashore first, then the ice cream machines, then the artillery."[56] Americans felt deprived if they did not have their ice cream, candy, coffee, and root beer or Coca-Cola.[57] They disliked New Zealand "sheep," labeling it "goat."[58] The Fijian fighters needed their *dalo* (taro), but settled for three times the bread issued to the Americans. Australians and New Zealanders needed their bread but in battle areas rarely fully enjoyed it, as they lacked good butter. They loathed the melt-resistant American substitute.[59] Above all, they craved their tea. Sergeant Les Clothier, fighting at Dobodura in 1943, noted sardonically in his diary, "Of course we had a cold meal and not even a cup of tea and slept in the mud. Nice country New Guinea."[60] Even when supplied with American rations, the New Zealanders

Figure 26. Aitutaki people put on feast of local food for Americans, March 1943 (EX. 111-SC-238513, NARA).

in New Caledonia had "New Zealand food"—extra tea, bread, and, where refrigeration existed, butter.[61]

These foods, associated with home, health, and social existence, were imported, as they were not part of the traditional indigenous diet. What many islanders perceived as "white man's" food appealed as much as a marker for their participation in the modern world as for its taste and convenience. Administrators rarely objected to the new foods; in the 1930s British administrators had endorsed meat eating, as they believed it helped islanders to resist tuberculosis.[62] In wartime, Tongans in the defense force became "partial to American food." Fijian commandos received American rations with the New Zealand supplement plus extra bread and cabin biscuits, and sampled novel foods such as cured bacon and cheese.[63] Desire for imported salted and preserved meat from the 1880s extended to a demand for fresh meat in places such as Fiji and the Samoas, where there were cattle herds and the "dollar" economy had boosted local incomes.[64] In Fiji, too, the consumption of canned meat and fish increased in 1943–1944 among both Indians and Fijians.[65] In the Samoas from about 1900, around the ports of Apia and Pago Pago, kegs of imported corned beef and canned fish as well as bread, rice, sugar, tea, and biscuits "had diversified ceremonial and even to some extent ordinary diet."[66] After the war, consumption soared.[67] On Upolu, where the Americans employed more than 2,400 men and hundreds of laundry ladies, what had been luxuries for the more sophisticated, affluent Samoans and part Samoans now came within reach of most. In 1942 there was a "sharp increase" in imports of "sugar, bacon and hams, biscuits, cheese, [white] flour, preserved meat" from Australia and New Zealand.[68] Introduced to canned meats in the 1880s, the Cook Islanders similarly expanded their consumption range, though the demand for sugar was as much for making "bush" beer as drinking with tea![69]

Tea heavily laced with dessertspoons of sugar, however, had already become part of the diet of prewar indentured labor, government employees, mission adherents, and sophisticated Polynesians, but it became more common among villagers in New Guinea during the war.[70] It would take years before ice cream got beyond the colonial towns, but many islanders had experienced it, and addiction to refined sugar came with the troops and their myriad gifts of candy, gum, sweet cookies, sweetened canned fruit, and "lolly water" (soft drinks) to both young and old.[71] Where few import controls prevailed in Western Samoa, merchants in 1942 tripled their prewar importation of confectionery, though some of this probably was sold to Americans.[72] Still, dental surveys in American Samoa in the early 1950s showed that dental caries increased the closer the children—whose second teeth were forming during the war—were to the naval base and the canteen.[73] By 1948, in parts of the New Hebrides, "[t]oothache now seems a new disease."[74] Local demand was such that by the 1950s, the first food factories were soft drink bottlers and bakeries.

Allied contact, especially American, intensified existing trends and introduced thousands to convenience foods, often overrefined and deficient in fiber and vitamins, but with added sugar and sodium as well as other preservatives. Not only teeth suffered. By 1950, medical researchers noted "the change from native to European food" on Rarotonga and the obesity of the population.[75] Today in Polynesia, where Spam, bully beef, and canned mutton prevailed in the war, this habit of eating fatty meat along with excessive sugar and refined carbohydrates is a significant factor in a complex leading to obesity, hypertension, coronary problems, and probably non-insulin-dependent diabetes mellitus (Type 2), with similar problems now emerging in Melanesia.[76] Equally disquieting, such food imports mean less self-sufficiency and increasing dependence on global linkages beyond the islanders' control.

Wartime military rations reinforced another consumer habit. Even more than for the Allies, tobacco signified the patriotic relationship of the warrior with the homeland, as one affronted Japanese confided. "You bloody Aussies [Australians] smoked the tobacco [from the dead] which was a gift from our Emperor." The Japanese so needed tobacco that they grew it in New Guinea.[77] For the Americans, the typical ration pack had four to nine cigarettes, and most soldiers smoked. Moreover, at the PX cigarettes sold extremely cheaply, the protected American tobacco industrialists being aware that their patriotic gesture recruited new customers seeking relief from tensions in war. To Melanesians, already addicted in the plantation-issue "twist" tobacco and their own homegrown leaf, there was no perceived risk in this, with mission sophisticates in the early 1910s using store-bought or tailor-made cigarettes like Europeans as a supposed remedy for asthma.[78] Wartime bartered cigarettes furthered reinforced consumption, as they did in the Gilbert and Ellice Islands.[79] Americans initiated Tongans into smoking and alcohol.[80] Similarly, in America Samoa the military provided "monthly smokers" gatherings at boxing matches to entertain chiefs and people where tailor-made cigarettes were freely offered, extending tobacco consumption from their home-grown leaf rolled like a cigarette to imported cigarettes.[81] For many islanders, smoking was sharing in the breath of the admired Americans, but, though it was unknown at the time, cigarettes gave a heavier dose of carcinogens and chemical residues than the cooler-burning local tobacco.[82]

Exploding the Conservation Myth?

Another kind of smoke came from fishing with explosives. These did great damage to reef structures and fish spawning grounds in the war, upsetting the ecology and perhaps causing ciguatera poisoning, with unrecorded deaths in areas of extreme disturbance.[83] Seeing labor recruiting and mission ships using explosives to fish in the 1880s, islanders adopted the practice when they could get dynamite. Few had any conception of the long-term results since, for example, they could not observe the micro-level of broadcast spawning and larval distribution on the reef. The local fish poisons, *Barringtonia* spp. and derris (*Derris elliptica*), did not damage the reef and sea-floor structures.[84] The Fiji and Cook Islands administrations had banned these from the 1920s along with dynamite, a method favored by Fijian hill people in river ponds and by the Chinese, Indians, and Japanese along the coast.[85] To supplement their own fish poisons, Cook Islanders, Samoans, and Fijians had eagerly adopted the more potent *Derris malaccensis* ("rakau Papua," "ava niukini," or "duva" respectively), probably brought home by indigenous missionaries who had worked in New Guinea.[86] Whenever they could get their hands on explosives, however, islanders had used them, a few losing those hands or hearing in the process. In New Caledonia, the governor banned explosives to prevent accidents, with nary a mention of fish stocks.[87] In the Solomons, however, the advisory council, with all European membership in 1921, wanted no dynamite licenses issued because "the use of dynamite for killing fish leads, in the course of time, to the extermination of an important food supply, in view of the numbers of immature fish which are killed."[88] By the 1920s, all administrations had made it illegal for local people to buy explosives.[89]

The war changed all that. Everywhere, particularly in the western islands, the invaders used explosives to fish.[90] The U.S. military in American Samoa saw dynamite fishing as an acceptable way to feed the people. ANGAU allowed its use to catch fish where the Japanese had destroyed native canoes and gear. On Santo, the Americans habitually used dynamite to fish for the officers' mess while New Hebrideans used grenades in river pools as a matter of course. In the western Solomons, the attitude was: "Spear too slow. Catch four, maybe five, fish. Hand grenade much quicker. Catch 100."[91] And Wilbert Chapman himself had no qualms about using dynamite in front of local residents. In wartime, administrators initially forbade the practice for fear of injury to islanders, not for conservation. Yet villagers in Papua and New Guinea, ambivalent about welcoming the indigenous strangers in the Pacific islands' regiment, reacted positively if they provided explosives for fishing.

Local people went to great lengths to get explosives. Once the AIF and the Japanese prisoners had moved out of Fauro in the western Solomons, Bougainvilleans crossed the strait, excavated buried dumps for canned rations and dynamite, and left the site in a dangerous state. Some New Hebrideans did a deal with U.S. servicemen to get TNT for fishing, but then got drunk and were found out.[92] In Western Samoa on north Upolu, fish were being killed with stolen explosives in 1943. The police observed that "explosives are the same to Samoans as liquor is to Marines"—true too, for most Pacific islanders.[93] Even when peace returned, any notions of preservation of fish habitat were forgotten when a big haul of fish was easy to get with wartime dynamite, though this was perhaps less true of people with fishing rights to the reefs.[94] In the New Hebrides, however, dynamite use continued, so much so that by the mid-1950s it had "done much harm on reefs and shallows as well as rivers and streams."[95]

At worst, conservation values in the Pacific, often limited to certain species, were susceptible to situational ethics; at best, bitter experience with new technology resulting in observable, rapid depletion was to be the islanders' only teacher. Even then, indigenous knowledge had its limitations because effect was not always attributed to human cause, such as when it was assigned to spiritual forces, or when the effect was thought to be human in origin, it was based on coincidence, in the case of bombing and the taro blight on Bougainville. As with every foreign fishing gear innovation, the people had no conservation strictures on this now readily available tool that enabled optimization of catch. Other social and organizational factors that came with Western influences eroded older practices that had limited exploitation.[96] Colonial rulers rarely understood the localized ways that enforced protection of the resources of the seas and the land. The most extreme, such as the French in New Caledonia, took property rights away, thus weakening native ways of usage and control. In spite of regulations, the rivers and lagoons were largely depleted of fish due to dynamite and fish poisons by the 1960s.[97] Often the effects of colonialism were more indirect. In Lau, Fiji, for example, master fishermen traditionally had protected the fisheries from exhaustion and controlled any large fishing parties. The British, while reinforcing the political power of the chiefs, had ignored the roles of the master fisherman as well as the *vaka vanua*, the custodian of the fruits and crops of the forest, devaluing their status. Combined with other social and economic changes, the power of such resource managers declined and their ability to protect the resource declined with it.[98] Everywhere, each new piece of fishing technology further challenged conservation, no matter how intact traditional environmental knowledge was. Moreover, in many islands, "traditional" conservation practices may have had attenuated development or been forgotten in the nineteenth and early twentieth centuries because of the often huge human depopulation from introduced diseases, with consequent recovery of some resources that earlier had been nearing their sustainable limits.

The military's demonstration effects were profound, but effects on the fishery can only be surmised because the baseline state of this was unknown to all but local communities, who have left no record. While little was known about the impact of military fishing, some saw in time that explosives and poisons had affected the fishery. The *Fono* (chiefly council) of American Samoa after the war decided that these were leading to the "gradual extinction of certain species of edible fish to the loss of the Samoan daily fare"[99] and so supported the administration's first major

> conservation measure . . . [which] prohibits the use of poisons and explosives for fishing. Since this law was passed in 1949, insufficient time has elapsed for any evaluation of the effectiveness of this measure.[100]

Unmeasured too, on uninhabited atolls, large bird populations, lightly hunted by islanders from distant islands, were decimated by airfield and garrison construction. Silent in the archives, their losses could have been comparable to Midway Island's, but no one was counting. Only in the 1990s, with the closing of Midway's garrison, have the bird populations revived. On the large high islands, however, with only a couple of years of peace, fauna recolonized their old habitats, though some of the former pet dogs of military units had crossed with the local dogs to produce wild, "repugnant creatures," unappealing to Western eyes.[101]

Whose Conservation?

In the midst of the war, some of the military had devised "conservation" plans, which did not sit well with their primary mission. Australia's General Blamey in November 1943 decided that the area between Hombron Bluff and the Laloki River in Papua should become a wildlife sanctuary with three purposes: to have an area near Port Moresby where flora and fauna would be preserved; where the troops could study the wildlife and presumably learn to survive in the jungle; and where "natural history" could be studied after the war.[102]

Ironically, all kinds of "development" work began in order to conserve—construction of a road around the lagoon, drainage, transplanting, and removal of silt from the lake, while one hundred plates of flora were prepared for the Melbourne herbarium. Soon problems arose. The local people persisted with the annoying habit of "continuing to roam the area from various directions." By mid-1944 several infantrymen wanted to transfer because they did not consider themselves "trained" for such work.[103] When the Australian government auditors came in December 1944, they were shocked:

> Apart from affording the manager opportunity to pursue his own horticultural vocation, the scheme has little to recommend it owing to the engineering necessary to construct an all type vehicle road and apparent excessive expenditure necessary for the upkeep of the reserve.[104]

When the war ended the idea did too.

In New Caledonia, FEA's Douglas Oliver believed that once the war was over and the Americans had taken all the fish they needed, they should present to the French government a plan to conserve the resource, as "the fish are a *ferae naturae*, and as such are definitely public property and charge: we are exploiting them in a foreign land."[105]

Conflicting Views and Aspirations

All the invaders were indeed exploiting resources in foreign lands. War can foreground assumptions that are moderated and even contested in peacetime. Among the Allied military, the silences in their voluminous records all declare one thing: They did not consider that indigenous people had property rights to the fish. A strong critic of colonial administrations, Wilbert Chapman extolled indigenous knowledge in relation to fish, but it did not occur to him that such knowledge implied rights. They certainly did, as both the Solomons and the Fijian administration always held. Disturbed conditions in the war zone and relocation of populations, however, meant that native claims were not easily made. Chapman and other experts even had ideas of exporting South Pacific fish to America during the war. If there were rights to fish, as Douglas Oliver hinted, they accrued to the "public," that is, the colonial state, though there is no evidence that Oliver or his superiors gave to any of these states the data he and Chapman had accumulated.[106]

In regard to the army farms, many of the same invaders did not consider that the native people had rights to the lands they occupied in forward areas, though they did consult colonial officials for advice. Since the Americans had farmed formerly "uncultivated" land, then, as they saw it, they had added value to the land rather than changing the ecology. When it came to conservation of "wildlife" in the peaceful Papuan reserve, the AIF did not consider that these lands, their fauna, and flora were in fact resources to the local people, including those who continued to "roam" across the area.

The war also revealed the long ecological shadow Australia's and New Zealand's agricultural and pastoral industries had cast on the tiny atolls of Ocean Island and the Mandate of Nauru. Britain, Australia, and New Zealand–controlled phosphate commission had supplied their prewar phosphate at cost. These atolls lost their vegetation and precious soil for a pittance.[107] Experts believed some of the residual fertility in the Australasian soils came from prewar superphosphate applications that had fed the Allies during the war.[108] In one sense then, these atolls had paid their debt and more to their tardy liberators, decades before they had incurred it.

War had accentuated attitudes to the seas and lands very different from the Pacific islanders' worldview. Some experienced colonial administrators knew this, and a few, like the forester McAdam, managed to get this across to the military.[109] In the Solomons and the New Hebrides when administrators considered local timber resource rights, it was an afterthought and one so complex that they largely ignored it. The French in New Caledonia had made the nice distinction that the local people had rights of usage but no property rights, and they do not appear to have consulted the locals when they allocated such rights to others.[110] The people were fully aware of their rights to these, yet in the war they seem largely silent. Never before had they witnessed modern warfare on an industrialized scale. Survival was more important than asserting rights. Why would they quarrel with invaders "who were quite capable of blowing them to pieces"?[111] Those who did ended up suffering or dead. Moreover, when friendly, the invaders usually brought largesse, new knowledge, and novel technologies that were worth the inconvenience of occupation, at least for a time. And, if treated well, the fabulous Americans might be coaxed into staying on.

With one exception, the inhabitants of war-damaged territories received some compensation in cash or goods from the Allies. But this introduced a novel perception: Loss of resources could be given a monetary or goods value, on a once-and-for-all basis. While concepts of compensation and reciprocity were common to Pacific societies, the idea that a government or a military force with no enduring social relationship could pay for resources reinforced the notion, already present in some areas in land transactions of the nineteenth century, that natural resources and their products, often of inestimable value in the long term, could be given a once-off cash equivalent. This commodification of resources reinforced the monetization of the economy that other aspects of the war, such as wider employment and sale of produce, intensified. The human inhabitants were modifying their perception of their environment and its resources, opening the way to later changes when decolonization loomed.

The war also highlighted fundamental weaknesses in localized indigenous knowledge. New techniques such as fishing with explosives, adopted across the islands with great alacrity, were not easily reconciled with conservation of fish or their habitat. In commercializing what had previously been mainly a clan and to some extent a community resource, such as timber, capitalism's cat was set among the subsistence exchange pigeons, challenging the value systems of these small societies, repeating in many respects the nineteenth-century process by which outsiders gained plantation land.

For the invading forces outside their own colonies, wartime occupation gave enormous scope to assess the fish and other potential resources, such as timber and minerals, of the southern Pacific islands. Those islands were small indeed in relation to the vast ocean. As Wilbert Chapman realized, it was this ocean, rather than the land, that held the greatest resource: the tuna fisheries. Under the prevailing Western notions of the law of the sea wherein states could only claim possession within the three-mile limit, this resource, this *mare nullius*, would be the most accessible to powerful foreigners.

From the Top Down

War in this oceanic world both demonstrated novel opportunities and created perils in the relationships its various human inhabitants had, and have, with their environment. War and its consequent geopolitical realignments catapulted the southern Pacific peoples into the trajectory of political independence in the 1960s through the 1980s. In 1945, powerful foreigners still dominated the islands, but when the war had begun to go in the Allies' favor, the powers nearest the islands thought of the islands' future. In 1944, Australia and New Zealand, reflecting partly the values of the Atlantic Treaty of 1941 and awareness of more international scrutiny of powers with colonial responsibilities, declared in the Canberra Pact a cooperative, planned approach for education, health, and agricultural research and knowledge dissemination for the entire region. This culminated in 1947 in the establishment of the South Pacific Commission in Noumea, supported by all colonial governments.[112] The war was eroding the barriers between the old colonial fiefdoms.

Before war ended, Australia's Labor government's minister for external territories, Eddie Ward, laid out plans for the future of TPNG, as did the secretary of the WPHC, H. Vaskess, for its territories. Overall, they had much in common: In TPNG, local government was to be a first step for the native people to learn to govern themselves beyond the limits of village and valley; major spending was to go to health and education; the public services were to be expanded and integrated between Papua and New Guinea and within the British territories; cooperatives were to be introduced or sustained; infrastructure was to be set in place; resources were to be found and assessed, and agriculture diversified with local participation and ownership.[113]

Such radical visions of native welfare and development of resources struck a hiatus the war itself had caused. War kills talent. Lack of suitable manpower in administrations hindered implementation. Some of Australia's liberal postwar policy also retarded recovery. The payment of war damages, back wages, and the abolition of the indenture system in October 1945 meant the people had little incentive to work, so the older money spinners of copra and rubber languished while plantations deteriorated even more. For the western Pacific territories of the Solomons, New Hebrides, and Gilbert and Ellice Islands as well as Fiji, Colonial Office scrutiny was a snag. Britain, unwilling to pay annual recurrent expenditure but agreeable to specific grants-in-aid, rejected or modified Fiji's plans in 1949. The New Hebrides, not officially a British possession, missed out on such grants, although the French considerably increased their spending for native health and education. Recovery to even prewar level was hard in the Solomons because of Maasina Rulu's isolationism, which kept most labor away from plantations until the early 1950s. Lack of war damage compensation did not help planters rebuild; many simply never returned. For all the information the war had brought, territory-wide surveys of resources—such as delineating native holdings as a prerequisite to commercial agriculture and forestry, as well as geological mapping—were needed, and much funding went to these essential building blocks of the economy.[114]

Such realities tempered the postwar enthusiasms of administrators, along with those of some Melanesians for a greater share in the modern world, glimpsed through war's window. Melanesian visions, however, remained embedded in enduring societal values. Thus when colonial governments, after resource surveys, allocated commercial rights to forests and minerals and even claimed lands for infrastructure siting, they faced peoples of complex and extensive kinship who believed that since they and their lands were one, they retained certain rights to them in perpetuity. So from at least the 1960s, various groups throughout much of Melanesia, wrestling with imposed programs for commodification of their environment on a large scale, opposed projected "development" of resources that would have helped the state's coffers, or wanted all royalties and even a major share of the profits, or favored negotiation on a continual basis for increasing returns for themselves or their local region rather than for the nation and for incoming and often disrespectful workers. Few of these approaches appealed to overseas investors, yet these groups of people concentrated their thinking on rent seeking rather than wealth-creating activities. Governments, both colonial and independent, found that such obduracy hindered their quest for major revenue sources.[115]

New Zealand, meanwhile, cooperated with the Western Samoans, who, as they had for decades, wanted to govern themselves. Under the United Nations from 1946, constitutional arrangements to achieve this were gradually put in place, along with significant training and localization of the public service, with independence in 1962. The Cook Islands were also independent in 1965, in free association with New Zealand. Tiny Nauru, like Samoa, was the other rare case of concerted indigenous lobbying for independence, its rich phosphate being seen as underwriting its future viability. Though Australia and New Zealand were reluctant to lose their cheap phosphate, this trust territory became independent in 1968. These precedents made gradual development needed in much of Melanesia less likely—all the more so with the United Nations preaching in 1960 that economic independence need not a prerequisite for political independence. Fiji, the wealthiest of the British possessions, continued to progress, untroubled by any serious push for independence, secure in the hope that Britain intended some form of free association with its smallest colonies.[116] But Britain, her eyes toward Europe, made it clear in the early 1960s that she was "in a leaving mood."[117] When it came to decolonization, Australia and New Zealand were obliged to be supportive because friendly stable islands governments in the region would mean their northern borders remained safe.

Movement Around and Up?

Wartime experiences began to alter islanders' visions for their futures. Employment and produce sales opportunities had brought considerable wealth—at least until 1946–47, when the bonanza began to peter out until resumed copra production provided some cash. The islanders found many new as well as familiar imported goods to spend their money on to make life easier or more socially pleasurable. Perhaps the least beneficial were Western foods, which in excess and in their refined and preserved forms have done little to improve indigenous health. Throughout, this "dollar prosperity" accelerated the transition from a predominantly subsistence to more of a money economy, stimulating aspirations for the future of more diverse wage employment and, especially in the eastern islands, of Western education and even migration to find the means to consolidate modernity.

In much of western Melanesia's emerging cash economy, the material wealth and organization of the Allies, particularly the Americans, accelerated the quest for new but multiple paths based on older epistemologies. Still, such paths were restricted to their own islands, since connections with their colonizers beyond were tenuous, severed from metropolitan centers by distance. More potent was the white labor union activism and racist assumptions in the early twentieth century against recruiting cheap Melanesian labor in Australia, a policy that had persisted to 2008, albeit for different reasons.[118] Beyond small, independent groups, there was little shared ideology or knowledge to build on to consolidate and articulate the new ideas and aspirations for modernity that wartime experiences had stimulated. Although in the immediate postwar period, Britain's and Australia's policies in the western Pacific were more development-oriented, "the vision of a bright phoenix-like future," as we have seen, faded with lack of manpower and infrastructure.[119] Western education, another door to modernity, had been slow to open for the area before the war, hindered by formidable geographical barriers, astounding linguistic and cultural diversity, and an unhealthy environment for outsiders. War indeed had left many Melanesians "adrift."[120] Several questioned why the technological superiority of the United States, as shown by rapid road construction and large-scale farming, had not been revealed by the prewar colonial administrations. Some created "cargo cults" that questioned the moral right of white men to possess wartime's vast wealth and technology, when Melanesians' ancestors were believed to be providers of all good things. In destabilizing and resisting colonial agendas, however, cults achieved little except perhaps psychological comfort. Others, galvanized by wider contact with their fellows, set up alternative localized governance structures, such as Maasina Rulu in the Solomons to assert identity, but they incurred colonial hostility when they sometimes used intimidation. Many sought to exploit new local government initiatives of the administration.[121] Not until the early 1960s did the means begin to show tentative signs of catching up to the aspirations. Government primary schools produced some young people for high school in Australia or Fiji. As new government secondary schools began to produce students, the University of Papua and New Guinea opened in 1965. A few New Caledonians began tertiary education in France, but with the franchise fully extended by 1953 following full citizenship in 1946, the population there and in the rest of the French Pacific voted in 1958 to stay with France.[122] Yet for western Melanesia, under cold war pressures, the United Nations' fashion for decolonization outran preparations and imposed it on peoples poorly equipped to advance the state-building process, including the wise use of high-value natural resources such as timber, minerals, and fish—as the past thirty years have shown.

In the eastern islands beyond Melanesia, where societies had been more familiar with foreign encounters[123] and where linkages with the world outside were several and more than three or four generations older, many Polynesians resumed the path of Western education. This equipped them to address the challenges of political independence in the 1960s and 1970s. In addition, as increasing postwar populations heavily pressured their small islands' resource base of soil, forest, and foreshore, Western education provided many with the skills needed to find work overseas. America-based Mormon Christianity, already active in Tonga and Samoa, attracted students who soon sought schooling in Hawai'i and Utah. Labor shortages in New Zealand provided opportunities for young Cook Islanders, including at least a hundred women, with three to four hundred migrating in wartime and hundreds more after, along with Western Samoans and Nuieans in the 1950s and 1960s. With the recovery of the education system, American Samoan ex-servicemen accepted the offer of further education at home. When the Fitafita disbanded in 1951, the men took the option of joining the navy in Hawai'i, with families following, an exodus of almost a thousand people, which guaranteed the securities of kinship. Reinforcing connections of those who served in the Maori Battalion, affiliated via church schools or by New Zealand capacity building, Western Samoans and Cook Islanders went to schools and universities in New Zealand on scholarships. Increasing numbers of Walliseans followed their predecessors to New Caledonia, while some Ellice Islands people went to Fiji for work and education. Some young Fijians gained scholarships overseas and ex-servicemen took up local ones. Tongans from the northern islands came to Tongatapu for schooling; by the mid-1950s hundreds of children were going overseas for further education.[124]

Wartime revelations renewed the Polynesians' curiosity for what was over the horizon, while still affirming the core values of their own societies in extending their social web. Just as they had sailed the Great Ocean in voyaging canoes, then ventured off on foreign whaling ships and steamers, the islanders after the war again were moving around, but on airplanes as well as ships. As one element in emotionally satisfying, reciprocal familial and cultural relationships, a significant proportion of their islands' wealth now comes in remittances from this mobile human resource. Arguably, their voyages have had happier social outcomes than their more homebound neighbors in the sunset lands to the west, withal the Melanesians' richer natural resources; but all are impelled by the desire for a better life that the war in part sowed and are propelled by the shrinking of resources relative to a population increase of 2.3 percent yearly, despite slowly declining fertility rates.[125]

War's legacy was profound, from seemingly minor changes, such as diet innovations, to great power realignments, dismantling of empire, visions of self-government, "development" of resources, and reassessments of the southern Pacific's role in geopolitics. The war tightened the global entanglements of the small with the great and meant the small have had to be particularly creative to negotiate their new world, where they were and still are largely perceived as a means to others' ends. The war that brought more than two million servicemen to the Great Ocean had triggered processes that soon saw the islanders and their environments further transformed, but for most of those exotic warriors, back in their homelands, the southern Pacific islands remained only a memory, frozen in wartime's frame.

PART IV

Embodying War's Environment

CHAPTER 12

Remembering Place

The Use of Souvenirs

There's nothing left for me
Of days that used to be
There's just a memory
Among my souvenirs.

The postwar fate of the islands' environment and people little concerned most servicemen. Their orientation was homewards, but they sought mementos of their experiences in these distant places on their journey to the future. On battlefields, collecting such things signaled hopes for a postwar existence. Men collected three types of souvenirs. One was the trophy, an item associated with the enemy: a water bottle or a body part. Another kind of souvenir was even more grounded in place: curios or native artifacts. The third bridged the gap between war and place. Starting at one end of the range were objects the men made themselves: ashtrays with a shell case for a base, and, closer to the natural world, shell jewelry and trinket boxes made from timber. At the other end were natural objects, such as shells and butterflies. To obtain all these the possessors had to be "somewhere in the Pacific," their address on letters home. If they obtained souvenirs and had not been there, their possession was hollow and without a voice, for it was within the personal and occasionally the public narrative of events that occurred in a specific place that such objects had meaning for their possessors and their home audience.

Spoils of the Battlefields

Almost all these souvenirs at the point of acquisition lost the use for which most were intended.[1] To their new possessors the provenance of these objects placed an exchange value on them, which was most pronounced with trophies of the enemy. With their own hierarchy of worth, some were more desired than others, and some, though desired, usually were forbidden because of a moral code their nation proclaimed as foundational to war's conduct. Even such savage activity developed conventions, and those not subscribing to such codes were deemed even more savage in the eyes of their foes. To the Allies, the Japanese were in that category because when they attacked Pearl Harbor they had not ratified the Geneva Convention of 1929.[2]

Soldiers wanted trophies. After all, much of warfare was like hunting and many had come from societies where hunting was still a masculine attribute. If not hunters and killers when they entered the services, their training made them so—or they would have no chance of surviving, let alone conquering. So in the dank jungles of the high islands and hot sands of atolls, men went stalking their human prey and trophies. Little differentiated the Allies in this quest, though the Australians believed the Americans the most enthusiastic.[3] As a battle-hardened sergeant told journalist Mack Morriss:

> If the Japs didn't know it before, they know now what the American Army's fighting for—it's souvenirs. Up there they'll shoot a Jap and he'll jump in the air and before he hits the ground they'll be all over him frisking him for souvenirs.[4]

Collecting had its challenges. First, the Allies soon learned that the only good Japanese was a dead one. Knowing that bodies would be searched, the Japanese sometimes rigged them with booby traps.[5] Secondly, relatively few soldiers were at the front where the dead were. One Australian at base in Port Moresby lamented, "It was hard . . . to get the stuff back to market as the only troops from the front line who went back were the sick and wounded and thus with nothing." Other means met the demand. Both the Australians in New Guinea and the Americans in the Solomons, for example, made their own Japanese flags and traded them with their unsuspecting fellows.[6] When the Australian infantrymen on their six shillings daily wage saw the U.S. demand for valued Japanese swords soar to £50,[7]

> one of our base workshops in Moresby started to manufacture swords, which by far were the most sought after articles. They did this in style with an assembly line and a weekly output target. The blades were made of car springs, beautifully shaped by the blacksmiths . . . often better and more beautifully finished than the genuine article.[8]

These blades were probably as good as the ordinary swords of the Japanese infantryman. In World War II, however, the Japanese had mass-produced swords from foundry steel without the adornment and strength of the hard-forged ones, the pride of ancient warriors and, from the sixteenth century until the Meiji restoration in 1868, the samurai class. Sword carrying by the Japanese soldier imbued him with the ethics of that warrior class. Antique swords of high quality were family heirlooms and were usually owned by Japanese commanders, though some officers had swords (*gendaito* or *kindaito*) made in the traditional way but produced during the war.[9]

Such swords were the ultimate trophies. After the surrender, the commander of the AIF 3rd Division, General Bridgeford, presented a sword surrendered by Colonel Takahashi of the 6th Japanese Division to the senior AIF chaplain, J. V. Robinson, at Torokina, Bougainville, along with "a Navy blade of a Commodore of the Japanese Marines" "as mementos of his appreciation." Fujiwara Mitsunaga Samura in c. 1595 had made the Takahashi sword and Rinshu Chogun Narisade made the other at about the same time. Other captured swords went to other chaplains in the division. For their new possessors these had a metonymic quality—the defeat of Japan, the triumph of good, the end of killing, all this distilled in weapons handed to Christian chaplains who had proclaimed the gospel amid battle. For Robinson, the gift of Takahashi's sword was the fitting coda to the war because the Japanese colonel had been among the perpetrators of the Rape of Nanking in 1937, when Japanese soldiers slaughtered between 260,000 and 400,000 Chinese and raped 20,000 to 80,000 women.[10] Australians knew about this atrocity and many invoked it like a mantra to keep fighting in the heat and slime of New Guinea, fearing what the Japanese would do to their own womenfolk.[11] And they knew about it because an enclave of Westerners, mainly Christian missionaries in Nanking, had taken photographs and written of the atrocities for the media.[12]

Orders stipulated that neither individuals nor units were to help themselves to these prized swords.[13] The AIF's chief of staff directed that swords taken at the surrender in the Southwest Pacific were to be accompanied by a written account of each ceremony, to be forwarded to the Australian War Memorial, in the capital, Canberra, across from the federal parliament. Allied photographers recorded the events.[14] When the Japanese surrendered in New Guinea, the Australians collected the weapons for distribution to units involved in engagements. At Rabaul, units received seven thousand weapons.[15] Some distributions saw swords dispatched to various military establishments in Australia.[16] The better quality trophies, often with their official mini-histories attached telling of how, when, and where they were obtained, became part of the public narrative about the war. Atop the hierarchy of exchange—rewards and prizes for outstanding individuals, units, and the nation—these swords of the Japanese are still retained by the victors.

As servicemen tried to obtain trophies, trade rapidly developed and market conditions prevailed. A Samoan marine traded his savings of $450 to a Seabee for a sword, his "one tangible contact with the great battles that had taken place to the west."[17] In the home of enterprise capital, the American magazine *Time* in June 1944 offered Pacific Market Notes, ranking "Samurai sword, fancy" high at $800 to $1,000 though a "[s]niper's rifle with telescope sight" was quoted at $700 to $1,000. Plain samurai swords went for $500 to $700 and a "Nambu machine gun" was going for $300 or six quarts of hard liquor. Collections of various Japanese small objects "were still going on New Britain" for "fresh eggs, steaks, oranges, canned goods."[18] Among themselves, the Allies were constantly trading such less valued trophies. Where the Japanese circulated their own currency, the Allied troops bartered with the native people for it. Money worthless as currency suddenly as souvenirs had higher value than Australian and American money, which must have been puzzling to those New Guineans with little experience of a cash economy. To underscore the worthlessness of the Japanese currency, the Australian army officers burned bundles of it in front of the people.[19]

Troops with desirable items could use them for other wants. On New Year's Eve 1942, friends of war correspondent Robert Miller deputized him to take a Japanese rifle to the HMAS *Hobart* at Guadalcanal to trade for alcohol.[20] Seabee entrepreneurs would buy Japanese souvenirs from enlisted men and sell them to others "at a profit, which is a common practice on the island [Guadalcanal]."[21] At Nissan, "one enterprising youth" in the New Zealand unit sold a Japanese antitank rifle to an American for $100.[22] Both New Zealanders and Americans cultivated relations with the Fijian commandos because they were "a ready source of highly prized Japanese souvenirs."[23]

Overenthusiastic marketing of souvenirs could threaten relationships between Allied commands, however. In October 1944, as the U.S. forces withdrew from New Guinea and handed over equipment to the Australians, the AIF command was concerned about troops frequenting American areas "offering trophies . . . for sale." They were told that "peddling of wares is to cease immediately."[24] Another command concern was the potential loss of intelligence when men scoured the battlefield for papers from dead Japanese. Diaries, maps, and notes could tell of the enemy's morale, strength, and plans. In the Munda campaign, "there was a large amount of traffic, bartering and selling of souvenirs," some of which the men attempted to post to areas outside the combat zone, to be foiled by the censors. English translations of material designed to "portray the moral [*sic*] of enemy troops" were reproduced and distributed to counteract the taking of documents.[25] In New Guinea after the Americans secured Manus, they seized a building full of

Japanese propaganda and twenty cases of documents for intelligence scrutiny, but they discovered that their men had taken other papers. Command found a compromise:

> The troops of the Division have been very cooperative in turning in documents, and by giving them something of this nature, which have no intelligence value, we have been to do away with the tagging of documents for return to them. Most of the propaganda material is obscene and definitely has no affect on our troops other than to give them a good laugh at the "corny" pictures and verses.

Though Japanese documents were genuine, their value to the soldier who hoped to tell a good story to the folks back home was lessened by the fact that no one could read them—whereas propaganda, in quaint English, combined entertainment value and authenticity.

So long as security was not compromised, officers and ranks shared the ancient military ethic that warriors had earned their spoils. During the March 1944 landing at Momote in Manus, U.S. Navy men hacked off parts of a Japanese Zero plane on the airstrip. Some went up and down the airstrip and coastline "as if obsessed, grabbing everything they could get their hands on."[26] An inquiry proved sympathetic to the culprits. The commander concluded that although offenders should be reprimanded, any material taken should be tagged, checked for intelligence purposes, and returned to them. Moreover,

> the Seabees as a whole may not be militarily trained or "souveniringly disciplined," but in the landing at Momote, they were instrumental in holding the beachhead. . . . These men had never been in a front fighting line before but they unhesitatingly went in, had casualties but held the enemy.[27]

When it came to trophies, the Japanese had been the same; they had collected photographs and field pieces from the dead American marines on Wake Island.[28] By 1944, however, many who survived in the Solomons and New Guinea had directed their vanishing energies to stripping the dead and foraging for food rather than for souvenirs. American troops too in extreme conditions, such as the first months after the Guadalcanal landing, looted "their own buddies";[29] if any souvenirs resulted they have become part of the silences of men who would rather forget what haunts some still.

Trophies were visible proofs of a rite of passage and many gloried in them. After the 9th Division of the AIF took Finschhafen in September 1943:

> The boys did well for souvenirs in Kakakog. Goodness knows they deserved to, after the fight they put up. There were few who didn't have their captured Jap rifle, water bottle, medical kit or gas mask. . . . Many chaps wandered about decked in captured marine uniforms, their pristine whiteness contrasting with the muddy stained dinginess of jungle uniforms.[30]

The authorities disallowed few Japanese objects, though any munitions had to be disabled and given a "souvenir stamp" so the men could keep them. The Americans did the same with certificates for "material trophies." Although shipping live munitions and arms to the homeland was forbidden, some slipped through.[31]

A few did not like taking souvenirs from dead Japanese, occasionally out of respect, but more often from detestation or repugnance of rotting flesh.[32] Usually such men had not been in battle or perhaps were concerned with the sensitivities of loved ones. As one corporal wrote to his wife:

> haven't collected any souvenirs as yet, not an easy job to collect, the idea of taking anything which the ugly yellow ### have no further use for is something I cannot bring myself to do.[33]

As with any valued object, men worried about their loss. Lieutenant Hauer of the small ships coy of the AIF had many opportunities at the war's end to collect souvenirs, but when he reached Lae he found:

> My gear arrived from Torokina. . . . I mean what was left of it, all my tortoise shell, and the wee gadgets I had made were missing, 4 Jap watches, a half a Jap parachute and a lot of other things, if I do get back to the unit there is sure going to be a row.[34]

When an engine of his plane cut out on his way to Hawai'i, one diarist's "first thought" was that "all the souvenirs which I had worked so hard to collect will be lost."[35]

Like Hauer, men had plans for their trophies, some not all that different in display terms from the national trophies of the fine Japanese swords. But the ordinary man pitched his personal narratives to the imagined future with himself in the center. This setting was less about the Japanese as about what the possessor of the souvenir had done in the Pacific. One man collected a clip of Japanese rifle ammunition and a map to send to his son.[36] Another told of how he found a Japanese flag in a box at General Kanda's headquarters on Bougainville. He assured his girlfriend in Australia that the emperor of Japan had presented it to Kanda after the Nanking conquest. The Australian planned a new use for the flag.

Figure 27. Australian going home from New Guinea with souvenirs (AWM 1944, 138).

> Maybe I'll let you make some pants out of it, you'd look lovely in 'em especially if you made 'em so the red spot would be at the rear, gee that would make a good target for me when I come home at nights.[37]

This souvenir gave his war experience authenticity and focused his thoughts on the extension of his prospective life. Eroticized in its new setting, it represented the life urge. The most intimate souvenirs of the Japanese, however, negated their life and represented destruction of their significance as social beings. Fijian infantryman Viliame Lomasalate tried to butcher two dead Japanese to share for eating with his companions, but was restrained. He later scooped out the eye from a dead Japanese and ate it, an annihilation of personal worth.[38] But this was not confined to atavistic reversion to pre-Christian Fijian traditions. Body parts and photographs of the Japanese dead were, for the American hunter, the perfect trophies. Just as Americans had mounted stag heads on their walls or were photographed beside a big fish catch at home, so they did with the enemy in the South Pacific.

In Australia's fighting history to the 1940s, no foe was as much despised as the Japanese; Americans and New Zealanders felt the same. The Japanese were fair game.[39] The taking of their body parts was what they deserved, unlike the other enemy, the Germans, who were considered far more human.[40] On Guadalcanal, "they [Marines] shot a sniper 100 yds from him and before he could get there they were kicking his teeth out for souvenirs. . . . At the 35th I saw a Jap ear passed around."[41] This was not an isolated incident, as a diary of an officer telling of the U.S. assault on the Japanese on Tulagi in August 1942 attests.

> Those troops of ours seem to have no discipline under fire. They were running around with half a dozen Japs' ears tied to their watch chains. One sailor had a Jap head that he wanted to shrink.[42]

Skulls, bones, and gold-filled teeth made their way home. Skulls stamped "Made in Japan" were sold at a souvenir outlet the Americans ran on Guadalcanal.[43] Such disrespect for the enemy was against the Geneva Convention, which the Allies supported. In 1943, *Life* magazine showed a photo of a soldier's girlfriend con-

Figure 28. Marine searching Japanese dead for souvenirs. Note canned stew is part of U.S. "C" rations, suggesting that the Japanese had taken this from the Americans (courtesy of Peter Flahavan).

templating a Japanese skull. When a well-wisher gave President Roosevelt a letter opener made from a Japanese bone, the president returned it and advised that it be given burial.[44] Grist to the Japanese propagandists, such reports incensed their population and produced "tears of indignation." In early 1944 the U.S. command reminded all units of the regulations for burial of enemy dead.[45] Australians had a better reputation in Japan for having respected the remains of the Japanese in a midget submarine that attacked shipping in Sydney Harbor in May 1942. But as censors picked up Japanese skulls and body parts coming into Australia, it was likely that the Japanese government could find out and take reprisals against Allied POWs. Intelligence "listening posts" monitored Japanese broadcasts to Australia that appealed to the mothers, questioning how they would like the remains of their dead to be so disrespected.[46]

Most remains went to the homelands in kit bags. Photographs were most portable. These ranged from showing "soldiers with skulls impaled on bayonets" and "atrocities," dead Japanese, and handcuffed prisoners of war. These and similar photographs, because of their content, violated the Geneva Convention and were censored. Originating at the front and usually involving the military's

Figure 29. American servicemen return from souvenir collection on battlefield at Kiligia, New Guinea, April 1944 (Australian War Memorial Negative No. 072100).

Figure 30. Marines cleaning a Japanese skull for a souvenir (courtesy of Peter Flahavan).

photographic units, men sold entire sets.[47] When the first sick returned to the U.S. Naval hospital in San Diego from Guadalcanal in 1942, similar photographs were found on them. In Auckland, U.S. Marines sold sets of eight to fifteen pictures for $10 to $15. RAAF personnel on Goodenough Island were selling to the Americans photos of captive Japanese taken at Milne Bay in 1944. Censors and intelligence officers did their best to clamp down on this, and the AIF court-martialed the men involved.[48]

The censor was at work too when, to raise money for the Comforts Fund for the AIF, an Adelaide store in 1943 organized a display of war photographs and souvenirs loaned by the public. He was ready to examine the photographs, but was surprised to learn that he was also responsible for checking parts of Japanese planes, munitions, and the like in case there might be something displayed that would breach security.[49] Hometown friends of U.S. servicemen also organized displays of souvenirs to applaud their courage and reinforce the country's will to win. Back from Guadalcanal, Joe Bernard, who had killed seven Japanese, lent his Japanese sword, flag, money, amulet, and photographs taken from the dead to the

Roosevelt Hotel in New Orleans, where they went on display, flanked by two marine guards.[50]

Samples of Island Places

Trophies of the enemy were a code signaling their conquest; they also implied the victor's survival of the threats of a foreign place. Yet in terms of their original purpose, the Japanese objects souvenired could have been obtained in Tokyo or Tulagi. What located them in place was the story of how they were obtained, which was personal to their new possessors. Curios or artifacts of the Pacific islands had more specificity. Made of local materials and even in the modified forms that were offered to the military, they spoke of their general provenance, an exotic, seductive place of natural and human danger. The climate, the terrain, the flora and fauna of the islands, made life difficult for foreigners. In the preconceptions of the invaders, the natives were at best primitive and at worst savage, but always strange, always "other." Amid Melanesia also lurked the enemy, infusing any benign aspects of the landscape with potential menace. Thus the native objects that went home were redolent of a simpler society as well as symbols of their possessors' survival outside their own familiar place. Obtained in war, they were far more suggestive than objects from the usual touristic experience, because no sane peacetime tourists are sent into battle, knowingly putting their own lives in peril and setting out to kill.[51] Soldiers who before the war had never left their home towns or farms knew these were potent objects: "These [souvenirs] were eventually mailed home by ship . . . to be admired and exclaimed over by those at home as being something our boy overseas had sent."[52]

From Bora Bora to Buna, from Tonga to Tarawa, the most sought-after object was the grass skirt.[53] To the invaders, fed by images of Hollywood's "hula" dancers, the skirt equaled the dancer, inviting and compliant, who in turn embodied the soft charm of some tame Pacific island in the deep oceans of the white man's imagination. In Tonga the grass skirt, *sisi pueka*, was worn for dance performances certainly, but few servicemen agreed that image was the daily reality once they had seen strapping Polynesian women in their cover-all dresses or watched a Melanesian woman smoking a pipe with a breast over her shoulder to feed a baby slung on her back.[54] But the home folks were not "somewhere in the Pacific," and they wanted grass skirts.

When Robert Miller visited a Nggela village his party was made welcome; "one woman with breasts down to her hips and wearing a grass skirt bought food into the house." He later crossed to north Guadalcanal going west, passing the abandoned battlefields and the devastated Visale mission and then sailed south to Wanderer Bay:

> The coming of the boat was a great occasion and everyone came down to the beach to welcome us. I got Shirley a grass skirt at Wanderer's [*sic*] Bay which she had been wanting for some time.[55]

Along with the erotic appeal, the grass skirt, at least in western Melanesia, also had an association with the primitive, the dangerous, and the scandalous. "Have a lot of natives around and am getting hold of grass skirts, war clubs, etc. We had one in today who told us about the last man he ate," so a jaunty John F. Kennedy wrote to his parents amid a discussion about the qualities of U.S. generals.[56]

So great was demand that a cottage industry sprung up near military camps. In the Morobe district of New Guinea, operations necessitated the relocation of Butibum, Kamkumung, Yange, and Angere villages. By mid-1944 in the composite community "a grass skirt factory was in full swing." Another "factory" was at nearby Wagam village. The skirts retailed at 2/-. An ANGAU officer, trying to balance the call for more laborers for the military and keeping the subsistence gardens going, found that this lucrative occupation was a new economic complication in a male-dominated society. He calculated the social effects when "an aged female native in her spare time can earn 15/- a week –£3 a month. . . . Her virile strapping son, at work with ANGAU, is getting 10/- p. m."[57] Further north near Finschhafen the situation was the same, with grass skirts and bows and arrows being mass-produced.[58]

Prices for skirts varied; different quality, naïveté of the purchasers, experience of the sellers, varying demand, and access were all factors.[59] Near Port Moresby in late 1944, a newcomer complained:

> Visited a native village and one of the boys tried to sell me a grass skirt for 10/-. They want money for everything. . . . The money is no good to them, they just like to have it. Some of them are worth hundreds.

Higher prices prevailed in the isolated Gulf district, where the AIF guarded the mouth of the Lakekamu River, the beginning of the overland supply route to Bulldog and Wau. The local headman, Jack, needed no instruction in monopolizing sales. He controlled the trade and "grass skirts were the most popular" at £1, or $2. "He got 15/- and the native who traded it 5/-. Probably the woman who made it got nothing."[60]

On Guadalcanal, with most of the fighting over in late 1944, Solomon Islanders were "selling grass skirts to G. I.'s at fabulous prices."[61] To meet demand on Mono (Treasury Island), the local people learned how to make them from Guadalcanal men in the SIDF, so clearly men had turned their hands to women's work for gain.[62] In order to get sales they added color. Around Munda they dyed them yellow using atebrin tablets.[63] In the New Hebrides, the administration, anxious to keep plantations producing, found that this low-paying work was no longer attractive to the men, who were busy retailing curios and grass skirts for $5 each.[64] In January 1944, the British resident went so far as to forbid the manufacture of native artifacts, which caused a stir because it interfered with local as well as U.S. trade networks. Grass skirt making was women's business and a major local trade item of women in the southern district, mainly Tanna, so this, the missionaries claimed, could not interfere with the supply of men offering to work.[65] The high commissioner in Suva disallowed the regulation, telling the resident that it was "harsh and intolerable and unjustifiably interferes with the liberty of the natives." More pertinent perhaps, it was "strongly objected by the United States authorities in the New Hebrides."[66]

The New Hebrides administration had tried briefly to force the native people not to make grass skirts and other curios. In Abemama in the Gilbert Islands, the Japanese forced the people to make curios for them. A native later told the British district officer, his understatement reflecting the depth of their suffering: "Most women in Abemama had little idea how to make mats, fans and baskets. That was altered. All women became skilled in native crafts."[67] Yet they turned their oppression to more rewarding pursuits when the Americans came buying and were keen to pay.[68]

In western Melanesia, where the demand remained high for extended periods, traditional art soon became "tourist art." Carvers produced "spurious native curios" that were less labor-intensive than they had been.[69] Carvings and masks were cruder in execution and often in subject matter. Prewar observers noted the change:

> Many of the natives are artists and craftsmen. The over flow of troops among the natives has not had a good effect among native craftsmen. The troops will buy anything and pay prices out of all proportion to the value of the work, so for the most part the craftsmanship is deteriorating.[70]

In the Trobriand Islands, Papua, where sexuality is less constrained than in most other Melanesian societies, the district officer on Kiriwina bemoaned the loss of "the fineness, artistry and originality" of the carvers. In its place, while the Americans were buying, "a twisted root will provide an inspiration, sometimes good—mostly pornographic . . . some of the vilest obscenities were exhibited in all sorts of places." After they left, "without interference they [carvers] have put off this evil except for a few examples of fornicating pigs."[71] Elsewhere too, the prewar quality soon reappeared because the bulk of such work had its own social and ritual meaning, often destined for internal trade networks that the war had disrupted.[72]

Neither fornicating pigs nor people were common subjects for carvers in the Polynesian islands that had long espoused Christianity. Islands such as Fiji, Tonga, Samoa, and Tahiti had traded artifacts with sailors since the first Europeans came to the Pacific, as had their counterparts in coastal Melanesia.[73] Before the war in Melanesia there had been some tourist trade along the routes of the steamer companies, such as Burns Philp Pty. Ltd., as they picked up copra and transported the white settlers.[74] As early as the 1870s several Christian missions had encouraged local craftwork to sell for a little cash for their followers' needs, including support of local churches.[75] New Caledonia, with its mobile population of military, colons, and liberated convicts, had a thriving trade in 1878. The convicts started to make their own curios of inscribed shell as the nineteenth century ended.[76] In Polynesia, curio making was underway for collectors swarming across the islands in the 1870s.[77] By the 1900s, steamships began bringing tourists to the main islands. They had little trouble buying souvenirs in towns such as Suva, Pago Pago, and Papeete, often retailed by middlemen—people of mixed descent, Europeans, the Indians in Fiji, or the Chinese. Mainly "tourist art," these war clubs or models of canoes, as well as pandanus mats, salad servers, napkin (serviette) rings, trays, food bowls, coconut shell buttons, cigarette cases, humidors, and trays, appealed to servicemen.[78] Under the naval administration, American Samoa had an organized craft cottage industry before the war to cater in part to more than fifty ships annually. When the price of copra continued low, as it did across the Pacific from 1929, this supplemented the earnings of the Samoans. Along with private merchants, the Department of Native Industry encouraged uniform prices and standards. Selling to visiting tourists declined when shipping fell off by a least a third with the outbreak of the war in Europe in 1939, but the bulk of Samoan craft found their duty-free markets in U.S. territory or bases in Honolulu, Guantanamo, and Panama. Though facilitated by the administration, much of this business was in the hands of private operators such as the E. W. Prichard Curio Trading Company, which sold *lauhala* (pandanus) mats and curios to Honolulu dealers.[79]

When the U.S. military base opened on Tutuila and American Samoa became a transit point for ships crossing the Pacific, the curio economy initially collapsed, the Department of Native Industry closing for the duration. Obtaining curios during the early war period was as difficult as getting the people to work their gardens because "defense work" paid far more and transportation was curtailed.[80] In the villages, women who had made the mats and baskets made a lot more money billeting U.S. marines and doing their laundry. By 1943, however, the production of "hula skirts," tapa, mats, and model canoes increased with the intensified transit of ships. But Samoans were playing a game with master traders. Increasing prices saw the military government introduce "a schedule of prices posted to protect service personnel."[81] This was aided by purchasing most curios for sale through the PX store, with the American units taking a 10 percent commission for their own "welfare."[82] In neighboring Western Samoa, Apia became the center of "the large-scale manufacture and sale of island souvenirs."[83]

In Tonga, Queen Sālote encouraged handcraft making to raise money for the Red Cross, Comforts Fund, and for the Spitfire Fund.[84] The American privates on about $10 daily were such high payers that the New Zealanders on seven shillings a day found it hard to compete. In spite of controls in the rest of the cash economy, artifact prices rose—less from the Tongans' demands and more from the Americans having no idea of the value and nowhere else to spend their money.[85] Greater familiarity reduced payment, but the New Zealanders still had to lobby to have a Red Cross bazaar postponed until the U.S. force had moved out so they could get curios at more affordable prices.[86] First-class handcraft, the fine mats were hard to obtain because of their significance in customary rituals. They represented much female labor as well as history. A new fine mat could cost 36/6, more than five times the New Zealand infantryman's daily wage.[87] Military leaders were keen to obtain quality souvenirs. Queen Sālote gave directions that some of her women were to make certain fine tapa (*ngatu*) pieces, which the Americans called "rugs," to give to Admiral Nimitz. When these did not appear when expected, the navy made inquiries and added to the order "two extra La Hala [*sic*] rugs" and "three rather simple pattern tapa mats, about the size of bedspreads for Fleet Admiral Nimitz," for which payment would be made.[88]

Elsewhere, other attempts were made to regulate the market. Crews of U.S. airplanes refueling at Aitutaki bartered so intensely with the locals that the command promised to control it by taking the goods off the crew when they reached Hawai'i, probably to get the islanders back to working their gardens.[89] When the Manihiki people learned that the Penrhyn people were selling the "shoddiest" curios, they made and shipped "several tons" of quality goods that the Americans on Penrhyn snapped up.[90] Cook Islands manufacturers also sent off bulk orders to their kin working in Auckland where Americans paid good prices.[91] In Fiji, the British introduced price controls, but New Zealand troops saw the price of store goods including curios in Indian shops go "sky high" when the Americans arrived.[92] In parts of western Melanesia, commanders, with the administration's backing, tried to control retailing with set prices for artifacts, but not solely to distribute curios or cash more equitably.[93] To keep natives out of bases and prevent U.S. personnel from stealing from villages, troubling the women, and pilfering supplies for bartering, the military set up "native trading centers" on Pavuvu, Russell Islands, and at Hombu Hombu Island, off Munda.[94] On Guadalcanal, trading in artifacts was confined to the "highway" during daylight on Sundays.[95] The administration assisted people distant from bases by purchasing artifacts to sell in government-run "trade" stores, making attempts to travel to centers like north Guadalcanal less likely.[96] In New Guinea, ANGAU mediated sales "where practicable."[97]

Lack of sales regulation in New Caledonia, however, threatened the relationship between the Americans and the administration. By 1943, French shopkeepers charged decreasing retail prices for souvenirs to U.S. officers, U.S. soldiers, and French servicemen respectively. Through their connection to Tahiti business firms, New Caledonian dealers imported curios. The army PX store also obtained supplies made in Tahiti. The military had the privilege of not paying import duty on articles from the U.S. sold in the PX. When the New Caledonian administration found that souvenirs from other Pacific islands were being sold, they complained that these should have incurred duties. Moreover, the PX prices undercut the importers of the Tahitian goods, forcing one New Caledonian company in September 1944 to cancel a contract with a Tahitian firm worth 280,000 francs. Realizing the political ramifications, the U.S. commander, Brigadier General Barnett, agreed to Governor Tallec's request to pay import duty.[98] In their correspondence, the French revealed that the souvenirs being retailed were created largely to fit the market's idea of what a native artifact was. These "articles de fantaisie en provenance des isles du Pacifique" were "tourist art," not the useful objects of daily or ritual life in Tahiti or elsewhere.[99]

Few servicemen worried about the authenticity of manufacture of such articles. James Michener's "Bloody Mary" was no literary figment.[100] In New Caledonia, New Hebrides, and Tahiti, French farmers and Tonkinese made "native" artifacts to sell. Chinese as well as Tahitians took boatloads of curios from Tahiti to the U.S. garrison on Bora Bora.[101] In Fiji, Indians made and sold some of the supposed Fijian artifacts; dealers imported Indian bangles into Western Samoa to sell to the Americans. On Makira in the Solomon Islands, the district officer in 1944 purchased artifacts to sell elsewhere to the Americans. He soon left middleman work to the displaced Solomon Islands' Chinese, who made artifacts as well as purchasing from the people. So brisk was their trade that they neglected their food gardens. These then sent "curios" by mail to Chinese employed by the U.S. forces on Guadalcanal, who were then able to sell direct to the troops—at a profit.[102] The American Seabees in the Solomons went one better: They manufactured the "native" artifacts, such as clubs and walking sticks, buffed them with black boot polish to give the appearance of "ebony," and found they could get a better price by selling them to "supposedly ignorant savages" who in turn retailed them at a profit to novice GIs.[103] As long as "artifacts" looked "Pacific" and exotic, purchasers were happy.

Few of the island curios had much practical value back in the homelands of the troops. Some ended up hanging on walls. One soldier from clothing-rationed New Zealand bought saris from Indians in Fiji for his fiancée's wedding dress and

Figure 31. American Elmer Williams at souvenir stall and newsstand with *Life* magazine, Noumea, New Caledonia (Album, Elmer J. Williams, 1Num 12 y, Collection, Archives of New Caledonia).

that of her bridesmaid.[104] But most souvenirs from the islands, once out of their origin, were mainly aids to memory, objects encapsulating an exotic experience within the context of wartime perils for formerly little-traveled young men, of value for display. Some experiences were deeper than others. Soldiers on garrison duty where mingling with the local people was possible had more chance and time to observe.[105] Malcolm Foord, writing from Tonga to his wife in New Zealand, told her that he had sent her a piece of tapa cloth. "What we're going to do with it heaven knows, but if we build a cottage like the Tongans do there would be plenty use for it." He detailed how tapa was used in Tongan homes and how and from what it was made.[106] In Foord's narration then, and more recently through memory, the possessor was reunited with place.[107]

Collecting the Native

On Manus some collectors donated native artifacts and Japanese gear to the base museum, which was well secured from thieves.[108] By and large, though, in the midst of a lush yet to them uncivilized landscape, the fighting men thought little of Western repositories of cultural objects. A few, however, brought their civilian interests with them, gathering artifacts and passing them on to U.S. museums.[109] Charles T. Downer, with prewar connections to the Cleveland Museum of Natural History, donated items from Papua New Guinea after the war.[110] The largest collection of artifacts amounted to several tons of material from the Solomon Islands and New Hebrides.[111] The collector was Lieutenant John Burke of New York, who was based in the Solomons. Before the war, he had lectured in history at the University of Columbia, with connections to anthropologists Margaret Mead and Harry Shapiro at the Museum of Natural History in New York. In 1943 he was involved in naval duties on Nggela in the Florida Islands. At six feet two inches tall, the ebullient Burke was for a time in charge of native labor, winning the confidence of the Melanesians and supposedly urging Malaitans to question British rule. He returned to lecture on labor relations at Princeton University in late 1944 and came back to the Solomons in early 1945 as staff historical officer, writing several base histories. He was to die in early April 1946 on Guadalcanal when the C-47 plane carrying him crashed.[112] As part of his historical work the navy had appointed him collector of Japanese and U.S. militaria for the projected naval museum in Washington D.C. Burke used this opportunity to collect native artifacts while the military artifacts became secondary.[113]

Timing was on Burke's side as by the second half of 1945 the United States was rapidly disposing of surplus. The navy command in the South Pacific encouraged donations to "hospitals, missions, etc.," and that they "might show their appreciations by donations to the new Museum . . . particularly appreciated will be old carvings of men or Gods, weapons, tapa cloth and any artifacts of daily life," to be shipped to Burke.[114] So Burke and his team donated medical and building equipment to missionaries and in return obtained artifacts from the people.[115] He also traveled extensively as an adviser to a congressional naval affairs subcommittee, with war disposal teams, and with parties searching for downed pilots. Through these connections he amassed a huge amount of material, some of it not seen by him until after collection. Burke fell out briefly with the British administration over his unauthorized seizure of munitions stored on Rennell Island, but an apology smoothed this breach, as the British saw the value of surplus to the local

Figure 32. Lt. John Burke with Kanak artifacts he was not able to acquire at Catholic Mission, St. Louis, New Caledonia (EX. 80-G-275588, NARA).

Figure 33. Artifacts made on request for John Burke, Ontong Java, Solomon Islands (EX. 80-G-275718, NARA).

people and missions. Although there were colonial policies to prevent the collecting of artifacts older than two years, the officials largely ignored Burke's activities as they too were keen to get surplus at good rates and thus did not want to make his collecting a political issue.[116]

Even though Burke's project to "collect carvings which are unique and which no American Museum has or which can obtain again" was successful, the naval museum did not want them.[117] Most went to the Museum of Natural History and some to the Peabody Museum of Salem. Burke also sent certain objects to Rene d'Harnoncourt at the Museum of Modern Art. The Museum of Modern Art later made the most of U.S. interest in the Pacific. From January to May 1946, it mounted an exhibition, Arts of the South Seas, with assistance from the Rockefeller Foundation. This later traveled elsewhere in the United States and included four of the pieces Burke collected.[118]

In the exhibition's catalogue, the organizers acknowledged that in an earlier time, these "distant islands of the South Seas" had evoked thoughts in Americans of

> a perilous paradise inhabited by picturesque children of nature. But recent reports from the men stationed in the Pacific theater of war struck a grimmer note. These men learned to know the islands the hard way—fighting and sweating it out in the suffocating heat of the damp jungles and in the desolation of god-forsaken specks of coral in a vast ocean.[119]

Aside from the aesthetic value of the objects and their influence on Western art styles, the exhibition aimed to show the "dramatic human content" of the islands and "the extraordinary achievement" of "primitive men" in creating a "series of rich cultures." Although it recognized that the U.S. servicemen and their allies learned "the hard way" about the islands, there is no mention of islanders learning anything. The exhibition attested to the creativity of "primitive men," but as represented, these were men still living timeless, uncomplicated lives in a distant place—even after the war. Thus while this and similar exhibitions may have portrayed the artistic talent of Melanesia, they also reinforced the illusion of a static Melanesia, echoing the fixed "ethnographic present" of many Pacific anthropologists.

Of all collections of cultural objects, those of societies having no written records of their past most easily can be classified according to the categories of collector, curator, or anthropologist. History, even more than usual, can be replaced by classification. As Susan Stewart has pointed out, "time is not something to be restored to an origin, rather, all time is made simultaneous or synchronous within the collection's world."[120] The museums, moreover, did not display and soon discarded "conspicuously culture-contacted objects" that embodied a history that Westerners might recognize, such as "trade tokens, as used by natives for money," "necklace, shells and pink yarn," "vase, made of 2 finely carved coconuts, riveted," and "grass skirt. Modern C. Polynesian type—yellow."[121] Never mind that most of the seemingly traditional and authentic artifacts had been made with introduced steel tools and for buyers like Burke, rather than for use within the society. Never mind too that each had a story of its context of production. Any use value of the objects within their own contexts or their exchange value for the discarded surplus of the industrialized United States were erased and reconstituted in terms of the aesthetic value of the collection to the observing culture.

In terms of artistic and cultural productions, the Arts of the South Seas exhibition, as Robert Welsch has noted, solidified the concept of discrete cultural and stylistic areas—Australia, Melanesia, Polynesia, and Micronesia—with impermeable boundaries and little internal variation.[122] In classification, curators put their own boundaries around their collections, arranging objects according to their own definitions. Yet this did not reflect the reality of the dynamic and mobile aspects of artistic ideas in this region. More significantly, in terms of the wider American public, the exhibition failed to address change in the Pacific. History, even as recent as the Pacific War, was erased. As Welsch states, these art objects were displayed "as timeless testaments to important art traditions."[123]

So collections and souvenirs served different purposes for their possessors, though to varying degrees both had and have their meanings reconstituted in any particular present. As classified by curators, the collection brought examples of the timeless natives of timeless islands to the U.S. museums for display and aesthetic pleasure. Even Burke, the historian of the changing war scene, who had seen some of these objects manufactured, neglected to assign any provenance to most of them. And if he recorded the circumstances of their production through his photographic record that the curators had seen, they ignored this.[124] Natives thus had no history; neither did their productions. In contrast, the native artifact as souvenir, rather than as museum piece, showed that the possessor had been to the place and it was a place that would remain part of the individual's history. This sample of native production tied the past to the present. The possessor could remember where he got it and often who sold or gave it to him, not a complete ethnographic record of course, but then the serviceman had the war to fight. His memory, awakened by the souvenir, would recreate in the future a record of people and events in the distant islands, but, as the individual and the circumstances of the recollection changed over time, so too would the story.

Troop Handicrafts

Most local artifacts out of their context rarely had use value to the troops. An exception was tortoiseshell jewelry, which, during the Victorian era, was useful as well as ornamental. In Tonga, a part-Tongan named James Hurrell made brooches, bracelets, necklaces, watchstraps, and letter openers from tortoiseshell, finding a market among the troops; similar articles sold well in Fiji.[125] This kind of artifact—local material formed to suit the use value of the visitors—bridged the cultural gap and many servicemen did the same as they tried their hands at craft. On Bora Bora, for instance, "soldier craftsmen" using mother-of-pearl shell made jewelry of "considerable artistry."[126]

More commonly though, as they had the tools at hand, they worked items from materials the invading industrialized culture had brought. In the latter category were ornaments made from disabled munitions, now called "trench art." Not plowshares from swords, but inkwells, ashtrays, bottle openers, picture frames, and rings from shell casings.[127] These were a counterpoint to war, foreshadowing the return to the icons of peace—the home and family. They also represented the breaking of the enemy's weapons and their own, so these gifts bundled memory and anticipation into the future. Skilled men could also make these for sale to their fellows or for gifts when Christmas came to the battlefields, a pastime which also aided their sanity. So avid were the AIF men at souvenir manufacture for self or sale, the authorities eventually had to stop them from using workshop equipment and material during working hours. A favored medium of the AIF as well as the NZEF was Perspex (Plexiglas), obtained from the canopies and windows of disabled aircraft. Often unit insignias set in Perspex "wings" of the airman became a brooch. The New Zealanders called these "foreigners" and sold them to the Americans who wanted gifts for their sweethearts.[128] Men made wooden trays of different local timbers and covered them in Perspex. Simpler items—an outline map of Australia, model planes, a Maori "tiki," or a letter opener—were common.[129]

Adventurous fellows obtained live baby crocodiles, which they killed and stuffed for souvenirs.[130] These appealed to children at home just as brightly colored mounted butterflies did.[131] In recreation and convalescent areas the services often provided instruction in how to make "handicrafts" to keep the men's minds occupied. A local craftswoman, Faailoilo, taught this to convalescents in American Samoa.[132] The Americans in the Solomons produced a booklet, "Guadalcanal Handicrafts," explaining how "native materials" such as "coconut leaf, lawyer [*sic*] cane, bamboo, whitewood, teak, giant clam shell, cowrie shells, tortoiseshell, ivory nut and clay" might be used.[133] Americans with little else to do went looking for pig's tusks as souvenirs from outlying islands in the New Hebrides, creating a dearth for local exchanges.[134] To relieve the monotony on Nissan in early

Figure 34. Guadalcanal souvenir sales. Native-made baskets for sale along with craft necklaces and watchbands made from local seashells and "trench art" of picture frames made by servicemen from discarded metal shells, November 1942 (EX. 127-GW-890-90660, NARA).

1944, the New Zealanders ran a shell "combine," systematically collecting, drilling, and threading shells for necklaces to sell to Americans for $10.[135] "Cats eyes" were popular as they could be made into bracelets and necklaces. A few Americans in New Guinea were so keen to obtain these that they traded gelignite for fishing with Melanesians, a dangerous exchange ANGAU soon curtailed.[136]

Shells were redolent of a tropical landscape and more appealing to womenfolk than stuffed crocodiles. Men from the RAAF in Goodenough Island:

> Got a couple of beautiful big shells each. They are light orange to pink white and to take one end and centre out would make very nice lampshades mounted on a stand of sorts. Now how the hell do we get them home? Mum [his wife] will love this.[137]

Shell souvenirs were for the women in the men's lives, envisaged as key figures for the return home. No ordinary tourists, navy men had this in mind as they rested in April 1944 at Majuro on their way to support the Allied landing at Hollandia, Dutch New Guinea:

> We climbed palm trees, and drank the milk from coconuts we shook down. We watched clouds in a blue inverted bowl overhead, and thought of loved ones so far away. Diving among the coral heads in the shallows of the reef we collected tropical shells—coweries [*sic*] and spider conchs, terribra, cats eyes and a dozen types of coral and sea urchins all to be fashioned into bracelets, rings and ear pendants for girl friends and wives an ocean away. It helped young men to forget that death might include them.[138]

Recollecting and Re-presentation

In war, souvenirs were never simply tourists' objects. Whether benign cats eyes or malign Japanese swords, they represented the exotic and the dangerous, but also life. The former represented why the men were fighting: protection and continuance of the fabric of their social selves with domestic relationships, loved ones, and home places. The latter did too: the obliteration of a hated foe, a threat to their way of life. The quest for souvenirs also brought welcome distraction and provided the currency for small comforts for men in testing conditions. Out of the battlefields, they were bearers of hope. Some, such as the best of the Japanese swords, had a high display value. And the grand collection of Melanesian artifacts that John Burke envisaged acquired an aesthetic value, in spite of its objects being emptied of both their use value and history in museums. Natural objects as souvenirs—the shell, the butterfly, the stuffed crocodile—and the products of those "close to nature," the Pacific islanders, all lost their atemporal quality and became historicized by the individual as part of his personal narrative. Even tiny objects, a tortoiseshell comb or a Perspex brooch, once given to a loved one, carried a personal and social significance beyond any cash or display value. All were icons of survival and triumph in the strange military landscape and alien environment; they were also talismans that betokened a return to normal life, home places, and a future.

Above all, the souvenir lent authenticity to the past as a prop and *aide memoire* to the individual who had stories to tell, representing to himself in reverie and to others how he coped with this strangeness, made even more threatening by a lethal enemy. Because they enveloped so much meaning as well as human emotion, souvenirs always begged for a narrator. The men understood this perfectly, as young Corporal H. P. Spindler wrote to his mother from New Guinea:

> I have collected quite a few things since coming here such as shells, stamps and several other small things which I am finding difficult to carry about with me. I

> am going to try to have it sent home if it will pass the censor so should a parcel arrive just open it & have a look & and leave it until I come home to tell you some storys [*sic*] about things which might seem to you to be useless.[139]

After over sixty years, such stories are now told less often. For many of the surviving participants, though they have their memories of probably the most exciting time of their youth if not their lives, souvenirs have ended up in attics, basements, or garages. Since, for example, American veterans are dying at a rate of almost 1,200 a day,[140] fewer and fewer people can share the intimacies of remembered experience in a foreign environment and relate to the participant's narrative. So the objects become less potent, bearing little message but their own presence. But in his lifetime they were rarely totally discarded. One man who served in Tonga remarked, "I think I brought back a grass skirt that was lying around here for many years. I don't know what happened to it then." His wife did, as she had kept it.[141] The value of the gift as a sign of hope and affection had not been lost to her. With death now recruiting the veterans, some donate souvenirs to museums. Here they have a new audience. They gain another cultural value when the participant's narrative accompanies the object; without the personal context, however, such objects can be no more than mute re-presentations of places "somewhere in the Pacific."[142] Perhaps for these veterans who carried souvenirs home and for their lost comrades who posted them home wrapped in love and hope but who never made it back alive, these objects, like their collectors, have faithfully completed their mission.

CHAPTER 13

Places of Memory, Sites of Forgetting

They could be in the seas, the fields, and the hills. There is nothing like somewhere.

The tropics rot everything, except memories.

Souvenirs embody place, but for comrades and those who have lost a loved one, two places in the geography of wartime memories evoke far more intense feelings. Like iron filings to a magnet, emotions adhere to where young men died and to where they are interred. Sudden and violent death magnifies the significance of the place where life left the body. Graves are visible inscriptions on landscape, a more permanent locus of grief and memory, marking where human remains lay in their individuality. But many are the war dead still far from their home soil, some with no known grave. Thus, for their families and friends, war memorials can be considered as collective cenotaphs or proxy graves. These memorials carry more texts than simply words; they are the foci of communal identity, political enactments, individual memories, and values as well as sacred places to commemorate loss and, paradoxically, to permit social forgetting.

Grave Matters: Locating Mortal Remains

When men died in battle they were buried almost where they fell. A chaplain or an officer might have an opportunity for a brief religious service, but rites of mourning often fell victim to operations. The first markers of graves commonly were crude crosses, fashioned by comrades. Burial parties marked the places on rough maps for later recall. Sometimes, with men in difficult terrain and under fire, few accurate records survived.[1]

Once the area was secure, the needs of the living dictated these burial places were not to be permanent. The psychology of group morale and discipline in battle made it incumbent on the military to gather its dead, a deep-seated value in most soldiers. Once battlefronts became rear positions, the Allies set about finding scattered remains for "consolidation" in larger cemeteries, in well-drained sites adjacent to bases where they could be maintained. The Australians considered future ease of access for relatives. With the precedent of their World War I dead in the Middle East, France, and Belgium, the Australian government anticipated that relatives of those buried in New Guinea would want to visit graves once peace came, so cemeteries needed to be near a port and likely accommodations.[2] So by early 1946, they consolidated remains from Madang, Kokoda, Salamaua, Jacquinot Bay, Finschhafen, and Milne Bay for interment at Bomana, and most New Britain burials to Bita Paka, with remains at Wewak being moved to Lae and, some years later, most at isolated Torokina on west Bougainville were reinterred at Bomana.[3]

In early 1945, U.S. temporary cemeteries were being closed and the dead relocated to Guadalcanal or Munda bases.[4] Dead from Western Samoa, Aitutaki,

Figure 35. Temporary cemetery at Tulagi, Solomon Islands, April 1944. Note the cross on entrance, a common American assumption of Christianity that did not account for the dead of the Jewish faith. These dead were later reinterred on Guadalcanal (EX. 127-GW-1023-61797, NARA).

Rarotonga, Bora Bora, Tongatabu, Upolu, Wallis, Tongareva, Funafuti, Nanomea, and Nukufetau were reburied in American Samoa. When in-theater consolidation of American dead from New Guinea ceased at Finschhafen, there were 9,559 graves. About 350 New Zealanders and Fijians and six British servicemen were exhumed from the Solomon Islands and removed to Bourail, New Caledonia. Four New Zealanders who died in Tonga were reinterred in Suva, along with other scattered burials.[5]

Before this, bodies had to be located. In Papua and New Guinea, body retrieval units owed much to the local people, whose "[r]emarkable eyesight allied to knowledge of jungle conditions enabled them to find what most white men would miss." The units often confronted atrocious conditions where the water table was so high that burial necessitated the corpse being weighed down to stop it from floating to the surface when the grave was filled in.[6] Likewise, even on an atoll such as Tarawa, finding the hundreds of American dead in the debris of fallen palms, smashed bunkers, artillery-gouged sand, and decaying Japanese was an appalling task, impossible without the help of the Gilbertese, who would "wade in dead Japs cleaning out fox-holes, dug-outs and buildings that white stomachs cannot stand."[7]

The keepers of these cemeteries, the Australian War Graves Maintenance Unit or the U.S. Quartermaster's Corps, created a landscape of visual neatness and disturbing tranquility—an imposed ordered geography to counter the random chaos of horror and death in battle. In the American cemetery at Munda, a large flag on a prominent rise marked a focal point of the cemetery's cruciform layout, amid row upon row of crosses or the Star of David.[8] Others respected Allied losses. On Guadalcanal, the Solomon Islands labor corps in September 1943 helped to construct a leaf memorial chapel for the dead.[9] When commemoration ceremonies took place in Tonga, Queen Sālote with characteristic empathy for grieving comrades, had each serviceman's grave covered in flowers, which touched American observers:

> our thoughts went out to the bereaved in the homeland and we could not help but feel that they would be comforted if they could but see the thoughtful care and remembrances that marked the last resting places of their lads.[10]

These were not to be their "last resting places," however. After World War I the American government gave families the option of having their dead repatriated. After World War II relatives were again given a choice, but American inability to maintain cemeteries scattered all over the Pacific meant that by 1946, they brought home all their Pacific dead for interment in either a national cemetery, such as Punchbowl near Honolulu, or in hometown cemeteries, depending on the family's wishes.[11]

Space as Homage

Even when remains were located not all the dead could be interred so easily. When the Australians took Rabaul they found a container of mixed ashes of seven RAAF and about twenty-one U.S. airmen the Japanese had cremated. They buried the ashes as if bodies were involved, with graves occupying the same area as a regular interment. The ashes were divided so that Australia's proportion in an urn:

> Would then be buried in the centre grave of a group of seven graves, and vacant graves left at either end of this group. . . . At the foot of the centre [grave] a notice board would be placed stating that this group of seven graves contains ashes, which represent the personnel whose names appear at the head of each grave.[12]

The Allies were working on a fundamental but virtually unarticulated premise.[13] The space the mortal remains would occupy in death was always to be the area a reclining man would fill, even when the body was cremated—at a time when cremation was uncommon in the West.[14] The same premise applied to the housing of the bodies. The flesh and small bones of thousands of the dead in the Pacific theaters—many buried two or three times before repatriation—were in most cases entirely decayed and certainly disarticulated. So bones, if bound together, would be no longer than the longest leg bones—the tibia, the fibula, and the femur. These would be less than two feet long with the skull, if extant, tied into it.[15] So a container to hold these would be at most about three feet in length and about one foot in breadth and depth.

Yet where a semblance of a set of human remains could be found, the American dead were placed in individual lined caskets of regular length, breadth, and depth.[16] The bones were put in their natural order in life and fixed tightly in a sheet and blanket and pinned, with packing and cross-ties to hold them in place within the casket. These were labeled and packed in individual crates, row upon row in specially fitted ships' holds for repatriation.[17]

Why normal caskets? The instructions do not tell, so fundamental is the assumption of the need to present to families and nation a returned warrior—a son, brother, father, and husband—as a whole individual person, even in death. Burial is so often about paying the last gestures of love to the dead and even of partial recovery of the loss of their being, the size of the coffin acknowledging the reality of their human substance. Space was homage to the absent beloved. What Allied government would have handed to a mother who had farewelled a healthy grown man in his prime such scant remains in a coffin no larger than the cradle in which she once lulled her baby son to sleep?

Once these coffins returned to America they each had a full-length grave, identical to their fellows, and, if in a national cemetery, with a headstone of a regular shape, size, and sober simplicity.[18] Australians and New Zealanders did the same. By 1949, their war dead came under the Commonwealth War Graves Commission, an institution set up in 1917 that maintains records of burial and 2,500 cemeteries of the dead of Britain, her former colonies, and dominions over several conflicts in many lands. Supported by continuing contributions from member governments, this commission recognizes the individual, but in death all are equal with the same type of permanent headstone inscribed with the name without distinction on account of "rank, race or creed." For each cemetery, a centerpiece of the "Sword of Sacrifice," a chivalric form which could also be perceived as an elongated cross, designed by Sir Reginald Blomfield, proved acceptable to practically all Christians, non-Christians, and atheists alike, a triumph of symbolic elision of the ecclesiastical and secular. Similar neutrality yet meaning was emplaced in the altar-like "Stone of Remembrance" in all cemeteries with more than a thousand graves. Designed by Sir Edward Lutyens, these carry the simple text: "Their name liveth for evermore" (Ecclesiasticus). To soften the bleakness of the cemetery, floriculture is emphasized with plantings of indigenous species.[19] Since these design fundamentals emerged in World War I, no subsequent argument has occurred. Wherever memorials, as opposed to cemeteries, were contemplated, however, such unanimity was to be rare.

Japanese Dead

The Japanese too did their best with their dead and when possible cremated them, as was customary, so the ashes and bone fragments could be sent home and their souls could rest.[20] In battle, cremation was difficult and once the Japanese began to retreat, their dead lay scattered hither and thither. Both sides often suffered from their noisome decay. Fighting at Gona mission, Australian private J. A. Milbourne saw Japanese wearing respirators because their dead were decomposing in bunkers. On burial duty, he "scraped Japs up" and lost his meal "a few times."[21]

What the AIF saw of shocking atrocities, including cannibalism, perpetrated by Japanese against captured Australians and Melanesians so enraged them that they were not overly bothered about the niceties of interring Japanese dead. They did so, rarely out of any respect but because of sanitation and military orders under the Geneva Convention of 1929, to which Australia subscribed.[22] Mass graves were common, but in some areas individuals had their own plots. At Sanananda, Papua, the Australian War Graves Maintenance Unit, when inspecting Japanese graves in 1944, found that ten nameplates had been removed. "One plate was recovered . . . about a mile from the cemetery." Some Australian troops made a sport of desecrating enemy graves, so "[p]rovost personnel will be on duty on Saturdays and Sundays to prevent further damage," but that failed to stop it completely.[23] For these soldiers, any trace of the identity of the Japanese was to be obliterated. The Americans felt no different. At Munda, New Georgia, the Japanese built an airstrip that the Americans captured. In spite of the bombing and artillery saturation of the area, a Japanese post to the dead remained standing upright, a lonely sentinel of memory. The only record of this is a photograph taken soon after the Americans landed. The inscription, partially illegible, reads in translation:

> At completion of Munda Airport by Masayoshi Morita:
> Confronting enemies . . .
> The omen of battles is cleared away at the runway.
> In the sky with long tracks of cloud, glitter the planes of my comrades,
> At the military base in the sea we weep together.[24]

Figure 36. Marine R. North inspects Japanese memorial post, Munda, Solomon Islands, September 1943 (EX. 127-GW 995-60486, NARA).

No more was seen of this memorial, reflecting, even if for a short time, the feelings of Japanese soldiers who had lost comrades in battle.

Signing Landscape

Another process of memorialization soon emerged, focused like this Japanese marker, on sites of death and battle. To comrades who shared the experience, particular ridges, beaches, or stretches of forest were no longer simply undistinguished terrain or nameless tropical landscape; they were places layered and permeated with shared meaning—of death, sacrifice, courage, and fear. The mind's cartography connected the internal and external. Just as the events in that place were mapped on the minds and hearts of those who fought there, so too did they want to inscribe their own text on it, to make their temporal experiences tangible on landscape. Soon, Allied units prepared about 160 memorial or battle boards recording who did what, where, and when.

Commanders had to balance the spontaneous grief of warrior comrades and likely postwar conditions. As leader, the Australian commander-in-chief, General Blamey, needed to maintain the morale of the living by honoring their courage and the memory of their dead mates. Blamey had seen examples of permanent markers when touring Gettysburg in the United States, and he wanted the same for significant locations. Lieutenant General Berryman, less attached to the significance of exact sites, advised:

> the number of signs should be governed by the following factors: (a) Number of troops engaged, (b) Length of time of active operations, (c) Intensity of the operations as measured by the losses inflicted upon the enemy and our own battle casualties. . . . Where possible the signs should be placed in accessible sites and arrangements made for the natives of the nearest village to look after their upkeep.[25]

By late 1945 the Australian government's Battlefields Memorial Committee found it had to deal with Blamey's awkward precedents:

> In New Guinea alone, more than fifty memorials were erected, by order of the then Commander-in-Chief, to commemorate the various battles in that area. The committee has expressed the opinion that, although many of the memorials were erected without government approval, the name of Australia is directly associated with them and the failure adequately to maintain them would be a reflection on the good name of Australia. . . . Elimination would only be

> effected when a memorial is located in such a place as would render impossible proper maintenance.[26]

Once Blamey left the committee the number of bronze plaques allowed was twenty-six. Governments knew that often the jungle swallowed such markers or the tropical sun and rain bleached and broke them on beaches. By 1960 several of these plaques had collapsed after their steel supports rusted. Some were moved from their sites to the Commonwealth War Cemeteries, but the Office of War Graves did not want the responsibility of maintaining the rest.[27] It seemed that by the late 1950s, along with plans for a major memorial in Port Moresby,[28] the Australian government was less interested in commemorating particular battle sites in its dependent territory, being more preoccupied with self-government issues there and with newer wars in Southeast Asia.

Unlike governments, those who lived through the experience have personal memories. When relatives of the dead came to Papua New Guinea, they visited one of the war cemeteries: Bomana, Lae, and Bita Paka. But the site of death continued to hold power. Soon after the war, relatives wanted to go to where their son, brother, or uncle had died, but often this was too costly, arduous, or simply uncertain.[29] Remembrance and pilgrimage still draw younger generations to cemeteries and battle sites, albeit with considerably more ease of access and accommodation than in the immediate postwar period.

Island Grave and War Memorial

When U.S. repatriation of their dead began, colonial powers felt the loss of graves as didactic texts on landscape. As at Munda, a British official commented,

> How much more fitting it would have been for these men to have been left where they fell, gathered into decent cemeteries where their crosses could stand as a perpetual reminder to the people of the Solomons of the price which America paid for their liberation.[30]

The American Battle Monuments Commission was told of the "psychological effect" a war cemetery in America's former colony of the Philippines would have on the people: as "permanent evidence of American sacrifice."[31] Memorials could play a similar instructive and political role. The Australian Battlefields Memorial Committee told parliament in 1947 that memorials were needed in New Guinea

> to remind those whom we term inferior peoples, and whom we are trying to uplift, that the white man fought for them as well as they fought for themselves against the barbaric Japanese.[32]

New meanings continued to attach to memorials. For a brief time the dual loading of the meaning of place as grave and memorial seemed to coalesce for the Americans. In December 1943, after the battle of Tarawa, Lord Halifax, the British ambassador in Washington, suggested that the king of England should present the atoll to the United States "as a tribute" to the dead and to reinforce American commitment to regaining Britain's Pacific territories.[33] So a gesture to remember the dead soon began to take on political overtones. Initially favorable, the British Foreign Office advised seeking the views of Australia's Curtin and New Zealand's Fraser. By this time, both were suspicious of U.S. territorial intentions in the southern Pacific. The Australian government replied that such an action "might easily lead to embarrassment and misunderstanding, and could be used to prejudice both Australian and New Zealand interests."[34] The New Zealand government thought "it will open a door to similar action in the Pacific in the case of other islands."[35] Fiji's Governor Mitchell had other concerns, stating, "We cannot give away 2 to 3000 British subjects without their consent, or obtain it without the most awkward publicity." Mitchell proposed a compromise—to give the Americans Betio, site of the landing. On his visit in December 1943 he had already assumed the area would be a massive cemetery and he had ordered that the people not be allowed back on its 560 acres. He advised the Colonial Office that this land could be purchased from the people and, like other planned resettlements of excess population, they could be moved to Fiji. He did not ask the owners what they thought, but he agreed it would give the United States "great pleasure" as "a national memorial."[36] Prime Minister Churchill, anxious not to upset the Australians and New Zealanders further when both were sore about having being left out of the top Allied war conferences, let the matter rest.

It came up again after the end of the Pacific War in September 1945 when the Foreign Office declared that "there might well be a suitable moment when we could make a gesture to the Americans." The Colonial Office did not agree but thought a memorial on Betio would be acceptable.[37] The question of handing over territory, rather than simply a site for a memorial, would not go away. By May 1946 when the Commonwealth prime ministers were to meet in Britain, two pieces of political maneuvering soon attached to the issue. First, the powerful U.S. Secretary of State, James Byrnes, indicated that the British appeal for a major loan before the U.S. Congress to prop up Britain's economy following the cancellation of lend-lease might be more favorably viewed if Tarawa were ceded to America. British prime minister Clement Attlee saw difficulties, since not only would the islanders' assent likely be needed, but also that of the British parliament, which was unlikely unless a wider strategic advantage were forthcoming. Second, the prime ministers of Australia and New Zealand, despite their fears in late 1943 of American designs on the southern Pacific, now were wanting a mutual regional defense agreement with the United States as well as with Britain. If this were forthcoming, Britain was ready to negotiate some kind of American control of Tarawa, perhaps under the United Nations.[38] Fiji's governor, A. Grantham, supported handing over Tarawa because it "would cost us little either in money or inconvenience."[39] But the Americans "were not interested in establishing any system of regional defense of the Southwest Pacific and their own defense interests lay further to the north" in Micronesia. Neither Britain nor Australia and New Zealand wanted to cede rights to Tarawa unless "the United States assumed some degree of obligation." While these parties were willing to discuss it further, the Americans were not.[40]

Some historians see the war as a turning point in the history of the Pacific, arguing that it contributed to decolonization. At this stage, however, the shift in Allied thinking was more about power rearrangements among themselves rather than power sharing with the indigenous people. What the island's significance was for Americans and their history and how this could be turned to British, Australian, and New Zealand strategic objectives, rather than what it had cost the islanders, prompted the contemplation of yet another arbitrary transfer of colonial control, a pattern that began in the late nineteenth century when Germany, America, and Britain traded islands as though they were commodities rather than communities. Thus Tarawa, of bitter loss and proud memory, had failed as a political bargaining chip. Tarawa was not to hold the American dead for long, because body repatriation soon began.[41]

Tarawa Teaches—Again

Partly a complex system, the tropical environment strives to negate the works of humans and, left to itself, will reassert its fluctuating ecology. Tarawa had shown the Americans that its tides were not to be trifled with in November 1943, and, helped again by human error, it would do the same to their efforts to mark their presence in the landscape. Once Tarawa became a minor garrison, the Americans under Commodore Erl C. B. Gould tidied cemeteries on Betio, set up new crosses on ordered lines of graves, and planted colorful shrubs. A sensitive gesture, this honored comrades and provided a pastime on a monotonous posting.[42]

Soon after the Quartermaster's Graves Registration Company began disinterring bodies at Betio in mid-1946, journalist Robert Sherrod, who had been at the landing in November 1943, returned to Tarawa. His story published in *Life* in

August 1946 upset both the naval authorities and the public alike. Not only had the wooden markers recording the events at various locales rotted or fallen down, there also were problems locating the dead. Sherrod wrote of a pile of human bones stacked unnoticed outside showers of officers' mess. Tarawa was a "bitter disappointment" as the object of his pilgrimage, because only "a few efforts have been made to do Tarawa's history justice."[43]

The Graves Registration Company had a difficult task when it reached Tarawa in March 1946. They found that the U.S. garrison's heavy equipment had not been maintained on the salt- and sand-laden atoll and was virtually useless. Thus, they were forced to resort to "manpower alone" and hire local labor.[44] Not only did they fail to find 51 percent of those recorded as missing, when it came to identifying those they did locate, several complications emerged. Working amid buried bombs and hand grenades, they found many bodies were without "dog tags" (identity discs). Many tags in graves were unreadable. The island literally ate these since the coral calcium carbonate had reacted with the metal. Poor records had been kept of burials. The tidy surface pattern of cemeteries bore little relation to the way the dead had been buried. At Betio, under the neat grid of one cemetery's rectangle, bodies were found placed diagonally in a mass grave. Armed with dental records, the units tried to find matches—but many of the dead had confusingly similar dental work, and lower jaws were frequently missing.[45] Sherrod's article and the navy's realization that of the only 49 percent of dead found, eight hundred could not be identified raised uncomfortable questions. Consequently, General A. Vandergrift, commandant of the Marine Corps, wanted a formal inquiry. To give this more publicity seemed impolitic, so a chaplain, Lt. Comdr. Joseph Wieber, was appointed to head a preliminary, closed inquiry for the naval inspector general.[46] As the evidence accumulated, mistakes emerged that simply could not be remedied, including lack of orders for the burial recording by the chaplains and Gould's well-intentioned beautification of cemeteries in 1944, which had destroyed whatever accuracy the first crude grave markings possessed. Moreover, the Graves Registration Company's inspection of cemeteries in 1946 was superficial, but the most unfortunate error was loss of original lists and diagrams showing the location of bodies. Weiber's report saw the naval inspector general close the inquiry with no further action because no one person or unit was to blame. A public inquiry would do no good and only hurt bereaved families.[47] At least plans were in train to change the metal composition of dog tags and to install bronze memorial plaques on Betio that, it was hoped, could cope with the salt and sand better than could wood.[48] For hundreds of American families, however, all they were told was their sons were missing or could not be identified. In national cemeteries, there are rows of the graves of such men, "known but to God."[49]

Bones of Contention

Once they were able, many Japanese wished to bring home their dead. Even with peace they had to face their former enemies' contempt. General Blamey's attitude reflected Australian opinion when he accepted the Japanese surrender at Morotai in September 1945 from General Teshima:

> In receiving your surrender I do not recognise you as an honourable and gallant foe, but you will be treated with due but severe courtesy in all matters. I recall the treacherous attack on our ally China in 1938. I recall the treacherous attack made on the British Empire and upon the United Stated of America in December 1941. . . . I recall the atrocities inflicted on the persons of our nationals as prisoners of war and internees, designed to reduce them by punishment and starvation to slavery.[50]

The Americans shared this view of an enemy with totally alien cultural patterns. The fighting ethic instilled from the top in the Japanese leadership and the military not only permitted but also encouraged unutterable cruelty, which troops in stressful situations frequently perpetrated on civilians and combatants alike.[51] The Rape of Nanking, the Bataan Death March of American prisoners, as well as wartime experiences, were burned into the brains of American troops, so the Japanese were seen as lower than animals. At most American bases billboards bore Halsey's words, "kill Japs, kill Japs, kill more Japs. You will help kill the little yellow bastards if you do your job well."[52] These anti-Japanese feelings, reinforced by what Allied troops witnessed or heard, made it impossible for them to set aside the bitterness. Revelations of Japanese treatment of internees and prisoners of war did nothing to change their opinions. Most never forgot or forgave.

Like their former enemies, the Japanese respected sites of comrades' deaths. To them, it was necessary to bring back remains and perform rituals where men died, to free the spirits so they could continue into an afterlife. Typically, parties of veterans came from Japan with Shinto and Buddhist priests and collected all bones in a particular area for cremation *in situ*. The Japanese government's Ministry of Health and Welfare as well as travel agents organized these bone-collecting expeditions and memorial tours to battle sites.[53]

When the high commissioner notified British colonial officials in the Solomons and the Gilbert and Ellice Islands that the first Japanese party was coming, they were unwilling to assist, as were many local people, so great was their abhorrence of the Japanese. But political realities forced them to reconsider, as did the fact that the British and Australian governments wanted their own dead respected in the Commonwealth War Cemetery in Yokohama.[54] This process, started in the early 1950s, continued well into the 1980s as new caches of bones were discovered, strewn around the jungle or uncovered by gardening.

For the Australian government these initial mortuary missions were equally worrisome. The first Japanese visits to TPNG were planned like major diplomatic operations to ensure the Japanese did not suffer rebuffs from Australian ex-servicemen and the natives.[55] Several villages now are host to small memorial stones erected by the Japanese veterans, but misunderstandings with villagers are common. The Japanese government, however, faces a daunting task of finding more than 1.16 million missing in all theaters, and, as relatives become old themselves, the impetus to pursue the quest is waning.[56]

Memorials: Domestic

When V-J day came on 15 August 1945, Arthur Gately, RAAF, was in Brisbane, Australia, after returning from New Guinea. His immediate reaction was to go to the site of the eternal flame and memorial to World War I in Anzac Square, a park in the city's heart.[57] Thousands of others had the same idea to be "at the centre of our homage, joy and participation." So great was the crowd he could not get near the memorial, so he moved along the street to King George Square plaza in front of the City Hall.[58] To Gately, these sites of public memory already were meaningful places to exult with his compatriots that the war had ended in victory.[59] And World War II's military roll soon found a place in this memorial area, depositing another generation's additions to the sediment of memory. Every year on 25 April, these same Brisbane sites see the Anzac Day parade of veterans of wars and often their descendants, wearing their father's, uncle's, or grandfather's medals.

Homeland memorials to the war dead, the survivors, and their collective deeds in battle, in that they represent communal significance, are not only the locus of intense personal emotions, but also of politics. That remains of Japanese from the Pacific and Southeast Asia were returned to a central shrine, Yasukuni Jinga in Kudan, Tokyo, seemed a fitting way to remember and respect the dead, but it also brought opprobrium on the Japanese government and prime minister for their participation from 1985 until 2006 in ceremonies at this religious institution. Former enemies, particularly China and Korea, express anger that known war criminals whose remains are there are shown respect and are elevated to *komi* status as national deities. Remains of Korean and even Chinese conscript workers are also there without the permission of their families. Another controversy is whether or not the state should financially contribute to the running of the Shinto shrine; this violates the constitution since Shinto is no longer the state religion. Several Japanese courts have ruled against official visits and the current prime minister does not visit the shrine, but the issue is not settled.[60] A subtext is that the divinity of the state is still upheld in Japan and those who died for it are worthy of remembrance, no matter their deeds in life. Unsurprisingly, outsiders who have suffered at the hands of the Japanese have difficulty accepting this rationale.[61]

The Americans have more than 60 percent of their war dead at home. As well as on special occasions, such as Veterans Day, families can visit graves any time. Many graves are now not so often visited for the very fact that their presence in the early postwar years enabled the bereaved to come to mourn and be with their dead and experience the "rituals of separation."[62] In time, for most this seems to have brought a form of closure and enabled them to turn more and more to the future. Grieving near the physical remains and remembering the deceased enabled the process of forgetting to begin, at least of the rawest loss. Paradoxically, forgetting or more truly resignation can only grow out of remembering. To begin this, there must be a sense of finality, born from a family having done all in their power to set their loved one's remains to rest—to have performed societal rituals befitting their passing. This impetus is revealed by discoveries of wartime human remains. When the U.S. Army exhumed nineteen of Carlson's raiders in 2000 on Makin Atoll, the DNA-identified remains were brought to the United States. For one of the dead, Mason Yarborough, his parents, deceased in the 1970s, had reserved his burial plot next to theirs. His siblings, as they had promised their parents, brought him "home" to Sikeston, Missouri, to be buried alongside his family.[63] Again and again, the same thoughts are expressed—here by a niece, Terri Knudsen, after the remains of her uncle Walter Knudsen were recovered in New Guinea in 2003 from a crashed B-24 Liberator and his identity confirmed by DNA, "It's unbelievable—62 years. We're so blessed to have him returned to us."[64] Remains returned to a family enable the lost member to have a place in his home soil and a family to find a sense of restoration and closure.[65]

America has several memorials relating to the Pacific War, such as the Iwo Jima Memorial near Arlington Cemetery in Washington that offended the Washington artistic establishment,[66] and the sunken "USS Arizona" in Pearl Harbor, Honolulu. But it has been slow to build a national one, probably because so many of the American dead came home. The most recent is part of a larger World War II memorial, opened in Washington in 2004 under the auspices of the American Battle Monuments Commission, an independent federal agency that cares for twenty-four permanent American burial grounds overseas and twenty-five separate memorials, monuments, and markers. The $183 million for this came "from hundreds of thousands of individual Americans, hundreds of corporations and foundations, veterans groups, dozens of civic, fraternal and professional organizations, states and one territory, and students in 1,200 schools across the country."[67] A circular design encompassing a pool with fountains, flanked by columns for each state and a pavilion for each major theater, the memorial echoes classical and modernist architecture. Its columns have a bronze oak wreath on one side backed by a wheat wreath on the rear and, front on, a suggestion of a cross in the short piece between the wreaths at right angles to the upright, but not an obvious enough suggestion, it seems, to offend Jewish people. The pavilions each incorporate a huge bronze American eagle holding a massive wreath.[68]

Yet its very grandeur creates impersonality. Dedicated to 400,000 dead, a wall of 4,000 gold stars, each representing a 100 dead, somehow reduces the impact of individual loss. Nowhere in stone are the names of the dead listed, unlike the Washington Vietnam memorial or the Australian War Memorial in Canberra. Thus it is more a memorial to collective and national memory than to the individual fighter. People feel this, as every day families leave behind photographs of their dead.

Few Australians and New Zealanders who lost their men in the Pacific could afford to visit their island graves in the immediate postwar decades; most did their mourning at home. On Anzac Day, a public holiday in Australia and New Zealand, they gather before daybreak, the time of the original Gallipoli landing in 1915, and on Armistice Day on 11 November when World War I ended, or other special anniversaries such as the day Japan surrendered, to remember those who served in this and other wars. The rituals of remembrance focus on ubiquitous statues of a World War One soldier atop a memorial base or obelisk in hundreds of small towns, on plaques at memorial halls or swimming pools in city suburbs, on large city monuments, or on the Australian War Memorial in Canberra or the War Memorial in Wellington. For most Australians and New Zealanders with their dead of the World Wars in distant places, such memorials are now more cenotaphs, surrogate but empty tombs where they can mourn.[69]

The potency of these memorials springs from the human heart and imagined places, far away where the dead lie. For those newly bereaved to have a son's or brother's name inscribed on a public memorial gives meaning to the deceased's short life and legitimizes its loss for the greater good. Distance, however, imposes an additional loss; such a remove from gravesites infuses its own poignancy. When the "Sword of Sacrifice" was to be unveiled in New Guinea's three war cemeteries in October 1953, mothers or widows of men buried or memorialized there could apply for a paid fare with the official party. Again and again, they expressed their wish to "see his grave."[70] Without such assistance, only a rare few could afford such a pilgrimage, for that is what it was to them.[71] For those who could not see a grave, the rituals performed at gravesites—touching the headstone, tracing with the fingers the engraved name, tidying the plot, placing flowers, prayer, and tears—all were emplaced closer to home in memorial structures. Few parents, lovers, or siblings of a dead man have ever forgotten their loved one, but grief can be channeled and supported by collective remembrance. Memorials enable this to occur.

Every mourner has an individual history of their dead; for some, the loss remains, for others attending, the memorial service is simply a mark of respect and gratitude. For descendants, often a new understanding of what that death meant to parents and grandparents comes,[72] so memorials instruct about the conflict and, at a deeper level, about the nature of war as loss, as destroyer, but also of family survival across the generations.

The ranks of Pacific War veterans, however, are thinning. Yet, after a drop in the numbers of people attending remembrance services in the late 1960s when the Vietnam War divided families and nation, since 1990 numbers have shot up in Australia and in New Zealand, but not apparently in the United States.[73] Is this because most American dead rest on home soil or because Americans draw their identity from other events? Local wars such as in Korea and Vietnam, just as they have added new names to old memorials, have brought new recruits to the circle of mourners, while children also swell attendances in Australia and New Zealand.[74] Given that the human species falls often to warfare, and that both Australia and New Zealand take a marker of national identity and their own unique relationship with each other from such wars,[75] these rituals of remembrance around memorials will continue. The remembrances will change with changing perceptions and recent interrogations of just what the Pacific War has meant and who contributed to the war effort, such as Australian Aboriginals, Pacific islanders, and women.[76] Although these stones may be static, war memorials paradoxically are active because they are continually invested with new meanings, often very different from those of their creators. In one sense these domestic memorials of the war are as much about present concerns and a message to the future as about the past.

Monumental Battles in Foreign Landscapes

At some sites, different readings of memorials have already emerged. History and social or collective memory diverge over the decades, and each is constantly in the process of revision as well as negotiation,[77] so that the meaning of war memorials near battle sites is never as fixed as the stone and bronze from which they are made. Memorials give solace to bereaved relatives, but such texts on foreign landscapes often become highly contested, revealing as much about current power struggles as about wartime events, beginning with the need some felt to show the native people the extent of Allied sacrifice, a subtext that lingers still. In Solomon Islands, old enemies want still to dominate the landscape, not with guns but with their definitive texts. In 1984, well before the fiftieth anniversary of the American landing on Guadalcanal, the Japanese had donated a peace memorial located on Mt. Austen/Hill 35, the scene of much fighting, in a dominant position in the landscape. Near it, sculpted by Seiichi Takahashi, who died in the war, a statue of a fisherman looks out to sea, donated by his home town.[78] A bruised Japan valued peace because it still lived with the horrors of the atomic bombing of Hiroshima and Nagasaki, now considered by some historians to be saber rattling by the United States to intimidate the rising Soviets, and certainly falsely presented to the public as a way to save thousands of American lives.[79] Yet to many American veterans, it was all very well for Japan to portray itself as peaceful, but this glossed over the nature of the conflict in which imperial Japan was the aggressor. By the time the fiftieth anniversary came around in 1992, Allied veterans of the Guadalcanal–Solomon Islands Memorial Commission had lobbied the American government for a massive memorial, a part circle containing four-foot-square, twenty-four-foot pylons with four independent blocks or "directional walls" indicating the events of major battles, Allied and Japanese losses of shipping, and participating aircraft units, to instruct the reader. Costing $500,000, this memorial is high up on the hill on Skyline Drive overlooking Honiara and Iron Bottom Sound.[80]

At the Skyline Memorial, history was being used to refresh social memory and to attempt to shape it, at least for some. Solomon Islanders, however, shared very different social memories to the foreign veterans who lived through the wartime events. Generations born after the war ended saw this monument-building competition as foolish waste, for these were purely commemorative structures with no other useful purpose, especially for the people of the land who endured someone else's war. As a former Solomons' prime minister noted,

> And yet again, at the height of Skyline Ridge we have yet to witness another battle between USA and Japan. Do we need them to do that yet again in our own soils? . . . I think that apart from the praise given to our people for their services during the war years, the Americans and British need to consider some forms of compensations to our local people. . . . I think we have already had enough of USA vs Japan during the last war.[81]

More was to come. In 1998 the Japanese who had built the terminal on Guadalcanal at Henderson's airport also donated a large sculpture, the "Gates of Nostalgia" by Ryokichi Mukai, to commemorate Japanese dead on Guadalcanal.[82] Following civil unrest in Solomons in 2000 and no airport maintenance, the Japanese government again funded refurbishing, since it was courting small Pacific states to win support in international bodies.[83]

At the same time, the Solomon Islands government announced it was about to rename the airport, built by the wartime Americans who captured its beginnings from the Japanese in 1942. Named after a U.S. war hero, Henderson Field has a memorial observation tower that American veterans groups have maintained over the past sixty years. To the Americans and their allies who flew in and out of it, this tower and the airfield embody wartime aviation and the pivotal role of the Guadalcanal campaign in turning the Japanese assault.[84] In 2003 when the airport terminal reconstruction was complete, the Solomons' government minister, Daniel Fa'afunua, announced that its name would be changed to Honiara International Airport. Newspaper reports indicated this was at the suggestion of the Japanese building consultants. An on-line petition brought more than eight thousand opponents of the idea and pleas from surviving veterans and families. Prime Minister Kemakeza, after being approached by U.S. diplomats, compromised and gave it the cumbersome name of Honiara International Airport–Henderson Field.[85]

As time passes, governments tend to forget memorials and their maintenance, unless they bear on current political matters. Veterans groups or close relatives of the dead, as with the American Memorial at Skyline, are usually the prime movers in having memorials in distant lands constructed or refurbished. This is easier when the countries have ongoing economic, social, and diplomatic ties, as is the case with Australia and PNG. To Australians, their operations there, especially the now almost mythical deeds on the Kokoda Track, are part of their definition of their own identity and nationhood.[86] By the time of the fiftieth and then sixtieth anniversaries of events of World War II, many of the plaques and memorials located in PNG had fallen into poor repair under the harsh tropical conditions, at a time when many Australians realized that the veterans were dying in greater numbers.[87] Thus, throughout the 1990s, patriotic individuals such as Ross Bastiaan, surviving veterans, and various Australian donors contributed to new bronze plaques in PNG locales.[88]

Astute politicians in Australia and PNG did not let this store of feeling lie untapped. They knew that such memorials, just like injuries that many of the Papua New Guineans suffered, can "be an ever-present reminder of where the war was—and where it could happen again."[89] In 1992, Prime Minister Paul Keating's moving speeches and symbolic gesture of kissing the foot of a memorial at Kokoda was part of his policy to focus Australia on the near north and Southeast Asia,[90] as much as reinforcing his support for republicanism by his declaration that Australians had fought and died in New Guinea "not in defence of the old world, but the new world. Their world."[91]

By the early 2000s, Papua New Guinea seemed like a "failing state" in the so-called "arc of instability" to Australia's north, vulnerable to terrorists, drug runners, and other global adventurers. Australia saw a need to prop up the government. In one of Australia's and Papua New Guinea's less heroic ventures, the Howard government (as it did in Nauru) persuaded the Papua New Guinea government to house some of these alleged threats, 356 "boat people," mainly Afghans who had tried to reach Australia by ship, on Manus Island in 2001 in return for more than $40 million. They would thus get neither a footing nor a hearing on Australian soil. In addition to the refurbishment of older Australian-built memorials, the construction of a new one was a major project for the Australian government, providing opportunities for Prime Minister Howard to appear in Papua New Guinea in 2002 to discuss the Manus solution, more aid to the Somare government, as well as the wartime anniversary.[92]

On the anniversary of Japan's surrender, the Australian government inaugurated an impressive memorial of four granite pillars each weighing 3.5 metric tons, each inscribed with a single word invoking values dear to Australian soldiers—"mateship," "courage," "endurance," and "sacrifice" respectively—in a circular pattern. The memorial was constructed at massive cost on a dominant knoll with a sweeping view across a great valley at Isuvura on the Kokoda Track, near the site where Private Bruce Kingsbury earned a posthumous Victoria Cross for valor. It also has ten information panels in English and Tok Pisin, so is meant to instruct both Australians and Papua New Guineans. Prime Minister Howard of Australia and Prime Minister Somare of Papua New Guinea, other dignitaries, and veterans were flown in by helicopter for the opening, and the speeches flowed, with Howard connecting the Anzacs of 1915 with the army at Kokoda in 1942.[93]

Historians argue that Keating and Howard have endowed the Kokoda campaign with undue importance as the victory that saved Australia.[94] But it suited their attempts to construct aspects of national identity for high policy reasons. Kokoda is geographically close to Australia and the campaign and its Academy Award–winning visual record shot by Damien Parer were already loaded with heroic qualities in Australia's social memory. Its limited strategic significance aside, the ambiguities of forced labor on the track, of who those laborers were, some ineffectual leadership, and of poorly trained Australian militiamen did not suit the unitary image of smooth cooperation of gallant warriors, so both Australian prime ministers dropped these ambiguities to remake social memory. As Hank Nelson argues, at these Papua New Guinea memorials, Keating wanted to emphasize Australia's regional significance and Howard wanted to link Kokoda to Gallipoli, the Anzac legend of heroism and the subtext of justifiable wars.[95] Thus, magnifying its importance was a vote catcher for Keating and Howard and an Australian aid catcher for Somare.

Unlike Solomons, there were no complaints from Somare regarding expenditure because this landmark memorial was yet another drawing card on the Kokoda Track for Australian war tourists, providing employment for local people and other practical outcomes, such as a scholarship fund for local students.[96] Since World War II, Australians at home have favored utilitarian or "living" memorials, rather than the purely monumental, so this was nothing novel.[97] Funded by both private groups such as Rotary and the Australian government, villages along the track have been recipients of several schools, a museum, hospitals, bridges, lighting and dam-raising projects, which provide utilitarian counterpoints to the narrow uses of war monuments.[98] Melanesians value relationships that are refreshed practically; deeds must follow the litanies of heroic rhetoric that remembrance evokes in visiting foreigners, especially politicians.

Ironically, even in doing this, the Australians have concentrated on the significance of the Kokoda Track to them as a place of battle, rather than on the local people involved in operations. Most of the benefits of recent interest by the Australian government and war tourists have been for the Orokaiva and Koiari who live beside the track, yet, as Hank Nelson has shown, most carriers and bearers who worked for the Australians were from areas well outside these places.[99] In 2007, Australia registered disquiet at proposed mining across "their" track, even though villagers there see this as a positive development.[100]

In Solomons and PNG, the Americans have left no utilitarian memorials. When veterans, gathered at Gizo in 1992, were asked to donate a building for public use, nothing came of it. America occasionally sends a group of servicemen to assist with disaster relief exercises, but this is simply overseas training.[101] Western Melanesia is of little strategic value to America, so such gestures are rare. Regional issues concerning the Western bloc there are left to the Australians and New Zealanders to address.

Eroding Memories

In the Pacific islands, near small villages and on remote foreshores, many memorials can be found, erected by the combatants. Some will not survive. Japanese memorials near Rabaul were largely buried by volcanic eruptions in 1994. In 1998, Asian loggers damaged a New Zealand memorial at Niarovai Bay, Vella Lavella. No islander notified any authority or the New Zealand high commission, but a war tourist happened to see it and reported it to the New Zealand government, which investigated and found the memorial very damaged, with a brass plaque missing. Further action was delayed by a tsunami in April 2007 that affected the site and saw New Zealand concentrating on relief projects in the Western Province.[102] Only those who want to remember will value such memorials, and they live in distant countries. Islanders have other places they value and other memories; this war that descended on the Pacific islands was rarely seen as theirs. What remains in the memory of the combatants and their kin is absent from the lived landscape of most islanders, unless new and beneficial relationships are made that are pivoted on such memorials. Consequently, in the Solomon Islands, Ewan Stevenson, who visits war sites often, testifies,

> The thing is we forget that these memorials in foreign countries are our history and not necessarily the locals. . . . The concept of "public" property doesn't exist in the Solomons either and public facilities are treated very badly. . . . The brass plaques on most of the American and Japanese WWII monuments a bit out of Honiara have been ripped off and discarded, so it's quite a common practice in the Solomons. My Dad was involved in the building of a number of these monuments and was always gutted when they were ripped off.[103]

In the former combatants' homelands, memorials have grown from the returned veterans groups and their wider local community. As Ken Inglis has so well shown, discussions about a memorial's wording, design, placement, and cost can involve community groups for years.[104] In the consensus or compromise reached, the community that bred the servicemen had a voice stronger than any government agency. Few of the memorials in the Solomons or the rest of the Pacific islands originated from such shared community discussion between islanders and the outside interested groups. Outsiders "consult," regarding siting and permissions, but only after the memorial concept has been metaphorically set in stone offshore. Thus these memorials are impositions on the landscape, reflecting foreign concerns.[105]

Changing human perception alone does not determine the fate of such memorials. The changing environment is taking its own inexorable toll. As sea levels rise from global warming, apparently a consequence of the industrialized nations' energy potlatch, several of the memorials on places like Tarawa could sink into the sea. What journalist Sherrod sixty years ago said of this place, which many veterans still consider sacred, is even truer now: "The inevitable erosion, of heroes as well as landmarks, has set in."[106]

"Stronger Than Stone"

For the living and generations to come, there can more efficacious memorials than those in stone. The process of remembering through dialogue and of moving to reconciliation can be a memorial in itself. Unlike Germany, the Japanese nation has found it difficult to confront its military history and war atrocities. Some steps toward greater honesty were made in the 1990s, however. Sponsored by the Australian War Memorial and the Japanese embassy, the Australia-Japan Research Project has involved scholars in Canberra, Japan, and PNG in a visionary project on the Pacific War.[107] From the early 1950s, when Japan as part of the anticommunist bloc became more dependent on America, the government entered decades of national amnesia about Japan's role in the Asian and Pacific wars.[108] In 1995, as part of a greater openness and the end of the cold war,[109] the Japanese government undertook this combined project, initiated by Prime Minister Murayama Tomiichi, to "to enable everyone to face squarely the facts of history." Over twelve years, various seminars, conferences, and publications have created many histories that reveal aspects of the war experience previously little examined.

Transcending geographical place and space, much of this is also in cyberspace and is thus freely available on websites, in English and Japanese.[110] The strongest features of the research are its humanity and honesty. The process of remembering and re-examining the war has been a powerful one and continues to be for the Japanese, Australians, and Papua New Guineans who have participated directly or as readers. Though both America and Japan respectively have recognized some of their inhumane acts in war, they have no parallel mutual project, perhaps because that could mean re-examination of the Japanese war crimes trials, atomic bombing, and abuses of Japanese civilians by occupying Americans after the war.[111] Remembering the events in an open forum between former protagonists acknowledges their different truths, the inestimable human suffering, and environmental waste this war entailed. Such a process respects the agency of all. For the living, there can be no other path to reconciliation. For the dead, as one of the first Japanese bone collectors of 1955, veteran Shiro Hara, believed, Melanesia's "savage lands" "are changing into paradise and the souls who died in these lands will repose in this paradise, forgetting utterly the difference of thought and nations."[112]

Conclusion

> And what is Earth's eye, tongue, or heart else, where
> Else, but in dear and dogged man?—Ah, the heir
> To his own selfbent so bound, so tied to his turn,
> To thriftless reave both our rich round world bare
> And none reck of world after, this bids wear
> Earth brows of such care, care and dear concern.
>
> —Gerard Manley Hopkins, "Ribblesdale"

Only death could reveal if those who perished in the islands found themselves in a true paradise, but during the war, a few brief months were usually enough to convince the naïve servicemen that their imagined hedonistic, earthly paradise was a figment of Hollywood. Both sides faced the reality of geography, terrain, climate, and the inhabitants, which for the Allies was not unpleasing in much of Polynesia, but generally challenging, if not repugnant, to most who fought in the western Melanesian islands. A totally alien landscape such as the swampy wilderness of south New Georgia exposed the psychological vulnerability of unseasoned and poorly led American troops in 1943. For the Japanese, the nature of the islands' environment and Allied strategy confirmed that in modern war, even in the fertile areas near Rabaul, they could not succeed by food alone, and elsewhere often starved for the lack of it.

Likewise, the western islands soon revealed the arsenal of diseases their environment could marshal against foreigners. The source was environmental, but more commonly the Allies personalized it to the "primitive" inhabitants, who were "seedbeds of infection" and, like the environment, had to be controlled. Major weapons in the fight against insect-borne diseases—freon aerosol-propelled containers and DDT, produced by chemical companies such as DuPont—were toxic right up the food chain and proved to be Trojan horses for the global environment. Another wartime weapon against disease was penicillin. After the war, this and other antibiotics saved thousands of lives in the islands and elsewhere, but they assisted the rapid growth of population that now presses hard on some island regions as it does on much of the planet, degrading soil fertility. Such weapons against diseases have proved to be two-edged swords.

For the military, their morale and thus their survival depended on effective medicine and psychological buttressing, including the maintenance of the emotional links with their homelands and loved ones. Regular mail, films, touring concert parties, and entertainers enabled men to move mentally for a time between their enervating island environment and home. They reinforced these links by sending home letters and souvenirs, tangibly joining their experience of the exotic and dangerous to the reassuring circle of domesticity as well as signaling hopes for their future life. But many thousands of servicemen never made it home. They became spiritually and often physically part of the environment where they died. Bound by the blood of battle, comrades marked this by trying to record on the landscape the events that had taken their companions, inscribing place to recall lives in and out of time. Back home, families grappled with bereavement through ritual over the remains and by attending services at war memorials. For those survivors who fought in the southern Pacific islands and those affected by war's loss down the generations, individual memories and meanings still claim attention and respect. As the years pass, however, collective memorialization has changed with shifting political and economic agendas.

Fighting and war may be hard-wired into the human species, but so too is cooperation, which was pivotal to Allied victory. Fighting qualities aside, New Zealand's and Australia's role as southern food baskets with extensive base facilities was probably as significant as the AIF's freeing the U.S. forces in New Guinea to advance north. Both southern governments also tapped a store of knowledge about their island possessions—the Allied terrain studies and the marshaling of native labor and local resources being examples—which proved invaluable to the waging of the war. The Japanese lacked this, but their nascent civil administration and attendant commercial companies based at Rabaul began to do just as they had in prewar Micronesia: find and develop resources for the betterment of Japan. Unlike the United States, they did not have to negotiate with colonial powers and had a free hand over land and people. Only their emerging isolation in 1943 dashed their designs.

Despite the Allies' cooperation, however, strains emerged. For four years from early 1942 until September 1945, Australia, New Zealand, the French and British administrations of the Western Pacific, and Tonga sacrificed considerable sovereignty for a then-unspecified duration to wage war alongside their powerful ally, America. Political reason prevailed over national and imperial hubris in a situation of extreme threat. Even so, the Free French administration remained guarded in relation to the "Americans' war" and American ambitions. Australia and New Zealand too were worried over America's postwar intentions and commercial aspirations in what these neighbors considered theirs and Britain's Pacific. America had sent its "economic commandos" to "new territory in the jungles" to make the most of the opportunities wartime necessity provided to reconnoiter the terrestrial and maritime resources of the southern Pacific (as well as other areas)[1] and attempted to corner much of the export market for certain tropical products. Not only did the Australian and New Zealand governments circumvent this whenever possible, but in 1944 bluntly stated that after the war the Americans should leave the islands they had occupied. Lest the United States claim rights from paying compensation, New Zealand paid such debts to islanders. Australia also compensated civilians in New Guinea.

The war catalyzed a range of changes, many relating to the use of the environment. In Melanesia, a greater awareness of the cash economy emerged, partly as a result of widespread employment of native labor and sale of curios and local produce. Military use of previously little-used resources and subsequent compensation consolidated this, inducing islanders to perceive such resources as commodities, a shift in their primary relationship with their environment. On islands that had a longer familiarity with the West, such as Fiji and Samoa, the war accelerated earlier processes that had slowed during the Great Depression. As Ratu Lala Sukuna said of Fijians, their indifference toward more intensive use of resources began to change with the war's "thousands of varied representatives of civilization."[2] After the war, resources were less used for direct societal subsistence and more often for sale to outsiders. The war also expanded demand for exogenous manufactured goods, creating dependency. To obtain these, cash was needed, which in turn meant expanded exchange of labor or local products. The islands' people had visions of their environment affording them a better living, but it would be from major transformations within it.

Parallel to these altering indigenous perceptions of resources, the colonial governments' visions of the islands' future, although hindered by the slow process of reconstruction, aimed to improve services and develop the human resource. Metropolitan funding gradually allowed for the assessment of natural resources with the aim of eliminating fiscal dependency as soon as feasible. Tropical timber seemed one sure money earner, with administrations pushing the extension of professional forestry to provide economic if not ecological sustainability, a policy that intensified as self-government and then independence loomed in the late 1950s and 1960s. The colonial vision of the future regarding this and other potential resources overlapped the indigenous vision, but there were vast areas of incongruity regarding who held the resource rights. This made for a tortuous and contested process when the colonial governments strove to develop the environment by the common "top down" approach to underwrite the creation of new small independent states in the 1960s and 1970s. Indigenous concepts of localized rights vis à vis the state's rights to resource revenue have been a continuing and contentious issue, all the more so since national rent-seeking policies seem easier and more appealing than wealth-creation policies. Their heirs, the governments of these independent states, have carried on these policies, but many would argue that because of inefficiency and corruption in some countries, such as Solomon Islands and PNG, that the returns to resource holders and the public have been no fairer than in colonial times. With this to contend with, most surviving "traditional" conservation practices, with their limited capacity to assign causation to depletion and thus to initiate corrective measures, have either faltered or have been discarded under commodification pressure for quick money, just as colonial measures to sustain resources have. For the forests, stable plantations systems along with their loss of biodiversity are only just beginning in much of Melanesia because many of scientific forestry's small gains made in the immediate lead-up to independence were lost in the spree of consumption by migratory foreign loggers that continues still. Even so, the rhetoric of conservation and sustainability is trotted out cyclically to obtain aid from foreign donors with short memories. Anathema to most prewar colonial powers, fiscal dependency on other countries has become etched on the islanders' mindset.

Islanders historically were much more engaged in using the inshore and lagoon fishery than using big timber trees of the forests. Thus they have long resisted attempts to take away their fishing rights, but in the war they had been either too intimidated or rewarded by occupiers to make an issue of it. Contrasting Western ideas about property and its use were shown in how armies used the land for their gardens and to extract aggregates as well as in Wilbert Chapman's proposed American exploitation of the deep-sea fishery for future profits. This began to happen in the early 1980s, later than Chapman thought, when the American Pacific fishing industry faltered because of two severe El Niño southern oscillations and cheap imports from Asia. American fishers entered the western Pacific to find others, including the Japanese, already there. Aided by cold war fears of Soviet influence, the Pacific states as members of the Pacific Forum, supported by Australia and New Zealand in 1987, gained American agreement to their legal rights for exclusive economic zones, domestically uncontested resources for governments since local fishers rarely had fished far out of sight of land.[3] These zones covered a two-hundred-mile radius from each state's shores, but because of an imprudent selling of license fees to foreign fishers, the islands and their clients may soon face the collapse of the huge tuna fishery through overfishing. Transfers of undersized catches to mother ships at sea and limited capacity to carry out surveillance and sanctions have also been factors.[4]

Wartime revision of islanders' perceptions was not restricted to natural resource use. Their contribution to the war effort increased their self-confidence in encountering modernity. Some women, even in male-dominated Melanesia, glimpsed new possibilities in the cash economy when they earned as much as or more than their men from the sale of goods and services. "Traditional" culture proved flexible when men taught others to make grass skirts, a female domain, and made carvings of subjects to suit soldiers' bawdy tastes. Nonetheless, in western Melanesia, fragmented small-scale social organizations, myriad languages, a dearth of Western education, and inability to access overseas work left them little able to capitalize on experiences the war brought. It did increase their aspirations to seek the benefits of the wider world, however, through incorporating the new knowledge into older systems of understanding their physical, political, and spiritual environment, and acting on these. Some took a path to the modern, or what they knew of the West, via "cargo cult" activities that failed to produce the desired results. Melanesians often also altered their ideas about one another. Wider regional identities or micro-nationalisms and incipient political movements found some outlet in the colonizers' own agenda for increased indigenous self-government; others met colonial obduracy when the administrations deemed that indigenous aspirations were too radical in the light of Melanesians' capacities at the time. In much of Polynesia, such aspirations were more readily actualized through greater educational and migrant labor opportunities along with an earlier history of successful epistemological harmonization of significant aspects of the modern world into their own archipelago-wide cultures.

The years of the Pacific War repeated, in an intensified manner, all the environmental processes and related resource contests that the southern Pacific had experienced previously. Just as when the first indigenous people arrived there, the military, in extreme situations, "overgrazed the range" and extracted timber, leaf for construction, aggregates, and fish for their own purposes with little regard for conservation. Both indentured and forced islander labor had existed before the war but had more disruptive correlates on a larger scale during the conflict, particularly in New Guinea. New waves of disease, such as dysentery, affected some communities, though most military medical units assisted the local people, if only to protect themselves and sustain goodwill. To control endemic diseases, especially insect-borne ones, the military made massive but localized changes to the ecology, moved native settlements away from camps, and even medicated the natives with potentially dangerous antimalarial drugs and sprayed the surroundings with DDT. Virtually in a matter of weeks in some places, the incoming armies with great machines such as "Carry-alls" and bulldozers, some never before seen in the islands, built mini–military cities peopled by men, with wharves and airfields far larger than prewar installations that had been assembled piecemeal over decades of Western contact. During the occupation by the United States, or "Uncle Sugar," imported foods such as canned beef, mutton, and fruit as well as various cookies, candy, soda, gum, and the like flooded into communities across the region, either introducing the inhabitants to something new or extending the range of tastes some had sampled before the war. Many islanders whose prewar clothing was either bark fiber or a lava lava/lap lap of calico found the discarded shirts and trousers of the Americans to their taste, just as they did their cigarettes. Add to all that the flooding of the islands with thousands of exotic, young, well-paid strangers in search of distraction, especially in rear bases, and within a year or so a few thousand part-American children were the result, continuing a process of biological hybridization begun when Europeans first entered the Pacific. Other exotics found niches too. Despite some vigilant administrations, new weeds and pests entered the islands to alter local ecologies, just as they had in the preceding 100 to 150 years.

There were other continuities, revealing that war and peace are not polar opposites but a continuum. The protagonists perceived the islands as part of their strategic landscape, a means to their ends, bastions of defense and bridges to advance and retreat across the Great Ocean, and as sites to bargain with. Palpable in war, this role continued into the peace. When postwar geopolitics became clearer, a weakened Britain considered capitalizing on the emotions of national grief and pride by trading off all or part of Tarawa as a cemetery and place of memory to court powerful America's support, first for a loan, then to help give Australia and New Zealand the regional security that Britain alone could not. Partly because of the Americans' plans to repatriate their dead and partly because they were strategically focused on former Japanese Micronesia, such support was unforthcoming. The Gilbertese had no idea their home was again a bargaining chip in a power game, repeating patterns set down by the great powers in the nineteenth century.

The war-weary American Congress and public, however, had not swallowed the militarists' bait of maintaining naval bases in the southern ocean to create a wide defense perimeter. They nonetheless accepted the acquisition of Micronesia, under a United Nations trusteeship, as a bastion at a far distance on their northwest that would presumably bear the brunt, as in the recent war, of environmental damage caused by conflict with any aggressor from that direction.[5] In terms of geopolitics, the isolation and distance from metropolitan centers that had made war in the Pacific islands so challenging logistically were pluses for further weapons development. America gained in Micronesia a faraway site in its defense bastion landscape for an extended series of tests of atomic and nuclear weapons as well as intercontinental missiles, which would have been less acceptable in the continental United States because of visible and potential damage to the environment, including humans. America did not waste much time putting its power brand on these "remote" islands to impress potential foes in the Communist bloc. The first American postwar atomic test, of sixty-six in the Pacific, was at Bikini in 1946, watched by forty thousand men, amid the towed hulks of captured Japanese ships and obsolete American battleships in the lagoon. The blast began an obscene litany of environmental and human crimes against guileless and powerless atoll dwellers and their descendants. War in the Pacific seemingly had taught America—and subsequently her cold war allies Britain and France, which also exploded many nuclear devices in the South Pacific—a way to protect their domestic environment while unleashing a global weapon, "the destroyer of worlds,"[6] whose ramifying effects even in the test phases were never totally contained in small, distant Pacific Islands.[7]

For the regional powers, the islands' best interests remained framed within their own. Japan did not consider paying reparations to the islands because the islands had counted for nothing in their calculations, but did so to Southeast Asia, whose raw materials it needed for reconstruction. Unsurprisingly, the war rekindled deeply held fears in Australia about the Asian menace to the north. Australia certainly delivered generous war damage compensation within New Guinea, but as part of a long-term strategic agenda to maintain a defense barrier to protect its domestic environment, in addition to its humanitarian concerns. Moreover, in 1945, domestic priorities saw the Australian government withdraw most of its army there before surveying abandoned war surplus. While the return of war-weary men appeased the Labor government's electorate, it was an opportunity wasted for New Guinea because much of the potential of Allied surplus could not be fully realized by the CDC before it deteriorated in the climate.

Beginning with extensive war damage compensation, Australia continued to court the few million people of PNG—to the tune of AU$15.5 billion in aid from 1975 to 2004—to retain a friendly buffer state between itself and possible northern threats,[8] just as, on a smaller scale, New Zealand does there and in southern Polynesia. Australian prime minister Kevin Rudd's government in 2008 was even considering a guest worker scheme that would include PNG.[9] The Australian government's motives today in maintaining war memorials near places of battle in PNG stem as much from the need to retain a visible presence there as from honoring the memory of its soldiers' and native carriers' sacrifice for Australian electors. For most Melanesians, the war with Japan was not theirs except in the worst possible way, as a battleground for exotic armies far from home, incurring "collateral damage" to them and their environment.

Politically and strategically, the islands of the southern Pacific were, and still are, pawns of the powers on their periphery. Despite this, since independence, peoples and their small nations think creatively and beyond their beaches. As in an extended family, individuals have "expanded the target" from their islands[10] to include lands of the Polynesian and the more recent Melanesian global diasporas, the former in sufficient numbers to be dynamic Pasifika communities in places from Sydney to Auckland, San Francisco, and Salt Lake City, linked with transnational kin via electronic communications and jet planes.[11] Beyond the boundaries of their original islands, such colonizing communities are creating their own cultural landscapes of neo-Samoas, Tongas, and Niues that, in turn, are influencing those homelands.

Following on innovative colonial cooperation that the war necessitated and continued in the South Pacific Commission of 1947, Pacific states in some cases have reaffirmed ancient connections among themselves. These connections are embodied in regional institutions under the umbrella of the Pacific Forum, which represents sixteen countries in the southern Pacific as well as Micronesia. Though creativity sometimes has spawned misguided "get rich quick" schemes—such as pyramid selling investments, passports for cash, or accepting dangerous waste for grants—young Pacific states now also have expanded their targets of more legitimate aid, investment plans, and educational access beyond former colonial rulers. Competing powers in the region, the Soviets in the 1980s and Taiwan and mainland China today, seek extended access to the resources of the region's ecosystems, challenging assumptions that the southern Pacific is largely an Australian–New Zealand sphere of influence and avoiding the latters' penchant for demanding good governance as part of their aid packages. Ironically, the recent instability of island governments and growing civil unrest is drawing more aid from the United States, a player that left that arena in the 1990s. Although island states can finesse the rules and external players may exchange places, the game still remains much the same, however. The islands' environment and future have been and are subject to forces that remain largely in the hands of those who do not live there: The islands were first a battlefield; then a test site for nuclear and missile testing, a defense bastion, and, in America's case in Guam, a forward military bridgehead; and since the 1960s a source of cheap tropical timbers, minerals, and fish for foreigners. The islands are also now becoming places for Chinese and Taiwanese settlement and investment, a development that many islanders distrust but which their governments permit in return for aid and other considerations. In the early 2000s, like the Pacific prisons for Europe's convict undesirables of the nineteenth century, the islands of Nauru and PNG served as Australia's barrier to unwanted "boat people" from Asia and the Middle East. Perhaps less exploitively, others will soon want Melanesia's islands as major loci of carbon sequestration by reforestation.

Politics and perceptions remained interdependent after the war. Dominant foreign interests began once again to remake the image of the islands into welcoming havens, another manifestation of their power to define other people and places. To those who fought the Japanese in Melanesia, the islands were no paradise and even the more equable and healthful Polynesia became depressing to many who had a long tour of duty there. As one commentator noted in 1947, "[t]he Pacific, like a woman when she has shortened her skirts, has lost most of its mystery."[12] Yet the old discourse of a fantasized Pacific was soon reasserted. Joan Beaumont shows that the Australian-American Association, as part of its commemoration of the Battle of the Coral Sea each year, began a series of balls in Melbourne for the social elite, including the military command. The décor of venues of these balls from 1946 on, as well as representing the sea, say by Neptune or mermaids, included "a Hawaiian atmosphere," with girls selling leis, "100 girls wearing sarongs," and a singer in "a real Hawaiian costume." In 1950, the venue was decorated as if it were a benign tropical island, a trope that remained dominant throughout the decade. A generic Polynesia had erased the realities of Melanesia's islands in the Coral Sea,[13] a translocation Australian infantrymen would have found bizarre.

Across the Pacific Ocean, a similar transformation occurred by the 1950s with the Hollywood film version of Rodgers and Hammerstein's stage musical *South Pacific*, a glamorized adaptation of some of James A. Michener's gritty, realistic short stories of the war, *Tales of the South Pacific*. What had been set primarily in Michener's wartime Santo was filmed in Kauai, in the Hawaiian islands.[14] The only unattractive aspect of island life shown was the racism revealed in the reaction of Nellie Forbush to the part-Polynesian children of planter Emile De Becque. The shortage of congenial female company was expressed in the song "There Is Nothing Like a Dame," but none of the "natives" in the film were recognizably Melanesians. All else was paradise to the eye.[15] With the addition of a few catchy songs, its genre was a return to images and discourse common before the war. Anyone who had fought in New Guinea's jungles or wiled away months in Santo's heat would have found themselves in an unfamiliar world in the pageantry of the Melbourne balls or the homogenized setting of *South Pacific*.

Yet those Americans who had found Hollywood's touchstone of island places and people on film so derisive in the Pacific theater and who knew that "Hollywood is wrong about the South Sea isles" seemed reticent once they reached home.[16] Before most wars, civilians share common perceptions. Before the Pacific War, the Hollywood fantasy had been supreme, but, although the perceptions of civilians at home and servicemen in the field diverged because of different experiences, the return home often forced veterans to conform to the civilian illusion of the Pacific.[17] Maybe these men wanted to forget the war's harsher realities and wasted lives in their desire to rebuild civilian life and fit in to their society. Some who fought in the Southwest Pacific had seen themselves or comrades become gleeful headhunters and the Japanese become cannibals—no different really from some Melanesians whom most of these exotic peoples considered uncivilized and primitive. Military hierarchies, war, and removing men from their home society's constraints can make them savage. This war in the Pacific with the Japanese confirmed that. Moreover, although many saw beauty in Melanesia, its remoteness, challenging terrain, climate, and arsenal of diseases made it a threatening environment to exotic armies. Any virtues of its black peoples were not easy to translate to a racist America. Perhaps as a counter, most servicemen preferred to evoke the older, ubiquitous, and gentler image of the welcoming olive-skinned island girl when they brought back grass skirts, shells, and beads for homefolk. Perhaps too, they were victims of their own society's dream of sexual and social freedom in a warm climate, where the island illusion won over reality. Depending on perspective, both "others," the Westerners and the Melanesians with their cargo cults, had a share of irrational fantasy and desire, the one seeking escape from modernity's moral confines and the other seeking modernity's moral parity. But the filmic image of "Polynesians dancing hulas" was so dominant that by the 1980s and 1990s even some Melanesians believed it.[18] Certainly, the tourist industry, especially out of Hawai'i, had no reason to attempt to correct this reasserting Western and indeed global social memory that both simplified and sanitized such representations with a Hollywood gloss. Even art museums in the United States chose to represent island societies as primitive, uniform over large areas, and uncomplicated by modernity. Their directors knew the war had happened, but they acted as if it had no effects on the islands, their people, and productions. Islands represented for the tourists and art consumers a "paradise" at best, or "simple" societies at worst, and remained a playground for the rich and powerful in more ways than one.

While Australians too may have been beguiled by a far paradise in a generic Polynesia, few were convinced it was to be found in western Melanesia. The enduring newsreel representations of New Guinea, its people, and their environment in wartime campaigns were well-known to the civilian population at the time and are often rerun on television programs, especially on Anzac Day and daily in the much-visited Australia War Memorial in Canberra. Moreover, unlike the Hawaiian Islands, at a distant front gate to the United States, PNG is on Australia's very threshold, a hundred miles across the Torres Strait and, as far as Australians are concerned, the site of the most arduous battles their men fought in the Pacific War. Australia's intense postwar association with the country, as a dependency and beyond independence in 1975, has provided continued reinforcement to thousands of Australians who worked there that, for all its beauty, it is no paradise and certainly its myriad societies are hardly simple. And these days, with considerable law-and-order problems, government corruption and mismanagement, and high HIV infection rate, PNG is not a place that most Australians, other than war tourists, often choose to visit for a Pacific holiday, preferring Fiji (when not actively in coup mode), Vanuatu, the Cook Islands, or Samoa.[19]

Politicians' and the tourist industry's agendas and imagined landscapes were one thing. To the military at the time, strategic and tactical assessment of resources and terrain had been vital. The American-devised strategy of the initial "ferry route" of island airfields, followed by island hopping during the offensive, was successful because the Japanese had spread their limited resources on a front from China to the South Pacific and could not maintain supplies when ships became main targets for Allied attack. Isolated, all the Japanese army could do was to cling to pockets on the islands of New Guinea and Micronesia while the industrialized might of an amply resourced America largely bypassed them and pushed north to fight more conclusive battles closer to Japan, with the AIF reducing the enemy in New Guinea.

Although the environment was a determining agent in military strategy and tactics in combat areas, the protagonists in western Melanesia saw it as largely empty of development, devoid of a cultural landscape. Rather than their war reducing the environment to wilderness as in parts of Europe, Americans, oblivious of the subtleties of the Melanesian humanized landscapes, believed their military activities had begun to domesticate wilderness and improve both the people and their "primitive areas." While they were less confident of any permanence of their intense, localized transformation of the environment to control insect-borne diseases, they saw their airfields, roads, and wharves along with their agricultural activities as positive achievements, the industrialized world's text inscribed on landscape. The tropics, however, do not tolerate built structures or even spectacular engineering feats for long without expert, expensive maintenance. Although some of their airfields and roads on coral bases, the odd network of clearance for a base, and the durable Nissan huts survived, for decades those maintained were just a small proportion of those left. The infrastructure that the uses of peace required was far more modest than that needed to cope with tens of thousands of soldiers and the excess reserves marshaled to wage modern war.

Few involved in the campaigns thought about possible damage to ecological systems—no different from the mass of the populations of their homelands even though the basics of ecology were better known there. But even if damage or degradation could have been measured, it remains subjective, and since human beings are doing the measuring, they are most likely to consider it from the perspective of their species and its needs. Certainly, colonial administrations tried to protect the indigenous human resource from harm, but in New Guinea villagers often were forced to supply labor. In regard to non-human resources, only where these had been paid for in the past and the colonial administrations acknowledged rights of use and/or ownership by the local people was any attempt made to compensate for loss. James McAdam in New Guinea led the way with timber trees, and ANGAU tried to educate military loggers about the value of food trees to the people. In the Solomons, all this was acknowledged, but with only a skeleton administration and no effective military force of their own, the British could only make belated efforts, in the face of the magnitude of the American forces, to protect resources valued by the people. Subsequently, unlike the Australians, the British made little effort to compensate for loss due to the war damage and military occupation. Outside the operational zone, in the Cook Islands, Tonga, Fiji, Samoa, and Bora Bora, administrators paid much more attention to this. The Americans cooperated, but they were obstinately deaf to French concerns about damaging their cattle herds by bringing the tick pest into New Caledonia. Though they had exterminated it from their homeland, the Japanese troops too thought only of their own needs when they brought in the giant African snail to New Guinea.

Anthropocentrism was supreme in war, as it had been in peace. Anything else was beyond contemplation because there was almost no available Western scientific knowledge of the ecology of lagoons or of tropical forests particular to the region. The little that there was, like the birds on Midway, fast fell victim to human needs in the emergency. Wilbert Chapman, sometime director of the School of Fisheries at the University of Washington, did not let his scientific knowledge of marine ecology interfere with his using explosives to bring in fish. Even the islanders, for all their localized traditional environmental knowledge, quickly took to promiscuous dynamiting of their fishing grounds, a habit which persists.[20]

This prewar lack of knowledge of ecosystems, even ones with potential cash value such as the tropical forests of Melanesia, precludes any exact quantification of environmental damage, some of which was unexpectedly transitory. Certainly, in places the structure and composition of forest re-establishing on logged areas appear different from the one cut out, but over millennia Melanesians too had altered forest composition by their bush fallow gardening practices. Cyclones often did the same in localized areas. So while this felling changed specific ecosystems, it was not novel. Many small trees were left anyway that could fill gaps in the canopy. If given time without further disturbance, the forests will recover. Several atolls and patches on the high islands lost productive land to drastic clearance and coral compaction for airstrips. Blasting of lagoon coral for infill or shipping access reduced marine life, though without subsequent disturbance and depending on the nature of dynamic reef communities, some may have recovered after twenty to fifty years. Moreover, cumulative overfishing poses a greater threat to the ecology; this long-term process has seen drastic loss of large marine vertebrates as well as smaller species such as pearl shell and clams.[21] At the time, however, this was a substantial loss for the islanders, for example, in some tiny islands in the Gilbert and Ellice groups as well as loss of garden land to airstrips on Emirau Island and the Trobriands. In Melanesia, little obvious damage to the terrain was inflicted as economic warfare, even when the aim was to destroy the enemy's access to locally grown food. Their scattered gardens certainly were bombed, but chemicals, other than explosives and occasionally diesel oil, were avoided.[22] Such bombing affected local people's subsistence, notably in New Britain and Bougainville, but relatively little lasting damage was done to the land. Perceptions of the ecology differed, however, because many Bougainvilleans attributed an upsurge in a taro blight to wartime bombing. Thus, while there were losses, they cannot be readily quantified, and trying to weigh these against gains for the humans, such as more airstrips, is as futile as comparing coconuts to apples.

Today, although with improved technology and detailed research we are more able to gauge losses in, say, the Second Indochina or Vietnam War (1961–1975)[23] and the Gulf War (1990–1991), considerable debate surrounds assessment and rectification, even where this can be enforced.[24] There is no doubt the use of chemical herbicides such as the dioxin "Agent Orange" on forests and crops and the large-scale destruction of mangroves have inflicted widespread gross insult on several ecological systems and caused continuing human suffering in Vietnam and indeed among the foreign troops, far greater than anything that happened in the Pacific islands in World War II.[25] Even setting aside the toxic nature of new weaponry, the difference in scale is astonishing. In the Pacific War, the Allies dropped about 656,400 tons of bombs, while bombing by the Allies in all theaters in World War II totaled only about 2.6 million tons.[26] In Indochina, the Americans dropped about 6.3 million tons of bombs up to the end of 1971, with four more years of war yet to come. After a war, rarely has an aggressor faced up to the task of amelioration of such huge environmental damage. In some cases it is not easy to discern where ultimate blame lies—we have yet to develop international legal institutions with this capacity to make such judgments. In the Pacific islands, once the armies left, any remaining obvious threats such as munitions became the responsibility of the colonial administrations, but these remained dependent on metropolitan governments to provide the requisite, costly expertise. Japan, the aggressor, and the United States, which dumped the most munitions, left others to clean up these dangerous deposits in the southern islands' environment. The potential of future contamination of the maritime and terrestrial environment with chemical discharge from dumped munitions and sunken ships and planes is unknown, but it remains a concern to contemporary governments with little ability to address such threats. More so than the brown tree snake that now overruns Guam and the weed called "American rope," many of the negative environmental impacts of the war take considerable time to become manifest.

Military operations hand in hand with conservation or protection of the environment is a non sequitur, even away from the battlefield, as General Blamey's experiment with setting up a nature reserve in Papua revealed. More recent wars—Vietnam and the Gulf—have demonstrated what World War II and the atom bomb prefigured, that at least for a time ecocide, like genocide, can result from modern weapons. Increasingly, such horrors have inspired legal specialists, diplomats, and ironically even the military to begin working their way toward some form of international commitment to protect the environment in war and war games, beyond the precedents of outlawing chemical and biological weapons.[27] Unlike earlier conflicts, television has brought the evidence of these wars' effects to the world, and now we learn even more via the ubiquitous blog on the Internet, telling the world about the fighting in Iraq. Moreover, in democracies, revelations of actual conflict in places far away can cause the invaders' civilian populations to resile from involvement. This and the precedents of banning certain weapons hint at the motivation that could make our species draw back from wars in the future. The self-interest that drives us to war may be harnessed to guide us away from it.

Sheer wishful thinking? Perhaps. Yet it is, after all, more than sixty years since we used atomic bombs as weapons. Yet more than ever before, our technology has delivered devastating "conventional" weapons that hurt civilians, animals, and probably certain flora: antipersonnel or land mines, cluster munitions, and radioactive artillery are but three. Already public opinion considers these unacceptable. These specific concerns could all be subsumed if we succeed in a new kind of world war going on right now, which, if we lose, will leave few victors and untold millions of vanquished. That is the war against global warming of the atmosphere. In this study, I have analyzed mainly local and regional environmental consequences of World War II in the southern Pacific islands. Yet there were global processes at work here too. Among the intangible or at least invisible at the time was the unnoted and uncalculated but huge burden of carbon dioxide thrown up into the atmosphere by the factories producing processed food, clothing, and war matériel, and by machines burning fossil fuels—ships, tanks, jeeps, bulldozers, and airplanes—from the lands of the protagonists. Herein lies the greatest silence of the archival record, a hiatus of scientific ignorance that only began to be closed in the 1950s.[28] World War II was a major building block in the process of global warming. Since the products of the Industrial Revolution began to make life easier for more and more Europeans, Americans, and Japanese, and more recently for Indians and Chinese, the Pacific islanders have been burdened involuntarily with a changing atmosphere which, if this process continues, could spell the end of their existence as their atolls drown, their watercourses and wetlands dry out, and their forests in the west burn under more extreme and more frequent El Niño events.

There is little doubt now that our Earth—not someone else's remote island, thousands of miles away—is heating up and that process could cause global mass extinctions and impoverish any human survivors. As I have argued throughout this study, the Earth is an actor on the stage of history. Thus, in a non-Western sense, all on and in it is alive. But it has no voice other than "dogged" humanity. Humanity might well consider a common Polynesian perception of our place in the order of things: As the last major creation we are the younger sibling of all else on the Earth; as such we owe respect to the rest.[29] Whether by evolution or creation, we—the human community—the last to come into the light, should not be its destroyer. We have only two choices: Either keep using fossil-based energy as we are and slaughter each other for diminishing resources such as oil and potable water, or clean up our act and the Earth. There are many precedents for the former, as Michael T. Klare warns, and indeed Japan's motives for entering the war included the desire for resource access.[30] Should we continue down that path, all we will achieve, besides immediate human suffering, is to bring on the process of global warming more rapidly. If we take the other path and alter the way we use energy to reduce carbon dioxide and other greenhouse gas emissions as well as reducing our population growth, our global environment could recover and our civilization could survive. As Tim Flannery clearly shows, we have through international cooperation done well in major skirmishes, such as control of acid rain and depletion of the ozone layer. So our species is quite capable of cleaning up our global mess.[31] Gradually, as the Earth's people witness devastating demonstrations of climate change and realize that more may be expected and suddenly, action on a global scale will not only be essential, but also likely because few can escape its consequences. It is this growing awareness developing from public and scientific opinion and, more important, the concomitant international political processes, such as the United Nations climate summit planned for 2009 in Denmark, which could lead us to oppose wars that consume enormous resources, spew forth carbon dioxide and other greenhouse gases at a huge rate, and inflict direct environmental damage and pollution at the battle sites.

Our human anthropocentrism may give our species the will not to destroy our myriad ecological systems in order not to destroy ourselves. Just as the Pacific War proved, we are capable of working together and of sacrificing narrow personal and national interests if the external threat is potentially fatal. That goal of the common good now must extend beyond old friends and neighbors to all the human community, because global warming has signed no Geneva Convention. It takes no prisoners, leaves no victors, and offers no reparations. Our biggest challenge is to simultaneously develop this normative consciousness of war's dangers as a major element of an environmental engineering of care for our Earth, because states—whether world powers, such as the United States and China, or minor ones, such as Cambodia and Vanuatu—left lagging behind may trigger disaster, perhaps for our entire species. The war for furthering this understanding is one we all can fight with our own prudent use of energy and by lobbying governments, locally and nationally. Unlike past ordinary wars, though sacrifices will be needed, this can ultimately produce a "win-win" result if we keep in front of us the common goal of global survival along with the past suffering those awful conflicts have inflicted on our species. That would be the finest memorial we could begin creating for the tragic waste of war and enable our successive generations to inherit a richer Earth and a sustaining environment.

Notes

Currency, Measurement, and Place-Names

1. Bank of New South Wales conversion table, rates of exchange prevailing on 10 Nov. 1943, enclosure, RG 313-58-3401, NARA SB.

Preface

1. McNeill 2000, 342–347.
2. One solely economic estimate of cost to the United States was $148 billion at 1940 prices. Harrison 2000, 115.
3. Tucker and Russell 2004, 2.
4. MacKenzie 1997, 215–228.
5. Levine 2004, 65–92.
6. Austin and Bruch 2000.
7. John Keats, "On first looking into Chapman's Homer," http://www.bartleby.com/126/24.html (accessed 1 Sept. 2007).
8. Kirch 1997, 193–226.
9. Kunitz 1994, 42–81.
10. Sahlins 1992, 57–82; Shineberg 1967, 29–81.
11. Worster 1990, 1091.
12. John Donne, "No man is an island," http://polyticks.com/home/Visions/NoManIsl.htm (accessed 1 Sept. 2007).

Prologue

1. Frost 1996, 58–79; Campbell 2003, 50–62.
2. Lissington 1972, 19–22; Weeks 1989, 185–200.
3. Ienaga 1979, 130–133, 153–180; Barnhart 1987, 148–161, 263–272: Hess 1987, 9–45; Marshall 1995, 2; Chouchi, North, and Yamakage 1992, 132–181; Gray 1997, 294.
4. Stuart 2002.
5. An exception was Micronesia, where the Japanese, with intense application,

subsidization, and investment, were making the islands into colonies of settlement, a market, and a resource supplier for Japan. By the late 1930s, they were economically a success—for the Japanese at least. Peattie 1988.

6. Stanner, Appreciation of current situation and problems of ANGAU, c. November 1943, AWM 43, 80/6/17, AWM.

7. Miller 1991.

Chapter 1: Imagining Landscapes

Epigraphs. Historical Narrative, Southwest Pacific, Chapter 11, Morale, c. 1946, Entry 183, RG 313, NARA; Montgomery cited in Bowd 2005, 93.

1. Smith 1984.

2. Arnold 2000, 6–18.

3. Paul Stanford, personal communication, 7 June 2001; John Vollinger, "World War II Memoirs," Jane Resture's Oceania Page, http://www.janesoceania.com/ww2_johann_memoirs (accessed 27 Sept. 2004); Bailey and Farber 2006, 641–645.

4. "Vintage South Seas Films, 1920–1939," http://www.myriahs.com/publishvideos/vintage1.html (accessed 10 Oct. 2005); "Silent era films," http://www.silentera.com/PSFL/data/A/AlohaOe1915.html (accessed 10 Oct. 2005); Quanchi 1996, 105–109; Johnson 1940; the Martin and Osa Johnson Museum, Kansas City, http://www.safarimuseum.com/their_movies.htm (accessed 18 Aug. 2005). To reinforce the visual representations, music of a *hapa haole* (mixed native and European ancestry) variety emphasizing an idealized and carefree island timelessness in the Hawaiian islands went out on the short wave as part of the "Hawai'i calls" radio program in the 1930s. Hopkins 1980, 329–338.

5. Melville 1892; O'Brien 1921; Knibbs 1929; Kushner 1984, 130. Australia's *Smiths Weekly* projected an idyllic Pacific. Quarterly Report, Medical War Diary, 7 Australian Division, 10 Jan. 1944, AWM 52, 11/1/49 AWM.

6. Herle, Stanley, Stevenson, and Welsch 2002, 2–6.

7. Weir 2003, 2, 249 footnote.

8. D. Shearer to Eric and Jess, 11 May 1943, PR 91/138, AWM.

9. Haugland 1944, 13.

10. Peattie 1998, 5–15; Jasper Sharp, "Pioneers of Japanese Animation," Part 2, Midnight Eye, www.midnighteye.com/features/pioneers-of-anime2.shtml (accessed 5 Sept. 2005); Young 1998, 362–373.

11. Hiromi 2004a, 28–40; Henry Frei, "Why the Japanese Were in New Guinea," Remembering the War in New Guinea Project, AWM, http://www.awm.gov.au/ajrp (accessed 2 Sept. 2005); Bergerud 1996, 135.

12. Treland, Notes on Army Engineer Operations in SWPA, May 1944, Entry 305C, RG 77, NARA.

13. Ashton 1998.

14. Annual Report, Chief Engineer, Southwest Pacific, 1942, Entry 305D, RG 77, NARA.

15. Annual Reports, Chief Engineer, Southwest Pacific, 1942, 1943, Entry 305D, RG 77, NARA; Casey, Mapping in SWPA, 29 Oct. 1943, Entry 43315, RG 338, NARA; Dod 1966, 188–191; Bowd 2005.

16. Morison 1975, 245–277.

17. Pacific Association Academic Committee 1943.

18. Bennett and Beckworth, The influence of medical factors in land campaigns in the South and Southwest Pacific, 19 Oct. 1944, Entry 1005, RG 52, NARA; Bergerud 1996, 128–129.

19. Metzger 1982, 28–30.

20. G. Long, Diary, 31 Oct. 1943, 47, AWM 67, 1/3; Hank Nelson, e-mail to author, 15 Sept. 2007; Tim Moreman, "Jungle, Japanese and the Australian Army: Learning the Lessons of New Guinea," Remembering the War in New Guinea Project, AWM, http://ajrp.awm.gov.au/ajrp/remember.nsf/pages/NT00002F06 (accessed 13 Oct. 2005).

21. Bergerud 1996, 210–212; Denfeld 1989, 44; Terry Donnelly, "A Sergeant at Arms," 13, MS No. 2003.38, AM; A 118, 64–43 Photos Fiji, Vol. II, 1944–45, 18.1, 22, 26, ANZ; Larsen 1946. Potted geographical, botanical, and semiethnographical guide booklets assisted survival. Henson 2000, 27–50; Merrill 1943, Kraemer 1944; [John Burke], "Solomon Islands Sketches," c. 1944, entry 178, RG 313, NARA; F. E. Williams, "Relations with the Natives of New Guinea in Wartime," 1 Dec. 1942, Records of Allied Operational and Occupation Headquarters, Entry 43452, RG 33I, NARA; U.S. Government, Army Service Forces 1943; George Elrick, "The Solomons," chapters 1–24, Misc. Papers, AM.

22. Powell 2003, 173–176.

23. Cranwell, Green, and Powell 1943; General Staff, Land Head Quarters Australia 1943; Merrill 1943.

24. Hitoshi Imamura, "The Tenor of My Life,"144, MSS 1089, AWM.

25. Bennett and Beckworth, The Influence of medical factors, 19 Oct. 1944, Entry 1005, RG 52, NARA.

26. Unidentified Japanese, Diary, 13 Oct. 1943, PR 00947, AWM.

27. Hisaeda Akiyoshi, Diary, 15 June 1942, PR 91/040, AWM.

28. Masatsugu 1992, 268.

29. Unidentified Japanese, Diary, 13 Oct. 1943, PR 00947, AWM.

30. Akogina, Diary, 28 Dec. 1942, A. E. Mexted Papers, ID 43276, NLNZ.

31. Unidentified Japanese, Diary, 14 Oct. 1942, Box 1, F, A12-2, RG 313-58-3283, NARA SB.

32. S. Okada, "The Lost Troops," 13, MSS 732, AWM.

33. A. J. Traill, Diary, 17 Aug. 1942, PR 00051, AWM.

34. A. Gately, Diary, 6 Mar. 1944, PR00756, AWM; A. P. Pirie, Letter, 14 Jan. 1943, PR00602, AWM; J. H. Leemon, "The body snatchers," 57, MSS 0811, AWM; F. O. Monk, "Taim Bifor," 73. MSS 1184, AWM; Jackson 1989, 51.

35. R. Miller, Diary, 20 Feb. 1943, PR00831, AWM.

36. Haugland 1944, 5.

37. Adam Bartlett, "Men of Moresby," John Williams Papers, PR 87/062, AWM.

38. Durham 2003, 88.

39. Reybold, Topics for discussion, 13 Nov. 1943, RG 77, NARA.

40. Report, Special Service activities on Espiritu Santo, 3 April 1946, Entry 427, RG 427, NARA.

41. W. Olsen, Letter, 7 Feb. 1944, PR90/094, AWM.

42. A. C. Bennett, "The rough infantry," 172, MSS1408, AWM.

43. Report, Special Service activities on Espiritu Santo, 3 April 1946, Entry 427, RG 427, NARA.

44. S. Okada, "The Lost Troops," 23, MSS 732, AWM.

45. A. Moore, "On active service with the Red Shield," 2 April, 16 July 1945, MSS 742, AWM.

46. G. K. Little, "Those were the days my friend," 150–151, MSS 1210, AM.

47. Inspection Report Aitutaki, 10 Apr. 1945, Entry 179, RG 313, NARA; Historical Narrative, Southwest Pacific, Chapter 11, Morale, c. 1946.

48. Parsons 1945, 62.

49. Priday, The Cook Islands, draft manuscript, 31 July 1944, Entry 183, RG 313, NARA.

50. Parsons 1945, 63–65, 225. "Technicolor" was a relatively new process and seen by many as representing fantasy rather than reality.

51. Kushner 1984, 116; Parsons 1945, 80–81, 224–225; Holmes to Air Dept. 2 Mar. 1945, AIR 127 3 (iii), ANZ.

52. Inspection Report Aitutaki, 10 Apr. 1945, Entry 179, RG 313, NARA; Historical Narrative, Southwest Pacific, Chapter 11, Morale, c. 1946, Entry 183, RG 313, NARA.

53. Cf. Morison 1968, 168.

54. Spector 1985, 260. G. H. Heyen was the compiler of *Sailing Directions on Navigation in between the Islands and Atolls of the Gilbert Islands* (Suva: Government Printer, 1937).

55. Dyer 1972; HyperWar Foundation, chapter 18, http://www.ibiblio.org/hyperwar/USN/ACTC/actc-18.html (accessed 3 Oct. 2005). A neap tide occurs just after the first and third quarters of the moon when there is the least difference between high and low water.

56. Holland cited in Macdonald 1982, 152–154; McQuarrie 2000, 120–131.

57. Dyer 1972.

58. Holland cited in McQuarrie 2000, 124–125.

59. Spector 1985, 114–118, 149–169, 263.

60. Macdonald 1982, 154.

61. Gregg 1984, 79, 161; Morison 1968, 89; Battle Experience bulletin No. 15, 15 July 1944, Entry 182, RG 313, NARA; Report on Galvanic Operations, Medical, 11 Jan. 1944, Entry 1005, RG 52, NARA. Amphtracs-track-driven amphibious vehicles, 25 feet long, 10 feet 8 inches wide.

62. *New York Times*, 1 Dec. 1943, cited in Macdonald 1982, 152–154.

63. P. Mitchell to SOS, 9 Dec. 1943, WO 106/5928, TNA.

64. Costello 1982, 437, 439.

65. Bergerud 1996, 350–355.

66. A. Moore, "On active service," Feb. 1945, MSS 742, AWM.

67. A. C. Bennett, "The rough infantry," 172, MSS 1408, AWM.

68. G. Long, Diary, 27 October 1943, 41, AWM 67, 1/3, AWM.

69. Fitch to Commanding General, 31 Dec. 1944, Entry 305c, RG 77, NARA; Parsons 1945, photograph facing pp. 78, 79.

70. G. Long, Diary, 14 Mar. 1945, AWM 67, 2/75, AWM.

71. Huie 1944, 27–59, 89–108; Jackson 1989, 42.

72. Bergerud 1996, 146–268.

73. Commander, South Pacific to South Pacific Force, 8 Dec. 1943, U.S. Navy Pamphlet, "Are you following through?" Memo of informal conference on South Pacific Traveling Inventory Board, 6 Dec. 1943, RG 313, NARA; A. Fitch to Allied Force Commanders, SW Pacific, 1 Mar. 1944, RG 77, NARA; C. Nimitz to Pacific Fleet and Shore Activities, 24 May 1944, Box 7 (v. 9700), F. A1, RG 313-58-3440, NARA SB; Disease Prevention Officer to Commander, 5 Sept. 1944, Box 3, F. A9-4, RG 313-58-3416 NARA SB.

74. Sill 1947, 193.

Chapter 2: Peopling the Southern Pacific

Epigraph: Service of Supply, Surgeons Section, n.d., c. 1945, Entry 44463, RG 338, NARA.

1. Broome 1982; Howe 1977; Denoon et al. 1997.

2. Berry, Diary, 21 Dec. 1942, PR 84/021, AWM; Hunt, Diary, 28 Nov. 1943, 3 DRL 6132, AWM; Shearer, Letter, 11 May 1943, PR 91/138, AWM; Parsonage, Diary, 31 July 1944, PR 90/80, AWM; Vernon, Diary, 3 Mar. 1943, 7 Feb., 24 Mar. 1944, PR 00787, AWM; Craig, Diary, 7 Aug. 1943, PR 00906, AWM; Lee, Letter, 19 Nov. 1944, PR 00961, AWM; Vernon, ANGAU Diary July–Nov. 1942, AWM 54, 253/5/8 Part 1, AWM.

3. J. Craig, Papers, 126, PR00906, AWM.

4. W. Olsen, Letter, 16 Jan. 1944, PR90/094, AWM.

5. Saito 1991, 208.

6. Public Relations Manual, n.d., C Service force, Manus, New Guinea, Box 8, F. 7th Flt, confidential S/L, RG 313-58-3416, NARA SB. Cf. Lindstrom 2001, 107–128.

7. *National Geographic* 81, June 1942, 691–722, 759–785; 86, Oct. 1944, 409–424, 451–476; 87, Feb. 1945, 129–162; Photograph 157096 and caption, General Records of the Department of the Navy, 1798–1947, RG 80, NARA; Photograph A43858 and caption, RG 342, NARA.

8. Report by the Joint Intelligence Committee, The situation in the Southwest Pacific, Memo no. 82, 22 June 1943, Geographic file, RG 218, NARA.

9. Masatsugu 1992, 273; Tamotsu 1992, 280; Waiko 1988, 45–59; Nelson 1979, 147–151; Powell 2003, 206–223.

10. Report on Operations by 31/51 AIF, Bougainville, Dec. 1944–Feb. 1945, AWM.

11. Powell 2003, 196–206.

12. J. Gatt, Recollections, PR 85/226, AWM; B. Love, Diary, 20 Dec. 1942, 3 DRL 7211, AWM; H. P. Spindler, Diary, 14 Jan. 1943, PR 83/171, AWM; Powell 2003, 240.

13. Charles W. Crary, "My life as a soldier: 1939–1945," http://www.memoriesofwar.com/veterans/crary.asp (accessed 19 Aug. 2005).

14. Navy Dept., Manual of Advanced Base Development, July 1943, Box 3 (v. 9666), F. A1, RG 313-58-3440, NARA SB; Durham 2003, 73–77.

15. H. P. Spindler, Diary, 14 Jan. 1943, PR 83/171, AWM; Shaw, Interview, 2 Sept. 1944, Entry 302, RG 112, NARA; Crary, "My life as a soldier: 1939–1945."

16. Gage, Interview, 15 Feb. 1945, Entry 302, RG 112, NARA.

17. Yoshihara Kane, "Southern Cross," Chapter 13, Remembering the War in New Guinea Project, AWM, http://www.awm.gov.au/ajrp (accessed 14 Sept. 2005).

18. Saito 1991, 209, 212.

19. Photograph A 43651 and caption, RG 342, NARA.

20. Commander to Commanding Officer, 7 July 1945, Box 1, F. P8-5, RG 313-58-3019, NARA SB.

21. French Islands of the Pacific, Feb. 1942, Records of the Adjutant General's Office, 1917 onwards, Entry 427, RG 407, NARA.

22. Shackelford, Interview, May 1944, Entry 302, RG 112, NARA.

23. Westlund to Commander General, 18 Aug. 1943, Reconnaissance of Utupua, RG 407, NARA.

24. J. Beattie to Commander, 22 Sept. 1945, enclosure, First Narrative of the Russell Islands Naval Command, c. Sept. 1945, Box 1, F. A12, RG 313-58-3019, NARA SB; Cf. Bennett 1993, 129–183.

25. Dr. Asiri [Aseri K. Manulevu], quoted in Report, Espiritu Santo, July 1945, RG 313, NARA.

26. Report, Espiritu Santo, July 1945, RG 313, NARA.

27. Sabel 1999, 197; Jackson 1989, 44, 72–76; Robert W. Conner, Diary, 2, 16 July, 6 Aug., 10, 19 Sept. 1944, 93rd Seabees Battalion, http://www.seabees93.net/memoirs.htm (accessed 20 Aug. 2005); Morriss 1996, 46–47; Lindstrom 1996, 32; Mead 1956; Lindstrom 1989, 395–414; Davenport 1989, 271–273.

28. Robinson 1979, 80; Zelenietz 1991, 11.

29. Sabel 1999, 94, 104, 109, 115, 119.

30. Benallack, Routine Orders, 16 Apr. 1945, HQ and No 1 Platoon, 2/2 Forestry Company (Nov. 1944–Apr. 1945), AWM 52 5/32/4; Nelson 1996, 203, 206–207; Sabel 1999, 151; Downer, Interview, 23 Jan. 1945, Entry 302, RG 112, NARA; Civil Affairs, c. 1945, Entry 183, RG 313, NARA.

31. Beattie to Commander, 22 Sept. 1945.

32. Chapman 1949.

33. Crary, "My life as a soldier: 1939-1945"; G. K. Little, "Those were the days my friend," MSS 1210, AWM.

34. Shibata quoted in Shaw 1991, 231.

35. James A. Donahue, Journal, http://www.guadalcanaljournal.com/ (accessed 19 June 2006).

36. *Suva Fiji Times,* 4 Oct. 1943, 4; *Report of Secretary for Fijian Affairs, 1945,* CP no. 4, Legislative Council of Fiji (Suva 1947), 9.

37. Dorman 1997.

38. Mikesell, Interview, c. 1943, Entry 302, RG 112, NARA; Williams, A Sergeant at arms, No. 2003.38, AM.

39. Mitchell to SOS, 22 July 1943, CO 225/333, Part 2, TNA.

40. Dorman 1997, 82.

41. G. Barrow, Outlying Interlude, 38, Mss Pac s. 43, RH.

42. Ashton 1998.

43. Price cited in Macgregor 1981, 110–111.

44. Ayson to Secretary, 3 Feb. 1943, EA 1, 86/18/2 Pt 1, ANZ; Garity, Report on visit to Rarotonga, 6 Aug. 1943, Entry 44463, RG 338, NARA.

45. [John Burke], United States Naval History of Tutuila, c. Aug. 1945, 1, Navy Yard Museum, Washington D.C.

46. Gunner Frederick Pearson Mager (492471), "The men that beat the Gun," Accession No. 2000. 438, AM.

47. Survey of Tonga, Mar. 1942, RG 313, NARA.

48. Priday, The Cook Islands, draft manuscript, 31 July 1944, Entry 183, RG 313, NARA.

49. Holder, Historical Narrative, Wallis Island, 28 June 1945, Entry 183, RG 313, NARA.

50. John Vollinger, "World War II Memoirs," Jane Resture's Oceania Page, http://www.janesoceania.com/ww2_johann_memoirs (accessed 27 Sept. 2004).

51. Metzger 1982, 32; Oppenheimer 1966, 3.

52. Parsons 1945, 124, 133–140, 152–156, 162–164; McKay 1968, 113; Metzger 1982, 35, 37.

53. J. T. Boone, Sexual Aspects of Military Personnel, Mar. 1941, Box 44, Entry 1009, RG 52, NARA.

54. T. Engelhorn, Report of Medical Department Activities, Aitutaki, 27 July 1944, Entry 302, RG 112, NARA.

55. Barrow, Outlying Interlude, Chapter IX, 5.

56. Lafitani 1998, 79; Margaret Armstrong, Visitors Book and memoirs, 129, Mss Pac. S.93, RH; Mageo 2001, 67.

57. History of Tongatapu, c. 1945, Entry 183, RG 313, NARA; History of Upolu, c. 1945, Box v. 13379, F. A12, RG 313-58B-3061, NARA SB; Thompson, Venereal disease–South Pacific Area, Sept. 1944–Oct. 1944, Entry 1012, RG 112, NARA; Gordon to Commander, 29 Oct. 1944, Box 8 (V.9701), RG 313-58-3440, NARA SB; Inspection report, Aitutaki, 28 Feb. 1945, RG 313, NARA; Priday, The Cook Islands, draft manuscript, 31 July 1944; Kushner 1984, 127, 140, 169, 173.

58. McKay 1968, 112.

59. Report U.S. Forces in Aitutaki, 10 Nov. 1943, IT 122/5/2 Part 1, ANZ; Annual Report Judicial Department, 30 June 1943, Governor's Office, Series no. 5, RG 284, NARA SB.

60. Annual Sanitary Report, Upolu, 1944, Box 18 (v. 9716), F.A9-1, RG 313-58-3440, NARA SB.

61. Moyer to Secretary of Navy, 30 June 1942 (draft letter), Governor's Office, Series no. 5, RG 284, NARA SB.

62. Spencer to Commander, South Pacific, 22 Mar. 1946, Island government files, Samoa, 1946, RG 284, NARA SB.

63. Parsons 1945, 117; Metzger 1982, 32; Kushner 1984, 127, 140, 169, 173; Priday, The Cook Islands, draft manuscript, 31 July 1944; Paul Sanford, personal communication, 7 June 2001; Vollinger, "World War II Memoirs."

64. Dunnigan and Nofi 1998, 73, 232, 309, 449; Robson 1942.

65. History of Upolu, c. 1945; Governor, Report on Western Samoa, 11 July 1945, RG 284, NARA SB.

66. Metzger 1982, 32. Cf. M. A. Bruner, *Newsletter of the Institute of Ethnic Affairs Inc.* 2, no. 2 (Feb. 1947): 4, enclosure, Records of the Governor, RG 284, NARA SB.

67. History of Tongatapu, c. 1945.

68. Frisbie 1948, 209.

69. Marsa Dodson, personal communication, 7 May 2008.

70. Macdonald 1982, 159; P. Mitchell to SOS, 18 Aug. 1944, and minutes, CO 83/243/1, TNA.

71. Carden to Trafford-Smith, 20 Aug. 1945, minute, CO 83/243/1, TNA.

72. Lindstrom and Gwero 1998, 188–199.

73. Oppenheimer 1966, 165; Priday, The Cook Islands, draft manuscript, 31 July 1944, Entry 183, RG 313, NARA; History of Tongatapu, c. 1945; Houser to Commander, 17 June 1946, AG's Office, RG 284, NARA SB; Tailby to Secretary, 10 Oct. 1944, IT 122/5/2, part I, ANZ.

74. Tailby to Secretary, 10 Oct. 1944.

75. Garity, Report on visit to Rarotonga, 6 Aug. 1943, Entry 44463, RG 338, NARA; Hickling, Report US forces on Aitutaki, 10 Nov. 1943, IT 122/5/2, Part I, ANZ; Priday, The Cook Islands, draft manuscript, 31 July 1944.

76. Kushner 1984, 125, 140. Mortality rate was calculated for children under one year. *Report of the Work of Research Expeditions* . . . c. 1953, 22.

77. Kushner 1984, 31–32; Irwin 1965, 87; Oppenheimer 1966, 165.

78. Tuiasosopo, Fono 1945, Series 4, RG 284, NARA SB.

79. Priday, The Cook Islands, draft manuscript, 31 July 1944.

80. Kushner 1984, 173.

81. "Feelings of affiliation" subhead: Historical Narrative, Southwest Pacific, Chapter 11, Morale, c. 1946, Entry 183, RG313, NARA.

82. Manchester 1980, 101. See *Hawaiian Buckaroo,* dir. Ray Taylor (Soo Lesser 1938), for Princess Luana.

83. F. E. Williams, "Relations with the Natives of New Guinea in Wartime," 1

Dec. 1942, Entry 43452, Records of Allied Operational and Occupation Headquarters, World War II, RG 33I, NARA; Treatment of Natives, Sept. 1942, ANGAU War Diary, AWM 52, 1/10/1, AWM; Benallack, Routine Orders, 16 Apr. 1945; Powell 2003, 200; Luski 1991, 19, 23–24, 29; Bowd 2005, 61; G. Long, Interview with Aitchinson and Whittaker, 7 Dec. 1943, Notebook 41, AWM 67, AWM; G. K. Little, "Those were the days my friend," 150–151, MSS 1210, AWM; Durham 2003, 85.

84. Thomas W. T. Mitchell, Papers, 34, PR87/134, AWM; Robinson 1979, 117–118.

85. Rodger to Commanding Officer, 10 Nov. 1943, Entry 178, RG 313, NARA; Commander to all Activities, 2 Sept. 1943, Box 7, F. P13, RG 313-58-3013, NARA SB.

86. Dishon, Patrol reports, Kotte area, 10–24 July 1944, PNG Patrol Reports, microfiche, A9844, NAA.

87. Extract from Faithorn, Patrol Report, Rigo Sub-district, 25 Aug.–3 Sept. 1943, ANGAU War Diary, AWM 52, 1/10/1, AWM; Robinson 1979, 103–104.

88. Lindstrom and Gwero 1998, 45–46, 68, 77, 104–195.

89. Green, Discussion, CO 2/9, 18 May 1943, War Diary, Medical, AWM 52, 11/1/49, AWM: Walker 1961, 467; Luski 1991; Beryl Maddock, Flight Sister, 75, Papers, AWM PR 98/23, AWM.

90. Laffin 1956, 24.

91. P. Carbaugh, Report of Medical Activities in New Guinea, 13 Sept. 1944, Entry 302, RG 112, NARA.

92. "American Minority Groups in World War II." en.wikipedia.org/wiki/American_Minority_Groups_in_World_War_II (accessed 25 Sept. 2007); Luski 1991; Munholland 2005, 151–115; Maddock, Flight Sister, 75; Commander Russell Islands to Commander, Marines, 8 May 1945, Box 7, F. A17-24, RG 313-58-3019, NARA SB.

93. Kirk et al., Report of Special Investigation, Number 6 Rue Paul Bart, 15 Sept. 1944, Entry 44463, RG 338, NARA. The fee was four to five dollars. Enlisted men were accommodated from 9:00 am to 7.30 pm, officers after that. The United States supplied prophylactics to its men. Tom Thomson's War Years, 17 Apr. 1945. www.netwalk.com/~vireo/TomsWarYears.html - 156k - (accessed 15 Aug. 2007); Richard Godin, e-mail to author, 17 Aug. 2007; Thompson, Report, Venereal Disease–South Pacific Area, Oct. 1945; Bill Rodman, e-mail, 6 Aug. 2007; Munholland 2005, 153; R. E. Gillespie, e-mail to author, 3 May 2001; Amelia Earhart forum, www.tighar.org/forum/Forum_Archives/200105.txt (accessed 6 Aug. 2007); Durham 2003, 32.

94. Quarterly Report, Medical War Diary, 7 Australian Division, 10 Jan. 1944, 8, AWM 52, 11/1/49, AWM.

95. W. Olsen, Letter, 30 Jan. 1944, PR90/094, AWM

96. M. G. Hauer, Letters, 22, 25 Nov. 1945, PR87/110, AWM.

97. Sabel 1999, 220; Durham 2003, 70.

98. Gillespie 1945, 81.

99. Shaw 1991, 228; Morris Low, "Japanese Perceptions of the Enemy," Remembering the War in New Guinea Project, AWM, http://www.awm.gov.au/ajrp (accessed 12 Sept. 2005).

100. Karundeng, Statement 18 Sept. 1944, ANGAU War Diary, Administration Reports Part 1, 1944, AWM 52, 1/10/1, AWM; Yoshiaki 2001; Ienaga 1979, 184, 190–191.

101. Tamotsu 1992, 280.

102. Nelson 1996, 158, 162, 207, 208, 212, 213, 226, 241, 283, 291–292.

103. Luski 1991, 13, 19, 95. Army nurses had ordinary ranks as well as officers.

104. Litoff and Smoth 1996, 61.

105. Sabel 1999, 120, 197; Crouch 1986.

106. "Dad's diary," 6 Mar., Dec. 1944, in writer's care.

107. Sabel 1999, 120; A. P. Pirie, Letter, 1 Nov. 1942, PR00602, AWM; S. Kildea, Diary, 2 Nov. 1942, PR00913, AWM; Morriss 1996, 78; R. Miller, Diary, 20 Feb. 1943, PR00831, AWM; A. Moore, "On Active Service with the Red Shield," 19 Mar. 1945, MSS 742, AWM.

108. A. Gately, Diary, 13 Oct. 1944, PR00756, AWM.

109. "Dad's diary," 31 Dec. 1943.

110. W. Olsen, Letter, 8 Mar. 1944, PR90/094, AWM.

111. A. Long, Diary, 20 Feb. 1943, PR00233, AWM.

112. Kushner 1984, 58; Parsons 1945, 225.

113. W. Olsen, Letter, 22 Jan. 1944, PR90/094, AWM.

114. Karl Shapiro, "Aside," in Tapert 1987, 214.

115. "Rabaul Ballad" http://www.geocities.jp/abm168/GUNKA/rabaul.html (accessed 28 Oct. 2007).

116. Yoshihara Kane, "Southern Cross," Chapter 16, Remembering the War in New Guinea Project, AWM, http://www.awm.gov.au/ajrp (accessed 17 Sept. 2005).

117. Shinto Miyako, Diary, 1943, Mexted Papers, No 43276, AWM; Cook and Cook 1992, 263–265.

118. "What the Soldier Thinks," Dec. 1943, RG 407, NARA.

119. Sabel 1999, 144–146; Conner, Letters, 6, 29 Aug. 1944.

120. Sontag 1977, 9.

121. Ahrens 2006.

122. Donahue, Journal.

123. R. Cattley, 22 Oct. 1942, 3DL/6105, AWM.

124. A. Long, Diary, 21 Aug. 1942, PR00233, AWM.

125. T. Neeman, Letters Jan. 1943–Jan. 1944, PR 01034, AWM; H. Dunkley, Letters, 1945, PR 84/35 AWM; W. Olsen, Letters, 13, 29 Mar., 1944, PR90/094, AWM; Letters to parents, 14 Mar., 26 Aug., 3 Oct. 1943, 14 Jan. 1944, Waterman family papers, MS 3907, NLNZ; Sabel 1999, 118, 128, 140, 158, 167, 170, 178.

126. W. Olsen, Letter, 14, 17, 30 Jan., 23 Feb. 1944, PR90/094, AWM.

127. A. P. Pirie, Letters, PR00602, AWM.

128. H. Dunkley, Letter, 23 Mar. 1943, PR 84/35, AWM.

129. J. Browne, 11, 23 Sept. 1942, MSS 1659, AWM.

130. W. Olsen, Letter, 23 Feb. 1944, PR90/094, AWM.

131. B. French, Diary, 1 Oct. 1945, PR 85/219, AWM; D. Cregan, 25 June 1943,

PR 84/264, AWM; Kushner 1984, 81; Monthly Report, CBMU, Mar. 1945, Box v. 9291, F.A9-4, RG 313-58-3401, NARA SB; Jones 1962, 427; Lidz 1946, 195.

132. Historical Narrative, Southwest Pacific, Chapter 11, Morale, c. 1946.

133. Conner, Diary, 2 Aug. 1944; Photograph, Jack Benny Show, 93rd CB, 26 Aug. 1944, RG 80-G-247191, NARA; Cox 1987, 107; T. Engelhorn, Report of Medical Department Activities, Aitutaki, 27 July 1944, Entry 302, RG 112, NARA.

134. Sabel 1999, 144–146; Conner, Letters, 6, 29 Aug. 1944.

135. Photograph, L. H. Edwards, Feb. 1945, 127-GU 1149, No 111575, Box 73, Marine Corps Records, RG 127-GW, NARA.

136. Parsons 1945, 187–190.

137. Conner, Letters, 24 Dec. 1943; Sabel 1999, 141; Christmas, Ugi Island, 1943, Photograph 236057, Navy Records, Box 699, RG 80-G, NARA; Christmas Finschhafen, 1943, SC 326530, Signal Corps, RG 111-SC, NARA; J. R. Hay, Airforce Interlude, 41, MSX 4862, NLNZ.

138. R. Miller, Diary, 25 Dec. 1942, PR00831, AWM.

139. J. R. Hay, Airforce Interlude, 42, MSX 4862, NLNZ.

140. G. H. Fearnside to Bob and Wendy, 1 Jan. 1945, PR85/071, AWM.

141. Gately, Diary, 7 Mar. 1944; V. O. Hunt, Diary, 31 Dec. 1943, DRL 6132, AWM; Trevor Thomas, Diary, 4 Jan. 1943, Mss 5143, NLNZ; Dorman 1997, 80–81; Waterworth 1960, 90; Historical Narrative, Southwest Pacific, Chapter 11, Morale, c. 1946.

142. Durham 2003, 85. By November 1944, in 533 theaters in the South Pacific Command alone, the U.S. Army screened 1,700 films a week, to say nothing of those screened by the U.S. Navy. Historical Narrative, Southwest Pacific, Chapter 11, Morale, c. 1946.

143. B. Love, 27 Jan. 1943, DRL 7211, AWM; V. Hunt, Diary, 13 Dec. 1944, 3DRL 6132, AWM; T. Engelhorn, Report of Medical Department Activities, Aitutaki, 27 July 1944, Entry 302, RG 112, NARA; Historical Narrative, Southwest Pacific, Chapter 11, Morale, c. 1946; "What the Soldier Thinks," Dec. 1943.

144. Historical Narrative, Southwest Pacific, Chapter 11, Morale, c. 1946.

145. "The internet movie database- IMDd," http://www.imdb.com/title/tt0036534/ (accessed 4 Oct. 2005).

146. Conner, Letter, 20 July 1945; Diary, 20 July 1945.

147. "The internet movie database- IMDd," http://www.imdb.com/title/tt0035553/ (accessed 4 Oct. 2005).

148. "Dad's diary," 13 Nov. 1943.

149. History of the 35 Battalion, Aug. 1945, n.p., MSS1107, AWM.

Chapter 3: Diseased Environments

Epigraph: Commander to South Pacific Force, 14 Feb. 1944, Box 14, v. 9699, F. P2, RG 313-58-3440, NARA SB.

1. Kunitz 1994, 43–81.
2. Robson 1942.

3. Bennett and Beckworth, The influence of medical factors in land campaigns in the South and Southwest Pacific, 19 Oct. 1944, Entry 1005, RG 52, NARA; Beckworth, Time Factor in the Development of Beriberi among Japanese Troops, 16 July 1943, Entry 44463, RG 338, NARA.

4. Cited in Harper, Lisansky, and Sasse 1947, 64–65.

5. Harper, Lisansky, and Sasse 1947, 5–9; Hairson, Bang, and Maier 1947, 800.

6. Harper, Downs, Oman, and Levine 1963, 413–414.

7. McCarthy and Carter c. 1967, 14.

8. Cited in Sweeney 2003, 16.

9. Harper, Downs, Oman, and Levine 1963, 400.

10. Buxton 1927.

11. Harper, Downs, Oman, and Levine 1963, 472.

12. This rebuff has also been attributed to commanders on Guadalcanal. Merillat 1982, 255.

13. Tully, Report on Malaria in the New Hebrides, 21 Aug. 1931, WPHC NHBS MP 187/31, WPA; Base Malaria and Epidemic Control, 1945, Entry 183, RG 313, NARA.

14. Downs, Harper, and Lisansky 1947, 73.

15. McCarthy and Carter c. 1967, 108; Bennett and Beckworth, The influence of medical factors.

16. Bennett and Beckworth, The influence of medical factors; Walker 1962, 84–88, 91–92, 95–96; Pilger 1993, 61; Bullard 2004, 203–220; Joy 1999, 196; Fenner 1998, 57–59.

17. Atebrin was also known as quinacrine and mepacrine.

18. N. Fairley, Malaria in the Western Pacific, 22 Dec. 1942, CO 83/238/85448, TNA. In late 1943, Fairley was responsible for finding the correct prophylactic dose of Atebrin at 100 mgs daily to prevent overt attacks of malaria; Hart and Hardenburgh 1963, 540; Walker 1962, 99; Joy 1999, 200, 204; Sweeney 2003, 27–35; Condon-Rall 1995, 99–105.

19. Walker 1962, 77–80.

20. Malaria at Cairns, 19 Dec. 1942, Entry 54A, RG 112, NARA; L. Schopick, Malaria and Endemic Diseases, South Pacific Area, n.d., c. 1945, Entry 1012, RG 112, NARA.

21. Walker 1962, 84–88, 99; Fairley, Malaria in the Western Pacific, 22 Dec. 1942, CO 83/238/85448, TNA; Joy 1999, 200, 204; Sweeney 2003, 35, 189, 239–241; Condon-Rall 2000, 51–70.

22. Joy 1999, 201.

23. Walker 1962, 98–100, 107–109.

24. Supplement to August report, 15 Sept. 1943, RG 313, NARA; Daggy 1945, 1–13.

25. Oman and Christenson 1947, 99; McCoy 1944, 538.

26. Walker 1962, 146–147.

27. Report, 3rd Malaria control detachment, 5 Oct. 1945, Entry 54A, RG112, NARA.

28. Report, Treasury Island, Mar. 1944, RG 38, NARA; Harper, Lisansky, and Sasse 1947, 42–56; Smith to Medical Officer, 5 Jan. 1943 and enclosures, Entry 179, RG 313, NARA; Hart and Hardenburgh 1963, 550–551; 11 AMCU Report Jan. 1944, Appendix 1, PR 00525, AWM.

29. Russell 2001, 116, figure 6.4.

30. Base malaria and epidemic control, New Hebrides, c. 1945, Entry 183, RG 313, NARA; Harper, Lisansky, and Sasse 1947, 1–67; Walker 1962, 107–109.

31. Jones, "A Volunteer's Story," 65, MSS 1168, AWM.

32. Harper, Monthly report for Dec., 31 Dec. 1943, Box 9, v. 9309, F. A9-2, RG 313-58-3401, NARA SB.

33. United States Bureau of Medicine and Surgery 1953, 73.

34. Russell 1963, 5.

35. Following prewar practice these laborers were not dosed, but treated for acute attacks. Black 1955, 27.

36. Powell 2003.

37. Black 1955, 27; Raphael Cilento, cited in Spencer 1994, 29; W. Tully, Malaria Survey, Draft to June 1931, WPHC NHBS 187/3/192, WPA; Gunther 1946, 510–511.

38. Benallack, Routine Orders Part 1, 16 Apr. 1945, HQ and No. 1 Platoon, 2/2 Forestry Coy, 5/32/4, AWM 52, AWM.

39. Malaria Newsletter No. 6, Dec. 1943, Box 7. F. P2, RG 313-58-3503, NARA SB; Schopick, Malaria and Epidemic Diseases–South Pacific area, c. 1945.

40. R. Murray, Laboratory Service in South Pacific Area, 1945, Entry 44463, RG 338, NARA.

41. Levine and Harper 1947, 121–123; Walker 1962, 95.

42. Downs, Harper, and Lisansky 1947, 88; Condon-Rall 2000, 59–63; Sweeney 2003, 62–86; Walker 1962, 117, 207, 234; War Diary, ADMS, 9 July 1944, July and August 1944 file, AWM 52, 11/1/49, AWM. The dosage increased to 0.7 grams for the Americans in November 1944. Harper, Lisansky, and Sasse 1947, 37.

43. Harper, Monthly Report for Dec., 31 Dec. 1943, Box v. 9309, F. A9-2, RG 313-58-3401, NARA SB. See also Parks, Monthly Malaria Reports, June 1943, 8 July 1943, Box v. 9309, F. A9-2, RG 313-58-3401, NARA SB; Harper, Lisansky, and Sasse 1947, 40.

44. Poole to Secretary to the Government, 24 Apr. 1944, Poole to Officer Commanding, 6 May 1944, Officer Commanding to SMO, 8 May 1944, Rutter to Secretary to the Government, 15 May 1944, Poole to CO, 19 June 1944, Bullen to Secretary to the Government, 22 June 1944, F 9/44 Part E, WPHC, WPA; Homewood to Breene, 27 Dec. 1942, Entry 44463, RG 338, NARA; Young, BSI, 4 Dec. 1942, WPHC F 9/43; Base Prevention Disease Officer to Commander, 5 June 1944, Box 1, F. A 9-4, RG 313-58–3416, NARA SB.

45. Sapero to Commanding General, 12 Sept. 1942, Entry 179, RG 313, NARA.

46. Sapero, Malaria hazard of Natives, 12 Sept. 1942, Entry 179, RG 313, NARA; Base and Epidemic Control, New Hebrides, c. 1945, 446–447, Entry 183, RG 313, NARA; Curtin to Commanding General, 10 Mar. 1943, RG 338, NARA; Malaria control at Base Button 1942, 17 Jan. 1943, Entry 179, RG 313, NARA; Mount, Malaria

Hazard of Tonkinese and Natives, 4 Oct. 4, 1943, Entry 179, RG 313, NARA; Harper, Lisansky, and Sasse 1947, 39.

47. Downs, Harper, and Lisansky 1947, 72; Lindstrom 1996, 19.

48. Bulletin 42, 24 Aug. 1944, F. G1, RG 313-58-3282, NARA SB.

49. Report cited in Efate History, 4 Apr. 1942–30 June 1943, Entry 427, RG 407, NARA.

50. Navy Dept., Manual for Advanced Base Development, 69, July 1943, Box 3 (v. 9666), F A1, RG 313-58-3440, NARA SB.

51. Gardiner, Quarterly History of Medical Activities, Emirau, 12 Oct. 1944, Entry 54A, RG 112, NARA; Officer in Charge, Manus to Commander, 5 May 1944, Box 1, F. A9-4, RG 313-58-3416, NARA SB; Wainwright to Chief Engineer, 26 Feb. 1944, Records of the Office of the Chief of Engineers, RG 77, NARA; Malaria and epidemic disease control, 6 June 1945, Box 1, F. A 9-4, RG 313-50-3019, NARA SB; Downs, Harper, and Lisansky 1947, 76–80; Harper, Downs, Oman, and Levine 1963, 400, 433.

52. Sketch Map of Hombu Hombu, c. 1944, WPHC BSIP 1/111/14/19.

53. Mikesell, Interview, May 1944, Entry 302, RG 112, NARA.

54. Hairson, Bang, and Maier 1947, 803; Levine and Harper 1947, 119–123.

55. The Third Division Histories Committee 1948, 115–125; Photographs 250846, 220016, 220040, 220013, RG 80, NARA; Observations on Green Island Reconnaissance, 31 Jan. 1944, Entry 427, RG 407, NARA; R. Murray, Laboratory Service in South Pacific Area, 1945, Entry 44463, RG 338, NARA; Murray to Commander, Return of Native inhabitants of Green Island, 17 August 1944; Administrative Report, ANGAU War Diary, Sept. 1944, AWM 52, 1/10/1, AWM; Leo Hannett, personal communication to author, 1971. This vulnerability of native people to infections outside their home area was well known before the war. Lambert 1949, 824.

56. Base Prevention Disease Officer to Commander, 5 June 1944 and minute, Box 1. F. A9-4, RG 313-58-3416, NARA SB. An upsurge in malaria was common when seeded units came from another area to a forward base. Malaria Officer to Officer in charge, 20 July 1944, Box 3, F. P 2, RG 313-58-3416, NARA SB.

57. Base Prevention Disease Officer to Commander, 5 Sept. 1944, Box 3, F. P2, RG 313-58-3416, NARA SB.

58. Unit History 116th Engineers, Dec. 1942, RG 305D, NARA; Cockburn to Casey, 21 Sept. 1943, RG 77, NARA.

59. Caption on Photograph 127-GW-1068, #69431, Malaria control series, RG 127, NARA.

60. Gibson, First Narrative of Russell Islands Naval command, 22 Sept. 1945, Box 1, F. A12, RG 313-58-3019, NARA SB.

61. Harper, Downs, Oman, and Levine 1963, 448.

62. United States Bureau of Medicine and Surgery 1953, 77.

63. Report on Malaria Prevention, Dobadura-Buna area, War diary, 20 Jan. 1943, AWM 52, 11/1/49, AWM.

64. Spencer 1994, 72; Harper, Lisansky, and Sasse 1947, 4.

65. Bullard 2004, 213–214; Black 1955.

66. Walker 1962, 161.

67. Appendix C, Quarterly Report 31 Jan. 1946, ANGAU Medical Services, Oct.–Dec. 1945, 481/12/136, AWM 54, AWM; Stout 1954, 528–543; Walker 1962, 127, 130, 154.

68. Spencer 1994, 72.

69. Mackerras, Notes on Malaria, c. 1943, AWM 54, 267/6/7, Part 145, AWM.

70. Baker 1963, 468.

71. Harper, Lisansky, and Sasse 1947, 59; Downs, Harper, and Lisansky 1947, 81–83.

72. Walker 1962, 118, 120–127; Alving 1955, 209. http://history.amedd.army.mil/booksdocs/KOREA/recad2/default.htm (accessed 3 May 2007).

73. Malaria and Epidemic Diseases control–South Pacific area, c. 1944, Entry 1012, RG 112, NARA.

74. Sweeney 2003, 151–155.

75. Horn 1933, 126–127; Manson-Bahr and Walters 1934, 15–16; Christophers 1940, 52–54; Cooper 1949, 717–721; Steck 1972, 23.168–23.169.

76. Malaria control, Guadalcanal, Reports for Dec., 31 Dec. 1943, Jan., 31 Jan. 1944, Box v. 9309, F. A9-2, RG 313-58-3401, NARA SB; Harper, Lisansky, and Sasse 1947, 41–42. Plasmochin (also known as pamaquine and plasmoquine) at this relatively high dosage in association with atebrin will destroy most vivax in the asexual stage (the liver cycle) as well as the gametocytes of *falciparum*. Cooper 1949, 725–726.

77. Tulagi-Florida, Report for Jan. 1944, Box v. 9288, F. P, RG 313-58-3401, NARA SB; Levine and Harper 1947,119–123.

78. Pringle and Avery-Jones 1966, 269–272; Voller and Wilson 1964, 551–552. Cf. Colborne 1955, 356–369; Archibald and Bruce-Chwatt 1956, 775–784.

79. Appendix C, Malaria in Base Areas, 33rd Meeting of Allied Malaria Control Conference, 17 May 1944, Medical War Diary, AWM 52, 11/1/49, AWM.

80. Final close out Report on Guadalcanal, 22 Oct. 1945–1 May 1946, Entry 44463, RG 338, NARA; Sapero 1949, 1129–1131.

81. [John Burke], United States Naval History of Tutuila, Navy Yard, Washington D.C., 1945, 119; Monthly sanitation report, 1 Oct. 1944, Box v. 13381, F. P 2, RG 313-58B-3061, NARA SB; Parsons 1945, 202, 204–209.

82. Engelhorn, Interview, 27 July 1944, Entry 302, RG 112, NARA.

83. Postwar research threw doubt on this. Jachowski and Otto 1952, 663–670.

84. Walker 1962, 208–210; Oman and Christenson 1947, 100–101.

85. Schopick, Malaria and Epidemic Diseases: South Pacific Area, 1945.

86. Perry 1950, 104–110.

87. Downs, Harper, and Lisansky 1947, 86.

88. Capps 1963, 62–63.

89. Downs, Harper, and Lisansky 1947, 86; Perry 1950, 105–110; Goldman and Eads, Dengue Fever on a South Pacific Base, n.d., c. 1944, Entry 179, RG 313, NARA.

90. Walker 1962, 172–173.

91. American Samoa Report 1950, 3, Annual Reports, RG 284, NARA SB: Commander to South Pacific Force, 14 Feb. 1944, Box v. 9699, F. P2, RG 313-58-3440, NARA SB; Walker, Meyers, Woodhill and McCulloch 1942, 227.

92. Commander South Pacific to all bases, 29 [month unclear] 1943, RG 313-58-3013, NARA SB.

93. [Burke], United States Naval History of Tutuila, 119; History of Upolu, c. 1945, Box v. 13379, F. A12, RG 313-58B-3061, NARA SB.

94. Hayman 1968, 142.

95. Engelhorn, Interview, 27 July 1944, Entry 302, RG 112, NARA.

96. American Samoa Report 1950, 3, Annual reports, RG 284, NARA SB: [Burke], United States Naval History of Tutuila, 54.

97. Inspection Report Aitutaki, 10 Apr. 1945, Entry 179, RG 313, NARA; Historical Narrative, Southwest Pacific, Chapter 11 Morale, c. 1946, Entry 183, RG 313, NARA; Morgan to RC, n.d., c. Feb. 1944; Hickling, U.S. Forces in Aitutaki, 10 Nov. 1943, IT112/5/2 Part 1, ANZ.

98. American Samoa Report 1950, 3, Annual reports, RG 284, NARA SB; Policy of the Filariasis Investigation and Control Board, Upolu, 18 Mar. 1943, Box v. 13379, P2, RG 313-58B-3061, NARA SB; Byrd and Amant, Filariasis among Marines, Tutuila, 1 July 1943, Box v. 13379, P2, RG 313-58B-3061, NARA SB.

99. Holder, Historical Narrative, Wallis Island, 28 June 1945, Entry 183, RG 313, NARA; John Vollinger, "World War II Memoirs," Jane Resture's Oceania Page. http// www.janesoceania.com/ww2_johann_memoirs (accessed 27 Sept. 2004).

100. Historical Narrative, Southwest Pacific, Chapter 11 Morale, c. 1946, Entry 183, RG 313, NARA.

101. Thompson, Native labor survey—New Caledonia and Dependencies, 17 Nov. 1942, Report on Franco-American relationship in New Caledonia, Report No. 432, 1945, Microfilm 323, Division of Pacific and Asian History, ANU, Canberra; Halsey to Acting Governor, 4 July 1943, Entry 183, RG 313, NARA.

102. Malaria Report, Jan. 1944, Box 3, F. A9-4, RG 313-58-3013, NARA SB.

103. Organization of Armed Forces in South Pacific Area, n. d., c. 1945, 35–38, RG 112, NARA.

104. May 1941, 449–450; Philip 1964, 341.

105. Philip 1964, 277–278, 309–322.

106. Zarafonetis and Baker 1964, 120.

107. Walker 1962, 178–181, 197–199; Crouch 1986, 80–82; Jones, A Volunteer's Story, 71, MSS 1168, AWM.

108. Philip 1964, 306, 343.

109. Zarafonetis and Baker 1964, 119–120; Walker 1962, 190.

110. Scrub Typhus in Forward area, Malaria newsletter No. 5, Nov. 1943; Newsletter No 9, Mar. 1944, Box v. 9309, F. A9-4, RG 313-58-3401, NARA SB.

111. Malaria and Epidemic Disease control reports for June 1944, Box1, F. A9-4, RG 313-58-3416, NARA SB; Zarafonetis and Baker 1964, 122, 142; Walker 1962, 191–195, 197.

112. Espiritu Santo Base History, c. 1945, 446, Entry 183, RG 313, NARA.

113. Russell 2001, 119–183.

114. Harper, Downs, Oman, and Levine 1963, 457.

115. Cited in Russell 1999, 788.

116. Espiritu Santo Base History, c. 1945, 446; Shields, Studies of airplane spraying, Hollandia, 28 Feb. 1945, Entry 54A, RG 112, NARA; Malaria and Epidemic Control Bulletin, No. 1, Mar. 1945, Box v. 3062, F. P2-3, RG 313-58D-3284, NARA RG; Harper, Lisansky, and Sasse 1947, 46–47; Walker 1962, 128–131: Harper, Downs, Oman, and Levine 1963, 460–461; Hart and Hardenburgh 1963, 548–550.

117. Espiritu Santo Base History, c. 1945, 446.

118. Photograph 061440 and caption, 18th Malarial Control Unit, AIF, AWM.

119. Walker 1962, 629–631; Pillsbury and Livingood 1968, 556–557, 574, 582–587, 651; Cox 1987, 134.

120. This was mainly Flexner's dysentery *(Shigella flexneri),* a form less severe than *S. dysenteriae.* Walker 1962, 16.

121. Walker 1962, 15–16; Bullard 2004, 215.

122. Allen 1983, 218–235; Burton 1983, 236–261.

123. Allan Walker, Binder of notes, c. 1944, 6, AWM 75, 228, AWM; Report, Medical Administration, 1944, ANGAU War diary, Part 2, AWM 52, 1/10/1, AWM.

124. Cole, Memo 49, 3 August 1945, Box v. 9294, F. P2, Commander to Base Commander, 22 August 1945, Box v. 9295, F. A2, Erni, Report of influenza epidemic, 18 August 1945, Box v. 9277, F. A9, RG 313-58-3401, NARA SB.

125. Station Order 10.44, 7 Apr. 1944, Box 1, S85, RG 313-58-3008, NARA SB; Larsen 1946, 36; *Suva Fiji Times,* 2 Oct. 1943, 10; Glover, Interview, 14 Aug. 1944, Entry 3103, RG 112, NARA.

126. Prime Minister to New Zealand Minister, Washington, 25 Feb. 1943, EA 1, 86/1/13, 1, ANZ.

127. *Suva Fiji Times,* 4 Oct. 1943, 4; *Report of Secretary for Fijian Affairs,* 1945, CP no. 4, Legislative Council of Fiji (Suva: Government Printing Office, 1947), 9.

128. Lala Sukuna, Minute, 28 Sept. 1944, F114/4, CSO FNA; Authority for evacuating Natives, 1942–1943, CSO N Series, 44/23, 44/23/11, FNA.

129. Wood-Ellem 1999, 53, 208; Page 2004, 68.

130. Station Order 10.44, 7 Apr. 1944, Box 1, F. S85, RG 313-58-3008, NARA SB; DO to DC, 29 July 1942, CSO F 9/55/1, FNA; *Annual Report of the Medical Department,* 1943, CP no. 17, Legislative Council of Fiji, 3; Prime Minister to New Zealand Minister, Washington, 25 Feb. 1943, EA 1, 86/1/13, 1, ANZ; Thompson, Report, Venereal Disease–South Pacific Area, Oct. 1945, RG 112, NARA; Page 2004, 68.

131. Thompson, Report, Venereal Disease–South Pacific Area, Oct. 1945; Engelhorn, Interview, July 27, 1944, Entry 302, RG 112, NARA; Brandt to Commandant, 22 August 1945, Box v. 3062, F. P6, RG 313-58D-3284, NARA SB; Spring 1998, 44; Cline 2002, 91.

132. Brandt to Commandant, 22 August 1945. Before the war the naval govern-

ment in American Samoa would not allow anyone with VD to enter the territory. Metzger 1982, 32.

133. Thompson, Report, Venereal Disease–South Pacific Area, Oct. 1945.

134. Gordon to Commandant, 23 Feb. 1945, Box v. 3062, F. P2, RG 313-58D-3284, NARA SB. See also Hickling to Tailby, 15 Nov. 1943, IT 122/5/2 Pt 1, ANZ; Hickling to RC, 20 August, 1 Sept. 1945 EA 1, 86/18/1, Pt 1, ANZ.

135. Security, New Caledonia, 24 Feb. 1942, Entry 427, RG 407, NARA. See also McCabe to Commander, 24 Nov. 1944, Box 9 (v. 9711), F. A9, Commanding Officer to Commander, 12 Sept. 1944, Box 17 (v. 9707), F. A1-1, RG 313-58-3440, NARA SB; Holder, Historical Narrative, Wallis Island, 28 June 1945, Entry 183, RG 313, NARA.

136. Holder, Historical Narrative, Wallis Island, 28 June 1945, Entry 183, RG 313, NARA.

137. Holder, Historical Narrative, Wallis Island, 28 June 1945; John Vollinger, "World War II Memoirs," Jane Resture's Oceania Page. http//www.janesoceania.com/ww2_johann_memoirs (accessed 27 Sept. 2004).

138. Noel to HC, 27 Sept. 1945, Waddell to HC, 10 Sept. 1945, WPHC 6/1, CF 29/29, WPA; G. Barrow, Outlying Interlude, Chapter XII, 12–13, Mss Pac S. 43, RH.

139. Hogbin 1946, 72.

140. History of Medical Activities, APO 717 [New Georgia], Jan. 1–Dec. 30, 1944, Entry 54A, RG 112, NARA: Data submitted to Sub-Committee House Naval Affairs Committee, Espiritu Santo, July 1945, Entry 179, RG 313, NARA; Quarterly History of Medical Activities, Green Island, July–Sept. 1944, Entry 302, RG 112, NARA; Gwynn, Interview, 23 May 1944, Entry 302, RG 112, NARA. Few local people in Melanesia had syphilis because they had gained immunity from having contracted yaws.

141. Boone 1941, 113–124 at RG 52, NARA.

142. H. Gwynn, Report on Medical Activities in SWPA, 23 May, Entry 302, RG 112, NARA.

143. Niemeier to Commander, South Pacific, 16 Sept. 1943 and enclosures, Investigation of Naval Personnel involved in Homosexual practices, 28 Dec. 1943, General courts, Entry 179, RG 313, NARA. Such men received harsh treatment in prisons. See Berube 1990, 204, 205, 216, 217, 219, 221.

144. A. P. Pirie to Melva, 27 Mar. 1943, PR 00602, AWM.

145. W. Burgess, Neuropsychiatry—South Pacific Area, 1945, Entry 1012, RG 112, NARA; CB 572 Unit report, 1 Nov. 1945, Russell Islands, Inspection report Aitutaki, 28 Feb. 1945, Entry 179, RG 313, NARA.

146. Parsons 1945, 80–81.

147. Rosner 1944, 770, 774.

148. G. Barrow, "Outlying Interlude," Chap 8, Mss Pac. s. 43, RH, Oxford.

149. Surgeon, XIV Corps to the Surgeon, 31 Oct. 1943, Memo re medical services, New Georgia Campaign, to the Surgeon, 31 Oct. 1943, RG 52, NARA.

150. P.O.W. Kato, Indoctrination Report 52, c. Feb. 1944, Box 3, F. Conf, A, RG 313-58-3500, NARA SB; Shinya 2001, 18–23, 26, 31–32.

151. Bennett and Beckworth, The influence of medical factors.

152. Callahan, Command History, Aug. 1942–Aug. 1945, Box v. 9304, A12, RG 313-58-3401, NARA SB.

153. Long 1973, 177–184.

154. Reybold, Topics for discussion with the Chief Engineer, 13 Nov. 1943, RG 77, NARA.

155. Report, Espiritu Santo, July 1945, Entry 178, RG 313, NARA. The association of race, primitiveness, and malaria as defining characteristics of Melanesians vis à vis Polynesians was a well-established colonial trope. See Eyre Hutson to Wilson, 1 Feb. 1927, CO 225/236/64224, TNA.

156. Malaria and Epidemic Control Officer to Commander, 4 Apr. 1945, Box 7, F. P3-P15, RG 313-58-3503, NARA SB.

Chapter 4: Local Resources: Living off Land and Sea

Epigraphs: Broadcast in "This other Eden," New Zealand Intelligence, Issue No. 89, 15 Feb. 1944, RG 313, NARA; Chapman 1949, 7.

1. "C" rations consisted of six cans: three contained a meat and vegetable and the other three had crackers, sugar, jam, powdered drinks, and cereals. Packed with 2,974 calories, "C" rations were considered too bulky for use by mobile troops. The "K" ration catered to the needs of paratroopers, tank crews, and other soldiers who depended on mobility for survival. Adopted in 1943, it consisted of breakfast (veal), dinner (Spam), and supper (sausage), with cheese, crackers, candy, gum, and powdered drinks. "US Army Rations World War Two." http://www.ww2incolor.com/forum/showthread.php?t=3551(accessed 20 Apr. 2007).

2. Morison 1968, 110.

3. Quarterly Report of the Chief Surgeon, Hollandia, 20 July 1944, Entry 54A, RG 112, NARA.

4. Horne to Chief of Bureau of Ordinance, et al., 10 Apr. 1942, TG 65.1, folder 866, Papers of Admiral Richard E. Byrd, Ohio State University.

5. Doughty to Vice Chief of Naval Operations. 10 Dec. 1942, TG 65.1, folder 866, Papers of Admiral Richard E. Byrd; F. Horne to A. Paul, 12 Sept. 1942, Entry 18, RG 169, NARA.

6. Doughty to Vice Chief of Naval Operations, 10 Dec. 1942; Perkins to Stettinius, 9 Jan. 1943; Stettinius to Perkins, 20 Jan. 1943; Palmer to SOS, 27 Jan. 1943, Entry 18, RG 169, NARA. The United States Commercial Company was responsible for the procurement of equipment, seeds, and the like and retained title to this equipment. Purnell, Vegetable growing Projects, 6 May 1944, enclosure, Entry 179, RG 313, NARA.

7. Crawford, Donald, Dowsett, and Williams 1954, 107–115.

8. Hall 1955; Milward 1977, 50–52; Baker 1965; Butlin and Schedvin 1955, 431–434; Hasluck 1970, 239–240, 437, 575–576; Commander Seventh Fleet to all stations, 27 June 1945, Box 4, F. A16-4, RG 313-58-3299, NARA SB; Base Medical Officer to Commander, 27 Feb. 1945, Box 2, F. P1-P2, RG 313-58-3401, NARA SB; Campaign History Bougainville, c. 1945, Entry 44463, RG 338, NARA.

9. Fullington et al., Annex Proceedings of Board of Officers Appointed for consideration of Supply of Food to Hospitals in the South Pacific Area, c. Sept. 1944, Entry 179, RG 313, NARA; M. H. Cloud, Interview, 8 July 1944, RG 112, NARA; A. Gately, Diary, 7 Mar. 1944, PR 00756, AWM; V. O. Hunt, Diary, 31 Dec. 1943, DRL 6132, AWM; Nelson 1996, 169; Trevor Thomas, Diary, 4 Jan. 1943, Mss 5143, NLNZ; Dorman 1997, 80–81; Waterworth 1960, 90; Cox 1987, 107, 111.

10. Historical Narrative, Southwest Pacific, Morale, Chapter II, c. 1946, 355–362, Entry 183, RG 313, NARA; History of the South Pacific Base, Book II, 1945, Entry 44463, RG 338, NARA; Twhigg, Complaints regarding food, 7 Jan. 1944, Barrowclough to PM, 5 August 1944, Barrowclough papers, 40440, AM.

11. [Oliver] Tahiti Survey, 15 May 1943, Oliver, Summary, South Pacific Project Report, First Quarter 1944, Bishop, FEA Activities in British Pacific Island Colonies, 10 Oct. 1944, RG 169, NARA.

12. Rose, Report on Agriculture Project, 18 August 1942–25 Jan. 1943, F. A9, RG 313-58-3394, NARA SB.

13. Ken Reardon, Interview, Feb. 1999; Wood-Ellem 1999, 210; Armstrong to HC, 1 Apr. 1942, WPHC TS SF 9/31, WPA; Tahiti Survey, 15 May 1943; Elizabeth Wood Ellem, personal communication, Nov. 2003; Rose, Report on Agriculture Project, 18 August 1942–25 Jan. 1943, F. A9, RG 313-58-3394, NARA SB; Priday [1945], 33–34.

14. Bennett 2001a, 270–271; Tahiti Survey, 15 May 1943, Oliver, Summary, South Pacific Project Report, First Quarter 1944, Bishop, FEA Activities in British Pacific Island Colonies, 10 Oct. 1944, RG 169, NARA; Fiji Islands, July–August 1944, Entry 427, RG 407, NARA; Port Operations, Fiji, June 1942–Jan. 1944, Entry 44463, RG 388, NARA; Supply and Production Board, Colony of Fiji, *Memorandum for the United States Board of Economic Warfare Mission* (Suva: Government Printer, Feb. 1943), 4.

15. Parsons 1945, 239–240.

16. Charge d'Affaires to Minister of External Affairs, 11 July 1943, Notes Vegetable Project, n.d., c. Oct. 1943, External Affairs to Administrator, 20 Dec. 1943, Charge d'Affaires to Minister of External Affairs, 5 Jan. 1944, Assistant Secretary to Director-General, 21 Jan. 1944, Secretary to Island Territories, 6 Apr. 1944, EA1, 86/17/5 pt 1, ANZ; AR Department of Agriculture, 30 June 1943, RG 313-58-3440, NARA SB; Oliver, Summary, South Pacific Project Report, First Quarter, 1944, Entry 173, RG 169, NARA; Priday [1945], 62; AR June 1942, June 1943, Governor's Office Series no. 5, RG 284, NARA SB: Moyer and Larsen, Island government order number nine, 8 June 1942, Governor's Office, Island government files 1944, RG 284,NARA SB; Analysis of Economic Status of native population, 1947, 46, Governor's Office Series no. 16, Sub Series no. 1, RG 284, NARA SB; [Patrick], Activities of Office of Economic Warfare and other U.S. activities in Samoa, 10 Nov. 1943, Patrick, Samoa: Programming of supplies, 4 Nov. 1943, EA1, 86/71/7 pt 1, ANZ; FEA, Sample Program with reference to the South and Central Pacific islands, c. Dec. 1944, Entry 173, RG 169, NARA.

17. AR, June 1942, June 1943, Governor's Office Series no. 5, RG 284, NARA SB: Moyer and Larsen, Island government order number nine, 8 June 1942; Governor's Office Series no. 16, Sub Series no. 1: Analysis of Economic Status of native population,

1947, 46, RG 284, NARA SB; Patrick to PM, 5 Nov. 1943, EA1, 86/71/7 pt 1, ANZ; [John Burke], United States Naval History of Tutuila, c. August 1945, Navy Yard, Washington D.C., 88, 107; Eustis 1979, 111.

18. Hickling, Report, U.S. forces in Aitutaki, 10 Nov. 1943, IT 122/5/2, pt 1, ANZ.

19. Bryan to Commander, SoPac, 24 Feb. 1945, Entry 183, RG 313, NARA. In the areas where d) was most common, New Caledonia and Fiji, most farmers were respectively French or Indian.

20. Raymaley, Food and forage in New Caledonia, 26 Nov. 1942 and enclosures, Entry 44463, RG 338, NARA; Priday [1945], 49; RC, Summary of events for the history of the war, 1 Jan.–31 Dec. 1943, WPHC NHBS 19/III, 7/20, WPA; History, Service of Supply, SPA, c. Mar. 1944, Entry 44464, RG 338, NARA; Annex No 1, Economic, 7 Jan. 1945, G-2 Periodic Intelligence Report, Entry 182, RG 313, NARA; FEA in South Pacific Project, Third quarter 1944, Sept. 1944, Entry 217, RG 234, NARA; Final close out Report on the South Pacific Command, 30 June 1946, Entry 44463, RG 338, NARA; Jackson 1989, 74; Service Command Bougainville, 23 Dec. 1943–Dec. 1944, Entry 427, RG 407, NARA; Oliver, Summary of the South Pacific Project Report, First Quarter of 1944, 7–9.

21. Jackson 1989, 71; Final close out South Pacific Base Command, 30 June 1946; Close to All Bases, SoPac, 29 Mar. 1945, Box 8, F. JJ7, RG 313-58-3503, NARA SB; Historical Narrative, Southwest Pacific, Morale, Chapter 11, c. 1946, 355–362; Annual Proceeding of the of Board of Officers Appointed re food to Hospitals in SoPac Area, n.d., c. late 1944, Entry 179, RG 313, NARA.

22. Schedule of prices for labor and commodities, 29 Feb. 1943, RG 313-58-3520, NARA SB; Trevor L. Thomas, Diary, Jan.–July 1943, MSX 5143, NLNZ; Gillespie 1954, 127; Hickling, Report, U.S. forces in Aitutaki, 10 Nov. 1943; Moon and Moon 1998, 56, 110, 114–115.

23. Acting British Resident to RC, 26 Sept. 1944, 5 Feb. 1945, NHBS 25/43, WPHC.

24. Kjar, Farms-General Policy, 14 May 1945 and enclosure, AWM 54, 337/7/10, AWM; Mair 1948, 197; G. H. Vernon, Diary, 2 August 1942, PR 00787, AWM.

25. A. S. Allen, Papers: Operations—7 Aust Division, Most Secret, c. Oct. 1942, 3 DRL 4142, AWM.

26. Baum to Commander General, 4 Dec. 1942, Bulcock to Forde, 30 Dec. 1942, Forde to Bulcock, 4 Jan. 1943 and enclosures, AWM 54, 337/3/4, AWM; New Guinea Vegetable Production, 1 Oct. 1943, AWM 54, 337/7/7, AWM; Crouch 1986, 92–93, 109.

27. ANGAU Report, May–Dec. 1944, AWM 54, 80/6/9, AWM. Prewar daily rations for indentured labor were 1.4 lbs. rice or equivalent (e.g. 7 lbs. taro or sweet potato); weekly 1.5 lbs. fresh or 0.75 lbs. canned meat or 1 lb. fish, along with salt, tea, sugar, and biscuits, amounting to 0.75 lb. Those in very heavy work such as mining or crewing ships received more, including double the canned meat quantity and the salt, tea, sugar, and biscuits. Mair 1948, 146–147, 193.

28. New Guinea Vegetable Production, 1 Oct. 1943, AWM 54, 337/7/7, AWM; Casey to Commander, 18 Mar. 1943, Entry 305C, RG 77, NARA.

29. Mair 1948, 196.

30. Photographs and captions, Nos 099615, 099610, AWM; ANGAU Report, May–Dec. 1944, AWM 54, 80/6/9, AWM.

31. Hicks, Kefford, and McKee, Report of food stores in New Guinea, c. June 1945, AWM 54, 337/7/10, AWM; Photographs and captions, Nos. 099599, 099603, 099610, AWM; ANGAU Report, May–Dec. 1944, AWM 54, 80/6/9.

32. Photographs and captions, Nos. 098597, 098598, 098591, 098602, 073500, 097114, 097118, 097125, 099505, AWM; G. K. Little, "Those were the days my friend," 146–152, MSS 1210, AWM; Cleland to Headquarters, 21 Sept. 1943 and enclosures, AWM 54, 337/7/1, AWM; Visit to New Guinea, 16 Apr.–7 May 1944, 18, 2396/12/134, E. J. Ward Papers, NLA; Mair 1948, 196.

33. J. H. Leeman, "The Body Snatchers," 53, MSS 0811, AWM; Photographs and captions, Nos. 073085, 073086, 073087, 073088, AWM; Judd, Kalinge, 12 Oct. 1944, PNG Patrol Reports, microfiche, A9844, NAA, Canberra.

34. Carruthers, Report on Morobe-Wau, 9 May 1944, PNG Patrol Reports, microfiche, A9844, NAA.

35. Photographs and captions, Nos. 073061, 073072, 073074, 073076, 075877, 073078, 076107, 073824, AWM; Nelson 1996, 166.

36. Baum to Commander General, 4 Dec. 1942, AWM 54, 337/3/4, AWM.

37. D. Shearer, letter 11 May 1943, PR 91/138, AWM.

38. Photograph and caption, No. 073314, AWM.

39. AR, Office of the Surgeon, Guadalcanal, 31 Dec. 1944, Entry 54A, RG 112, NARA.

40. Engelhorn, Report of Medical Department, Aitutaki, 27 July 1944, Entry 302, RG 112, NARA.

41. Photographs and captions, Nos. 073081, 075877, 075882, AWM; William Sabel, "Bringing new knowledge to the South Pacific," http://www.memoriesofwar.com/veterans/sabel.asp (accessed 28 Aug. 2005).

42. Gardens, Oct. 1943, AIR 127 3X2121/1/W, ANZ; M. H. Cloud, Interview, 8 July 1944, RG 112, NARA; Gillespie 1945, 47, 48–49, 69; Mary Wilson, 28 Aug. 1943, Ms Ref no. 91-268, NLNZ; Waterworth 1960, 116.

43. Jackson 1989, 74.

44. History of the Medical department hospital dietician, 17 Oct. 1945, Entry 44463, RG 338, NARA.

45. Activities of the Army Veterinary Service in the Pacific Ocean Areas: 7 Dec. 1941–30 Jan. 1945, Document 88A, Entry 1012, RG 112, NARA; Historical Narrative, Southwest Pacific, Morale, Chapter 11, c. 1946, 355–362; South Pacific Base Command, Office of Surgeon, Annual Report, 1945, Entry 312, RG 112, NARA; Bennett 2001a, 271; Thompson and Adloff 1971, 396.

46. Alailima 1988, 234–239; Eustis 1979, 109.

47. AR, Office of the Surgeon, Guadalcanal, 31 Dec. 1944, Entry 54A, RG 112,

NARA; Activities of the Army Veterinary Service in the Pacific Ocean Areas, 7 Dec. 1941–30 Jan. 1945, Documents 148–150, Entry 1012, RG 112, NARA; Noel to Commanding General, 15 Apr. 1944, WPHC CF 29/20 Vol. I, WPA; Farm Manager to Secretary to Government, 25 May 1950, WPHC F48/52, WPA; R. Berry, Diary, 9 Sept. 1942, PR 84/021, AWM; RC to HC, 9 Mar. 1944, WHPC F32/65/, WPA; Crichlow to Secretary to Government, 3 June 1944 and enclosures, WPHC BSIP 1/111, F 15/5, Part 1, NASI; DO, Tour of Arosi, July 1945, WPHC BSIP 9/1, F1-51, NASI. Cf. Larsen 1946, 99.

48. Jack Craig, Diary, 10 Sept. 1943, PR 00 906, AWM.

49. J. Goode, Notes on food supply, Funafuti, 23 Dec. 1942, Papers, Mss Pac s.112, RH.

50. Saito 1991, 211.

51. Cited in Belshaw 1950, 144. Cf. Ravuvu 1988, 33.

52. Iwamoto Hiromitsu, "Japanese Occupation of Rabaul, 1942–1945" Pacific War in Papua New Guinea: Perceptions and Realities, Symposium, Division of Pacific and Asian History, ANU, 1–9 Sept. 1999); *The United States Strategic Bombing Survey (Pacific): The Allied Campaign against Rabaul*, 23–25.

53. H. P. Spindler, Diary, 18 Nov. 1942, PR 83/171, AWM.

54. McLeod, 3–28 August 1944, Witu group, PNG Patrol Reports, microfiche, A9844, NAA.

55. Prisoner of war interrogation Reports, 332 (Taketoshi Nagaoka), Box v. 9287, F. A16-2, RG 313-38-3401, NARA SB; [illegible name] Bogia to Watam, Macgregor to DO, ANGAU, 2 July 1944, Leger, Bagasin Sub District, 4 August 1944, Monk, Karkar Island, June 1944; Doonar, Bogati area, 25 May–10 June 1944, [Illegible name] Watut area, Bloxham to DO ANGAU, 9 May 1944; Robinson, Munum-Ngasawapum area, 10–14 Sept. 1943; Leydon, Uruwa-Yupna area, 13 August–16 Sept. 1944, PNG Patrol Reports, microfiche, A9844, NAA; Kami Kesen, Interview, Remembering the war in New Guinea Project, AWM, http://ajrp.awm.gov.au/ajr/remember.nst/WebPrinter/FO 11E5; Charles W. Crary, "My life as a soldier: 1939–1945," 31, http://www.memoriesofwar.com/veterans/crary.asp (accessed 19 August 2005); Barry, Hogbin and Taylor, Compensation to the natives of Papua and New Guinea, July 1945, 1956/1096, A 463/17, NAA.

56. A. Macdonald, Memoirs, 1–8, PR 83/220, AWM; Long 1963, 102–103; Oliver 1991, 6, 47.

57. B. H. Macdougal, Letter, 20 May 1945, 3 DRL/457, AWM.

58. Powell 2003, 90; R. W. Flew, Diary, 27 Dec. 1944, PR 00526, AWM; Excerpts from captured Japanese diary, 4 Nov. 1942, WO 106/5928, TNA; Lawrence 1964, 110.

59. Foley, Komba, Selepe, 7–18 Mar. 1944, PNG Patrol Reports, microfiche, A9844, NAA; Holmes to Air Dept, 16 Mar. 1945, AIR 127, 3(iii), ANZ; J. F. Goldie, Correspondence 1922–1951, Goldie to Scriven 13 Mar. 1946, Methodist Records, Microfilm, PMB 925; Objective folder, Part 1 and 2, Rendova Island, 27 May 1943, Records of U.S. Army Command, RG 338, NARA.

60. Hitoshi Imamura, "The tenor of my life," 151, 153–154, MSS 1089, AWM;

H. A. Dye, "Fish by the ton," *The Quartermaster Review* (Mar./Apr. 1944), enclosure, Entry 217, RG 234, NARA.

61. Emery, 30 Jan.–24 Mar. 1945, Aola, Talasea, Slattery, n.d., c. 11 Jan. 1944, Kumbun Island, PNG Patrol Reports, microfiche, A9844, NAA.

62. McMullen to ANGAU HQ, 1 June 1944, Morobe-Finschhafen District, PNG Patrol Reports, microfiche, A9844, NAA.

63. Larsen 1946, 99.

64. A. A. Jones, "A Volunteer's Story," 66, MSS 1168, AWM.

65. Evan, Report on Kolombangara, c. Dec. 1943, Entry 179, RG 313, NARA; U.S. Marine Photograph 127GW 1046 (58417), 8 Jan. 1943, RG 127-CW, NARA; Cited in Navy Dept., Manual of Advanced Base Development, July 1943, 112, Box 3(v. 9666), F. A1, RG 313-58-3440, NARA SB.

66. Report 30 Jan.–5 Feb. 1944, Box 2, F. A9, RG 313-58B-3254, NARA SB.

67. Alfred Weinzierl, personal communication, 6 May 2004; Silverio Ilaha, Interview with author at Maleai village, Shortland Island, 1976; Monk, Karkar Island, June 1944, PNG Patrol Reports, microfiche, A9844, NAA; Diary of Akogina, 28 Dec. 1942, Mexted Papers, Id 43276, AM; Walton, Tabar Island Group Reconnaissance, 24 May 1944, RG 33, NARA; Eliab Kaplimut, Interview, Remembering the war in New Guinea Project, AWM, http://ajrp.awm.gov.au/ajr/remember.nst/Web-Printer/82E32C2 (accessed January 2005); Naval operational force, Patrol of 14 May 1944, RG 313, NARA.

68. Shaw 1991, 226–230.

69. Evans, Intelligence Report, c. Dec. 1943, Entry 179, RG 313, NARA; Kami Kesen, Interview, Remembering the war in New Guinea Project, AWM, http://ajrp.awm.gov.au/ajr/remember.nst/Web-Printer/F0C11E5 (accessed January 2005); Ellis 1946, 81–85; McQuarrie 1994, 135.

70. Sugar to How, telegram, 26 Feb. 1945, Entry 43350, RG 338, NARA; Long 1963, 151–152, 154–155, 186; M. G. Hauer, Letter, 6 Nov. 1945, PR 87/110, AWM; Packard 1975, 48; Prisoner of war interrogation Reports, 327 (Yamamoto Tsunea), 329 (Katayama Takeyoshi), Box v. 9287, F. A16-2, RG 313-38-3401, NARA SB.

71. Long 1973, 556–557; Alfred Weinzierl, personal communication, 6 May 2004; Peter Lait, Joseph Tokankan, Interviews, Remembering the war in New Guinea, AWM, http://ajrp.awm.gov.au/ajrp/remember.nsf/ (accessed January 2005).

72. Hitoshi Imamura, "The tenor of my life," 151, 153–154; Dye, "Fish by the ton."

73. Peter Lait and Ruben Lamasisi, Interviews, Remembering the war in New Guinea Project, AWM, http;//ajrp.awm.gov.au/ajrp/remember.nsf (accessed January 2005); Alfred Weinzierl, personal communication, 6 May 2004; Hitoshi Imamura, "The tenor of my life," 151, 153–154, MSS 1089, AWM; Dye, "Fish by the ton," Entry 217, RG 234, NARA.

74. Long 1973, 557; Hiromi 2004b, 138–152.

75. Intelligence, Daily Digest, Nos. 513–538, May 1944, Entry 179, RG 313, NARA; Garden spraying Bougainville [c. June 1944], AIR 127 9C, ANZ.

76. Report on a visit to the SW Pacific area, Nov. 1944–Feb. 1945, Entry 213, RG 175, NARA; J. W. Hanley, Diary, 13 Sept. 1944, PR 00774, AWM.

77. "Correcting Great Tragedies" subhead after Sackville-West 1946; S. Okada, "The Lost Troops" (translation), 7, 19–29, MSS 732, AWM.

78. Oliver, Summary of the South Pacific Project Report, First Quarter of 1944, Entry 173, RG 169, NARA.

79. J. Crouch, "A special kind of service," 57, 64, MSS 1038, AWM; Photographs Nos. 070526, 073415, 074645, AWM; Report Medical Activities, Second Quarter, Finschhafen, 1944, Entry 54A, RG 112, NARA; A. Moore, "On active service with the Red Shield," 2 Apr., 2 Sept. 1945, MSS 742, AWM.

80. Gillespie 1945a, 125.

81. V. O. Hunt, Diary, Oct. 1943–20 Apr. 1945, DRL 6132, AWM.

82. Photographs and captions, Nos. 016795, 016802, 016938, 071866, 073295, 073299, 073303, 073305, 073645, 073646, 073651, 073664, 100450, AWM.

83. Allied Geographic Section 1942, 17; Thune 1989, 244.

84. B. Macdougal, Letter, 20 May 1945, DL/457, AWM.

85. Ostrom, Report on the Leeward Group, 13 July 1942 and enclosures, RG 179, NARA; Priday [1945], 71–72; Kushner 1984, 190.

86. Glore to Commanding General, 15 Oct. 1942 and enclosures, F. A9, RG 313-58-3394, NARA SB; Ramsey Main to HC, 22 June 1944, CSO F 115/131, FNA.

87. Raymaley to President, U.S. Joint Purchasing Board, 16, 30 Nov. 1945, Entry 44463, RG 338, NARA; Gillespie 1945a, 69; David Gald, Diary, 24 July 1943, Micro MS 583, NLNZ.

88. Chapman to Miller, 4 Apr. 1945, Entry 217, RG 234, NARA; Chapman 1949, 33; Palmer to SOS, 27 Jan. 1943, Entry 18, RG 169, NARA; Tahiti Survey, 15 May 1943; Fiedler to McDonald, 20 July 1943; Ryerson to Chapman, 4 Oct. 1943, Entry 217, RG 234, NARA.

89. Lissington 1972, 19–22; Rottman 2002, 53–54.

90. Fiedler to Ryerson, 24 July 1943, Entry 217, RG 234, NARA.

91. Chapman, Report on Fishing possibilities, Canton Island, Oct. 1943, Chapman to Ryerson, 31 Oct. 1943 and enclosures, Entry 217, RG 234, NARA.

92. Oliver, The Fishing Industries of the South Pacific Islands, c. 20 June 1942, RG 234, NARA; Chapman to Oliver, 15 Dec. 1943 and enclosures, Box v. 9269, F. A1, RG 313-58-3401, NARA SB.

93. Oliver, Summary, South Pacific Project Report, First Quarter 1944, NARA; FEA in South Pacific Project, Third quarter 1944, Sept. 1944, Entry 217, RG 234, NARA; Chapman 1949, 29–30.

94. FEA in South Pacific Project, Third quarter 1944, Sept. 1944, Smith, New Caledonia Fishing Program, 24 May 1945, Entry 217, RG 234, NARA; Chapman 1949, 134–136; Priday [1945], 49–50.

95. FEA in South Pacific Project, Third quarter 1944, Sept. 1944, Dye, "Fish by the ton," Entry 217, RG 234, NARA; FEA, Outline of Report on FEA Activities during the months of Feb. 1945, Entry 173, RG 169, NARA; Smith, New Caledonia Fishing Program, 24 May 1945.

96. Smith, New Caledonia Fishing Program, 24 May 1945; FEA, Outline of

Report, Feb. 1945; Seethorn, Observations by Force Veterinarian, in Glore, Report on Experimental fishing Project, 18 Oct. 1942, F. A9, RG 313-58-3394, NARA SB.

97. Smith, New Caledonia Fishing Program, 24 May 1945, Entry 317, RG 234, NARA.

98. FEA, Outline of Report Feb. 1945.

99. FEA Activities in British Pacific Island Colonies, 10 Oct. 1944, British Empire Geographic file, RG 169, NARA; FEA, Sample Program with reference to the South and Central Pacific Areas, c. Dec. 1944; Smith to Bryan, 20 Dec. 1944, Entry 217, RG 234, NARA.

100. Chapman 1949, 8.

101. Chapman 1949, 78–82, 91, 99–101, 117, 128, 131, 133–134, 146–147, 156, 179, 185–189, 206–208, 241–246; Chapman to Oliver, 15 Dec. 1943 and enclosure, Box v. 9269, F. A1, RG 313-58-3401, NARA SB.

102. FEA Activities in British Pacific Island Colonies, 10 Oct. 1944.

103. Smith to Bryan, 20 Dec. 1944; Chapman to Miller, 4 Apr. 1945 and enclosure, Entry 217, RG 234, NARA.

104. Michiharu Shinya, "The Path from Guadalcanal" trans. by E. H. Thompson, chapter 3, 1, MS 1763, NLNZ.

Chapter 5: Taking Stock: Building for Battle

Epigraphs: Treland, Notes on Army Engineer Operations in SWPA, May 1944, Entry 305C, RG 77, NARA; "Build with Native Materials," Apr. 1943, Box v. 3248, F. N19, RG 313-58-3377, NARA SB.

1. Planning for the defense of the Philippines, the Americans' "air ferry" routes avoided the territories of Midway, Wake, and Guam, near the Japanese-mandated islands of Micronesia. Airfields for heavy bombers, the B-17s or Flying Fortresses, and fighter aircraft, were to be built on the southern route to link Hawaii, the Line Islands (Christmas Island), the Phoenix Islands (Canton Island), Fiji, New Caledonia, and Australia with the Philippines. An alternate route further south was activated in May 1942 once the Japanese had captured the Philippines and begun their advance southwards. It spanned Christmas Island, Penrhyn, Aitutaki, Tongatapu, and Norfolk Islands to link to Australia. Fitzgerald 1992, 47–64.

2. Richardson, Army Corps of Engineers, Historical Review, c. 1946, RG 77, NARA; Fitzgerald 1992, 47–64.

3. Morgan to RC, n.d., c. Feb. 1944, IT 122/5/2, Part 1, ANZ.

4. Richardson, Army Corps of Engineers, Historical Review, c. 1946; Fitzgerald, "Air Ferry Routes," 47–64.

5. McQuarrie 1994, 38, 144–147.

6. Report of Post war Development Board, n. d., c. May 1946, Box 1, F. A1, RG 313-58-3300, NARA SB.

7. Gibson, First Narrative of Russell Island Command, 22 Sept. 1945, Box 1, F. A12, RG 313-58-3019, NARA SB.

8. Serial 381, Conservation of Coral, Kukum Beach, 6 Aug. 1943, Box v. 3242, RG 313-58-3377, NARA SB.

9. Treland, Notes on Army Engineer Operations in SWPA, May 1944, Entry 305C, RG 77, NARA.

10. Kiersch 1998, 144–145, 148–150.

11. Final close out Report on Guadalcanal, Oct. 1945–May 1946, 9, 11, Entry 44463, RG 338, NARA.

12. Agreement between United States and New Zealand, 16 Feb. 1944, Entry 178, RG 313, NARA; Base Camp Order 49, Sand, firewood, bamboo, etc.-procurement of, 2 May 1943, Entry 179, RG 313, NARA; Minutes of Construction Executive Committee, Nov. 1942, Entry 44463, RG 338, NARA.

13. Haseman, Analysis of timber requirements and local production, 21 June 1944, Entry 305C, RG 77, NARA.

14. Bennett 2001a, 267; Priday, Report 1 Jan. to 31 Aug. 1944, Report, 6 Dec. 1944, Entry 183, RG 313, NARA.

15. Robson 1942, 372–373.

16. *Reports to the League of Nations of the Administration of the Territory of New Guinea, 1924–1940.*

17. Healy 1967, 112–113; Jonas 1985, 46; Essai 1961, 139; McAdam to Lane-Poole, 22 Feb., 1 July 1938; Lane-Poole to Secretary, PM's Dept., 4 Feb. 1941; McAdam to Lane-Poole, 7 Feb. 1941, A452, 59/6/29, NAA; Robson 1942, 236; *Australian Dictionary of Biography,* Vol. 15, 147–148; Lane-Poole 1925; Bennett 2000, 66–67, 94, 107, 110; Kajewski 1930, 172–180; *The Forests of the colony of Fiji,* CP No. 9, Legislative Council of Fiji, 1933 (Suva: Government Printer, 1933); *Annual Report of the Forestry Department, 1939,* Legislative Council of Fiji (Suva: Government Printer, 1940); Priday, Draft, re New Caledonia [submitted to military censor], 6 Dec. 1944, Entry 183, RG 313, NARA; Gillespie 1945, 40.

18. Bennett 2000, 6–8.

19. [Oliver], Tahiti Survey, 15 May 1943, FEA, Sample Program, c. Dec. 1944, Entry 173, RG 169, NARA; Frank, FEA Activities in the British Pacific Island colonies, 10 Oct. 1944, British Empire Geographic file, RG 16, NARA; Burton to Blandy, 10 Mar. 1944, WPHC NHBS MP 21/4, WPA.

20. Watson, Lumber possibilities on the Island of Savaii, 17 Jan. 1943, Officer in Charge to Commanding General, 15 Nov. 1943, Box v. 13379, RG 313-58B-3061, NARA SB; Sando to Timber Controller, c. Sept. 1943; Shanahan to PM, 28 Feb. 1944, and enclosures, IT 1, 14/4, pt. 1, ANZ.

21. Port Operations Fiji Islands, June 1942–Jan. 1944, Entry 44463, RG 388, NARA; Bennett 2001a, 267–268; [Oliver], Tahiti Survey, 15 May 1943, Entry 173, RG 169, NARA.

22. [Oliver], Tahiti Survey, 15 May 1943, FEA, Sample Program, c. Dec. 1944; Activities of Divisions HQ SOS SPA, Aug. 1944, Entry 44463, RG 338, NARA; Hagen, Labor question, 17 June 1943, Breene, Labor for Aneityum Logging Company, 19 June 1943, Entry 183, RG 313, NARA; Annex No. 1 to G-2 Intelligence Report No. 85,

Economic, 12 Aug. 1944, Entry 4463, RG 313, NARA; Kauri timber, A.L.C., Customs declarations, July 1942–July 1945, WPHC NHBS MP 21/1, WPA; Minute in Vaskess to British RC, 24 Jan. 1944, WPHC NHBS MP 21/4, WPA.

23. Powell, Report of Inspection of timber in the Nepui Valley, 27 Feb. 1943, Box v. 9658, F. A9, RG 313-58C-3290, NARA SB; Carter to Commanding Officer, 8 Mar. 1943, Henkle to Commanding Officer, 9 Mar. 1943, Box v. 9654, RG 313-58A-3490, NARA SB; Summary South Pacific Project Report, First Quarter 1944, Oliver to Chief, 28 Jan. 1944, Entry 173, RG 169, NARA; Summary South Pacific Project Report, Third Quarter 1944, Entry 217, RG 234, NARA; Priday, Report 1 Jan. to 31 Aug. 1944, Entry 183, RG 313, NARA; Sando, Report of Inspection of islands between 160 degrees and 170 degrees east, Sept.–Oct. 1943, WPHC F 45/2/1, WPA; Blandy to HC, 26 Apr. 1944, WPHC NHBS MP 21/4, WPA.

24. Saville 1974, 174, 176.

25. Healy 1967, 113.

26. Sando, Report of Inspection of islands, Sept.–Oct. 1943.

27. Hiromitsu 1999.

28. Hamilton, Extract from Diary, 8 Aug. 1945, AIR 118 77V, ANZ.

29. Hiromitsu 1999; Maitland to Steigrad, 5 Nov. 1945, AWM 67, 2/75, AWM; Charlesworth, Report on inspection of Japanese sawmills in the Gazelle Peninsula, Oct. 1945, AWM 54, 609/7/5, AWM.

30. Noel to Commanding General, 15 Apr. 1944, WPHC CF 29/20 Vol. 1, WPA; Sinclair to HC, 1 Mar. 1945, WPHC F 45/2/1, WPA; Final close out Report, Guadalcanal, Oct. 1945–1 May 1946.

31. R. J. B. to Rose, 18 May 1943, Entry 305C, file 192, RG 77, NARA.

32. Wright, Lumber to advanced base, 24 Apr. 1943, Teale to Chief Engineer, 6 Apr. 1943, Casey to Johnson, 5 Apr. 1943, St. Clair to Hobbs, 14 May 1943, Robinson to Chief Engineer, 29 Mar. 1943, Sverdrup to Base Engineer, 29 June 1943; Sverdrup to Drake-Brockman, 2 July 1943; R. J. B to Rose, 18 May 1943, Kramer, Notes of Timber Production meeting at Victoria Barracks, July 1943, Entry 305C, file 192, RG 77, NARA; Robinson to Teale, 21 July 1943 and encls., Entry 345, RG 77, NARA.

33. Status of lumber production, 21 May 1942, Entry 305C, file 192, RG 77, NARA; L. J. S. to Chief Engineer, 10 July 1943; L. T. R. to Chief Engineer, 13 July 1943; McAdam, Report, July 1943; Lieutenant-General, Development of timber resources, 11 Nov. 1943, AWM 52, 5/32/2 (Mar.–Nov. 1944), AWM.

34. Kramer, Notes of Timber Production meeting at Victoria Barracks, July 1943, Entry 305C, file 192, RG 77, NARA.

35. Ostrander to Commanding General, 8 Sept. 1943; AMW 52, 5/32/2 (Mar.–Nov. 1944), AWM: Dawson, Raising of Forestry units, 2 Mar. 1942; Military Secretary, Tranfers to Forestry units, 10 Mar. 1942, Cockburn, Forestry Policy for New Guinea, 5 May 1944 and encls., Entry 305C, file 193, RG 77, NARA; McAdam, Timber Production resources of Milne Bay, 11 Jan. 1944, Entry 305C, file 194, RG 77, NARA; Carron 1985, 298.

36. Bennett 2003, 111–113.

37. McAdam, Report of sawmill operations, 10 Apr. 1944, Entry 305H, file 348, RG 77, NARA.

38. Hewitt to Chief Engineer, 30 Mar. 1944, Wright, Lumber production in forward areas, 9 Aug. 1944; H. J. C., Policy, furnishing information to NG force on timber production, 24 Apr. 1944; Allen, Lumber production in forward areas, 4 June 1944, Entry 305H, file 193, RG 77, NARA.

39. Haseman, Analysis of timber requirements and local production, 21 June 1944.

40. No 3 Platoon 2/2 Forestry Coy (Sept. 1945–Jan. 1946); HQ and No. 1 Platoon 2/2 Forestry Coy (Sept. 1945–Jan. 1946), AWM 52, 5/32/4, AWM; McAdam, Report on Sawmilling Operations in Australian New Guinea, 10 Apr. 1944, Entry 305H, file 348, RG 77, NARA; Frisby, 1613 Engineer Forestry Company: Historical summary, 10 May 1945, NARA RG 77, entry 305H, file 364; 1 Commander Royal Engineers, NGFR (1943–1945), AWM 52, 5/32/2 AWM.

41. Bennett 2003, 114–115, 118.

42. McAdam, Monthly report, 2 June 1944, AWM 52, 5/32/2 (1944), AWM. I have calculated this figure from averages for much of 1942 and early 1943 as well as more specific returns from c. mid-1943. Its accuracy is reinforced by the comparable total cited for production to 30 Sept. 1944 of 41,605,102 board feet. Steele to LGA, 5 Nov. 1944, AWM 52, 5/32/2 (1943–1944), AWM.

43. NGFR, 1 CRE, AWM 52, 5/32/2 (1944), AWM.

44. Steele to LGA, 5 Nov. 1944, NGFR, 1 CRE, AWM 52, 5/32/2 (1943–1944), AWM. Essai calculates the actual sawed timber at 80 million super feet, but he does not cite his sources. This has been cited by Jonas in cubic meters, but the conversion seems to have been done to board feet true measure rather than superficial feet Hoppus measure, the accepted measure during the war. Essai 1961, 140; Jonas 1985, 47.

45. NGFR, 1 CRE, Hebblethwaite, Sawmill returns, 1 June 1944, Sawmill report, 3 Aug. 1944, AWM 52, 5/32/2 (1944), AWM.

46. Legg 1963.

47. McAdam, Report, 23 July 1943, Entry 305C, file 192, RG 77, NARA.

48. Saville 1974, 147.

49. Commander in Chief, Directive, n. d., c. Jan. 1944, NGFR, 1 CRE, AWM 52, 5/32/2 (1944 Mar.–Nov.), AWM. The Australian minister for external territories, E. Ward, in Sept. 1944 first enunciated the Australian government's intention to pay compensation. Ward to [?], 20 Sept. 1944, Ward to Barry, 26 Oct. 1944, A518/1, A320/3/1 Pt 1, NAA; Cf. Nelson 1999, 26–27.

50. Karkar Island, 4 of 1944/45, Hamilton to Headquarters, Northern Region, 17 July 1944, PNG Patrol Reports: microfiche, A9844, NAA; 2/2 Forestry Company, 16 July 1944, AWM 53, 5/32/4 (Sept. 1943–Oct. 1944), AWM.

51. Chapman to LHG, 11 Aug. 1944, Fitch, Timber Production in forward areas, 8 Oct. 1944, Entry 305C, file 194, RG 77, NARA.

52. Manus: Naval Base order, no 93, 9 Nov. 1944, Box 1, RG 313-58-3300, NARA SB.

53. 2 Platoon 2/2 For. Co., 20 Nov. 1944, AWM 52 5/32/4 (Jan. 44–May 45), AWM.

54. Lieutenant-General, Development of timber resources, 11 Nov. 1943, NGFR, 1 CRE, AWM 52, 5/32/2 (Mar.–Nov. 1944), AWM.

55. Frisby, 1613 Engineer Forestry Company: Historical summary, 10 May 1945, Entry 305H, file 364, RG 77, NARA.

56. Lieutenant-General, Development of timber resources, 11 Nov. 1943.

57. Les T. Carron, interview with author, Canberra, 21 Jan. 2002.

58. Essai 1961, 141; Jonas 1985, 47; Carron, interview, 21 Jan. 2002; 1 CRE New Guinea Forest Reports, AWM 52, 5/32/2 (1944, Jan.–Feb., Mar.–May, June–Aug., Sept.–Nov. 1945), AWM; 1 Forestry Survey Coy, AWM 52, 5/32/6 (May–Aug. 1944, Sept.–Dec. 1944, Jan.–June, July–Oct., Nov. 1945–Jan 1946), AWM; 2 Forestry Survey Coy, AWM 53, 5/32/7 (May–Sept. 1944, Oct. 1944–Apr. 1945, May–Nov. 1945), AWM.

59. Activities Reports of the 61st USNCB for July 1943, Aug. 1943, Box v. 9280, F. A4-3, RG 313-58-3401, NARA SB; Walker 1948, 3, 183.

60. Final close out Report, Guadalcanal, Oct. 1945–1 May 1946; Bennett 2000, 118–119; Haseman, Analysis of timber requirements and local production, 21 June 1944; Lanzoni, Memo to Public Works Officer, 23 Apr. 1944, Box v. 9289, F. N35, RG 313-58-3401, NARA SB.

61. Bennett 2000, 124–125; Lanzoni, Memo to Public Works Officer, 23 Apr. 1944; Sabel 1999, 163–167.

62. "Operation Roll-up": The history of surplus property disposal in the Pacific Ocean, 35, Microfilm No. H-108, Navy Yard, Washington D.C.

63. Bennett 2003, 116–117.

64. Goodsir to RC, 31 Aug. 1945, BSIP F28/12-1, NASI; Bennett 2000, 118 and cf. 141.

65. Strength Report, Solomon Islands, 14 Mar. 1944, RG 313-58-3503, NARA SB.

66. Sando, Report of Inspection of islands . . . Sept.–Oct. 1943.

67. HC to RC, 2 Oct. 1943, BSIP F 28/12-1, NASI; Vaskess to RC, 22 Jan 1944, WPHC NHBS MP 21/4, WPA.

68. Sinclair to HC, 1 Mar. 1945, WPHC F 45/2/1, WPA.

69. Vaskess to RC, 24 Jan. 1944.

70. A. J. Bradshaw, Folder 2, 135–136, MS-3900-2, NLNZ.

71. Bennett 2000, 133–135.

72. Walker to RC, 15 July 1945, WPHC BSIP 28/12-1, NASI; No 1 Islands Works Squadron to Air Dept., 26 Mar. 1945, Billings Papers, MBL.

73. Vaskess, notes, 23 July 1945, WPHC F45/2/1, WPA.

74. These take about twenty years to fruit and fifty years to reach maximum productivity.

75. Walker to RC, 15 July 1945, WPHC BSIP 28/12-1, NASI.

76. Ramsay Main, Palmer, and Kisch, Meeting at CO, 15 July 1948, Ramsay Main, Palmer, Stapleton, Armitage-Smith, and Kisch, Meeting at CO, 20 July 1948, [Illegible] to Kisch, 26 Aug. 1948, Russell-Edmonds, Bentley, Ramsey Main, and Kisch, Meeting at

Treasury, 26 Aug., 1948, Russell-Edmonds to Kisch, 27 Aug. 1948, CO 225/343/86167B, TNA.

77. Final close out Report on Guadalcanal, Oct. 1945–1 May 1946.

78. Walker 1948, 4, 26, 83–84; Bennett 2000, 133–141; Walker to [illegible], 2 Sept. 1945, WPHC BSIP F 28/12-1, NASI.

79. Gibson, Command History, 22 Sept. 1945, Box 1, F. A12, RG 313-58-3019, NARA SB.

80. Notes on Army Engineer Operations in SWPA, Entry 305C, RG 77, NARA; Sandars to Officer commanding, Apr. 1943, Commanding Officer to Quartermaster, 6 Jan. 1945, Box 1, F. L1-15, RG 313-58-3520, NARA SB; Operations Order 34-43, 6 June 1943, Serial 2350 for LCT 327, 1 Oct. 1943, Box 9395, Serials, Commander to Commander Guadalcanal, 3 Feb. 1943, Box 9306, Serials, RG 313-58-3401, NARA SB. A fathom is six feet in length.

81. Mossman, Samarai, 2–10 Nov. 1944, PNG Patrol Reports, microfiche, A9844, NAA.

82. Bloxham, Salamaua, 29 June–6 Oct. 1944, Niall to Headquarters, 16 Oct. 1944, PNG Patrol Reports, microfiche, A9844, NAA.

83. FG 2, Periodic reports, Co-operative marketing, Fijian farmers, 15 July 1944, Entry 44463, RG 338, NARA SB; Gillespie 1945, 136.

84. Officer in charge to Chief Secretary, 9 June 1942, CSO F115/79/1, FNA.

85. Acker to Waitt, 15 May 1944, Entry 62B, RG 175, NARA.

86. Parker, Notes on Engineer Operations in Buna Area, 12 Jan. 1943, Entry 305C, RG 77, NARA.

87. Brewer, Misima report, 5–17 July 1943, PNG Patrol Reports, microfiche, A9844, NAA.

88. Haseman, Analysis of timber requirements and local production, 21 June 1944.

89. Steele, memo, 5 Nov. 1944, NGFR, 1 CRE, AWM 5/32/2 (1943–1945), AWM.

90. Commander, New Britain to Reciprocal Aid Officer, 14 July 1945, Box 4, F. A16-4, RG 313-58-3299, NARA SB; Haseman, Stumpage royalty New Guinea, 15 May 1944; Casey, Stumpage royalty, 21 May 1944; Cockburn, Stumpage for New Guinea timber, 23 May 1944, Entry 305C, file 194, RG 77, NARA.

91. Gillespie 1945b, 41; The Corps of Engineers in the South Pacific, c. 1946, Entry 477, RG 407, NARA.

92. R. W. Flew, Diary, 27 Jan. 1944, PR 00526, AWM.

93. Heberle 1996, 333–338; Bayliss-Smith, Hviding, and Whitmore 2003, 346–352.

94. Commander to Commander, Service Squad, 30 May 1944, Box v. 9306, Serials, RG 313-58-3401, NARA SB; Lumber Production Navy 811, 31 Aug. 1944 and enclosures, Entry 305C, RG 77, NARA; Whitehouse, Trobriand Patrol Report, 8 Sept. 1943, Ross, Samarai Patrol Report, 23 Oct. 1943, PNG Patrol Reports, microfiche, A9844, NAA; Bennett 2000, 1–35; Lincoln to Commanding Officer, 17 Apr. 1943, Entry 179, RG 313, NARA; Bennett 2001a, 277.

95. Lobban and Schefter 1997, 195–202; Report of 44th Construction Battalion activities, Manus, 1944, RG 313, NARA; Richardson, Army Corps of Engineers, Historical Review, c. 1946, passim, RG 77, NARA.

96. Rottman 2002, 9.

97. Belshaw and Stace 1955, 33; McQuarrie 1994, 147.

98. Jones 1951, 392.

99. RC to HC, 14 Mar. 1947, WPHC F 58/55, WPA.

100. Sando, Report of Inspection of islands . . . Sept.–Oct. 1943.

Chapter 6: Resources for the Metropole: Trade for the Periphery

Epigraphs: Fiji Times, 12 Jan. 1944, 6; C. B. C. to Chairman, 27 Apr. 1944, Item 42, CP 637/1, NAA.

1. Copra Marketing, Vol. I–Vol. VII, WPHC CF 33/6, WPA; Supply and Production Board, Fiji, Memorandum for the US BEW Mission, Feb. 1943, Entry 416, RG 169, NARA; Margaret Armstrong, memoirs, 79, Mss Pac s. 93, RH; A proposed basis for US Economic Policy in the Pacific Islands, c. Jan. 1945, Entry 217, RG 234, NARA; Buckley and Klugman 1983, 344–345, 350, 357.

2. Fiji Government, *Memorandum for the United States Board of Economic Warfare Mission, Feb. 1943* (Suva: Government Printer, 1943), 11; Frank, FEA Activities in the British Pacific Island colonies, 10 Oct. 1944, British Empire Geographic file, RG 16, NARA; Bennett 2001a, 273–274. Australia produced ample sugar for its own needs.

3. Bennett 2001a, 257, 272–274.

4. ARs 1942, 1943, 1947, American Samoa, Governor's Office, Series 5, RG 284, NARA SB; Armstrong to HC, 2 July 1942, WPHC TS: SF 33/1, WPA; Fox-Strangeways to HC, 15 May 1944, WPHC GEIC: CF 62/13 Vol. 1, WPA; Blandy to HC, 19 Oct. 1943 and enclosures, WPHC NHBS 1491, WPA; RC to District Agent, 11 Dec. 1943, and enclosures, WPHC 24/1944, WPA; [Patrick], Activities of US BEW, 13 Aug. 1943, EA1, 86/18/4 pt 1, ANZ.

5. Armstrong to HC, 2 July 1942, Copra Marketing.

6. Glore, Report on Experimental Fishing Project, 15 Oct. 1942, F. A9, RG 313-58-3394, NARA SB.

7. Buckley and Klugman 1983, 357, 358, 362.

8. FEA, Sample Program with reference to the South and Central Pacific Islands, c. Dec. 1944, Entry 173, RG 169, NARA; Blandy, Summary of events for the history of the war, 1 Jan.–31 Dec. 1943, WPHC NHBS 19/III, 7/20, WPA; Combined Administrative Committee, Copra for the Southwest Pacific, c. July 1944, Entry 2, RG 218, NARA; G-2 Periodic Intelligence Report, Annex No 1, Economic, 7 Jan. 1945, Entry 182, RG 313, NARA; Meetings of Chamber of Commerce, Vol. 17, 2 Feb. 1943, ANC 145W, 12, ANC.

9. Meetings of Chamber of Commerce, Vol. 19, Jan. 1945, ANC 145W, 12, ANC; Jack to Vaskess, 27 July 1940, Copra Marketing, Vol. I, PM, Australia to HC, 23 Dec.

1940, Vol. II, WPHC CF 33/6, WPA; FEA, Sample Program c. Dec. 1944; Blandy, Summary, 1 Jan.–31 Dec. 1944.

10. Oliver to Commander, Sept. 1944, Oliver, FEA Administration South Pacific Project, Third quarter 1944, Sept. 1944, Entry 217, RG 238, NARA; Stettinius to Perkins, 14 Dec. 1942, Entry 18, RG 169, NARA.

11. Mitchell to Noel, 12 July 1944, WPHC CF 62/13 Vol. I, WPA.

12. Mitchell to Newton, 16 Aug. 1944, WPHC CF 29/20 Vol. 1, WPA.

13. Combined Administrative Committee, Copra for the Southwest Pacific, c. July 1944, Entry 2, RG 218, NARA.

14. A proposed basis for US economic policy in the Pacific islands, c. Jan 1945, Entry 217, RG 234, NARA.

15. Thompson to Monson, Counter-espionage survey, 21 Dec. 1942, Entry 179, RG 313, NARA; G-2 Periodic reports, HQ Island Command, Annex No. 1, 1944–1945, Annex No. 2, 1944–1945, Annex No. 3, 1944–1945, Annex No. 4, 1943–1945, Entry 398-USAFISPA (formerly RG 338, Entry 44463), RG 494, NARA; Weeks 1989, 185–200; Henningham 1994, 35–38.

16. The Economy of New Caledonia, 9 Jan. 1942, Series A981/4, New C16, NAA; H. Evatt, Background paper, Australia and New Zealand conference, Jan. 1944, Series M1942/1, 7, NAA; Lawrey 1982; Thompson and Adloff 1971, 267–275; Priday [1945], 42.

17. Thompson and Adloff 1971, 413; G-2 Periodic reports, Annex No. 1, 29 July, 29 Sept. 1944, 24 Mar., 21 July 1945, Entry 398-USAFISPA (formerly RG 338, Entry 44463), RG 494, NARA; Crowley to McCarthy, 1 Feb. 1944, Entry 129, RG 169, NARA; A proposed basis for US economic policy, c. Jan. 1945.

18. British Empire File, n.d., c. July 1943, Entry 150, RG 169, NARA; [No signature] to AGWAR, 18 Apr. 1942, Sykes to Tompkins, 18 Aug. 1942, Handy to Munitions Assignments Board, 6 Nov. 1942, Entry 11, RG 218, NARA; Nickel Production Representative, Sept. 1943, Organizational History, Service of Supply HQ, July–Sept. 1943, Entry 44463, RG 338, NARA; Bryan to Commander, 24 Feb. 1945, Entry 183, RG 313, NARA.

19. The Corps of Engineers in the South Pacific, c. Sept. 1945, Entry 477, RG 407, NARA.

20. Geiger, Final Progress Report, Mineral Exploration, 15 Nov., 4 Dec. 1943, 8 Jan. 1944, Entry 44463, RG 338, NARA.

21. Ashley to HC, 15 Mar. 1939 and enclosures, WPHC 2839/39, WPA; Woodford to HC, 14 Feb. 1912 and enclosures, WHPC 525/12, WPA; The Corps of Engineers in the South Pacific, c. Sept. 1945.

22. Mitchell to SOS, 6 June 1944, WPHC NHBS 24/1944, WPA.

23. Bennett 1987, 262.

24. Stanley to HC, 28 Jan. 1944, WPHC CF 53/7; Gent to Mitchell, 24 Aug. 1944 and enclosures, WPHC NHBS 24/1944, WPA; Vaskess 1943; Bennett 2000, 133–141.

25. Noel to Vaskess, 28 Sept. 1944, WPHC CF 59/8, WPA; SOS to HC, 26 October 1948, NHMP 24/1944, WPA; Geiger, Progress report for Apr. 1944, Mineral Explora-

tion Guadalcanal, May 1944, Entry 427, RG 407, NARA; Buck Slip, Officer of Engineers, SOS SPA, 17 Aug. 1944, in The Corps of Engineers in the South Pacific, c. Sept. 1945.

26. No. 59862, Photographic records Marine Corps, Guadalcanal, RG Series 127 GW 911, NARA.

27. G. K. Little, "Those were the days my friend," 245–246, AWM MSS 1210, 419/49/27, AWM.

28. Forde, Statement, Recapture of Nauru and Ocean Islands, 12 June 1944, Geographic file, RG 218, NARA; Baker 1965, 109, 112, 114, 195, 196, 303; Butlin 1955, 107–109; PM's Department to HC, 9 July 1943 and enclosures, Series A518, K112/6/3, Part 2, NAA.

29. Forde, Statement, Recapture of Nauru and Ocean Islands, 12 June 1944.

30. Barrowclough to HQ, 30 Oct. 1944, EA 1, 86/1/13, 1, ANZ; McQuarrie 2000, 161–167.

31. Seward to Miller, Aug. 1942, Historical File, RG 169, NARA.

32. Bryan to Commander, Sopac, 24 Feb. 1945, Entry 183, RG 313, NARA.

33. Hasluck 1970, 291–292.

34. [Oliver], Tahiti Survey, 15 May 1943, RG 169, NARA.

35. Blandy, Summary, 1942; Fiji Government, *Memorandum for the United States Board of Economic Warfare Mission, Feb. 1943.*

36. Armstrong to HC, 2 July 1942, WPHC TS CF33/1, WPA; [Oliver], Tahiti Survey, 15 May 1943; Armstrong to CS, 15 Sept. 1944, WPHC TS 39/42, WPA; Franks to Stettinius, 23 Sept. 1942 and enclosures, Entry 416, RG 169, NARA; Meetings of Chamber of Commerce, Vol. 17, Jan. 1944, ANC 145W, 12, ANC; FEA, South Pacific Project, Third Quarter of 1944, c. Sept. 1944, Entry 217, RG 234, NARA.

37. Annex No. 1 to G-2 Intelligence Reports, Nos. 75–134, 1944–1945, Entry 44463, RG 338, NARA; Blandy, Summary, 1942–1944, WPHC NHBS 19/III, 7/20, WPA; Mitchell to the PM, 29 Sept. 1943 and enclosures, Series A 989, Item 1943/655/9, NAA; Civil Affairs History, c. 1945, Entry 183, RG 313, NARA; Buckley and Klugman 1983, 356–357.

38. South Pacific Project, 30 June 1943, Entry 18, RG 169, NARA; FEA, South Pacific Project, Third Quarter of 1944, c. Sept. 1944.

39. SOS to British Colonies Supply Mission, 7 Apr. 1943, SOS to Mitchell, 7 Apr. 1943, Mitchell to SOS, 23 Apr. 1943, WO 106/3342, TNA; FEA Report on FEA activities, Feb. 1945, Entry 173, RG 169, NARA.

40. FEA, South Pacific Project, First Quarter of 1944, Apr. 1944, Entry 173, RG 169, NARA; A proposed basis for US Economic Policy, c. Jan. 1945; [Illegible] to PM, 10 Nov. 1943, EA1, 86/71/7 pt 1, ANZ.

41. McKinnon 1993, 50–51.

42. McCarthy, Aitutaki compensation claims, 26 June 1943, Secretary to Assistant Secretary, 2 Nov. 1944, [Shanahan], Penhryn and Rarotonga–claims to native lands, 13 Sept. 1943, IT 122/5/2 pt 1, ANZ.

43. [Patrick] to PM, 13 Aug. 1943, EA1, 86/18/4 pt 1, ANZ; Garity, Report on visit to Rarotonga, 6 Aug. 1943, Entry 44463, RG 338, NARA.

44. Kushner 1984, 126–127, 169, 172, 190; Ostrom to Commanding General, 12 Apr. 1942, 26 July 1942, Entry 179, RG 313, NARA. Selling from the commissary was policy to establish good relations in areas where no alternatives existed. Navy Dept., Manual of Advanced Base Development, July 1943, Box 3 (v. 9666), F. A1, RG 313-58-3440, NARA SB.

45. Vrigneaud to Governor-General, Hanoi, c. July 1941, Straw area commander to CINCPAC, telegram 080450, June 1942, Entry 179, RG 313, NARA; Commander to Commander, Tutuila, 6 Sept. 1943, Box 2 (v. 9683), F. JJ56, RG 313-58-3440, NARA SB.

46. Cf. Stanner 1953, 328–329.

47. Patrick, Investigations in Samoa, 11 Nov. 1943, EA1, 86/71/7 pt 1, ANZ; Tailby to Minister, 1 Apr. 1943, ITI, ex 4/16/1 pts 9810, ANZ; Stanner 1953, 338–339.

48. Tailby to Minister, EA, 12 Aug. 1942, and enclosures, ITI, 4/16/23 pt 1, ANZ; Tailby to Acting Minister, EA, 1 Apr. 1943, ITI, ex 4/16/ 1 pts 9 & 10, ANZ; Peter McQuarrie, personal communication, 26 Aug. 2004; Patrick, Import Control, Samoa, 4 Nov. 1943, EA1, 86/71/7 pt 1, ANZ.

49. Patrick, Samoa, Programming of Supplies, 4 Nov. 1943, EA1, 86/71/7 pt 1, ANZ.

50. Patrick, Import Control, Samoa, 4 Nov. 1943, EA1, 86/71/7 pt 1, ANZ.

51. Memo, The Samoa Import Control Order, 1943, 21 Oct. 1943, EA1, 86/71/7 pt 1, ANZ; Rottman 2002, 90.

52. Patrick, Samoa, Programming of Supplies, 4 Nov. 1943, Patrick to PM, 11 Nov. 1943, EA1, 86/71/7 pt 1, ANZ.

53. Field 1984; Campbell 1999, 92–100; Western Samoa Intelligence, 14 Mar. 1943, WA II, 2 Box 32, Secret files 42-42, ANZ.

54. McKay to Secretary, 5 Nov. 1943, Patrick, Samoa, Programming of Supplies, 4 Nov. 1943; Buckley and Klugman 1983, 357–358.

55. FEA, South Pacific Project, Third Quarter of 1944, c. Sept. 1944.

56. A proposed basis for US economic policy, c. Jan. 1945.

57. Anon, Draft, Department of Island Territories War History 1939/45, ITI W2439 69/9/6, ANZ.

58. Leahy, Native trade in New Guinea, 7 May 1943, Entry 305C RG 77, NARA.

59. Prospectors Michael and Dan Leahy had constructed the first airstrip in the highlands in this manner in the 1930s.

60. Sverdrup to Chief Engineer, 22 Mar. 1943 and enclosures, Entry 305C, RG 77, NARA; Kiersch 1998, 172.

61. Leahy to Heiberg, 27 Sept. 1943, Entry 43315, RG 338, NARA.

62. Dept of External Territories, Australian New Guinea PCB, ANGAU, 15 Mar. 1944, Item 42, CP 637/1, NAA; Commerce Member, Report on Operations of the Australian New Guinea PCB for year ending 30 June 1944, Item 43, CP 637/1, NAA; C. B. C. to Chairman, 2 Mar. 1944, Schedules A and B, CP 637/ 1, NAA.

63. C. B. C. to Chairman, 2 Mar. 1944.

64. C. B. C. to Chairman, 27 Apr. 1944, Item 42, CP 637/ 1, NAA.

65. C. B. C. to Chairman, 2 Mar. 1944.

66. Dept of External Territories, Australian New Guinea Production Control Board; ANGAU, 15 Mar. 1944, Item 42, CP 637/1, NAA.

67. Affeld, Report, Civil administration Gilbert Islands, 16 Jan. 1944, Geographic file, RG 218, NARA; Newton to Commander in Chief, 18 Jan. 1944 and enclosures, Box 12, F. A14/A17, RG 313-58-3503, NARA SB; Marchand, Notes on Solomons, 12 July 1943, CO 225/333, Part 2, TNA.

68. Morison 1968, 111; Affeld, Report, Civil administration Gilbert Islands, 16 Jan. 1944; Fox-Strangeways to HC, 15 May 1944.

69. Mitchell to Newton, 16 Aug. 1944, WPHC F 29/20 Vol. 1, WPA; ARs, Eastern District, 1943, 1944, WPHC BSIP 9/111/1, NASI.

70. FEA, South Pacific Project, First Quarter of 1944, Apr. 1944, Entry 173, RG 169, NARA; Jones, Annex No. 2 to G-2 periodic Report, 20 Jan. 1944, Entry 44463, RG 338, NARA.

71. Noel to HC, 23 Apr. 1944 and enclosure, WPHC CF 62/19, WPA.

72. FEA, South Pacific Project, First Quarter of 1944, Apr. 1944; Simmons to *Chicago Tribune,* 12 Dec. 1944, RG 313-58-3401, NARA SB; FEA, Report on FEA activities, Feb. 1945, Entry 173, RG 169, NARA.

73. Oliver to Commander, Sopac, 5 Sept. 1944, Entry 217, RG 234, NARA.

74. Mitchell to Newton, 16 Aug. 1944, WPHC CF 29/20, Vol. 1, WPA; FEA, South Pacific Project, Third Quarter of 1944, c. Sept. 1944, Entry 217, RG 234, NARA; Bryan to Commander, Sopac, 24 Feb. 1945; Oliver to Commander Sopac, 5 Sept. 1944, Entry 217, RG 234, NARA; Noel to Vaskess, 29 Sept. 1944, WPHC CF59/8, WPA; FEA, Report on FEA activities, Feb. 1945, Entry 173, RG 169, NARA; *Annual Report BSIP, 1948,* 13; Jones, Annex No 2 to G-2 Periodic Report, 20 Jan. 1944, Entry 44463, RG 338, NARA.

Chapter 7: The Human Resource

Epigraph: Caption on U.S. Navy photograph, Pentecost Island, New Hebrides, 1943, RG 80, G157096, NARA.

1. "Operation Roll-Up": The History of Surplus Property Disposal in the Pacific Ocean, I-3, Navy Yard, Washington, D.C.

2. Robinson to AG, 15 Sept. 1944, AG's office, 1944, RG 284, NARA SB; Winslow 1990, 111–116; Bennett 1987, 162–164, 210–214; Mair 1948, 78–79. In Fiji taxes could be paid in kind on a district basis, so indenture was uncommon among Fijians.

3. Newbury 1975, 25–38; Moore, Leckie, and Munro 1990.

4. Memorandum notes on a conference, USS Argonne, 7 Oct. 1942, Box 1, F. A12, RG 313-58-3394, NARA SB; P. Mitchell, Fiji and Tonga Local Forces, 29 Sept. 1942, Entry 179, RG 313, NARA.

5. Ravuvu 1988, 8–14.

6. Gillion 1977, 174–180.

7. Howlett 1948, 13, 159, 177–267.

8. Terry Donnelly, "A Sergeant at Arms," 13, No. 2003.38, AM.

9. Minute, c. 1945, A. L. Armstrong Papers, Mss Pac r. 4, RH; Brownlees to Armstrong, 6 Feb. 1942, WPHC TS SF 9/25 Vol. IV, WPA; Wood-Ellem 1999, 191–221; History of Tongatapu, c. 1945, Entry 183, RG 313, NARA; [Cooper] 1946, 78–79.

10. Ata to Johnson, 10 May 1945, Johnson, Demobilisation of the Tonga Defense Force, 19 Sept. 1945, WPHC SF 9/25, Vol. VI, WPA.

11. Michener to Commander, 1 Oct. 1945, Entry 178, RG 313, NARA.

12. Larsen 1946, 80–84, 97–98, 99–100, 161; Feldt 1967, 81, 86, 113; G. Barrow, "Outlying Interlude," 6–11, 28, Mss Pac s. 43, RH; Young, Memo, 4 Dec. 1942, WPHC BSIP 9/44, WPA; White, et al., 1988, 176–196; *O'o: A Journal of Solomon Islands Studies* 4 (1988): 122–124; Donnelly, "A Sergeant at Arms," 23–24; George 1947, 96.

13. White et al. 1988, 133–148; Josselyn, Coastwatching 1941–1943. There were other such Coastwatching groups. Horton 1970; Feldt 1946; Tonkin-Covell 2000.

14. Zelenietz 1991, 9.

15. Skinner, Notes on Recruiting and discharge of natives, 5 Jan. 1945 and enclosures, Entry 43451, RG 331, NARA; Griffin, Nelson, and Firth 1979, 98; Long 1963, 83.

16. Nelson 1980, 202–216.

17. Nelson 1980, 202–216; Long 1963, 263–265; Wolfers 1975, 46–48.

18. Garvin to Long, Feb. 1943, Entry 44463, RG 338, NARA.

19. Josselyn, Coastwatching 1941–1943.

20. *Fiji Times,* 23 Nov. 1943, 6.

21. General Sturdee, cited in Long 1963, 263.

22. Larsen 1946, 151.

23. Bergerud 1996, 112–114; Potts, Historical narrative Fiji Islands, c. 1945, Entry 183, RG 313, NARA; Page 2004, 67; [Cooper] 1946, 75, 79; Larsen 1946, 23, 28, 87, 100–101, 151; Ravuvu, 1988, 13–16; Wood-Ellem 1999, 192–193.

24. Larsen 1946, 24–26, 67, 89, 151; [Cooper] 1946, 55–61; *Fiji Times,* 10 Jan. 1944, 6.

25. Butler, Minesweeping operations, 20 May 1944, Box 1, F. S81, RG 313-58-3394, NARA SB.

26. Appendix to Annex No. 1-Economic, c. July 1943: Report on Franco-American relationship in New Caledonia, Report No. 432, 1945, Microfilm 323, Division of Pacific and Asian History, ANU.

27. Thompson and Adloff 1971, 268–269; Appendix to Annex No. 1-Economic: Report on Franco-American relationship, 1945; Price to Commander, 7 May 1943, Entry 183, RG 313, NARA; McColl, Notes on Ouvea Atoll, 28 Nov. 1942, Entry 427, RG 409, NARA.

28. Assistant HC to CO, 9 Mar. 1941, CO 968/22/6.

29. Quarterly Summaries of events, 1 Apr.–30 June 1940, 30 June–31 Dec. 1940 and enclosures, Summary of events, 1 Jan.–31 Dec. 1941, WPHC NHBS MP 19/III 7/20, WPA.

30. Summaries of events, 1 Jan.–31 Dec. 1942, 1 Jan.–31 Dec. 1943, 1 Jan.–31 Dec. 1944, WPHC NH BS 19/III 7/20, WPA; DeRoode, Living in the Jungle, May 1943, Entry 427, RG 407, NARA; Moon and Moon 1998, 15, 31; Gwero 1988, 39.

31. Defense of Cooks, 11 Dec. 1941, Ayson to Secretary, 3 Feb. 1943, EA 1, 86/18/2 Pt 1, ANZ.

32. Administrator to External Affairs, 22 Feb. 1941, EA 1, 86/17/1, 1, ANZ; Department of Island Territories, War History 1939–1945, ITI W2439 69/9/6, ANZ. Some Samoans in Germany had joined Hitler's forces.

33. Louise Mataia, "'Odd men from the Pacific': The participation of Pacific Island men in the 28th Maori Battalion, 1939–45," MA thesis, University of Otago, 2007, 126.

34. Franco 1989, 376–393; Oppenheimer 1966, 141–142; Anon., "History of First Samoan Battalion, U.S. Marine Corps Reserve," 28 June 1945, 3–9, cited at http://www.asg-gov.com/historicalcalendar_july.htm (accessed 29 Sept. 2004).

35. Memorandum notes on a conference, USS Argonne, 7 Oct. 1942; P. Mitchell, Fiji and Tonga Local Forces, 29 Sept. 1942, Entry 179, RG 313, NARA.

36. P. Mitchell to SOS, 25 Oct. 1943, WO 106/5928, TNA.

37. Governor to SOS, 29 July 1942, CSO CF36/13, NAF; Port operations, Fiji Islands, June 1942–Jan. 1944, Entry 44463, RG 338, NARA. Before the war, Fijians were also the best paid. Stanner 1953, 393.

38. Bennett 2001a, 273–274.

39. Governor to PM, 26 Jan. 1943, Nimitz to Halsey, 31 Jan. 1943 and enclosures, Entry 179, RG 313, NARA. The number seems to have been 7,336 in Nov. 1942 according to the Manpower Board. *Report on Manpower,* 1942, Fiji Legislative CP No. 17, 3.

40. Nicoll to Commanding General, 2 May 1944, Entry 179, RG 313, NARA. Cf. Ravuvu 1988.

41. *Report of the Secretary of Native Affairs, 1945,* Fiji Legislative CP No. 4 of 1947, 6; Fiji Times, 20 Mar. 1944, 6.

42. Homewood to Breene, 27 Dec. 1942, Entry 44463, RG 338, NARA. See also Young, BSI, 4 Dec. 1942, WPHC BSIP 9/43, WPA.

43. Bennett 1987, 151–191.

44. Garvin to Long, Feb. 1943, Entry 44463, RG 338, NARA.

45. Strength Report 15 Mar. 1944, Box 1, F. A9-4, RG 313-58-3503, NARA SB; Widdy to RC, 18 July 1944, WPHC BSIP 9/43, NASI; Bennett 1987, 222; I. Hogbin, Preliminary Report to Trench, 1 Oct. 1943, Noel to Officer Commanding, 19 Nov. 1943, Note on file, Report on recruiting Native labor on Guadalcanal, 10 Dec. 1943, RC to DC Malaita, 21 July 1944 and enclosures, WPHC BSIP 9/43, NASI.

46. Burgess, Memo, Native Labor, 7 Oct. 1943, Box 2, F. A3, RG 313-58-3377, NARA SB; Roberts to DMI, 11 Nov. 1943, RG 331, NARA.

47. White, Memo, Native Labor, 29 Mar. 1943, Box 2, F. F. LL, RG 313-58-3520, NARA SB; Strength Report 15 Mar. 1944, Box 1, F. A9-4, RG 313-58-3503, NARA SB.

48. For prewar situation see Bennett 1993.

49. RC to DC, 13 Oct. 1950, Russell, Matters Discussed at Ata, 9 Sept. 1950, WPHC BSIP 9/44, NASI; Laracy and White 1988, 110; Russell 2003, 41.

50. Memo, c. Oct. 1943, WPHC BSIP F9/44 Part E, NASI; Ngwadili and Gafu 1988, 202–215.

51. Desertion of D. Steinhardt, 7 Apr. 1945, Box v. 9275, F. P13, RG 313-58-3401, NARA SB; Santa Cruz AR, 1944, WPHC BSIP 9/111/2, NASI; Archer to Parkinson, 9 July 1945 and enclosures, WPHC BSIP F 28/14 Pt 1, NASI; Suggested demobilization scheme, 1945–46, WPHC BSIP 9/91, NASI. Cf. Davenport 1989, 270–273.

52. Bennett 1987, 177; Noel to District Agent, 24 May 1945, WPHC NHBS 33/14.

53. HC to SOS, 16 Feb. 1945, Johnson, Statement, 12 June 1945, Office in Charge to HC, 8 June 1945, HC to SOS, 16 June 1945, SILC, Total man days, 21 Sept. 1945, Acting RC to HC, 26 Jan. 1946, WPHC BSIP 9/44, NASI. The British did not present this account to the United States for refund via reverse lend-lease. Final close out Report on Guadalcanal, 22 Oct. 1945–1 May 1946, Entry 44463, RG 338, NARA.

54. SILC costs exclude the officers' wages. This is based a basic monthly wage of $50 for an enlisted man. Combatants received $10 more. The average rate seems to have been $64 in the South Pacific, but with officers it was about $150. Some sources reckon the rates respectively to have been $73 and $203. This did not include sustenance. Oppenheimer 1966, 144; www.nationalww2museum.org/education/education_numbers .html (accessed 18 Mar. 2007).

55. Fox-Strangeways to Island Commander, 29 Jan. 1943, Affeld, Report, Civil administration Gilbert Islands, 16 Jan. 1944, Geographic file, RG 218, NARA; Newton to Commander, 18 Jan. 1944, Box 12, RG 313-58-3503, NARA SB.

56. Fox-Strangeways to Commander, 28 Dec. 1943, RG 218, NARA.

57. Affeld, Report, Civil administration Gilbert Islands, 16 Jan. 1944, RG 218, NARA.

58. Cf. McQuarrie 1994, 117.

59. Fox-Strangeways to Commander, 28 Dec. 1943.

60. Affeld, Report, Civil administration, 16 Jan. 1944; McQuarrie 1994, 123; Marama and Kaiuea 1984, 128–146. Cf. White and Lindstrom 1989.

61. Nicoll to Commanding General, 2 May 1944, Entry 179, RG 313, NARA.

62. RC to HC, 9 Aug. 1945, WPHC BSIP F9/91, NASI; 4th Special US Naval Construction Battalion, Training of Natives, c. 1945 and enclosures, Commander to Commander South Pacific Fleet, c. Aug. 1945, Box v. 9291, F. A9-4, RG 313-58-3401, NARA SB; Strength Reports, APO 709, Sept. 1944–July 1945, Box 1, F. A9-4, RG 313-58-3503, NARA SB; Murray to Commander, 21 July 1945 and enclosures, Entry 178, RG 313, NARA; Jacob, History of Guadalcanal Beaches and Army Port Growth, 1 Mar. 1946, RG 112, NARA.

63. W. E. H. Stanner, Appreciation of current situation and problems of ANGAU, AWM 54, 80/8/17, AWM.

64. Ian Hogbin, Report, 10 Oct. 1943, WPHC BSIP 9/43, NASI.

65. G. O'Donnell, Extracts from AR for the Fly River, 1942, ANGAU War Diary, Nov.–Dec. 1942, AWM 52, 1/10/1, AWM.

66. Ryan 1969, 531–548; NARA; Leahy to Robinson, 22 June 1943 and enclosures, Methods of Carrier transport in New Guinea, c. 1943, Entry 305 c, RG 77, NARA; Native Labor Records Procedure, 11 Sept. 1944, Entry 43451, RG 331, NARA; Summary of relief and rehabilitation, c. Sept. 1944 and enclosure, A9373, Item 1, NAA; Campaign History, Bougainville, c. 1944, Entry 44463, RG 338, NARA; Downs 1980, 6–7, 38–39; Stanner 1953, 80–81.

67. Mair 1948, 200, 202.

68. Hiromitsu 1999, 8–12; Tabar Island report, 1 July 1944, Entry 43452, RG 331, NARA.

69. Summary of events, 1 Jan.–31 Dec. 1942; Bonnemaison 1994, 225–226.

70. D. W. Kralovec, Naval History of Espiritu Santo, 1945, Navy Yards Archives, Washington D.C., microfilm NRS II-231, 328.

71. Joint Order No. 61, July 1942, Collet to French District Agent, 26 Oct. 1942, Blackwell to Northern District Agent, 30 Nov. 1942, Otto to Call, 12 Dec. 1942, WPHC NHBS MP 14/43, WPA; Civil Affairs, c. 1945, Entry 183, RG 313, NARA; Bonnemaison 1994, 225–227; Worsley 1957, 157–169; Lindstrom 1989, 404–406.

72. Wyman to Commanding Officer, 13 Sept. 1944, Entry 44463, RG 338, NARA.

73. Dubois, Extensive Employment of Natives, 22 June 1942, Thompson, Native labor, 17 Nov. 1942, Appendix to Annex No. 1-Economic: Report on Franco-American relationship in New Caledonia, report No. 432, 1945.

74. Wyman to Commanding Officer, 13 Sept. 1944.

75. Winslow 1990, 112–116.

76. Wyman to Commanding Officer, 13 Sept. 1944, Transportation Corps, New Caledonia, 28 Jan. 1943–31 Mar. 1945, Entry 44463, RG 338, NARA; [Ballard] to External Affairs, 17 Nov. 1943, A989/1, Item 43/735/310/3, NAA; Thompson, native labor survey, 17 Nov. 1942; Halsey to Acting Governor, 4 July 1943, Entry 183, RG 313, NARA; *PIM*, Aug. 1947, 77; Price to Poncet 15 May 1943 and enclosures, Entry 183, RG 313, NARA. About sixty Walliseans were already in New Caledonia in 1940. Videai and Cotter 1960, 174; Shineberg 1999, 71, 245–246.

77. Halsey to Acting Governor, 4 July 1943, Entry 183, RG 313, NARA.

78. Priday [1945], 66.

79. John Vollinger, "World War II Memoirs," Jane Resture's Oceania Page, http://www.janesoceania.com/ww2_johann_memoirs (accessed 27 Sept. 2004). See also Commanding Officer, Wallis to Commander, 12 Sept. 1944, Box v. 9707, F. A1-1, RG 313-58-3440, NARA SB; Historical Narrative Wallis Island, 28 June 1945, Entry 183, RG 313, NARA.

80. McCabe to Commander, 24 Nov. 1944, Commanding Officer to Commander, 12 Sept. 1944, Box v. 9707, F. A1-1, RG 313-58-3440, NARA SB; Holder, Historical Narrative, Wallis Island, 28 June 1945, Entry 183, RG 313, NARA.

81. Connell 1987, 98–99; Lawrey 1982, 85; Thompson and Adloff 1971, 403; Kobayashi 1992, 152–157.

82. G-2 Economic Periodic report, 7 Jan. 1945, Entry 182, RG 313, NARA; Civil Affairs, c. 1945; Stead, Appendix A to Annex no. 2-Political, 18 Dec. 1943, Entry 183,

RG 313, NARA; Report on Franco-American relationship in New Caledonia, Report No. 432, 1945; Passenger arrivals, 27 July 1943 and enclosures, Box 1, F. P32, RG 313-58-3282, NARA SB; McGinnis, Javanese Situation, 25 Mar. 1944, Entry 179, RG 313, NARA; Henningham 1994/95, 151–183; Bennett 2004, 283–307; Munholland 1991, 543–553.

83. Shafroth to Commander, 26 Jan. 1944 and enclosures, Entry 179, RG 313, NARA; Henningham 1994/95, 166–167; Munholland 1991, 545–546.

84. [John Burke], United States Naval History of Tutuila, c. Aug. 1945, Navy Yards Museum, Washington D.C., 107; Franco 1989, 379–393; Woodbury 1946, 235; Denfeld 1989, 36–48; Anon., "History of [the] First Samoan Battalion, U.S. Marine Corps Reserve," 28 June 1945, 3–4 cited at http://www.asg-gov.com/historicalcalendar_july.htm (accessed May 2006).

85. High Chiefs to President of the USA, 10 Dec. 1948, Series 6, Governor's Office, RG 284, NARA SB.

86. [Burke], United States Naval History of Tutuila, 13; Robson 1942, 63.

87. Patrick, Import Control, Samoa, 4 Nov. 1943, EA1, 86/71/7 pt 1, ANZ.

88. Notes on Samoan matters, Oct. 1943, EA1, 86/71/7 pt 1, ANZ; History of Upolu, c. 1945, Box v. 13379, F. A12, RG 313-58B-3061, NARA SB; Historical Narrative Wallis Island, June 1945, Entry 183, RG 313, NARA; Franco 1985, 221, 223.

89. Watson to the Administrator, 5 Oct. 1943, McCulloch to Dept. of Island Territories; Telegram No 511, 5 Nov. 1943, EA1, 86/17/3 pt 1, ANZ; Patrick to PM, 11 Nov. 1943, Patrick, Programming of supplies, 4 Nov. 1943, EA1, 86/71/7 pt 1, ANZ; Dept. of Island Territories, War History 1939/45, ITI W2439 69/9/6, ANZ; Employment of Samoan Labor by U.S. forces, 7 Oct. 1943–26 Sept. 1944, EA-1, 86/17/3 pt 1, ANZ.

90. Priday [1945], 62; Watson to the Administrator, 5 Oct. 1943, McCulloch to Dept. of Island Territories; Telegram No 511, 5 Nov. 1943, EA1, 86/17/3 pt 1, ANZ; Patrick to PM, 11 Nov. 1943, Patrick, Programming of supplies, 4 Nov. 1943, EA1, 86/71/7 pt 1, ANZ; Shanahan to Nash, 17 Dec. 1943, Shanahan, Minute for file, 17 Dec. 1943, Shanahan to Department of Island Territories, 28 Jan. 1944, EA1, 86/17/3 pt 1, ANZ; Shanahan to McKay, 13 Jan. 1944; McCulloch to Dept. of Island Territories, 10 Jan. 1944, EA1, 86/17/3 pt 1, ANZ.

91. Peter McQuarrie, personal communication, 26 Aug. 2004; Hooper and Huntsman 1991, 124–130; Notes of Discussion with the Administrator and the Secretary to Western Samoa Administration, Oct. 1943, EA1, 86/17/1, ANZ.

92. Frisbie 1948, 201–207; Ayson to Secretary, 3 Feb. 1943, EA1, 86/18/2 pt 1, ANZ; Report U.S. Forces in Aitutaki, 10 Nov. 1943, IT 122/5/2 pt 1, ANZ; Aitutaki, 10 Apr. 1945, Entry 178, RG 313, NARA; [Patrick], Activities of U.S. Board of Economic Warfare, 13 Aug. 1943, EA1, 86/18/4 pt 1, ANZ; New Zealand representative to Acting PM, 24 Aug. 1942, EA1, 86/18/1, pt 1, ANZ; Gilson 1980, 192; Notes of discussion Administrator and Secretary, Western Samoa, Oct. 1943.

93. Armstrong to CS, 15 Sept. 1944, WPHC TS 39/42, WPA; Gilliam to Commander, 16 Sept. 1943 in History of Tongatapu, c. 1945, Entry 183, RG 313, NARA; Wood-Ellem 1999, 200–221.

94. Kushner 1984, 126–127; Shaforth to Secretary of the Navy, 26 Feb. 1942, Box 1, F. A13–A16, RG 313-58-3233, NARA SB; Ostrom to Commanding General, 12 Apr. 1942, 26 July 1942, Entry 179, RG 313, NARA.

95. Gropman 1997, 3 fn 6; Strength Report, Solomon Islands, 14 Mar. 1944, Box 1, F. A9-4, RG 313-58-3503, NARA SB; Sabel 1999, 129.

96. Stauffer 1956, 243–245.

97. Nelson 1996, 161, 270; G-2 Periodic Intelligence Report, 8 Jan. 1945, Annex No 1, Entry 182, RG 313, NARA; Fifi'i 1989, 50–57.

98. Belshaw 1950, 99.

99. Mead 1956; Lindstrom 1989, 395–414; Davenport 1989, 271–273; Gina 2003, 34–35.

100. *Fiji Times,* 13 Apr. 1944, 7.

101. South Pacific Strategy, Delegate J. R. Farrington, Confidential No 8, c. 1945, Entry 183, RG 313, NARA; Strahan 2005, 28; McQuarrie 2000, 149–157; Macdonald 1982, 157–159; Russell 2003, 42; Mitchell to Shafroth, 7 Sept. 1943, Entry 183, RG 313-58-3233, NARA SB; Baker to Commander, 26 Aug. 1946, RG 407, NARA; Shaforth to Mitchell, 23 Sept. 1943 and encls., WPHC CF 10/17, WPA.

102. Fifi'i 1989, 51–90; Lepowsky 1989, 217–225; Moon and Moon 1998, 86–87; Lindstrom 1989, 404–414.

103. J. M. Clift, *PIM,* Oct. 1946, 39.

104. Feuer, Unrest in the South Pacific, 16 Mar. 1945, Entry 183, RG 313, NARA; Feuer 19 June 1946; Feuer Aug. 1946, 264–267; Mair 1948, 204–212; Stanner 1953, 46–56, 131–142.

105. HC to Acting RC, 21 Sept. 1943, WPHC BSIP F9/55, NASI.

106. Williams, "Relations with the Natives of New Guinea in Wartime," 1 Dec. 1942, Entry 43452, RG 331, NARA. F. E. Williams was the Papuan government's anthropologist.

107. Franco 1985, 220–222.

108. Robinson, Memo, 4 Jan. 1944, AG's Office, 1944, 8H-12483 [2 of 2], RG 284, NARA SB; Ludwig, Political Conditions, 14 Apr. 1945, Reports Governor's office, RG 284, NARA SB; Wood-Ellem 1999, 210; BEW report cited in Patrick, Samoa, Programming of supplies, 4 Nov. 1943, EA1, 86/71/7 pt 1, ANZ; Report US Forces in Aitutaki, 10 Nov. 1943, IT 122/5/2 pt 1, ANZ; Stanner 1953, 326–327, 340–342, 393, 396; McKay 1968, 99, 112–113. The Ellice Islanders are Polynesians; the Gilbertese are related to other peoples of Micronesia.

109. Gray to Secretary, 5 Nov. 1943, IA 1, 16/17/1, ANZ

110. Wood-Ellem 1999, 135, 210, 222–227; Campbell 2001, 156–158; Lal 1992, 112; McQuarrie 1994, 151–155; Priday [1945], 29; Woodbury 1946, 231; Gilson 1980, 177; Parsons 1945, 104–108; Gunner Frederick Pearson Mager (492471) "The men that beat the Gun," Accession No. 2000.438, AM; Keesing 1934, 414–449; Oppenheimer 1966, 19, 24; World War II, Photograph no. WH 650, NLNZ; McQuarrie 2000, 182; R. Crocombe, "Tribute to a Polynesian RenaissanceMan," http://archives.pireport.org/archive/2007/July/07-26-comm1.htm (accessed 7 Aug. 2007).

111. Parsons 1945.

112. History of Tongatapu, c. 1945.

113. Macdonald 1982, 159–160.

114. *AR of the Secretary for Fijian Affairs, 1950,* CP 8 of 1952 9, F108/34/1, FNA.

115. *Western Samoa: Report to the Trusteeship Council by United Nations Mission to Western Samoa.*

116. McKay 1968, 112–114; Stanner 1953, 328; Louise Mataia, personal communication, June 2006.

117. Parsons 1945, 118–119.

118. Kiste 1994, 246–247.

119. Frisbie 1948, 225–226; Gilson 1980, 193–209.

120. Gina 2003, 34–35; Gwero 1988, 40; Lawrence 1964, 130; Silata 1988, 66–67; Mead 1956, 172–179; Connell 1987, 123.

121. Powell 2003, 178; Lawrence 1964, 123–124, 126, 132.

122. Final close out Report on Guadalcanal, 22 Oct. 1945–1 May 1946, Entry 44463, RG 338, NARA.

123. Zelenietz 1991, 1–19.

124. Lepowsky 1989, 218–220; Lawrence 1964, 123–124; Lindstrom 1989, 404–414; Davenport 1989, 271–276; G. F. R., 1946: 381–382; Robinson 1979, 186–187.

125. Shlomowitz 1982, 49–67; Bennett 1987, 173; Bennett 1993, 132, 144–145.

126. *PIM,* 16 (1), 1945, 24, 15(12), 1945, 23; Bennett 1987, 173–175; Tommy Elkington, interview with author, 1976.

127. Robinson 1979, 182–183; Belshaw 1950, 47–48, 92; Lawrence 1964, 98–236; Mead 1956; Maher 1961; Gwero 1988, 40–43; Bennett 1987, 297–310; Mair 1948, 219–226; Fifi'i 1989; Lindstrom and White 1989; Bonnemaison 1994, 225–227; Thompson and Adloff 1971, 497–500; Bhabha 1994.

Chapter 8: Paying for the Damages

Epigraphs: Karotu, cited in McQuarrie 2000, 173; Kisch to Burns, 30 Nov. 1949, CO 225/343/86167/B, TNA.

1. Foreign Claims Commission: Instructions and Regulations for Administration thereof, 12 May 1943, Bulletins, Entry 179, RG 313, NARA. The only other way such claims could be brought was against the U.S. government in the United States Court of Claims. Halsey to Cox, 16 Nov. 1942, Entry 179, RG 313, NARA.

2. BSIP Defence (Compensation) Regulation 1940, Defence (Compensation) Amendment Regulation 1940, CO 225/343/86167/B, TNA.

3. Aerodrome Sites, 1939, Air 118 33, ANZ; RNZAF-Works, Fiji aerodromes, Feb 1942–July 1943, CSO F37/187, FNA; *PIM,* 15 Sept. 1938, 6, 15 Dec. 1939, 33.

4. Emergency Powers (Defence) Act 1939.

5. A. Potts, History of Fiji, Island File, n.d., c. Nov. 1945, 6, Entry 183, RG 313, NARA; Fitzgerald 1992, 47–64.

6. This was extended subsequently. Order, 27 Jan. 1943, CSO F37/210 Pt. 1, FNA; Howlett 1948, 23.

7. A. Potts, History of Fiji, Island File, n.d., c. Nov. 1945, 6–16.

8. Director of Lands, Notes 13 Nov. 1946, Notes, 30 Dec. 1946, CSO F37/292 Pt 1, FNA; Wise to Judd, 26 May 1942 and enc, CSO NAD 44/12/24, FNA.

9. CSR to CS, 17 Apr. 1946, CSO F115/71/3, NARA; Stanner 1953, 197–198.

10. CSO F37/210, CSO F115/71, CSO F115/71/1, CSO F115/71/2, CSO F115/28, CSO F37/292, CSO F37/292/2, FNA; Minutes of Nadi Provincial Council, Nov. 1943, CSO NAD62/8/12, FNA; *Fiji Legislative Council Debates,* 17 May 1943 (Suva: Government Printer, 1944), 21, 37.

11. Charlton, Director of Lands to CS., 27 Feb. 1942, CSO F37/210 Pt 1, NARA; *ARs Agriculture Department,* 1940, 1945; AJ, Suva (1943), 14, 3, 85–87; AJ (1942), 14, 4, 98–99; AJ (1944), 1, 1, 23–24; AR, Northern District, 1946, CSO F62/303, NARA.

12. Harlan to Director of Lands, 31 Mar. 1943, DO, Nadi to DC, Western, 3 Apr. 1943, DC, Western to CS., 9 Apr. 1943, Petition 15 Apr. 1943, Weekly reports on payment of Compensation, May–Nov. 1943, CSO F115/71/1, FNA; Minutes of Nadi Provincial Council, Nov. 1943, CSO NAD62/8/12, FNA; CSR to CS., 17 Apr. 1946, CSO F115/71/3, FNA.

13. Rottman 2002, 66

14. Agreement for the Use, Administration and Operation of a Naval Base on Tongatabu, History of Tongatabu, c. Aug. 1945, Entry 183, RG 313, NARA; Agreement between the United Kingdom and the U.S. regarding the Defense of Tonga, 15 Aug. 1942, Entry 176, RG 313, NARA.

15. Ata to Captain, 6 Dec. 1944, Final close out Report on the South Pacific Bases, Entry 44463, RG 338, NARA.

16. Olsen to Commanding Officer, 1 Feb. 1943, Curley to Commanding Officer, 18 June 1943, Box 1, F. L0, L10, & L13, RG 313-58-3394, NARA SB. The army left the island in early 1943, so the navy took over.

17. Curley to Commanding Officer, 18 June 1943.

18. Ata to Captain, 6 Dec. 1944, Final close out Report on the South Pacific Bases; Olsen to Commanding Officer, 1 Feb. 1943; Foreign Claims Commission: Instructions and Regulations for Administration thereof, 12 May 1943, Bulletins, Entry 179, RG 313, NARA.

19. Vaskess to the Chief of Staff, 16 June 1943 and encls., Nimitz to Chief of Naval operations, 8 Dec. 1943 and encls., Entry 176, RG 313, NARA; Margaret Armstrong, Visitors Book and memoirs, 149–150, Mss Pac. S. 93, RH.

20. History of Tongatabu, c. Aug. 1945, Entry 183, RG 313, NARA; Ian Campbell, personal communication, May 2003.

21. Rottman 2002, 86.

22. Bivens to Governor, 12 June 1946, AG's Office, RG 284, NARA SB.

23. Tasi to Superintendent, CBs, 27 Oct. 1942, AG's Office, RG 284, NARA SB.

24. Ingram, Statement, 12 Jan. 1944, AG's Office, RG 284, NARA SB.

25. Robinson to PW Officer, 21 Feb. 1944, Robinson to Donnahue, 28 June 1944,

Mrs. Maletoa to AG, 6 Aug. 1944, Utu to General, 12 Nov. 1944, Viamasima Molio'o to Commandant, 25 Apr. 1944, Electricity for civilians, 12 Oct. 1945, AG's Office, RG 284, NARA SB; Aua village, no. 18 and Pauu to AG, 28 Jan. 1944 and enclosures; Fatu Palu to Governor, 28 Mar. 1944, Hobb to Fatu Palu, 22 Apr. 1944 and enclosures, War Damage claims, RG 284, NARA SB.

26. Hungerford to Ladner, 23 Aug. 1945, Uma Taimi to Governor, 3 Mar. 1944, Alo claim, 24 July 1942, Report of Claims Commission, 18 Dec. 1945, *O le Fa'atonu,* No. 1, Vol. XLIII, 1946, War Damage claims, AG's Office, RG 284, NARA SB.

27. High Chiefs to U.S. President, 10 Dec. 1948, RG 284, NARA SB.

28. Nu'uli, no 49 (c), 5 Jan. 1953, War Damage claims, RG 284, NARA SB; Rottman 2002, 87; Vaitoga village, no. 62, 15 June 1953, Pago Pago village, no. 51, Max Haleck, claim, 15 May 1953, War Damage claims, RG 284, NARA SB; Libby to Draney, 25 Sept. 1953, Love to Libby, 19 Nov. 1953, Macquarie to Libby, 27 Apr. 1954, Lowe to Strand, 25 Oct. 1954, AG's Office, RG 284, NARA SB.

29. Vaitoga village, no. 62, 15 June 1953, War Damage claims, RG 284, NARA SB; Chairman supplemental Land and Claims Commission, 16 Aug. 1950, Records of Governor's Office, series no. 16, RG 284, NARA SB; Tuuga Laufasa, 8 Jan. 1946, War Damage claims, RG 284, NARA SB; File.

30. Lissington 1972, 19–23; Wood 1958, 74–76, 79.

31. Commanding General to Commander, 20 May 1942, History of Upolu, Western Samoa, c. Nov. 1945, Box v. 13379, F. A12, Barrett to Administrator, 1 June 1942, Manager to Commanding Officer, USMC, 13 Apr. 1944, Sec. to Administrator, 18 Apr. 1944, Turnbull to Andruska, 12 Sept. 1944, Box v. 13381, F. Misc., RG 313-58B-3061, NARA SB; McKay 1968, 105–107.

32. Final close out Report on Upolu, 28 Jan. 1946 and enclosures, Entry 178, RG 313, NARA; Shanahan to Sec., 22 Feb. 1944, IA 1, 86/17/1, ANZ.

33. Naval base Aitutaki, 10 Apr. 1945, Entry 178, RG 313, NARA; Final close out, South Pacific Base, 30 June 1946, Entry 44463, RG 338, NARA.

34. McCarthy, Aitutaki compensation claims, 26 June 1943, Secretary to Assistant Secretary, 2 Nov. 1944, IT 122/5/2 pt 1, ANZ.

35. Kay 1972.

36. [Shanahan], Penrhyn and Rarotonga—claims to native lands, 13 Sept. 1943, IT 122/5/2 pt 1, ANZ.

37. Buckeridge to Minister, 28 Feb. 1946, Land Taken for Airfield, New Zealand Island Territories, c. July 1946, IT 122/5/2, ANZ.

38. Evatt, Papers for ANZ conference, Jan. 1944, M1942/1, Item 7, NAA.

39. Train to Commander South Pacific 5 Aug. 1942, Entry 179, RG 313, NARA; McCormack to Naval Claims Commission, 21 Jan. 1943, 44 W 705, ANC; Guindon to Governor, 26 Oct. 1942, 44 W 682, ANC; Director of the Muéo Society to Verges, 28 June 1944, 44 W 707 (212), ANC; Patch to Montchamp, 2 Nov. 1942, 44 W 709, ANC.

40. Patch to Montchamp, 30 Oct. 1942, 44 W 709, ANC.

41. Montchamp to Lincoln, 3 Dec. 1942, 44 W 514, ANC; Lincoln to Montchamp,

22 May 1943, Henkle to Governor's Cabinet, 26 June 1943, 44 W 520, ANC; Verges to Governor, 25 May 1943, 44 W 707, ANC; Gillespie 1954, 126.

42. Tixier to Atherton, 24 Dec. 1941, Atherton to Tixier, 15 Jan. 1942, Commanding Officer, Bora Bora to Commander South Pacific, 6 Aug. 1945 and enclosures, Shaforth to Secretary of the Navy, 26 Feb. 1942 and enclosure, Box 1, F. A13–16, RG 313-58-3233, NARA SB; McColm to Commander South Pacific, 5 Mar. 1945, Entry 178, RG 313, NARA; Hendren and Burgess to the Governor of French Oceania, 25 Jan. 1946, Entry 183, RG 313, NARA; Barnett to Tallec, 26 Jan. 1945, 44 W 707 (212), ANC; Tallec to Hendren, 21 Jan. 1946, Entry 183, RG 313, NARA.

43. Minute, 20 Nov. 1952; Acting RC to HC, 4 Mar. 1953, WPHC NH BS 32/59, WPA; Lee, Adjusting report, lend-lease, Mar. 1946, Entry 183, RG 313, NARA; Agreement for transfer of surplus property, 28 May 1946, Entry 400, RG 59, NARA; History of SOS SPA, c. Mar. 1944, Entry 44463, RG 338, NARA.

44. Wallin to Chief of Bureau of Yards and Docks, 18 July 1942, Entry 183, RG 313, NARA; Final close out report on Wallis, 30 Nov. 1945, McGhee to Commanding General South Pacific, 10 Oct. 1945 and enclosures, Entry 178, RG 313, NARA; Munster to Commander South Pacific, 4 Aug. 1945 and enclosures, Box 1, F. L4-L5, RG 313-58-3233, NARA SB; Burgess, Final close out Report on South Pacific Base Command, Annex C, 30 June 1946, Entry 44463, RG 338, NARA.

45. Secretary to Secretary, Commerce and Agriculture Dept., 2 Jan. 1948; Memo for Secretary, External Affairs Dept., 14 Aug. 1948 and enclosure, Notes on Australian Policy, A1838, A1838/2, Item 324/1/2, NAA; French debt in New Caledonia, A1838/1, Item 324/1/3, NAA.

46. Gillespie 1954, 132.

47. Robson 1942, 140–141, 145; Acting RC, Compensation for coconut trees, 21 Nov. 1944, WPHC CF 29/20 Vol. I, WPA.

48. Memo on acquisition of land for RAAF bases, n.d., c. Oct. 1941; Blandy to Colardeau, 8 Sept. 1941 and enclosures, WPHC NHBS MP 149/1941, WPA; Summary of events for the History of the War, 1 Jan.–Dec. 31 1941, WPHC NHBS 19/III 7/20, WPA.

49. RC to HC 30 July 1942, British Judge to Lieutenant Commander Hepburn, 24 Aug. 1942, Egan, Minutes, 26 Aug. 1942, 2 Sept. 1942, HC to RC, 20 Nov. 1942, Egan, Minutes, 27 May 1943, 1 June 1943, 23 June 1943, Blandy to HC, 4 Sept. 1943, SOS to HC, 25 Dec. 1943 and enclosures, WPHC NHBS MP 33/2, WPA; Wilkinson to Commander, South Pacific, 1 June 1943, Entry 182, RG 313, NARA. See also CO 968/86/5, CO 968/151/2, WO 106/2621, TNA.

50. Mitchell to Shaforth, 11 Jan. 1944, WPHC NHBS MP 33/2, WPA.

51. SOS to HC, 25 Dec. 1943, Mitchell to Shaforth, 11 Jan 1944, Shaforth to Mitchell, 23 Jan. 1944, SOS, 17 Mar. 1944, WPHC NHBS MP 33/2, WPA.

52. Egan, Minute, 29 Apr. 1943, Egan, Minute, 8 May 1943. Egan, Minute, 25 Sept. 1943, WPHC NHBS MP 32/59, WPA; Egan, Minute, 25 Oct. 1943, Blandy and Fourcade to Commanding Officer, 13 Dec. 1943, WPHC NHBS MP 32/9, WPA; Civil Affairs: Establishment of a Civil Affairs Office, c. Nov. 1945, Entry 183, RG 313, NARA.

53. Johnson to Blandy, 16 Apr. 1943, WPHC NHBS MP 32/7, WPA; Commissioners to Commanding Officer, c. Oct. 1943, Egan, Minute 11 Oct. 1943, Blandy to French HC, 13 Dec. 1943, Blandy and Fourcade to Commanding Officer, 13 Dec. 1943, WPHC NHBS MP 32/9, WPA.

54. Blandy to HC, 26 Feb. 1944, WPHC NHBS MP 32/9, WPA.

55. Civil Affairs: Establishment of a Civil Affairs Office, c. Nov. 1945; Rottman 2002, 78–79.

56. Civil Affairs: Establishment of a Civil Affairs Office, c. Nov. 1945.

57. Acting RC to HC, 4 Mar. 1953, WPHC NHBS MP 32/59, WPA.

58. RC, Summary of events for the History of the War, 1 Jan.–31 Dec 1943.

59. Civil Affairs: Establishment of a Civil Affairs Office, c. Nov. 1945.

60. Summary of events for the History of the War, 1 Jan.–31 Dec 1942, WPHC NHBS 19/III 7/20, WPA.

61. Civil Affairs: Establishment of a Civil Affairs Office, c. Nov. 1945; RC, Summary of events for the History of the War, 1 Jan. 1941–31 Dec. 1943.

62. Egan, Minutes, 20 Aug. 1943; 2 Sept. 1943, Blandy, Minute 33, 2 Nov. 1943, Copy of Minute from Main, War damage claims, 3 Nov. 1947, WPHC NHBS MP 32/59, WPA; Acting RC, Compensation for coconut trees, 21 Nov. 1944, WPHC CF 29/20 Vol. I, WPA.

63. Organizational History of SOS in SPA, c. 1943, Entry 444633, RG 338, NARA; Civil Affairs: Establishment of a Civil Affairs Office, c. Nov. 1945; Acting RC, Compensation for coconut trees, 21 Nov. 1944, WPHC CF 29/20 Vol. I, WPA; Shaforth to South Pacific Area, 28 Dec. 1943, Box 21 (v. 9699), F. L11, RG 313-58-3440, NARA SB.

64. Stout, Status of Leases and Claims at Espiritu Santo, 3 Apr. 1946, Entry 427, RG 407, NARA.

65. Howie to Commanding Officer, 31 Dec. 1944, Entry 444633, RG 338, NARA.

66. Stout, Status of Leases and Claims at Espiritu Santo, 3 Apr. 1946; RC, Summary of events for the History of the War, 1 Jan.–31 Dec 1944; 1 Jan.–Dec. 1945, WPHC NHBS 19/III 7/20, WPA; Commander South Pacific to Field Commissioner South Pacific, 31 Jan. 1946 [date unclear] and enclosures; US Naval Base Order 187, 19 Feb. 1945, Box v. 319812, F. A2-11(2), RG 313-58A-3254, NARA SB. This process of goods in lieu of cash settlement had started unofficially before June. Howie to Commanding General, 1 May 1945, Entry 44463, RG 338, NARA; Commander to Commanding Officers, 29 June 1945, Box 7, F. L11, RG 313-518-3503, NARA SB.

67. Acting RC to HC, 23 Nov. and enclosures, WPHC NHBS SF 9/31/5, WPA.

68. Macquire and Kuter to L'Abbe, 15 Nov. 1944, WPHC NHBS SF 9/31/5, WPA; Shaw to Commanding officer, 7 Dec. 1944 and enclosures, Entry 178, RG 313, NARA.

69. Egan, Minutes, 20 Dec. 1944, WPHC NHBS MP 33/2 Part II, WPA; Commander South Pacific to Field Commissioner South Pacific, 31 Jan. 1946 [date unclear] and enclosures; U.S. Naval Base Order 187, 19 Feb. 1945, Box v. 319812, F. A2-11(2), RG 313-58A-3254, NARA SB.

70. Egan, Minutes, 20 Dec. 1944; Claims of the Société Française des Nouvelles Hebrides and Comptoirs Francaises des Nouvelles Hebrides, 29 June 1945 and enclo-

sures, Commander South Pacific to Field Commissioner South Pacific, 31 Jan. 1946 [date unclear] and enclosures; U.S. Naval Base Order 187, 19 Feb. 1945, Box v. 319812, F. A2-11(2), RG 313-58A-3254, NARA SB; Howie to Commanding Officer, 31 Dec 1944, Activities of Divisions HQ SOS SPA, Aug. 1944, Entry 44463, RG 338, NARA.

71. Minute, 20 Nov. 1952, Acting RC to HC, 4 Mar. 1953, WPHC NHBS MP 32/59, WPA; Leger, Report to the Assembly of France, No. 35, 11 Feb. 1954 and enclosures, 109W, 278, ANC.

72. Thomas to Officer Administering, 27 Sept. 1947 and enclosure, Copy of Minute from Main, War damage claims, 3 Nov. 1947; Acting HC to British RC, 4 Nov. 1947 and enclosures, WPHC NHBS MP 32/59, WPA.

73. Blackwell to Kuter, 23 Jan. 1943, WPHC NHBS MP 32/7, WPA; Acting RC to HC, 25 Mar. 1953, Hill, Statement of claims, Apr. 1944 and enclosures, Acting RC, 4 Mar. 1953, NHBS MP 32/59, WPA; Hill to Claims Officer, 29 Dec. 1943 and enclosures, WPHC CF 29/20 Vol. II, WPA; [Illegible] to Hill, 14 Apr. 1953; Acting RC to [Illegible], 6 May 1953, WPHC NHBS MP 32/7, WPA.

74. RC, Summaries of events for the History of the War, 1 Jan. 1942–31 Dec. 1944, WPHC NHBS 19/III 7/20, WPA.

75. RC, Summaries of events for the History of the War, 1 Jan. 1944–31 Dec. 1945, WPHC NHBS 19/III 7/20, WPA.

76. Civil Affairs: Establishment of a Civil Affairs Office, c. Nov. 1945; Memo for Officer in charge, re Peronnet, 27 Oct. 1943, Box 1, F. A8-2, RG 313-58-3285, NARA SB.

77. Acting RC to HC, 4 Mar. 1953, WPHC NHBS MP 32/59, WPA; Egan, Minute, 20 Dec. 1944; RC, Summary of events for the History of the War, 1 Jan.–31 Dec. 1943, WPHC NHBS MP 33/2 part II, WPA.

78. War Damage Reports, Gilbert and Ellice Islands and Solomon Islands, c. 1946, CO 225/336, TNA.

79. Mitchell to SOS for Colonies, 4 Oct. 1943, WPHC CF82/18/1, Vol. I, WPA.

80. Maude to HC, 3 Mar. 1947, WPHC SF 9/31/2, Vol. I, WPA; McQuarrie 2000, 172; Goode, Notes on food supply at Funafuti, 23 Dec. 1942, Papers, Mss Pac s.112, RH.

81. Maude to Sec., WPHC, 13 Mar. 1943, WPHC SF 9/31/2, Vol. II, WPA.

82. Mitchell to SOS, 17 June 1944, WPHC SF 9/31/2, Vol. II, WPA; McQuarrie 2000, 149–157; Macdonald 1982, 157–159.

83. Mitchell to SOS, 17 June 1944.

84. SOS to HC, 21 Aug. 1944, WPHC SF 9/31/2, Vol. II, WPA.

85. Maude to HC, 3 Mar. 1947; Nicoll to SOS, 16 Apr. 1947, RC to HC, 15 Apr. 1950, WPHC SF 9/31/2, Vol. 11, WPA; Robson 1942, 157.

86. War Damage Reports, Gilbert and Ellice Islands and Solomon Islands, c. 1946, CO 225/336, TNA; Ramsay Main, Report of the War Damage Claims Commission, Aug. 1947–Apr. 1948 and enclosures, CO 225/343/86167/B, TNA.

87. HC to RC, 25 Mar. 1954 and enclosures, WPHC CF 29/87, WPA; *PIM*, Jan. 1954, 56–57; Highland 1991, 111–112.

88. Mitchell to Newton, 16 Aug. 1944, WPHC CF 29/20 vol. 1, WPA.

89. Final close out Report, South Pacific Command, 30 June 1946, Annex C, Entry 44463, RG 338, NARA.

90. AR, Guadalcanal Sub-base, 31 Dec. 1941, RG 218, NARA.

91. Commander South Pacific to All Stations South Pacific, 2 May 1944 and enclosures, Entry 178, RG 313, NARA; Commander to Commander, South Pacific, 23 July 1945, Grinnel to Ladner, 22 Aug. 1945, Entry 178, RG 313, NARA; Final close out Report on Guadalcanal, May 1946, 5–9, Entry 44463, RG 338, NARA; Commanding Officer to Commander, South Pacific, 1 May 1945, Commanding Officer to Commander, South Pacific, 1 June 1945 and enclosed photographs, Box 6, F. L11, RG 313-58-3503, NARA SB.

92. Final close out Report on Guadalcanal, May 1946, 21.

93. Mitchell to SOS, 18 Jan. 1943, WO 106/3342, TNA.

94. Frost 1992, 144.

95. Mitchell, Diary, 28 Feb., 14, 15 Mar., 21–29 Aug. 1944, MSS. Afr. r. 101, RH; Mitchell to SOS, 18 Aug. 1943, CO 968/86/5, TNA; Mitchell to SOS, 18 Jan. 1943, WO 106/3342, TNA; Mitchell to SOS, 31 Aug. 1944, WO 106/5928, TNA.

96. *PIM,* 15 Mar. 1946, 8; WPHC F. 32/21/1; Commander to Commander, South Pacific, 23 July 1945, Entry 178, RG 313, NARA; Egan, Minute, 8 Sept. 1952, WPHC NHBS MP 32/59, WPA.

97. RC to HC, 10 Aug. 1942, WPHC SF 9/1/1 Vol. II, WPA; RC to HC, 25 Sept. 1945 and minutes of 15, 20 Sept. 1945, Bentley to Sec. to the Government, Honiara, 1 July 1945, WPHC SF 9/1/1 Vol. VI, WPA.

98. Final close out Report on Guadalcanal, May 1946, 7–9; Noel to the Commanding General, 15 Apr. 1944, WPHC CF 29/40 Vol. I, WPA; Personal communication, James Tedder, 2002.

99. Noel to HC, 10 Aug. 1942, WPHC SF9/1/1 Vol. III, WPA.

100. Final close out report on South Pacific Base command, Grantham to the Commanding Officer, 16 Jan. 1946, enclosure, Entry 44463, RG 338, NARA; List of Claims in BSIP, 2 June 1944, and enclosures, WPHC F 32/21/1, WPA; Claims, 9 Sept. 1947, WPHC CF 29/87, WPA; Notes, 25 Mar. 1954, WPHC CF 32/21/3, Vols. 1 and Vol. 2, WPA; Ramsay Main, Report of the War Damage Claims Commission, Aug. 1947–Apr. 1948.

101. War Damage Reports, Gilbert and Ellice Islands and Solomon Islands, c. 1946.

102. Final close out report on South Pacific Base command, Grantham to the Commanding Officer, 16 Jan. 1946, enclosure, Entry 44463, RG 338, NARA; Charles, Minute, 4 Aug. 1949, WPHC CF 29/20 Vol. 1, WPA.

103. Burke to Flag Sec. 14 Nov. 1945, Entry 183, RG 313, NARA.

104. Baddeley to the Claims Officer, Oct. 1945, Baddeley to Claims Officer, 5 Jan. 1946, Entry 183, RG 313, NARA.

105. Thomson to the Bishop of Melanesia, 29 Jan. 1946, Entry 44463, RG 338, NARA; Commanding Officer to Sale Officer, 28 Aug. 1945, Box 1, F. A11, RG 313-59-3496, NARA SB.

106. [Sando], Excerpt from Report on Inspection of Islands, 23 Sept.–30 Oct. 1944, WPHC NHBS MP 21/4, WPA; Correspondence to Vanikoro, Sept. 1939–Aug. 1943, Boye to Sec., 19 Feb. 1942, Wilson to Boye, 20 July 1943, Boye to Sec., 27 Oct. 1944, Vanikoro Timber Co. records, Business and Labor Archives, University of Melbourne; Newton to Johnson, c. Jan. 1945, Adjutant General to Sweeney, 9 Oct. 1945, Entry 178, RG 313, NARA.

107. Noel, Statement, 11 Oct. 1944, and enclosures, Vaskess, Minutes, 19 June 1945, WPHC F 45/1, Vol. IV, WPA.

108. HC to SOS, 12 Sept. 1945, Vaskess, Minute, 15 Sept. 1945, HC for UK in Australia to HC, Suva, 21 Nov. 1945, WPHC SF 9/1/1 Vol. VI, WPA.

109. Freeston to SOS, 11 June 1948, CO 225/343/86167B, TNA.

110. Ramsay Main, Palmer, and Kisch, Meeting at CO, 15 July 1948, CO 225/343/86167B, TNA.

111. Ramsay Main, Palmer, and Kisch, Meeting at CO, 15 July 1948, Ramsay Main, Palmer, Stapleton, Armitage-Smith, and Kisch, Meeting at Colonial Office, 20 July 1948, [Illegible] to Kisch, 26 Aug. 1948, Russell-Edmonds, Bentley, Ramsey Main, and Kisch, Meeting at Treasury, 26 Aug., 1948, Russell-Edmonds to Kisch, 27 Aug. 1948, CO 225/343/86167B, TNA.

112. [Illegible] to HC, n.d. draft, c. Oct. 1948, CO 225/343/86167B, TNA.

113. *PIM,* Aug., 7, Sept., 10, 21, Nov. 1949, 29; HC to RC, 25 Mar. 1954 and enclosures, WPHC CF 29/87, WPA.

114. Letter from the Secretary to the BSIP government, cited in *PIM,* Jan. 1954, 56.

115. List of Claims in BSIP, 2 June 1944 and enclosures, WPHC F 32/21/1, WPA; Claims, 9 Sept. 1947, WPHC CF 29/87, WPA; Notes, 25 Mar. 1954, WPHC CF 32/21/3, Vols. 1 and Vol. 2, WPA; Bennett 1987, 303.

116. Zoloveke 1988, 77.

117. *PIM,* June 1949, 25.

118. Gill to SOS, 3 June 1948, Harper to Churchill, 2 Nov. 1949, CO 225/343/86167B, TNA.

119. *PIM,* Sept. 1949, 21, Nov. 1949, 29.

120. Zelenietz 1991, 1–19.

121. Nelson 1999, 26; Mair 1948, 219–224; Stanner 1953, 87, 118–119, 129; Downs 1980, 40–42.

122. Nelson 1979, 147–151; Beruel Panu and Eliab Kaplimut, Interviews, Remembering the war in New Guinea Project, AWM, http://ajrp.awm.gov.au/ajrp/remember.nsf. (accessed 16 May 2006).

123. Williams, "Relations with the Natives of New Guinea in wartime," 1 Dec. 1942, Entry 43452, RG 331, NARA.

124. Nelson 1979, 147–151; Nelson 1999, 4–26; Mair 1948, 198–203.

125. J. L. Taylor, Paper on Native welfare, Conference of Officers of HQ and Officers of Districts staff, 7–12 Feb 1944, Papers and discussions, Vol. 11, AWM 254, 6, AWM; Mead 1956, 171–172.

126. J. Gatt, Recollections, PR 85/226, AWM; B. Love, Diary, 20 Dec. 1942, 3DRL 7211, AWM.

127. H. "Bert" Beros, "The Fuzzy Wuzzy Angels," *Women's Weekly,* 9 Jan. 1943.

128. Ward, Item 2396/12/585, External Territories of the Commonwealth, NLA.

129. Ward to [Illegible], 20 Sept. 1944, A 518/1 A320/3/1 Part 1, NAA.

130. Barry, Hogbin, and Taylor, Compensation to the natives of Papua and New Guinea, July 1945, 1956/1096, A 463/17, NAA.

131. McAdam, Report, 23 July 1943, file 192, entry 305C, RG 77, NARA; L. Austen, Paper on Native welfare, Conference of Officers of HQ and Officers of Districts staff, 7–12 Feb. 1944, Papers and discussions, Vol. 11, AWM 254, 6, AWM; Ward to Barry, 26 Oct. 1944, A 518/1 A320/3/1 Part 1, NAA.

132. Barry, Hogbin, and Taylor, Compensation to the natives of Papua and New Guinea, July 1945.

133. Summary of relief and rehabilitation, c. Sept. 1944 and enclosure, A9373, Item 1, NAA; Downs 1980, 38–39; Stanner, Appreciation of current situation and problems of ANGAU, AWM 54 (80/8/17), AWM; Mair 1948, 186–198.

134. Barry, Hogbin, and Taylor, Compensation to the natives of Papua and New Guinea, July 1945; Ward, Memo for Cabinet, 5 Dec. 1945, Appendix, Compensation to Natives, Appendix A, 5 Dec. 1945, A9816 (A9816/3), Item 1944/580, NAA; Bennett 1987, 281.

135. Barry, Hogbin, and Taylor, Compensation to the natives of Papua and New Guinea, July 1945.

136. Halligan, Memo, Compensation to Natives, 26 June 1945 and enclosures, Curtin, Ford, and Chifley documents, 1941–1949, CRS A 6006, NAA; Humphries to Sec. of External Territories, 3 Oct. 1945 and enclosures, A518/1, A320/3/1 Part I, NAA; Downs 1987, 189, 191–192; Clarke, Baniara Patrol Report, no. 1 of 1948–1948, 29 July to 5 Aug. 1947, Bamford, Finschhafen, Hube Subdivision, 31 Mar.–15 May 1950, Sharp, West Nakanai Subdivision, Cape Hoskins, 2 Aug.–2 Sept. 1954, PNG Patrol Reports, microfiche, A9844, NAA; *ARs of the Territory of New Guinea, 1947–1961* (Port Moresby: Government Printer, 1948–1962); *ARs of Papua, 1948–1961* (Port Moresby: Government Printer, 1948–1962). (Copies in the Australian Parliamentary Papers, 1949–1962).

137. Downs 1980, 40–42.

138. *ARs of the Territory of New Guinea, 1947–1961; ARs of Papua, 1948–1961;* Humphries to Sec., Dept. of External Territories, and encls., A518/1, A320/3/1/Part 1, NAA; Barry Report, A463/17, item 1956/1096, NAA; Ward, Cabinet Memo, 5 Dec. 1945 and enclosures, A9816 (A9816/3), Item 1944/580, NAA; Summary of relief and rehabilitation, c. Sept. 1944 and enclosure, A9373, Item 1, NAA; Robson 1942, 229, 268, 269; Mair 1948, 4; Stanner 1953, 87, 118–119, 129; Downs 1980, 40–42; Nelson 1999, 27; Iwamoto Hiromisu, "Patrol Reports: Sources for assessing war damage in Papua New Guinea," *Remembering the War in New Guinea,* Symposium (Canberra: Australian War Memorial, Oct. 2000), 1–17, http://www.awm.gov.au;8000/ajrp/remember.nsf/pages/NT00002A52 (accessed June 2005).

139. ANGAU, Report for Feb. 1942–Sept. 1944, A9373, item 1, NAA; Mair 1948, 191; Robson 1942, 241, 278. In the period from 1947 to 1950, £1,770,753 went to administrative spending. For the same period, compensation amounted to £1,076, 611. Downs 1980, 68.

140. Humphries to Sec. Dept. of External Affairs, 3 Oct. 1945, A 518/1 A320/3/1 Part 1, NAA.

141. Ramsay Main, Palmer, and Kisch, Meeting at Colonial Office, 15 July 1948, CO 225/343/86167B, TNA.

142. An analysis of policy, *PIM*, Jan. 1943–June 1944, Item 12/164–176, E. J. Ward, Papers, NAA; Mair 1948, 222–223.

143. *Angels of War*, Canberra: Ronin Home Video, 1984.

144. Powell 2003, 256.

145. Tenison 1942, 26; Molloy to Deputy Controller, 9 Nov. 1945, 3 July 1945; Alderman to Headquarters ANGAU, 16 May 1945, SP423/3, Item S101-S300, NAA, Sydney; Todd, construction of airstrips, 2 Dec. 1943, Item Legal opinion, SP423/4, NAA, Sydney; Minutes of the War Damage Commission, 7 Jan. 1944, SP302/2, Item Vol. 2, NAA, Sydney; Todd, Secondary growth on plantations, 28 Mar. 1945, Item Legal opinion, SP423/4, NAA, Sydney; Minutes of the War Damage Commission, 24 May 1944, Chifley, Press statement, c. Dec. 1944, Item Vol. 2, SP302/2, NAA, Sydney; Doig, Notes for the PM, 14 Sept. 1944, A9816 (A9816/3), Item 1944/580, NAA.

146. Australia House of Representatives, *Hansard*, 6 Oct. 1943, Vol. 176, 212; 25 Feb. 1948, Vol. 196, 209; Archer to Custodian 29 Mar. 1947; Coles to Custodian, 29 Mar. 1947, A518/1, Item 1320/3/2, NAA.

147. Hank Nelson, e-mail to writer, 16 September 2007.

148. Tachibana 1996, 171.

Chapter 9: Close Out: Quitting the Islands

Epigraph: White 1965, 140.

1. For U.S.A., see Gropman 1997.

2. Halsey to Sopac Area, 8 Dec. 1943, Box v. 13381, F. N/A3-1, RG 313-58B-3061, NARA SB.

3. "Operation roll-up," 1, microfilm H-108, Navy Yards, Washington, D. C.

4. Treland, Notes on Army Engineer Operation in SWPA, n. d., c. May 1944, Entry 305C, RG 77, NARA; Ashton 1998, 4.

5. Rodeick, 19 Dec. 1942, cited in Report, The Corps of Engineers in the South Pacific, c. 1945, Entry 477, RG 407, NARA.

6. Lademan to Halsey, 21 Dec., cited in Potts, Historical Narrative, Fiji Islands, c. 1946, Entry 183, RG 313, NARA.

7. Nimitz, Pacific Fleet Letter 31L-55, 24 May 1944, Box 7 (v. 9700), F. A1, RG 313-58-3440, NARA SB.

8. Nimitz to Commander, 15 Apr. 1943; Halsey to Sopac and SWP, 8 Dec. 1943, Entry 179, RG 313, NARA; Barnett, Memo no. 113, Salvage and Battlefield Reclama-

tion Plan South Pacific Area, 27 Aug. 1943, Box v. 13381, F. A1, RG 313-58B-3061, NARA SB; Army Service Force Circular 69, 2 Sept. 1943, Entry 109, RG 160, NARA.

9. Straub, Memo, 16 July 1943, Box 320651, L11-1, RG 313-58-3061, NARA SB.

10. Commanding Officer to Commandant, 19 Sept. 1944, Box 17 (v. 9707), F. A1-1, RG 313-58-3440, NARA SB.

11. Navy Dept., Manual of Advanced Base Development and Maintenance, July 1942, 112, Box 3 (v. 9666), F. A1, RG 313-58-3440, NARA SB; Pinsof, Monthly reports of progress, Material recovery unit no. 7 [South Solomons], Jan.–1 May 1945, Box v. 9291, F. A9, RG 313-58-3401, NARA SB; "Operation roll-up," microfilm H-108.

12. Commander to Chief of Naval Operations, 6 Feb. 1944, Commander to All Advanced Bases, 28 Feb. 1944, Box v. 9289, F. S94, RG 313-58-3401, NARA SB.

13. [John Burke], United States Naval History of Tutuila, c. Aug. 1945, Navy Yard Museum, Washington, D.C., 131.

14. Denfeld 1989, 44.

15. Barnett, Memo 113, Salvage and battlefield reclamation plan South Pacific Area, 27 Aug. 1943, Box v. 13381, F. A1, RG 313-58B-3061, NARA SB; Office of Procurement and Material, Property Disposition Directive No. 3, 17 Apr. 1945, Harris, Salvage and Obsolete Material, Disposition of, 27 Apr. 1945, Box 1, F. A3, RG 313-58-3517, NARA SB.

16. HC to RC, 21 Sept. 1945, WPHC CF 58/28/4 Vol. 1, WPA.

17. CP No. 26, 2 Dec. 1944, *Legislative Council of Fiji*, 1944, 1, 8, 9; Commander to Colonel Secretary, 31 Oct. 1945, CSO F37/210/pt 2, FNA; CP No. 12, 17 Mar. 1947, *Legislative Council of Fiji*, 1947, 1, 2, 8.

18. Calhoun, Rolling up the South Pacific, 15 Sept. 1945, Entry 178, RG 313, NARA; Commander in Chief to All Units, 3 May 1945, Box 5, F. A2-4, RG 313-58-3416, NARA SB.

19. Summary of 4 June Conference on SOPAC roll-up, June 1945, Box v. 9658, F. A9, RG 313-58D-3290, NARA SB; Commander Service Squadron to Commanding Officers, 29 June 1945, Box 7 (v. 9658), F. A9, RG 313-58-3503, NARA SB.

20. Alexis to Commander, 8 Sept. 1945, Box 4, RG 313-58-3300, NARA SB; Boak to Commanding Officer, Naval Base, 20 Mar. 1945, Box 8, F. S82, RG 313-58-3416, NARA SB; Carter to Commandants, 18 Sept. 1945, Box 1, F. L11, RG 313-58-3517, NARA SB; Sec. of Navy to Commanding Officer, 26 Sept. 1945, Box 4, F. A16, RG 313-58-3416, NARA SB; "Operation roll-up," microfilm H-108.

21. "Operation roll-up," microfilm H-108.

22. History of the South Pacific Base Command, c. July 1946, Entry 44463, RG 338, NARA.

23. Hofmann, Survey of surplus disposal problem in South and Southwest Pacific base areas, 20 July 1945, Entry 400, RG 59, NARA.

24. History of the South Pacific Base Command, c. July 1946; Narrative of South Pacific Area and Force, 1 Sept. 1945–1 Oct. 1946, Entry 183, RG 313, NARA; Summary of 4 June Conference on SOPAC roll-up, June 1945; Commander to Staff, 19 Oct. 1945, Box 1, F. L11, RG 313-58-3517, NARA SB; Executive Order No. 9630, Redistribution of

foreign economic functions and functions with respect to surplus property in foreign areas, 29 Sept. 1945 and enclosures, Box 1, RG 313-58-3233, NARA SB; Pilgert 1949, 26.

25. "Operation roll-up," microfilm H-108; Martin, Naval Base Order 118-45, 22 Oct. 1943, RG 313-58-3300, NARA SB.

26. Comservpac to all bases, Pacific, 14 Oct. 1945, Box 1, RG 313-58-3300, NARA SB; "Operation roll-up," microfilm H-108.

27. "Operation roll-up," microfilm H-108.

28. Final close out Report on Guadalcanal, Oct. 1945–May 1946, Entry 44463, RG 338, NARA; Barrett to Commander, 27 Sept. 1945, Box v. 9278, F. L8, RG 313-58-3401, NARA SB; Parsonage to Aubin, 20 Oct. 1945, Roman Catholic Mission Records, Solomons: Reel 6, PMB 1120; Thrift 2003, 13; Richter 2005, 5–6.

29. Final close out report on Russell Islands, 30 Oct. 1945, Entry 178, RG 313, NARA; Logue to Gillan, 1 Apr. 1946, Entry 183, RG 313, NARA; Rottman 2002, 120; "Operation roll-up," IV-34-36, microfilm H-108.

30. [No author], Memo, n.d., Entry 183, RG 313, NARA; First Narrative of Russell Islands Naval Command, 22 Sept. 1945, Box 1, F. A12, RG 313-58-3019, NARA SB.

31. [No author], Memo, n.d.

32. Sabben-Clare to Wailes, 16 Nov. 1948, Entry 400, RG 59, NARA.

33. Minutes to HC, 25 May 1953, WPHC CF 58/28 Vol. VII, WPA.

34. Blandy, Summary of events for a history of the war, 1944, WPHC NHBS 19/III, 7/20, WPA.

35. Final Inspection of APO evacuated by Army personnel, 14 Dec. 1944, Entry 44463, RG 388, NARA.

36. Reece Discombe, personal communication, 11 Sept. 2003; Status Report of Espiritu Santo, 3 Apr. 1946, RG 313, NARA.

37. Wood-Ellem 1999, 216–217.

38. *Congressional Record,* 79th Congress, 1st Session, Jan.–Dec. 1945, Appendix A5236; *Congressional Record,* 79th Congress, 2nd Session, Jan.–Aug. 1946, Appendix A1411–A1412, A2217–A2218; J. R. Hay, "Airforce Interlude," 42, MSX-4862, NLNZ; G. K. Little, "Those were the days my friend"—the story of the 3rd Australian Light Wireless Telegraph Section, 426, AWM 419/59/27, MSS 1210, NAA; Commander, Pacific to all units, 26 Jan. 1946, RG 181-58-3037, NARA; Logue to Comsopac, May 1946 and enclosures, Entry 183, RG 313, NARA.

39. "War Department policies and assumptions government the demobilization of the Army," n. d., c. 1946, Entry 109, RG 160, NARA.

40. Special Planning Division, Progress Report, 28 Aug. 1943, Material Demobilization Emergency Plan No. 2, 27 Sept. 1943, Entry 109, RG 160, NARA; Acting HC to SOS, 24 Jan. 1956, CO 1036/154, TNA; "Operation roll-up," microfilm H-108; Robert W. Eigell, cited in Durham 2003, 136.

41. Commander, Sopac to State Dept., FEA, American Red Cross, other U.S. governmental agencies representatives, South Pacific, 25 Oct. 1945, Entry 178, RG 313,

NARA; Burgess to CS, 16 Mar. 1946, CSO F37/210/pt 2, FNA; NARA Narrative of South Pacific Area and Force, 1 Sept. 1945–1 Oct. 1946, Entry 183, RG 313, NARA; Commander Service Force to Commander, 21 Oct. 1945, Entry 178, RG 313, NARA.

42. History of the South Pacific Base Command, c. July 1946; Office of the FLC, Survey of surplus disposal problem in South and Southwest Pacific base areas, 18 Dec. 1945, Entry 400, RG 59, NARA.

43. The navy commander in mid-December 1945 moved his staff from Noumea to USS *Vincennes.* In Mar. 1946, the navy headquarters in the South Pacific moved to Tutuila. The South Pacific Base Command ceased on 30 June 1946, and the U.S. Army in New Caledonia took over, while agencies such as FLC operated from Noumea until May 1947. Narrative of South Pacific Area and Force, 1 Sept.–1 Oct. 1946, Entry 183, RG 313, NARA; Final close out, South Pacific Base Command, 30 June 1946, Entry 44463, RG 338, NARA; Field Commissioner, History of FLC, Noumea, 23 May 1947, RG 319.1, NARA.

44. "Operation roll-up," microfilm H-108.

45. Phillip Mitchell, Diary, May 1944, Mss Afr. r. 101, Wm 0950/02, RH; Vaskess to HC, Minute, 11 Nov. 1945, WPHC CF 58/28/3, WPA.

46. History of FLC Noumea, 23 May 1947, RG 59, NARA; Wallin to Chief of Bureau and Docks, c. 18 July 1947, Entry 183, RG 313, NARA; Report of Disposal of Surplus Property at Upolu, Funafuti, Aitutaki, Bora Bora, Penrhyn, June 1946, RG 59, NARA; Close out Report Aitutaki, Agreement, 15 Aug. 1946, Entry 44463, RG 338, NARA.

47. History of FLC Noumea, Jan. 1947, 23 May 1947, RG 59, NARA; Murphy to Field Commissioner for Australia, 26 Dec. 1947, Entry 400, RG 59, NARA; Minute, 6 Sept. 1946, CSO F37/210/pt 2, FNA.

48. Final close out Report on Guadalcanal, Oct. 1945–May 1946; History of the South Pacific Base Command, July 1946; Wade to Commander, Sosols, 116 Aug. 1945, Box v.9296, F. L11-4, RG 313-58-3401, NARA SB.

49. Goldie to Scrivin, 29 Nov. 1945, Methodist Mission, Correspondence, microfilm, PMB 925, Pacific Manuscripts Bureau, Canberra.

50. Noel to HC, 29 Sept. 1944, WPHC F10/14 Vol. 1, WPA; History of the South Pacific Base Command, July 1946; "Operation roll-up," microfilm H-108.

51. RC to HC, 7 Nov. 1946 and Notes, WPHC CF 58/28/3 Vol. III, WPA.

52. Acting RC to HC, 6 Dec. 1945, 25 Dec. 1945, 25 May 1946, DO to Secretary, 5 June 1946, HC to Acting HC, 8 Aug. 1946, Stead to Secretary, 9 Nov. 1946, WPHC CF 58/28/4 Vol. 1, WPA.

53. Acting RC to HC, 28 Dec. 1946, 6, 30 Jan., 16 June 1947; HC to SOS, 9 Jan. 1947, WPHC CF 58/28/4 Vol. 1, WPA.

54. Acting RC to HC, 17 July 1947 and minutes, 21 July 1947, WPHC CF 58/28/4 Vol. 1, WPA.

55. Acting RC to HC, 25, 26 July, 29 Aug., 15 Oct., 5 Nov., 8, 31 Dec. 1947, Officer in charge to HC, 4 Oct. 1947, WPHC CF 58/28/4 Vol. 1, WPA; Peck, History of Sale, 24 Jan. 1948, WPHC CF 58/28/4 Vol. II, WPA.

56. Logue to Commander, Noumea, Apr. 1946, Entry 183, RG 313, NARA; McMorrow to Grantham, 12 July 1946, WPHC CF58/28/3 Vol. I, WPA; Logue to Comsopac, Apr. 1946 and enclosures; Wellings to Comsopac, 8 June 1947 and enclosure, Entry 183, RG 313, NARA.

57. Andrews to Commander, 16 Jan. 1947 and enclosure, Huber to Commander 29 Jan. 1948, Entry 183, RG 313, NARA; Bursley, History of FLC Noumea for Jan. 1947, Entry 400, RG 59, NARA; Bivens to Governor, n.d., c. Jan. 1946, AG's Office, Island Files, RG 284, NARA SB; Alailima 1988, 250–253.

58. History of the South Pacific Base Command, July 1946; U.S. Naval Base Order No. 187, 19 Feb. 1945, Box v. 319812, F. A2-11(2), RG 313-58A-3254, NARA SB.

59. Reece Discombe, personal communication, 11 Sept. 2003.

60. Field Commissioner, Personal report, 22 Oct. 1946, Field Commissioner to Department of State, 8 Jan. 1946, Entry 400, RG 59, NARA; "Operation roll-up," microfilm H-108.

61. Bell 1977, 144–172; Long 1963, 19–20.

62. Howie, Report on alleged unsatisfactory features covering the disposal of surplus war materials in the Territory of New Guinea, Nov. 1950, A518, Item F809/1/1, NAA.

63. Long 1963, 19–25; Beaumont 1996, 33–34.

64. Long 1963, 555, 581, 583; Howie, Report on alleged unsatisfactory features, Nov. 1950.

65. Office of the FLC, Survey of surplus disposal problem in South and Southwest Pacific base areas, 18 Dec. 1945, Entry 400, RG 59, NARA; "Operation roll-up," microfilm H-108.

66. Alexis to Commander, 8 Sept. 1945, Box 4, RG 313-58-3300, NARA SB; Office of the FLC, Survey of surplus disposal problem in South and Southwest Pacific base areas, 18 Dec. 1945; "Operation roll-up," microfilm H-108.

67. Scharmach to Secretary of External Territories, 1 July 1946, A518/1 (A518/1) AF838/1, NAA.

68. Office of the FLC, Survey of surplus disposal problem in South and Southwest Pacific base areas, 18 Dec. 1945.

69. Hofmann, Survey of surplus disposal problem in South and Southwest Pacific base areas, 31 July 1945.

70. Office of the FLC, Survey of surplus disposal problem, 18 Dec. 1945.

71. Wallen to Commissioner, 23 Aug. 1948, Entry 400, RG 59, NARA.

72. "Operation roll-up," microfilm H-108; Strachan 2005.

73. Wallen to Commissioner, 23 Aug. 1948, Entry 400, RG 59, NARA.

74. Evacuation of New Guinea by U.S. Forces, July 1945, Lend Lease transfers, AWM 54 no. 16/2/11 file No. 1, NAA; Butlin and Schedvin 1977, 794–798.

75. Howie, Report on alleged unsatisfactory features, Nov. 1950; Present position, Rabaul, on evacuation of CDC, c. May 1947, Chifley to Ward, 25 Oct. 1948, A518, Item F809/1/1, Part 1, NAA.

76. Downs 1987, 191–192; Howie, Report on alleged unsatisfactory features, Nov. 1950; Howie to Secretary, 15 Sept. 1948, A518, Item F809/1/1, Part 1, NAA.

77. Hank Nelson, e-mail to writer, 16 Sept. 2007.

78. Howie, Report on alleged unsatisfactory features, Nov. 1950; 13th Aust Small Ships Coy AIF, AWM PR87/110, NAA; Lt M. G. Hauer, Papers, 8 July 1946, AWM file 419/60/47, NAA; Phillips to Davis, 7 Dec. 1946, A518, Item F809/1/1, Part 1, NAA; Downs 1980, 22–23.

79. Howie to Secretary, 5 Aug. 1948 and enclosures, A518, Item F809/1/1, Part 1, NAA; Downs 1987, 191–192; Howie to Secretary, Dept. of Territories, 11 Apr. 1947, Notes of a conference held with Administrator, New Guinea, 21 May 1947, Ashley to Chifley, 9 July 1947, Chifley to Ashley, 7 Aug. 1947, Binns to Assistant Secretary, 2 Dec. 1948, Chifley to Ward, 25 Oct. 1948, Murray to Secretary, Department of External Territories, 24 Apr. 1950, Spender to Beale, 17 July 1950, A518, Item F809/1/1, Part 1, NAA; Cf. Downs 1987, 23.

80. Ashley to Chifley, 9 July 1947, A518, Item F809/1/1, Part 1, NAA.

81. Newman, Notes of Meeting, 22–23 Nov. 1949, A518, Item F809/1/1, Part 1, NAA; "Operation roll-up," microfilm H-108; Binns, Acquisition of U.S. rights, Manus and elsewhere, 2 Dec. 1948, Newman, Notes of Meeting, 22–23 Nov. 1949, A518, Item F809/1/1, Part 1, NAA.

82. Murray to Secretary, Department of External Territories, 24 Apr. 1950; Spender to Beale, 17 July 1950, A518, Item F809/1/1, Part 1, NAA; Howie, Report on alleged unsatisfactory features, Nov. 1950.

83. CWS, Notes for the Minister, 28 Nov. 1950, A518, Item F809/1/1, Part 1, NAA.

84. HC to RC, 12 Jan., 3 Feb. 1948, Bryant to Stapleton, 30 Jan. 1948, Martin and Acting HC, 30 Jan. 1948, Treasury Form, Purchase of U.S. War Assets, 31 Dec. 1947, Mitchell to Secretary, 2 Mar., 12 June, 18 Aug. 1948, Chief Secretary to Morris, Hedstrom, 25 Mar., 6 Apr. 1948, Mayo-Gaskell to Chief Secretary 14 Apr. 1948 and enclosures, Cronin, Equipment at Funafuti and Tarawa, 11 June 1948, Mitchell and Chief Secretary, Draft contract, July 1948, Allison to Chief Secretary, 20 Aug. 1948, WPHC CF 58/28/4 Vol. II, WPA; Allison and Chief Secretary, Contract, 20 Aug. 1948, Acting RC to HC, 3 Dec. 1951, 18 July, 13 Sept. 1952, Minute, 18 Aug. 1952, [Illegible] to Chief Secretary, 19 Sept. 1952; Parnell to WPHC, 4 Nov. 1952; RC to Acting HC, 20 July 1955, WPHC CF 58/28/4 Vol. III, WPA.

85. McMorrow to Grantham, 12 July 1946; Bursley to HC, 31 Aug. 1946, WPHC CF 58/28/3 Vol. 1, WPA.

86. Chief Secretary, Minute, 31 Aug. 1948, Note for file, n.d., WPHC CF 58/28/3 Vol. III, WPA.

87. HC to SOS, 1 Sept. 1948, WPHC CF 58/28/3 Vol. III, WPA; Officer in Charge to HC, 12 Feb. 1949, WPHC CF 58/28/3 Vol. IV, WPA.

88. Acting RC to HC, 18 Oct. 1949; Tatchell and Newman to Secretary to the Government, 17 Aug. 1949, Germond and Westhoven, Agreement, 29 Dec. 1949; Dyett

to Acting RC, n.d., c. Sept. 1952; Acting RC to HC, 20 Nov. 1952; Minutes, 25 May 1953; Hughes to Westhoven, 21 Dec. 1953; DC to Chief Secretary, 2 Apr. 1957, WPHC CF 58/28/3 Vol. V, WPA; Note, Brass shipped on behalf Ayrton Metal Co. and enclosure, n.d., c. 1952, WPHC CF 58/28/3 Vol. VII, WPA.

89. RC to HC, 10 May 1951, WPHC CF 58/28/3 Vol. V, WPA; Maitland to Beeley, 9 Nov. 1953, Beeley to Maitland, 8 Dec. 1953, WPHC CF 58/28/3 Vol. III, WPA; RC to HC, 10 May 1951, WPHC CF 58/28/3 Vol. V, WPA; Hearth to Carpenter, 26 Oct. 1957, WPHC CF 127/9/11, WPA.

90. Assistant HC to Acting RC, 2 Nov. 1949, WPHC CF 58/28/3 Vol. II, WPA.

91. Minutes, 7 Dec. 1951, WPHC CF58/28/14 Vol. VI, WPA.

92. Hughes to Westhoven, 21 Dec. 1953, WPHC CF58/28/14 Vol. II, WPA.

93. *Annual Reports, British Solomon Islands Protectorate, 1948, 1953–1967* (Honiara: Government Printer, 1949, 1954–1968).

94. Thrift 2004, 20.

95. Macdonald 1982, 159.

96. Moon and Moon 1998, 22, 38, 46, 54, 112.

97. *Fiji Times,* 25 Aug. 1943, 6.

98. Larsen 1946, 99; Lasaqa 1972, 252–253.

99. Gwero 1988, 42–43; Ngwadili and Gafu 1988, 213; Counts 1989, 198–199.

100. Mamaloni c. 1993, 15.

101. Laracy and White 1988, 107–115; Counts 1989, 191–192, 200–201; Gegeo 1989, 353–371.

102. White and Lindstrom 1989, 26, 27; Michener 1951, 213–214; Hilder 1961, 144–145, 188–189.

103. Wilson 1969, 69; Denfeld 1989, 46.

104. Notes on discussion, the Administrator and the Secretary to Western Samoa Administration, Oct. 1943, EA 1, 86/17/1, ANZ.

105. *American Samoa Bulletin,* Aug. 1945, Vol. 10, No. 1, enclosure, AG's Office, Island government, 1945, 9B-11G 485, RG 284, NARA SB; Hilder 1961, 144–145, 189.

106. Laffin 1956; Michener 1951, 188, 396.

Chapter 10: Leavings on Landscape

Epigraph: Gillespie 1945, 149.

1. Spennemann 1998, 1–42.

2. Intelligence Officer to Director of Naval Intelligence, 7 Nov. 1921, Nillack (?), Memo for Commander Walker, 15 Mar. 1940, Entry 47, RG 181, NARA.

3. Fisher 1949, 103–110; Baker 1946, 205–213.

4. McQuarrie 1994, 151.

5. Jones 1951, 393–394; Highland 1991, 111–112.

6. Michener 1951, 187.

7. Gillespie 1945.

8. Bennett 2000, 128.

9. Hogbin 1946, 72.

10. Glenn Summerhayes, personal communication, 5 Feb. 2008.

11. Gillespie 1945, 24–25 and photographs opposite p. 16.

12. Potts, Historical narrative, Fiji Islands, c. 1945, Entry 183, RG 313, NARA.

13. Tommy Elkington, interview by writer, 1976.

14. Laffin 1956, 85.

15. Cited in Belshaw 1950, 143.

16. Dorsey 2004, 252–256, 258.

17. Potts, Historical Narrative: Fiji Islands, c. Dec. 1945, Entry 183, RG 313, NARA.

18. Callahan, Command History Southern Solomons, Aug. 1942–Aug. 1945, Box v. 9304, F. A12, RG 313-58-3401, SB NARA; Chapter 9, Manual of Anti-Submarine Warfare for Small Craft, Box 1, F. A16, RG 313-58-3377, SB NARA.

19. Olsen, Minefields on Bleacher, 4 Aug. 1942, Box 1, F. S75-S76, RG 313-58-3394, NARA SB.

20. Butler, Minesweeping operations, 20 May 1944, Box 1, F. S81, RG 313-58-3394, NARA SB.

21. Dorsey 2004, 257

22. Leland, G-2, Economic Intelligence, Annex No 1, Report 121, 21 Apr. 1945, Entry 44463, RG 338, NARA.

23. Meetings of Chamber of Commerce, Vol. 19, 26 Nov. 1945, 145W, 12, ANC.

24. Noumea diary, 1 Nov. 1943, folder 179, RG 313, NARA.

25. The Reduction of Rabaul, 19 Feb.–15 May 1944, Box 4, F. A2-13, RG 313-58-3368, NARA SB.

26. Assistant Ordnance Officer, Inspection of installations, Guadalcanal, 3 Apr. 1944, Box 3, F. A9-8, RG 313-58-3368, NARA SB; Commanding Officer, Airfield construction, Koli area, 16 Nov. 1943, Box v.9280, F. A1, RG 313-58-3401, NARA SB.

27. Final close out Report on Guadalcanal, c. June 1946, Entry 44463, RG 338, NARA; Anon, "Dad's diary" (New Zealand), 30 Nov. 1943, copy in writer's care; Trevor Thomas, Diary, 3 Sept. 1943, Msx 5143, NLNZ; NARA World War II Diaries, Russell Islands, RG 38, NARA; Explosives report, No. 30 Banika, 18 Oct. 1945, Nos. 101 and 102, Sun Valley, 26 June 1944, RG 334, NARA; Report on Hell's Point Area, Jan. 1953, MP 927/1, Item A 11/13/19, NAA; Hills, Supplementary Progress Report, Aug. 1951, MP926/1, Item 3378/118/9, NAA.

28. Air Central Coordinator to Commander Fleet Air, 8 June 1944, Box v. 319773, F. L11-1, RG 313-58-3525, NARA SB; Officer in Charge, Bomb Disposal Unit Report, 13 July, 5 Aug. ? Sept. 1943, 7 Feb. 1944, Box 2, F. S81, RG 313-58-3377, NARA SB; Commander Task Force 31 to Commanding General, 23 Nov. 1943, Box 2, F. S81, RG 313-58-3503, NARA SB; Commander to Commander, 21, 26 Sept. 1944, Box 2, F. S78, RG 313-58-3250, NARA SB.

29. Wallis, Report of No, 2 BD Section, 1 Aug. 1950–17 Apr. 1952, 19 Apr. 1952, MP927/1 Item A11/13/19, NAA; Hills, Supplementary Progress Report, Aug. 1951 and encl., map of Banika, MP926/1 Item 3378/118/9, NAA.

30. Chapman 1949, 178–180; Bennett 1987, 305; Officer in charge, Tonga, to Chief of Naval Operations, 20 May 1944, Box 1, F. S81, Commanding Officer, Tonga to Commanding Officer, Fiji, 1 Mar. 1945, Box 1, F. S75, RG 313-58-3394, NARA SB; *PIM,* Mar. 1948, 19 Mar. 1944, 15 Mar. 1945; Port Regulations for Munda, addenda, 29 Oct. 1943, Box 1, F. H1-H7, RG 313-58-3503, NARA SB.

31. Survey Request and report, Tutuila, 7 Dec. 1945, Box v. 3062, F. S76-S80, RG 313-58D-3284, NARA SB.

32. Bulletin No. 37, Guadalcanal, 16 Feb. 1945, Box v. 9294, F. A1, RG 313-58-3401, NARA SB.

33. *PIM,* Mar. 1948, 19.

34. History of South Pacific Base command, c. June 1946, Entry 444637, RG 338, NARA.

35. Long 1963, 558–559.

36. Final close out Report, c. June 1946, Entry 44463, RG 338, NARA.

37. Noel to Howie, 22 Oct. 1945, enclosure in Final close out Report, c. June 1946, Entry 44463, RG 338, NARA.

38. Noel to HC, 29 Sept. 1944, WPHC F10/14 Vol. I, WPA; Bryant to Secretary, 24 Aug. 1948, WPHC F32/74, Vol. I, WPA; Report of the Activities of the 1st Australian Bomb Disposal Section, c. Dec. 1948, MP927/1, Item A11/13/16, NAA; Secretary to Press Relations Officer, 8 Feb. 1949; Cleary, Bomb Disposal—Papua New Guinea, 30 Mar. 1949, MP691/1 Item 3395/15/2, NAA.

39. Brigadier to Army HQ, 25 Mar. 1947 and enclosures, MP 742/1/0, Item 11/1/1113, NAA; Sinclair to Halligan, 19 Dec. 1947, MP691/1 Item 3395/15/2, NAA.

40. Sabastian, Activities of 1 Aust Bomb Disposal Section, Aug. 1951, 10 Sept. 1951, MP927/1, Item A11/13/32, NAA.

41. Wallis, Report of No. 2 BD Section, 1 Aug. 1950–17 Apr. 1952, 19 Apr. 1952, MP927/1 Item A11/13/19, NAA; Hills, Supplementary Progress Report, Aug. 1951, MP926/1 Item 3378/118/9, NAA; RC to HC, 31 Oct. 1951, WPHC F32/74, Vol. I, WPA; Chamberlain to Sidebothom, 21 Dec. 1951, WPHC F32/74, Vol. II, WPA.

42. Croft to Naval Board, 25 June 1951, MP926/1, Item 3378/118/9, NAA.

43. Acting RC to HC, 20 Nov. 1952, WPHC CF 58/28/3 Vol. VI, WPA.

44. Richter 2005, 5–6.

45. Acting RC to HC, 11 Aug. 1952, WPHC F32/74 Vol. II, WPA; Proclamation, No. 1 of 1953, WPHC F32/74/2, WPA; Acting HC to Sec of State, 11 Apr. 1953, Harry to Acting RC 11 June 1953, WPHC F32/74 Vol. III, WPA; Herron, Monthly Progress Report, July 1952, 1 Aug. 1952, Herron, Report on Hell's Point Area, Jan. 1953, MP927/1, Item A11/13/19, WPA.

46. Moffat, Monthly Progress report, June 1954, July 1954, MP927/1, Item A11/13/19, NAA.

47. Harry to Acting RC 11 June 1953, WPHC F32/74 Vol. III, WPA.

48. "WWII Bombs still a threat on Guadalcanal," http://archives.pireport.org/archive/2004/march/03%2D23%2D15.htm (accessed 3 Feb. 2006); John Ravelo, "WWII

weapons explode in San Jose, Saipan," http://archives.pireport.org/archive/2001/Sept./09-07-17.htm (accessed 3 Feb. 2006).

49. John Bull, "Congress to investigate chemical-weapons dumping in oceans," http://www.centredaily.com/mld/centredaily/news/nation/13159811.htm (accessed 15 Nov. 2005); Pete Harrison, "Where the real nasties lurk," http://www.divernet.com/safety/nasty598.htm (accessed 20 Nov. 2002); Byran Bender, "International Response; Abandoned Chemical Weapons pose Continuing challenge for OPCW," http://www.nti.org/d_newswire/issues/2002/12/10/8p.html (accessed 3 Feb. 2006).

50. Lewis et al., 1996, 36–47; Jenks 2007, 552–577.

51. Hank Nelson, e-mail to writer, 16 Sep. 2007.

52. T. N. T. Mitchell, Memoirs, PR 87/134 AWM; Maria Berg, "Historical Chemical Weapons sites in the Asia-Pacific region," http://www.bicc.de/weapons/chemweap/asiapac/austra.html, (accessed 20 Nov. 2002).

53. Halsey to Commanding General, 16 Jan. 1943, Box 21, F. S77, RG 313-58-3440, NARA SB; Waitt and Jarvis, Waite and Jarvis, Report of trip, 24 Sept.–21 Nov. 1944, 14 Dec. 1944, RG 175, NARA; Maria Haug, "Allied Chemical Weapons in the Asia-Pacific Theatre during World War II," http://www.opcw.org/synthesis/html/s7/p20prt.html (accessed 3 Feb. 2006); Geoff Plunkett, "Chemical Warfare Agent (CWA) Sea Dumping off Australia," www.hydro.gov.au (accessed Jan. 2000); Goodwin 1998, 17–20. Other gases such as the choking agent phosgene and chloropicrine, a tear gas, were stored for use.

54. Affidavit of Edward Z. Fang, 21 Apr. 1945, Entry 2 B, RG 175, NARA; Waitt and Jarvis, Report of trip, 24 Sept.–21 Nov. 1944, 14 Dec. 1944, RG 175, NARA; Ienaga 1979,188–189; Haug, "Allied Chemical Weapons"; Harris 2002; Daws 1994.

55. Acker to Waitt, Report, 21 May 1944, Entry 62 B, RG 175, NARA.

56. Report of a visit to Southwest Pacific Area, Feb. 1945, Entry 2B, RG 175, NARA.

57. Acker to Waitt, Reports, 15, 21 May 1944, Entry 62 B, RG 175, NARA.

58. Gorrill, An Appreciation of the potentialities of a C. W. attack in tropical climates with particular reference to the jungle-covered areas of the Southwest Pacific, 20 Dec. 1943, Entry 4c, RG 175, NARA; Maria Haug, "Allied Chemical Weapons in the Asia-Pacific."

59. T. N. T. Mitchell, Memoirs, PR 87/134, AWM; Maddock to Harvey, 18 Sept. 1981, PR 89/23, AWM; Bridget Goodwin, "Mustard Gas," 7.30 *Report,* ABC-TV, 12 June 1987; "Keen as Mustard," ABC-TV, *True Stories,* 31 Aug. 1989; Goodwin 1998. See also, Berg, Historical Chemical Weapons sites.

60. T. N. T. Mitchell, Memoirs, PR 87/134, AWM. This was probably the orange-footed scrubfowl, *Megapodius reinwardt.*

61. Geoff Plunkett, "Chemical Warfare Agent (CWA) Sea Dumping off Australia," www.hydro.gov.au (accessed Jan. 2000).

62. Michael J. Field, "More than Ghosts Haunt the Pacific 60 years on," http://archives.pireport.org/archive/2000/may/05%2D15%@D14.hrm (accessed 2

Feb. 2006); "Chemical Warfare Agent Found on Guam may be moved to Johnson Atoll," http://archives.pireport.org/archive/1999/august/08-18-01.html (accessed 3 Feb. 2006); Mary-Louise O'Callaghan, "US to destroy Solomons Weapons," The Age, 18 May 1991; Haug, "Allied Chemical Weapons in the Asia-Pacific"; "Seeing through Steel: INEEL Developed Technologies Identifies Chemical Weapons," 16 Oct. 1998, http://search.netscape.com/ns/boomframe.jsp?query=mustard+gas (accessed 3 Feb. 2006).

63. Stockholm International Peace Research Institute 1980, 166–167.

64. Cervi 1999, 351–399; Maharaj 1999, 7–24; Jameson 1975, 109–113; "Solomons urged to clean up Iron Bottom Sound." http://pidp.eastwestcenter.org/pireport/2007/June/06-29-rel2.htm (accessed 2 July 2006).

65. Cervi 1999.

66. Fosberg 1953, 233.

67. Parham to Senior Agriculturalist, 15 Aug. 1947, WPHC F33/59, WPA.

68. Guillaumin 1953, 82; H. Dunkley, Letter, 24 Mar. 1943, PR 84/35, AWM. See also, E. Chick, Letter, 11 Dec. 1943, PR 00938, AWM.

69. Fosberg 1953.

70. Institute of Pacific Islands Forestry, "Pacific Island Ecosystems at Risk," http://www.hear.org/Pier/ (accessed 4 Apr. 2006).

71. Parham 1941, 81; Whistler 1995, 17; Institute of Pacific Islands Forestry, "Pacific Island Ecosystems at Risk," http://www.hear.org/Pier/ (accessed 4 Apr. 2006); McKay 1968, 97.

72. Turbott 1949, 37; Parsons 1945, 83.

73. Institute of Pacific Islands Forestry, "Pacific Island Ecosystems at Risk," http://www.hear.org/Pier/ (accessed 4 Apr. 2006).

74. Warea Orapa, "The Status of Chromolaena ororata on Papua New Guinea," http://www.ehs.edu.edu.au/choromoleana/fourth/orapa.htm (accessed 15 June 2005).

75. Mead 1961, 23.

76. District Officer, Patrol report, Madang-Bogia, Sept.–Nov. 1946, PNG Patrol Reports, microfiche, A9844 NAA.

77. *PIM,* Aug. 1946, 68, Sept. 1946, 22.

78. *PIM,* Sept. 1946, 76, Nov. 1946, 76.

79. *PIM,* Dec. 1946, 30.

80. *PIM,* Jan. 1947, 71.

81. G. S. Dun, cited in Mead 1961, 181.

82. *PIM,* July 1949, 7. See Mead 1961, 180–182.

83. *PIM,* Sept. 1947, 33.

84. *PIM,* Jan. 1948, 71, July 1948, 40, Nov. 1948, 15–16, Jan. 1949, 55–56; June 1949, 90; Downs 1980, 52; Mead 1961, 142.

85. M. K. Carter, "A Small Ship's Saga," MSS 1259, AWM.

86. Mead 1961, 7, 11–13, 14.

87. Mead 1961, 5.

88. Hitoshi Imamura, "The Tenor of my Life," 153, MSS 1089, AWM.

89. "*Achatina fulica,*" http://www.issg.org/database/species/ecology.asp?si=64&ver=print (accessed 27 Apr. 2006) *A. fulica* is also a vector of the rat lungworm *Angiostrongylus* cantonensis (which causes eosinophilic meningitis in humans and neurological disease in other animals) and the bacterium *Aeromonas hyfrophila.*

90. Watson 1985, 7–10; James Planck, "Giant African Snail: Watch out for the world's worst snail pest," http://www.dpi.qld.au/health/5613.html (accessed 14 Mar. 2003).

91. Satoshi Chiba, "Species Diversity and Conservation of Mandarina, a land snail of the Ogasawara Islands," 2003, http://www.airies.or.jp/publication/ger/pdf/07-01-04.pdf (accessed 19 June 2006).

92. See re people, Holmes to Air Dept., 16 Mar. 1945, AIR 127, 3(iii), ANZ.

93. *Agricultural Journal* (Fiji), Vol. 18, 3 (1947), 80.

94. See Kirsch 1997, 150–152.

95. Connell 1978, 445–452; Packard 1975; Brooks 2000, 50.

96. Rodda et al. 1999; Fritts and Rodda 1998, 113–140; Perry and Morton, 1999, 125–142; Jaffe 1997.

97. Buxton 1927, 67, 72.

98. *Annual Report of Medical Department, 1938,* CP no. 40, Legislative Council of Fiji, 1939; Director of Medical Services to Sec. of WPHC, 12 June 1939, WPHC 2040/39, WPA.

99. Buckley and Klugman 1983, 352–353.

100. Armstrong to Tyner and Olsen, 30 July 1942, WPHC TS, MP 65/1942, WPA.

101. Consul to HC, 30 July 1942, WPHC TS, MP 65/1942, WPA.

102. HC to Cdr., South Pacific, 11 Aug. 1942, WPHC TS MP 65/1942, WPA.

103. Dearing to Chief of Staff, 11 Sept. 1942, Sopac, Entry 179, RG 313, NARA.

104. PRO Sec. of S to Mitchell, 2 Feb., 27 Mar., 25 May, 21 July 1943, CO, 83/238/85448, TNA; Post war reconstruction: Fiji and the Western Pacific, CP 2 and 3, Legislative Council of Fiji, 1944.

105. Joy 1999, 199; United States Army Medical Service 1963, 435–437; Mitchell to Sec. of S, 5 Mar. 1943, telegrams 131 and 132, CO 83/238/85448, TNA.

106. Magath to Commander, SoPac, 31 Mar. 1943, Entry 179, RG 313 NARA; Manual of Advanced Base Development, July 1943, 79, Box 3 (v. 9666), F. A1, RG 313-58-3440, NARA SB; SoPac confidential letter #9=44, 10 Nov. 1944, Box 1, F. P1-P5, RG 313-58-3150, NARA SB; Towers to Pacific Fleet, 27 Nov. 1944, Box 8 (v. 9701), F. P2, RG 313-58-3440, SB NARA.

107. *Annual Report of Medical Department, 1938,* CP no. 40, Legislative Council of Fiji, 1939; Director of Medical Services to Sec. of WPHC, 12 June 1939, WPHC 2040/39, WPA; *Annual Report of Medical Department, 1940,* CP no. 6, Legislative Council of Fiji, 1941; Buxton to Smart, 20 Jan. 1942; Smart to Buxton, 28 Jan. 1942, Smart to McGusty, 9 Feb. 1942, CO 83/238/85448, TNA.

108. Shineberg 1999, 29–30, 239–240; Laird 1956, 189–190; Perry 1950, 104.

109. Arrêté No. 1000, 10 Août 1946, 44 W 367, ANC.

110. Verges 1944, 5–6; L. L. (Bill) Callow, personal communication, 13 Feb. 2001; ANC Verges, Rapport, 7 Avr. 1944, 107W, ANC; Desquesnes 1988, 55.

111. Verges to Governor, 24 June 1942, Bourgeau to Sebree, 26 June 1942, Sebree to Bourgeau, 26 June 1942, Tallec to Rose, 28 Oct. 1944, 44 W 709 (212), ANC.

112. Fredine, Report on the Investigation of Cattle Ticks in New Caledonia, 13 Jan. 1945, Legg, Memo to Director-General of Health, 28 July 1944, Baker to USASOS HG, 4 Nov. 1944, Entry 178, RG 313, NARA; Cumpston to Secretary, Dept. of External Affairs, 11 July 1944, A989, Item 1944/610/11/1, NAA.

113. Tallec to Rose, 28 Oct. 1944, 44 W 709 (212), ANC.

114. NARA English translation of extract from *La France Australe,* 1 Mar. 1945, Entry 178, RG 313, NARA; Smith, Annex 2 to Political Report No. 115, 10 Mar. 1945, Entry 44463, RG 338, NARA; 17; Fredine, Report on the Investigation of Cattle Ticks in New Caledonia, 13 Jan. 1945, Entry 178, RG 313, NARA.

115. Arrêté No. 399, 3 May 1944, 44 W 365, ANC.

116. Guindon to Governor, 26 Oct. 1942, 44 W 682, ANC; Montchamp, Rapport au Conseil d'administration, 7 Dec. 1942, 44 W 718, ANC; Dubusson à Gouverneur, 28 Dec. 1942, 44 W 709, ANC; Pour la Sociéte de Muéo, à Verges, 28 June 1944, 44 W 707 (211), ANC; Le Gouverneur à [illegible], 23 Dec. 1942, 44 W 514, ANC; Map of tick infestation; Fredine, Report on the Investigation of Cattle Ticks in New Caledonia, 13 Jan. 1945, Entry 178, RG 313, NARA; Smith, Annex No. 1 to Economic Reports, Nos. 75, 83, 84, 85, 100, 101, Entry 44463, RG 338, NARA; NARA Map of tick infestation; Fredine, Report on the Investigation of Cattle Ticks in New Caledonia, 13 Jan. 1945, Entry 178, RG 313, NARA; Smith, Annex No. 1 to Economic Reports, Nos. 75, 83, 84, 85, 100, 101, Entry 44463, RG 338, NARA.

117. Cumpston to Secretary, Dept. of External Affairs, 5 Sept. 1944, A989, Item 1944/610/11/1, NAA; Forsyth to Australian Representative, 11 Sept. 1944, A6445, Item 36/1946, NAA; Verges, Rapport, 12 Apr. 1944, Tallec à Commandant Supérieur des troopes, 19 Apr. 1944, 107W, ANC; Registre copie des correspondence de la bregade de gendameries de La Foa, 1944–1948, Cote S J 29, ANC; ATNC Tallec, Rapport au Conseil d'administration, 10 July 1944, 44 W 718, ANC; Verges 1944; Smith, Annex to Economic Report No. 85, 12 Aug. 1944, Smith, Annex to Economic Report No. 83, 5 Aug. 1944, Entry 44463, RG 338, NARA. Arsenical tickcides were not completely effective and resistance soon built up in the ticks. In about 1947, Rucide (DDT-based) began to be used and by the 1950s other chlorinated hydrocarbons were used. In 1973, the organic phosphate ethion was the main chemical used. L. L. (Bill) Callow, personal communication, 13 Feb. 2001; Brun, Wilson, and Daynes 1983, 17; Desquesnes 1988, 32.

118. Smith, Annex No. 1 to Economic Reports, Nos. 75, 83, 84, 85, 100, 101, Annex No. 2 to Political Reports, Nos. 82, 104, 112, 115, Entry 44463, RG 388, NARA.

119. Fredine, Report on the Investigation of Cattle Ticks in New Caledonia, 13 Jan. 1945, Entry 178, RG 313, NARA; Fredine to Gabillon, 12 Sept. 1944, Fonds de la Commune de Houailou, ANC.

120. Legg to Ferdine, 28 Oct. 1944, Fredine, Report on the Investigation of Cattle Ticks, 13 Jan. 1945, Entry 178, RG 313, NARA.

121. Island Command, Base Memo No. 28, Importation of Animals, 10 July 1949, Entry 179, RG 313, NARA; Island Command, Base Memo No. 1, Importation of Animals, 11 Feb. 1945, Entry 178, RG 313, NARA. The neighboring New Hebrides introduced the same prohibition. Reynolds, Restriction in landing of animals, 2 July 1944 and encls., WPHC NHBS MP 58/29, WPA.

122. Barnett to Tallec, 27 Apr. 1945, 107 W, ANC.

123. Agreement for transfer of surplus property, 28 May 1946, Entry 400, RG 59, NARA.

124. Faivre, Poirier, and Routhier 1955, 175; Thompson and Adloff 1971, 276, 476.

Chapter 11: Legacies and Visions

Epigraphs: Gina 2003, 34; E. Ward, Australia's policy in Pacific Territories, n.d., c. June 1945, 2396/12/348, Ward papers, External Territories of the Commonwealth, NLA.

1. Keesing 1979, 46–73.

2. Macdonald 1982, 159–160; Campbell 2001, 160–161.

3. Campbell 2003, 257–281; Firth 1997, 311–322.

4. Vasey 1981, 17–29; McKillop and Firth 1981, 85–103; Butchart to Sandy, 24 Nov. 1952, American Samoa GO, 1872–1961, Series 16, AR, 1952, American Samoa, GO, Series 5, RG 284, NARA SB; Bennett 1987; Pollock 1992, 135–157.

5. Agricultural reports, 1935, 1936, 1940, American Samoa GO, Series 5, RG 284, NARA SB.

6. Campbell 2001, 141, 162–164; Cottrell-Dormer, Working plan: Agriculture in Tonga, 7 Nov. 1939, CO 225/326, TNA.

7. Marchand to Acheson, 22 Aug. 1940 and enclosures, CO 225/332, TNA.

8. Bennett 2001a.

9. Raymaley, Food and Forage Production in New Caledonia, 26 Nov. 1942, Entry 44463, RG 338, NARA; Raw statistics on herds and crops, 1937–1945, 37 W 542, ANC; Connell, 1987, 98–123; Historical sketch U.S. Naval Advanced Base, Noumea, c. 1 Dec. 1945, Entry 6303, RG 313, NARA; Thompson and Adloff 1971, 378–379, 382–383, 385–386; Gargominy 1993; Waterworth 1960, 96–97.

10. Soil Survey, Lunga and Kookoom Estates, n.d., c. 1938, Entry 182, RG 313, NARA.

11. Final close out Report on Guadalcanal, Oct. 1945–May 1946, Entry 44464, RG 338, NARA.

12. Donald, The Development of Guadalcanal Plain, c. May 1948, WPHC F33/41 Vol. I, WPA.

13. Alfred C. Wright, Journal, c. 1943, 38, MSX 5967, NLNZ.

14. Final close out Report on Guadalcanal, Oct. 1945–May 1946; Donald, The Development of Guadalcanal Plain, c. May 1948; Senior Agricultural Officer to Secretary to Government, 9 July 1951 and enclosures, WPHC F33/41 Vol. IV, WPA; Lasaqa 1972, 48–49.

15. Bennett 2000, 128–132.

16. Denoon and Snowden 1981, 113–122, 143–168.

17. Lepowsky 1989, 210–217, 221, 226–227. Paradoxically, the low-protein diet may have given infants and young children some protection against malaria. Lepowsky 1985, 105–126.

18. Bennett 2001, 270–271, 277.

19. Thompson and Adloff 1971, 383.

20. FEA South Pacific Project, third quarter of 1944, Sept. 1944, Entry 217, RG 234, NARA; Kjar, New Guinea Farms, 10 Apr.–14 May 1945, 14 May 1945, AWM 54, 337/7/10, AWM.

21. Final close out Report on Guadalcanal, Oct. 1945–May 1946.

22. Donald, The Development of Guadalcanal Plain, c. May 1948; RC to HC, 11 Aug. 1952, WPHC F33/41 Vol. VI, WPA; Lasaqa 1972, 45–58; Bennett 1987, 315.

23. Packard 1975, 48; William Sabel, "Bringing new knowledge to the South Pacific," http://www.memoriesofwar.com/veterans/sabel.asp (accessed 28 Aug. 2005).

24. Wyman, Native Labor Camp Joe Louis, 13 Sept. 1944, Entry 44463, RG 338, NARA; British District Agent to the British and French RCs, 2 Apr. 1948 and enclosures, WPHC NHBS 24/1944, WPA; ARs 1951, 1952, GO Series no. 5, RG 284, NARA SB.

25. Lever to Acting RC, 17 Aug. 1936, WPHC 1001/36, WPA; Bennett 1987, 227–228; Administrator to Peron, 4 Nov. 1947, IT1, 14/9/1, ANZ; Reid, Report, c. 1921, IT1, 14/5, ANZ; Lever 1933, 253–256; Butchart, Memo: Management Survey, 25 Sept. 1951, 19, America Samoa GO, Series No 15, RG 284, NARA SB; Administrator to Peron, 4 Nov. 1947, IT1, 14/9/1, ANZ.

26. Hicks, Kefford, and McKee, Report of food stores in New Guinea, c. June 1945, Kjar, Farms, General Policy 14 May 1945 and enclosure, AWM 54, 337/7/10, AWM.

27. Gordon to Governor, 1 May 1945, Colvin, Memo re visit to Swain's Island, 26 Mar. 1947, GO 1872–1961, Coded Administration Records, RG 284, NARA SB; ARs, 1946, 1947, 1949, GO, RG 284, NARA SB.

28. Carson 1962; Spencer 1992, 36–52; Peters 1962, 20–31; Macgregor 1966, 69–78; Dotto and Schiff 1978.

29. Walker 1948, 4; Pleydell 1970, 61.

30. Jonas 1985, 45–59; Bennett 1987, 162–185, 209–235.

31. Bennett 2001, 265–269; Trenaman to Allan, 2 Dec. 1965, WPHC NHBS CF 218/3/1, WPA; Angus, 1957, 2–3; *AR Forestry Department 1970,* Parliamentary Paper No. 22 of 1971 (Suva, 1971); Scarr 1968, 176–215, 218–251; Trenaman, Forestry on Erromanga, Sept. 1961, and encls., WPHC NHBS CF 218/3/1, WPA; Wilkie to Allan, 15 Jan. 1962, and minute 17, 18 June 1962, WPHC NHBS 618/61/1, Part 1, WPA.

32. Marshall 1950; Colin Marshall, Notes on Forestry in Tonga, c. Mar. 1959, WPHC TS 4/50, WPA.

33. Belshaw 1950, 69 fn; Laracy and White 1988, 110.

34. Bennett 1987; Lewis 1996, 296–303; Dennis 1981, 238, 242.

35. Keesing 1934, 338, 341; Macdonald 1982, 142.

36. Jackson 1997, S23–32.

37. Firth 1946, ix; Peattie 1988, 138–141, 152.

38. Hornell 1940.

39. E. Corlette, Report, 10 June 1935 and encls., WPHC 683/1935, WPA; Hornell 1940; Bennett 2001, 274–275; Priday [1945], 71–72; Acting HC to SOS, 16 Nov. 1936, WPHC 1001/36, WPA; DO to Secretary to Government, 28 June 1940 and encls., WPHC BSIP 1/111, F28/10, NASI; Oliver, The Fishing Industries of the South Pacific Islands, c. 20 June 1942, RG 234, NARA.

40. Cooke 1983, 290; Iwamoto 1999a, 199–217; Kobayashi [1992], 152–170; Japanese Nationals, Fiji c. Dec. 1942, AD 1, 336/1/27, ANZ.

41. Hornell 1940, 35; Krämer 1995, 196–237, 464–502; Legand, Present position of existing fisheries in New Caledonia, 13 May 1952, F108/43 Part 1, FNA; Van Pel 1956, 4.

42. Chapman 1949, 62–71, 118–129.

43. Noumea Chamber of Commerce, Meetings, Vol. 5, 19 Nov. 1909, 17 Jan. 1914, 12 Apr. 1915, Vol. 6: 12 Jan. 1916, 11 May 1918, 145W, ANC; Corlette to Blandy, 20 June 1935 and encl., WPHC NHBS 1/1, MP 91/1935, WPA; Lever to Acting RC, 17 Aug. 1936, Muller to Acting Premier, 17 July 1936, WPHC 1001/36, WPA; *Trocas shell fishing with Modern Diving Equipment,* 12 Oct. 1934, Legislative Council of Fiji, CP no. 51; Oliver, The Fishing Industries of the South Pacific Islands, c. 20 June 1942; Salvat 1980, 131–148; Rapaport 1995, 39–52.

44. Chapman to Miller, 4 Apr. 1945, Entry 217, RG 234, NARA.

45. Chapman to Heimburger, 26 Sept. 1945, Entry 217, RG 234, NARA.

46. Chamberlain to Hickling, 4 Apr. 1948 and encls., F108/20, Pt 1, FNA.

47. Ross 1964, 167–168; Bennett 2001b, 8; Shineberg 1999, 148–151; Murray Young, Report on Cervical Adenitis in the Gilbert Islands, 31 Mar. 1930, CO 225/241/74166, TNA.

48. Early 1998, 141–143; Iremonger 1948; Deacon to Haddon, Oct 1926, Envelope 16006, HP.

49. Seward to Muller, Aug. 1942, Historical file, RG 169, NARA.

50. Beattie to Commander, 22 Sept. 1945, enclosure, First Narrative of Russell islands Naval Command, c. Sept. 1945, Box 1, F. A12, RG 313-58-3019, NARA SB.

51. ANGAU, Summary of relief and rehabilitation already carried out, c. Sept. 1944, A 9373, Item 1, NAA.

52. Wyman, Native Labor Camp Joe Louis, 13 Sept. 1944; Moon and Moon 1998, 56, 93, 110; Robinson 1979, 126.

53. Office of Strategic Services, The Gilbert Islands and the War, Report No. 92, 17 Nov. 1942, RG 169, NARA; Island Commander to Air Commander, 16 Jan. 1944, Geographic file, RG 218, NARA.

54. Trafford-Smith, Minute, 17 Nov. 1944, CO 225/338/86516/3, TNA; J. Goode, Notes on food supply at Funafuti, 23 Dec. 1942, Papers, Mss Pac s.112, RH; Highland 1991, 111–112.

55. Turbott 1949, 44.

56. Dorman 1997, 80.

57. Survey of Welfare and Recreation and Educational Services in the Pacific Ocean Areas, 28 Feb.–31 Mar. 1945, Box v. 9275, F. P10, RG 313-58-3401, NARA SB; Jim to Pa and Ma, 30 May 1950, T. I. Mills Papers, MS 7007-18, NLNZ; Heinz to Commander, 23 Mar. 1945, Box v. 3062, F. P21, RG 313-58D-3284, NARA SB; History of Tongatapu, c. 1945, Entry 183, RG 313, NARA; Cox 1987, 111, 141.

58. John Vollinger, "World War II Memoirs," Jane Resture's Oceania Page, http://www.janesoceania.com/ww2_johann_memoirs (accessed 27 Sept. 2004); Jackson 1989, 45.

59. Dorman 1997, 81; Cox 1987, 107; Wales to Army HQ, 26 Apr. 1943, EA1, 86/1/4 pt 1, ANZ; Barrowclough to PM, 5 Aug. 1944, Barrowclough papers, No 40440, AM; A. J. Traill, Diary, 22 Sept. 1942, PR 00051, AWM.

60. Les Clothier, Diary, 16 Dec. 1943, PR 00588, AWM.

61. Wales to Army HQ, 26 Apr. 1943, Avery to Nash, 1 May 1943, EAI, 86/1/4 pt 1, ANZ; J. R. Hay, "Airforce Interlude," 42, MSX-4862, NLNZ; Mary Wilson, 28 Aug. 1943, MS Ref no. 91-268, NLNZ; Gillespie 1945, 104–107.

62. Pearce to HC, 24 Feb. 1931 and enclosures, CO 225/247, TNA; O'Brien, Minute, 25 Aug. 1932, CO 225/264/93699, TNA.

63. History of Tongatapu, c. 1945, Entry 183, RG 313, NARA; Larsen 1946, 33; Wales to Army HQ, 26 Apr. 1943, EA1, 86/1/4 pt 1, ANZ; Fiji Government, Supply and Production Board, *Memorandum for the United States Board of Economic Warfare Mission*, 3.

64. Ross 1964, 167–168; Bennett 2001a, 271; ARs 1942, 1943, American Samoa, GO, Series 5, RG 284, NARA SB; PIM, Aug. 1943, 12, July 1945, 31.

65. *Fiji Times and Herald* Supplement, 22 Nov. 1943, extract in *Agricultural Journal of Fiji* 15, no. 1 (1944): 30.

66. Keesing 1934, 322; ARs, Underwood, AR, 1904, American Samoa, GO, Series 5, RG 284, NARA SB; Grattan 1948, 83; Metzger 1982, 31.

67. Parsons 1945, 138, 146; Collector of Customs, *Returns of the Trade, Commerce, and Shipping of the Territory of Western Samoa*, 1930–1956 (Wellington: Government Printer, 1931–1957).

68. BEW report cited in Patrick, Samoa, Programming of supplies, 4 Nov. 1943, EA1, 86/71/7 pt 1, ANZ; Collector of Customs, *Returns of the Trade.*

69. Hickling, Report, U.S. forces in Aitutaki, 10 Nov. 1943, IT 122/5/2, pt 1, ANZ; Garity, Report on visit to Rarotonga, 6 Aug. 1943, Entry 44463, RG 338, NARA; Frisbie 1948, 206, 210, 225; Lange 1982, 88–89.

70. Brittain 1888, 28, in Codrington Papers, Mss Pac, s. 9, RH; *Melanesian Mission AR, 1901* (London: W. H. Smith, 1902), 52; Shineberg 1999, 151; Moore 1985, 218; Young, Report on Cervical Adenitis in the Gilbert Islands, 31 Mar. 1930; Robinson 1979, 161.

71. Page 2004, 66; Parsons 1945, 62–63, 139, 157–158, 171–172, 193–194; Gina 2003, 34.

72. ANZ Patrick to PM, 4 Nov. 1943, EAI, 86/71/7 pt 1, ANZ.

73. Neubarth 1954.

74. Philip Ilo to RC, 28 Mar. 1948, WPHC 9/11 F 52/20 Vol. II, WPA.

75. Report of the Work of Research Expeditions sent to Western Samoa, Rarotonga and Pukapuka during 1948 to 1953, c. 1953, 44.

76. Wood-Ellem 1999, 209; Noel to HC, 20 Aug. 1945, WPHC F33/26/1. Vol. 1, WPA; Robert Keith-Reid, "Yes, many Pacific Island people are eating themselves to death," *Pacific Magazine,* 1 Oct. 2001, http://www.pacificislands.cc/pm102001/pmdefault.php?urlarticleid=0034 (accessed 13 Oct. 2003); World Health Organization 2002.

77. Unidentified Japanese, Diary, 19 Oct. 1944, PR 00927, AWM.

78. Koehler, *Special Rations for the Armed Forces, 1946–1953* (Washington D.C.: Historical Branch, 1948) QMC Historical Studies, Series II, No. 6; http://www.qmfound.com/army_rations_historical_background.htm (accessed 19 Mar. 2007); Bennett 1987, 94, 171–172; Pantutun to Rivers, 10 Jan., 17 Mar. 1910, HP, 12043.

79. Wyman, Native Labor Camp Joe Louis, 13 Sept. 1944; Affled, Report, 4 Mar. 1944, Geographic file, RG 218, NARA; McQuarrie 1994, photograph on p. 118; Cox 1987, 107.

80. Wood-Ellem 1999, 209, 219.

81. [John Burke], United States Naval History of Tutuila, c. Aug. 1945, Navy Yard Museum, Washington D.C., 145. By 1900, Samoans grew tobacco and smoked it in a leaf, but it was not a common habit. Krämer 1995, 153, 161, 192 fn 9; Spennemann 2007, 29, 89; Mary Prichard, "Siapo.com," http://www.siapo.com/maryprichard.html (accessed 20 Mar. 2008).

82. Scrimgeour and Jolley 1983, 1414–1416.

83. Ruff 1989, 203.

84. Foale 2006, 129–137; Bice 1881, 45, Bice 1883, 49, in Codrington Papers, Mss Pac s. 10, RH; Mangaia Ordinance No. 7, 1927, F108/43 Part 1, FNA; DeRoode, Report, Living in the Jungle, May 1943, Entry 427, RG 407, NARA.

85. Mangaia Ordinance No. 7, 1927; Acting HC to SOS, 16 Nov. 1936, WPHC 1001/36, WPA; [Illegible] to Inspector General, 23 June 1925 and enclosures, CSO 1709/25, FNA; Hornell, Diary, 27 Aug. 1939, HP 10065.

86. Mangaia Ordinance No. 7, 1927, F108/43 Part 1, FNA; Gatty 1953, 154; AR June 1950, ARs, Records of the GO, RG 284, NARA SB; Toganivalu to Acting Under Secretary, 31 Jan. 1922, CSO MP 4784/21, FNA; Hornell, Diary, 19 Sept. 1939, HP 10065.

87. Woodford 1890, 231; Cooke 1983, 252–253; Buckland to RC, 19 Nov. 1929 and enclosures, WPHC NHBS 403/1929, WPA; Toganivalu to Acting Under Secretary, 31 Jan. 1922, CSO MP 4784/21, FNA; Hviding 1996, 55, 209, 220–221, 278, 310, 328, 390; Orders of Council, No. 559, 12 June 1911, ANC 44W, 308, ANC; Acting HC to SOS, 16 Nov. 1936, WPHC 1001/36, WPA; [Illegible] to Inspector General, 23 June 1925 and enclosures, CSO 1709/25, FNA.

88. Advisory Council of the BSIP, Paper No. 1, 30 Sept. 1921, CO 225/183, TNA.

89. Acting HC to SOS, 16 Nov. 1936, WPHC 1001/36, WPA; Jones, Petition in Ashley to HC, 22 May 1933, WPHC 1936/33, WPA.

90. David Gadd, Diary, 24 July 1943, Micro MS 583, NLNZ; Gillespie 1945, 106; Holmes to Air Department, 16 Mar. 1945, AIR 127 3 (iii), ANZ.

91. Sabel 1999, 122, 126.

92. [Burke], United States Naval History of Tutuila, c. Aug. 1945, 88; DeRoode, Report-Living in the Jungle, May 1943, Entry 427, RG 407, NARA; Base notice, Tulagi, No.75-43, 21 Dec. 1943, Box 1, F. A1, Commanding Officer to Antiaircraft Artillery Batts, 11 Feb. 1944, Box 12, F. S81, RG 313-58-3013, NARA SB; Burke, Report of Siassi Island, May 1945, PNG Patrol Reports, microfiche, A9844, NAA; Record of Proceedings of investigation conducted at Naval Base 3205, Manus, Dec. 1945–Jan. 1946, A17-25, JAG, Navy Yards, Washington D.C.; DO, Manus, ANGAU report, 30 Jan. 1945, Box 5, F. A2, RG 313-58-3299, NARA SB; Emery, 19 Nov. 1944, Witu group, Ryall, May 1945, Siassi district, Cowley, 20–28 Sept., Goodenough Island, PNG Patrol Reports, microfiche, NAA; Nelson 1980, 208; DC to Secretary to the Government, 1 July 1946, WPHC SF 9/1/1, Vol. VI, WPA; Hoggatt to Commanding Officer, 17 July 1945, enclosure, WPHC MP 26/43, WPA; District Agent to RC, 17 Apr. 1943 and enclosures, WPHC NHBS MP 22/19, WPA; Moon and Moon, 1998, 46.

93. Inspector to Administrator, 31 Mar. 1943, Box v. 13380, RG 313-58B-3061, NARA SB; American Samoa Bulletin, 10 Sept. 1944, 2, AG's Office, Island Government files, 1945, 9B-11G 485, RG 284, NARA SB; Metzger 1982, 31.

94. Police vs. Alosio, 12 Aug. 1949, WPHC F40/3/33, WPA; Sentence on Aseri of Ugele, 1 Sept. 1949, WPHC F40/3/34, WPA; Page 2004, 45.

95. Van Pel 1956, 4.

96. Johannes 1978, 354; Lieber 1994, 131–163; Hornell, Diary, 8 Sept. 1939, HP 10065.

97. Foale 2006, 129–137; Thompson and Adloff 1971, 339.

98. Thompson 1949, 260–261; Lieber 1994, 131–163.

99. AR June 1950, ARs, Records of the GO, RG 284, NARA SB.

100. Darden to Secretary General of IUPN, 5 July 1950, Records of the GO 1872–1961, Series 16, RG 284, NARA SB.

101. Michener 1951, 185.

102. Blamey to Quartermaster, 3 Nov. 1943, AWM 54, 337/3/1, AWM; Marshall, Report on flora and fauna reserve, Loloki Valley, c. Oct. 1944, folder 7-3, box 30, MS 7132, A. J. Marshall Papers, NLA, Canberra.

103. Root to Quartermaster General, 23 Dec. 1943,Veale to New Guinea Force, 2 July 1944, Root to Quartermaster General, 20 July 1944, AWM 54, 337/3/1, AWM; Marshall, Report on flora and fauna reserve, c. Oct. 1944.

104. Chief Auditor to ANGAU, 31 Dec. 1944 and enclosures, AWM 54, 337/3/1, AWM.

105. FEA. South Pacific Project, Third quarter 1944, Sept. 1944, Entry 217, RG 234, NARA. *Ferae naturae* means animals that are wild or generally found at liberty. As such, they were not capable of being stolen unless first reduced to possession. Thus, Western law held that no one owned these fish, but of course national claims to their own *ferae naturae* would probably hold in the face of claims by a foreign state or group.

106. DO to RC, 22 Aug. 1933 and enclosures, WPHC 1515/33, WPA; Thompson 1949, 261; R. H. Lister, "Fiji society and war psychology," 19 July 1944, 6, MS 96529, NLNZ; Ashley to HC, 25 Sept. 1933 and minutes, CO 225/276/18858,TNA; Hornell 1940, 34–45, 84; Legand, Present position of existing fisheries in New Caledonia, 13 May 1952, F108/43 Part 1, FNA; Hickling, Report on the fisheries of Fiji, 1947 and enclosures, F108/20 Part 1, FNA.

107. Weeramantry 1992, 201–264.

108. Ross 1954, 266.

109. Humphries to Sec., Dept. of External Territories, and encls., A518/1, A320/3/1/Part 1, NAA; Barry Report, 87, A463/17, item 1956/1096, NAA.

110. Vaskess to RC, New Hebrides, 24 Jan. 1944, Blandy to HC for New Hebrides, 26 Apr. 1944, WPHC NHBS MP 21/4, WPA; Orders for native reserve, No. 1181, 8 Dec. 1899, ANC 44W, 283, ANC.

111. Report, Espiritu Santo, July 1945, Entry 178, RG 313, NARA.

112. Kay 1972.

113. Downs 1980, 13–61; Essai 1961, 46–52; Vaskess 1943.

114. Campbell 2003, 263–271; Bennett 1987, 301–302.

115. Bennett 1987, 330–336; Bennett 2000, 163–360; Denoon et al. 1997, 383–389; Hyndman 2001, 33–54.

116. Campbell 2003, 271–273, 286–289,

117. Cited in McKinnon 1993, 256. Pitcairn is the only exception.

118. Parnaby 1964, 180–199.

119. G. Barrow, "Outlying Interlude," Chap 12, Mss Pac. S. 43, RH.

120. J. M. Clift, *PIM*, Oct. 1946, 39.

121. Laracy 1983; Downs 1980, 62–65; Lawrence 1964, 98–165, 179–221, 224–232; Mead 1956.

122. Henningham 1992, 23–24, 47–48.

123. D'Arcy 2006, 118–143.

124. Lal 1992, 134–137, 158–159; Bennett 2001a, 276–288; Irwin 1965, 103; Gilson 1980, 177, 191–192, 212–215; Challis 1953, 1–8; Kolokesa Māhina-Tuai, e-mail to author, 29 Oct. 2007; Report of the Work of Research Expeditions sent to Western Samoa, Rarotonga and Pukapuka during 1948 to 1953, 1953, 15; Report 1949, ARs GO, RG 284, NARA SB; Butchart, Memo, 25 Sept. 1951, Reports GO, Series 15, RG 284, NARA SB; Analysis of the Economic Status of native population of American Samoa, c. 1947, Records of the GO, 1972-1961, RG 284, NARA SB; Commanding Officer to Commandant, 10 May 1944, RG 313-58-3440, NARA SB; McKay 1968, 138–140; Lewthwaite, Mainzer, and Holland 1973, 133–140; Franco 1985, 217, 219–229; Stanner 1953, 326–327; Ravuvu 1988, 55; McQuarrie 1994, 155; Macdonald 1982, 159; Campbell 2001, 181–183; Helu 1998 31–32, 36–37; Wood-Ellem 1999, 220, 222–226.

125. Lafitani 1998, 82; Connell and Brown 2005, 1–13; Gerald Haberkom, "Pacific population dynamics and recent trends," http://www.spc.int/demog/en/index .html (accessed 30 Oct. 2006); World Bank, "Opportunities to Improve Social Services Human Development in the Pacific Islands," http://www.wds.worldbank

.org/external/default/WDSContentServer/WDSP/IB/2007/05/17/000310607_20070517100419/Rendered/PDF/397780EAP0P0791Development01PUBLIC1.pdf (accessed 2 Aug. 2007).

Chapter 12: Remembering Place

Epigraph: "Among my souvenirs," words and music by Horatio Nicholls and Edgar Leslie, 1927. The lyrics were sung in *The Best Years of Our Lives,* 1946, RKO, Samuel Goldwyn Company, directed by William Wyler, a film about three returning servicemen adjusting to civilian life.

1. For parts of this discussion, I have drawn on Stewart 1993, 132–166.
2. Brackman 1987, 249–250.
3. Jack Craig, Papers, 10 Sept., 1 Oct. 1943, PR 00906, AWM; History of Admiralty Islands campaign, 29 Feb.–18 May 1944, AWM 54 80/6/6, AWM.
4. Morriss 1996, 39.
5. J. A. Milbourne, Papers, 1942–1943, 33, PR 87/221, AWM; Manus Base Order No. 2, 12 Apr. 1944, Box 1. f. A1, RG 313-58-3300, NARA SB; Jackson 1989, 104.
6. A. C. Bennett, "The Rough Infantry," 218, MSS 1408, AWM; Chapman 1949, 76.
7. C. L. Pender, Diary, 24 Jan. 1943, PR 83/180, AWM.
8. A. C. Bennett, " The Rough Infantry."
9. "Japanese Military Swords," http://home.earthlink.net/~steinrl/military.htm (accessed 23 Apr. 2007).
10. J. V. Robinson, Papers, 7 Oct. 1945, PR 84/216, AWM; Chang 1998, 6, 102; John G. Rennie, Memoirs, No. 1999.721, AM.
11. M. G. Hauer, Papers, 2 Nov. 1945, PR 87/110, AWM; T. J. Farrell, Papers, file 3, Talk on morale, PR82/74, AWM.
12. Chang 1998, 106–139, 153–157.
13. Review of operations of RNZAF, Bougainville, at Buin, 12–21 Sept. 1945, Entry 183, RG 313, NARA.
14. Dougherty, 5 Oct. 1945 and enclosures, AWM 54, 320/3/48, AWM.
15. Photo and caption No. 098687, AWM.
16. Dougherty, 5 Oct. 1945 and enclosures, AWM 54, 320/3/48, AWM.
17. Oppenheimer 1966, 141.
18. Market Notes, *Time,* 19 June 1944, http://www.time.com/time/archive (accessed 25 June 2005).
19. Monk, Patrol on Karkar Island, June 1944, PNG Patrol Reports, microfiche, A9844, NAA; Photos and captions, Nos. 059282-059285, AWM.
20. R. Miller, Papers, 31 Dec. 1942–1 Jan. 1943, PR 01389/1, AWM.
21. Higden to Commander, 2 July 1943, Box v. 9281, F. P13, RG 313-58-3401, NARA SB; Durham 2003, 91–96.
22. Gillespie 1945, 79.
23. Terry Donnelly, "A Sergeant At Arms," No. 2003.38, AM.

24. 1 CRE New Guinea Forest Reports, Routine orders 28 Oct. 1944, AWM 53 5/33/2, AWM.

25. Higgenbotham to Commander, 28 July 1944, Box 1, F. A2-7, RG 313-58-3019, NARA SB.

26. Frederick to Chief, 12 Mar. 1944, Box 1, F. A12-1, RG 313-58-3416, NARA SB.

27. Christoph to Commander, 28 Mar. 1944, box 2, F. A17/P13-5, RG 313-58-3416, NARA SB.

28. Tapert 1987, 72.

29. Merillat 1982, 154.

30. Peter Hemery, "Kakakog Kate and other souvenirs," AWM 54 773/4/91, AWM.

31. 1 CRE Forest Reports, Routine orders, 3 June 1944, AWM 53 5/32/2, AWM; Souvenir Retention Certificates 1946–1947, Box 2, F. A4-2, RG 313-58-3300, NARA SB.

32. "Dad's diary," 17 Oct. 1942.

33. Tom Neeman, Letters, 3 Jan. 1943, PR 01034, AWM.

34. M. G. Hauer, Papers, 1 Feb. 1946, PR 87/110, AWM.

35. R. Miller, Papers, 30 Aug. 1942, PR 01389/1, AWM.

36. C. L. Pender, Diary, 23 Jan. 1943, PR 83/180, AWM.

37. M. G. Hauer, Papers, 2 Nov. 1945.

38. Ravuvu 1988, 49–50.

39. Durham 2003, 87–89.

40. Jarvis 2004, 129–130.

41. Morriss 1996, 67; "Dad's diary," 17 Oct. 1942.

42. Anon., Diary, 5 Aug. 1942, 45, America Samoa, GO, Series 3, RG 284, NARA SB.

43. Durham 2003, 90, 95.

44. Weingartner 1992, 53–67.

45. Commission of Inquiry into Breaches of the Rules of Warfare, 14 Sept. 1944 and enclosures, A989 (A989/1), 54 883/1/6, AWM; Pacific Fleet Letter, 27 Jan. 1944, Box v. 319814, F. P6, RG 313-58A-3254, NARA SB.

46. Commission of Inquiry into Breaches of Rules of Warfare, 1944 and enclosures.

47. Muehleisen to Intelligence Officer, 7 June 1944, Entry 179, RG 313, NARA; Holt to Commander, SPA, 22 Mar. 1945, U.S. military censorship, 0-313, 24 Feb. 1945, Jones to Commander, SPA, 28 Mar. 1945 and enclosures, Entry 78, RG 313, NARA; "Dad's diary," 5–6 Mar. 1943; V. O. Hunt, 28 Mar. 1944, 3 DRL 6132, AWM; B. French, Diary, 6 June 1945, PR 85/219, AWM.

48. Commission of Inquiry into Breaches of the Rules of Warfare, 14 Sept. 1944 and enclosures, 54 883/1/6, AWM; Muehleisen to Intelligence Officer, 7 June 1944, Entry 179, RG 313, NARA.

49. Maut to Chief Publicity Censor, 27 Jan. 1943 and enclosures, SP 109/3, 336/08, NAA.

50. Joseph Bernard, http://carol_fus.tripod.com/photo_mc_jbernard.html (accessed 25 Sept. 2003).

51. Cf. Bailey and Farber 2006, 641–660; Gordon 1998, 616–638.

52. Ashton 1998, 1.

53. Kushner 1984, 126; Wood-Ellem, 1999, 208;

54. A. M. Patterson, interview with Aaron Fox, Dunedin, 27 Jan. 1999.

55. R. Miller, Papers, Jan.–Feb. 1943, PR 01389/1, AWM.

56. Tapert 1987, 90.

57. Pitt, Huon area, 15–29 July 1944, PNG Patrol Reports, microfiche, A9844, NAA.

58. Rees, Finschhafen sub-district, 4 Aug.–6 Sept. 1944, PNG Patrol Reports, microfiche, A9844, NAA.

59. Durham 2003, 91–92.

60. G. K. Little, "Those were the days my friend," 306, MSS 1210, AWM.

61. Simmons to "Chicago Tribune," 12 Dec. 1944, Box v. 9285, F. P9, RG 313-58-3401, NARA SB.

62. Laracy and White 1988, 110–111.

63. Sabel 1999, 160.

64. Acting British District Agent to RC, 26 Sept. 1944, WPHC NHBS MP 25/43, WPA.

65. Blandy to RC, 19 Oct. 1943 and encls., WPHC NHBS MP 30/15, WPA.

66. HC to RC, 19 Feb. 1944, WPHC NHBS MP 30/15, WPA. Cf. Lindstrom 1996, 21.

67. Holland to RC, 10 Dec. 1943, WPHC CF 10/26, WPA; Como-Parkinson, Memo, 17 Sept. 1945, FO 371/44623, TNA.

68. Island Commander to Air Commander, 16 Jan. 1944, Geographic file, RG 218, NARA.

69. Haggard, Patrol Report Siassi Islands, 25 Aug.–30 Oct. 1946, PNG Patrol Reports, microfiche, A9844, NAA.

70. Austen, Native Welfare, Conference Port Moresby, 7–12 Feb. 1944, 10, AWM 254, AWM.

71. Whitehouse, Patrol Report for Kitava Island villages, Kiriwina, 1 May, 1944, 5–15 July 1946, PNG Patrol Reports, microfiche, A9844, NAA.

72. Haggard, Patrol Report Siassi Islands, 25 Aug.–30 Oct. 1946.

73. Viel 1974, 238–240.

74. Douglas 1996.

75. Mossman, Report, Samarai district, 2–3 Nov. 1943, PNG Patrol Reports, microfiche, A9844, NAA; Early 1998, 279; Codrington to Tom, 10 Apr. 1872, 17 Sept. 1873, Melanesian Mission Papers 2/1, SOAS, London; *Melanesian Mission Annual Report, 1902* (London: W. H. Smith, 1903), 31; *Melanesian Mission Annual Report, 1908* (London: W. H. Smith, 1909), 23.

76. Viel 1974; Captions on photographs on display, Musée de Ville, Noumea, Jan. 2006.

77. Gardner 2006, 142.

78. Kushner 1984, 58, 127, 171; Ashton 1998, 10; Milne to Stengels, 10 Dec. 1937, Listed stock, 15 Mar. 1939, American Samoa, GO, Series 5, RG 284, NARA SB.

79. Governor to Secretary of the Navy, 6 Aug. 1936, AR, 1938, AR, 1940, American Samoa, GO, Series 5, RG 284, NARA SB; Intelligence Officer to Governor, 4 Oct. 1942, America Samoa, GO, Series 3, RG 284, NARA SB; Mary Prichard, "Siapo.com," http://www.siapo.com/maryprichard.html (accessed 20 Mar. 2008).

80. Moyer to Sec. of Navy, Report, 30 June 1943, American Samoa, GO, Series 5, RG 284, NARA SB; Prichard, "Siapo.com."

81. AR to June 1943, 9, American Samoa, GO, Series 5, RG 284, NARA SB. See also Analysis of Economic Status of native population, 1947, 41, GO Series no. 16, Sub Series no. 1, RG 284, NARA SB; [John Burke], United States Naval History of Tutuila, Museum, Navy Yards, Washington D.C., 135; Parsons 1945, 174, 225

82. [Burke], United States Naval History of Tutuila, 144; Parsons 1945, 169.

83. Priday [1945] 62, 64; Alailima 1988, 242.

84. Margaret Armstrong, Visitors Book and memoirs, 154, MSS Pac. S. 93, RH; Wood-Ellem 1999, 210.

85. The average U.S. serviceman was paid $71.33 a week, with officers about three times that. "World War Two by the Numbers," http://the.honoluluadvertiser.com/peaceinthepacific/numbers (accessed 13 Mar. 2007); Armstrong to Colonial Secretary, 15 Sept. 1944, WPHC TS 39/42, WPA.

86. Ken Reardon, interview with Aaron Fox, Auckland, 22 Feb. 1999; History of Tongatapu, c. 1946, Entry 183, RG 313, NARA; Armstrong to Colonial Secretary, 15 Sept. 1944, WPHC TS 39/42, WPA.

87. Foord 1996, 54.

88. Calhoun to Hardy, 24 May 1945, Entry 183, RG 313, NARA. "La Hala" probably means "Lauhala," the common name for pandanus mats in Hawaii (Adrienne Kaeppler, personal communication, 30 Sept. 2003). In Samoa "lauhala" also refers to the pandanus leaf used in weaving. Two months later, Vice Admiral Calhoun paid for a subscription to *Life* magazine for Queen Sālote. NARA Calhoun to Brownlees, 15 July 1945, Entry 179, RG 313, NARA.

89. Hickling to Tailby, 15 Nov. 1943, and enclosures, IT, 122/5/2 pt 1, ANZ.

90. Frisbie 1948, 209, 211, 225.

91. Gilson 1980, 191.

92. Trevor L. Thomas, Diary, 18 Jan., 8, 15 Feb. 1942, MSX 5141, NLNZ; James W. Allison, Diary, 11 Mar. 1943, No. 1999.1717, AM.

93. Benallack, Routine Orders, 16 Apr. 1945; Chapman 1949, 77; Schedule of prices for labor and commodities, 29 Mar. 1943, Box 1, F. LL, RG 313-58-3520, NARA SB.

94. Witt, Memo 43, 14 Aug. 1944, Box 1, F. A2-11, RG 313-58A-3244, NARA; Jones, Annex No. 2 to G-2 periodic Report, 20 Jan. 1944, Entry 44463, RG 338, NARA.

95. Air Command Order, 3 Jan. 1945, Box 7, F. A2-11, RG 313-58-3377, NARA SB.

96. ARs, eastern District, 1943, 1944, WPHC BSIP 9/111/1, WPA.

97. Benallack, Routine Orders, 16 Apr. 1945.

98. Pridey [1945], 51; Stead, Annex No. 1 to G-2 Report No. 46, 13 Nov. 1943, Entry 182, RG 313, NARA; Annex No. 1 to G-2 Report No. 91, 23 Sept. 1944, Entry 44463, RG 338, NARA; Tallec to Governor, 6 Feb. 1945 and encls., Entry 183, RG 313, NARA; Guilleux to President of Chamber of Commerce, 9 Sept. 1944 and encls., 145W, 18, ANC.

99. Tallec to Barnett, 10 Feb. 1945, 44 W 520, ANC.

100. Michener 1947, 155–208.

101. Munholland 1991, 545; Report on Franco-American Relationship in New Caledonia, c. 1945, 21, Microfilm 323, Department of Pacific and Asian History, ANU; G-2 Periodic Intelligence Report, Annex No. 1, Economic, 7 Jan. 1945, Entry 182, RG 313, NARA; Kushner 1984, 58.

102. 1 Mar. 1945–30 Sept. 1945, Quarterly reports, CSO CF8/38/6 Pt 2, FNA; PIM, Aug. 1945, 15; Alailima 1988, 241; AR, Eastern District, 1943, Folder E, AR, 1944, Folder E2, WPHC BSIP 9/111/1, WPA.

103. Chapman 1949, 76; Durham 2003, 63.

104. Ashton 1998, 18.

105. Parsons 1945.

106. Foord 1996, 52–53.

107. Malcolm Foord, interview with Aaron Fox, Dunedin, 20 Jan. 1999. Foord's book *The Fortunate Soldier* was based largely on his wartime letters home.

108. Photos, G380455 and G38456, RG 80, NARA.

109. Kaeppler and Stillman 1985, 15, 72,177, 192, 243, 281.

110. Charles Downer, Statement, 23 Jan. 1945, RG 218, NARA; Virginia Krumholz and Sharon Dean May, personal communication, Cleveland Museum, June 2003.

111. Burke to Weitzner, 18 Oct. 1945; Burke to Shapiro, 7 Mar. 1946, Division of Anthropology Archives, AMNH.

112. Noel to HC, 27 Sept. 1945, WPHC 6/1, CF 29/20, WPA; Crispell, Letter, 2 Dec. 1944, Cooper to Commanding Officer, 17 Jan. 1945, Kalbfus to Bill, 30 May 1945; Burke to Flag Secretary, 14 Nov. 1945, Entry 183, RG 313, NARA; Quigley to Commander, 23 June 1944, Box v. 9289, F. S85, RG 313-58-3401, NARA SB; Burke to Mead, 30 July, 18 Oct. 1945, Mead to Burke, 5 Sept. 1945, Mead Papers, Library of Congress, Washington; Michener 1951, 185–186.

113. Burke, 26 June 1945, Box 1, F. A4-A5, RG 313-58-3233, NARA SB.

114. Regulations for the disposal of excess government property, 25 July 1945 and encls., WPHA NHBS MP 26/43, WPA.

115. Barrett to Commander, 27 Sept. 1945, Box v. 9278, F. L8, RG 313-58-3401, NARA SB; Parsonage to Aubin, 20 Oct. 1945, Roman Catholic Mission, Solomons, PMB 1120, Reel 6.

116. RC to HC, 28 Aug. 1945, WPHC CF 58/28/3 Vol. 1, WPA; Noel to HC, 27 Sept. 1945, Waddell to HC, 10 Sept. 1945, WPHC 6/1, CF 29/29, WPA; Maino to Chief

of Staff, 13 Nov. 1945, Entry 178, RG 313, NARA; Acting RC to HC, 12 Nov. 1946 and minutes, WPHC 6/1, CF 29/29, WPA.

117. Burke to Commander, 14 Jan. 1946 and enclosure, Entry 183, RG 313, NARA.

118. Shapiro to Turnbull, 17 May 1946, AMNH; Kristen Mable, personal communication, Museum of Natural History, 8 Feb. 2001; Christina Hellmich, personal communication, Peabody Essex Museum, 1 Nov. 2002, and accession cards 11576, 11770, 11791, 11966, Peabody Museum; Fetchko 1974, 54–57.

119. Linton and Wingert, in collaboration with D'Harnoncourt c. 1946. Walter H. Deihl of the Buffalo Museum of Science aided the preparation of this exhibition, with artifacts from the collection at that museum.

120. Stewart 1993, 151.

121. Accession catalogue, 80.1, numbers 289–348, 495–533, 20–21, 26–27, AMNH.

122. Herle et al., 2002, 2–3.

123. Herle et al., 2002, 6.

124. Burke to Commanding Officer, n.d., Burke to Naval Medical museum, 12 Sept. 1945, Entry 178, RG 313, NARA; Burke to Shapiro, 9 Feb. 1946, AMNH.

125. [Illegible] to Widdowson, 18 Jan. 1946, WPHC TS 8/46, WPA. *Fiji Times,* 12 Apr. 1944, 4.

126. Kushner 1984, 108.

127. Durham 2003, 62, 91–96.

128. In New Zealand slang, work done out of working hours was called "foreigner."

129. B. French, Diary, 8 Feb. 1945, PR 85/219, AWM; Ron Berry, Diary, 25 Sept. 1942, PR 84/021, AWM; AWM Photos nos. 061241, 076909, 092697, AWM; 1 CRE Forest Reports, Routine Orders, 15 Sept., 10 Oct. 1944, AWM 53 5/32/2, AWM; A. M. Patterson, interview with Aaron Fox, Dunedin, 27 Jan. 1999; John Rennie Memoirs and Geoffrey Bentley, " The men behind the fliers," encl., No. 43195, AM; Terry Donnelly, "A Sergeant At Arms," No. 2003.38, AM; Durham 2003, 63, 64, 94.

130. Photo No. 016873 and caption, AWM.

131. L. A. Paton, Diary, 19 Mar. 1944, AWM PR 85/245, AWM; Pat Lee, Letter, 19 Nov. 1944, AWM PR 00961, AWM; Gavan Long, Diary, no. 2, 99, AWM 67 1/3, AWM; Folder 2, A. J. Bradshaw, Memoirs, 128, MS 3871, NLNZ; Dorothy Page, personal communication, June 2003.

132. Parsons 1945, 172–174.

133. Guadalcanal Handicraft, n.d., Box v. 9275, F. P10, RG 313-58-3401, NARA SB.

134. Geslin 1956, 273; Adam to Blandy, 21 Mar. 1943 and encls., WPHC NHBS MP 22/19, WPA.

135. Gillespie 1945, 85, 126, 148.

136. *Fiji Times,* 20 Apr. 1944, 2; Benallack, Routine Orders, 16 Apr. 1945; Burke, Report of Siassi Island, May 1945, PNG Patrol Reports, microfiche, A9844, NAA.

137. V. O. Hunt, 12 May 1944, 3 DRL 6132, NAA.

138. Charles W. Frank, "From Philly to Tokyo: The saga of the USS New Jersey, BB 62 in WW II," http://alumni.nrotc.tulane.edu/Philly_to_Tokyo/Philly_to_Tokyo_ch03.htm (accessed 23 Sept. 2003).

139. H. P. Spindler, Letter, 3 July 1942, PR 83/171, AWM.

140. "Belated tribute to Veterans," www.buzzle.com/editorials/5-28-2004-54802.asp (accessed 11 Mar. 2007).

141. Ken Reardon, interview with Aaron Fox, Auckland, 22 Feb. 1999.

142. Bill Brewster, personal communication, Sept. 2003; Windsor Jones, personal communication, 25 Nov. 2003.

Chapter 13: Places of Memory, Sites of Forgetting

Epigraphs: Anonymous woman's comment at the reinterment of New Zealand's Unknown Warrior in Wellington, 11 Nov. 2004, Radio New Zealand National broadcast; Laffin 1956, 124.

1. G. Long, Diary, Nov. 1943, 99, AWM 67, 1/3, AWM; Stauffer 1956, 248–254.

2. Two of the Australian overseas dead in the Great War came home: the commander of the First Division of the AIF, W. T. Briggs, buried at Duntroon in 1915, and the Unknown Australian Soldier reinterred in the Australian War Memorial, Canberra, on 11 Nov. 1993. Inglis 1998, 75, 453.

3. HQ War Graves Group NG Feb. to Dec. 1946, Houghton, Report AWGS, 3 Mar 46, AWM 52, 21/1/6, AWM; Brown to Gavin Long, 19 Aug. 1953, AWM 93, 50/9/2/4/2.

4. J. M. Ross (Commanding Officer) to Commander South Pacific, 25 Jan. 1945, Box 3, F. P6, RG 313-58-3503, NARA SB; John L. Stewart to Commanding Officer, 30 Aug. 1944, Box 2, F. P6, RG 313-58-3496, NARA SB.

5. R. W. Sidway, Certificate, 7 Dec. 1945, encl., Agreement, USA and New Zealand re Surplus Property, 15 Aug. 1946, Entry 44463, RG 338, NARA; [L. G. Allan], Index of cemeteries, c. Oct. 1946, Entry 2110, RG 92, NARA; Chiefs of Staff Representative to Commanding General, 29 Apr. 1945, J. Heenan to Secretary of External Affairs, 8 Jan. 1946 and enclosures, EA 1, 87/14/4/6 Pt 1, ANZ; Lee to Colonial Secretary, 14 Feb. 1949 and encls., F115/173 Pt 1, FNA.

6. Jack Leemon, "The Body Snatchers," MSS 0811, AWM.

7. F. O. Affeld to Island Commander and Air Commander, 16 Jan. 1944, RG 218, NARA.

8. War Graves Maintenance Unit, NG Reports, Sept. 1943–Nov. 1944, AMW 52, 21/3/5, AWM; Leemon, "The Body Snatchers"; Photograph, Noumea Cemetery, Elmer Williams, Tour of Duty Collection, ANC; No. A43 600, War Theatre, Munda, U.S. Air Force Photos, Series FH, RG 342, NARA.

9. History of Cemetery, 8 Nov. 1945 and encl., Final close out Report Guadalcanal, Oct. 1945–1 May 1946, Entry 44463, RG 338, NARA.

10. P. G. Polowniak, "Memorial Day Services May 30th 1945 Tongatabu," U.S. Naval Advanced Base Report Tongatabu, 1945, 138, Entry 183, RG 313, NARA.

11. Henry Wolfe to Quartermaster General, 12 Sept. 1945 and encls., Entry 2110, RG 92, NARA; Wernham to Commanding Officer, 15 Mar. 1946, Naval Inspector General's report of investigation of Burial of deceased Marine Corps personnel on Tarawa, Bnd # 40350, Torts and Claims records, JAG, Navy Yard, Washington D.C. Cemeteries of war dead in the United States are the responsibility of the National Parks Service; Edward Steere, "National Cemeteries and Memorials in Global Conflict," www.qmfound.com/national_cemeteries_and_memorials_in_global_conflict.htm (accessed 21 Jan. 2007). There are U.S. war cemeteries in the Philippines, Alaska, and Hawai'i.

12. HQ War Graves—Recovery of Ashes of Allied Personnel, Rabaul, 1946, AWM54, 135/1/2, AWM.

13. Cf. Inglis 1998, 258–259.

14. Cremation rates to deaths were 3.7 percent in the United States and about 10 percent in Australia. Prothero 2001, 163–164; Inglis 1987, 245–246.

15. Manual, Repatriation Plan AGRS-PTA, 1946, 58, Entry 2110, RG 92, NARA.

16. The cost of each repatriation was reckoned at $1,000. *PIM*, Feb. 1948, 26.

17. Manual, Repatriation Plan AGRS-PTA, 1946, 51, 67–75, Entry 2110, RG 92, NARA.

18. War Department 1946, 15; Department of Army 1947, 3–9.

19. Yukio Toyoda, "Consoling the Dead: Japanese memorial tours in Papua New Guinea," in The Pacific War in New Papua New Guinea: Perceptions and Realities Symposium, 1–2 Sept. 1999, Canberra, Australian National University. http://www.cwgc.org/ (accessed 22 Jan. 2007); Winter 1997, 107; Inglis 1998, 253–255.

20. Spot report 27, 25 Dec. 1945, WO 106/5928, TNA; Robinson 1979, 142.

21. Milbourne's memoirs, Aug. 1942, 32, Papers of Pte J. A. Milbourne and Sgt. George Routledge, AWM PR 87/221, AWM.

22. Mark Johnston, "'Yet they're just as human as we are': Australian attitudes towards the Japanese in the South-west Pacific" (Symposium paper), http://ajrp.awm.gov.au/ajrp/remember.nsf/pages/NT00002B0E (accessed 23 Jan. 2007).

23. War Graves Maintenance Unit NG Reports, Sept. 1943–Nov. 1944, AWM 52, 21/3/5, AWM.

24. Photograph 60476, September 1943, Marine Corps, RG 127-GW, NARA. Translation provided by Takashi Shogiman.

25. Berryman to Ogle, 23 Oct. 1944, AWM PR 84/370, AWM.

26. McBride, Notes for Cabinet, C 8 Australian Battlefields Memorials Committee—policy, 20 Dec. 1949, A4940 A4940/1, NAA.

27. Reid 2001, 47–51.

28. Notes on Cabinet Submission No. 367, National War Memorials, December 1955, A4906/1, 367, NAA.

29. See for example Laffin 1956, 23, 87–88.

30. G. Barrow, "Outlying Interlude," 87, Mss Pac s. 43, RH.

31. General George Marshall, cited in Piehler 1995, 130.

32. Australia, Parliamentary Debates, Hansard (Canberra: Government Printer, 1947), vol. 192, 9 May 1947, 2181.

33. Halifax to Foreign Office, 15 Dec. 1943, DO 35/2124, TNA.

34. Australian government to Dominion Office, 28 Dec. 1943, DO 35/2124, TNA.

35. New Zealand government to Dominion Office, 28 Dec. 1942, DO 35/2124, TNA; File A 989, 1944/43/655/12, NAA.

36. Mitchell to Secretary of State, 20 Dec. 1943, DO 35/2124, TNA.

37. Memo for Colonial Office, 3 May 1946, DO 35/2125, TNA.

38. Conclusions of Meeting, 3 May 1946, Minutes of Meeting, 3 May 1946, Minutes of 12th Meeting of Prime Ministers, 6 May 1946, Secretary of State to Grantham, 23 May 1946, DO 35/2125, TNA.

39. Grantham to Secretary of State, 29 May 1946, DO 35/2125, TNA.

40. Secretary of State to Grantham, 23 May 1946, DO 35/2125, TNA.

41. Mansell and Rogers, Minute, 29 Mar. 1946, FO 115/4199, TNA.

42. J. W. Roper to Erl C. B. Gould, 16 May 1947, Naval Inspector General's report, JAG; Photo GW 1208, RG 127, NARA; Philip Mitchell, Diary, 12 June 1944, MSS. Afr. r. 101, RH. I consulted the JAG material in 2000, but the file was recorded as lost as of 27 June 2007 in a letter to me from R. A. Leonard, deputy assistant judge.

43. Robert Sherrod, "Tarawa Today," *Life,* 5 Aug. 1946, encl. A in Julien Marshall to Commanding General, 5 Oct. 1946, Naval Inspector General's report, JAG.

44. I. Eisensmith to Chief, 3 July 1946, Naval Inspector General's report, JAG.

45. Naval Inspector General to Secretary of the Navy, 11 Mar. 1947, Naval Inspector General's report, JAG.

46. A. Vandegrift to Secretary of the Navy, 12 Nov. 1946, Sherrod, "Tarawa Today," *Life,* 5 Aug. 1946, encl. A in Julien Marshall to Commanding General, 5 Oct. 1946, Hewlett Thebaud to Chief of Naval Operations, 18 Dec. 1946, Naval Inspector General's report, JAG.

47. Facts and excerpts from testimony of Joseph Weiber and others, Enclosure A in Naval Inspector General to Secretary of the Navy, 11 Mar. 1947, Naval Inspector General's report, JAG.

48. I. Eisensmith to Chief, Memorial Branch, 3 July 1946, St Julian Marshall to Commanding General, 3 Oct. 1946, Naval Inspector General's report, JAG.

49. American Battle Monuments Commission, "History," http://www.abmc.gov/commission/history.php (accessed 22 Mar. 2007).

50. T. Blamey, 9 Sept. 1945, enclosure in Lt. Gen. Sir F. H Berryman's papers, PR 84/370 (419/9/9), AWM.

51. Ienaga 1979, 129–192

52. Photograph 56176, 26 May 1943, Marine Corps, RG 127-GW, NARA; Ahrens 2006, 12.

53. Yukio Toyoda, "The war in New Guinea as portrayed in Japanese newspapers," ajrp.awm.gov.au/ajrp/remember.nsf/pages/NT00002442 (accessed 14 Feb. 2007); Yukio Toyoda, "Consoling the Dead"; mdn.mainichi-msn.co.jp/features/archive/news/2005/08/20050812p2g00m0fe031000c.html (accessed 13 Apr. 2007).

54. *Asahi Shimbun,* 12 Jan. 1955, British Ambassador to the Ministry for Foreign Affairs, 20 Aug. 1954, A518, G016/2/1 Part 1, NAA.

55. T. Eckersley to Secretary, 2 Sept. 1953 and enclosures, A518, G016/2/1 Part 1, NAA; D. Cleland to Secretary, 1 Mar. 1955, A518, G016/2/1 Part 2, NAA. See also War graves, Japan visit 1965, A1838/399, 1510/3/38/3 Part 2, NAA.

56. Toyoda, "Consoling the Dead."

57. Anzac is the acronym for Australian and New Zealand Army Corps, a force fighting together with considerable effect after landing in the wrong place following British command at Gallipoli, Turkey, in 1915. The Turks eventually drove them off.

58. Arthur Gately, "A call to Arms: War Service with the RAAF," 183, PR 00756, AWM.

59. Powell 2003, photograph AWM 089058, opposite p. 54.

60. Martin Fackler, "Abe's gift to the Yasukuni war shrine in Japan is scrutinized," www.iht.com/articles/2007/05/08/news/japan.php (accessed 21 May 2007).

61. "Shrine Opposition," http://www.geocities.com/gatoesmuchogor/opposition.html (accessed 24 Jan. 2007); Andrew McGreevy, "Arlington National Cemetery and Yasukuni Jinja," www.zmag.org/content/showarticle.cfm?ItemID=8491 (accessed 14 Feb. 2007); Tachibana 1996, 173.

62. Winter 1997, 113.

63. Pacific Islands Report, http://pidp.ewc.hawaii.edu/Pireport/2000/Dec./12-19-19.htm (accessed 20 Dec. 2000).

64. "Missing World War II men are identified," www.freerepublic.com/focus/f-news/1656754/posts (accessed 14 Feb. 2007); Randall Dorton to Donald Jackson, 30 Jan. 1960, Entry 1898C, RG 92, NARA.

65. "Remains returned," www.pownetwork.org/remret2.htm (accessed 22 Mar. 2007).

66. The Commission of Fine Arts, the National Sculpture Society, and the Artist's Guild of Washington disliked the sculpture based on the famous Joseph Rosenthal photograph of raising the flag, and they also questioned the character of the sculptor, Felix DeWeldon. Piehler 1995, 135–138, 152–153.

67. American Battle Monuments Commission, http://www.abmc.gov/home.php (accessed 1 Mar. 2007).

68. National WWII Memorial, http://www.wwiimemorial.com/ (accessed 1 Mar. 2007).

69. Inglis 1998, 474. The Australians record all who served on memorials, mainly because the AIF was largely voluntary. They had few conscripts, who initially were confined to Australia. In February 1943, these Militiamen became liable for overseas service but all served either in New Guinea or in Dutch New Guinea. Thus the AIF outside New Guinea was entirely voluntary. New Zealanders, who had some conscripts, record those who died in service.

70. Ethel Pedina to Secretary, 14 Sept. 1953, I. O'Reilly to Secretary, 23 Sept 1953, Mary Wright to Prime Minister's Department, 25 Sept. 1953, Eileen McKnight to

Sir, 22 Sept. 1953, A462, 827/2/24 Part 2, NAA. The Australian government called the Sword a Cross, reflecting a cultural perspective.

71. Ethel Pedina to Secretary, 20 Nov. 1953, I. O'Reilly to Secretary, 1 Dec. 1953, L. Watkins, 29 Oct. 1953, A462, 827/2/24 Part 2, NAA.

72. Inglis 1998, 473.

73. Record attendances were noted on Anzac Day 2007.

74. Inglis 1998, 427, 435–439; Maclean and Phillips 1990, 161.

75. "New Zealand memorial a tribute to the Anzac Relationship, say PM," www.beehive.govt.nz/ViewDocument.aspx?DocumentID=10309 (accessed 15 Mar. 2007).

76. Inglis 1998, 444–471; Mataia 2007.

77. Muller, 2002, 21.

78. "Hill 35, Guadalcanal," http://www.pacificwrecks.com/provinces/solomons_gifu.html (accessed 28 Jan. 2007).

79. Ienaga 1979, 200–202; Alperovitz 1995. For a historiographical overview, see Walter 1996, 11–37.

80. "Guadalcanal American Memorial," http://www.abmc.gov/memorials/memorials/gu.php, (accessed 13 Feb. 2007). I was present for the lead-up to the fiftieth anniversary and spoke to American veterans regarding this.

81. *Solomon Star,* 28 Apr. 1989, 7, cited in White 1996, 55.

82. "Japanese sculptor's work dedicated at Guadalcanal's Henderson Airport," http://archives.pireport.org/archive/1998/june/06%2D09%2D11.htm (accessed 11 Mar. 2007).

83. For examples of Japan's campaign to resume whaling in the South Pacific, see Pacific Islands Report, http://archives.pireport.org/archive/2003/Sept./09%2D29%2Dtcp1.htm; http://archives.pireport.org/archive/2001/july/07%2D19%2D15.htm; http://archives.pireport.org/archive/2001/Feb./02%2D21%2D08.htm; http://archives.pireport.org/archive/2002/may/05%2D23%2D11.htm (accessed 17 Feb. 2007).

84. Pacific Islands Reports, http://archives.pireport.org/archive/1998/june/06%2D09%2D11.htm; http://archives.pireport.org/archive/1998/Feb./02%2D20%2D03.html; http://archives.pireport.org/archive/2003/june/06%2D17%2D13.htm; http://archives.pireport.org/archive/2003/may/05%2D19%2D21.htm (accessed 17 Feb. 2007).

85. World War II Marine Raiders, http://www.usmarineraiders.org/Henderson01.htm (accessed 17 Feb. 2007).

86. "Battle of Isurava and Milne Bay Sixtieth Anniversary," http://www.parliament.nsw.gov.au/prod/parlment/hansart.nsf/V3Key/LC20020827120 (accessed 18 Feb. 2007).

87. Department of Veterans Affairs, "Isurava memorial," www.dva.gov.au/commem/oawg/png.htm (accessed 26 Jan. 2007).

88. Australian Bronze Commemorative Plaques, www.plaques.satlink.com.au/misc/supporters.htm (accessed 14 Feb. 2007).

89. Laffin 1956, 124.

90. Max Walsh, "A New Asian Gleam in the Australian Leader's Eyes," www.iht.com/articles/1992/05/29/max_.php (accessed 13 Feb. 2007).

91. Cited in Inglis 1998, 444.

92. Shane McLeod, "John Howard visits war memorial," http://www.abc.net.au/am/stories/s648181.htm (accessed 13 Apr. 2007); Nic Maclellan, "The Pacific 'non solution,'" *Pacific Journalism Review* 8 (2002): 145–154, www.asiapac.org.fj/PJR/issues/next/2002refugees.pdf (accessed 13 Apr. 2007).

93. Dept. of Veterans Affairs, "On line travel diary, Sogeri and Owers Corner," http://www.dva.gov.au/commem/png/diary/pngdiary3.htm; Dept of Veterans Affairs, "Isurava memorial," www.dva.gov.au/commem/oawg/png.htm (accessed 24 Jan. 2007).

94. Nelson 2006, 109–126; Tony Jones, "History wars surround Kokoda Campaign," www.abc.net.au/lateline/content/2006/s1623611.htm (accessed 13 Apr. 2007).

95. Nelson 2006, 125–126.

96. The Kokoda Track Foundation, www.kokodatrackfoundation.org/programs.html (accessed 13 Feb. 2007).

97. Inglis 1998.

98. Kokoda Memorial Foundation, www.kokodamemorialfoundation.com.au/; John Phillips, "The Kokoda Memorial," www.rotarnet.com.au/Magazine/articles/sep2002/16.html (accessed 13 Feb. 2007).

99. Nelson 2007, 73–88.

100. "No to mining along PNG's historic Kokoda Trail," 6 Nov. 2007, http://archives.pireport.org/archive/2007/november/11%2D06%2D (accessed 20 Feb. 2008).

101. Naval Construction Division, "Leadership," www.necc.navy.mil/components/seabees/leadership.htm (accessed 14 Feb. 2007).

102. Alistair Crozier, Ministry of Foreign Affairs, New Zealand, 31 May 2006, e-mail to author; Michelle McGillivray, Ministry of Foreign Affairs, 21 May 2007, e-mail to author.

103. Ewan Stevenson, personal communication, 30 May 2006.

104. Inglis 1998; Maclean and Phillips 1990, 82.

105. "Guadalcanal Veterans: Martin Clemens," http://guadalcanal2.homestead.com/canalvets.html (accessed 13 Feb. 2007).

106. Sherrod, "Tarawa Today," *Life*, 5 Aug. 1946, encl. A in Julian Marshall to Commanding General, 5 Oct. 1946, Naval Inspector General's report, JAG.

107. Steven Bullard, personal communication to author, 21 Feb. 2007; Steven Bullard, "The Australia-Japan Research Project," http://ajrp.awm.gov.au/ajrp/ajrp2.nsf/WebI/Chapters/$file/Introduction.pdf?OpenElement, (accessed 22 Feb. 2007). The heading above refers to a Turkish proverb: "Man is harder than iron, stronger than stone and more fragile than a rose."

108. Ienaga 1979, 247–256; Tachibana 1996, 169–173.

109. Tachibana 1996, 169–174.

110. Australia-Japan Research Project, http://www.awm.gov.au/ajrp (accessed 12 Feb. 2007).

111. Ienaga 1979, 236–238; Tachibana 1996, 173–174; Alperovitz 1995, 623;

Ministry of Foreign Affairs, Japan, "Statement by Prime Minister Tomiichi Murayama on the 'Peace, Friendship, and Exchange Initiative,'" http://www.mofa.go.jp/announce/press/pm/murayama/state9408.html (accessed 22 Feb. 2007).

112. Shiro Hara to Sir [D. Cleland], 5 Mar. 1955, A518, GO 16/2/1, Part 2, NAA.

Conclusion

Epigraph: Hopkins 1918, 54.

1. Executive Director, U.S. Board of Economic Warfare, 1 June 1943 and other files at Bureau of Areas and Geographic file of Administrator, 1939–1946, RG 169, NARA.

2. *Annual Report of the Secretary for Fijian Affairs*, 1950, CP 8 of 1952 9, CSO F108/34/1, FNA.

3. Waugh 1992, 171–178; D'Arcy 2006, 102.

4. Robert Keith-Reid, "Fishy tuna money," www.pacificmagazine.net/issue/2003/02/01/fishy-tuna-money; "The Real Problems in the Pacific," www.oceans.greenpeace.org/en/the-expedition/news/problems-in-the-Pacific (accessed 10 May 2007).

5. Gale 1979, 47–88.

6. "Robert Oppenheimer," www.en.wikiquote.org/wiki/Robert_Oppenheimer (accessed 10 Mar. 2007).

7. Firth 1997, 324–357. Permanent genetic damage (chromosome shift) has been proven among New Zealand men on ships near Britain's test sites in the Pacific as recently as April 2007.

8. White 2004, 8.

9. "PNG hopes for best," 6 Nov. 2007, http://archives.pireport.org/archive/2007/november/11%2D27%2D (accessed 20 Feb. 2008).

10. Lewis 1972, 153–180.

11. "Diaspora" is used in the older sense of the word, of seeding and scattering.

12. *PIM*, January 1947, 36.

13. Newspaper reports cited in Beaumont 2004, 74–75.

14. *South Pacific* (1958), Magna Theatre Corporation, Samuel Goldwyn Company, directed by Joshua Logan. The tourist industry in the French Pacific claims Moorea in the Society Islands as the site of these events. http://www.tahiti-tourisme.com/islands/moorea/moorea.asp (accessed 20 Oct. 2008).

15. "James Albert Michener," www.kirjasto.sci.fi/michene.htm (accessed 15 Apr. 2007).

16. E. McCleary, US NCB MU 533, History of U.S. Naval Advanced Bases, Guadalcanal, 1942–1945, 9, Box v. 9304, 313-58-3401 NARA SB.

17. Linderman 1987, 1–3. I thank Russell Johnson for this reference.

18. Jully Makini, personal communication, June 2006, and Tarcisius Tara Kabutaulaka, personal communication, 2 October 2007.

19. "Australia warns citizens traveling to PNG," http://pidp.eastwestcenter.org/pireport/2007/June/06-06-04.htm (accessed 7 June 2007). Scott 2005, 15–16, 28,

33–34, 43–49; Papua New Guinea ranks high in corruption according to Transparency International. http://www.transparency.org/news_room/in_focus/2007/cpi2007/cpi_2007_table (accessed 2 Oct. 2007). Since 1987 Fiji has experienced four coups, but little bloodshed.

20. In Nggela, Solomon Islands dolphins are caught to send to Saudi Arabia, and the islanders use explosives to gather the ten kilos of fish per day needed to feed a dolphin. Paul Roughan, e-mail to author, 24 October 2007.

21. Grigg and Dollar 1990, 439–452; Charles Birkeland, "Status and Issues of Coral Reefs: Statement to the US Commission on Ocean Policy," 14 May 2002, www.oceancommission.gov/meetings/may13_14_02/birkeland_testimony.pdf (accessed 13 Sept. 2007); Jackson 2001, 629–636.

22. Roberts 2000, 53–55.

23. Stockholm International Peace Research Institute 1980, 89–98.

24. Omar, Briskey, Misak, and Asem 2000, 317–337, 338–352.

25. Hay 2000, 402–425.

26. "US Strategic Bombing Survey," http://zfacts.com/p/679.html (accessed 12 Apr. 2007); Littauer and Uphoff 1972, 9, 203.

27. Quinn, Evans, and Boock 2000, 156–170.

28. Flannery 2005, 25, 40–44, 83–94.

29. Tui Atua Tupua Tamasese Ta'isi Efi, "Bio-ethics and the Samoan Indigenous Reference" Keynote Address, UNESCO Bio-ethics Conference, Samoa, 13 November 2007.

30. Klare 2001.

31. Flannery 2005, 159–160, 214–221.

Bibliography

Abdulraheem, Mahmood Y. 2000. "War-Related Damage to the Marine Environment in the Ropme Sea Area." In *The Environmental Consequences of War: Legal, Economic, and Scientific Perspectives*, ed. Jay E. Austin and Carl E. Bruch, 338–352. Cambridge: Cambridge University Press.

Accession cards. Nos. 11576, 11770, 11791, 11966, Peabody Museum, Salem, Massachusetts.

Agricultural Journal of Fiji, 1941–1947. 1942–1948. Suva: Government Printer.

Ahrens, Prue, ed. 2006. *Tour of Paradise: An American Soldier in the South Pacific.* Bayswater, Victoria: Vulgar Press.

Akogina. Diary, Dec. 1942, Mexted Papers, Id 43276, New Zealand Army Memorial Museum, Waiouru, New Zealand.

Alailima, Fay. 1988. *Aggie Grey: A Samoan Saga.* Honolulu: Mutual Publications.

Allen, Bryant J. 1983. "A Bomb or a Bullet or the Bloody Flux? Population Change in Aitape Inland, Papua New Guinea, 1941–1945." *Journal of Pacific History* 18, no. 3–4: 218–235.

Allied Geographic Section. 1942. *Terrain Studies, No. 24, Talasea, New Britain.* Australia: Allied Geographical Section, Southwest Pacific Area.

Allied Geographical Section. 1942. *Terrain Study No. 28, Main Routes Across New Guinea.* Australia: Allied Geographical Section, Southwest Pacific Area.

Allied Geographical Section. 1944. *An annotated bibliography of the Southwest Pacific and adjacent area, Southwest Pacific Area,* vol. 2. Australia: Allied Geographical Section, Southwest Pacific Area.

Allison, James W. Diary, No. 1999. 1717. New Zealand Army Memorial Museum, Waiouru, New Zealand.

Alperovitz, Gar. 1995. *The Decision to Use the Atomic Bomb and the Architecture of an American Myth.* London: Harper Collins.

Alving, Alf S. 1955. "Clinical Treatment of Malaria." In *Recent Advances in Medicine and Surgery (19–30 April 1954),* Vol. II, ed. Walter Reed Army Institute of Research, 209–218. Washington: Army Institute of Research.

ANC, Territorial Archives of New Caledonia, Noumea, 107W, 109W, 145W, 44 W 365, 44 W 367, 44 W 514, 44 W 520, 44 W 682, 44 W 705, 44 W 707, 44 W 709, 44 W 718, 44 W 283, 44 W 308, Cote S J 29.

Angels of War, Canberra: Ronin Home Video, 1984.

Angus, J. R. 1957. *Evolution of a Policy Related to Planned Land Use and the Forest Estate.* British Commonwealth Forestry Conference, 1957. Suva: Government Printer.

Annual Reports of Papua, 1948–1961. Port Moresby: Government Printer, 1948–1962.

Annual Reports of the Territory of New Guinea, 1947–1961. Port Moresby: Government Printer, 1948–1962.

ANZ, Archives New Zealand, Wellington. Files of Army, Air Force, Defence Office, External Affairs, Internal Affairs, Island Territories.

Archibald, H. Munro, and Leonard J. Bruce-Chwatt. 1956. "Suppression of Malaria with Pyrimethmine in Nigerian Schoolchildren." *Bulletin of the World Health Organisation* 15: 775–784.

Armstrong, A. L. c. 1952. Papers, Mss Pac r. 4. Rhodes House Library, Oxford.

Armstrong, Margaret. Visitors Book and memoirs, Mss Pac. s. 93, Rhodes House Library, Oxford.

Arnold, David. 2000, "'Illusory Riches': Representations of the Tropical World, 1840–1950." *Singapore Journal of Tropical Geography* 21, no. 1: 6–18.

Ashton, W. R. 1998. "An Enjoyable War?" Unpublished manuscript, writer's copy.

Austin, Jay E., and Carl E. Bruch, eds. 2000. *The Environmental Consequences of War: Legal, Economic, and Scientific Perspectives.* Cambridge: Cambridge University Press.

Australian Dictionary of Biography, Vol. 15, 1966–2002 [Melbourne], London, New York: Melbourne University Press, Cambridge University Press.

Australian War Memorial. 1945. *Jungle Warfare: With the Australian Army in the SW Pacific.* Canberra: Australian War Memorial.

AWM, Australian War Memorial, Canberra. Personal records, letters, manuscripts, and memoirs; AWM 43, 52, 54, 67, 93, 254.

Bailey, Beth, and David Farber. 2006. "The Fighting Man as Tourist: The Politics of Tourist Culture in Hawaii during World War II." *Pacific Historical Review* 65, no. 4: 641–660.

Baker, Benjamin. 1964. "The Suppression of Malaria." In *Internal Medicine in World War II, Vol. II: Infectious Diseases,* ed. John Boyd Coates, 465–476. Washington, D.C.: Office of the Surgeon General, Department of the Army.

Baker, J. V. T. 1965. *The New Zealand People at War: War Economy.* Wellington: Department of Internal Affairs.

Baker, R. H. "Some Effects of the War on the Wildlife of Micronesia." *Transactions of the Eleventh North American Wildlife Conference, 1946.* Washington, D.C.: American Wildlife Institute.

Barnhart, Michael. 1987. *Japan Prepares for Total War.* Ithaca, N.Y.: Cornell University Press.

Barrowclough Papers, New Zealand Army Memorial Museum, Waiouru, New Zealand.

Barrow, G. c. 1946. "Outlying Interlude," Mss Pac s. 43, Rhodes House, Oxford.

Bayliss-Smith, Tim, Edvard Hviding, and Tim Whitmore. 2003. "Rainforest Composition and Human Disturbance in Solomon Islands." *Ambio* 32, no. 5 (Aug): 346–352.

Beaumont, Joan. 1996. "Australia's War: Asia and the Pacific." In *Australia's War 1939–45*, ed. Joan Beaumont, 26–53. St. Leonards, Sydney: Allen and Unwin.

———. 2004. "Australian Memory and the US Wartime Alliance: The Australian-American Memorial and the Battle of the Coral Sea." *War and Society* 22, no. 1 (May): 69–87.

Bell, Roger J. 1977. *Unequal Allies: Australian American Relations and the Pacific War.* Melbourne: Melbourne University Press.

Belshaw, Cyril S. 1950. *Island Administration in the South West Pacific.* London and New York: Royal Institute of International Affairs.

Belshaw, H., and V. D. Stace. 1955. *A Programme for Economic Development in the Cook Islands.* Prepared for 1955 Session of the Cook Islands Legislative Council. Wellington: Government Printer.

Bennett, Judith A. 1987. *Wealth of the Solomons: A History of Trade, Plantations and Society 1800–1978.* Honolulu: University of Hawaiʻi Press.

———. 1993. "'We do not come here to be beaten': Resistance and the Plantation System in the Solomon Islands to World War II." In *Plantation Workers: Resistance and Accommodation,* ed. Brij V. Lal, D. Munro, and E. D. Beechert, 129–183. Honolulu, University of Hawaiʻi Press.

———. 2000. *Pacific Forest: A History of Resource Control and Contest in Solomon Islands, c. 1800–1997.* Cambridge, Leiden: White Horse Press, Brill Academic Press.

———. 2001a. "War, Emergency and the Environment: Fiji, 1939–1946." *Environment and History* 7, no. 3: 255–287.

———. 2001b. "Germs or Rations: Beriberi and the Japanese Labour Experiment in Colonial Fiji and Queensland." *Pacific Studies* 24, no. 3/4: 1–18.

———. 2003. "Local Resource Use in the Pacific War with Japan: Logging in Western Melanesia." *War and Society* 21, no. 1 (May): 83–118.

———. 2004. "Fears and Aspirations: US Military Intelligence Operations on the South Pacific, 1941–1945." *Journal of Pacific History* 39, no. 3: 283–307.

Bentley, Geoffrey. "The Men behind the Fliers," No. 43195, New Zealand Army Memorial Museum, Waiouru, New Zealand.

Bergerud, Eric. 1996. *Touched with Fire: The Land War in the South Pacific.* New York: Penguin Books.

Beros, H. "Bert." 1943. "The Fuzzy Wuzzy Angels." *Women's Weekly*, Sydney. 9 Jan.

Berube, Allan. 1990. *Coming Out Under Fire: A History of Gay Men and Women in World War Two.* New York: Free Press.

Bhabha, Homi. 1994. *The Location of Culture.* New York: Routledge.

Bice, C. 1881. *The Island Voyage, 1880.* Ludlow, U.K.: The Melanesian Mission.

———. 1883. *Melanesian Mission Report for 1883.* Ludlow, U.K.: The Melanesian Mission.

Billings Papers, Macmillan Brown Library, Christchurch, New Zealand.

Black, Robert H. 1955. *Malaria in the South-West Pacific.* Noumea: South Pacific Commission.

Bonnemaison, Joël. 1994. *The Tree and the Canoe: History and Ethnography of Tanna.* Honolulu: University of Hawai'i Press.

Boone, Joel T. 1941. "The Sexual Aspects of Military Personnel." *Journal of Social Hygiene* 27, no. 3 (March): 113–124.

Bowd, Reuben R. E. 2005. *A Basis for Victory: The Allied Geographic Section 1942–1946.* Canberra: Strategic and Defence Studies Centre, Australian National University.

Brackman, Arnold C. 1987. *The Other Nuremberg, The Untold Story of the Tokyo War Crimes Trials.* New York: Morrow.

British Solomon Islands Protectorate government.

1948, 1953–1958. *Annual Report on the British Solomon Islands for the year(s) . . .* London: HMSO.

1959–1967. *Annual Report on the British Solomon Islands for the year(s) . . .* Honiara: BSIP/London: HMSO.

Brittain, A. 1888. *Report of the Island Voyage for 1887.* Ludlow, U.K.: The Melanesian Mission.

Brooks, Fred. 2000. *Cultivar Resistance to Taro Leaf Blight Disease in American Samoa.* Technical report No. 33. Pago Pago, American Samoa: American Samoa Community College Land Grant Program.

Broome, Richard. 1982. *Aboriginal Australians: Black Responses to White Dominance, 1788–1980.* Sydney: George Allen and Unwin.

Brun, Luc-Olivier, J. T. Wilson, and A. Daynes. 1983. "Ethion Resistance in the Cattle Tick (Boophilus microplus) in New Caledonia." *Tropical Pest Management* 29, no. 1: 16–22.

Buckley, K., and K. Klugman. 1983. *The Australian Presence in the Pacific: Burns Philp 1914–1946.* Sydney: George Allen and Unwin.

Bullard, Steven. 2004. "'The great enemy of humanity.' Malaria and the Japanese Medical Corps in Papua, 1942–43." *Journal of Pacific History* 39, no. 2: 203–220.

Bullard, Steven, and Tamura Keiko, eds. 2004. *From a Hostile Shore: Australia and Japan at War in New Guinea.* Canberra: Australian War Memorial.

Burke, John. Correspondence: Burke to Weitzner, 18 Oct. 1945, Burke to Shapiro, 7 Mar. 1946, and Accession catalogue, 80.1, numbers 289–348, 495–533, pp. 20–21, 26–27, Division of Anthropology Archives, American Museum of Natural History.

[Burke, John]. 1945. United States Naval History of Tutuila, c. Aug., Microfilm NRS II-387, Navy Yard Museum, Washington, D.C.

Burton, John. 1983. "A Dysentery Epidemic in New Guinea and its Mortality." *Journal of Pacific History* 18, no. 3–4: 236–261.

Butlin, S. J. 1955. *War Economy, 1939–1942.* Canberra: Australian War Memorial.

Butlin, S. J., and C. B. Schedvin. 1977. *War Economy, 1942–1945.* Canberra: Australian War Memorial.

Buxton, P. A. 1927. *Researches in Polynesia and Melanesia: An Account of Investigations in Samoa, Tonga, the Ellice Group, and the New Hebrides, in 1924, 1925, Parts I–IV.* London: London School of Hygiene and Tropical Medicine.

Byrd, Admiral Richard E. Papers, The Ohio State University Archives.

Campbell, I. C. 1999. "New Zealand and the Mau in Samoa: Reassessing the Cause of a Colonial Protest Movement." *New Zealand Journal of History* 33, no. 1: 92–100.

———. 2001. *Island Kingdom: Tonga Ancient and Modern.* Rev. ed. Christchurch: Canterbury University Press.

———. 2003. *Worlds Apart: A History of the Pacific Islands.* Christchurch: Canterbury University Press.

Capps, Richard B. 1963. "Dengue." In *Internal Medicine in World War II, Infectious Diseases, Vol. II,* ed. John Boyd Coates, 59–78.Washington, D.C.: Office of the Surgeon General, Department of the Army.

Carron, L. T. 1985. *A History of Forestry in Australia.* Canberra: Australian National University Press.

Carson, Rachel. 1962. *Silent Spring.* Boston: Houghton Mifflin.

Cervi, Gregg Anthony. 1999. "War Wrecks and the Environment: Who's Responsible for the Legacy of War? A Case Study: Solomon Islands and the United States." *Journal of Environmental Law and Litigation* 14: 351–399.

Challis, R. L. 1953. *Social Problems of Non-Maori Polynesians in New Zealand.* Noumea: South Pacific Commission.

Chang, Iris. 1998. *The Rape of Nanking: The Forgotten Holocaust of World War II.* Ringwood, Victoria: Penguin.

Chapman, Wilbert M. 1949. *Fishing in Troubled Waters.* Philadelphia: Lippincott.

Chouchi, Nazli, Robert C. North, and Susumu Yamakage. 1992. *The Challenge of Japan before World War II and After.* New York: Routledge, Chapman and Hall.

Christophers, S. Rickard. 1940. "The Treatment of Malaria and Some Points about the Drugs in Use against This Disease." *Transactions of the Royal Society of Tropical Medicine and Hygiene* 36: 49–59.

Cline, Dennis. 2002. *Skeeter Beaters: Memories of the South Pacific, 1941–1945.* Rogers, Minn.: DeForest Press.

Codrington, R. H. Papers. Mss Pac, s. 9, Rhodes House Library, Oxford, England.

Colborne, M. J. 1955. "The Effect of Malaria Suppression in a Group of Accra School Children." *Transactions of the Royal Society of Tropical Medicine and Hygiene* 49, no. 4 (July): 356–369.

Collector of Customs. 1931–1957. *Return of the Trade, Commerce, and Shipping of the Territory of Western Samoa, 1930–1956.* Wellington: Government Printer.

Condon-Rall, Mary Ellen. 1995. "The Role of the US Army in the Fight against Malaria, 1940–1944." *War and Society* 13, no. 2 (Oct.): 99–105.

———. 2000. "Malaria in the Southwest Pacific in World War Two." In *Science and the Pacific War,* ed. Roy M. McLeod, 51–70. Dordrech: Springer.

Connell, John. 1978. "The Death of Taro: Local Response to a Change of Subsistence Crops in the Northern Solomon Islands." *Mankind* 11, no. 4: 445–452.

———. 1987. *New Caledonia or Kanaky? The Political History of a French Colony.* Canberra: National Centre for Development Studies, Australian National University.

Connell, John, and Richard P. C. Brown. March 2005. *Remittances in the Pacific: An Overview.* Manila: Asian Development Bank.

Cook, Haruko Taya, and Theodore F. Cook. 1992. *Japan at War: An Oral History.* New York: New Press.

Cooke, John. 1983. *Working in Papua New Guinea 1931–1946.* Upper Mt. Gravatt, Brisbane: Lahara Publications.

[Cooper, Harold]. 1946. *Among Those Present: The Official Story of the Pacific Islands at War.* London: H.M.S.O.

Cooper, W. Clark. 1949. "Summary of Antimalarial Drugs." *Public Health Reports* 64, no. 23 (10 June): 717–721.

Costello, John. 1982. *The Pacific War 1941–1945.* New York: Quill.

Counts, David. 1989. "Shadows of War: Changing Remembrance through Twenty Years in New Britain." In *The Pacific Theater: Island Representations of World War II,* ed. Geoffrey M. White and Lamont Lindstrom, 187–203. Honolulu: University of Hawai'i Press.

Cox, Bryan. 1987. *Too Young to Die: The Story of a New Zealand Fighter Pilot in the Pacific War.* Auckland: Century Hutchinson.

Crawford, J. G., C. M. Donald, C. P. Dowsett, and D. B. Williams. 1954. "Wartime Agriculture in Australia, 1939–1950." In *Wartime Agriculture in Australia and New Zealand 1939–1950,* ed. J. G. Crawford, C. M. Donald, C. P. Dowsett, D. B. Williams, and A. A. Ross, 107–115. Stanford, Calif.: Stanford University Press.

Cranwell, L. M., J. E. Green, and A. W. B. Powell, 1943. *Food Is Where You Find It: A Guide to Emergency Foods of the Western Pacific.* Auckland: Auckland Institute and Museum.

Crouch, Joan. 1986. *A Special Kind of Service: The Story of the 2/9 Australian General Hospital, 1940–1946.* Chippendale, N.S.W.: Alternative Publishing Co-operative Ltd.

"Dad's diary" (New Zealand), 1942, copy in writer's care.

Daggy, Richard H. 1945. "The Biology and Seasonal Cycle of *Anopheles farauti* on Espiritu Santo, New Hebrides." *Annals of the Entomological Society of America* 38, no 1: 1–13.

D'Arcy, Paul. 2006. *The People of the Sea: Environment, Identity, and History in Oceania* Honolulu: University of Hawai'i Press.

Davenport, William H. 1989. "Taemfaet: Experiences and Reactions of Santa Cruz

Islanders during the Battle for Guadalcanal." In *The Pacific Theater: Island Representations of World War II*, ed. Geoffrey M. White and Lamont Lindstrom, 257–278. Honolulu: University of Hawai'i Press.

Daws, Gavan. 1994. *Prisoners of the Japanese: POWS of World War II in the Pacific.* New York: William Morrow.

Denfeld, Duane Colt. 1989. "Guarding the South Pacific: American Samoa Bases." *Journal of the Council on America's Military Past* 15, no. 4 (Jan.): 36–48.

Dennis, Maxine. 1981. "Plantations." In *A Time to Plant and a Time to Uproot: A History of Agriculture in Papua New Guinea*, ed. Donald Denoon and Catherine Snowden, 219–248. Port Moresby: Department of Primary Industry and Institute of New Guinea Studies.

Denoon, Donald, and Catherine Snowden, eds. 1981. *A Time to Plant and a Time to Uproot: A History of Agriculture in Papua New Guinea.* Port Moresby: Department of Primary Industry and Institute of New Guinea Studies.

Denoon, Donald, Stewart Firth, Jocelyn Linneken, Malama Meleisea, and Karen Nero, eds. 1997. *The Cambridge History of the Pacific Islanders.* Cambridge: Cambridge University Press.

Department of History, University of Papua and New Guinea. 1972–1979. *Oral History.* Boroko: University of Papua and New Guinea.

Desquesnes, Marc. 1988. "Boophilus Microplus, Biologie et Modes de Lutte, Applications à la Nouvelle-Calédonie." Thèse, Doctorat Vétérinaire, Ecole Nationale Vété rinaire d'Alfort, France.

Dod, Karl C. 1966. *US Army in World War II: The Corps of Engineers: The War against Japan.* Washington, D.C.: U.S. Government Printing Office.

Donnelly, Terry. "A Sergeant at Arms," No. 2003.38, New Zealand Army Memorial Museum, Waiouru, New Zealand.

Dorman, T. E. 1997. *The Green War.* Christchurch: Caxton Press.

Dorsey, Kurk. 2004. "Compromise and Conservation: World War Two and American Leadership in Whaling Diplomacy." In *Natural Enemy, Natural Ally: Toward an Environmental History of War*, ed. Richard Tucker and Edmund Russell, 252–269. Corvallis: Oregon State University Press.

Dotto, L, and H. Schiff. 1978. *The Ozone War.* New York: Doubleday.

Douglas, Ngaire. 1996. *They Came for Savages: 100 Years of Tourism in Melanesia.* Lismore, N.S.W.: Southern Cross University.

Downs, Ian. 1980. *The Australian Trusteeship Papua New Guinea 1945–1975.* Canberra: Australian Government Publishing Service.

———. 1987. *The Last Mountain: A Life in Papua New Guinea.* St. Lucia, Brisbane: University of Queensland Press.

Downs, W. G., P. A. Harper, and E. T. Lisansky. 1947. "Epidemiology of Insect Borne Diseases in Army Troops." *Supplement to the American Journal of Tropical Medicine* 27, no. 3 (May): 69–89.

Dunnigan, James F., and Albert A. Nofi. 1998. *The Pacific War Encyclopedia.* New York: Checkmark Books.

Durham, J. Frank. 2003. *You Only Blow Yourself Up Once.* As Told to Doug Hay. New York: iUniverse.

Dyer, George C. 1972. *The Amphibians Came to Conquer: The Story of Admiral Richmond Kelly Turner.* Washington, D.C: U.S. Dept. of the Navy.

Early, Lisa. 1998. "'If we win the women': The Lives and Work of Female Missionaries at the Methodist Mission in Solomon Islands, 1902–1940." PhD dissertation, University of Otago, New Zealand.

Ellis, Albert. 1946. *Mid-Pacific Outposts.* Auckland: Brown and Stewart.

Elrick, George. n.d. "The Solomons," chapters 1–24. Misc. Papers, Army Museum, Waiouru, New Zealand.

Essai, Brian. 1961. *Papua and New Guinea: A Contemporary Survey.* Melbourne: Melbourne University Press.

Eustis, Nelson. 1979. *Aggie Grey of Samoa.* Adelaide: Hobby Investments.

Faivre, J.-P., J. Poirier, and P. Routhier. 1955. *La Nouvelle-Calédonie: Géographie et histoire economie, demographie.* Paris: Nouvelles editions latines.

Feldt, Eric. 1967. *The Coast Watchers.* Sydney: Angus and Robertson.

Fenner, F. 1998. "Malaria Control in Papua New Guinea in the Second World War: From Disaster to Successful Prophylaxis and the Dawn of DDT." *Parassitologia* 40: 57–59.

Fetchko, Peter J. 1974. "The Pacific Collections of the Peabody Museum of Salem." *South Pacific Bulletin* (Fourth Quarter): 54–57.

Feuer, Lewis S. 1946a. "Cartel Control in New Caledonia." *Far Eastern Survey* 15, no. 12 (19 June): 184–187.

———. 1946b. "End of Coolie Labour in New Caledonia." *Far Eastern Review* (Aug.): 264–267.

Field, Michael J. 1984. *Mau. Samoa's Struggle against New Zealand Oppression.* Wellington: A. H. & A. W. Reed.

Fifi'i, Jonathan. 1989. *From Pig-Theft to Parliament: My Life Between Two Worlds.* Translated and edited by Roger Keesing. Suva: Institute of Pacific Studies and the Solomon Islands Extension Centre of University of the South Pacific.

Fiji Government.

Annual Reports 1941–1946. 1942–1947. Department of Agriculture. Suva: Government Printer.

Annual Report of the Forestry Department, 1939. 1940. Suva: Government Printer.

Annual Report of the Medical Department, 1940. 1941. Suva: Government Printing Office.

Annual Report of the Medical Department, 1943. 1944. Suva: Government Printing Office.

Annual Report of the Secretary for Fijian Affairs, 1950. 1952. Suva: Government Printer.

Council Paper No. 51, 12 Oct. 1934. 1934. Legislative Council. Suva: Government Printer.

Council Paper No. 1, 31 Oct. 1943. 1944. Legislative Council. Suva: Government Printer.

Council Papers Nos. 2 and 3, 1944. 1944. Legislative Council. Suva: Government Printer.

Council Paper No. 26, 2 Dec. 1944. 1944. Legislative Council. Suva: Government Printer.

Council Paper No. 12, 17 Mar. 1947. 1947. Legislative Council. Suva: Government Printer.

Legislative Council Debates, 17 May 1943. 1944. Suva: Government Printer.

Memorandum for the United States Board of Economic Warfare Mission. February 1943. Supply and Production Board. Suva: Government Printer.

Report on Manpower, 1942. Suva: Government Printer.

Report of Secretary for Fijian Affairs, 1945. 1947. Suva: Government Printer.

The Forests of the Colony of Fiji. 1933. Suva: Government Printer.

Trocas Shell Fishing with Modern Diving Equipment. 12 Oct. 1934. Suva: Government Printer.

Fiji National Archives (FNA).

Series Colonial Secretary Office, Suva.

Fiji Times. 1942–1946. Suva.

Firth, R. 1946. *Malay Fishermen: Their Peasant Economy.* London: K. Paul, Trench and Trubner and Co. Ltd.

Firth, Stewart. 1997a. "The War in the Pacific." In Donald Denoon, Stewart Firth, Jocelyn Linneken, Malama Meleisea, and Karen Nero, eds., *The Cambridge History of the Pacific Islanders,* 311–322. Cambridge: Cambridge University Press.

———. 1997b. "Nuclear Pacific." In Donald Denoon, Stewart Firth, Jocelyn Linneken, Malama Meleisea, and Karen Nero, eds., *The Cambridge History of the Pacific Islanders,* 324–357. Cambridge: Cambridge University Press.

Fisher, Harvey I. 1949. "Populations on Midway and the Man-Made Factors Affecting Them." *Pacific Science* 3 (April): 103–110.

Fitzgerald, Donald T. 1992. "Air Ferry Routes Across the South Pacific." In *Builders and Fighters: US Army Corps of Engineers,* ed. Barry W. Fowle, 47–64. Fort Belvoir, Va.: Office of History.

Flannery, Tim. 2005. *The Weather Makers: The History and Future Impact of Climate Change.* Melbourne: Text Publishing.

Foale, Simon. 2006. "The Intersection of Scientific and Indigenous Ecological Knowledge in Coastal Melanesia: Implications for Contemporary Marine Resource Management." *International Social Science Journal* 58, no. 187 (March): 129–137.

Foord, Malcolm. 1996. *The Fortunate Soldier: With the New Zealand Army on Tongatabu 1943.* Dunedin: Published by the author.

Fosberg, F. R. 1953. "The Naturalized Flora of Micronesia and World War II." *Eighth Pacific Science Congress.* Manila: University of the Philippines Campus.

Franco, Robert W. 1985. "Samoan Perceptions of Work: Moving Up and Moving Around." PhD dissertation, University of Hawai'i.

———. 1989. "Military Work and International Movement from Samoa." In *The Pacific Theater: Island Representations of World War II*, ed. Geoffrey M. White and Lamont Lindstrom, 379–393. Honolulu: University of Hawai'i Press.

Frisbie, Florence (Johnny). 1948. *Miss Ulysses from Puka-Puka: The Autobiography of a South Sea Trader's Daughter.* Macmillan: New York.

Fritts, Thomas H., and Gordon H. Rodda. 1998. "The Role of Introduced Species in the Degradation of Island Ecosystems: A Case History of Guam." *Annual Review of Ecological Systemics* 29: 113–140.

Frost, Alan. 1996. "The Antipodean Exchange: European Horticulture and Imperial Designs." In *Visions of Empire: Voyages, Botany, and Representations of Nature*, ed. David Philip Miller and Peter Hanns Reill, 58–79. Cambridge: Cambridge University Press.

Frost, Richard. 1992. *Enigmatic Proconsul: Sir Philip Mitchell and the Twilight of Empire.* London and New York: Radcliffe Press.

Gald, David. 1943. Diary, Micro MS 583, National Library of New Zealand, Wellington.

Gale, Roger W. 1979. *The Americanization of Micronesia: A Study in the Consolidation of U. S. Rule in the Pacific.* Washington D.C.: University Press of America.

Gardner, Helen Bethea. 2006. *Gathering for God: George Brown in Oceania.* Dunedin: Otago University Press.

Gargominy, Olivier. 1993. *Les introductions d'especes animales et vegetales en Nouvelle--Calédonie.* Rennes: Ecole Nationale Superieure Agronomique et ORSTROM.

Gatty, Harold. 1953. "The Use of Fish Poison Plants in the Pacific." *Fiji Society of Science and Industry* 3: 152–159.

Gegeo, David. 1989. "World War II Experiences." In *The Pacific Theater: Island Representations of World War II*, ed. Geoffrey M. White and Lamont Lindstrom, 353–371. Honolulu: University of Hawai'i Press.

General Staff, Land Head Quarters Australia, 1943. *Friendly Fruits and Vegetables.* Melbourne: General Staff, Land Head Quarters.

George, J. B. 1947. *Shot Fired in Anger.* Plantersville, S.C.: Small Arms Technical Publishing Company.

Geslin, Yves. 1956 "Les Américains aux Nouvelle-Hébrides." *Journal de la Société des Océanistes* 12, no. 12 (Dec): 245–286.

G. F. R. 1946. "New Caledonia and the War." *Pacific Affairs* 19, no. 4 (Dec.): 373–383.

Gillespie, Oliver A. 1945a. *Shovel, Sword and Scalpel.* [Wellington, N.Z.]: A.H. and A.W. Reed for the Third Division Histories Committee.

———, ed. 1945b. *Pacific Pioneers.* Wellington: A. H. and A. W. Reed.

———. 1954. "Les Néo-Zélandais en Nouvelle-Calédonie pendant la seconde guerre mondiale." *Journal de la Société des Océanistes* 10, no. 10 (Dec.): 111–132.

Gillion, K. L. 1977. *The Fiji Indians: Challenge to European Dominance, 1920–1946.* Canberra: Australian National University Press.

Gilson, Richard. 1980. *The Cook Islands 1820–1950.* Edited by Ron Crocombe. [Wellington]: Victoria University Press in association with the Institute of Pacific Studies of the University of the South Pacific.

Gina, Lloyd Maepeza. 2003. *Journeys in a Small Canoe: The Life and Times of a Solomon Islander.* Edited by Judith A. Bennett with Khyla J. Russell. Canberra: Pandanus Press.

Goode, James. Papers, Mss Pac s. 112, Rhodes House Library, Oxford.

Goodwin, Bridget. 1998. *Keen as Mustard: Britain's Horrific Chemical Warfare Experiments in Australia.* St. Lucia, Brisbane: University of Queensland Press.

Gordon, Bertram M. 1998. "Warfare and Tourism: Paris in World War II." *Annals of Tourism Research,* 25, no. 3, 616–638.

Grattan, F. J. H. 1948. *An Introduction to Samoan Custom.* Apia: Samoa Printing and Publishing Co.

Gray, Anthony W. 1997. "Joint Logistics in the Pacific Theater." In *The Big L: American Logistics in World War II,* ed. Alan Gropman, 293–338. Washington, D.C.: National University Press.

Great Britain, National Archives. Colonial Office Series 83, 225, 968, 1036; Foreign Office Series 115, 371, 375; War Office Series 106; Dominions Office Series 35. Kew, London.

Gregg, Charles T. 1984. *Tarawa.* New York: Stein and Day.

Griffin, James, Hank Nelson, and Stewart Firth. 1979. *Papua New Guinea: A Political History.* Melbourne: Heinemann Educational Australia.

Grigg, Richard W., and Steven J. Dollar. 1990. "Natural and Anthropogenic Disturbance on Coral Reefs." In *Ecosystems of the World 25 – Coral Reefs,* ed. Z. Dubinky, 439–452. Amsterdam: Elsevier.

Gropman, Alan, ed. 1997. *The Big L: American Logistics in World War II.* Washington, D.C.: National University Press.

Guillaumin, A. 1953. "L'Evolution de la flore Néo-Calédonienne." *Journal de la Société des Océanistes* 9, no. 9 (Dec.): 78-85.

Gunther, Carl. 1946. "New Conceptions of Malaria Control." *Medical Journal of Australia* (April): 510–512.

Guthrie, Margaret W. 1979. *Misi Utu: Dr. D.W. Hoodless and the Development of Medical Education in the South Pacific.* Suva, Fiji: Institute of Pacific Studies, University of the South Pacific in association with the South Pacific Social Sciences Association.

Gwero, James. 1988. "Oral Histories of World War II from Northern Vanuatu." *O'o: A Journal of Solomon Islands Studies* 4: 37–43.

Haddon Papers, Cambridge University Library, Cambridge.

Hairson, N. G., F. B. Bang, and J. Maier. 1947. "Malaria in the Natives of New Guinea." *Transactions of the Royal Society of Tropical Medicine and Hygiene* 40, no. 6 (July): 795–807.

Hall, H. Duncan. 1955. *History of the Second World War: North American Supply.* London: HMSO.

Harper, P. A., E. T. Lisansky, and B. E. Sasse. 1947. "General Aspects and Control Measures." *Supplement to the American Journal of Tropical Medicine* 27, no. 3: 1–68.

Harper, Paul A., Wilber G. Downs, Paul W. Oman, and Norman D. Levine. 1963. "New Hebrides, Solomon Islands, Saint Matthias Group, and Ryukyu Islands." In *Preventive Medicine in World War II, Communicable Diseases, Malaria,* Vol. VI, ed. John Boyd Coates, Jr. et al., 399–495. Washington, D.C.: Office of the Surgeon General, Department of the Army.

Harris, Sheldon H. 2002. *Factories of Death.* Rev. ed. New York and London: Routledge.

Harrison, Mark. 2000. *The Economics of World War II.* Cambridge: Cambridge University Press.

Hart, Thomas A., and William A. Hardenburgh. 1963. "The Southwest Pacific Area." In *Preventive Medicine in World War II, Communicable Diseases, Malaria,* Vol. VI, ed. John Boyd Coates, Jr. et al., 513–578. Washington D.C.: Office of the Surgeon General, Department of the Army.

Hasluck, Paul. 1970. *The Government and the People 1942–1945.* Canberra: Australian War Memorial.

Haugland, Vern. 1944. *Letter from New Guinea.* London: Hammond, Hammond and Co. Ltd.

Hawaiian Buckaroo, dir. Ray Taylor. Soo Lesser, 1938.

Hay, Alistair W. M. 2000. "Defoliants: The Long-Term Health Implications." In *The Environmental Consequences of War: Legal, Economic, and Scientific Perspectives,* ed. Jay E. Austin and Carl E. Bruch, 402–425. Cambridge: Cambridge University Press.

Hay, J. R. "Airforce Interlude." MSX-4862, National Library of New Zealand, Wellington.

Hayman, Joseph M. 1968. "Filariasis," In *Internal Medicine in World War II, Infectious Diseases and General Medicine,* Vol. III, ed. John Boyd Coates, Jr. et al., 123–144. Washington, D.C.: Office of the Surgeon General, Department of the Army.

Healy, A. M. 1967. *A History of the Development of the Bulolo Region, New Guinea.* New Guinea Research Bulletin, No 15. Canberra: Australian National University.

Heberle, Simon. 1996. "Explanations for Palaeoecological Changes in the Northern Plains of Guadalcanal, Solomon Islands: The Last 3200 years." *The Holocene* 6, no. 3: 333–338.

Helu, I. F. 1998. "Changing Values and Changed Psychology of Tongans During and Since World War II." In *Echoes of Pacific War,* ed. Deryck Scarr, Niel Gunson, and Jennifer Terrell, 31–37. Canberra: Division of Pacific and Asian History, Australian National University Press.

Henningham, Stephen. 1992. *France and the South Pacific: A Contemporary History.* Honolulu: University of Hawai'i Press.

———. 1994. "The French Administration, The Local Population, and the American Presence in New Caledonia," *Journal de la Societé des Océanistes* 1: 21–42.

———. 1994/95. "Labour Resistance and a Challenged Colonial Order: The Asian Workforce in New Caledonia and the New Hebrides at the Time of the Second World War." *Journal of Pacific Studies* 18: 151–183.

Henson, Pamela M. 2000. "The Smithsonian Goes to War: The Increase and Diffusion of Scientific Knowledge in the Pacific." In *Science and the Pacific War*, ed. M. MacLeod, 27–50. Dordrecht, Boston, and London: Springer.

Herle, Anita, Nick Stanley, Karen Stevenson, and Robert L. Welsch. 2002. *Pacific Art: Persistence, Change and Meaning.* Honolulu: University of Hawai'i Press.

Hess, Gary. 1987. *The United States' Emergence as a Southeast Asian Power.* New York: Columbia University Press.

Heyen, G. H., comp. 1937. *Sailing Directions on Navigation in between the Islands and Atolls of the Gilbert Islands.* Suva, Fiji: Government Printer.

Highland, Sam. 1991. "World War II in Kiribati." In Geoffrey M. White, ed. 1991. *Remembering the Pacific War*, 109–112. Honolulu: Center for Pacific Studies, University of Hawai'i.

Hilder, Brett. 1961. *Navigator in the South Seas.* London: Percival Marshall and Co.

Hiromi, Tanaka. 2004a. "Japan in the Pacific War and New Guinea." In *From a Hostile Shore: Australia and Japan at War in New Guinea*, ed. Steven Bullard and Tamura Keiko, 28–40. Canberra: Australian War Memorial.

———. 2004b. "Japanese Forces in Post-Surrender Rabaul." In *From a Hostile Shore: Australia and Japan at War in New Guinea*, ed. Steven Bullard and Tamura Keiko, 138–152. Canberra: Australian War Memorial.

Hiromitsu, Iwamoto. 1999. "Japanese Occupation of Rabaul, 1942–1945." Paper pre sented at Pacific War in Papua New Guinea: Perceptions and Realities, Symposium, Division of Pacific and Asian History, ANU, 1–9 Sept.

Hogbin, H. I. 1946. "The Trobriand Islands, 1945." *Man* XLVI, no. 48–69 (May–June): 72.

Hooper, Anthony, and Judith Huntsman, trans. 1991. *Matagi Tokelau: History and Traditions of Tokelau.* Suva and Apia: Institute of Pacific Studies and Office for Tokelau Affairs.

Hopkins, Gerard Manley. 1918. *Poems of Gerard Manley Hopkins.* Edited with notes by Robert Bridges. London: Humphery Milford.

Hopkins, J. 1980. "Hawaiian Music and Dance." In *Hawaii*, ed. L. Lueras, 329–338. Hong Kong: Apa.

Horn, Arthur E. 1933. "The Control of Disease in Tropical Africa: Part II." *Journal of the Royal African Society* 32, no. 127 (April): 123–134.

Hornell, James. 1940. *Report on the Fisheries of Fiji.* Suva, Fiji: Government Printer.

Horton, D. C. 1970. *Fire over the Islands.* Sydney: Reed.

Howe, K. R. 1977. *Race Relations: Australia and New Zealand: A Comparative Survey 1770s–1970s.* Wellington: Methuen.

Howlett, R. A., comp. 1948. *The History of the Fiji Military Forces, 1939–1945.* Suva, Fiji: Government Printer.

Hughes, Helen, and Gauvai Sodhi, 2006. *Should Australia and New Zealand Open their*

Doors to Guest Workers from the Pacific? St. Leonards, Sydney: Centre for Independent Studies.

Hughes, William. 1942. "The Treatment of Malaria in a Hyperendemic Zone." *Transactions of the Royal Society of Tropical Medicine and Hygiene* 36, no. 2: 60–74.

Huie, William Bradford. 1944. *Can Do! The Story of the Seabees.* New York: Dutton.

Hviding, Edvard. 1996. *Guardians of Marovo Lagoon.* Honolulu: University of Hawai'i Press.

Hyndman, David. 2001. "Academic Responsibilities and Representation of the Ok Tedi Crisis in Postcolonial Papua New Guinea." *The Contemporary Pacific* 13, no. 1: 33–54.

Ienaga, Saburō. 1979. *Japan's Last War: World War II and the Japanese, 1931–1945.* Oxford: Basil Blackwell.

Inglis, K. S. 1987. "Passing Away." In *Australians 1938*, ed. Bill Gammage and Peter Spearritt, 235–253. Broadway, N.S.W.: Fairfax, Syme and Welden.

———. 1998. *Sacred Places: War Memorials in the Australian Landscape.* Melbourne: Melbourne University Press.

Iremonger, Lucille. 1948. *It's a Bigger Life.* London: Hutchinson.

Irwin, George. 1965. *Samoa: A Teacher's Tale.* London: Cassell.

Iwamoto, Hiromitsu. 1999a. Japanese Occupation of Rabaul, 1942–1945. Paper presented at The Pacific War in Papua New Guinea: Perceptions and Realities, Symposium, International Research Project, Canberra: Australian National University, Sept.

———. 1999b. *Nanshin: Japanese Settlers in Papua and New Guinea.* Canberra: Journal of Pacific History.

Jachowski, Leo A., and Gilbert Otto. 1952 "Filariasis in American Samoa." *American Journal of Tropical Medicine and Hygiene* 1: 663–670.

Jackson, Donald. 1989. *Torokina: A Wartime Memoir, 1941–1945.* Ames: Iowa State University Press.

Jackson, J. B. C. 1997. "Reefs since Columbus." *Coral Reefs* 16, Supp.: S23–32.

Jackson, Jeremy B. C., et al. 2001. "Historical Overfishing and the Recent Collapse of Coastal Ecosystems." *Science* 293 (12 July): 629–637.

Jaffe, Mark. 1997. *And No Birds Sing: A True Ecological Thriller Set in a Tropical Paradise.* New York: Barricade Books, Incorporated.

Jameson, S. C. 1975. "Toxic Effect of the Explosive Depth Charge Chemicals From the Ship Sankisan Maru on the Coral Reef Fish *Dascyllus aruanus.*" *Micronesia* 11 no. 1: 109–113.

Jarvis, Christina. 2004. *The Male Body at War: American Masculinity during World War II.* DeKalb: Northern Illinois University Press.

Jenks, Andrew. 2007. "Model City USA: The Environmental Cost of Victory in World War II and the Cold War." *Environmental History* 12, no. 3: 552–577.

Johannes, R. E. 1978. "Traditional Marine Conservation Methods in Oceania and their Demise." *Annual Review of Ecology and Systematics* 9: 349–364.

Johnson, Osa. 1940. *I Married Adventure: The Lives and Adventures of Martin and Osa Johnson.* London: Hutchinson.

Jonas, W. J. 1985. "The Commercial Timber Industry in Colonial Papua New Guinea." *Pacific Studies* 8, no. 2 (Spring): 45–60.

Jones, James. 1962. *The Thin Red Line.* New York: Charles Scribner.

Jones, K. Westcott. 1951. "Tarawa Atoll." *The Fortnightly* 175 (June): 391–397.

Joy, Robert J. T. 1999. "Malaria in American Troops in the South and Southwest Pacific in World War II." *Medical History* 43, no. 2: 192–207.

Judge Advocate General (JAG), Naval Yard, Washington D.C. Inspector General's report of investigation of bural of dceased Marine Corps personnel on Tarawa, File A17-25, torts and claims records.

Kaeppler, Adrienne L., and Amy Ku'uleialoha Stillman. 1985. *Pacific Island and Australian Artifacts in Public Collections in the United States and Canada.* Paris: UNESCO.

Kajewski, S. Frank. 1930. "A Plant Collector's Notes on the New Hebrides and Santa Cruz Islands." *Journal of the Arnold Arboretum* 11: 172–180.

Kay, Robin, ed. 1972. *The Australia-New Zealand Agreement 1944.* Wellington: Historical Publications Branch.

Keesing, Felix M. 1934. *Modern Samoa: Its Government and Changing Life.* London: George Allen and Unwin.

Keesing, Roger M. 1978. "Politico-Religious Movements and Anticolonialism on Malaita: Maasina Rule in Historical Perspective." Pt. I, *Oceania* 48: 241–261.

———. 1979. "Politico-Religious Movements and Anticolonialism on Malaita: Maasina Rule in Historical Perspective." Pt. II, *Oceania* 49: 46–73.

Kiersch, George A. 1998. "Engineering Geosciences and Military Operations." *Engineering Geology* 49: 123–176.

Kirch, Patrick Vinton. 1997. *The Lapita Peoples: Ancestors of the Oceanic World.* Cambridge, Mass: Blackwell.

Kirsch, S. 1997. "Indigenous Response to Environmental Impact along the Ok Tedi." In *Compensation for Resource Development in Papua New Guinea,* ed. S. Toft, 143–155. Port Moresby and Canberra: Law Reform Commission and National Centre for Development Studies, Australian National University.

Kiste, Robert C. 1994. "United States." In *Tides of History: The Pacific Islands in the Twentieth Century,* ed. K. R. Howe, Robert C. Kiste, and Brij V. Lal, 227–257. St. Leonards, N.S.W.: Allen and Unwin.

Klare, Michael T. 2001. *Resource Wars: The New Landscape of Global Conflict.* New York: Henry Holt and Co.

Knibbs, S. G. C. 1929. *The Savage Solomons As They Were and Are.* London: Seeley, Service.

Kobayashi, Tadao. 1992. *Les Japonais en Nouvelle Calédonie: Histoires des émegres sous contrat.* Noumea: Societe d'Etudes Historique de la Nouvelle-Calédonie.

Koehler, Franz A. 1948. *Special Rations for the Armed Forces, 1946–1953.* Washington D.C.: Historical Branch, Quartermasters Corps, Historical Studies, Series II, No. 6.

Kraemer, J. H. 1944. *Native Woods for Construction Purposes in the Western Pacific Region.* Washington: U.S. Government Printing Office.

Kralovec, D. W. comp. 1945. Naval History of Espiritu Santo, Microfilm NRS II-231, Naval Yards Archives, Washington D.C.

Krämer, Augustin. 1995. *The Samoa Islands, Vol. II, Material Culture.* Translated by Theodore Verhaaren. Honolulu: University of Hawai'i Press.

Kunitz, Stephen, ed. 1994. *Disease and Social Diversity: The European Impact on the Health of Non-Europeans.* Oxford: Oxford University Press.

Kushner, Ervan F. 1984. *Bogged Down in Bora Bora.* Paterson, N.J.: Ervan F. Kushner Books.

Laird, Marshall. 1956. *Studies of Mosquitoes and Freshwater Ecology in the South Pacific.* Wellington: Royal Society of New Zealand.

Laffin, John. 1956. *Return to Glory.* Sydney: Angus and Robertson.

Lafitani, Siosuia F. Pouvalu. 1998. "New Behaviours and Migration Since World War II." In *Echoes of Pacific War,* ed. Deryck Scarr, Niel Gunson, and Jennifer Terrell, 76–86. Canberra: Australian National University Press.

Lal, Brij V. 1992. *Broken Waves: A History of the Fiji Islands in the Twentieth Century.* Honolulu, University of Hawai'i Press.

Lambert, Sylvester M. 1949. "Malaria Incidence in Australia and the South Pacific." In *Malariology: A Comprehensive Survey of All Aspects of This Group of Diseases From a Global Standpoint.* Vol. II, ed. Mark F. Boyd, 820–830. Philadelphia: W. B. Saunders Company.

Lane-Poole, C. E. 1925. *The Forest Resources of the Territories of Papua and New Guinea.* Melbourne: Commonwealth of Australia.

Lange, Raeburn T. 1982. "A History of Health and Ill-Health in the Cook Islands." PhD dissertation, University of Otago, Dunedin.

Laracy, Hugh, ed. 1983. *Pacific Protest: The Maasina Rule Movement, Solomon Islands, 1944–1952.* Suva: Institute of Pacific Studies.

Laracy, Hugh, and Geoffrey White, eds. 1988. "Of Food and Friendship: Selected Comments." *O'o: A Journal of Solomon Islands Studies* 4: 107–115.

Larsen, Colin R. 1946. *Pacific Commandos: New Zealanders and Fijians in Action.* Wellington: A. H. & A. W. Reed.

Lasaqa, I. Q. 1972. *Melanesians' Choice: Tadhimboko Participation in the Solomon Islands Cash Economy.* Port Moresby and Canberra: Australian National University Press.

Lawrence, Peter. 1964. *Road Belong Cargo; A Study of the Cargo Movement in the Southern Madang District New Guinea.* Melbourne: Melbourne University Press.

Lawrey, John. 1982. *The Cross of Lorraine in the South Pacific: Australia and the Free French Movement 1940–1942.* Canberra: Journal of Pacific History.

Leckie, J. 2004. "Modernity and the Management of Madness in Colonial Fiji." *Paideuma* 50: 551–574.

Legg, Frank. 1963. *The Eyes of Damien Parer.* Adelaide: Rigby Ltd., Adelaide.

Lepowsky, Maria. 1985. "Food Taboos, Malaria and Dietary Change: Infant Feeding and Cultural Adaptation on a Papua New Guinea Island." *Ecology of Food and Nutrition* 18: 105–126.

Lepowsky, Maria. 1989. "Soldiers and Spirits: The Impact of World War II on a Coral Sea Island." In *The Pacific Theater: Island Representations of World War II*, ed. Geoffrey M. White and Lamont Lindstrom, 205–230. Honolulu: University of Hawai'i Press.

Lever, R. J. A. W. 1933. "Status of Economic Entomology in the British Solomon Islands." *Bulletin of Entomological Research* 24: 253–256.

Levine, Norman D., and Paul Harper. 1947. "Parasitological Observations on Malaria in Natives and Troops, and on Filariasis in Natives." *Supplement to the American Journal of Tropical Medicine* 27 No. 3 (May): 119–129.

Levine, Roger S. 2004. "'African Warfare in All Its Ferocity': Changing Military Landscapes and Precolonial and Colonial Conflict in Southern Africa." In *Natural Enemy, Natural Ally: Toward an Environmental History of War*, ed. Richard Tucker and Edmund Russell, 65–92. Corvallis: Oregon State University Press.

Lewis, D. C. 1996. *The Plantation Dream: Development British New Guinea and Papua, 1884–1942.* Canberra: The Journal of Pacific History.

Lewis, David. 1972. *We the Navigators.* Canberra: Australian National University Press.

Lewis, Michael, Peter McVay, Grant Caine, and Ian Gaze. 1996. *Environmental Management of Commonwealth Land: Site Contamination and Prevention.* Audit Report no. 31 1995–1996. Canberra: Australian Government.

Lewthwaite, Gordon R., Christine Mainzer, and Patrick J. Holland. 1973. "From Polynesia to California: Samoan Migration and its Sequel." *Journal of Pacific History* 8: 133–140.

Lidz, T. 1946. "Psychiatric Casualties on Guadalcanal." *Psychiatry* 9 (Aug.): 193–213.

Lieber, Michael. 1994. *More Than a Living: Fishing and Social Order on a Polynesian Atoll.* Boulder, Colo.: Westview.

Linderman, Gerald F. 1987. *Embattled Courage: The Experience of Combat in the American Civil War.* New York and London: The Free Press and Collier Macmillan.

Lindstrom, Lamont. 1989. "Working Encounters: Oral Histories of World War II Labor Corps from Tanna, Vanuatu." In *The Pacific Theater: Island Representations of World War II*, ed. Geoffrey M. White and Lamont Lindstrom, 395–414. Honolulu: University of Hawai'i Press.

———. 1996. *The American Occupation of the New Hebrides Vanuatu.* Christchurch: Macmillan Brown Centre.

———. 2001. "Images of Islanders in Pacific War Photographs." In *Perilous Memories: The Asia-Pacific Wars*, ed. T. Fijitani, Geoffrey M. White, and Lise Yoneyama, 107–128. Durham, N.C.: Duke University Press.

Lindstrom, Lamont, and James Gwero, eds. 1998. *Big Wok, Storian blong Wol Wo Tu long Vanuatu.* Suva, Fiji; and Christchurch, New Zealand: Institute of Pacific Studies, University of the South Pacific and University of Canterbury.

Lindstrom, Lamont, and Geoffrey M. White. 1989. *The Pacific Theater: Island Representations of World War II.* Honolulu: University of Hawai'i Press.

———. 1990. *Island Encounters: Black and White Memories of the Pacific War.* Washington, D.C.: Smithsonian Institution Press.

Linton, Ralph, and Paul S. Wingert, c. 1946. *Arts of the South Seas.* In collaboration with Rene D'Harnoncourt. New York: Museum of Modern Art.

Lister, R. H. 1944. "Fiji Society and War Psychology." MS 96529, National Library of New Zealand, Wellington.

Lissington, M. P. 1972. *New Zealand and the United States 1840–1944.* Wellington: Government Printer.

Litoff, Judy Barrett, and David C. Smoth. 1996. "The Wartime History of the Waves, Spars, Women's Marines, Army and Navy Nurses." In *A Woman's War Too: US Women in the Military in World War II,* ed. Paula Nassen Poulas, 47–70. Washington, D.C.: NAPA Trust Fund Board.

Littauer, Raphael, and Norman Uphoff, eds. 1972. *The Air War in Indochina.* Ithaca, N.Y.: Cornell University Press.

Lobban, Christopher S., and Maria Schefter. 1997. *Tropical Pacific Island Environments.* Mangilao: University of Guam Press.

Long, Gavin. 1963. *The Final Campaigns.* Canberra: Australian War Memorial.

———. 1973. *The Six Years War: A Concise History of Australia in the 1939–45 War.* Canberra: Australian War Memorial and the Australian Government Publishing Service.

Luski, Walter A. 1991. *A Rape of Justice: MacArthur and the New Guinea Hangings.* Lanham, Md.: Madison Books.

McCarthy, D. D. and D. G. B. Carter c. 1967. "The Control of Filiariasis in Western Samoa: An Interim Report on an Assessment Survey, 1967." Presented to the Medical Research Council of New Zealand [Auckland, New Zealand].

McCoy, O. R. 1944. "Malaria and the War." *Science* 100, no. 2607 (15 Dec.): 146–147.

Macdonald, Barrie. 1982. *Cinderellas of the Empire: Towards a History of Kiribati and Tuvalu.* Canberra: Australian National University Press.

Macgregor, J. D. 1966. "Malaria in the Island Territories of the South Pacific." MD thesis, St. Andrews University, Scotland.

Macgregor, Morris. 1981. *Integration of the Armed Forces, 1940–1960.* Washington: Center of Military History, United States Army.

McKay, C. G. A. 1968. *Samoana: A Personal Story of the Samoan Islands.* Wellington: A. H. & A. W. Reed.

MacKenzie, John M. 1997. "Empire and the Ecological Apocalypse: The Historiography of the Imperial Environment." In *Ecology and Empire: Environmental History of Settler Societies,* ed. Tom Griffiths and Libby Robin, 215–228. Melbourne: Melbourne University Press.

McKinnon, Malcolm. 1993. *Independence and Foreign Policy: New Zealand in the World Since 1935.* Auckland: Auckland University Press.

McKillop, R., and S. G. Firth. 1981. "Foreign Intrusion: The First Fifty Years." In *A Time to Plant and a Time to Uproot: A History of Agriculture in Papua New Guinea,* ed.

Donald Denoon and Catherine Snowden, 85–103. Port Moresby: Department of Primary Industry and Institute of New Guinea Studies.

Maclean, Chris, and Jock Phillips. 1990. *The Sorrow and the Pride, New Zealand War Memorials.* Wellington: Historical Branch, GP Books.

McNeill, J. R. 2000. *Something New under the Sun: An Environmental History of the Twentieth-Century World.* New York and London: W. W. Norton and Co.

McQuarrie, Peter. 1994. *Strategic Atolls: Tuvalu and the Second World War.* Christchurch and Suva: Macmillan Brown Centre, University of Canterbury, New Zealand, and Institute of Pacific Studies University of the South Pacific.

———. 2000. *Conflict in Kiribati: A History of the Second World War.* Christchurch: Macmillan Brown Centre.

Mageo, Janette Marie. 2001. "The Third Meaning in Cultural Memory: History, Identity, and Spirit Possession in Samoa." In *Cultural Memory: Reconfiguring History and Identity in the Postcolonial Pacific,* ed. Janette Marie Mageo, 58–80. Honolulu: University of Hawai'i Press.

Mager, Frederick Pearson (492471). "The Men that Beat the Gun," Accession No. 2000.438, AMW.

Maharaj, Russell J. 1999. *Contamination Risk Assessment from WWII Armoury in Iron Bottom Sound Solomon Islands, SOPAC Technical Report 280.* Suva, Fiji: South Pacific Commission.

Maher, Robert F. 1961. *New Men of Papua: A Study in Culture Change.* Madison: University of Wisconsin Press.

Mair, L. P. 1948. *Australia in New Guinea.* London: Christophers.

Mamaloni, Solomon. c. 1993. "The Road to Independence." In *Independence, Dependence, Interdependence: The First 10 Years of Solomon Islands Independence,* ed. Ron Crocombe and Esau Tuza, 7–18. Honiara: Government Printing Press.

Manchester, W. 1980. *Goodbye Darkness: A Memoir of the Pacific War,* New York: Dell.

Manson-Bahr, P. H., and A. H. Walters. 1934. "Selective Action of Atebrin and Plasmoquine on the Subtertian Malaria Parasite." *The Lancet* 226 (6 Jan): 15–16.

Marama, Biritake, and Sister Tiura Kaiuea. 1984. "Awakening: The Gods of War in the Atolls." In *Kiribati: Aspects of History,* ed. Sister Alaima Talu et al., 128–146. Tarawa: University of the South Pacific and Ministry of Education, Training and Culture, Kiribati Government.

Marshall A. J. Papers, National Library of Australia, Canberra.

Marshall, Colin. 1950. *Forestry in Western Samoa: A Report.* Wellington, Government Printer.

Marshall, Jonathan. 1995. *To Have and Have Not: Southeast Asian Raw Materials and the Origins of the Pacific War.* Berkeley: University of California Press.

Masatsugu, Ogawa. 1992. "The 'Green Desert' of New Guinea." In *Japan at War: An Oral History,* ed. Haruko Taya Cook and Theodore F. Cook, 267–276. New York: New Press.

Mataia, Louise. 2007. "'Odd men from the Pacific:' The Participation of Pacific Island Men in the 28th Maori Battalion, 1939–45." MA thesis, University of Otago.

May, A. J. 1941. "Endemic Typhus in Papua." *The Medical Journal of Australia* (12 April): 449–450.

Mead, Albert. 1961. *The Giant African Snail: A Problem in Economic Malacology.* Chicago: University of Chicago Press.

Mead, Margaret. 1956. *New Lives for Old: Cultural Transformation—Manus, 1928–1953.* London: Victor Gollancz.

Mead, Margaret. Papers, Library of Congress, Washington.

Melanesian Mission Annual Report, 1901. 1902. London: W. H. Smith.

Melanesian Mission Annual Report, 1902. 1903. London, W. H. Smith.

Melanesian Mission Annual Report, 1907. 1908. London: W. H. Smith.

Melanesian Mission Annual Report, 1908. 1909. London, W. H. Smith.

Melanesian Mission Report, 1883. 1884. Ludlow, U.K.: The Melanesian Mission.

Melanesian Mission. Papers 2/1. School of Oriental and African Studies, London.

Melville, Herman. 1892. *Typee: A Real Romance of the South Seas.* New York: U.S. Book Co.

Methodist Mission. Records, PMB 925, Microfilm, Pacific Manuscripts Bureau, Canberra.

Merillat, Herbert Christian. 1982. *Guadalcanal Remembered.* New York: Dodd, Mead and Co.

Merrill, E. D. 1943. *Emergency Food Plants and Poisonous Plants of the Islands of the Pacific.* Washington: War Department.

Metzger, Louis. 1982. "Duty Beyond the Seas." *Marine Corps Gazette* 66, no. 1 (Jan): 28–37.

Michener, James A. 1947. *Tales of the South Pacific.* New York: Corgi Books.

———. 1951. *Return to Paradise.* London: Secker and Warburg.

Miller, Edward S. 1991. *War Plan Orange: The US Strategy to Defeat Japan, 1897–1945.* Annapolis, Md.: Naval Institute Press.

Mills T. I. Papers, MS 7007-18, National Library of New Zealand.

Milward, Alan S. 1977. *War, Economy and Society 1939–1945.* London: Allen Lane.

Mitchell, Philip. 1943–1944. Diary, Miss Afr. 101, Rhodes House Library, Oxford.

Miyako, Shinto. 1943. Diary, Mexted Papers, No. 43276, New Zealand Army War Museum, Waiouru, New Zealand.

Moon, Margaret, and Bruce Moon, recorders. 1998. *Ni-Vanuatu Memories of World War II.* Christchurch, N.Z.: Private Printing.

Moore, Clive. 1985. *Kanaka: A History of Melanesian Mackay.* Port Moresby: Institute of Papua New Guinea Studies and the University of Papua New Guinea.

Moore, Clive, Jacqueline Leckie, and Doug Munro, eds. 1990. *Labour in the South Pacific.* Townsville, Queensland: James Cook University.

Morison, Samuel Eliot. 1968. *History of United States Naval Operations in World War II.* Vol. VII, *Aleutians, Gilberts and Marshalls, June 1942–April 1944.* Boston: Little, Brown.

———. 1975. *History of United States Naval Operations in World War II.* Vol. IV, *Coral Sea, Midway and Submarine Actions, May 1942–August 1942.* Boston: Little, Brown.

Morriss, Mack. 1996. *South Pacific Diary 1942–1943.* Edited by Ronnie Day. Lexington: University Press of Kentucky.

Muller, Jan-Werner, ed. 2002. *Memory and Power in Post-War Europe: Studies in the Presence of the Past.* Cambridge: Cambridge University Press.

Munholland, Kim. 1991. "World War II and the End of Indentured Labor in New Caledonia." *Proceedings of the Annual Meeting of the Western Society for French History* 18: 543–553.

———. 2005. *Rock of Contention: Free French and Americans at War in New Caledonia, 1940–1945.* New York: Berghahn Books.

National Archives of Australia, records relating to war in Papua New Guinea, 1939–1960. Canberra and Sydney.

National Archives of New Zealand, records of Departments of Air, External Affairs, Island Territories, and Internal Affairs. Wellington.

NATI, National Archives of Solomon Islands, Honiara, British Solomon Islands Protectorate Series (BSIP).

NARA, National Archives of the United States, College Park, Maryland:

RG 33, Extension Service
RG 52, Bureau of Medicine and Surgery
RG 59, General Records of the Department of State
RG 77, Office of the Chief of Engineers
RG 80, General Records of the Department of the Navy, 1798–1947
RG 92, Office of Quartermaster General
RG 112, Office of the Surgeon General (Army)
RG 127, U.S. Marine Corps
RG 160, Headquarters Army Service Forces
RG 169, Foreign Economic Administration
RG 175, Chemical Warfare Service
RG 179, War Production Board
RG 181, Naval Districts and Shore Establishments
RG 218, U.S. Joint Chiefs of Staff
RG 234, Reconstruction Finance Corporation
RG 313, Naval Operating Forces
RG 319.1, Record of Army Staff. Administrative History
RG 331, Allied Operational and Occupation
RG 338, U.S. Army Commands, 1942–
RG 342, U.S. Air Force Commands, Activities, and Organizations
RG 407, Adjutant General's Office
RG 494, U.S. Army Forces in the Middle Pacific

NARA SB, National Archives of the United States, San Bruno, California:

RG 284, Government, American Samoa

RG 313, Base records: 313-58-3008-Fiji, 313-58-3013-Tulagi, 313-58-3019-Russell Islands, 313-58-3061-Upolu, 313-58-3233-Bora Bora, 313-58-3282-Espiritu Santo, 313-58-3283-Espiritu Santo, 313-58-3299-Noumea, 313-58-3300-Manus, 313-58-3368-Guadalcanal, 313-58-3377-Tulagi, 313-58-3394-Tonga, 313-58-3401-South Solomons, 313-58-3416-Manus, 313-58-3440-Tutuila, 313-58-3496-Tulagi, 313-58-3502-Tulagi, 313-58-3503-Tulagi, 313-58-3517-Tulagi, 313-58-3520-Tulagi, 313-58A-3244-Russell Islands, 313-58A-3254-Noumea, 313-58A-3490, 313-58B-3061-Upolu, 313-58C-3290-Noumea, 313-58D-3284-Tutuila, 313-58D-3290-Noumea.

National Geographic 81 (June 1942); 86 (Oct. 1944); 87 (Feb. 1945).

Nelson, Hank. 1979. "The Swinging Index: Capital Punishment and British and Australian Administrations on Papua and New Guinea." *The Journal of Pacific History* 13, nos. 3–44: 130–152.

———. 1980. "Hold the Good Name of the Soldier." *Journal of Pacific History* 15, nos. 3–4: 202–216.

———, ed. 1996. *The War Diaries of Eddie Allan Stanton.* St. Leonards, Victoria: Allen and Unwin.

———. 1999. "Pay Back: Australian Compensation to Wartime New Guinea." Paper, The Pacific War in Papua New Guinea: Perceptions and Realities Symposium, International Research Project, Canberra: Australian National University, Sept.

———. 2006 "Kokoda: The Track from History to Politics." *Journal of Pacific History* 38, no. 1: 109–126.

———. 2007. "Kokoda: And Two National Histories," *Journal of Pacific History* 42, no. 1 (June).

Neubarth, Raymond G. 1954. *Dental Caries in School Children of American Samoa.* South Pacific Commission Technical Paper 64. Noumea: South Pacific Commission.

Newbury, Colin. 1975. "Colour Bar and Labour Conditions on the New Guinea Goldfields 1935–41." *Australian Journal of Politics and History* 21, no 3: 25–38.

Ngwadili, Arnon, and Isaac Gafu. 1988. "Malaita Refuge. Guadalcanal Labour Corps." In *The Big Death: Solomon Islanders Remember World War Two*, ed. Geoffrey M. White, David Gegeo, Karen Ann Watson-Gegeo, and David Akin, 197–215. Suva, Fiji: Institute of Pacific Studies, Solomon Islands Extension Centre of the University of the South Pacific and Solomon Islands College of Higher Education.

O'Brien, Frederick. 1921. *Mystic Isles of the South Seas.* New York: Century Co.

O'Callaghan, Mary-Louise. 1991. "US to Destroy Solomons Weapons." *The Age*, 18 May.

Oliver, Douglas, 1992. *Black Islanders: A Personal Perspective of Bougainville 1937–1991.* South Yarra, Victoria: Hyland House.

Oman, P. W., and L. D. Christenson. 1947. "Entomology." *Supplement to the American Journal of Tropical Medicine* 27, no. 3 (May): 91–117.

Omar, Samira A. S., Ernest Briskey, Raafat Misak, and Adel A. S. O. Asem. 2000. "The Gulf War Impact on the Terrestrial Environment of Kuwait: An Overview." In *The Environmental Consequences of War: Legal, Economic, and Scientific Perspectives,* ed. Jay E. Austin and Carl E. Bruch, 316–337. Cambridge: Cambridge University Press.

O'o: A Journal of Solomon Islands Studies 4 (1988). Honiara.

"Operation Roll-up." The history of surplus property disposal in the Pacific Ocean, Microfilm No. H-108, Naval Yards, Washington D.C.

Oppenheimer, Harold L. 1966. *March to the Sound of the Drums.* Danville, Ill.: Wabash Press.

Pacific Islands Monthly. 1938–1954. Sydney: Pacific Publications.

Packard, Jerry. 1975. "The Bougainville Taro Blight." MA thesis, University of Hawai'i.

Pacific Association Academic Committee. 1943. *The Solomon Islands and Their Vicinity: Geography and People.* Tokyo: Taiheiyo Kyokai Shuppanbu (Japanese text).

Page, Patricia. 2004. *Across the Magic Line: Growing Up in Fiji.* Canberra: Pandanus Press.

Patrol reports, Papua and New Guinea, 1941–1949, microfiche, National Archives of Australia, Canberra.

Parham, B. E. V. 1941. "Notes on the Alien Flora of Fiji." *Transactions of the Fiji Society for Science and Industry*: 76–88.

Parnaby, O. W. 1964. *Britain and the Labor Trade in the Southwest Pacific.* Durham, N.C.: Duke University Press.

Parsons, Robert P. 1945. *MOB 3: A Naval Hospital in a South Sea Jungle.* New York: Bobbs-Merrill Co.

Peattie, Mark R. 1998. *Nanyo: The Rise and Fall of the Japanese in Micronesia, 1885–1945.* Honolulu: University of Hawai'i Press.

Perry, Gad, and John M. Morton. 1999. "Regeneration Rates of Woody Vegetation on Guam's Northwest Field Following Major Disturbance: Land Use Patterns, Feral Ungulates and Cascading Effects of the Brown Tree Snake." *Micronesica* 32, no. 10: 125–142.

Perry, W. J. 1950. "The Mosquitoes and Mosquito-Borne Diseases on New Caledonia, An Historic Account: 1885–1946." *American Journal of Tropical Medicinal Hygiene* 30, no. 1 (Jan.): 103–114.

Peters, W. 1962. "A Critical Survey of the Results of Malaria-Eradication and Control Programmes in the South West Pacific." *Annals of Tropical Medicine and Parasitology* 56, no. 1: 20–31.

Philip, Cornelius B. 1964. "Scrub Typhus and Scrub Itch." In *Preventive Medicine in World War II: Communicable Diseases,* Vol. VII, ed. John Boyd Coates, 275–347. Washington, D.C., Office of the Surgeon General, Department of the Army.

Piehler, G. Kurt. 1995. *Remembering War the American Way.* Washington and London, Smithsonian Institution Press.

Pilger, Alison. 1993. "Courage, Endurance and Initiative: Medical Evacuation from the Kokoda Track, August–October 1942." *War and Society* 11, no. 1 (May): 52–75.

Pilgert, Henry R. 1949. *The History of Foreign Surplus Property Disposal, 1945–1949.* Washington, D.C.: Office of the Foreign Liquidation Commissioner.

Pillsbury, Donald M., and Clarence S. Livingood, 1968. "Dermatology." In *Internal*

Medicine in World War II: Infectious Diseases and General Medicine, Vol. III, 543–673. Washington D.C.: Office of the Surgeon General, Department of the Army.

Pleydell, G. J. 1970. *Timbers of the British Solomon Islands*. London: United Africa Co.

Pollock, Nancy. 1992. *These Roots Remain: Food Habits of the Central and Eastern Pacific since Western Contact*. Honolulu: University of Hawai'i Press.

Powell, Alan. 2003. *The Third Force: ANGAU's New Guinea War 1942–1946*. South Melbourne: Oxford University Press.

Priday, H. E. Lewis. [1945]. *The War from Coconut Square: The Story of the Defence of the Island Bases of the South Pacific*. Wellington: Reed.

Pringle, G., and S. Avery-Jones. 1966. "Observations on the Early Course of Untreated Falciparum Malaria in Semi-Immune African Children Following a Short Period of Protection." *Bulletin of the World Health Organisation* 34, no. 2: 269–272.

Prothero, Stephen. 2001. *Purified by Fire: A History of Cremation in America*. Berkeley: University of California Press.

Quanchi, Max. 1996. "Photography, Representation and Cross-Cultural Encounters: Seeking Reality in Papua, 1886–1930." PhD dissertation, University of Queensland.

Quinn, John P., Richard T. Evans, and Michael J. Boock, 2000. "United States Development of Operational-Environmental Doctrine." In *The Environmental Consequences of War: Legal, Economic, and Scientific Perspectives*, ed. Jay E. Austin and Carl E. Bruch, 156–170. Cambridge: Cambridge University Press.

Rapaport, Moshe. 1995. "Oysterlust: Islands, Entrepreneurs and Colonial Policy over Tuamotu Lagoon." *Journal of Pacific History* 30, no. 1: 39–52.

Ravuvu, Asesela. 1988. *Fijians at War 1939–1945*. Suva, Fiji: Institute of Pacific Studies.

Reid, Richard. 2001. "'Quite Pathetic to See.' The Australian Army's Permanent Recording Notices in Papua New Guinea." In *A Century of Service: 100 Years of the Australian Army*, ed. Peter Dennis and Jeffrey Grey, 41–51. Canberra: Army History Unit.

Rennie, John. Memoirs, enclosure, No. 43195, New Zealand Army Memorial Museum, Waiouru, New Zealand.

Report of the Island Voyage for 1887. 1888. Ludlow, U.K.: The Melanesian Mission.

Report of the Work of Research Expeditions Sent to Western Samoa, Rarotonga and Pukapuka during 1948 to 1953, New Zealand Medical Research in the Pacific. N.d., c. 1953. Dunedin.

Report on Franco-American relationship in New Caledonia, Report No. 432. 1945. U.S. Forces, Microfilm, Division of Pacific and Asian History, Canberra.

Reports to the League of Nations of the Administration of the Territory of New Guinea, 1924–1940. 1925–1941. Canberra: Commonwealth of Australia.

Richter, Ray. 2005. "Betikama Missionary School." *Journal of Pacific Adventist History* 5, no. 1 (June): 4–9.

Roberts, Adam. 2000. "The Law of War and Environmental Damage." In *The Environmental Consequences of War: Legal, Economic, and Scientific Perspectives,* ed. Jay E. Austin and Carl E. Bruch, 47–86. Cambridge: Cambridge University Press.

Roberts, Stephen H. 1927. *Population Problems of the Pacific.* London: George Routledge and Sons.

Robinson, Neville K. 1979. *Villagers at War: Some Papuan Experiences in World War II.* Canberra: Australian University Press.

Robson, R. W., comp. and ed. 1942. *Pacific Islands Yearbook 1942.* Sydney: Pacific Publications.

Rodda, G. H., Y. Sawai, D. Chiszar, and H. Tanaka, eds. 1999. *Problem Snake Management: The Habu and the Brown Treesnake.* Ithaca, N.Y.: Cornell University Press.

Roman Catholic Mission. Records, Solomon Islands, PMB 1120, Microfilm Reel 6, Canberra.

Rosner, A. A. 1944. "Neuropsychiatric Casualties from Guadalcanal." *American Journal of Medical Science* 207 (June): 770–776.

Ross, A. A. 1954. "Wartime Agriculture in New Zealand, 1939–1950." In *Wartime Agriculture in Australia and New Zealand 1939-1950,* ed. J. G. Crawford C. M. Donald, C. P. Dowsett, D. B. Williams, and A. A. Ross, 243–324. Stanford, Calif.: Stanford University.

Ross, Angus. 1964. *New Zealand's Aspirations in the Pacific in the Nineteenth Century.* Oxford: Oxford University Press.

Rottman, Gordon L. 2002. *World War II Pacific Island Guide: A Geo-Military Study.* Westport, Conn: Greenwood Press.

Ruff, Tilman A. 1989. "Ciguatera in the Pacific: A Link with Military Activities." *The Lancet* (28 June): 201–205.

Russell, Edmund. 1999. "The Strange Career of DDT: Experts, Federal Capacity, and Environmentalism." *Technology and Culture* 40, no. 4 (Oct.): 770–796.

———. 2001. *War and Nature: Fighting Humans and Insects with Chemicals from World War I to 'Silent Spring.'* Cambridge: Cambridge University Press.

Russell, Paul F. 1963. "Introduction." In *Preventive Medicine in World War II, Communicable Diseases, Malaria,* Vol. VI, 1–10. Washington D.C: Office of the Surgeon General, Department of the Army.

Russell, Tom. 2003. *I Have the Honour to Be.* Spennymoor, U.K.: Memoir Club.

Ryan, Peter. 1969. "The Australian New Guinea Administrative Unit ANGAU." In *The History of Melanesia,* ed. K. S. Inglis, 531–548. Canberra: Australian National University Press.

Sabel, William O. 1999. *Seeds of Hope: An Engineer's World War II Letters.* West Lafayette, Ind.: Purdue University Press.

Sackville-West, Vita. 1946. *The Garden.* Garden City, N.Y.: Doubleday Publishers.

Sahlins, Marshall. 1992. *Historical Ethnography. Vol. 1, Ahahulu: The Anthropology of History in the Kingdom of Hawai'i,* ed. Patrick Kirsh and Marshall Sahlins. Chicago: University of Chicago Press.

Saito, Hisafumi. 1991. "Barefoot Benefactors: A Study of Japanese Views of Melanesians." In *Remembering the Pacific War,* ed. Geoffrey M. White, 207–222. Honolulu: Center for Hawaiian, Asian and Pacific Studies, University of Hawai'i.

Salvat, B. 1980. "The Living Marine Resources of the South Pacific—Past, Present and Future." In *Population-Environment Relations in Tropical Islands: The Case of Eastern Fiji,* ed. H. C. Brookfield, 131–148. Paris: UNESCO.

Sapero, James J. 1949. "Prevention of Malaria Infections by Drug Prophylaxis." In *Malariology: A Comprehensive Survey,* ed. Mark F. Boyd, 1129–1131. Philadelphia and London: W. B. Saunders and Co.

Saville, Gordon. 1974. *King of Kiriwina: The Adventures of Sergeant Saville in the South Seas.* With John Austin. London: Leo Cooper.

Sayers, E. G. 1943. *Malaria in the South Pacific: With Special Reference to the Solomon Islands.* Wellington: Government Printer.

Scarr, Deryck, 1968. *Fragments of Empire: A History of the Western Pacific High Commission, 1877–1914.* Canberra and Honolulu: Australian National University Press and University of Hawai'i Press.

Scrimgeour, E. M., and D. Jolley. 1983. "Trends in Tobacco Consumption and Incidences of Associated Neoplasms in Papua New Guinea." *British Medical Journal* 286: 1414–1416.

Shapiro, Karl. 1987. "Aside." In *Lines of Battle: Letters from American Servicemen, 1941–1945,* ed. Annette Tapert, 214. New York: Times Books.

Shaw, Basil. 1991, "Yukio Shibata and Michael Somare: Lives in Contact." In *Remembering the Pacific War,* ed. Geoffrey M. White, 223–237. Honolulu: Center for Pacific Studies, University of Hawai'i.

Shineberg, Dorothy. 1967. *They Came of Sandalwood: A Study of the Sandalwood Trade in the South-West Pacific, 1830–1865.* Melbourne: Melbourne University Press.

———. 1999. *The People Trade: Pacific Island Laborers and New Caledonia, 1865–1930.* Honolulu: University of Hawai'i Press.

Shinya, Michiharu. N.d. "The Path from Guadalcanal." Translated by E. H. Thompson, MS 1763, National Library of New Zealand.

———. 2001. *Beyond Death and Dishonour: One Japanese at War in New Zealand.* Auckland: Castle Publishing.

Shlomowitz, Ralph. 1982. "The Profitability of Indentured Melanesian Labour in Queensland." *Australian Economic History Review* 22: 49–67.

Silata, Walingai Patrick B. 1988. "Oral Accounts of the Second World War Experiences of the People of the Huon Peninsula, Morobe Province, Papua New Guinea." *O'o: A Journal of Solomon Islands Studies* 4: 63–74.

Sill, Van Rensselaer. 1947. *American Miracle.* New York: Odyssey Press.

Smith, Bernard. 1984. *European Vision and the South Pacific.* 2nd ed. Sydney: Oxford University Press.

Sontag, Susan. 1977. *On Photography.* New York: Anchor Books.

South Pacific, dir. Joshua Logan (Magna Theatre Corporation, Samuel Goldwyn Company, 1958).

Spector, Ronald H. 1985. *Eagle Against the Sun: The American War with Japan*. New York: The Free Press.

Spencer, Margaret. 1992. "History of Malaria Control in the Southwest Pacific Region, with Particular Reference to Papua New Guinea and the Solomon Islands." *Papua New Guinea Medical Journal* 35: 36–52.

———. 1994. *Malaria: The Australian Experience, 1943–1991*. Townsville: Australian College of Tropical Medicine.

Spennemann, Dirk H. R. 1998. "Japanese Economic Exploitation of Central Pacific Seabird Populations, 1898–1925." *Pacific Studies* 21, no. 1/2 (Sept.): 1–42.

———. 2007. *"Gedruckt in Samoa." A Bibliographic Analysis of the Samoanisches Gouvernements-Blatt and other Printing in German Samoa (1901–1914)*. Albury, N.S.W.: Heritage Futures.

Spring, Ira. 1998. *An Axe, a Camera and a Jar of Peanut Butter*. Seattle: Mountaineers Books.

Stanner, W. E. H. 1953. *The South Seas in Transition: A Study of Postwar Rehabilitation and Reconstruction in Three British Dependencies*. Sydney: Australasian Publishing Co.

Stauffer, Alvin P. 1956. *US Army in World War II: The Technical Services: The Quartermaster's Corps*. Washington, D.C.: Center for Military History, U.S. Army.

Steck, E. A. 1972. *The Chemotherapy of Protozoan Diseases*. Washington, D.C.: Walter Reed Institute of Research.

Stewart, P. J., and A. Strathern. 2002. *Gender, Song, and Sensibility: Folktales and Folksongs in the Highlands of New Guinea*. Westport, Conn.: Praeger.

Stewart, Susan. 1993. *On Longing: Narratives of the Miniature, the Gigantic, the Souvenir, the Collection*. Durham, N.C.: Duke University Press.

Stockholm International Peace Research Institute. 1980. *Warfare in a Fragile World: Military Impact on a Fragile Environment*. London: Taylor and Francis.

Stout, Duncan M. 1954. *War Surgery and Medicine*. Wellington: New Zealand Government.

Strahan, Lachlan. 2005. *Day of Reckoning*. Canberra: Pandanus Books.

Stuart, Annie. 2002. "Parasites Lost? The Rockefeller Foundation and the Expansion of Health Services in the Colonial South Pacific, 1923–1939." PhD dissertation, University of Canterbury, New Zealand.

Sweeney, Tony. 2003. *Malaria Frontline: Australian Army Research During World War II*. Melbourne: Melbourne University Press.

Tachibana, Seiitsu. 1996. "The Quest for a Peace Culture: The A-bomb Survivors' Long Struggle and the New Movement for Redressing Foreign Victims of Japan's War." In *Hiroshima in History and Memory*, ed. M. J. Hogan, 168–186. Cambridge: Cambridge University Press.

Tamotsu, Ogawa. 1992. "Soldiers' Deaths." In *Japan at War: An Oral History*, ed. Haruko Taya Cook and Theodore F. Cook, 276–281. New York: New Press.

Tapert, Annette, ed. 1987. *Lines of Battle: Letters from American Servicemen, 1941–1945*. New York: Pocket Books.

Tenison, M. C. 1942. *War Damage Legislation.* Sydney: Butterworth and Co., Australia.

The Best Years of Our Lives, dir. William Wyler (RKO, Samuel Goldwyn Company, 1946).

The Third Division Histories Committee. 1948. *Pacific Service.* Wellington: A. H. and A. W. Reed for the Third Division Histories Committee.

Thomas, Trevor L. 1942. Diary, MSX 5141, National Library of New Zealand.

Thompson, Laura. 1949. "The Relations of Men, Animals, and Plants in an Island Community (Fiji)." *American Anthropologist* 51, no. 2: 253–267.

Thompson, Virginia, and Richard Adloff. 1971. *The French Pacific Islands.* Berkeley and London: University of California Press.

Thrift, Lyndon. 2003. "Post-War Batuna." *Journal of Adventist History* 3, no. 2 (Dec.): 13–18.

———. 2004. "Exciting Yet Purposeful: A New Venture in the Solomon Islands." *Journal of Pacific Adventist History* 4, no. 1 (June): 18–21.

Thune, Carl E. 1989. "Making History on Normanby Island." In *The Pacific Theater: Island Representations of World War II*, ed. Geoffrey M. White and Lamont Lindstrom, 231–256. Honolulu: University of Hawai'i Press.

Tonkin-Covell, John. 2000. "The Collectors: Naval, Army and Air Intelligence in the New Zealand Armed Forces during the Second World War." PhD dissertation, University of Waikato, New Zealand.

Tucker, Richard, and Edmund Russell, eds. 2004. *Natural Enemy, Natural Ally: Toward an Environmental History of War.* Corvallis: Oregon State University Press.

Turbott, I. G. 1949. "Diets, Gilbert and Ellice Colony." *Journal of the Polynesian Society* 58: 36–46.

United States of America Government.

Army Service Forces. 1943. *Melanesian Pidgin English Guide.* Washington, D.C.: Government Printing Office.

Congressional Record, 79th Congress, 1st Session, Jan.–Dec. 1945.

Congressional Record, 79th Congress, 2nd Session, Jan.–Aug. 1946.

Department of Army, 1947. *Information Regarding Interments, Headstones and Monuments in National Cemeteries.* Washington, D.C.: U.S. Government Printing Office.

United States Army Medical Service. 1963. *Preventive Medicine in World War II, Vol. VI.* Washington, D.C.: Office of the Surgeon General, Department of the Army.

United States Bureau of Medicine and Surgery. 1953. *History of the Medical Department of the United States Navy in World War Two: A Narrative and Pictorial Volume*, Vol. 1. Washington, D.C.: Government Printing Office.

The United States Strategic Bombing Survey (Pacific): The Allied Campaign against Rabaul. 1946. Washington, D.C.: Naval Analysis Division.

War Department, 1946. *Disposition of World War II Armed Forces Dead.* Washington, D.C.: U.S. Government Printing Office.

Vanikoro Timber Co. Records, Business and Labor Archives, University of Melbourne.

Van Pel, H. 1956. *A Survey of the Fisheries of the New Hebrides with Preliminary Recommendations for their Development.* Noumea: South Pacific Commission.

Vasey, Daniel. 1981. "Agricultural Systems in Papua New Guinea: Adapting to the Humid Tropics." In *A Time to Plant and a Time to Uproot: A History of Agriculture in Papua New Guinea,* ed. Donald Denoon and Catherine Snowden, 17–29. Port Moresby: Department of Primary Industry and Institute of New Guinea Studies.

Vaskess, H. 1943. *Memorandum: Post War Policy, Reconstruction, and Re-organisation of Administration.* Suva: Government Printer.

Verges, J. 1944. *Les Tiques du bétail.* Nouméa: Imprimeries Réunies.

Videai, D., and C. Cotter. 1963. "Walliseans en Nouvelle-Calédonie." *Journal de la Société des Océanistes* 19, no. 9 (Dec.): 173–187.

Viel, Phillipe. 1974. "Recherche et prix des 'curios' de la Nouvelle Calédonie en 1878." *Journal de la Société des Océanistes* 30, no. 44 (Sept.): 238–240.

Voller A., and H. Wilson. 1964. "Immunological Aspects of a Population under Prophylaxis against Malaria." *British Medical Journal* (29 Aug.): 551–552.

Waiko, John D. 1988. "'Damp Soil My Bed: Rotten Log My Pillow': A Villager's Experience of the Japanese Invasion." *O'o: A Journal of Solomon Islands Studies* 4: 45–59.

Walker, Allan S. 1952. *Clinical Problems of War.* Third reprint, 1962. Canberra: Australian War Memorial.

———. 1961. *Medical Services of the RAN and RAAF.* Canberra: Australian War Memorial.

Walker, A. S., E. Meyers, A. R. Woodhill, and R. N. McCulloch. 1942. "Dengue Fever." *The Medical Journal of Australia* 2, no. 11 (Sept): 223–228.

Walker, F. S. 1948. *The Forests of the British Solomon Islands Protectorate.* London: Crown Agents.

Walter, J. Samuel. 1996. "The Decision to Use the Bomb." In *Hiroshima in History and Memory,* ed. M. J. Hogan, 11–37. Cambridge: Cambridge University Press.

"War Medicine and Surgery." 1943. *Medical Journal of Australia* 21, no. 7 Supplement (7 Aug.): 81–84.

Ward, E. J. Papers, National Library of Australia, Canberra.

Waterworth, G. E. 1960. *One Man in His Time.* Christchurch: Whitcomb and Tombs.

Watson, J. 1985. "The Giant African Snail in Australia: Pest or Nuisance." *Queensland Agricultural Journal* (Jan.–Feb.): 7–10.

Waugh, Geoffrey. 1992. "The Politics and Economics of Fisheries in the South Pacific." In *Resource Development and Politics in the Pacific Islands,* ed. Stephen Henningham and R. J. May, 171–178. Bathurst, N.S.W.: Crawford House Press.

Weeks, Charles J. 1989. "An Hour of Temptation: American Interests in New Caledonia." *Australian Journal of Politics and History* 35, no. 2: 185–200.

Weeramantry, Christopher. 1992. *Nauru: Environmental Damage under International Trusteeship.* Melbourne: Oxford University Press.

Weingartner, James J. 1992. "Trophies of War: US Troops and the Mutilation of Japanese War Dead, 1941–1945." *The Pacific Historical Review* 61, no. 1 (Feb.): 53–67.

Weir, Christine Helen. 2003. "The Work of Mission: Race, Labour and Christian Humanitarianism in the South-west Pacific, 1870–1930." PhD dissertation, Australian National University.

Western Pacific Archives (WPA) collection, Auckland University:

Inwards Correspondence Western Pacific High Commission (WPHC).

Western Pacific High Commission, New Hebrides, British Service. Office of the High Commissioner (NHBS).

Tonga Series (T), Great Britain. Agent and Consul Tonga.

Gilbert and Ellice Series (CEIC).

Solomon Islands Series (BSIP).

Western Samoa: Report to the Trusteeship Council by United Nations Mission to Western Samoa. 1947. Wellington: Department of External Affairs.

Whistler, W. A. 1995. *Wayside Plants of the Islands.* Honolulu: Isle Botanica.

White, Geoffrey M., David Gegeo, Karen Ann Watson-Gegeo, and David Akin, eds. 1988. *The Big Death: Solomon Islanders Remember World War Two.* Suva, Fiji: Institute of Pacific Studies, Solomon Islands Extension Centre of the University of the South Pacific and Solomon Islands College of Higher Education.

White, Geoffrey M., and Lamont Lindstrom, eds. 1989. *The Pacific Theater: Island Representations of World War II.* Honolulu: University of Hawai'i Press.

White, Geoffrey M., ed. 1991. *Remembering the Pacific War.* Honolulu: Center for Pacific Studies, University of Hawai'i.

White, Geoffrey. 1996. "War Remains: The Culture of Preservation in the Southwest Pacific." *CRM* 19, no. 3: 52–56.

White, Hugh. 2004. *Strengthening our Neighbour: Australia and the Future of Papua New Guinea.* Canberra: Australian Strategic Policy Institute.

White, Osmar. 1965. *Parliament of a Thousand Tribes.* London: Heinemann.

Wilson, Mary. Papers and letters, Ms Ref no. 91-268, National Library of New Zealand, Wellington.

Wilson, S. D. 1969. "Cook Islands Development 1946–1965." In *New Zealand's Record in the Pacific Islands in the Twentieth Century,* ed. Angus Ross, 60–114. Auckland: Longman Paul.

Winslow, Donna. 1990. "Workers in Colonial New Caledonia to 1945." In *Labour in the South Pacific,* ed. Clive Moore, Jacqueline Leckie, and Doug Munro, 111–116. Townsville, Queensland: James Cook University.

Winter, Jay. 1997. *Sites of Memory, Sites of Mourning: The Great War in European Cultural History.* Cambridge: Cambridge University Press.

Wolfers, Edward P. 1975. *Race Relations and Colonial Rule in Papua New Guinea.* Sydney: Australia and New Zealand Book Co.

Wood, F. L. W. 1958. *The New Zealand People at War: Political and External Affairs.* Wellington: War History Branch, Department of Internal Affairs.

Woodbury, David O. 1946. *Builders for Battle: How the Pacific Naval Bases were Constructed.* New York: Dutton and Co.

Wood-Ellem, Elizabeth. 1999. *Queen Sālote of Tonga: The Story of an Era, 1900–1965.* Auckland: Auckland University Press.

Woodford, Charles Morris. 1890. *A Naturalist Among the Head-Hunters.* London: George Philip and Son.

World Health Organization. 2002. *Report: Workshop on Obesity Prevention and Control Strategies in the Pacific, Apia, Samoa, 26–29 September 2000.* Manila: World Health Organization.

Worsley, Peter. 1957. *The Trumpet Shall Sound: A Study of "Cargo" Cults in Melanesia.* London: Macgibbon and Kee.

Worster, Donald. 1990. "Transformations of the Earth: Toward an Agroecological Perspective in History." *Journal of American History*, 76, no. 4: 1097–1106.

Wright, Alfred C. c. 1943, Journal, MSX 5967, National Library of New Zealand, Wellington.

Yoshiaki, Yoshimi. 2001. *Comfort Women: Sexual Slavery in the Japanese Military During World War II.* Translated by Suzanne O'Brien. New York: Columbia University Press.

Young, Louise. 1998. *Japan's Total Empire: Manchuria and the Culture of Wartime Imperialism.* Berkeley: University of California Press.

Zarafonetis, Chris J. D., and Myles P. Baker. 1964. "Scrub Typhus." In *Internal Medicine in World War II, Infectious Diseases*, Vol. II, ed. John Boyd Coates, 111–142. Washington, D.C.: Office of the Surgeon General, Department of the Army.

Zelenietz, Marty. 1991. "Invisible Islanders: Melanesians and American War Mythology." *Man and Culture in Oceania* 7: 1–19.

Zoloveke, Gideon. 1988. "The War Is Not Our War." *O'o: A Journal of Solomon Islands Studies* 4: 75–78.

Index

Page numbers in **boldface** type refer to illustrations.

aerosol can, for spraying, 64, 215, 223, 291
African Americans, 29, 32, 33, 36–38, 40, 67
agriculture, xxiii, 5, 13, 43, 76–86, 96, 115, 132, 146, 164, 195, 210, 220–222, 225, 234–236, 301; American reconnaissance, 132; Board of Economic Warfare, xxv, 76; cinchona, 82; coffee, 17, 32, 79, 82, 86, 145, 220–221; and colonial administrations, 115–116, 121; intensive farming, 221; mechanization, 220; rice, 83, 86, 88–89, 221
aid: and conservation, 233, 294; and dependency, 6, 286; development, 6, 220, 233–240, 297, 298
airfields: American claims for, 2, 163; American Samoa, 161; Canton Island, 2, 93, 97; construction of, 2, 27, 97, 99, 103, 119, 140, 169, 180, 296, 301; Cook Islands, 163; environmental affects of, 199–203, 210, 232; Fiji, 158, 186, 201; Nauru, 122; New Caledonia, 119; New Guinea, 103, 128, 171, 176, 191, **207**; New Hebrides, 145, **204**; post-war, 196; Solomon Islands, **24**, **55**, 90, 114, 140, 171, 203, 206, 285; Tarawa, **200**; Western Samoa, 62, 200. *See also* aviation
Aitutaki, Cook Islands, 19, 35–36, 62, 67, 78, 80–81, 84, 117, 124–125, 147, 152, 163, 187, **228**, 257, 269, 332n.1
American Samoa, 19, 31, 60, 62, 100, 124, 185, 211, 229, 231, 270; administration, 152, 159, 222, 224, 232, 256, 324n.132; America, 14, 34–36, **34**, 159, 264; defense force, 128, 239; food, 78, **162**, 167, 220, 222, 256; trade, 116, 124
ANGAU (Australian New Guinea Administrative Unit): civilians, 57, 66, 11, 121, 176, 189, 211, 226, 254, 265; disease, 54, 60, 66, 70; district officers, 15, 30, 175; food production, 30, 82–83, 144, 221, 231; forest products, 103–106, 111; labor, 30, 32, 82, 128–130, 137, 142–143, 149, 151, 153; military, 37, 57, 60, 70, 111, 142, 188, 258, 302
anthropologists, 12, 262; American, 76, 260; Australian, 37, 175; and ethnographic present, 262
ANZAC (Australian and New Zealand Army Corps) pact. *See* Canberra pact
armaments, 7, 119, 198; deep sea mines, 137, 202, 205; affects on homelands, 208, 218; excavated for militias, 208. *See also* munitions
army, Australian, 14, 16, 26, 30, 32, 35, 37, 44, 51–52, 54–55, 58–59, 63, 65, 68, 82–83, 88, 91, 96, 102–103, 105, 111, 121, 128, 137–138, 175–177, 188–190, 201, 209, 231, 234, 245–248, 252, 254, 264, 272, 292, 301, 384n.2, 387n.69; Colonel Neil Hamilton Fairley, 50, 52, 318n.18; General Sir Thomas Blamey, 52, 105, 137, 190, 233, 274–275; and Japanese, 4, 12–13, 14, 43, 51–52, 301; operational areas, 15, 28, 33, 59, 66, 77, 79–81, 84, 99, 103–104, 117, 127,

129–130, 133, 178, 180, 214, 302; and United States, 15, 26, 32, 68, 101, 168, 216, 281, 317n.142, 361n.43
Army-Navy Liquidation Commission. *See* Foreign Liquidation Commission
Asians, 28–29, 66, 122, 134, 149, 151, 165, 287, 297; Chinese, 33, 36, 78, 82–83, 88, 93, 148, 178, 220, 230, 245, 256, 258, 280, 298, 304; growers, 78, 140; Indians, 36, 66, 78, 117, 127, 135, 140, 151–152, 158, 225, 230, 256–258, 304, 327n.19; Javanese, 146; Koreans, 36, 280; retailers, 93, 148; Taiwanese, 298; Tonkinese, 56, 165, 258; Vietnamese, 146–147
Atlantic Charter, 6
atolls, 22, 113, 115, 130, 171, 193, 199, **200**, 201, 209, 227, 281, 297; Betio, 19, 114, 186–187, 193, 276–278; bird life, 199, 232, 302; affects of construction upon, 98, 113; Midway, 98, 199, 232; Tarawa, xxiii, 19–22, 114, 131, 142, 169, 186, **200**, 253, 270, 276–278, 288, 296
Australian Department of External Affairs, 130, 192–193
Australian Department of External Territories, 128–130, 236, 335n.49
Australian Imperial Forces (AIF). *See* army, Australian
Australian War Memorial, 245, 282, 288, 384n.2
aviation, 2, 15, 65, 75, 107, 110, 204, 285; "Air ferry" route, 2, 158, 332n.1; New Zealand's concerns, 2, 163; Roosevelt's aims, 2, 163; seaplanes, 2, 98, 147; and spraying of chemicals, 65, 90, 222. *See also* airfields

barter, 83–89, 122, 134, 230, 246; American policy, 147, 226, 246, 257; New Guinea, 246. *See also* trade; money
bases, 4, 32–33, 36–37, 40, 44, 46–48, 67–68, 70, 76–77, 102, 103, 127, 180, 200, 203–204, 269, 273, 292; American, 1, 6, 7, 19, **20**, **24**, 25, 26, 27, 32, 34, 36, 50, 56–57, 61–62, 65–66, 67, 71, 76, 81, 85, 93, 98–99, 103, 107, 109–110, 119, 124–125, 128, 136, 139, 146–147, 150, 152, 158–159, 163, 165–166, 169, 180, 182, 184–191, 200, 202, 205, 211, 213, 226, 229, 256–257, 260, 269, 279, 296, 301, 361n.43; Australian, 51, 54, 83, 91, 138, 165, 176, 190, 196, 244; cost of Noumea, 187–188; location of, 26, 50, 158; Manus, **20**; Munda, **24**; rainfall at, 50
battlefields, xxiv, 7, 48, 103, 243, 246, 251, 253, 264, 266, 274–275, 298, 303; conditions, 54, 58, 88, 102
Betio, Gilbert Islands, 19, 114, 186–187, 193, 199, **200**, 276–278
Blamey, General Sir Thomas, 52, 105, 137, 190, 233, 274–275, 279, 303
Board of Economic Warfare (BEW), xxv, 76–77, 100–102, 117–126, 130–132, 172; vegetable growing projects, 76–77
boards, 182–183; compensation, 159; marketing, 116; production, 117–118, 128, 181, 224; supply, xxv, 76, 93, 123, 181
bombing, 53, 91, 98, 102, 119, 165, 175, **204**, **207**, 231, 273, 284, 289, 304; affects of, on gardens, 90, 169, 175–176, 289; on marine life, 90, 202; on people, 43, 49, 87, 122, 200, 206; on soils, 201; tonnage, 203, 303; on vegetation, 169, 213
bombs. *See* munitions
Bora Bora, Society Islands, 28, 35–37, 61–62, 67, 93, 125, 148–149, 164–165, 186, 202, 253, 258, 264, 270, 302
botany, 100, 107, 223; herbarium, 107, 233; surveys of, 100–101, 104, 106–107, 109, 220, 223, 236
Bougainville, 1, **23**, 79; food, 81, 84–85, 87–88, 176, 213, 222, 303; forests, 104, 107; indigenous people, 31, 70, 143, **144**, 231; Nissan, 47, 57, 95; operations, 135, 137, 140, 248; Torokina, 206, **207**, 245, 269
Britain: and America, 76, 163, 168, 205, 276–277, 296; and Australia, 104, 208–209, 276–277, 292, 296; as imperial power, 1–3, 6, 29, 77, 135, 152, 168, 170–171, 220, 234, 236–238, 272, 276–277, 296–297, 390n.7; imports,

116–117; Ministry of Food, 116–118, 125; and New Zealand, 163, 293, 296
British Phosphates Commission, 121–122
Buna-Gona, Papua, 4, 14, 37, 52, 63, 82, 103, 111, 144, 253, 272
Burke, Lieutenant John, 153, 172, 260–263, **261**, 266
Buxton's line, 70, 214, **217**

campaigns, 53, 68, 70, 137, 246; Buna-Gona, 14, 51–52, 63, 82, 272; Coral Sea, 12, 51, 119, 180, 299; Guadalcanal, 15–16, 54, **55**, 69–70, 103, 140, 180, 184, 285; Kokoda Track, 14–15, 26, 43, 51, 65, 82, 86, 91, **174**, 285–287; Midway, 12, 119, 180; Milne Bay, xix, 51–52, 137; Munda, 56, 246; Owen Stanley Mountains, 15, 17, 43–44, 51, 63, **174**; Tarawa, xxiii, 19–22, 26, 114, 142, 169, **200**, 270, 276
Canberra pact, 6, 124, 235
cannibalism, 12, 272; and Japanese, 272, 299; and Melanesians, 87
cargo cults. *See* indigenous peoples
Carson, Rachel, xx, 222
celebrations, 48
Chapman, Wilbert, 32, 75, 94–96, 225–226, 233–235, 294, 302
Chemicals: DDT, 64–65, 70, 222–223, 291, 295, 370n.117; DEET, 64; experiments in Queensland, 208–209; fungicides, 222; and gardening, 89, 222; gases, xx, 208–209, 367n.53; insecticides, 52–56, 64, 118, 214, 222; stores of, 208, 367n.53; warfare agents, 90, 111, 198, 203, 208–209, 303, 367n.53
Christianity, 12; church buildings, 172; of indigenous people, 134, 151, 173, 195, 239, 256; of military, 45, 269. *See* also missions
climate, xxi, xxiv–xxv, 13–16, 19, 47, 50, 76, 82–84, 158, 185, 187, 189, 197, 203, 209, 253, 291, 297, 300, 305; dry season, 56; rain shadow, 51; wet season, 21, 50, 61
Cold War, 238, 288; allies, 288, 294, 297
colonial administrations, xxi, 2, 12–13, 100, 103, 121, 123, 158, 169, 293; attempts to control spread of pests, 198, 210–218, **217**, 222, 296; attitudes of, xxvi, 4–5, 67, 109, 132, 167, 219, 224, 238, 294–295; attitudes of, to each other, xxiv, 77, 108–109, 116, 119, 292–293; attitudes of, to indigenous people, xxiv–xxv, 4, 29, 31–32, 36, 55, 66, 105, 110, 115, 121, 125, 134, 151–152, 157–164, 168–178, 231–238, 255–257, 276–277, 295, 301; attitudes of, to military, xxiv, 31, 66, 75, 77, 99, 108, 115, 121, 134, 138, 151, 234; and crops, 77–78, 82–83, 115–118, 134, 220–222, 234, 238, 255; disposal of war surplus and scrap, xxi, 180–197, 203, 206, 214, 303; education provided, 152–154, 177, 216, 219, 235–239, 295; and environment, 75, 98, 113–114, 179, 198, 203, 232, 234, 294; and fisheries, 225–226, 232–233; labor supply, 31–32, 55, 86, 115, 125, 131–134, 139–151, **143**, **144**, 175–177, 224, 301; postwar planning, 219, 223, 235–236, 293; revenue for, 5, 121–122, 125–126, 134, 170, 173, 195, 225, 237, 296
Colonial Office (Britain): and Fiji, 214, 236, 276; and Western Pacific territories, 168–173, 236, 276; and part-American children, 36
Colonial Sugar Refinery (CSR), 117, 140, 158
commands, military, 299; American, 25, 27, 33, 44, 52, 54–56, 60–61, 68, 70, **79**, 81–82, 93, 104, 110, 118, 120–121, 134, 141, 170–172, 208, 214, 218, 251, 257, 260, 317n.142; Australian, 52, 104–105, 153, 170, 246–247; Japanese, 88, 102; regions, **13**, **18**, 111–112, 153, 170, 181–182, 188, 205
Commonwealth Disposals Commission, Australia (CDC), 190–193, 297
Communications: "care" packages, 44; mail, 41–44, 243, 292
Communists, New Caledonia, 146
compensation, xxi; America, 99, 104, 110, 159–162, 170–172, 293; Australia, 105,

172–177, 297, 335n.49; Britain, 109, 165–173; cash, xxi, xxvi, 224, 234–236; Fiji, 109, 158–159; France, 164–168; for Islanders, xxvi, 105, 148, 157, 178, 284, 293; Japan, 170, 173, 178, 297; in kind, xxvi, 234; New Zealand, 124–125, 163–164, 293; for settlers, xxvi, 178; and social memory, 177
concert parties, 44, **46**, 292
conservation, xx; of environment, 199, 303; indigenous attitudes toward, 230–231, 235, 294; of matériel, 27, 180–181; of resources, 27, 179–181, 222, 230–232; and war, 179, 303
construction: engineers, 25, 27, 53, 97–99, 103–104, 107, 111–113, 120, 128, 180, 200, 203, 301; materials, 99–103, 106, 112, 119, 163, 180–182, 184, 223–224, 295; prefabricated buildings, 109–110; units, 25, 29, 57, 104, 107, 113, 142, 181. *See also* resources
consumer goods. *See* trade
convicts, 1, 256
Cook, Captain James, xxii, 1
Cook Islands, 147, 148, 301; America, 19, 33–36, 78, 124, 147–148, 229, 257; environment, 98, 113, 211, 230; New Zealand, 2, 29, 33, 78, 138, 152, 163–164, 187, 230, 237, 239, 302
cooperatives, 78, 131, 221, 235–236; Fiji, 78, 224–225; Gilbert and Ellice Islands, 225
copra, 6; and Depression, 5, 116; exports, 116, 118; indigenous production of, 6, 117, 127; in Island economies, 6, 32, 116, 145, 168, 170, 224; prices, 116–117, 125, 255; uses, 116. *See also* plantations

damage: to ecological systems, xxi, xxvi, 113, 170, 198, 209, 213, 218, 220, 222, 230, 296–297, 301–303, 305; war, xxi, 81, 86, 99, 109–110, 114, 124, 157–178, 186, 189, **200**, 205, 211, 216, 218, 234, 236, 273, 297, 302–303. *See also* compensation
decolonization, 235, 277; and Australia, 208, 235–237; and Britain, 236–237; and independence, 152, 208, 223, 235–237, 239, 293–294, 297, 300; by New Zealand, 235–237; resource surveys, 236; self-government, 218, 275, 293, 295; and United Nations, 223, 237–238. *See also* development of islands
de Gaulle, Charles, 2, 76, 116
demobilization, xxv, 107, 135, 177, 185, 189
departure of military, 110, 179–197
depopulation. *See* population
development of islands: Colonial Development and Welfare Act, 214, 220; by colonial governments, 6, 109, 194–195, 219, 237; desire for, 220, 237; education for, 219, 235–236, 238–239, 295, 298; funding of, 214, 220, 237; lack of, 232, 301
development of islands, plans for: by Australia, 174, 233, 238, 294, 297; by Britain, 109, 238; by France, 238; by New Zealand, 237, 239, 294; by United States, **20**, 21, 180, 220, 222, 224, 232, 256. *See also* colonial administrations
diet, 49, 75, 78, 82–85, 91, 144, 147, 212, 221, 222, 225–226, **228**, 372n.17; American, 222, 226, 228–229; change, 228–229, 240; affects of imported foods, 84, 89, 228–229; polished rice, 51, 69, 131, 226; vitamins, 1, 83–84, 221, 229. *See also* food
disease, xxiii–xxiv, 7, 32, 35, 47, 49–71, 133, 176, 232, 292, 295; affects of, on Americans, 70; affects of, on Australians, 70; affects of, on Japanese, 70; beri–beri, 70; carriers, xxvi, 49, 61; and DDT, 222–223, 291, 295; and demalarialization, 59; dengue fever, 17, 33, 50, 60–61, 321n.89; dental, 84, 229; dermatitis, 65; and drug therapy, 52–60, 64–65, 70, 90, 295, 318n.18; dysentery, 57, 63, 65–66, 70, 177, 295, 323n.120; and environment, 49, 69–70, 291, 300–301; epidemics, 51–52, 54, 56, 58, 61, 65–67, 177, 215,

318n.13, 319nn.30, 39, 46, 320n.51, 321nn.73, 85, 322n.111, 323nn.116, 124, 325n.156; and epidemiology, 51–52, 58–59; epidemiology of venereal disease, 35, 66–67; filariasis, 33, 60–62, 67, 70, 146, 222, 322n.98; gonorrhea, 66–67; and infection rates, 52, 56, 58–59, 320n.56, 325n.155; influenza, 57, 66, 323n.124; and insecticides, 57, 64–65, **64**, 214–215, 222, 295; and insects, xxi, 50–53, 59, 64, 214, 223, 291, 295, 301; malaria, 16–17, 50–63, 68–70, 191, 214–215, 221, 372n.17; malarial control units, 27, 53–58, **64**, 65, 71; and military attitudes, 16, 51–53, 58; and mortality, 50–51; and mosquitoes, 51–53, 56–61, 63, 214–215, 221; and "native seedbed," 31, 50, 54–59, 62, 67, 70–71, 291; pneumonia, 57, 66; and prevention, 52–58, 61–62, 70, 214–215, 222, 295; scrub typhus, 50, 63–64, 322n.110; and semi-immunity, 51, 60; and spread of, 51–52, 58–60, 320n.56; syphilis, 66, 67, 324n.140; and treatment of civilians, 31, 54–60; and treatment of military, 27, 52–60; and types of, 50–51, 58–60; venereal, 35, 66–68, 313n.57, 315n.93, 323nn.130, 131, 324nn.132, 133; venereal disease treatment, 66–67; and World Health Organization, 222, 375n.76; yaws, 54, 67, 324n.140
drugs. *See* medicine
Dutch New Guinea, 13, 37, 63, 91, 189, 266, 387n. 69

economy, 12, 32, 117, 119, 122, 126, 134, 149, 157, 168, 179, 185, 246, 256–257, 276, 293, 295; and Depression, 3, 5, 116, 134, 149, 168, 220, 224, 293; inflation, 123, 125, 141; postwar, 185, 224, 227–228, 235–238, 276; price control, 122–126, 257. *See also* barter; trade
Efate, New Hebrides, 22, 32, 51, 56, 59, 61, 79, 80, 101, 165, 168, 184, 211
entertainment. *See* celebrations; concert parties; films
environment: as agent, xxi, 179, 301; Allied perceptions of, xxvi, 5, 11–19, 26, 47, 94, 301; as ally, 58, 69–71, 137, 185; and atolls, 22, 198–200; and birds, 198–200; damage to, xx–xxi, xxvi, 157, 198–202, **200**, 213, 296–297, 303, 305; difficulties of, xxi, 69, 191; affects of blasting coral, 113–114, 198–200; as enemy, 15–16, 20–24, 49–51, 53, 69–71, 238, 291, 300; on equipment, 191; and forests, xxii, 106–110, 113–114, 223–224, 234, 236; and high islands, 112, 196, 200–201, 232; Japanese perceptions of, 12–19, 48; of logging, 113–114; on munitions, 202–205, 303; of natural events, 112–113; and reefs, 113–114; on surplus disposal, xxvi, 179, 191, 202–210, **207**, 303; at Tarawa, 19–26
erosion, 113, 288; as a result of cultivation, 220–221
Espiritu Santo, New Hebrides, 16–17, 32, 38, 56, 61–65, 79, 81, 101, 120, 123, 145–146, 165–168, 181, **204**, 205, 211, 231, 299
Europeans, xxii–xxiii, 1, 3, 5, 11, 27, 29, 38, 49, 60, 66, 115, 117, 133–138, 150–153, 168, 171–174, 178, 191, 195, 230, 256, 296, 304, 308n.4

Fairley, Colonel Neil Hamilton, 50–52, 318n.18
farms. *See* gardens
fertility. *See* population
fertilizers, 122, 220–221; corpses, 16, 142, 199, 270; and military farms, 220–221; nightsoil, 88; phosphate, 5, 84, 121–122, 147, 169–170, 226, 234, 237, 370n.117; rice growing, 88
Fiji, 28, 97, 108–109, 127, 134, 149, 152, 186, 205, 210–211, **217**, 220–225, 228, 230, 232–233, 239, 256, 264, 270, 277, 293, 301, 332n.1, 391n.19; administration, 22, 66, 77, 99, 108–109, 116, 131, 138–140, 158–159, 186, 197, 215,

230, 232, 236–238, 257, 277, 302; and Allies, 15, 19, 32–33, 35, 101, 112, 117, 123–124, 131, 134, 135–136, 140, 152, 158, 181, 214, 246; Chinese, 78, 134, 220, 230, 256; disease, 61, 66, 214; Fijians, 15, 32, 36, 66–67, 78, 85, 97, 111, 117, 135–137, 140, 148, 151–152, 158–159, 223, 228, 230, 239, 249, 270, 293, 342n.2, 344n.37; food, 77–78, 80–81, 85, 158, 221; forests, 99–101, 111, 112–113, 211, 223; Indians, 66, 78, 117, 135, 140, 151–152, 158–159, 225, 228, 230, 256–258, 327n.19; Japan, 225, 230; Phillip Mitchell, 22, 36, 134, 139–140, 142, 159, 214, 218, 276; resources, 5, 97, 116–118, 120; Sukuna, Lala, 32, 66, 134, 139, 148, 152, 293; views of British, 135, 237

Fijian Military Force, 85–86, 134–138, 227–228, 246, 249, 270; attitudes toward, 85–86, 137; composition of, 134–135; conditions of enlistment, 134; environmental knowledge, 135, 137; as fighting force, 32, 85, 135–137; New Zealand role in, 35, 134–136; in Solomon Islands, 32, 85–86, 135; Tongans in, 135; training of, 15, 135–136, 148; Victoria Cross awarded, 137

films: and indigenous people, 12, 175, 299; Hollywood's representations, 11–12, 16, 19, 34, 35, 299–300; images of the Pacific, 12, 299, 308n.4, 378; influence of, 292; and mosquitoes, 53, 56; showing of, 43, 46–47, 145, 317n.142

fish, xxv, 131, 171, 233–235, 239, 249, 295, 298, 327n.27, 376n.105; affects of explosives on, 94, 113, 225, 230–232, 234; exotic species, 53, 61, 70, 230; for hospital patients, 91, 93, 95; poisoning of, 111, 209–210, 230, 232; shellfish, xxiii, 202, 225; threats to, 202, 209–210, 230, 232, 391n.20

fishing, xxiii, 57, 76, 91–96, **92**, 225–226, 228, 229, 294, 302; advice from native people, 94–96; by Americans, 93–95, 226, 231, 294; by Australians, 91–93, 96; boats, **87**, 95; commercial, 95, 225; deep-sea, 93, 202, 225, 294; in exclusive economic zones, 294–295; in-shore, 6, 199, 225–226, 294; by Japanese, 86–90, **87**, 225, 294; kits, 93–95; methods of, 6, 88, 90–95, 170, 206, 230–232, 234, 302, 391n.20; surveys by Americans, 93–95, 225; and Wilbert Chapman, 32, 75, 94–96, 225–226, 231, 233–235, 294, 302

Florida Island, Solomon Islands, 37, 61, 66, 71, 108, 120, 172, 260

food: American, 15, 43, 76–78, **79**, **80**, 85, 96; from Australia, 76, 82, 96, 121–122, 227–229, 292, 296; Australian vegetable growing projects, 76, 83, **84**; bartered and sold to military, 77–78, 81, 83–91, 128, 226; beer, 46, 68, 127, 181, 229; canned, 76, 78, 82, 83, 85, 122, 125, 131, 148, 226, 228–229, 231, 246, **275**, 296, 327n.27; cattle and other livestock, xxi, 85, 114, 116, 119, 120,164, 170, 215–217, 220–221, 228, 302, 370n.112; chickens, 78, 85–87, 89; Coca-Cola, 46, 227; coffee, 17, 32, 79, 82, 86, 131, 142, 145, 220, 221, 227; fruit, xxv, 15, 17, 32, 43, 59, 76–78, 82–84, 88, 96, 100–101, 126, 141, 160, 162, 229, 296, 336n.74; Giant African Snail, 89, 211, 212, 302, 369n.90; for hospitals, 78, 82, 85, 91, 93–95; imported, 84, 89, 228–229; increased diversity of, 226–229; indigenous, 14–15, **14**, 50, 77–78, 106, **208**, 302; of Japanese, 15, 43, 75–76, 85, 89, 247, 291, 303; losses to indigenous people, 86–87, 110–111, 113, 169, 175–176, 221; melons, 79, 160, 162, 222; military rations, 57, 75–77, 82–85, 111, 131, 136–137, 141–143, 144, 145–146, 161, 170, 186, 201, 226–231, **250**, 325n.1, 327n.27; milk, 82, 84, 216, 226; and morale, 43, 68, 76–77, 91, 96; from New Zealand, 76, 80, 96, 185, 121–122, 227–229, 292, 296; from New Zealand exchanged for equipment, 185; of New Zealanders, 81, 84–85; pigs, 1, 83, 85–89, 128, 171, 175, 255–256, 264; production in

islands, 81, 140; rice, 30, 51, 69, 82–83, 86, 88–89, 124, 131, 146, 148, 221, 226, 229, 327n.27; root beer, 227; supplied by indigenous people, 77–78, 81, 83, 161; sweet potato, 17, 88–89, **160**, 212, 222, 327n.27; truck crops, 222. *See also* fish
Foreign Economic Administration (FEA), 76, 78–81, 93–96, 100–101, 107, 117–118, 123–124, 127, 130–132, 181, 376n.105
Foreign Liquidation Commission (FLC), 182–189, 193, 361n.43
forests, xxii, xxiv, 14, **20–21**, 63, 97, 223–224; carbon sequestration, 298; colonial policies toward, 293; commercial exploitation, 99–100, 109; development potential, 223–224; Fiji departments of forests, 100, 223; food trees, 106, 110, 114; forestry and logging units, 106; indigenous perceptions of, 223–224, 232, 293; information about, 100–104; logging of, 103–104, 113, 223, 294; and modern equipment, 100–101; New Caledonia, 100; New Guinea, 100, 223; non-timber products, 110–111; palms, 103–105, 110–111, 114, 163, 169, 176, 222; reforestation, 106, 223–224, 298; rights to, 103; Solomon Islands, 223; surveys, 100–109, 223, 236. *See also* timber
France, 1–3, 77, 119, 123, 165, 168, 238, 269, 297; Charles de Gaulle, 76, 116, 138; Free French, 2, 76, 116, 119, 122, 123, 138, 164, 216, 218; Vichy, 2, 119, 123, 125, 138
freon. *See* aerosol can
Funafuti, Ellice Islands, 86, 98, 169, 186, 193, 199, 270

gardens, 17, 19, 37, 57, 113, 157, 171, 200, **204**, 221, 256–258, 294, 302–303; American, 78–79, 140–143, **144**, 147, 220; Australian, 82–84; bombing of, 90, 175–176, 213, 303; demonstration affect, 96, 221; flower, 91; Guadalcanal plains, **79**; Japanese, 75, 86–89, **89**, 90, 212–213; Maasina Rulu, 221, 236, 238; and morale, 78, 90–91; postwar, 206, 220, 280; for subsistence, 86–89, 175, 254; Tongans, 77; types of vegetables grown, 17, 77, 79, 83–84
Geneva Convention 1929, 244, 250–251, 272
geographic regions: commands, **13**; Melanesia, xxii, xxv, 28, 263, 325n.155; Micronesia, 28, 263, 348n.108; Polynesia, xxii, 28, 36, 263, 325n.155, 348n.108
geology, 50, 97, 99, 119, 120, 132; data about, 119–120, 132, 236; and drainage, 50, 53, 70, 203; and engineers, 97–99, 120; and Metal Reserves Corporation, 120; minerals, 3, 5, 116, 118–122, 124, 235–236, 239, 298; US Corps of Engineers, 203, 120. *See also* soils
Germany, 2–3, 119, 135, 277, 288, 344n.32
Ghormley, Vice Admiral, 139, 214–215
Gilbert and Ellice Islands, 4, 348n.108; administration, 152, 168–170, 171, 173, 178, 186, 193, 236, 279; America, 19, 36, 114, 122, 132, 169, 195, **227**, 230; environment, 96, 188, 199, 302; food, 171; Japan, 169, 255; labor, 66, 93–94, 142, **143**, 149, 226, 270; trade, 130, 225. *See also* Tarawa
global warming, xxvi, 288, 304–305
Guadalcanal, Solomon Islands, 15–16, 41, 43–44, 47, 51, 53–57, **55**, 65, 68–70, 79, **79**, 81, 85, 88, 91, 95–96, 99, 101, 103–104, 107–111, 114, 120–121, 135, **136**, 140–143, **143**, 150, 153, 171, 180–188, **183**, 193–195, 200–206, 220–222, 246–247, 250–254, 257–264, **264**, 269–270, **269**, 283–285, 318n.12
Gulf War (first), xxi, 303

Halsey, Admiral William, 179, 215, 279
Hawai'i, xxiii, 1, 3, 5, 12, 19, 95, 131, 134, 171, 180, 208, 210, 213, 239, 248, 257, 299–300, 308, 332n.1, 381n.88, 385n.11
health, xxiv, 49, 54, 65, 67, 68, 69–71, 96, 219, 222, 228, 235, 299; Americans, 27,

51–71; Australians, 51–59, 63, 65–71; education, 177; and environmental transformation, 221; hospitals, 27, 41, 65–68, 78, 85, 91–95, 143, 186, 191, 203, 252; indigenous people, 54–58, 62, 69–71, 146, 236–237; Japanese, 49, 51–52, 58–59, 65, 69–70, 90, 279; and quarantine, 66, 213–218; and sanitation, 53–54, 62, 65, 146, 272

Hell's Point, Guadalcanal, Solomon Islands, 203, 206–208

Honiara, Solomon Islands, 186, 196, 206, 221, 284, 288

Horii, Major General, South Seas Force, 15, 17, 51, 86

horticulture, 212, 220, 233; indigenous methods, 6, 96, 220. *See also* gardens

impact of the West, xxii, 28, 122, 150, 198, 226, 235–239, 293–295; geographic spread, 154, 225, 231–232; temporal differences, 78, 148, 238–239, 294–296

indenture, 6, 29, 130, 133–134, 146, 148, 174–175, 220, 226, 229, 295, 327n.27, 342n.2; abolished, 151, 178, 224, 236

indigenous peoples: American perceptions of, 16, 28, 31–37, **38**, **40**, 56, 59, 62, 67, 70, 71, 133, 136, 141–142, 145–146, 153, 262–263, 266; aspirations, 152–153, 236–240, 295; attitudes to Americans, 34–37, 66–67, 77, 150, 152, 195, 230, 234, 238, 260; attitudes to Australians, 30, 188, 175; attitudes to Japanese, 86–87, 175, 255, 279; attitudes to New Zealanders, 126, 134–135, 152; Australian perceptions of, 28–29, 39–40, **40**, 137, 140, 143, 153; cargo cults, 150, 221, 238, 295, 300; carriers, 30, 32, 105, 107; common names for, 28–29, 31; formal education, 152, 154, 219, 235–239, 295, 298; friendships with, 32–35; gender roles, 33, 254, 255, 295; indigenous politics, 153, 239, 295; Japanese perceptions of, 31, 40–41; Jon Frum, 145; knowledge, 154, 231–232, 233, 235, 295, 302; Maasina Rulu, 221, 236, 238; migration, xxii, 238–239; New Zealand perceptions of, 32–33, 39, **39**, 41, 137; perceptions of environment, xxv, 201, 293–295; perceptions of money, 77, 115, 151–152, 117, 176–177, 224, 237–238, 246, 254, 293; perceptions of selves, 153, 295; perceptions of wartime, 151–152, 237–238; sexual relations with military, 37–41, **38**, **39**, **40**, 67; socio-political organization, xxiii, 28, 134, 137, 140, 148, 152, 153, 232, 236–237, 254, 287, 295, 300; soldiers, 32, 153. *See also* sexual relations; women

Industrial Revolution, xx; and global warming, 304

infrastructure: affects on biota, 301; colonial, 169–170, 189, 196, 223, 236; lack of, 6, 15, 99, 103, 238; military, 97, 159, 165, 185, 218–219

intelligence, 54; American, 119, 132, 216, 252; Australian, 128, 251; from Japanese documents, 246–247

Japanese, xix, xxii, xxv, **87**, **89**; Allied views of, 28, 53, 86, 244, 249–252, **250**, **251**, **252**, 272–274, **273**, 279; expansion, 2–4; as fighters, 22, 68, 69; and indigenous people, xxv, 12, 29–32, 36, 39, 75–76, 87, 137

Kokoda, Papua, 14, 15, 26, 43, 51, 65, 82, 86, 91, **174**, 269, 285–287

Labor Corps, 32, 134, 139–148; for Australians, 143–144, **174**, 286; conscription, 143–145, 151; diet, 82, 137, 144, 227, 229, 327n. 27; efficiency, 140; Fijian, 134–135, 139–140; and forced labor, 30, 144, 151, 175, 286, 295; Gilbert and Ellice Islands, 131, 142; and Gilbert and Ellice Islands Dock Company, 66, **143**; for Japanese, 144; and motives, 141; New Caledonia, 62, 145–146; New Guinea, 57, 60, 143–145; New Hebrides, 56, 145; and origins, 141;

and reputation in Australia, 30, 105, 175; and reputation among Americans, 142; and reputation in Australia, 140; Solomon Islands, 32, 54–56, 131, 140, 270; and strikes, 141, 149; Tonga, 147–148. *See also* laborers

laborers, 29, 86, 91, 117, 122, **129**, 133–134, 206; Asian, 36, 78, 117, 134, 146, 149, 151, 220; conscripted, 143–145, 146; health, 54–56, 62, 66, 85, 146; incentives for, 75, 122, 125, 128, 132; indentured, 6, 29, 130, 133–134, 146, 148, 151, 174–175, 178, 220, 224, 226, 229, 236, 295, 327n.27, 342n.2; malaria control among, 27, 54–56, 58–60, **64**, 319n.35; occupations of, 6, 26, 30, 54, 58, 77–83, **79**, 88, 93, 103, 133, 136–137, **143**, 144, **144**, 145–146; payment of, 86, 115, 122–123, **126**, 128, **129**, 131, 141, 144–145, 147–148, **149**, 152–153; rations, 82–83, 111, 131, 144–145, 327n.27; relations, 30–31, 146–148; replacements for military, 117, 140, 145, 254; segregation of, 54–56, 70; supply, 32, 123, 151, 177; unions, 152; women, 143, 146, 149

Lamour, Dorothy, 12, 16, 37

land, 29, 36, 49, 169, 171, 180, 199, 220–222, 292, 303; American perceptions of, 220, 234; Australian perceptions of, 26; colonial perceptions of, 276, 294; indigenous perceptions of, 137, 161, 163, 169, 170, 176, 199–200, 232, 235, 237, 302; leased, 165–166, 168; loss, 98, 158, 163; value added by use, 168, 234

landscape, xxi–xxiii, 13, 16, 26, 27, 41, 47, 91, 153, 200, 265–266, 268–270, 274–277, 283, 287–288, 295–296, 301

lend-lease, 76, 99, 104, 108, 109, 112, 118, 122–123, 127, 141, 147, 151, 159, 163–169, 171, 181–182, 185–186, 190, 218, 276, 345n.53; and Australia, 76, 112, 122, 127, 190; and British Commonwealth, 76, 123, 166, 169, 171, 276, 345n.53; and Fiji, 99, 108–109, 112, 118, 123, 181; and France, 76, 164–167, 186, 218; and New Zealand, 76, 99, 122, 147, 164, 185

MacArthur, General Douglas, 12, 15, 69, 188

McAdam, Major James, 104–105, 223, 234, 302

Malaita, Solomon Islands, 31–32, 110, 136, 140–141, 153, 171, 221, 260

Manus Island, New Guinea, **20**, 26, 27, 41, 57, 79, 104, 106–107, 184, 189–192, 206, 213, 246–247, 260, 286

Maori, 29, 33, 264; Maori Battalion, 138, 148, 239

maps, xxii, 13–14, **13**, **18**, **20**, **23**, **24**, 26, 53, **55**, **57**, **92**, **102**, 121, **204**, **207**, **217**, 246, 248, 264, 268; Allied Terrain Studies, 14; colonial, 13–14, 107, 110; field sketches, 13–14, 24

marriage: in Islands, 35, 37, 40, 67, 175

Mau movement, Western Samoa, 29, 126

medicine, xxiv; Atebrin (Atebrine), 52, 53, 54–60, 64, 255, 318n.17, 318n.18, 321n.76; Plasmochin (Plasmoquin), 52, 59–60, 321n.76; Quinine, 52, 58, 59, 82, 90

memorials, war, xxvi, 268–289, 300, 306; and American Battle Monuments Commission, 275, 281; and Australian Battlefields Memorial Committee, 274–275; and boards, 274–275; and commemoration at, 268, 270, 274–275, 284, 285–286, 299; and domestic, in Australia, 280, 282, 387nn.69, 70; and foreign, in Papua New Guinea, 274–276, 282, 285–287; in Japan, 280–281; and maintenance of, 274–275, 278; and meanings of, 276, 279–283, 286–287; in New Zealand, 282, 387n.69; and perceptions of, 283–285; and politics of, 169–170, 276, 285–286, 296; in Solomon Islands, 270, 273, 275–276, 283–285, 287–288; and Tarawa as, 276–277, 296; on Tarawa, xxiii, 19–22, 26, 142, 169, 276–278; in United States, 281–282, 387n.66. *See also* war

memory, 19, 41, 243, 259–260, 263–264; social, 150–151, 175, 177, 195, 201, 284, 286–287, 289, 300; of war dead, xxi–xxii, xxvi, 268–289. *See also* war
merchants, 123; Burns, Philp, and Co. Ltd, 85, 117, 123, 125, 127, 129, 214, 256; copra trade, 116–117, 256; Gilbert and Ellice Islands, 130, 225; Morris, Hedstrom, and Co., 117, 126, 127, 193; New Caledonia, 117, 202; New Hebrides, 123; supplies of goods, 123; Western Samoa, 229; W. R. Carpenter, 116, 117, 186
Micronesia, 28, 179, 210, 263, 298, 348n.108; Americans in, 33, 124, 131, 212, 277; Japanese in, 2, 12–13, 86, 180, 212, 225, 292, 296, 301, 307n.5, 332n.1
military: ethic, 245, 247, 279; training of, 13–15, **14**, 52, 56, 62, 68, 90, 133, 135, 244, 287; training of indigenous people by, 135–138, 148, 153, 208
military island defense units: American Samoa, 33, 138, **139**, 161, 239; Cook Islands, 138; Fiji, 86, 134; New Guinea, 148; New Hebrides, 138, 145; New Zealand Maori Battalion, 138, 148, 239; Nuie, 138; Solomon Islands, 136–137, **136**, 148, 254; Tonga, 134–135, 147–148, 228; Western Samoa, 138, 152
Milne Bay, Papua, xix, 31, 40, 51–52, 85, 91, 101, 103, 107, 111, 113, 137, 191–192, 252, 269
mines (armaments), 137, 202, 205, 304; and whales, 202
mining, 6, 17, 101, 119–121, 133, 146, 174, 226
missions, Christian, xxv, 12, 31, 85, 103, 154, 170, 171, 172–175, 178, 184, 185, 191, 222, 229, 230; and artifacts, 255–262, **261**; Catholic, 186, 189, 206; Melanesian Mission (Anglican), 172; Methodist, 99; Seventh-day Adventists, 108, 207; at Visale, 253
Mitchell, Sir Philip (governor of Fiji and high commissioner), 22, 36, 118, 120, 134, 139, 140, 142, 166, 169–171, 214, 218, 276
money, 128, 150, 171, 173, 227, 236, 246, 252, 277, 293–294; and Polynesians, 77–78, 115, 117, 135, 141, 151, 176–177, 206, 237, 246, 254, 256–257, 263
morale, 27, 30, 35, 65, 68–69, 91, 96, 179, 246, 274; entertainment, 44–48, **46**, 292; and mail, 41–44, 292; and mental disease, 44, 68–69; and military experience, 7, 68–69, 269, 292; in Pacific theatres, 44
Munda, New Georgia, Solomon Islands, **24**, 25, 27, 56, 95, **98**, 99, 107, 200, 205, 208, 254, 257, 269–270, 273, **273**, 275; campaign, 56, 246
munitions, 182, 188, 202, 248, 252, 260, 264, 303; affects on environment, 200–202, 270, 303–304; artillery, 200–201, **204**, 227, 273; bombs, **24**, 25, 43, 49, 53, 87, 90–91, 102, 119, 122, 165, 169, 171, 175–176, 200–201, 204–205, **204**, 213, 273, 278, 284, 289, 303–304; disposal, xxv–xxvi, 179–182, 185–190, 204–208, 214, 260, 303; dumping at sea, **183**, 203, 205, 208–209, 303; dumps on land, xxv, 53, 203–208, **204**, 210; dynamite, 53, 93–94, 230–232; hand grenades, xix, 88, 201, 206, 231, 278; military disposal units, 188–189, 206–208, **207**, 260; nuclear weapons testing, 296–298. *See also* mines; bombing
museums, 27, 260, 287; collectors for, 260–263, **261**, 266, 267; and ethnographic present, 12, 262–263; Pacific artifacts in, 12; representations of Pacific peoples, 12, 262–263, 300, 383n.119

Nanking, Rape of, 245, 248, 279
natives. *See* indigenous peoples
Nauru, 122, 131, 169; and boat people, 285, 298; independence, 237; and Japanese, 88, 122, 245; phosphate, 5, 121, 170, 234, 237
navy: American, 22, **24**, 27, 29, 37, 40, 60–61, 68, 77–81, 93, 95, 106, 123, 125,

131, 146, 157–164, 172, 181–189, 194, 214, 220–223, 239, 247, 257, 260, 265–266, 350n.16, 361n.43; Australian, 19, 206; Japanese, 4, 6, 12, 49, 86, **89**
neurosis. *See* morale
New Britain, New Guinea, 15, 40, 75, 84, **87**, 101–102, **102**, 104, 107, 144, 176, 212, 246, 269, 303
New Caledonia, xxi, 5, 28, 38, **39**, **42**, 43, 109, 119–120, 124, 134, 138, 148–149, 154, 202, 208, 210, **217**, 226, 238–239, 256, 258–259, **259**, **261**, 270, 327n.19, 332n.1; administration, 113, 119–120, 123, 137, 145, 146, 164–165, 186, 214, 215–218, 225, 230, 232, 234, 258, 302; America, 2, 3, 38, 61–62, 68, 93–95, 99, 119–120, 124, 145–146, 151, 164–165, 182, 185–186, 214–218, 220, 258, 293, 361n.43; Australia, 2, 119, 122, 165; environment, 17–18, 79, 185, 210; food, 79–81, 84–85, 93, 95, 124, 220–222, 228; forests, 100–101, 112, 113; Kanaks, 35, **38**, 81, 137–138, 145, 148; women, 38
New Guinea, xix, 2, 4–5, 7, 44, 50, 52, 55, 59, 66, 82, **102**, 130–131, 140, 151, 167, 173, 180–182, 195–197, 210, 213, 221, 230, 238, 246, **251**, 258, 260, 274–275, 286, 289, 391n.19; America, 15, 37–38, 56, 57, 188–190, 246–247, 265–266, 270, 281, 292, 295; Australia, 29, 30, 31, 174–178, 209, 219, 269, 274, 297; Australian military forces, 26, 32, 35, 54, 66, 91, 96, 121, 127–128, 149, 153, 188, 197, 208, 236, 244, 245, **249**, 254, 266, 280, 282, 285–286, 293, 301; conditions in, 15–17, 43, 59–63, **64**, 65–68, 70, 82, 127–128, 227; and conditions of enlistment, 136–137; environment, 53, 201, 205, 211–213, 231, 300; environmental knowledge, 137, 270; food, 82–83, **84**, 85, 88, 91; forests, 99, 101–107, **102**, 110–113, 223, 302; Japan, 31, 36, 42, 49, 59, 70, 86–88, 91, 230, 245; labor, 57, **64**, 134, 142–145, 226, 295, 301; Pacific Islands Regiment, 30, 136–137, 231; perceptions of, 12–13, 15–17, 26, 29, 39, 40, **40**, 43–44, 227, 299; provisional administration, 189–193; resources, 5, 99, 116, 118. *See also* ANGAU; Papua
New Hebrides, xxiii, 28, 50–56, 152–153, 168, 171, 173, 211, 215, 226, 229, 231, 258, 371n.121; administration, 123, 138, 165–166, 167–168, 178, 236, 255; America, 15, 36–37, 56, 60–61, 76, 117, 120, 145, 166, 184, 187, 208, 214, 260, 264; food, **14**, 79, **80**, 81, 123, 222, 226; forests, 100–101, 109, 112, 222–223, 234; labor, 134, 141, 145–146, 149; perceptions of, 16, 28, 31
Nimitz, Admiral Chester, 15, 22, 69, 122, 180, 257
Noel, Resident Commissioner (Solomon Islands), 118, 121, 131, 172
Noumea, New Caledonia, 37, 68, 94, 165, 168, 181, 185–189, 196, 203–205, 225, 236, **259**, 361n.43
Nuie, 29, 138, 239

Oliver, Douglas, 76, 81, 94, 118, 124–125, 131, 172, 233–234
Owen Stanley Ranges, Papua, 15, 17, 26, 43–44, 51, 63, **174**
ozone layer, 223, 305

Pacific Forum, 294, 298
Pacific Islanders. *See* indigenous peoples
Papua, xiii–xiv, xix, 128, 219, 230, 231, 260, 275; administration, 5, 29, 236, 348n.106; America, 38, 67, 255; Australia, 173–177, 190; Australian military forces, 32, 51, 136, 233, 234; food, 82, 221, 226; forests, 15, 101, **102**, 103, 104–107, 110, 113; Japan, 17, 272; labor, 143, **174**, 270; perceptions of, 29, 31, 32. *See also* New Guinea
Parer, Damien, **174**, 175, 286
pastoralism, xxiii, 234; in Fiji, 221; in New Caledonia, 5, 164, 221
Pearl Harbor, 1–2, 119, 165, 184, 244, 281
Penrhyn, Cook Islands, 28, 35–36, 67, 98, 147, 163, 211, 257, 270, 332n.1
perceptions, xxii–xxiv, 1, 121, 219, 283,

298–299; of environment, xxi, xxvi, 26, 47, 201, 219, 235, 288, 303, 305. *See also* indigenous people
pests, 198, 211–218, 221, 222, 296; biological controls, 222; brown tree snake, 213–214, 303; cattle tick, xxi, 164, 215–218, **217**, 221, 302, 370n.117; Giant African Snail, 211–213, 302; rat, xxii, 199, 369n.89; of taro, 213, 231, 303
photographs, 245, 273, 282, 387n.66; aerial, 107, 110; for home, 43; and Kodak culture, 43; as propaganda, 29–30; as souvenirs, 247, 249, 251–252, 263
places, xxii, 17, 33, 70; commemorated, 268, 270, 274–275, 280, 284, 299; meaning of, xxii, xxiv, xxvi, 26, 41–48, 266, 272, 276; and memory, 243–289; naming of, 26, 27; as sites of battle, xxvi, 197, 201, 243, 246, 274–275, 283–287, 297
plantations, 21, 85, 99,115–116, 122, 125, 174, 178, 193, 212, 236, 294; Australian Production Control Board, 128, 130, 143, 191; coconut, 17, 103; coffee, 17; control of, 29, 167, 224, 235; laborers, 6, 29, 56, 117, 133–134, 143, 146, 148, 153, 226, 230, 236, 255; New Guinea, 29–30, 63, 103, 130, 191; oil palm, 116, 184, 222; sago palm, 88, 106, 111–113; Solomon Islands, 85, 99, 172–173, 184, 220; Western Samoa, 147
politics, 157, 197; American ambitions in Pacific, 94, 127, 199; Australian policies, 6, 124, 127, 188, 209, 235; British policies, 169–170; failing state, 286; of memorials, 268, 275–277, 280, 281–282, 283–286, 292; New Zealand policies, 6, 124–127, 147, 150, 163–164, 196, 235, 237; proposed transfer of Tarawa to United States, 276–277, 296. *See also* colonial administrations; indigenous peoples
population, xxi, xxiii, xxiv, 6, 14, 34–35, 37, 49–50, 56–57, 65, 87, 98, 133, 135, 142, 146, 148, 169, 292; Fiji, 78, 140, 220; Indian compared to Fijian, 135
Port Moresby, Papua, 37, 51, 82, 91, 93, 103, 127, 177, 190–191, 233, 244, 254, 275
Price, Major General Charles, 33, **139**
Production Control Board (PCB), Australia, 128, 130, 143, 191

quarantine, 66, 213, 214; in New Caledonia, 215–218

Rabaul, New Britain, New Guinea, 15, 39, 42, 51, 58, 83, 86–90, **87**, **89**, **102**, 117–119, 127, 189–191, 196, 203, 208, 211–212, 225, 245, 271, 287, 291–292
race: attitudes toward, 12; depictions of, 29; Islanders' views of African Americans, 32–33, 37; Polynesians and Melanesians compared, 28, 30–33, 325n.155
Red Cross, 41; curio sales, 257
Reparation Estates, Western Samoa, 85, 100, 125, 147
resources, xx, xxii–xxvi, 1, 3–4, 5, 12–13, 14, 49, 70, 75–96, 132, 153, 178–179, 233–237, 239–240, 292, 293–294, 298, 301, 302; and aggregates, 97–99; commodification of, xxiii, 219, 223–225, 235–237; fisheries, xxiii–xxv, 201–202, 225–226, 232; indigenous human, xxiii, 122–123, 132–133; minerals, 118–122. *See also* copra; fish; food; forests; land; soils; sugar; trade
reverse lend-lease. *See* lend-lease
roll-up. *See* departure of military
Roosevelt, President Franklin D., 2, 124, 251
Russell Islands, Solomon Islands, 31–32, **45**, 56, 81, 85, 99, 108, 170, 184, 193, 203, 205, 257

Sālote, Queen, 77, 147–148, 381n.88; role in Tonga, 257
salvage, 25, 195, 207; environmental factors in, 183, 185; Material Salvage Units, 108, 182, 184; policies of America, 180–182, 185, 188, 189; policies of Australia, 189, 192, 193; redeployment, 181, 183, 185, 188, 194–195, 206; rights to, 192, 194; sales of, 187,

189, 191–192, 193, 195; Transco Agreement, 181. *See also* conservation; surplus
Salvation Army, 26, 91
Samoa. *See* American Samoa; Western Samoa
scrap. *See* salvage
Seabees. *See* construction
settlers, xxii, xxvi, 1, 4–5, 29, 49, 101, 122, 138, 166, 174, 212, 225, 256; and compensation, 166–168, 173, 177–178; farms, 5, 79; plantations, 122
sexual relations, 33–41, 66–68; brothels, 37–38; "comfort" women, 39; and disease, 62; and drug therapy, 53–54; homosexuals, 67–68, 324n.143; Rennell Island, 67; Trobriand Islands, 40, 67, 255
shipping, 4, 15, 27, 31, 78, 81–82, 98, 109, 113, 116–117, 121–124, 141, 158, 181–187, 192–194, 248, 251, 256, 284, 302; space, 75, 80, 97, 103, 112, 126
soils, xxii, 7, 50, 63, 177, 200–201, 210, 222, 234, 239; chemical composition, 84, 113, 220; fertility of, 5, 17, 84, 121–122, 201, 220, 234, 292; as resource, 50, 78, 115, 220; types of, 50, 88, 115. *See also* geology; land
Solomon Islands, xix, 2, 5, 28, 50–51, 54, 56, **57**, 60–63, 70, **79**, 94–96, 117–121, 154, 158, 170–173, 175–176, 178, 184, 205–208, 218, 224, 283–284, 287, 294, 391n.20; administration, 184–186, 193–196, 209, 220, 230–231, 233–234, 236, 238, 302; America, 27, 31–32, 35–37, 67, 68, 70, 136, 150–151, 184, **196**, 202, 205, 208–209, 226, 244, 258, 260, **261**, 264, **269**, 275, 284–285, 287–288; Australia, 208; environment, 13–15, 113, 200, 203, 210–211, 213; Fiji, 32, 86, 135, 270; forests, 100–101, 108–113, 223–234; Japan, 14, 15, 49, 59, 87–88, 102–103, 135, 188, 205, 247, **273**, 279, 284–285; labor, 31–32, 134, 139–142, 151, 270; New Zealand, 36, 270; Solomon Islands Defense Force, 153, 134–136, **136**, 137; trade, 118, 130–131, 254, 258, **261**
South Pacific (musical), 299
South Pacific Commission, 209, 236, 298
souvenirs, xxi–xxii, xxvi, 148, 195, 226, 243–267, **249**, **250**; artifacts, 243, 253–266, **261**; barter of, 246, 257; body parts, 195, 243, 249–251, **251**, **252**; carvings, 255–256; curios, 243, 253–258, 293; demand for, by Americans, 244, 246–251, **252**, 255–258, **259**, 260–261, 264–265; demand for, by Australians, 244–248, **249**, 251–252; demand for, by Japanese, 247, 255; demand for, by New Zealanders, 246, 250, 257; factors in production of, 256, 263; grass skirts, 253–255; handicrafts, 243, 256, 264–266, **265**; manufacture of, 148, 244, 255–258, 263–264; meaning of, xxvi, 253; natural objects, 243; price control, 256–257; retailers of, 257–258; and role of censor, 246, 251–253, 267; sale of, 258, **259**; tourist art, 255–258, 266; trade in, 226, 244–246, 254–265; trench art, 264–265, **265**; trophies, 243–253; value of, 243–248, 255, 257–267
strategic materials: copra, 118; minerals, 119–121, phosphates, 121–122; reserves, 103–104, 120, 123, 179–181, 301; sugar, 116–117
strategy: combat, 2, 4, 15, 69, 97, 122, 158, 174, 291, 301, 332n.1; defense, 3–4, 58; economic, of America, xxiv, xxv, 76, 119–120, 127, 293, 132, 146; economic, of Australia and New Zealand, xxiv, 119, 127, 132; mobile base organization, 15, 27, 180; perceptions of islands, 1–2, 3, 4, 5, 178, 296; principle of overwhelming strength, 179–180; striking mobility, 180
sugar: in diet, 78, 82, 131–132, 142, **160**, **162**, 229, 296, 325n.1, 327n.27; production, 5, 115, 116–117, 132, 140, 151, 158, 221, 338n.2
Sukuna, Major Ratu Lala, 32, 66, 134, 139, 148, 152, 293

surplus, war: abandonment, 204–205; of American Samoa, 187; and Army-Navy Liquidation Commission, 182, 189; buyers, 181, 184, 186–187, 189, 192, 193; and colonial administrations, 180, 185; and Commonwealth Disposals Commission, 190–192; and complaints about, 192–193; of Cook Islands, 182–183, 188, 197; difficulties of disposal, xxv, 182–183, 188, 197; disposal processes, 150, 159, 185–186, 187; dumps, 183, **183**, 184–185, 202–203, 205, 209; of Fiji, 181, 186; and Foreign Liquidation Commission, 189; of Gilbert and Ellice Islands, 186–187, 193; goods given away, xxvi, 141, 159, 152, 171, 187, 260; Islanders' perceptions of, xxv–xxvi, 150, 195–196; Islanders' uses of, 195, 224; maintenance of, xxv, 187, 188, 189–190, 297; and Million Dollar Point, Efate, 184–185; of New Caledonia, 182, 185–186, 221; of New Guinea, 188–193; of New Hebrides, 167, 184, 187; policies of America, 167, 181–182, 185, 205; of Solomon Islands, 184, 186, 193–195, 260, 262; and Surplus Property Board, 182; of Tonga, 159, 185; waste of, 185; of Western Samoa, 187

tactics, xxi, 26; of Americans, 4, 14, 22, 30, 54, 301; of Australians, 14; of indigenous fighters, 14, 137, 153; of Japanese, 69, 301
Tarawa, Gilbert Islands, xxiii, 19–22, 26, 114, 131, 142, 169, 186, **200**, 253, 270, 278, 288; suggested transfer of, 276–277, 296
tides, xxi, 21, 70, 310n.55; Tarawa, 19–22, 277
timber: Australian policy, 103–107; and civilian needs, 99–100, 102, 109–111; and construction, 99–101, 103, 107; and crates, 100–101, 107; and dunnage, 100; and exports, 99–101, 115, 223–224; and furniture, 100, 110, 112; and imports, 111–112; and local building, 97, 103, 109–111, 224; and production, 103–109; and sawmills, 25, 100–108, **102**, 146, 223; and sources, 99–114, 223; and species, 99–101, 107, 109, 114; and supply rationalization, 103; traditional uses of, 294, 302; value, 224, 302. *See also* forests
tobacco, 30, 88, 111, 128, 130–131, 142, 226, 229; cigarettes, 128, 230; local supplies, 86, 230, 375n.81
Tokelau Islands, 29, 125, 147, 151
Tonga, xix, 7, 19, 28, 100, 152, 195, 202, 239, 270, 298; administration, 76, 135, 185, 214, 220, 257, 292, 302; America, 33, 35–36, 66, 76, 77–78, 93, 159, 161, 185, 208, 214–215, 228–230, 253, 257; Defense Force, 134, 135, 147, 228; environment, 19, 137, 215; food, 77–78, **80**, **92**, 93, **160**; labor, 147–148; New Zealand, 33, 78, 138, 148, 159, 259; trade, 116–118, 123, 253, 256–257, 264, 267
Tongareva. *See* Penrhyn
tourists, 256, 258, 286–287, 300, 301, 390n.14; military as, 43, 253, 255, 265
trade, 3, 115–132, 133, 173, 225, 255–256; availability, 117; exports, 76, 100, 115–118, 123–127, 223; global implications, 3, 100, 115–119, 124, 126–127, 132; imports, 78, 122–127, 130–132, 227; as incentive, 30, 75, 111, 115, 125, 128, 130, 132–134, 147, 151; indigenous valuables, 128, 255; and lend-lease, 123, 127; regional variation in demand, 127–128, 129–130, 141; retail, 123, 125, 131, 148, 258; role of military, 81, 88, 93, 115–116, 118, 120–121; significance to Islanders, 111, 115, 117, 122, 125, 127–128, 147; supplies, 111, 122, 124, 126, 128, 130–131; types of goods, 14, 34, 59, 76, 86, 93, 100, 116–122, 125, 128–131, **129**, 226; and wages, 117, 125, **126**, **129**, 130–131, 255. *See also* barter
transformation of landscape, xxi–xxiii, 11, 19, 153, 198–218; airstrips, 2, 6,

98, 158, 187, 199–200, 273, 302–303, 341n.59; *babai* or *pulaka* pits, 98, 169, 226; borrow pits, 53, 98–99, 200; islets, 56–57, 98, 201; roads, 6, 13, 15, 17, 19, 21, 55, 97, 99, 101, 106, 120, 147, 159, 168, 187, 191, 196, 199, 200, 203, 210, 233, 238, 301; swamps, 53, 58, 70
Trobriand Islands, Papua, 40, 67, 113, 200, 255, 303

United Nations Organization, 6, 190, 223, 237–238, 277, 296, 305
United States Commercial Company (USCC), 95, 325n.6
United States Department of Agriculture, 78, 81, 85

Vietnam War, xxi, 283, 303–304; and bombing, 303; and chemical herbicides, 303
villagers, 7, 37, 54, 56, 59–60, 67, 81, 83, 86, 88, 90, 93, 111, 153, 174–175, 229, 231, 280, 287, 301; relocation of, 57, 67, 142–143, 158, 163
villages, 13, 19, 23, 31–32, 37, 54, 56–57, 59, 61–62, 70, 83, 87, 99, 110, 120, 130, 138–139, 141–143, 151, 158, 161–162, 171, 175, 176–177, 195, **196**, 200, 221, 236, 253–254, 256–257, 274, 280, 287
Vouza, Sergeant Major Jacob, 136, 153

wages, 123, 125, **126**, **129**, 130, 135, 137, 141–142, 144–152, **149**, 170, 178, 190, 224, 236, 238, 244, 257, 345n.54; geographic variation, 146–152, **149**; meaning of, 149. *See also* money
Wallis Island, 33–36, 62, 67, 70, 80, 125, 138, 146, 151, 165, 181, 239, 270, 346n.76
war: and body retrieval units, 270–271; and burial, 142, 199, 251, 268–272, 277, 278, 281, 385n.11; cemeteries, **24**, 269–272, **269**, 275–282, 296, 385n.11; coffins, 271; consolidation of remains, 269–270; cremation, 271–272, 279, 385n.14; criminals, 188, 128; dead, xxvi, 19, 38, 49, 70, 86, 88, 89, 142, 197, 203, 230, 234, 246–249, 251–252, 268–270, **269**, 277, 296, 384n.2, 385n.11; death and soil fertility, 199; and death ritual, 268, 271–272, 279, 280–283, 292; design of cemeteries, 270; and global warming, xxvi, 288, 304–306; graves, 268–282; graves at Tarawa, 170, 278, 385n.11; and hunting, 244; locating the dead, 270, 278; and mass burials, 199, 201, 272, 278; and modernity, xxv, 6, 153–154, 174, 195, 238, 295–300; and Quartermaster's Corps, 270, 277; repatriation of remains, 270–271, 275–277, 279–280, 281, 296, 384n.2, 385n.16; size of disarticulated bodies, 271; and War Graves Maintenance Unit, 270. *See also* memorials
weeds, 53, 178, 196, 210–211, 221, 296, 303
Western Pacific High Commission (WPHC), 116, 123, 131, 159, 173, 185, 194, 236
Western Samoa, 36, 100, 138, 152, 231, 239, 269; America, 36, 62, 78, 85, 163; food, 78, 228–229; labor, 146–147, 148, 222; New Zealand, 29, 99, 125, 127, 152, 187, 200, 237; trade, 78, 85, 229, 257, 258
women, 42, 44, **45**, 46–47, 78, 195, 201, 248, 250, 265–266, 283; "comfort," 39; craft workers, 255–257; indigenous, 12, 19, 33–42, **38**, **39**, **40**, 66–67, 86, 111, 117, 124–125, 143, **144**, 146, 149, 239, 253–255, 295, 299–300; lack of, 41, 68; laundresses, 125, 142, 147–148, 256; nurses, 37–38, 40–41, 63, 91, 316n.103; nurses and gardening, 91; protection of military, 37–38, 40–41, 66; rape of, 37–38, 137, 245; self-perception, 149; sex workers, 35, 40, 67; traditional work, 255–257, 295; waitresses, 66

About the Author

Judith Bennett is an Australian who has lived for over two decades in the wonderful country of New Zealand where she teaches Pacific history at the University of Otago, Dunedin. Her major books have been on the Solomon Islands; the award-winning *Wealth of the Solomons* (Honolulu, 1987) and *Pacific Forest* (Cambridge and Leiden, 2000). She also edited with Khyla J. Russell *Journeys in a Small Canoe: The Life and Times of a Solomon Islander*, by Lloyd Maepeza Gina (Canberra, 2003). She is currently researching colonial forest policy in the South Pacific as well the long-term demographic impact of World War II.

Production Notes for Bennett | *Natives and Exotics*

Cover design and text composition by Santos Barbasa Jr.

Text design by University of Hawai'i Press production staff
with display type in Raleigh and text type in Minion

Printing and binding by The Maple-Vail Book Manufacturing Group

Printed on 50 lb. Glatfelter Offset D37, 400 ppi.